**W9-AHF-388**

For Exams Scheduled After June 30, 2018

# CPA EXAM REVIEW
# BUSINESS

**UPDATES AND ACADEMIC HELP**
Click on Customer and Academic Support under CPA Resources at
http://www.becker.com/cpa-review.html

**CUSTOMER SERVICE AND TECHNICAL SUPPORT**
Call 1-877-CPA-EXAM (outside the U.S. +1-630-472-2213)
or click Customer and Academic Support under CPA Resources at
http://www.becker.com/cpa-review.html

This textbook contains information that was current at the time of printing.
Your course software will be updated on a regular basis as the content
that is tested on the CPA Exam evolves and as we improve our materials.
Note the version reference below and click on Customer and Academic
Support under CPA Resources at http://www.becker.com/cpa-review.html
for a list of available updates or to learn if a newer version of this book is
available to be ordered.

**BECKER**
PROFESSIONAL EDUCATION®

V 3.1

## COURSE DEVELOPMENT TEAM

Timothy F. Gearty, CPA, MBA, JD . . . . . . . . . . . . . Editor in Chief, Financial/Regulation (Tax) National Editor

Angeline S. Brown, CPA, MAC . . . . . . . . . . . . . . . . . . . . . . . . . . . . . . . . . . . . . Sr. Director, Product Management

Valerie Funk Anderson, CPA . . . . . . . . . . . . . . . . . . . . . . . . . . . . . . . . . . . . Sr. Manager, Accounting Curriculum

Stephen Bergens, CPA . . . . . . . . . . . . . . . . . . . . . . . . . . . . . . . . . . . . . . . . . . . Manager, Accounting Curriculum

Patrice W. Johnson, CPA . . . . . . . . . . . . . . . . . . . . . . . . . . . . . . . . . . . . . . Sr. Manager, Accounting Curriculum

Tom Cox, CPA, CMA . . . . . . . . . . . . . . . . . . . . . . . . . . . . . . . . . . . . . . Financial (GASB & NFP) National Editor

Steven J. Levin, JD . . . . . . . . . . . . . . . . . . . . . . . . . . . . . . . . . . . . . . . . . . . . Regulation (Law) National Editor

Pete Console . . . . . . . . . . . . . . . . . . . . . . . . . . . . . . . . . . . . . . . . . Sr. Director, Educational Technologies

Brian Cave . . . . . . . . . . . . . . . . . . . . . . . . . . . . . . . . . . . . . . . . . . . . Sr. Manager, Software Development

Dan Corrales . . . . . . . . . . . . . . . . . . . . . . . . . . . . . . . . . . . . . . Sr. Manager, Curriculum Quality Assurance

Danita De Jane . . . . . . . . . . . . . . . . . . . . . . . . . . . . . . . . . . . . . . . . . . . Director, Course Development

Anson Miyashiro . . . . . . . . . . . . . . . . . . . . . . . . . . . . . . . . . . . . . . . . . . Manager, Product Development

John Ott . . . . . . . . . . . . . . . . . . . . . . . . . . . . . . . . . . . . . . . . . . . . . . . . . . . . Manager, Visual Design

Tim Munson . . . . . . . . . . . . . . . . . . . . . . . . . . . . . . . . . . . . . . . . Team Lead, Product Development

Linda Finestone . . . . . . . . . . . . . . . . . . . . . . . . . . . . . . . . . . . . . . . . . . . . . . . . . . Sr. Course Editor

Naomi Oseida . . . . . . . . . . . . . . . . . . . . . . . . . . . . . . . . . . . . . . . . . . . . . . . . . . Product Development

Eric Vasquez . . . . . . . . . . . . . . . . . . . . . . . . . . . . . . . . . . . . . . . . . . . . . . . . . . Product Development

## CONTRIBUTING EDITORS

| | |
|---|---|
| Teresa C. Anderson, CPA, CMA, MPA | Peter Olinto, JD, CPA |
| Katie Barnette, CPA | Sandra Owen, CPA, MBA, JD |
| Jim DeSimpelare, CPA, MBA | Michelle M. Pace, CPA |
| Melisa F. Galasso, CPA | Jennifer J. Rivers, CPA |
| Holly Hawk, CPA, CGMA | Josh Rosenberg, MBA, CPA, CFA, CFP |
| Julie D. McGinty, CPA | Jonathan R. Rubin, CPA, MBA |
| Sandra McGuire, CPA, MBA | Michael Rybak, CPA, CFA |
| Stephanie Morris, CPA, MAcc | Denise M. Stefano, CPA, CGMA, MBA |
| Michelle Moshe, CPA, DipIFR | Elizabeth Lester Walsh, CPA, CITP |

## LICENSE AGREEMENT—TERMS & CONDITIONS

**DO NOT DOWNLOAD, ACCESS, AND/OR USE ANY OF THESE MATERIALS (AS THAT TERM IS DEFINED BELOW) UNTIL YOU HAVE READ THIS LICENSE AGREEMENT CAREFULLY.  IF YOU DOWNLOAD, ACCESS, AND/OR USE ANY OF THESE MATERIALS, YOU ARE AGREEING AND CONSENTING TO BE BOUND BY AND ARE BECOMING A PARTY TO THIS LICENSE AGREEMENT ("AGREEMENT").**

**The printed Materials provided to you and/or the Materials provided for download to your computer and/or provided via a web application to which you are granted access are NOT for sale and are not being sold to you.  You may NOT transfer these Materials to any other person or permit any other person to use these Materials.  You may only acquire a license to use these Materials and only upon the terms and conditions set forth in this Agreement.  Read this Agreement carefully before downloading, and/or accessing, and/or using these Materials.  Do not download and/or access, and/or use these Materials unless you agree with all terms of this Agreement.**

**NOTE: You may already be a party to this Agreement if you registered for a Becker Professional Education CPA program (the "Program") or placed an order for these Materials online or using a printed form that included this License Agreement.  Please review the termination section regarding your rights to terminate this License Agreement and receive a refund of your payment.**

**Grant:** Upon your acceptance of the terms of this Agreement, in a manner set forth above, Becker Professional Development Corporation ("Becker") hereby grants to you a non-exclusive, revocable, non-transferable, non-sublicensable, limited license to (as defined below) the Materials by downloading them onto a computer and/or by accessing them via a web application using a user ID and password (as defined below), and any Materials to which you are granted access as a result of your license to use these Materials and/or in connection with the Program on the following terms:

During the Term (as defined below) of this Agreement, you may:

- use the Materials for preparation for one or more parts of the CPA exam (the "Exam"), and/or for your studies relating to the subject matter covered by the Program and/or the Exam), and/or for your studies relating to the subject matter covered by the Materials and/or the Exam, including taking electronic and/or handwritten notes during the Program, provided that all notes taken that relate to the subject matter of the Materials are and shall remain Materials subject to the terms of this Agreement;
- download the Materials onto any single device;
- download the Materials onto a second device so long as the first device and the second device are not used simultaneously;
- download the Materials onto a third device so long as the first, second, and third device are not used simultaneously; and
- download the Materials onto a fourth device so long as the first, second, third, and fourth device are not used simultaneously.

The number of installations may vary outside of the U.S.  Please review your local office policies and procedures to confirm the number of installations granted—your local office's policies and procedures regarding the number of allowable activations of downloads supersedes the limitations contained herein and is controlling.

You may not:

- use the Materials for any purpose other than as expressly permitted above;
- use the downloaded Materials on more than one device, computer terminal, or workstation at the same time;
- make copies of the Materials;
- rent, lease, license, lend, or otherwise transfer or provide (by gift, sale, or otherwise) all or any part of the Materials to anyone;
- permit the use of all or any part of the Materials by anyone other than you; or
- reverse engineer, decompile, disassemble, or create derivate works of the Materials.

**Materials:** As used in this Agreement, the term "Materials" means and includes any printed materials provided to you by Becker, and/or to which you are granted access by Becker (directly or indirectly) in connection with your license of the Materials and/or the Program, and shall include notes you take (by hand, electronically, digitally, or otherwise) while using the Materials relating to the subject matter of the Materials; any and all electronically-stored/accessed/delivered, and/or digitally-stored/accessed/delivered materials included under this License via download to a computer or via access to a web application, and/or otherwise provided to you and/or to which you are otherwise granted access by Becker (directly or indirectly), including, but not limited to, applications downloadable from a third party, for example Google® or Amazon®, in connection with your license of the Materials.

**Title:** Becker is and will remain the owner of all title, ownership rights, intellectual property, and all other rights and interests in and to the Materials that are subject to the terms of this Agreement. The Materials are protected by the copyright laws of the United States and international copyright laws and treaties.

**Use of Navigator 2.0:** If your employer or college/university has instructed Becker to use its Navigator 2.0 to track your studies, the following will occur: a) once you have activated your software (course log-in), you will be asked to set up your study planner. In order to do this, you may be required to provide information about yourself as part of the Program registration process, or as part of your continued use of the Materials. You agree that any registration information you give to Becker will be shared by Becker with your employer or college/university ; and b) once that is done, Navigator 2.0 will automatically track if you are behind in your studies based on your study planner, your office location, your service line within the firm, your college/university course, which course parts were purchased (Audit and Attestation, Financial Accounting and Reporting, Business Environment and Concepts, and Regulation), what format are you using (online, live, self-study), your course progress, study time details (hours/min in course, # of log-ins, last log in), exam progress details including: whether you applied to take the exam, and if so, the state to which you applied; whether you received your NTS (notice to schedule), and if so, its expiration date; whether you scheduled your exam, and if so, the date; whether you received any scores and what they were; and the number of attempts to pass each of the four parts.

**Navigator 2.0 Liability Provisions:** You hereby waive any claims, causes of action, and damages, and agree to hold harmless and indemnify Becker and its affiliates, officers, agents, and employees from any claim, suit or action arising from or related to your use of the Materials, the sharing of any of your information by Becker with your employer or violation of these terms, including any liability or expense arising from claims, losses, damages, suits, judgments, litigation costs and attorneys' fees.

SUBJECT TO THE OVERALL PROVISION ABOVE, YOU EXPRESSLY UNDERSTAND AND AGREE THAT BECKER, ITS PARENT CORPORATION, SUBSIDIARIES AND AFFILIATES, AND THE OFFICERS, AGENTS AND EMPLOYEES OF THOSE ENTITIES, SHALL NOT BE LIABLE TO YOU FOR ANY LOSS OR DAMAGE THAT MAY BE INCURRED BY YOU, INCLUDING BUT NOT LIMITED TO LOSS OR DAMAGE AS A RESULT BECKER SHARING YOUR INFORMATION WITH YOUR EMPLOYER OR COLLEGE/UNIVERSITY.

THE LIMITATIONS ON BECKER'S LIABILITY TO YOU IN THE PARAGRAPHS ABOVE SHALL APPLY WHETHER OR NOT BECKER HAS BEEN ADVISED OF OR SHOULD HAVE BEEN AWARE OF THE POSSIBILITY OF ANY SUCH LOSSES ARISING.

**Termination:** The license granted under this Agreement commences upon your receipt of these Materials. This license shall terminate the earlier of: (i) ten (10) business days after notice to you of non-payment of or default on any payment due Becker which has not been cured within such 10-day period; or (ii) immediately if you fail to comply with any of the limitations described above; or (iii) upon expiration of the period ending eighteen (18) months after you log-in to access the Materials, that is, the first time you visit the Becker Program homepage at https://online.becker.com and log-in using your user identification and password; or upon expiration of the twenty-four (24) month period beginning upon your purchase of the Material, whichever of these periods first transpires (the "Term"). In addition, upon termination of this license for any reason, you must delete or otherwise remove from your computer and other device any Materials you downloaded, including, but not limited to, any archival copies you may have made. The Title, Exclusion of Warranties, Exclusion of Damages, Indemnification and Remedies, Severability of Terms and Governing Law provisions, and any amounts due, shall survive termination of the license.

**Your Limited Right to Terminate this License and Receive a Refund:** You may terminate this license for the in-class, online, and self-study Programs in accordance with Becker's refund policy as provided at http://www.becker.com/cpa-review/resources/cpa-exam-review-policy and as listed below.

**Cancellations and Refunds:** To cancel your enrollment and receive a refund, contact Becker Professional Education at 800-868-3900.

Textbooks should be returned within 10 days of notification of withdrawal. Students should contact Becker for a "Return Materials Authorization" number prior to shipping returns. Students should ship materials by certified mail or an alternative traceable method. Flashcards and the material license fees for the Becker Promise are non-refundable. The cost to return materials is the responsibility of the student. Refunds will be made within 30 days from the date of cancellation. Non-receipt of shipment disputes must be made with 90 days of original purchase date.

All returns must be sent to: Becker Professional Education.
Attn: Becker Returns, 200 Finn Ct., Farmingdale NY, 11735

For **Online CPA Exam Review Course and CPA Final Review course students\***, a full tuition refund (less any applicable savings and fees) will be issued within 10 days of initial purchase or first login, whichever comes first.

For **Live Format and Cohort Program CPA Review students\***, a full tuition refund (minus all applicable savings) will be issued to students who withdraw on or before the 5th business day or if students do not attend any part of the course (no-shows) after the start date of the scheduled section and provided that electronic course materials are not accessed. Thereafter, no refund will be issued as full access to course content has been granted.

Under certain circumstances, a live class may be cancelled up to 5 days in advance of the scheduled start date. Students will be provided with rescheduling options which could include access to self-study materials when live courses are not available. If rescheduling efforts are not successful, a refund for the cancelled course section may be issued and access suspended provided that the section content has not been accessed.

**No Shows** are students who never attend a live/live online class and do not access any portion of the course software/electronic materials.

For **Atlanta Intensive and Final Review students\***, a full tuition refund (minus all applicable savings) will be issued to students who withdraw on or before the 2nd class of the first scheduled part. Thereafter, no refund will be issued as full access to course content has been granted.

For **SkillMaster Workshops:** A full refund will be issued to students who withdraw at least 10 business days before the scheduled workshop. Thereafter, no refund will be issued.

(\*Applicable in all states except those noted below.)

**The following cancellation policy is applicable for students in Alabama, Arkansas, District of Columbia, Kansas, Kentucky, Louisiana, Nebraska, Nevada, New Hampshire, New Mexico, Oklahoma, West Virginia:**

If cancellation occurs within 3 business days of registration, all monies paid by the student will be refunded even if classes have already started.

A full tuition refund (minus all applicable savings and fees) will be issued to students who withdraw on or before the 5th business day after the start date of the first scheduled section; thereafter, students are entitled to a prorated refund (minus all applicable savings and fees) for the unused portion through 60% of the part taken (75% in Arkansas and DC).

For example, the refund for a candidate who withdraws after completing 12 hours (3 sessions) of Audit classes will be calculated as follows:

- Amount Paid $1131.00
- Amount to be Prorated $1131.00
- 8 Hours Cancelled / 20 Hours Scheduled × $1131.00 = $452.00 (Amount Refunded)
- Residents are not required to submit written notification of withdrawal.

**New Hampshire Students:** Any buyer may cancel this transaction by submitting written notification of withdrawal any time prior to midnight of the third business day after the date of this transaction.

**Oklahoma Students:** Becker Professional Education is licensed by Oklahoma Board of Private Vocational Schools, 700 N. Classen Blvd. #250, Oklahoma City, OK, 73118.

**Classroom Locations:** University of Oklahoma, 307 West Brooks, Room 200, Norman, OK 73019, Oklahoma Christian University, 2501 E Memorial Rd., Edmond, OK 73136, and Oklahoma State University, 108 Gunderson Hall, Stillwater, OK 74078.

**Tennessee Students:** At a minimum, refunds are calculated as follows:

| Date of Withdrawal During: | Percent Refund of Tuition (Less Administrative Fee) |
| --- | --- |
| First day of scheduled classes | 100% |
| Balance of week 1 | 90% |
| Week 2 | 75% |
| Weeks 3 and 4 | 25% |
| Weeks 5–8 | 0% |

Refunds are to be prorated as of last day of actual attendance, notification is not required. All monies paid by an applicant will be refunded if requested within three days after signing an enrollment agreement and making an initial payment.

Holder in Due Course Rule: Any holder of this consumer credit contract is subject to all claims and defenses which the debtor could assert against the seller of goods and services obtained pursuant hereto or with the proceeds hereof. Recovery hereunder by the debtor shall not exceed that paid by the debtor. (This Federal TradeCom Regulation became in effect 5/14/75.)

Becker Professional Education is licensed by Oklahoma Board of Private Vocational Schools, 700 N. Classen Blvd. #250, Oklahoma City, OK, 73118.

**NON-REFUNDABLE ITEMS:** Charges for Flashcards, Supplemental Multiple-Choice Questions, 0% APR* Financing Processing Fee and the Becker Promise material license fee are non-refundable.

*Annual Percentage Rating

**Attendance:** To review Becker's attendance policy, please visit http://www.becker.com/cpa-review/resources/cpa-exam-review-policy

**Exclusion of Warranties:** YOU EXPRESSLY ASSUME ALL RISK FOR USE OF THE MATERIALS. YOU AGREE THAT THE MATERIALS ARE PROVIDED TO YOU "AS IS" AND "AS AVAILABLE" AND THAT BECKER MAKES NO WARRANTIES, EXPRESS OR IMPLIED, WITH RESPECT TO THE MATERIALS, THEIR MERCHANTABILITY OR FITNESS FOR A PARTICULAR PURPOSE AND NO WARRANTY OF NONINFRINGEMENT OF THIRD PARTIES' RIGHTS. NO DEALER, AGENT OR EMPLOYEE OF BECKER IS AUTHORIZED TO PROVIDE ANY SUCH WARRANTY TO YOU. BECAUSE SOME JURISDICTIONS DO NOT ALLOW THE EXCLUSION OF IMPLIED WARRANTIES, THE ABOVE EXCLUSION OF IMPLIED WARRANTIES MAY NOT APPLY TO YOU. BECKER DOES NOT WARRANT OR GUARANTEE THAT YOU WILL PASS ANY EXAMINATION.

**Exclusion of Damages:** UNDER NO CIRCUMSTANCES AND UNDER NO LEGAL THEORY, TORT, CONTRACT, OR OTHERWISE, SHALL BECKER OR ITS DIRECTORS, OFFICERS, EMPLOYEES, OR AGENTS BE LIABLE TO YOU OR ANY OTHER PERSON FOR ANY CONSEQUENTIAL, INCIDENTAL, INDIRECT, PUNITIVE, EXEMPLARY OR SPECIAL DAMAGES OF ANY CHARACTER, INCLUDING, WITHOUT LIMITATION, DAMAGES FOR LOSS OF GOODWILL, WORK STOPPAGE, COMPUTER FAILURE OR MALFUNCTION OR ANY AND ALL OTHER DAMAGES OR LOSSES, OR FOR ANY DAMAGES IN EXCESS OF BECKER'S LIST PRICE FOR A LICENSE TO THE MATERIALS, EVEN IF BECKER SHALL HAVE BEEN INFORMED OF THE POSSIBILITY OF SUCH DAMAGES, OR FOR ANY CLAIM BY ANY OTHER PARTY. Some jurisdictions do not allow the limitation or exclusion of liability for incidental or consequential damages, so the above limitation or exclusion may not apply to you.

**Indemnification and Remedies:** You agree to indemnify and hold Becker and its employees, representatives, agents, attorneys, affiliates, directors, officers, members, managers, and shareholders harmless from and against any and all claims, demands, losses, damages, penalties, costs or expenses (including reasonable attorneys' and expert witnesses' fees and costs) of any kind or nature, arising from or relating to any violation, breach, or nonfulfillment by you of any provision of this license. If you are obligated to provide indemnification pursuant to this provision, Becker may, in its sole and absolute discretion, control the disposition of any indemnified action at your sole cost and expense. Without limiting the foregoing, you may not settle, compromise, or in any other manner dispose of any indemnified action without the consent of Becker. If you breach any material term of this license, Becker shall be entitled to equitable relief by way of temporary and permanent injunction without the need for a bond and such other and further relief as any court with jurisdiction may deem just and proper.

**Confidentiality:** The Materials are considered confidential and proprietary to Becker. You shall keep the Materials confidential and you shall not publish or disclose the Materials to any third party without the prior written consent of Becker.

**Use of Your Data:** You understand that you will be providing personal information if you register for the Program and that the following will occur: (a) once you have registered, logged in, and activated your account, you will be asked to provide information about yourself as part of the registration process, or as part of your continued use of the Materials. You agree that any registration information you give to Becker will be used and stored by Becker. By using the Materials, you hereby consent to Becker retaining your personal information for purposes of the Program and for future purposes in marketing to you regarding other Becker Products.

**Waiver of Liability:** You hereby waive any claims, causes of action, and damages, and agree to hold harmless and indemnify Becker and its affiliates, officers, agents, and employees from any claim, suit, or action arising from or related to your use of the Materials, the use and storing of any of your information by Becker, or violation of these terms, including any liability or expense arising from claims, losses, damages, suits, judgments, litigation costs, and attorneys' fees.

SUBJECT TO THE OVERALL PROVISION ABOVE, YOU EXPRESSLY UNDERSTAND AND AGREE THAT BECKER, ITS PARENT CORPORATION, SUBSIDIARIES AND AFFILIATES, AND THE OFFICERS, AGENTS, AND EMPLOYEES OF THOSE ENTITIES, SHALL NOT BE LIABLE TO YOU FOR ANY LOSS OR DAMAGE THAT MAY BE INCURRED BY YOU, INCLUDING BUT NOT LIMITED TO LOSS OR DAMAGE AS A RESULT OF BECKER USING OR STORING YOUR INFORMATION WITH YOUR PROFESSOR OR COLLEGE/UNIVERSITY.

THE LIMITATIONS ON BECKER'S LIABILITY TO YOU IN THE PARAGRAPHS ABOVE SHALL APPLY WHETHER OR NOT BECKER HAS BEEN ADVISED OF, OR SHOULD HAVE BEEN AWARE OF, THE POSSIBILITY OF ANY SUCH LOSSES ARISING.

**Severability of Terms:** If any term or provision of this license is held invalid or unenforceable by a court of competent jurisdiction, such invalidity shall not affect the validity or operation of any other term or provision and such invalid term or provision shall be deemed to be severed from the license. This Agreement may only be modified by written agreement signed by both parties.

**Governing Law:** This Agreement shall be governed and construed according to the laws of the State of Illinois, United States of America, excepting that State's conflicts of laws rules. The parties agree that the jurisdiction and venue of any dispute subject to litigation is proper in any state or federal court in Chicago, Illinois, USA. The parties hereby agree to waive application of the UN Convention on the Sale of Goods. If the State of Illinois adopts the current proposed Uniform Computer Information Transactions Act (UCITA, formerly proposed Article 2B to the Uniform Commercial Code), or a version of the proposed UCITA, that part of the laws shall not apply to any transaction under this Agreement.

**NOTICE TO STUDENTS: ACCET COMPLAINT PROCEDURE**

This institution is recognized by the Accrediting Council for Continuing Education & Training (ACCET) as meeting and maintaining certain standards of quality. It is the mutual goal of ACCET and the institution to ensure that educational training programs of quality are provided. When problems arise, students should make every attempt to find a fair and reasonable solution through the institution's internal complaint procedure, which is required of ACCET accredited institutions and frequently requires the submission of a written complaint. Refer to the institution's written complaint procedure which is published in the institution's catalog or otherwise available from the institution, upon request. Note that ACCET will process complaints which involve ACCET standards and policies and, therefore, are within the scope of the accrediting agency.

In the event that a student has exercised the institution's formal student complaint procedure, and the problem(s) have not been resolved, the student has the right and is encouraged to take the following steps:

1. Complaints should be submitted in writing and mailed, or emailed to the ACCET office. Complaints received by phone will be documented, but the complainant will be requested to submit the complaint in writing.

2. The letter of complaint must contain the following:

   a. Name and location of the ACCET institution;

   b. A detailed description of the alleged problem(s);

   c. The approximate date(s) that the problem(s) occurred;

   d. The names and titles/positions of all individual(s) involved in the problem(s), including faculty, staff, and/or other students;

   e. What was previously done to resolve the complaint, along with evidence demonstrating that the institution's complaint procedure was followed prior to contacting ACCET;

   f. The name, email address, telephone number, and mailing address of the complainant. If the complainant specifically requests that anonymity be maintained, ACCET will not reveal his or her name to the institution involved; and

   g. The status of the complainant with the institution (e.g., current student, former student, etc.).

3. In addition to the letter of complaint, copies of any relevant supporting documentation should be forwarded to ACCET (e.g., student's enrollment agreement, syllabus or course outline, correspondence between the student and the institution).

4. **SEND TO:**
   ACCET
   CHAIR, COMPLAINT REVIEW COMMITTEE
   1722 N Street, NW
   Washington, DC 20036
   Telephone: (202) 955-1113
   Fax: (202) 955-1118 or (202) 955-5306
   Email: complaints@accet.org
   Website: www.accet.org

Note: Complainants will receive an acknowledgement of receipt within 15 days.

# BUSINESS
*Program Attendance Record*

Student: _____     Location: _____

| BUSINESS 1 | BUSINESS 2 |
|---|---|
| Attendance Stamp | Attendance Stamp |

| BUSINESS 3 | BUSINESS 4 |
|---|---|
| Attendance Stamp | Attendance Stamp |

| BUSINESS 5 | BUSINESS 6 |
|---|---|
| Attendance Stamp | Attendance Stamp |

## IMPORTANT NOTES TO STUDENTS REGARDING "THE BECKER PROMISE"

- The attendance sheet must be stamped at the end of each class attended. This is the only acceptable record of your classroom attendance.
- An overall percentage correct of 90% or higher is required on MCQs and simulations to qualify for The Becker Promise.
- Please e-mail documentation to beckerpromise@becker.com or fax to 866-398-7375 no later than 45 days following the completion of each section.
- For Becker Promise redemption policies and procedures, visit becker.com/promise.

## NOTES

# BUSINESS
*Table of Contents*

# Introduction
# BEC

## NOTES

# Business Environment and Concepts (BEC) Overview

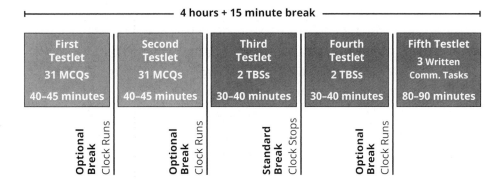

## BEC Exam—Summary Blueprint

| Content Area Allocation | Weight |
|---|---|
| Corporate Governance | 17–27% |
| Economic Concepts and Analysis | 17–27% |
| Financial Management | 11–21% |
| Information Technology | 15–25% |
| Operations Management | 15–25% |
| **Skill Allocation** | **Weight** |
| Evaluation | — |
| Analysis | 20–30% |
| Application | 50–60% |
| Remembering and Understanding | 15–25% |

The complete BEC exam blueprint appears in the back of the book.

## Written Communication—Lecture

For the Business section of the CPA Exam, candidates will be required to complete three written communication tasks. The written communication tasks will appear in the fifth and final testlet of the exam.

- Each written communication will give you a situation, a request for a response, and a series of instructions. Your answer will be typed in the designated response area using a simple word processor.

- For additional guidance on the written communication task, view the written communications lecture in your CPA Exam Review course.

## Becker's CPA Exam Review—Course Introduction

Becker Professional Education's CPA Exam Review products were developed with you, the candidate, in mind. To that end we have developed a series of tools designed to tap all of your learning and retention capabilities. The Becker lectures, comprehensive texts, and course software are designed to be fully integrated to give you the best chance of passing the CPA Exam.

Passing the CPA Exam is difficult, but the professional rewards a CPA enjoys make this a worthwhile challenge. We created our CPA Exam Review after evaluating the needs of CPA candidates and analyzing the CPA Exam over the years. Our course materials comprehensively present topics you must know to pass the examination, teaching you the most effective tactics for learning the material.

## Becker Customer and Academic Support

The Becker Customer and Academic Support area is your source for course updates, supplemental materials, and academic support. Just click on Customer and Academic Support under CPA Resources at:

http://www.becker.com/cpa-review.html

You can access customer service and technical support from Customer and Academic Support or by calling 1-877-CPA-EXAM (outside the U.S. + 1-630-472-2213).

## The Uniform CPA Exam—Overview

### Exam Sections

The CPA Examination consists of four sections:

#### Financial Accounting and Reporting

The *Financial* section consists of a four-hour exam covering financial accounting and reporting for commercial entities under U.S. GAAP, governmental accounting, not-for-profit accounting, and the differences between IFRS and U.S. GAAP.

#### Auditing and Attestation

The *Auditing* section consists of a four-hour exam. This section covers all topics related to auditing, including audit reports and procedures, generally accepted auditing standards, attestation and other engagements, and government auditing.

## Regulation

The *Regulation* section consists of a four-hour exam, combining topics from business law and federal taxation, including the taxation of property transactions, individuals, and entities.

## Business Environment and Concepts

The *Business* section consists of a four-hour exam covering general business topics, such as corporate governance, economics, financial management, information technology, and operations management, including managerial accounting.

### Question Formats

The chart below illustrates the question format breakdown by exam section.

| Section | Multiple-Choice Questions | | Task-Based Simulations or Written Communication Tasks | |
|---|---|---|---|---|
| | Percentage | Number | Percentage | Number |
| Financial | 50% | 66 | 50% | 8 TBSs |
| Auditing | 50% | 72 | 50% | 8 TBSs |
| Regulation | 50% | 76 | 50% | 8 TBSs |
| Business | 50% | 62 | 50% | 4 TBSs/3 WC |

Each exam will contain testlets. A testlet is either a series of multiple-choice questions, a set of task-based simulations, or a set of written communications. For example, the Business examination will contain five testlets. The first two testlets will be multiple-choice questions, the third and fourth testlets will contain task-based simulations, and the last testlet will contain three written communication tasks. Each testlet must be finished and submitted before continuing to the next testlet. Candidates cannot go back to view a previously completed testlet or go forward to view a subsequent testlet before closing and submitting the earlier testlet. Our mock exams contain these types of restrictions so that you can familiarize yourself with the functionality of the CPA Exam.

### Exam Schedule

The computer-based CPA Exam is offered during the first two months and 10 days of each calendar quarter. Candidates can schedule an exam date directly with Prometric (www.prometric.com/cpa) after receiving a notice to schedule.

### Eligibility and Application Requirements

Each state sets its own rules of eligibility for the examination. Please visit www.becker.com/state as soon as possible to determine your eligibility to sit for the exam.

### *Application Deadlines*

With the computer-based exam format, set application deadlines generally do not exist. You should apply as early as possible to ensure that you are able to schedule your desired exam dates. Each state has different application requirements and procedures, so be sure to gain a thorough understanding of the application process for your state.

### *Grading System*

You must pass all four parts of the examination to earn certification as a CPA. You must score 75 or better on a part to receive a passing grade and you must pass all four exams in 18 months or you will lose credit for the earliest exam that you passed.

# Corporate Governance and Financial Risk Management

## Module

# Internal Control Frameworks

## 1 Introduction to COSO

The Committee of Sponsoring Organizations (COSO), an independent private sector initiative, was initially established in the mid-1980s to study the factors that lead to fraudulent financial reporting. The private "sponsoring organizations" include the five major financial professional associations in the United States: the American Accounting Association (AAA), the American Institute of Certified Public Accountants (AICPA), the Financial Executives Institute (FEI), the Institute of Internal Auditors (IIA), and the Institute of Management Accountants (IMA).

In 1992, COSO issued *Internal Control—Integrated Framework* ("the framework") to assist organizations in developing comprehensive assessments of internal control effectiveness.

In 2013, the framework received an update to deal with changes in technology, business models, globalization, outsourcing, and regulatory environment. One significant enhancement to the 2013 update was the formalization of fundamental concepts that were part of the original 1992 framework. Specifically, these fundamental concepts have evolved into 17 principles that have been categorized within the five major internal control components. COSO's framework is widely regarded as an appropriate and comprehensive basis to document the assessment of internal controls over financial reporting.

## 2 COSO Internal Control Framework

The framework is used by company *management* and its board of directors to obtain an initial understanding of what constitutes an effective system of internal control and to provide insight as to when internal controls are being properly applied within the organization. The framework also provides confidence to external stakeholders that an organization has a system of internal control in place that is conducive to achieving its objectives.

### Pass Key

An effective system of internal control requires more than adherence to policies and procedures by management, the board of directors, and the internal auditors. It requires the use of judgment in determining the sufficiency of controls, in applying the proper controls, and in assessing the effectiveness of the system of internal controls. The principles-based approach of the framework supports the emphasis on the importance of management judgment.

## 2.1   Definition of Internal Control

Internal control is a process that is designed and implemented by an organization's management, board of directors, and other employees to provide reasonable assurance that the organization will achieve its operating, reporting, and compliance objectives.

## 2.2   Application to Management and Board

The framework assists an entity's management and board of directors in the following areas:

- Effectively applying internal control within the overall organization, on a divisional (operating) unit level or at a functional level.

- Determining the requirements of an effective system of internal control by ascertaining whether the components and principles exist and are functioning properly.

- Allowing judgment and flexibility in the design and implementation of the system of internal control within all operational and functional areas of the organization.

- Identifying and analyzing risks and then developing acceptable actions to mitigate or minimize these risks to an acceptable level.

- Eliminating redundant, ineffective, or inefficient controls.

- Extending internal control application beyond an organization's financial reporting.

## 2.3   Application to Stakeholders

The framework also provides value to external stakeholders and other parties that interact with the organization by providing:

- Greater understanding of what constitutes an effective system of internal controls.

- Greater confidence that management will be able to eliminate ineffective, redundant, or inefficient controls.

- Greater confidence that the board has effective oversight of the organization's internal controls.

- Improved confidence that the organization will achieve its stated objectives and will be capable of identifying, analyzing, and responding to risks affecting the organization.

## 2.4   COSO Cube

The 2013 framework continues to use a cube to depict the relationship between an entity's objectives, integrated internal control components, and organizational structure. The three categories of *objectives* (operations, xreporting, and compliance) are shown as columns on the cube, and the five *internal control components* (control environment, risk assessment, control activities, information and communication, and monitoring activities) are depicted as rows. Additionally, the entity's *organizational structure* (entity level, division, operating unit, and function) is shown on the cube as a third dimension.

*Internal Control—Integrated Framework,* © 2013 Committee of Sponsoring Organizations of the Treadway Commission (COSO). Used with permission.

## 2.5    Framework Objectives

There are three *categories of objectives* within the framework.

**1.    Operations Objectives**

*Operations objectives* relate to the effectiveness and efficiency of an entity's operations. This category includes financial and operational performance goals as well as ensuring that the assets of the organization are adequately safeguarded against potential losses.

**2.    Reporting Objectives**

*Reporting objectives* pertain to the reliability, timeliness, and transparency of an entity's external and internal financial and nonfinancial reporting as established by regulators, accounting standard setters, or the firm's internal policies.

**3.    Compliance Objectives**

*Compliance objectives* are established to ensure the entity is adhering to all applicable laws and regulations.

## 2.6    Components of Internal Control (**CRIME**)

The updated framework retained the original five integrated *components* of internal control, including the control environment, risk assessment, information and communication, monitoring activities, and (existing) control activities. These components and the 17 related fundamental principles are needed to achieve the three *objectives* of internal control.

Each of the 17 principles is intended to be suitable to all entities and is presumed to be relevant. However, management may determine that a principle is not relevant to a component.

In addition, the framework introduces 81 points of focus. Some points of focus may not be suitable or relevant, and others may be identified. They are intended to facilitate designing, implementing, and conducting internal control by providing examples. They are not intended to be used as a checklist, and there is no requirement to separately assess whether points of focus are in place.

### Pass Key

The COSO framework does not prescribe which controls an entity should implement for effective internal control. Instead, an organization's selection of controls requires management's judgment based on factors unique to the entity.

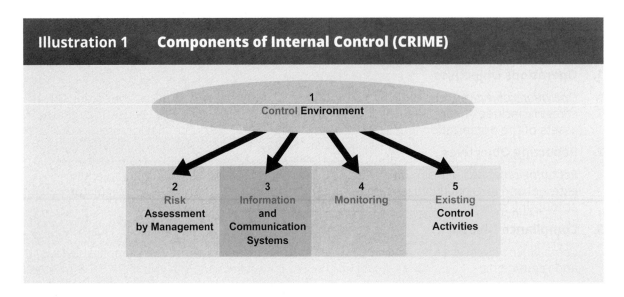

**Illustration 1    Components of Internal Control (CRIME)**

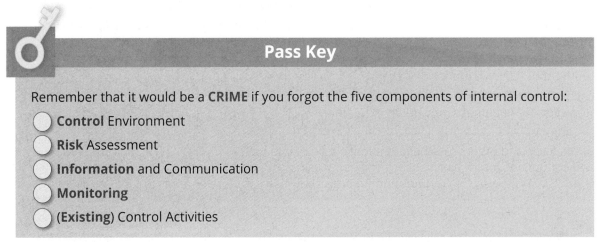

## Pass Key

Remember that it would be a **CRIME** if you forgot the five components of internal control:

- **Control** Environment
- **Risk** Assessment
- **Information** and Communication
- **Monitoring**
- **(Existing)** Control Activities

### 2.6.1   Control Environment

The control environment includes the processes, structures, and standards that provide the foundation for an entity to establish a system of internal control. The importance of internal control and expected standards of conduct is established through a "tone at the top" approach taken by the senior management and board of directors of an entity. The five principles related to the control environment are:

1.  **Commitment to Ethics and Integrity:** There is a commitment to ethical values and overall integrity throughout the organization. Points of focus include setting the tone at the top, establishing standards of conduct, evaluating adherence to standards of conduct, and addressing deviations in a timely manner.

2.  **Board Independence and Oversight:** The board is independent from management and oversees the development and performance of internal control. Points of focus include establishing oversight responsibilities and providing oversight for the system of internal control.

3.  **Organizational Structure:** Management establishes an organizational structure. Points of focus include establishing reporting lines, as well as defining, assigning, and limiting authorities and responsibilities that are appropriate to the organization's objectives.

4. **Commitment to Competence:** There is a commitment to hire, develop, and retain competent employees. Other points of focus include evaluating competence and addressing shortcomings in addition to succession planning.

5. **Accountability:** Individuals are held accountable for their internal control responsibilities. Points of focus include establishing performance measures, incentives, and rewards, and evaluating those for ongoing relevance while considering excessive pressures.

### 2.6.2 Risk Assessment

Risk assessment is an entity's identification and analysis of risks to the achievement of its objectives. The four principles related to risk assessment are:

1. **Specify Objectives:** The organization creates objectives that allow for identification and assessment of the risks related to those objectives. Points of focus include identifying objectives that reflect management's choices while complying with applicable accounting standards, laws, and regulations.

2. **Identify and Analyze Risks:** The organization identifies risks across the entity and analyzes risks in order to determine how the risks should be managed. Points of focus include analyzing internal and external factors, involving appropriate levels of management and determining how to respond to risks.

3. **Consider Potential for Fraud:** The organization considers the potential for fraud in assessing risks. Points of focus include assessing incentives and pressures, opportunities and attitudes, and rationalizations.

4. **Identify and Assess Changes:** The organization identifies and assesses changes that could significantly affect the system of internal control. Points of focus include assessing changes in the external environment, business model, and leadership.

### 2.6.3 Information and Communication

Information and communication systems support the identification, capture, and exchange of information in a timely and useful manner. The three principles related to information and communications are:

1. **Obtain and Use Information:** The organization obtains or generates and uses relevant, high-quality information to support the functioning of internal control. Points of focus include management identifying and defining information requirements within the internal control component level.

2. **Internally Communicate Information:** The organization internally communicates information necessary to support the functioning of internal controls, including relevant objectives and responsibilities. Points of focus include the flow of information up, down, and across the organization using a variety of methods and channels.

3. **Communicate With External Parties:** The organization communicates with external parties regarding matters that affect the functioning of internal control. Points of focus include management having open, two-way external communication channels using a variety of methods and channels.

### 2.6.4 Monitoring Activities

Monitoring is the process of assessing the quality of internal control performance over time by assessing the design and operation of controls on a timely basis and taking the necessary corrective actions. The two principles related to monitoring activities are:

1. **Ongoing and/or Separate Evaluations:** The organization selects, develops, and performs ongoing and/or separate evaluations to ascertain whether the components of internal control are present and functioning. One point of focus is to consider establishing baseline understandings.

2. **Communication of Deficiencies:** The organization evaluates and communicates internal control deficiencies in a timely manner to parties responsible for taking corrective action. One point of focus is monitoring corrective actions.

### 2.6.5   (Existing) Control Activities

Control activities are set forth by an entity's policies and procedures to ensure that the directives initiated by management to mitigate risks are performed.

Control activities may be detective or preventive in nature and may include automated and manual activities (e.g., approvals, reconciliations, verifications). Segregation of duties is usually part of the control activities developed by an organization, and when not practical, management should develop alternative controls. The three principles related to control activities are:

1. **Select and Develop Control Activities:** The organization selects and develops control activities that contribute to the mitigation of risks to acceptable levels. Points of focus include integrating with risk assessment when selecting activities and considering entity-specific factors.

2. **Select and Develop Technology Controls:** The organization selects and develops general control activities over technology to support the achievement of objectives. Points of focus include determining dependencies between the use of technology in business processes and establishing relevant technology infrastructure control activities.

3. **Deployment of Policies and Procedures:** The organization deploys control activities through policies that establish what is expected and procedures that put policies into action. Points of focus include establishing responsibility and accountability for executing policies and procedures and taking corrective action.

## Pass Key

The candidate should be familiar with the five components of internal control (in bold) and each of the 17 principles within the components.

**Control Environment**

- Commitment to ethical values and integrity
- Board independence and oversight
- Organizational structure
- Commitment to competence
- Accountability

**Risk Assessment**

- Specify objectives
- Identify and analyze risks
- Consider the potential for fraud
- Identify and assess changes

(continued)

(continued)

**Information and Communication**

- Obtain and use information
- Internally communicate information
- Communicate with external parties

**Monitoring Activities**

- Ongoing and/or separate evaluations
- Communication of deficiencies

**(Existing) Control Activities**

- Select and develop control activities
- Select and develop technology controls
- Deploy through policies and procedures

---

### Illustration 2    COSO Application

- **Risk:** Management is unaware of risks that could affect the company.

  — **Component:** Risk assessment.

  — **Principle:** The company identifies risks to achieving its objectives and analyzes risks to determine how the risks should be managed.

  — **Control Activity:** Periodic risk assessments are reviewed by management, including internal audit assessments.

- **Risk:** Employees act in an unethical or unlawful manner.

  — **Component:** Control environment.

  — **Principle:** The company demonstrates a commitment to integrity and ethical values.

  — **Control Activity:** A code of conduct or ethics policy exists and includes provisions about conflicts of interest, related party transactions, illegal acts, and the monitoring of the code by management, the audit committee, and board of directors.

## 2.7 Effective Internal Control

### 2.7.1 General Requirements

The framework indicates that an effective system of internal control provides reasonable assurance that the entity's objectives will be achieved. Under the framework, an effective system of internal control requires:

- All five components and 17 principles that are relevant to be both *present* and *functioning*.

    - **Present (Design):** The term "present" means that the components and relevant principles are included in the design and implementation of the internal control system.

    - **Functioning (Operating Effectively):** The term "functioning" demonstrates that the components and relevant principles are currently operating as designed in the internal control system.

- That all five components operate together as an *integrated* system in order to reduce, to an acceptable level, the risk that the entity will not achieve its objectives.

### 2.7.2 Specific Requirements

To be considered an effective system of internal control, senior management and the board must have reasonable assurance that the entity:

- Achieves effective and efficient operations when:

    - external threats are considered unlikely to have a significant impact on the achievement of objectives; or

    - the organization can reasonably predict and mitigate the impact of external events to an acceptable level.

- Understands the extent to which operations are managed effectively and efficiently when:

    - external events may have a significant impact on the achievement of objectives; or

    - the organization can reasonably predict and mitigate the impact of external events to an acceptable level.

- Complies with all applicable rules, regulations, external standards, and laws.

- Prepares reports that are in conformity with the entity's reporting objectives and all applicable standards, rules, and regulations.

### Pass Key

The framework requires judgment in designing, implementing, and conducting internal control and in assessing the effectiveness of internal control.

### 2.7.3 Ineffective Internal Control: COSO

Internal control deficiencies are shortcomings in a component or components and relevant principles that reduce the likelihood of an entity achieving its objectives.

Although U.S. GAAS uses the terms "significant deficiency" and "material weakness," the COSO framework uses the term "major deficiency."

A major deficiency represents a material internal control deficiency, or combination of deficiencies, that significantly reduces the likelihood that an organization can achieve its objectives.

When a major deficiency is identified pertaining to the presence and functioning of a component or relevant principle, or with respect to the components operating together in an integrated manner, the entity may not conclude that it has met the requirements for an effective internal control system under the COSO framework.

## 2.8 Internal Control (Framework) Limitations

Although internal control provides reasonable assurance that a firm will achieve its stated objectives, it does not prevent bad decisions or eliminate all external events that may prevent the achievement of the entity's operational goals. The following are inherent limitations that may exist even in an effective internal control system:

- Breakdowns in internal control due to errors or human failure
- Faulty or biased judgment used in decision making
- Issues relating to the suitability of the entity's objectives
- External events beyond the control of the entity
- Circumvention of controls through collusion
- Management override of internal controls

| Question 1 | CPA-06748 |
|---|---|

The external auditors for the Horace Company assess the achievement of internal control objectives each year and communicate the assessment to management and the board. Communication by the external auditor illustrates which principle of the information and communication component of the Committee of Sponsoring Organizations' Integrated Framework?

    **a.** Financial Reporting Information

    **b.** Internal Control Information

    **c.** Internal Communication

    **d.** External Communication

| Question 2 | CPA-06483 |
|---|---|

A company that retains a CPA with the appropriate knowledge, skills, and abilities to prepare timely and effective financial reporting is applying the ideas from which principle of effective internal control over financial reporting?

    **a.** Integrity and ethical values

    **b.** Management philosophy and operating style

    **c.** Accountability

    **d.** Financial reporting competencies

# 3   Applying the Internal Control Framework

The COSO framework may be used to manage the application of internal controls, evaluate their effectiveness, and serve as a basis for management's assertions regarding the existence or absence of internal control deficiencies. Inherent in both the concept and application of the framework is the existence of risk to achievement of objectives and the implementation of controls to mitigate risk. Applying the COSO internal control framework is intended to reduce assessed risk to acceptable levels.

## 3.1   Using the COSO Framework Document

Management will logically compile and document the internal control assessment using the following steps as supported by the COSO framework guidance:

- **Overall Assessment:** Overall assessments are supported by component evaluations.

- **Component Evaluation:** Component evaluations are supported by principal evaluations.

- **Principal Evaluation:** Principal evaluations serve as the source for isolating and defining internal control deficiencies.

- **Summary of Internal Control Deficiencies (if any):** Internal control deficiencies are summarized and impact the overall assessment.

This overall assessment may trigger a reevalution of the components.

## 3.2   Common Risks Identified Using the COSO Framework

### 3.2.1   Material Omission or Misstatement

Management identifies risks that could individually or in combination result in material omissions or misstatements of the financial statements. The process for evaluating risk is dynamic and ongoing. Risks vary as entities operate in:

- Multiple industries, markets, and geographic areas

- Multiple regulatory environments with different standards

- Transactional environments with numerous contracts

- An active merger, acquisition, and divestiture environment

- A dynamic technological environment

- A high executive turnover environment

### 3.2.2   Fraud

The risk of fraud is typically characterized by either fraudulent financial reporting (intentional misstatements of financial reports designed to deceive users) and misappropriation of assets (theft).

Specific risks encountered include:

- Management bias in exercising judgment

- The degree of estimates and judgments underlying accounting and reporting

- Incentives for fraud (e.g., bonuses)

- Attitudes and rationalizations by individuals
- Unusual transactions
- Vulnerability to management override

A system of internal control over external financial reporting is designed and implemented to prevent or detect in a timely manner any material omissions within or misstatements of the financial statements due to error or fraud.

### 3.2.3 Management Override

Management override refers to actions taken by management in an attempt to override controls for personal gain. Management override of controls can lead to fraud.

## Pass Key

Management intervention is not the same as management override. It represents the fully appropriate involvement of management in unusual transactions.

### 3.2.4 Illegal Acts

Illegal acts represent violations of government regulations that could have a material impact on the financial statements. Assessments of potential illegal acts include:

- Existence of investigations
- Reports of regulatory examiners
- Payments for unspecified services
- Delinquent tax returns

## 3.3 Controls

Management considers how the risk of material omissions and misstatements should be managed across the entity. Management selects, develops, and deploys controls to effectively apply principles within each component to respond to assessed risk. As part of its response, management considers:

- Laws, rules, regulations, and standards that apply to the entity
- The nature of the entity's business and the markets in which it operates
- Scope and nature of the operating model
- Competence of personnel
- Use and dependence on technology

### 3.3.1 Selection and Development of Controls

The selection and development of controls can include any of the following approaches:

- Use workshops or control activity inventories to map risks to controls.
- Implement control activities over outsourced functions.
- Consider the types of control activities.

◼ Consider alternative control to segregation of duties.

◼ Identify incompatible functions.

### 3.3.2 Selection and Development of General Controls Over Technology

The selection and development of general controls over technology can include any of the following approaches:

◼ Use risk-control matrices to document technology dependencies.

◼ Evaluate end-user computing.

◼ Implement or monitor control activities when outsourcing IT functions.

◼ Configure the IT infrastructure to support restricted access and segregation of duties.

◼ Configure the IT system to support the complete, accurate, and valid processing of transactions and data.

◼ Administer security and access.

◼ Apply a system development life cycle over packaged and internally developed software.

### 3.3.3 Deploying Controls Through Policies and Procedures

Deploying controls through policies and procedures may include any of the following approaches:

◼ Develop and document policies and procedures.

◼ Deploy control activities through the business unit of functional leaders.

◼ Conduct regular and ad hoc assessments of control activities.

# 1 Introduction to Enterprise Risk Management

In 2004, COSO issued *Enterprise Risk Management (ERM)—Integrated Framework* ("the framework") to assist organizations in developing a comprehensive response to risk management. In recognition of the changing complexity of risk, the emergence of new risks, and the enhanced awareness of risk management by both boards and executive oversight bodies, COSO published *Enterprise Risk Management—Integrating With Strategy and Performance* in 2017.

According to COSO, "Risk is the possibility that events will occur and affect the achievement of strategy and business objectives."

## 1.1 Value

The underlying premise of ERM is that every entity exists to provide value for stakeholders and that all entities face risk in the pursuit of value for their stakeholders. Management decisions will affect the development of value, including its *creation, preservation, erosion, and realization*.

### Pass Key

Value is defined by the type of entity.

**For-profit commercial entities:** Value is usually shaped by strategies that balance market opportunities against the risks of pursuing those opportunities.

**Not-for-profit and governmental entities:** Value may be shaped by delivering goods and services that balance the opportunity to serve the broader community against any associated risk.

### 1.1.1 Value Creation

Value is created when benefits of value exceed the cost of resources used. Resources may include people, financial capital, technology, process, and brand (market presence).

### Illustration 1    Value Creation

Silky & Shiny & Smooth Skin Products has a full line of skin care products. The company decides to develop shampoos and conditioners using a companion product line. The successful and profitable launch of the new product line represents value creation.

Material from *Enterprise Risk Management—Integrating With Strategy and Performance,* © 2017 Committee of Sponsoring Organizations of the Treadway Commission (COSO). Used with permission.

### 1.1.2 Value Preservation

Value is preserved when ongoing operations efficiently and effectively sustain created benefits. High customer satisfaction with profitable product lines is evidence of value preservation.

### 1.1.3 Value Erosion

Value is eroded when faulty strategy and inefficient/ineffective operations cause value to decline.

---

**Illustration 2     Value Erosion**

Silky & Shiny & Smooth Skin Products has a full line of skin care products. The company decides to develop shampoos and conditioners using a companion product line. The unsuccessful launch of the new product line represents value erosion. Not only are financial resources lost, but the brand name suffers as well.

---

### 1.1.4 Value Realization

Value is realized when benefits created by the organization are received by stakeholders in either monetary or nonmonetary form.

---

**Illustration 3     Value Realization**

Value realization is illustrated by increased profitability and stock prices for company owners, increased customer satisfaction, consistent product and brand usage, market leadership, and consistent innovation that not only enhances the company but improves the economy.

---

## 1.2 Mission, Vision, and Core Values

Mission, vision, and core values define what an entity strives to be and how it wants to conduct business.

### 1.2.1 Mission

Mission represents the core purpose of the entity. The mission represents why the company exists and what it hopes to accomplish.

### 1.2.2 Vision

Vision represents the aspirations of the entity and what it hopes to achieve over time.

### 1.2.3 Core Values

Core values represent an organization's beliefs and ideals about what is good or bad, acceptable and unacceptable, and they influence the behavior of the organization.

Each enterprise is unique. The ERM framework helps identify the individual features that make an enterprise stand out.

# 2    Definition of Enterprise Risk Management

As defined by COSO:

> Enterprise risk management is the *culture, capabilities, and practices, integrated with strategy-setting and performance*, that organizations rely on to *manage risk* in creating, preserving, and realizing *value*.

## 2.1    Culture

Culture represents the collective thinking of the people within an organization. Individuals have unique points of reference that influence how they identify, assess, and respond to risk. Culture plays an important role in shaping decisions regarding risk.

### Pass Key

Core values correlate with culture.

## 2.2    Capabilities (Competitive Advantage)

Competitive advantage produces value for an entity. Exploitation of competitive advantage and adaptation to change are skill sets embedded within ERM.

## 2.3    Practices

ERM is an organizational practice continually applied to the entire scope of activities of the business. It is part of management decisions at all levels of the entity. It is neither static nor is it an adjunct or add-on to the business.

## 2.4    Integration With Strategy-Setting and Performance

Strategy is set in a manner that aligns with mission and vision. Business objectives flow from strategy. Business objectives drive the activities of all business units and functions.

ERM integrates with strategy-setting and operating activities to promote an understanding of how risk potentially affects the entity overall.

### Pass Key

Mission and vision correlate with strategy and business objectives.

## 2.5    Managing Risk Linked to Value

ERM practices are intended to provide the management and the board with a reasonable expectation that the organization's overall strategy and business objectives can be achieved. Reasonable expectation means the amount of risk of achieving strategy and business objectives is appropriate for that entity.

An organization must continually review and manage the types and amounts of risk it is willing to accept in its pursuit of value.

### 2.5.1    Risk Appetite

Risk appetite represents the types and amounts of risk, on a broad level, that an organization is willing to accept in pursuit of value. Risk appetite is a range rather than a specific limit and provides guidance on the practices an organization is encouraged to pursue or not pursue.

- Risk appetite is expressed first in mission and vision.

- Risk appetite varies between products, business units, or over time in line with changing capabilities for managing risk and must be flexible enough to adapt to changing business conditions without approvals.

### 2.5.2    Relationship of Value and Risk Appetite

Managing risk within risk appetite enhances an organization's ability to create, preserve, and realize value. ERM seeks to align anticipated value creation with risk appetite and capabilities for managing risk over time.

# 3    Enterprise Risk Management Themes and Terms

Enterprise Risk Management encompasses numerous themes and uses very specific terminology.

An entity's culture, driven by core values, defines a mission to create value and recognizes that an inventory of risks exist that threaten the achievement of the mission and the creation of value. The application of ERM is intended to provide management with a reasonable expectation of success.

- **Risk Inventory:** All risk that could impact an entity.

- **Reasonable Expectation:** The amount of risk of having strategy and business objectives that is appropriate for an entity, recognizing that no one can predict risk with precision.

Core values affect the amount of risk an organization is willing to accept within the context of the business. The organization makes overall decisions regarding risk appetite and, based on that determination, assesses its risk capacity and develops a risk profile.

- **Business Context:** The trends, events, relationships, and other factors that may influence, clarify, or change an entity's current and future strategy and business objectives.

- **Risk Capacity:** The maximum amount of risk that an entity is able to absorb in the pursuit of strategy and business objectives.

- **Risk Profile:** A composite view of the risk assumed at a particular level of the entity or aspect of the business that positions management to consider the types, severity, and interdependencies of risk and how they may affect performance relative to the strategy and business objectives.

Although risk is evaluated at a departmental and divisional level, entity-wide risks use a portfolio view. Related ideas include the ability of the entity to absorb risk and its ongoing management efforts.

- **Portfolio View:** A composite view of risk the entity faces which positions management and the board to consider the types, severity, and interdependencies of risk and how they may affect the entity's performance relative to its strategy and business objectives.

- **Organizational Sustainability:** The ability of an entity to withstand the impact of large-scale events.

- **Performance Management:** The measurement of efforts to achieve or exceed the strategy and business objectives.

# 4   Enterprise Risk Management Interrelationships

Enterprise Risk Management is depicted as a series of sequential yet intertwined components that drive an organization toward enhanced value.

The tone at the top and communication are linked, and weave into the similarly linked efforts to develop overall strategy, specific business objectives, and manage performance to the achievement of value.

Mission, vision, and values drive the process but are also affected by performance, as management constantly reviews its risks and its ability to create value.

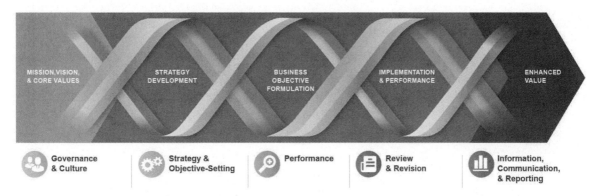

*Enterprise Risk Management—Integrating With Strategy and Performance,* © 2017 Committee of Sponsoring Organizations of the Treadway Commission (COSO). Used with permission.

# 5   Components of Enterprise Risk Management

Enterprise risk management is defined by five interrelated components and is supported by 20 risk management principles. The components somewhat resemble the COSO cube for internal control but address the broader issues of risk as it impacts an entity.

1. Governance and Culture

2. Strategy and Objective-Setting

3. Performance

4. Review and Revision

5. Information, Communication, and Reporting (Ongoing)

## Pass Key

Knowing the logical order of the enterprise management framework has been a topic of released questions. Memorize the five components as you **GO PRO** with ERM.

**G**overnance and Culture
Strategy and **O**bjective-Setting
**P**erformance
**R**eview and Revision
Information, Communication, and Reporting (**O**ngoing information-gathering and feedback)

## Pass Key

The five components of ERM are supported by 20 principles. Recollecting which principles support which components is a potential source of multiple-choice points, summarized below:

| Governance and Culture | Strategy and Objective-Setting | Performance | Review and Revision | Information, Communication, and Reporting (Ongoing) |
|---|---|---|---|---|
| DOVES | SOAR | VAPIR | SIR | TIP |

| | | |
|---|---|---|
| Governance and Culture | D | Defines desired culture |
| | O | Exercises board oversight |
| | V | Demonstrates commitment to core values |
| | E | Attracts, develops, and retains capable individuals (employees) |
| | S | Establishes operating structure |
| Strategy and Objective-Setting | S | Evaluates alternative strategies |
| | O | Formulates business objectives |
| | A | Analyzes business context |
| | R | Defines risk appetite |
| Performance | V | Develops portfolio view |
| | A | Assesses severity of risk |
| | P | Prioritizes risk |
| | I | Identifies risks (events) |
| | R | Implements risk responses |
| Review and Revision | S | Assesses substantial change |
| | I | Pursues improvement in Enterprise Risk Management |
| | R | Reviews risk and performance |
| Information, Communication, and Reporting (Ongoing) | T | Leverages information and technology |
| | I | Communicates risk information |
| | P | Reports on risk, culture, and performance |

## 5.1    Governance and Culture (**DOVES**)

Governance and culture together form a base for all other components of enterprise risk management.

- Governance sets the entity's tone at the top, serves to endorse the importance of enterprise risk management, and establishes oversight responsibilities for ERM.

- Culture is reflected in decision making.

### 5.1.1    Exercises Board **O**versight

The board of directors provides oversight for an entity's strategy and carries out governance responsibilities to support management in achieving strategy and business objectives. The board is expected to have the skills, experience, and business knowledge to understand the entity's strategy; stay informed on relevant issues; and maintain an active and accountable role that is independent and conscious of potential bias.

| Illustration 4      Board Oversight |
| --- |
| Active and accountable board oversight is often characterized by frequent conversations with management to determine the suitability of ERM design and effectiveness in enhancing value. |

### 5.1.2    Establishes Operating **S**tructure

Operating structures are established to pursue strategy and business objectives. Operating structures describe how an entity organizes and carries out its day-to-day operations and contributes to the alignment of risk management practices with core values.

### 5.1.3    Defines **D**esired Culture

The organization defines the desired behaviors that characterize the entity's desired culture. An entity's culture influences how the organization identifies risk, what types of risk it accepts, and how it manages risk. Culture is a spectrum that progresses from Risk Averse to Risk Neutral and extends to Risk Aggressive.

| Pass Key |
| --- |
| The ability of an organization to successfully achieve its strategy and business objectives is impeded when the behaviors and decisions of the organization (culture) do not align with its core values. |

### 5.1.4    Demonstrates Commitment to Core **V**alues

The organization demonstrates a commitment to the entity's core values. Without support from the top of the organization, risk awareness can be undermined and risk-inspired decisions may be inconsistent with those values.

### 5.1.5  Attracts, Develops, and Retains Capable Individuals (Employees)

Commitment to building human capital in alignment with the strategy and business objectives is a principle of the governance and culture component. The ultimate accountability for development and retention of capable individuals starts with the board and its selection of executive leadership. The selection of team members is typically delegated to appropriate levels of management. Human resources professionals assist management in assembling competent team members through consideration of the following factors:

- Knowledge, skills, and experience

- Nature and degree of judgment and limitations of authority to be applied to a specific position

- The costs and benefit of different skill levels and experience

The ongoing process of attracting, developing, and retaining individuals includes attracting or seeking out competent individuals and training them, then mentoring, evaluating, and ultimately retaining them with appropriate incentives and rewards.

No less important than maintenance of the current talent pool is preparation for succession, a process that may involve identifying more than one person who could fill a crucial role.

## 5.2  Strategy and Objective-Setting (**SOAR**)

Enterprise risk management is integrated into the entity's strategic plan through the process of setting strategy and business objectives that considers both internal and external factors and their effect on risk framed by business context.

- An organization sets its risk appetite in conjunction with strategy-setting.

- The business objectives allow strategy to be put into practice and shape the entity's day-to-day operations and priorities.

### 5.2.1  Analyzes Business Context

Consideration of the potential effects of business context on risk profile is a principle supporting the strategy and objective-setting component. Business context may be dynamic, complex, and even unpredictable. Business context usually considers both external and internal environments.

### 5.2.2  Defines Risk Appetite

The organization defines risk appetite in the context of creating, preserving, and realizing value.

- Entities consider risk appetite in qualitative terms, while others may be quantitative. The best approach for an entity is one that aligns with the analyses used to assess risk in general, whether that is qualitative or quantitative.

- General terms such as "low appetite" or "high appetite" are sufficient expressions of risk appetite. Referencing "targets," "ranges," "ceilings," or "floors" may also be used.

Ultimately, risk appetite is expressed in the context of objectives.

### 5.2.3  Evaluates Alternative Strategies

Evaluation of alternative strategies and the potential effect on risk profile is a principle supporting the strategy and objective-setting component. Strategy is evaluated from two perspectives:

- The possibility that the strategy does not align with the mission, vision, and core values of the entity

- The implications from the chosen strategy

Misaligned strategies may impede achievement of the mission and fulfillment of the entity's mission.

The implications of each strategy include risks and opportunities of each strategy. Identified risks collectively form a risk profile and serve as the basis for developing and evaluating alternative strategies.

- The development of alternative strategies considers the supporting assumptions relating to the business context, resources, and capabilities. The level of confidence associated with each supporting assumption will affect the risk profile of each of the strategies.

- Development of a risk profile for a strategy enables consideration of the types and amount of risk faced by the organization.

Successful strategy is carried out within the organization's risk appetite. Strategy may change as the evaluation of risk or the ability to perform changes.

### 5.2.4   Formulates Business Objectives

Business objectives are the measurable steps that an organization makes to achieve its strategy. The alignment of business objectives to strategy supports the entity in achieving its mission and vision.

- Business objectives are developed that are specific, measurable or observable, attainable, and relevant (to the achievement of strategy).

- Business objectives may relate to financial performance, customer aspirations, operational efficiency, compliance obligations, or innovation.

The organization sets targets to monitor the performance of the entity and support the achievement of its business objectives.

Monitoring performance includes the concept of tolerance. Tolerance is the range of acceptable outcomes related to achieving a business objective within the risk appetite. Tolerance is also referred to as the acceptable variance in performance.

## 5.3   Performance (VAPIR)

Identification and assessment of risks that may affect an entity's ability to achieve its strategy and business objectives represent the performance component.

- Organizations identify and assess risks that may affect the achievement of strategy and business objectives.

- Risk is prioritized according to severity and in consideration of the entity's risk appetite.

- The organization then selects risk responses and monitors performance for change.

- The resulting portfolio view describes the amount of risk the entity has assumed in the pursuit of its strategy and entity-level business objectives.

### 5.3.1   Identifies Risks

Organizations identify risks that affect their performance in achieving strategy and business objectives. New and emerging risks are identified, and currently assessed risks are reevaluated using various techniques.

### 5.3.2  Assesses Severity of Risk

The severity of risk is evaluated after it has been identified. Resources and capabilities are deployed to keep the risk within the entity's risk appetite based on the assessment.

The severity of a risk is assessed at multiple levels (across divisions, functions, and operating units) in line with the business objectives it may affect. Risks deemed severe at the operating level may be less of a concern at the division or entity level.

Severity measures relate to impact (result or effect of the risk) and likelihood (possibility of the risk occurring). Likelihood may be expressed qualitatively or quantitatively.

Risk assessment includes the concepts of inherent risk, target residual risk, and actual residual risk.

- Inherent risk is the risk to an entity in the absence of any direct or focused actions by management to alter its severity.

- Target residual risk is the amount of risk that an entity prefers to assume in the pursuit of its strategy and business objectives knowing that management will implement or has implemented direct or focused actions to alter the severity of the risk.

- Actual residual risk is the risk remaining after management has taken action.

The organization strives to identify triggers that will prompt a reassessment of severity when required.

### 5.3.3  Prioritizes Risk

Prioritization of risk as a basis for determining risk response is a principle underlying the performance component. Risks that result in the entity approaching the risk appetite for specific business objectives are typically given higher priority.

### 5.3.4  Implements Risk Responses

Risk responses are generally classified as:

- **Accept:** No action is taken to change the severity of the risk. Acceptance is most appropriate as a risk response when risk to strategy and business objectives is within the entity's risk appetite.

- **Avoid:** Action is taken to remove the risk (leaving a line of business, etc.). Avoidance is appropriate when an entity cannot devise a risk response that will mitigate the risk to objectives.

- **Pursue:** Action is taken that accepts increased risk to achieve improved performance. Pursuit of risk is appropriate when management understands the nature and extent of any changes required to achieve desired performance while not exceeding the boundaries of acceptable tolerance.

- **Reduce:** Action is taken to reduce the severity of the risk. Management designs risk mitigation techniques to reduce risk to an amount of severity aligned with the target risk profile and risk appetite.

- **Share:** Action is taken to reduce the severity of the risk. Sharing risk with such techniques as outsourcing and insurance lower residual risk in alignment with risk appetite.

Risk responses may trigger a review of strategic and business objectives.

### 5.3.5 Develops Portfolio View

The organization develops and evaluates a portfolio (entity-wide) view of risk. A portfolio view allows management and the board to consider the type, severity, and interdependencies of risks and how they may affect performance and align with the overall risk appetite.

## 5.4 Review and Revision (SIR)

By reviewing enterprise risk management capabilities and practices, and the entity's performance relative to its targets, an organization can consider how well the enterprise risk management capabilities and practices have increased value over time and will continue to drive value in light of substantial changes.

### 5.4.1 Assesses Substantial Change

The entity identifies and assesses changes that may substantially affect strategy and business objectives; it is a principle supporting the review and revision component. Assessments may include identifying internal and external environmental changes related to the business context as well as changes in culture.

### 5.4.2 Reviews Risk and Performance

The organization reviews entity performance and considers risk, including the capabilities and practices of the organization. Evaluations may relate to potentially incorrect assumptions, poorly implemented practices, entity capability, or cultural factors.

### 5.4.3 Pursues Improvement in Enterprise Risk Management

The organization pursues improvement of enterprise risk management. Opportunities to revisit and improve efficiency and usefulness may occur in any area.

## 5.5 Information, Communication, and Reporting (Ongoing) (TIP)

Communication is the continual, iterative process of obtaining information and sharing it throughout the entity.

- Management uses relevant information from both internal and external sources to support enterprise risk management.

- The organization leverages information systems to capture, process, and manage data and information. By using information that applies to all components, the organization reports on risk, culture, and performance.

### 5.5.1 Leverages Information and Technology

The organization leverages the entity's information and technology systems to support the organization with relevant information. Relevant information helps the organization be more agile in its decision making and provides a competitive advantage.

---

**Illustration 5  How Information Supports Decisions**

Different types of information support different levels of the decision making:

**Governance and culture-related practices.** The organization may need information on the standards of conduct and individual performance in relation to those standards.

**Strategy and objective-setting practices.** The organization may need information on stakeholder expectations about risk appetite.

**Performance-related practices.** Organizations may need information on their competitors to assess changes in the amount of risk.

**Review and revision-related practices.** Organizations may need information on emerging trends in enterprise risk management.

---

Information is generally characterized as structured (e.g., database files, etc.) and unstructured (e.g., volumes of e-mail, photos, etc.). The ability to accumulate and analyze data effectively is constantly evolving. Classifying information using common risk categories helps with risk assessment (e.g., information from internal audit, information management, etc.)

Data management is integral to risk-aware decisions. Effective data management considers three key elements:

- Data and information governance promote standardization of high-quality data.

- Processes and controls promote data reliability.

- Data management architecture refers to the fundamental design of the technology. Design is driven by value defined by management's needs.

### 5.5.2 Communicates Risk Information

The organization uses communication channels to support enterprise risk management. Communications are made to internal and external stakeholders and with the board of directors. Communication techniques vary widely. Communication methods must be evaluated for effectiveness.

### 5.5.3 Reports on Risk, Culture, and Performance

The organization reports on risk, culture, and performance at multiple levels and across the entity. Reporting may be either quantitative or qualitative and be made to a wide range of users, including management, risk owners, assurance providers, external stakeholders, and others.

Types of reports include:

- Portfolio view of risk (outlining the severity of risk at the entity level)

- Profile view of risk (outlining the severity of risk at different levels within the entity, e.g., a division, etc.)

Reporting on culture seeks to measure and provide feedback on behavior and attitudes. Reporting can be complex and may be embodied by:

- Analytics of cultural trends
- Benchmarking to other entities or standards
- Compensation schemes and the potential influence on decision making
- "Lessons learned" analysis
- Reviews of behavioral trends
- Surveys of risk attitudes and risk awareness

The frequency of reporting should be commensurate with the severity and priority of risk.

| Question 1 | CPA-06480 |
| --- | --- |

According to the Committee of Sponsoring Organizations (COSO) of the Treadway Commission, which of the following components of enterprise risk management addresses an entity's commitment to core values?

    **a.** Governance and Culture

    **b.** Strategy and Objective-Setting

    **c.** Performance

    **d.** Review and Revision

| Question 2 | CPA-06754 |
| --- | --- |

Able Corporation owns numerous businesses along the coast of Florida. The company's management has identified business interruption events as a potential risk resulting from storm damage caused by hurricanes. The company elects to not only insure its properties but to "buy down" standard deductibles with additional premium. Able's response to potential risks is known as:

    **a.** Avoidance

    **b.** Reduction

    **c.** Sharing

    **d.** Acceptance

# 1 Introduction to the Sarbanes-Oxley Act of 2002

The Sarbanes-Oxley Act of 2002 has had a profound effect on the financial reporting requirements of public companies. In particular, there are numerous provisions for expanded disclosures by corporations and specific representations required by officers of public companies that must accompany published financial statements. Key provisions of the act related to those disclosures are described in Title III and Title IV of the act. Title VIII and Title IX describe penalties for violating the act. Title XI covers guidelines for rules and punishments concerned with fraudulent corporate activities.

# 2 Title III (Corporate Responsibility)

The corporate responsibility section of the act relates to the establishment of an audit committee and the representations made by key corporate officers, typically the chief executive officer (CEO) and the chief financial officer (CFO).

## 2.1 Public Company Audit Committees

- Public companies are responsible for establishing an audit committee that is directly responsible for the appointment, compensation, and oversight of the work of the public accounting firm employed by that public company (also referred to as an issuer).

  - The auditor reports directly to the audit committee.

  - The audit committee is responsible for resolving disputes between the auditor and management.

- Audit committee members are to be members of the issuer's board of directors but are to be otherwise independent. Independence criteria are as follows:

  - Audit committee members may not accept compensation from the issuer for consulting or advisory services.

  - Audit committee members may not be an affiliated person of the issuer. (Affiliation means a person having the ability to influence financial decisions).

- Audit committees must establish procedures to accept reports of complaints regarding audit, accounting, or internal control issues (whistle-blower hotlines).

  - Procedures must accommodate confidential, anonymous reports by employees of the issuer.

  - Procedures must accommodate receipt and retention of complaints as well as a method to address those complaints.

## 2.2    Corporate Responsibility for Financial Reports

Corporate officials, typically the CEO and CFO, must sign certain representations regarding annual and quarterly reports, including their assertion that:

- They have reviewed the report.

- The report does not contain untrue statements or omit material information.

- The financial statements fairly present in all material respects the financial condition and results of operations of the issuer.

- The CEO and CFO signing the report have assumed responsibility for internal controls, including assertions that:

    - Internal controls have been designed to ensure that material information has been made available.

    - Internal controls have been evaluated for effectiveness as of a date within 90 days prior to the report.

    - Their report includes their conclusions as to the effectiveness of internal controls based on their evaluation.

- The CEO and CFO signing the report assert that they have made the following disclosures to the issuer's auditors and the audit committee:

    - All significant deficiencies and material weaknesses in the design or operation of internal controls which might adversely affect the financial statements.

    - Any fraud (regardless of materiality) that involves management or any other employee with a significant role in internal controls.

- The CEO and CFO signing the report must also represent whether there have been any significant changes to internal controls.

## 2.3    Improper Influence on the Conduct of Audits

No officer or director, or any person acting under the direction thereof, may take any action that would fraudulently influence, coerce, mislead, or manipulate the auditor in a manner that would make the financial statements materially misleading.

## 2.4    Forfeiture of Certain Bonuses and Profits

If an issuer is required to prepare an accounting restatement due to material noncompliance with any financial reporting requirement under the securities laws, the CEO and CFO may be required to reimburse the issuer for:

- bonuses or incentive-based or equity-based compensation.

- gains on sale of securities during that 12-month period.

# 3   Title IV (Enhanced Financial Disclosures)

The enhanced financial disclosures associated with issuer reports include additional details regarding the financial statements, internal controls, and the operations of the audit committee.

## 3.1   Disclosures in Periodic Reports (Generally Quarterly or Annually)

Financial statement disclosures are intended to ensure that the application of GAAP reflects the economics of the transactions included in the report and that those transactions are transparent to the reader. Enhanced disclosure requirements include the following:

- All material correcting adjustments identified by the auditor should be reflected in the financial statements.

- The financial statements should disclose all material off-balance sheet transactions:

  - Operating leases

  - Contingent obligations

  - Relationships with unconsolidated subsidiaries

- Conformance of pro forma financial statements to the following requirements:

  - No untrue statements

  - No omitted material information

  - Reconciled with GAAP basis financial statements

- Use of special purpose entities (SPEs).

## 3.2   Conflict of Interest Provisions

Issuers are generally prohibited from making personal loans to directors or executive officers.

- Exceptions apply if the consumer credit loans are made in the ordinary course of business by the issuer.

- Exceptions apply if the terms offered to the officer are generally made available to the public under similar terms and conditions with no preferential treatment.

## 3.3   Disclosure of Transactions Involving Management and Principal Stockholders

- Disclosures are required for persons who generally have direct or indirect ownership of more than 10 percent of any class of most any equity security. Disclosures are made by filing a statement.

- Statements are filed at the following times:

  - At the time of registration

  - When the person achieves 10 percent ownership

  - If there has been a change in ownership

## 3.4    Management Assessment of Internal Controls

The assessment of internal controls is commonly referred to as Section 404. Each annual report is required to contain a report that includes the following:

▣    A statement that management is responsible for establishing and maintaining an adequate internal control structure and procedures for financial reporting.

▣    An assessment, as of the end of the most recent fiscal year of the issuer, of the effectiveness of the internal control structure and procedures for financial reporting.

The auditor must attest to management's assessment of internal control.

## 3.5    Certain Exemptions

Investment companies are exempt from this act.

## 3.6    Code of Ethics for Senior Officers

▣    Issuers must disclose whether the issuer has adopted a code of conduct for senior officers (e.g., CEO, CFO, controller, and chief accountant). If no code of conduct has been adopted, the issuer must disclose the reasons.

▣    The code of ethics contemplates standards that promote:

- Honest and ethical conduct (including handling of conflicts of interest).

- Full, fair, accurate, and timely disclosures in periodic financial reports.

- Compliance with laws, rules, and regulations.

▣    Changes to or waivers from the code must be reported on a Form 8-K.

## 3.7    Disclosure of Audit Committee Financial Expert

At least one member of the audit committee should be a financial expert. Financial reports of the issuer must disclose the existence of a financial expert on the committee or the reasons why the committee does not have a member who is a financial expert.

▣    A financial expert qualifies through education, past experience as a public accountant, or past experience as a principal financial officer, controller, or principal accounting officer for an issuer.

▣    Knowledge of the financial expert should include:

- Understanding of GAAP.

- Experience in the preparation or auditing of financial statements for comparable issuers.

- Application of GAAP.

- Experience with internal controls.

- Understanding of audit committee functions.

## 3.8    Enhanced Review of Periodic Disclosures by Issuers

The Securities and Exchange Commission (SEC) is required to review disclosures made by issuers, including those in Form 10-K, on a regular and systematic basis for the protection of investors. When scheduling reviews, the SEC should consider the following:

▣    Issuers that have issued material restatements of financial results.

▣    Issuers that experience significant volatility in their stock prices when compared to other issuers.

- Issuers with the largest market capitalization.

- Emerging companies with disparities in price-to-earning ratios.

- Issuers whose operations significantly affect any material sector of the economy.

# 4    Title VIII (Corporate and Criminal Fraud Accountability)

## 4.1    Criminal Penalties for Altering Documents

- Individuals who alter, destroy, mutilate, conceal, cover up, falsify, or make false entry in any record, document, or tangible object with the intent to impede, obstruct, or influence an investigation will be fined, imprisoned for not more than 20 years, or both.

- Auditors of issuers should retain all audit and review workpapers for a period of seven years from the end of the fiscal period in which the audit or review was conducted. Failure to do so will result in a fine, imprisonment for not more than 10 years, or both.

## 4.2    Statute of Limitations for Securities Fraud

The statute of limitations for securities fraud is no later than the earlier of two years after the discovery of the facts constituting the violation, or five years after the violation.

## 4.3    Whistle-Blower Protection

An employee who lawfully provides evidence of fraud may not be discharged, demoted, suspended, threatened, harassed, or in any other matter discriminated against for providing such information. An employee who alleges discharge or other discrimination for providing evidence of fraud may file a complaint with the Secretary of Labor and may be provided with compensatory damages, including:

- reinstatement with the same seniority status that the employee would have had;

- back pay with interest; and

- compensation for any special damages as a result of the discrimination including litigation costs, expert witness fees, and reasonable attorney fees.

## 4.4    Criminal Penalties for Securities Fraud

An individual who knowingly executes, or attempts to execute, securities fraud will be fined, imprisoned not more than 25 years, or both.

# 5    Title IX (White-Collar Crime Penalty Enhancements)

## 5.1    Attempt and Conspiracy

An individual who attempts (conspires) to commit any white-collar offense will be subject to the same penalties as those who commit the offense, as predetermined by the United States Sentencing Commission. The penalties for mail and wire fraud were increased from 5 years to 20 years. The penalties for violating ERISA were increased from not more than $5,000 to not more than $100,000 and from not more than 1 year to not more than 10 years for individuals. (Either or both of the fine and the sentence may be imposed.) Fines imposed upon persons who are not individuals cannot exceed $500,000.

## 5.2 Amendment to Sentencing Guidelines Related to Certain White-Collar Offenses

▣ The United States Sentencing Commission ("Sentencing Commission") will review and amend, as needed, the Federal Sentencing Guidelines and policy statements to carry out the provisions of the Attempt and Conspiracy Act. This includes ensuring that the sentencing guidelines and policy statements take into account the nature of any offense and that the corresponding penalties are commensurate with the provisions of the act. In the event the Sentencing Commission determines a growing trend of a particular offense, it will review to determine whether any modifications to the Sentencing Guidelines or policy statements are necessary.

▣ The Sentencing Commission will review any additional aggravating or mitigating circumstances for a particular offense that could justify an exception to the existing sentencing ranges.

## 5.3 Failure of Corporate Officers to Certify Financial Reports

▣ Any issuer periodic report which contains financial statements that is filed with the SEC must be accompanied by the following:

- A written statement that the periodic report fully complies with the Securities Exchange Act of 1934.

- A written statement that the information contained in the report fairly presents, in all material respects, the financial condition and operating results of the issuer.

- The written statements above must be signed by the chief executive officer and chief financial officer (or equivalent) of the issuer (who bear responsibility for these statements).

▣ Any party that certifies the periodic financial report and/or its content knowing that it does not satisfy all the requirements shall be fined and/or imprisoned. Specifically, a party who:

- *certifies* any statement knowing that it does not comply with all requirements will be fined not more than $1,000,000 and/or imprisoned not more than 10 years; or

- *willfully* certifies any statement knowing that it does not comply with all requirements will be fined not more than $5,000,0000 and/or imprisoned not more than 20 years.

# 6 Title XI (Corporate Fraud Accountability)

## 6.1 Tampering With Record or Impeding an Official Proceeding

Any individual who alters, destroys, or conceals a document (record) with the intent to modify the document and its integrity or the availability of the document in an official proceeding shall be fined and/or subject to not more than a 20-year prison term.

## 6.2 Temporary Freeze Authority for the SEC

If during an investigation pertaining to potential violations of federal securities laws by an issuer of publicly traded securities (or a director, officer, or employee acting on its behalf) the SEC determines it is likely that the issuer will be required to make penalty payments, the SEC may petition a federal district court to require the issuer to escrow the payments in an interest-bearing account for 45 days.

## 6.3 Authority of the SEC to Prohibit Persons From Serving as Officers or Directors

For any cease-and-desist proceedings, the SEC may issue an order to conditionally or unconditionally prohibit an individual from serving as an officer or director of the issuer for a stipulated period (or permanently) if that individual has violated securities rules and regulations and the SEC determines that this individual is unfit to serve as an officer or director of an issuer.

## 6.4 Retaliation Against Informants

Any individual who knowingly takes any harmful action against another person with the intent to retaliate for that person providing truthful information to the SEC regarding a possible federal offense shall be fined and/or imprisoned for not more than 10 years.

| Question 1 | CPA-07014 |
|---|---|

Which of the following is necessary to be an audit committee financial expert, according to the criteria specified in the Sarbanes-Oxley Act of 2002?

- **a.** A limited understanding of generally accepted auditing standards.
- **b.** Education and experience as a certified financial planner.
- **c.** Experience with internal accounting controls.
- **d.** Experience in the preparation of tax returns.

| Question 2 | CPA-06491 |
|---|---|

Conflict-of-interest provisions of the Sarbanes-Oxley Act of 2002 generally prohibit the directors or executive officers of an issuer from:

- **a.** Owning more than 10 percent of common stock.
- **b.** Owning more than 10 percent of any form of equity.
- **c.** Receiving a personal loan from the issuer not in the ordinary course of business.
- **d.** Receiving perquisite compensation.

## NOTES

# 1 Trade-offs Between Risk and Return

## 1.1 Definitions

Risk and return are a function of both market conditions and the risk preferences of the parties involved.

▪ **Risk:** May be defined as the chance of financial loss. More formally, the term "risk" may be used interchangeably with the term "uncertainty" to refer to the variability of returns associated with a given asset.

▪ **Return:** May be defined as the total gain or loss experienced on behalf of the owner of an asset over a given period. Typically, greater risk yields greater returns. The seller of financial securities compensates the buyer of financial securities with increased opportunity for profit by offering a higher rate of return.

## 1.2 Risk Preferences

Different managers have varying attitudes toward risk. Three basic risk preference behaviors exist:

▪ **Risk-Indifferent Behavior:** reflects an attitude toward risk in which an increase in the level of risk does not result in an increase in management's required rate of return.

▪ **Risk-Averse Behavior:** reflects an attitude toward risk in which an increase in the level of risk results in an increase in management's required rate of return. Risk-averse managers require higher expected returns to compensate for greater risk. Most managers are risk-averse.

▪ **Risk-Seeking Behavior:** reflects an attitude toward risk in which an increase in the level of risk results in a decrease in management's required rate of return. Risk-seeking managers are willing to settle for lower expected returns as the level of risk increases.

# 2 Types of Risk

Measurements of risk attempt to capture the multiple dimensions of risk. Risk exposures include interest rate, market, default, credit, liquidity, and price risk.

## 2.1 Interest Rate Risk (or Yield Risk)

*Interest rate risk* (or yield risk) is often used in the context of financial instruments and represents the exposure of the owner of the instrument to fluctuations in the value of the instrument in response to changes in interest rates.

---

**Illustration 1     Interest Rate Risk**

Thayer Thermodynamics Inc. owns a five-year, $10,000 Duffy International coupon bond purchased at a discount. Recently, the market rate of interest increased 1 percent, causing the market value of the bond to decline to $9,610. Assuming the bond's carrying value on the financial statements was $9,840 at the time the market rate of interest abruptly increased, Thayer Thermodynamics suffered a $230 market loss in bond value as a result of its exposure to interest rate risk.

## 2.2    Market/Systematic/Nondiversifiable Risk

The exposure of a security or firm to fluctuations in value as a result of operating within an economy is referred to as *market risk*. Market risk is sometimes referred to as *nondiversifiable risk* because it is a risk inherent in operating within the economy. Nondiversifiable risk is attributable to factors such as war, inflation, international incidents, and political events.

---

**Illustration 2     Market Risk**

The prices on publicly traded stocks generally increase and decrease together with overall market activity. Although the prices may not increase or decrease identically, they often move in the same direction. A technology company's stock, for example, might increase in value on a given day from $37.00 per share to $37.75 per share. This increase in the stock price is consistent with the overall 2 percent increase in the NASDAQ on that trading day.

## 2.3    Unsystematic/Firm-Specific/Diversifiable Risk

*Diversifiable risk* (which is also referred to as *nonmarket, unsystematic,* or *firm-specific risk*) represents the portion of a firm's or industry's risk that is associated with random causes and can be eliminated through diversification. Diversifiable risk is attributable to firm-specific or industry-specific events (e.g., strikes, lawsuits, regulatory actions, or the loss of a key account).

**Pass Key**

It is important to be able to classify risk into two broad categories:

**D    Diversifiable** risk

**U        Unsystematic** risk (nonmarket/firm-specific)

**N    Nondiversifiable** risk

**S        Systematic** risk (market)

Remember the mnemonic **DUNS** to keep these risk types and their alternative names clear.

## 2.4    Credit Risk

*Credit risk* affects borrowers. Exposure to credit risk includes a company's inability to secure financing or secure favorable credit terms as a result of poor credit ratings. As credit ratings decline, the interest rate demanded by lenders increases, collateral may be required, and other terms are generally less favorable to the borrower.

| Illustration 3    Credit Risk |
| --- |

Duffy International seeks to borrow $10,000 for five years, but the company has a history of late payments and displays a high debt-to-income ratio and high debt-to-equity ratio (measurements discussed later). Although market rates of interest are 7 percent, lenders may only loan money to Duffy International at an 8 percent rate, require a lien on the company's inventory as collateral, and insist on shortening the term of the loan to three years. Duffy International's inability to borrow the funds it needs at the market rate of interest and under favorable terms illustrates the company's exposure to credit risk and demonstrates the creditors' attempt to mitigate default risk (see below).

## 2.5    Default Risk

*Default risk* affects lenders. Creditors are exposed to default risk to the extent that it is possible that its debtors may not repay the principal or interest due on their indebtedness on a timely basis.

| Illustration 4    Default Risk |
| --- |

Thayer Thermodynamics Inc. (TTI) holds $100,000 worth of $1,000 face value bonds recently issued by Duffy International. During the third quarter of the year, Duffy fails to make its quarterly interest payment on its outstanding bond issue. The loss incurred by TTI results from the company's exposure to default risk or the possibility that the debtor will not make its debt service payments as outlined in the bond agreement (indenture).

## 2.6    Liquidity Risk

*Liquidity risk affects lenders (investors).* Lenders or investors are exposed to liquidity risk when they desire to sell their security, but cannot do so in a timely manner or when material price concessions have to be made to do so.

| Illustration 5    Liquidity Risk |
| --- |

Smithfield Company holds several fixed-income securities of Johnson Manufacturing Company. Due to its current operational needs, Smithfield attempts to sell $250,000 of Johnson's 10-year bonds but is unsuccessful in attracting willing buyers at current market prices. As the company's working capital requirements increase, Smithfield significantly discounts the bonds to obtain the proceeds from the Johnson bond investments. Smithfield is exposed to liquidity risk, as evidenced by its inability to sell the bonds on a timely basis and the need to make concessions to attract willing investors.

## 2.7　Price Risk

*Price Risk* represents the exposure that investors have to a decline in the value of their individual securities or portfolios. Factors unique to individual investments and/or portfolios contribute to price risk, which becomes an even greater concern with increased market volatility. Price risk is related to diversifiable (unsystematic) risk.

# 3　Computation of Return

Return compensates investors and creditors for assumed risk. Return is often stated or measured by interest rates. Interest can be expressed as either a cost (interest expense) to debtors or income (interest income) to investors.

## 3.1　Stated Interest Rate

- **Definition:** The *stated interest rate* (sometimes referred to as nominal interest rate) represents the rate of interest charged before any adjustment for compounding or market factors.

- **Computation:** The *stated interest rate* is the rate shown in the agreement of indebtedness (e.g., a bond indenture or promissory note).

| Example 1 | Stated Interest Rate |
|---|---|

**Facts:** A $10,000 promissory note states that payments will be made quarterly at a 10 percent interest rate per annum.

**Required:** Calculate the stated interest rate. *Hint:* You do not need a calculator.

**Solution:** Stated rate = 10 percent

## 3.2　Effective Interest Rate

- **Definition:** The *effective interest rate* represents the actual finance charge associated with a borrowing after reducing loan proceeds for charges and fees related to a loan origination.

- **Computation:** Effective interest rates are computed by dividing the amount of interest paid based on the loan agreement by the net proceeds received.

| Example 2 | Effective Interest Rate |
|---|---|

**Facts:** A $10,000 promissory note has a stated rate of 10 percent per annum and is due in one year. The bank charges a loan origination fee of $75 and the state in which the loan is made levies a $50 documentary stamp charge. Taxes and fees are taken from loan proceeds.

**Required:** Compute the effective interest rate.

**Solution:**

| | |
|---|---:|
| Interest paid (10,000 × 10%) | $ 1,000 |
| Divided by net proceeds (10,000 − 75 − 50) | ÷ 9,875 |
| Effective interest rate | 10.13% |

## 3.3   Annual Percentage Rate

▪ **Definition:** The *annual percentage rate* of interest represents a noncompounded version of the effective annual percentage rate described and computed below. The annual percentage rate is the rate required for disclosure by federal regulations.

▪ **Computation:** Annual percentage rates are computed as the effective periodic interest rate times the number of periods in a year. Annual percentage rate emphasizes the amount paid relative to funds available.

---

| Example 3 | Annual Percentage Rate |
|---|---|

**Facts:** A $10,000 promissory note displays a stated rate of 8 percent with interest to be paid semiannually. The bank charges a $75 loan origination fee and a documentary tax of $50 is assessed by the state.

**Required:** Calculate the annual percentage rate.

**Solution:**

**Step 1:** Compute the effective periodic interest rate (as per above)

| | |
|---|---:|
| Interest paid (10,000 × 8% × 6/12) | $   400 |
| Divided by available funds (10,000 − 75 − 50) | ÷ 9,875 |
| Effective periodic interest rate | 4.05% |

**Step 2:** Multiply the effective periodic interest rate by the number of periods in a year

| | |
|---|---:|
| Effective periodic interest rate | 4.05% |
| Periods in a year | ×      2 |
| Annual percentage rate | 8.10% |

---

## 3.4   Effective Annual Percentage Rate

▪ **Definition:** The *effective annual percentage rate* represents the stated interest rate adjusted for the number of compounding periods per year. The effective annual percentage rate is abbreviated APR.

▪ **Computation:** The effective APR is computed as follows:

$$\text{Effective annual interest rate} = [1 + (i/p)]^p - 1$$

$i$ = Stated interest rate

$p$ = Compounding periods per year

| Example 4 | Effective Annual Percentage Rate |
|---|---|

**Facts:** A note has an 8 percent stated rate of interest compounded semiannually (two times per year).

**Required:** Compute the effective annual percentage rate or APR.

**Solution:**

Effective annual interest rate = $[1 + (i/p)]^p - 1$

Effective annual interest rate = $[1 + (0.08/2)]^2 - 1$

Effective annual interest rate = $[1 + (0.04)]^2 - 1$

Effective annual interest rate = $1.0816 - 1$

Effective annual interest rate = 8.16%

## 3.5 Simple Interest (Amount)

- **Definition:** Simple interest is the amount represented by interest paid only on the original amount of principal without regard to compounding.

- **Computation:** Simple interest is formulated as follows:

$$SI = P_0(i)(n)$$

$P_0$ = Original principal

$i$ = Interest rate per time period

$n$ = Number of time periods

| Example 5 | Simple Interest |
|---|---|

**Facts:** A $10,000 promissory note bears simple interest at 8 percent for two years.

**Required:** What is the simple interest on this obligation?

**Solution:**

$SI = P_0(i)(n)$

$SI = \$10,000(8\%)(2)$

$SI = \$1,600$

## 3.6    Compound Interest (Amount)

- **Definition:** Compound interest is the amount represented by interest earnings or expense that is based on the original principal plus any unpaid interest earnings or expense. Interest earnings or expense, therefore, compounds and yields an amount higher than simple interest.

- **Computation:** Compound interest is computed as a future value as follows:

$$FV_n = P_0(1 + i)^n$$

$P_0$ = Original principal

$i$ = Interest rate

$n$ = Number of periods

---

### Example 6    ▶    Compound Interest

**Facts:** A promissory note for $10,000 carries an interest rate of 8 percent for two years, compounded annually.

**Required:** Compute the maturity value of the promissory note.

**Solution:**

$FV_n = P_0(1 + i)^n$

$FV_n = \$10,000 (1 + 0.08)^2$

$FV_n = \$10,000 (1.1664)$

$FV_n = \$11,664$

---

## 3.7    Required Rate of Return

The required rate of return is calculated adding the following risk premiums to the risk-free rate:

- **Maturity Risk Premium (MRP):** Is the compensation that investors demand for exposure to interest rate risk over time. This risk increases with the term to maturity.

- **Purchasing Power Risk or Inflation Premium (IP):** Is the compensation investors require to bear the risk that price levels will change and affect asset values or the purchasing power of invested dollars (e.g., real estate).

- **Liquidity Risk Premium (LP):** Is the additional compensation demanded by lenders (investors) for the risk that an investment security (e.g., junk bonds) cannot be sold on a short notice without making significant price concessions. Liquidity is defined as the ability to quickly convert an asset to cash at fair market value.

- **Default Risk Premium (DRP):** Is the additional compensation demanded by lenders (investors) for bearing the risk that the issuer of the security will fail to pay interest and/or principal due on a timely basis.

---

### Illustration 6     Default Risk Premium

A bank desires to purchase a corporate bond for its investment portfolio. Given the characteristics of the bond issue/issuer and current financial market conditions, a required rate of return of 8 percent is deemed appropriate for the bond issue, as follows:

|   | | |
|---|---|---|
| | Real rate of return | 3% |
| + | Inflation premium (IP) | 2% |
| | Nominal rate of return | 5% |
| + | Risk premium: | |
| | Interest rate risk (MRP) | |
| | Liquidity risk (LP) | |
| | Default risk (DRP) | 3% |
| | Required rate of return | 8% |

---

# 4   Mitigating and Controlling Financial Risk

Business entities must be able to not only identify and assess various financial risks, but also implement strategies to mitigate and control the impact these risks can have on their operations and finances.

## 4.1   Diversification

Diversifiable risk represents the portion of a single asset's risk that is associated with random causes and can be eliminated through diversification. Diversification is the process of building a portfolio of investments of different and offsetting risks. Although diversification can reduce certain risks, business are exposed to risks that cannot be managed through diversification (i.e., nondiversifiable risks). A diversified investor should be concerned only with nondiversifiable (systematic) risk because, in theory, an investor can create a portfolio of assets that eliminates all (or virtually all) diversifiable risk.

## 4.2   Strategies to Mitigate and Control Specific Financial Risks

Companies use many different strategies to reduce their exposure and vulnerability to the various financial risks.

### 4.2.1   Mitigating Interest Rate Risk

An investor can mitigate interest rate risk by investing in floating rate debt securities, which do not change in value when interest rates change and also generate higher coupon payments when interest rates rise. Derivatives such as forward rate agreements (FRAs) or interest rate swaps, in which the investor pays a fixed interest rate and receives a floating interest rate, can also be used to mitigate interest rate risk.

## Illustration 7      Interest Rate Swap

East Company has invested in $1,000,000 of 8 percent fixed rate bonds. East expects interest rates to increase during the next 12 months. On January 1, East Company enters into an interest rate swap with West Company in which East Company agrees to make to West Company a series of future payments equal to the fixed interest rate of 8 percent on the principal amount of $1,000,000. In exchange, West Company agrees to make to East Company a series of future payments equal to a floating interest rate of LIBOR* + 1 percent on the principal amount of $1,000,000.

Underlying:               East Company—8%, and West Company—LIBOR + 1%

Notional amount:          $1,000,000

Initial net investment:   $0 (no cost to enter into the swap contract)

Settlement amount:        East Company—8% × $1,000,000 = $80,000, and West Company—(LIBOR + 1%) × $1,000,000

On the first settlement date, LIBOR was 8.5 percent and the following amounts were exchanged:

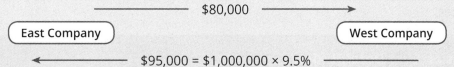

Derivatives generally have multiple settlement options. This derivative could be settled in the following ways:

**1.** East Company could pay $80,000 to West Company, and West Company could pay $95,000 to East Company.

**2.** West Company could pay $15,000 ($95,000 − $80,000) to East Company. This is a net settlement and is the most likely form of settlement in this example.

*LIBOR (London Interbank Offered Rate) is a benchmark rate that some of the world's leading banks charge each other for short-term loans.

### 4.2.2   Mitigating Market Risk

Market risk, because it is inherent in the marketplace and overall economy, is not as easy to mitigate. Market risk cannot be mitigated through diversification. One way to control market risk is to invest in derivatives that provide gains to the investor when the market declines. Short selling (selling an investment in the hopes of buying it back at a lower price later) is another strategy that provides returns when the market declines.

## Illustration 8      Short Sale

The CFO of Dillon Bank is concerned that falling oil prices may lead to an overall stock market decline in the coming months. In order to protect the bank's investment portfolios against a market decline, the CFO opens several short positions in index funds designed to track the S&P 500. She will earn a profit if the market does decline, as she can buy back the funds at lower prices. However, if the market rises, she will eventually have to buy back the funds at higher prices than the original sale price.

### 4.2.3 Mitigating Unsystematic Risk

Unsystematic risk can be minimized through diversification. If an investor has a broad portfolio of investments, then an event that has a negative effect on one firm, industry, or investment type would have less of an effect on the value of the portfolio as a whole.

### 4.2.4 Mitigating Credit Risk

Credit risk is managed through improvements in credit ratings, which are assigned at entity and individual debt levels. When credit ratings are higher, borrowing can occur at more favorable terms (such as lower interest rates). Factors evaluated in determining credit ratings include overall economic outlook, industry conditions, cash flow measures, leverage, capital structure, management strength, historical performance, and financial ratios measuring solvency, liquidity, profitability, etc. Management has various degrees of control over these factors, but awareness of them and understanding of how changes can affect credit ratings are crucial to controlling this risk.

### 4.2.5 Mitigating Default Risk

Default risk can be mitigated in several ways. As a lender, an entity may choose to lend only to borrowers with low risk of default. Another option is to adjust the interest rates charged to better reflect the risk of each borrower, such that higher-risk borrowers will pay higher interest rates.

---

**Illustration 9    Default Risk**

Miller Inc. wants to reduce its default risk and is considering two plans. Miller can either reduce the population of potential customers by extending credit to customers with credit ratings only above a certain threshold, or it can continue extending credit to all customers but charge higher interest rates to borrowers that pose greater risks of not paying back money owed.

---

### 4.2.6 Mitigating Liquidity Risk

Liquidity risk is higher for investments that don't have active markets (e.g., forward contracts, limited partnerships). Liquidity risk is mitigated by allocating a greater percentage of capital to investments that trade on active markets, such as equities, corporate bonds, futures contracts, and options.

### 4.2.7 Mitigating Price Risk

Price risk can be minimized through diversification. Price risk also can be mitigated through short selling or derivatives, such as put options.

## Illustration 10    Put Option

Roberts Company owns 10,000 shares of Buy Big Inc. stock. Roberts plans to sell the stock during January and is concerned that the price of the stock will fall below the current price of $75/share. On January 1, Roberts purchased a put option on the stock of Buy Big. The option gives Roberts the right to sell the 10,000 shares of Buy Big stock at $75/share during the next 30 days. Roberts paid a premium of $2/share to enter into the option. Roberts exercises the option when Buy Big stock was selling for $69/share.

| | |
|---|---|
| Underlying: | $75/share |
| Notional amount: | 10,000 shares of Buy Big stock |
| Initial net investment: | $2/share × 10,000 shares = $20,000 |
| Settlement amount: | $75/share × 10,000 shares = $750,000 |

Derivatives generally have multiple settlement options. This derivative could be settled in the following ways:

1.  Roberts could deliver 10,000 shares of Buy Big stock to the option writer in exchange for $750,000. Roberts would realize a gain of $60,000 [($75/share exercise price − $69/share market price) × 10,000 shares. The option writer would realize a loss of $60,000 because the option writer must pay $75/share for stock with a market value of $69/share.

2.  The option writer could pay Roberts $60,000 to settle the contract. This is a net settlement.

Because $20,000 was paid to purchase the put option, Roberts will report a net gain of $40,000 ($60,000 gain − $20,000 premium). If the stock price had remained above $75/share during the 30-day period, Roberts would not have exercised the option and would have sold the stock for the market price.

---

### Question 1                                                                    CPA-05788

A company has an outstanding one-year bank loan of $500,000 at a stated interest rate of 8 percent. The company is required to maintain a 20 percent compensating balance in its checking account. The company would maintain a zero balance in this account if the requirement did not exist. What is the effective interest rate of the loan?

    a.   8 percent
    b.   10 percent
    c.   20 percent
    d.   28 percent

# 1 Currency Exchange Rate Risk

Within domestic environments, a single currency defines the value of assets, liabilities, and operating transactions. In international settings, the values of assets, liabilities, and operating transactions are established not only in terms of the single currency, but also in relation to other currencies. Exchange rate (FX) risk exists because the relationship between domestic and foreign currencies may be subject to volatility.

## 1.1 Factors Influencing Exchange Rates

Circumstances that give rise to changes in exchange rates are generally divided between trade-related factors (including differences in inflation, income, and government regulation) and financial factors (including differences in interest rates and restrictions on capital movements between companies).

### 1.1.1 Trade Factor (Relative Inflation Rates)

When domestic inflation exceeds foreign inflation, holders of domestic currency are motivated to purchase foreign currency to maintain the purchasing power of their money. The increase in demand for foreign currency forces the value of the foreign currency to rise in relation to the domestic currency, thereby changing the rate of exchange between the domestic and foreign currency.

---

**Illustration 1    Relative Inflation Rates**

Assume that the U.S. dollar is relatively stable while the Mexican peso is suffering from sudden inflationary pressures. As the Mexican peso buys less in the domestic Mexican economy, Mexicans and their banking institutions seek the safe haven of the U.S. dollar to maintain the purchasing power of their liquid resources. The demand for U.S. dollars created by Mexicans buying them with Mexican pesos makes the U.S. dollar more valuable in terms of the peso and drives up the exchange rate. The U.S. dollar commands more pesos in an exchange of currency.

---

### 1.1.2 Trade Factor (Relative Income Levels)

As income increases in one country relative to another, exchange rates change as a result of increased demand for foreign currencies in the country in which income is increasing.

**Illustration 2     Relative Income Levels**

The income level in the United States increases significantly in the second quarter. Americans flock to Mexico City on vacation to buy piñatas. The increased supply of American dollars seeking to buy pesos to purchase Mexican goods causes the value of the American dollar to fall in relation to a stated number of pesos. The exchange rate is thus affected by relative income levels and the associated demand for foreign currency created by higher domestic income.

### 1.1.3   Trade Factor (Government Controls)

Various trade and exchange barriers that artificially suppress the natural forces of supply and demand affect exchange rates.

**Illustration 3     Government Controls**

A tariff on imported piñatas would have the effect of discouraging the purchase of imports, thereby reducing demand for the peso and maintaining the exchange rate.

### 1.1.4   Financial Factors (Relative Interest Rates and Capital Flows)

Interest rates create demand for currencies by motivating either domestic or foreign investments. The forces of supply and demand create changes in the exchange rate as investors seek fixed returns. The effect of interest rates is directly affected by the volume of capital that is allowed to flow between countries.

**Illustration 4     Relative Interest Rates and Capital Flows**

Assume that returns on institutional investments in Mexico skyrocket in the third quarter while returns on comparable institutional investments remain significantly lower in the United States. U.S. investors find the opportunity to earn high returns with similar risks in Mexican financial institutions irresistible. The demand for pesos increases as American investment increases. The exchange rate changes as the peso commands more U.S dollars.

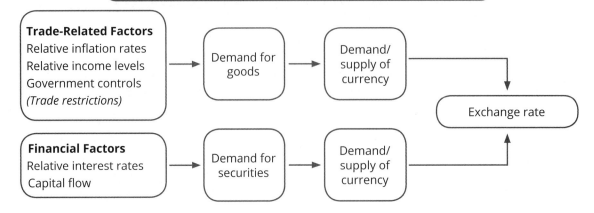

**Summary Chart: Circumstances That Impact Exchange Rates**

**Trade-Related Factors**
Relative inflation rates
Relative income levels
Government controls
*(Trade restrictions)*
→ Demand for goods → Demand/supply of currency →

**Financial Factors**
Relative interest rates
Capital flow
→ Demand for securities → Demand/supply of currency →

Exchange rate

## 1.2    Risk Exposure Categories

### 1.2.1    Transaction Exposure

Exchange rate risk is defined, in part, by *transaction exposure*. Transaction exposure is defined as the potential that an organization could suffer economic loss or experience economic gain upon settlement of individual transactions as a result of changes in the exchange rates. Transaction exposure is generally measured in relation to currency variability or currency correlation. Measurement of transaction exposure is generally done in two steps:

**1.**    Project foreign currency inflows and foreign currency outflows.

**2.**    Estimate the variability (risk) associated with the foreign currency.

---

**Illustration 5    Transaction Exposure**

Seattle Import/Export, a U.S. import/export company, imports commodities from Canada that it pays for in Canadian dollars and exports commodities to Canada for which it receives Canadian dollars. If Seattle Import/Export anticipated that it would export C$10,000,000 to Canada over the next year while importing C$8,000,000 over the same period, the net exposure in Canadian dollars is a C$2,000,000 inflow (receivable).

If the current exchange rate is $0.75/C$1, the net exposure in U. S. dollars is $1,500,000 (C$2,000,000 × 0.75). If the rate is anticipated to fluctuate five cents, between $0.70 and $0.80, the total U.S. dollar fluctuation exposure would be expected to be between $1,400,000 and $1,600,000.

---

### 1.2.2    Economic Exposure

In addition to transaction exposure, exchange rate risk is defined, in part, by *economic exposure*. Economic exposure is defined as the potential that the present value of an organization's cash flows could increase or decrease as a result of changes in the exchange rates. Economic exposure is generally defined through local currency appreciation or depreciation and is measured in relation to organization earnings and cash flows.

■    **Currency Appreciation and Depreciation**

*Currency appreciation (depreciation)* refers to the strengthening (weakening) of a currency in relation to other currencies.

•    **Effect of Currency Appreciation**

As a domestic currency appreciates in value or becomes stronger, it becomes more expensive in terms of a foreign currency. As a currency appreciates, the volume of outflows tends to decline as domestic exports become more expensive. However, the volume of inflows tends to increase as foreign imports become less expensive.

•    **Effect of Currency Depreciation**

As a domestic currency depreciates in value or becomes weaker, it becomes less expensive in terms of a foreign currency. As a currency depreciates, the volume of outflows tends to rise as domestic exports become less expensive. However, the volume of inflows tends to decline as foreign imports become more expensive.

The economic exposure created by domestic currency appreciation or depreciation with respect to a foreign currency depends on the net inflow or outflow of foreign currency.

---

### 1.2.3    Translation Exposure

In addition to the transaction and economic exposures, exchange rate risk is defined in part by *translation exposure*. Translation exposure is the risk that assets, liabilities, equity, or income of a consolidated organization that includes foreign subsidiaries will change as a result of changes in exchange rates. Translation exposure is generally defined by the degree of foreign involvement, the location of foreign subsidiaries, and the accounting methods used and measured in relation to the effect on the organization's earnings or comprehensive income.

▪ **Degree of Foreign Involvement**: Translation exposure increases as the proportion of foreign involvement by subsidiaries increases.

---

#### Illustration 6    Translation Risk

Domestic International Inc. has no foreign subsidiaries but is deeply involved in exporting to neighboring countries. Global International Inc. has 12 foreign subsidiaries which, combined, make up 65 percent of consolidated revenues. Domestic International has less translation exposure than Global International because it has no foreign subsidiaries. Domestic's international business does expose the company to exchange rate risks, however, in terms of both transaction and economic exposure.

Because of Global International's extensive foreign operations, the parent company has significant exposure to foreign currency translation exposure, and depending on the entity's export/import activity, Global International may also be exposed to foreign exchange transaction and economic risks.

---

▪ **Locations of Foreign Investments:** Measurements of financial results of foreign investments frequently occur in the foreign currency in which the investee company operates. The exposure of the parent company to translation risk is affected by the stability of the foreign currency in comparison to the parent's domestic currency. The more stable the exchange rate, the lower the translation risk. The more volatile the exchange rate, the higher the translation risk.

## 2    Mitigating and Controlling Transaction Exposure

Businesses have various methods of managing the transaction exposure associated with exchange rate risks. The use of financial instruments and hedging attempts to mitigate the effect of exchange rate fluctuations on individual transactions. The following discussion analyzes hedging as it relates to foreign currency transactions.

### 2.1    Measuring Specific Net Transaction Exposure

Net transaction exposure is the amount of gain or loss that might result from either a favorable or an unfavorable settlement of a transaction.

### 2.1.1  Selective Hedging

Hedging is a financial risk management technique in which an organization, seeking to mitigate the risk of fluctuations in value, acquires a financial instrument that behaves in the opposite manner from the hedged item. In effect, hedging is a process of reducing the uncertainty of the future value of a transaction or position (e.g., asset, liability, income) by actively engaging in various derivative investments.

---

**Illustration 7     Hedging**

Worldwide Sweet Peaches buys shipping crates for its product from Mexico. The company incurs liabilities denominated in pesos that it satisfies in pesos bought with U.S. dollars at the time of transaction settlement. The company incurs a significant liability in pesos at a spot rate of $0.10. Worldwide management expects that the peso will strengthen to $0.20 by the time the bill is due and thereby double its cost. To mitigate this perceived transaction risk, the company decides to hedge its position by locking in the current peso spot rate of $0.10.

---

### 2.1.2  Identifying Net Transaction Exposure

Consolidated entities consider their net transaction exposure prior to considering hedge strategies. Net transaction exposure considers the effect of transaction exposure on the entity taken as a whole rather than on individual subsidiaries. Although exchange rate issues might adversely affect one subsidiary, they might favorably affect another. The net transaction exposure is the aggregate exposure associated with a particular foreign currency for a particular time and is computed as follows:

**1.**  Accumulate the inflows and outflows of foreign currencies by subsidiary.

**2.**  Consolidate the effects on the subsidiary by currency type.

**3.**  Compute the net effect in total.

### 2.1.3  Adjusting Invoice Policies

International companies may hedge transactions without complex instruments by timing the payment for imports with the collection from exports.

## 2.2  Mitigating Transaction Exposure: Futures Hedge

A *futures hedge* entitles its holder to either purchase or sell a particular number of currency units of an identified currency for a negotiated price on a stated date. Futures hedges are denominated in standard amounts and tend to be used for smaller transactions.

### 2.2.1  Accounts Payable Application

- Accounts payable denominated in a foreign currency represents a potential transaction exposure to exchange rate risk in the event that the *domestic currency weakens* in relation to the foreign currency. Should the domestic currency weaken relative to the foreign currency, more domestic currency will be required to purchase the foreign currency, thereby increasing the company's cost of settling the liability. If management does not hedge this liability exposure, the company will incur a foreign exchange transaction loss.

- A *futures hedge contract* to buy the foreign currency at a specific price at the time the account payable is due will mitigate the risk of a weakening domestic currency.

---

**Illustration 8     Futures Contract**

Worldwide Sweet Peaches buys crates from Mexico. On the date that Worldwide Sweet Peaches buys crates and incurs a significant liability in pesos, the spot rate is $0.10. Because the company fears that the peso will strengthen to $0.20 by the time the bill is due in 30 days, the company enters into a futures contract that will allow it to purchase the pesos needed to pay the liability for $0.10 per peso in 30 days.

---

### 2.2.2  Accounts Receivable Application

- Accounts receivable denominated in a foreign currency represent a potential transaction exposure to exchange rate risk in the event that the *domestic currency strengthens* in relation to the foreign currency. Should the domestic currency strengthen, less domestic currency (than originally anticipated from the sale that created the receivable) can be purchased with the foreign currency received. An exchange loss will result.

- A *futures hedge contract to sell* the foreign currency received in satisfaction of the receivable at a specific price at the time the accounts receivable is due will mitigate the risk of a strengthening domestic currency.

---

**Illustration 9     Futures Hedge Contract**

Running Apparel International, a U.S.-based retailer, has international retail operations in several countries, including significant business in Japan. Company management expects that the Japanese retail operations will generate and liquidate a significant amount of its accounts receivables in 30 days. Although the current $/¥ spot rate is $1/¥98.02, company management expects the $/¥ spot rate to be $1/¥102.09 in 30 days. To mitigate this expected foreign exchange loss caused by the appreciation of the U.S. dollar (relative to the Japanese yen), the company enters into a futures contract to sell yen at the current spot rate ($1/¥98.02) in 30 days, thereby locking in the current value of these foreign receivables.

---

## 2.3  Mitigating Transaction Exposure: Forward Hedge

A *forward hedge* is similar to a futures hedge in that it entitles its holder to either purchase or sell currency units of an identified currency for a negotiated price at a future point. Although futures hedges tend to be used for smaller transactions, forward hedges are contracts between businesses and commercial banks and normally are larger transactions. Although a futures hedge might hedge a particular transaction, a forward hedge would anticipate a company's needs to either buy or sell a foreign currency at a particular point.

### 2.3.1  Accounts Payable Application

- Accounts payable denominated in a foreign currency represent a potential transaction exposure to exchange rate risk in the event that the *foreign currency strengthens*.

- A *forward hedge contract to buy* the foreign currency at a specific price at the time accounts payable are due for an entire subsidiary will mitigate the risk of a weakening domestic currency.

### 2.3.2   Accounts Receivable Application

■   Accounts receivable denominated in a foreign currency represent a potential transaction exposure to exchange rate risk in the event that the *domestic currency strengthens*.

■   A *forward hedge contract to sell* the foreign currency received in satisfaction of the receivables at a specific price at the time the accounts receivable are due or on the monthly cycle of a particular subsidiary will mitigate the risk of a strengthening domestic currency.

## 2.4   Mitigating Transaction Exposure: Money Market Hedge

A *money market hedge* uses international money markets to plan to meet future currency requirements. A money market hedge uses domestic currency to purchase a foreign currency at current spot rates and invest them in securities timed to mature at the same time as related payables.

### 2.4.1   Money Market Hedge: Payables (Excess Cash)

Firms with excess cash use money market hedges to lock in the exchange rate associated with the foreign currency needed to satisfy payables when they come due. Money market hedges for payables satisfaction include the following steps:

**1.**   Determine the amount of the payable.

**2.**   Determine the amount of interest that can be earned prior to settling the payable.

**3.**   Discount the amount of the payable to the net investment required.

**4.**   Purchase the amount of foreign currency equal to the net investment required and deposit the proceeds in the appropriate money market vehicle.

---

### Illustration 10   Money Market Hedge: Payables (Excess Cash)

Duffy's Discount Piñatas has a payable due to its Mexican suppliers in the amount of 1,000,000 pesos in 90 days. The current exchange rate is $0.08 per peso and Mexican interest rates are 16 percent. Duffy has $100,000 in excess cash and elects to use a money market hedge to mitigate transaction exposure to exchange rate risk. Duffy performs the following steps:

**1.**   Determine the required investment in pesos at Mexican interest rates: 1,000,000 / 1.04 = 961,538.

  (**Note:** A 16 percent annual interest rate for 90 days is equal to approximately 4 percent).

**2.**   Purchase 961,538 pesos with $76,923 (961,538 pesos × 0.08).

**3.**   Invest pesos at Mexican interest rates and satisfy payables upon maturity of the investment.

Duffy has secured the satisfaction of its current $80,000 payable for $76,923.

---

### 2.4.2   Money Market Hedge: Payables (Borrowed Funds)

Firms that do not have excess cash follow the same basic procedure for a money market hedge on payables, except that they first borrow funds domestically and invest them internationally to satisfy the payable denominated in a foreign currency.

### Illustration 11    Money Market Hedge: Payables (Borrowed Funds)

Duffy's Discount Piñatas has a payable due to its Mexican suppliers in the amount of 1,000,000 pesos in 90 days. The current exchange rate is $0.08 per peso, Mexican interest rates are 16 percent, and U.S. interest rates are 6 percent. Duffy computes that it must borrow $76,923 to use a money market hedge to mitigate transaction exposure to exchange rate risk consistent with the first money market hedge example, but has no excess cash. Duffy borrows the needed amount for 90 days in the United States.

Duffy has secured the satisfaction of its current $80,000 payable for $78,077 (76,923 × 1.015 or 6% for 90 days).

### 2.4.3   Money Market Hedge: Receivables

A money market hedge used for receivables denominated in foreign currencies effectively involves factoring receivables with foreign bank loans. Foreign currency amounts are borrowed in discounted amounts that are repaid in the ultimate maturity value of the receivable denominated in the foreign currency. Borrowed foreign currency amounts are converted into the domestic currency.

### Illustration 12    Money Market Hedge: Receivables

Duffy's Discount Piñatas has a receivable from a Mexican customer in the amount of 1,000,000 pesos due in 90 days. The current exchange rate is $0.08 per peso and Mexican interest rates are 16 percent. Duffy needs available cash and cannot wait to receive $80,000 in 90 days. Because Duffy needs the money now, the company elects to use a money market hedge technique to expedite collection and mitigate any transaction exposure to exchange rate risk.

Duffy computes that it can borrow 961,538 pesos and convert them to $76,923 consistent with the first money market hedge example. Duffy borrows the pesos from Mexican financial institutions.

Duffy will be able to meet whatever its current cash requirements are in the United States with the $76,923, and when the 90-day discounted note for 961,538 pesos matures for 1,000,000 pesos, Duffy will satisfy it with the collections from the foreign accounts receivable.

## 2.5   Mitigating Transaction Exposure: Currency Option Hedges

*Currency option hedges* use the same principles as forward hedge contracts and money market hedge transactions. However, instead of requiring a commitment to a transaction, the currency option hedge gives the business the option of executing the option contract or purely settling its originally negotiated transaction without the benefit of the hedge, depending on which result is most favorable.

### 2.5.1   Currency Option Hedges: Payables

A call option (an option to buy) is the currency option hedge used to mitigate the transaction exposure associated with exchange rate risk for payables.

- Similar to a futures contract or forward contract, the business plans to buy a foreign currency at a low rate in anticipation of the foreign currency strengthening in comparison to the domestic currency in order to ensure that it can settle its liability at the predicted value.

■ The business has the option (not the obligation) to purchase the security at the option (strike or exercise) price. The business evaluates the relationship between the option price and the exchange rate at the settlement date. Generally, if the option price is less than the exchange rate at the time of settlement, the business will exercise its option. If the option price is more than the exchange rate at the time of settlement, the business will allow the option to expire. Although option premiums are used to compute any net savings associated with option transactions, they are a sunk cost and are irrelevant to the decision to exercise the options.

| Example 1 | Currency Option Hedge: Payables |
| --- | --- |

**Facts:** Gearty International owes its Mexican supplier 1,000,000 pesos due in 30 days. Although the peso is currently exchanged for the U.S. dollar at $0.08, the company is fearful that the Mexican peso will strengthen in comparison to the dollar before the settlement to as much as $0.10. Gearty International pays a $0.005 option premium to secure a call option to buy 1,000,000 pesos in 30 days for $0.08/peso.

**Required:** Compute Gearty's net savings, assuming that Gearty is correct in its assessment of international exchange rates and the exchange rate at the time of the settlement (the spot rate) increases as predicted.

**Solution:**

| Spot Rate at Settlement | Option Price | Premium | Total Option | Settlement Cost for 1,000,000 Pesos |
| --- | --- | --- | --- | --- |
| $0.10 | – | – | – | $100,000 |
| – | $0.08 | $0.005 | $0.085 | (85,000) |
| Net savings | | | | $ 15,000 |

Gearty's consideration for the option, the $0.005 option premium, is $5,000 and is paid regardless of whether the option is exercised. The gross savings of $20,000 [(0.10 − 0.08) × 1,000,000 pesos] is reduced by the $5,000 option premium to reflect a $15,000 net savings. Because the option premium is a sunk cost, it does not affect the company's decision to exercise the call option.

**Facts:** Same as above

**Required:** Calculate Gearty's loss, assuming that Gearty is incorrect in its assessment of international exchange rates, the exchange rates stay constant at $0.08, and the company allows its option to expire.

**Solution:**

| Spot Rate at Settlement | Option Price | Premium | Total Option | Settlement Cost for 1,000,000 Pesos |
| --- | --- | --- | --- | --- |
| $0.08 | – | – | – | $80,000 |
| – | $0.08 | $0.005 | $0.085 | (85,000) |
| Loss | | | | $ (5,000) |

Exercising the option is actually equal to simply settling the transaction at the spot rate. Gearty will likely buy pesos at the spot rate regardless of the loss associated with the premium.

### 2.5.2 Currency Option Hedges: Receivables

A put option (an option to sell) is the currency option hedge used to mitigate the transaction exposure associated with exchange rate risk for receivables.

▪ Similar to a futures contract or forward contract, the business plans to sell a foreign currency at a higher rate, in anticipation of the foreign currency weakening in comparison to the domestic currency, to ensure that it can capitalize on receivable collections at a stable or predicted value.

▪ The business has the option (not the obligation) to sell the collected amount of the foreign currency from the receivable at the option (strike or exercise) price. The business evaluates the relationship between the option price and the exchange rate at the settlement date. Generally, if the option price is more than the exchange rate at the time of settlement, the business will exercise its put option. If the put option price is less than the exchange rate at the time of settlement, the business will allow the put option to expire. Although premiums are used to compute any net preserved value associated with option transactions, they are a sunk cost and irrelevant to the decision to exercise the options.

---

| Example 2 | Currency Options Hedge: Receivables |
|---|---|

**Facts:** Gearty International is owed 1,000,000 pesos due in 30 days from its Mexican customer. Although the peso is currently exchanged for the U.S. dollar at $0.08, the company is fearful that the Mexican peso will weaken in comparison to the dollar before the settlement to as little as $0.06. Gearty International pays a $0.005 put premium to secure a put option to sell 1,000,000 pesos in 30 days for $0.08.

**Required:** Compute the net preserved value assuming that Gearty is correct in its assessment of international exchange rates and the exchange rate at the time of the settlement (the spot rate) decreases.

**Solution:**

| Spot Rate at Settlement | Option Price | Premium | Total Option | Settlement Cost for 1,000,000 Pesos |
|---|---|---|---|---|
| $0.06 | – | – | – | $(60,000) |
| – | $0.08 | $0.005 | $0.075 | 75,000 |
| Net preserved value | | | | $ 15,000 |

Gearty's consideration for the put option, the $0.005 put premium, is $5,000 and is paid regardless of whether the put option is exercised. The gross value "preserved" of $20,000 [(0.08 − 0.06) × 1,000,000 pesos] is reduced by the $5,000 put premium paid to reflect a net $15,000 preserved receivable value. Because the put premium is a sunk cost, it is not included in the decision to exercise the option.

(continued)

---

(continued)

**Facts:** Same as above

**Required:** Calculate Gearty's loss, assuming that Gearty is incorrect in its assessment of international exchange rates, the exchange rates stay constant at $0.08, and Gearty allows the put option to expire.

**Solution:**

| Spot Rate at Settlement | Option Price | Premium | Total Option | Settlement Cost for 1,000,000 Pesos |
|---|---|---|---|---|
| $0.08 | – | – | – | $(80,000) |
| – | $0.08 | $0.005 | $0.075 | 75,000 |
| Loss | | | | $ (5,000) |

Exercising the put option would actually be equal to simply settling the transaction at the spot rate when the receivables are received. Gearty will likely sell pesos at the spot rate regardless of the loss associated with the premium.

## 2.6    Mitigating Transaction Exposure: Long-Term Transactions

The following hedge transactions are used to mitigate exchange rate risk presented by transaction exposure.

### 2.6.1   Long-Term Forward Contracts

Mechanically, *long-term forward contracts* deal with the same issues as any other forward contracts. Long-term forward contracts are set up to stabilize transaction exposure over long periods. Long-term purchase contracts may be hedged with long-term forward contracts.

### 2.6.2   Currency Swaps

Transaction exposure associated with exchange rate risk for longer-term transactions can be mitigated with *currency swaps*.

▪ **Two Firms**

Two firms with coincidental needs for international currencies may agree to swap currencies collected in a future period at a specified exchange rate. The two entities essentially swap their currencies in an exchange negotiation completed years in advance of their receipt of the currencies.

▪ **Financial Intermediaries**

Typically, financial intermediaries are contacted to broker or to match firms with currency needs.

▪ **Parallel Loan**

Two firms may mitigate their transaction exposure to long-term exchange rate loss by exchanging or swapping their domestic currencies for a foreign currency and simultaneously agreeing to re-exchange or repurchase their domestic currency at a later date.

## Example 3 | Currency Swap

**Facts:** In order to hedge its future raw material purchases for its operations, in Poland, a U.S. manufacturing firm (U.S. counterparty) agrees to enter into a currency swap with a Polish multinational firm (foreign counterparty) whereby the U.S. counterparty agrees to provide the following quarterly notional amounts in U.S. dollars to the foreign counterparty in exchange for the following quarterly notional amounts in Polish zlotys.

| Quarter End | U.S. Counterparty Receives | Foreign Counterparty Receives |
|---|---|---|
| 1 | 1,500,000 zloty | 500,000 USD |
| 2 | 900,000 zloty | 300,000 USD |
| 3 | 750,000 zloty | 250,000 USD |
| 4 | 1,800,000 zloty | 600,000 USD |

Assume that the exchange rates are 3.25 zloty/1.0 USD and 2.85 zloty/1.0 USD at the end of quarter 1 and quarter 2, respectively.

**Required:** Calculate the U.S. manufacturing firm's foreign currency gain or loss recorded at the end of the first and second quarters on the currency swap.

**Solution:** The U.S. manufacturing firm (U.S. counterparty) entered into a fixed notional amount currency swap with a foreign counterparty when the exchange rates were 3.0 zloty/1.0 USD. Because the contractual quarterly payments made in U.S. dollars to the Polish firm are fixed at that exchange rate throughout the swap, any movement up or down of these two exchange rates will result in a foreign currency gain or loss.

In the first quarter, the U.S. dollar appreciates versus the Polish zloty, so the U.S. counterparty incurs a foreign currency loss. Under the terms of the currency swap, the U.S. counterparty pays 500,000 U.S. dollars and receives 1,500,000 zloty (based on an exchange rate of 3.0 zloty/1.0 USD). The 1,500,000 zloty received are worth only 461,538 U.S. dollars based on the end of quarter exchange rate of 3.25 zloty/1.0 USD:

    1,500,000 / 3.25 = 461,538 USD

Paying 500,000 U.S. dollars and receiving zloty worth only 463,538 U.S. dollars represents a loss of 38,462 U.S. dollars:

    500,000 – 461,538 = 38,462 USD

In the second quarter, the U.S. dollar depreciates versus the Polish zloty. As a result of the swap, the U.S. counterparty incurs a foreign currency gain. The U.S. counterparty pays 300,000 U.S. dollars and receives 900,000 zloty. The value in U.S. dollars of 900,000 zloty based on the end of quarter exchange rate of 2.85 zloty/1.0 USD is 315,789 U.S. dollars.

    900,000 / 2.85 = 315,789

Paying 300,000 U.S. dollars and receiving zloty worth 315,789 U.S. dollars represents a gain of 15,789 in U.S. dollars:

    315,789 – 300,000 = 15,789 USD

## 2.7 Mitigating Transaction Exposure: Alternative Hedging Techniques

The following hedge transactions are used to mitigate exchange rate risk presented by transaction exposure.

### 2.7.1 Leading and Lagging

*Leading and lagging* represent transactions between subsidiaries or a subsidiary and a parent. The entity that is owed may bill in advance if the exchange rate warrants (leading) or possibly wait until the exchange rate is favorable before settling (lagging).

### 2.7.2 Cross-Hedging

The technique known as *cross-hedging* involves hedging one instrument's risk with a different instrument by taking a position in a related derivatives contract. This is often done when there is no derivatives contract for the instrument being hedged, or when a suitable derivatives contract exists but the market is highly illiquid.

### 2.7.3 Currency Diversification

The simplest hedge for long-term transactions is to diversify foreign currency holdings over time. A substantial decline in the value of one currency would not affect the overall dollar value of the firm if the currency represented only one of many foreign currencies.

## 3  Mitigating and Controlling Economic and Translation Exposure

Businesses have various methods of managing the economic and translation exposure associated with exchange rate risks. Generally, the use of organization-wide solutions related to the entity itself and related reporting requirements are included in the approach.

### 3.1  Assessing Economic Exposure

Economic exposure is defined by the degree to which cash flows of the business can be affected by fluctuations in exchange rates. The extent to which revenues and expenses are denominated in different currencies could seriously affect the profitability of an organization and represents economic exposure.

---

**Illustration 13   Economic Exposure**

Pete's Primo Piñatas manufactures piñatas in Mexico. The company's expenses paid to local suppliers are denominated in the peso. The company exports nearly 80 percent of its product to the United States and receives revenues denominated in U.S. dollars from upscale Mexican theme-party planners. If the peso were to strengthen in relation to the dollar, then import revenues could be significantly less than domestic expenses. Pete's Primo Piñatas would suffer economic losses as a result of its economic exposure to exchange rate risk.

---

### 3.2  Techniques for Economic Exposure Mitigation

Economic exposures typically relate to organization-wide issues and can usually only be mitigated with organization-wide approaches that involve restructuring and adjustments to the business plan.

### 3.2.1  Restructuring

Economic exposure to currency fluctuations can be mitigated by restructuring the sources of income and expense to the consolidated entity.

- **Decreases in Sales**

  A company fearful of a depreciating foreign currency used by a foreign subsidiary may elect to reduce foreign sales to preserve cash flows.

■ **Increases in Expenses**

A company anticipating a depreciating foreign currency may elect to increase reliance on those suppliers to take advantage of paying for raw materials or supplies with cheaper currency.

### 3.2.2 Characteristics of Restructuring and Economic Exposure

Restructuring tends to be more difficult than ordinary hedges. Economic exposures to exchange rate fluctuations are viewed as more difficult to manage than transaction exposures.

| Question 1 | CPA-05860 |
|---|---|

If the dollar price of the euro rises, which of the following will occur?

- **a.** The dollar depreciates against the euro.
- **b.** The euro depreciates against the dollar.
- **c.** The euro will buy fewer European goods.
- **d.** The euro will buy fewer U.S. goods.

| Question 2 | CPA-05590 |
|---|---|

What is the effect when a foreign competitor's currency becomes weaker compared with the U.S. dollar?

- **a.** The foreign company will have an advantage in the U.S. market.
- **b.** The foreign company will be disadvantaged in the U.S. market.
- **c.** The fluctuation in the foreign currency's exchange rate has *no* effect on the U.S. company's sales or cost of goods sold.
- **d.** It is better for the U.S. company when the value of the U.S. dollar strengthens.

| Question 3 | CPA-05767 |
|---|---|

Platinum Co. has a receivable due in 30 days for 30,000 euros. The treasurer is concerned that the value of the euro relative to the dollar will drop before the payment is received. What should Platinum do to reduce this risk?

- **a.** Buy 30,000 euros now.
- **b.** Enter into an interest rate swap contract for 30 days.
- **c.** Enter into a forward contract to sell 30,000 euros in 30 days.
- **d.** Platinum cannot effectively reduce this risk.

# Financial Management

## Module

# 1 Capital Structure Components

An entity's capital structure is the mix of debt (long-term and short-term) and equity (common and preferred) used to finance operations and growth.

## 1.1 Debt Financing

Entities use various forms of short-term and long-term debt in their capital structures. Common forms of short-term debt include short-term notes payable, commercial paper, and line-of-credit arrangements. Long-term debt may include long-term notes payable, debentures, bonds, and capital leases.

### 1.1.1 Commercial Paper

Commercial paper is an unsecured, short-term debt instrument issued by a corporation. Commercial paper matures in 270 days or less (the threshold above which commercial paper must be registered with the SEC) and typically matures in 30 days. The proceeds from commercial paper must be used to finance current assets such as account receivable or inventory, or to meet short-term obligations.

### 1.1.2 Debentures

A debenture represents an unsecured obligation of the issuing company. In the event of default, the holder of a debenture has the status of a general creditor. Risks associated with debentures may be mitigated by a negative-pledge clause that stops a company from pledging assets to additional debt.

### 1.1.3 Subordinated Debentures

A subordinated debenture is a bond issue that is unsecured and ranks behind senior creditors in the event of an issuer liquidation. Subordinated debentures command higher interest rates than debentures to allow for additional risk.

### 1.1.4 Income Bonds

Income bonds represent securities that pay interest only upon achievement of target income levels. Income bonds represent a risky bond that typically only is used in reorganizations.

### 1.1.5 Junk Bonds

Junk bonds are characterized by high default risk and high return. Junk bonds are classified as "noninvestment grade" bonds by the major credit rating agencies given their more likely default on principal and/or interest payments by the issuer. Junk bonds are frequently used to raise capital for acquisitions and leveraged buyouts.

**Illustration 1      Junk Bonds**

Rust Belt Industries is looking to close its machinery plant in the small town of Oxidation, Ohio. The company is the only major employer in Oxidation. To preserve their way of life, employees have decided to buy the company from its current owners. The group of employees completed a leveraged buyout of the owners by issuing noninvestment grade (junk) bonds.

### 1.1.6   Mortgage Bonds

A mortgage is a loan that is secured by residential or commercial real property. Mortgages are usually pooled together and issued as mortgage bonds, with bondholders protected from default by a lien on the pooled real property assets. A distinguishing feature of mortgage bonds is that trustees act on behalf of bondholders to foreclose on mortgage assets in the event of default.

### 1.1.7   Leasing

A lease represents a contractual agreement in which the owner of an asset, the lessor, allows another party, the lessee, to use the property (asset) in exchange for periodic lease payments.

- **Operating Lease**

    *Operating leases* are those instances in which a property is rented over an insignificant portion of the asset's useful life with no obligation (or opportunity) to assume ownership of the property. Operating leases are considered off-balance sheet financing for the lessee, as there is no balance sheet effect with the periodic rent payments reflected as rent expense on the income statement. Companies that use operating leases (versus capital leases) will have stronger financial ratios because liabilities are lower (debt off-balance sheet) and, in the early years of the lease, rent expense is lower than the combined depreciation expense and interest expense reported under a capital lease.

- **Capital Lease**

    *Capital (or finance leases per IFRS)* are analogous to a lessee buying an asset and financing it with debt. The lessee records the present value of the minimum lease payments as an asset on its balance sheet as well as the corresponding current and long-term lease obligations. Instead of recording rent expense on the income statement, the lessee records both depreciation expense and interest expense under a capital lease. Generally, (lessee) firms that desire to report higher periodic operating cash flows prefer using capital leases over operating leases because the principal portion of the capital lease payment is reported as a financing cash outflow, while the entire (rent) payment under an operating lease is reported as an operating cash outflow. In order to classify a lease as a capital lease, a lessee must meet one of the following four criteria:

- • **Ownership** transfer at the end of lease

- • **Written** option for bargain purchase

- • **Ninety** (90) percent of lease property FV ≤ PV of lease payments

- • **Seventy-five** (75) percent or more of the asset's economic life is committed in the lease term

    If none of the above criteria are met, the lessee must treat the lease as an operating lease.

---

### Illustration 2 Leasing

Phillips Manufacturing Company is working on its strategic plan for the upcoming year. Due to increased product demand, the company must expand its manufacturing by either constructing a new building or leasing an existing manufacturing facility for the next five years.

Management carefully weighs both options and recommends leasing the facility using an operating lease based on the following factors:

1. There are tax advantages offered by leasing, given Phillips' existing marginal tax rates;

2. The company has high financial leverage, and an operating lease structure will be used to keep additional debt off-balance sheet;

3. The use of an operating lease will improve the company's return on invested capital ratios; and

4. Local real estate prices have been highly volatile. Leasing provides additional flexibility, allowing management to reassess the lease-versus-buy decision and the level of product demand in five years.

## 1.2 Equity Financing

Equity financing involves the issuance of equity (stock) securities that represent different forms of ownership of the company. A distinguishing feature of equity securities is the rights of shareholders to a firm's assets in a bankruptcy (liquidation) are less than that of both secured and unsecured bondholders.

### 1.2.1 Preferred Stock

Preferred stock is a hybrid equity security that has features similar to both debt and equity. Preferred shares offer or require a fixed dividend payment to their holders, which is similar to coupon payments made on debt instruments. They are like equity because the timing of the dividend payment is at the discretion of the board of directors (not mandatory) and the dividend payments are not tax deductible. Preferred shares may have the following features and uses:

■ **Cumulative Dividends**

A cumulative provision on preferred stock may require that (unpaid) *dividends in arrears* on preferred stock from a prior period be paid prior to the distribution of common stock dividends.

■ **Participating Feature**

Preferred shares may participate in declared dividends along with common shareholders to the extent that undistributed dividends exist after satisfying both preferred dividend requirements and common shareholder requirements at the preferred dividend rate.

■ **Voting Rights**

In rare circumstances, preferred shares are given voting rights. Usually these situations are associated with dividends in arrears for significant periods.

### 1.2.2 Common Stock

*Common stock* represents the basic equity ownership security of a corporation. Common stock includes voting rights with optional dividend payments by the issuer. Most common stock is issued with a stated par value. When the common stock is issued at a given market price, the proceeds received by the issuer are separated between the common stock account (i.e., par value times the number of shares issued) and the additional paid-in capital account. A negative feature of common equity is that common shareholders have the lowest claim to a firm's assets in a liquidation.

## Pass Key

The following table summarizes some of the general characteristics of debt and equity financing:

|  | Debt | Equity |
|---|---|---|
| Flexibility | No | Yes |
| Tax deductibility | Yes | No |
| EPS dilution | No | Yes |
| Increased financial risk | Yes | No |
| Security issuance costs | Low | High |
| Investor return | Fixed | Variable |

# 2    Weighted Average Cost of Capital

The *weighted average cost of capital* (WACC) serves as a major link between the long-term investment decisions associated with a corporation's capital structure and the wealth of a corporation's owners. The weighted average cost of capital is the average cost of all forms of financing used by a company. WACC is often used internally as a hurdle rate for capital investment decisions. The theoretical optimal capital structure is the mix of financing instruments that produces the lowest WACC.

## Pass Key

The value of a firm can be computed as the present value of the cash flow it produces, discounted by the costs of capital used to finance it. The mixture of debt and equity financing that produces the lowest WACC maximizes the value of the firm.

## 2.1    Computing the Weighted Average Cost of Capital (WACC)

The *weighted average cost of capital* (WACC) is the average cost of debt and equity financing associated with a firm's existing assets and operations.

### 2.1.1    Formula

The weighted average cost of capital is determined by weighting the cost of each specific type of capital by its proportion to the firm's total capital structure.

> WACC  =  Cost of equity multiplied by the percentage equity in capital structure  +  Weighted average cost of debt multiplied by the percentage debt in capital structure

- The percentage equity and percentage debt in the capital structure is calculated using the market values of the outstanding debt and equity, if market values are available.

---

### Example 1    Calculating WACC

**Facts:** Assume that the cost of equity capital for XYZ Company is 17.8 percent. Also assume a weighted average interest rate of 10 percent and a targeted capital structure composed of 75 percent equity and 25 percent debt. Finally, assume a tax rate of 30 percent.

**Required:** Compute XYZ's WACC.

**Solution:**

1.  Cost of debt (after tax):

    =  Interest rate × (1 − Tax rate)

    =  10% × (1 − 30%)

    =  10% × 70%

    =  7%

2.  WACC = (17.8% × 75%) + (7% × 25%) = 15.1%

If XYZ is using its WACC as the hurdle rate, then it should invest in any project that will yield a return higher than 15.1 percent.

---

### 2.1.2    Individual Capital Components

*Individual capital components* include both long-term and short-term elements of a firm's permanent financing mix.

- **Long-Term Elements:** *Long-term elements* include long-term debt, preferred stock, common stock, and retained earnings.

- **Short-Term Elements:** *Short-term elements* may include short-term interest-bearing debt (e.g., notes payable). Other forms of current liabilities (e.g., accounts payables and accruals) are rarely, if ever, included in the cost-of-capital estimate, because they generally represent interest-free capital.

- **After-Tax Cash Flows:** In evaluating the cost of the components of capital structure, *after-tax cash flows* are the most relevant. The cost of debt is computed on an after-tax basis because interest expense is tax deductible.

## 2.2    Weighted Average Cost of Debt

The relevant cost of *long-term debt* is the after-tax cost of raising long-term funds through borrowing. Sources of long-term debt generally include issuance of bonds or long-term loans. Debt costs are generally stated as the interest rate of the various debt instruments. In some cases, debt costs are stated according to basis points above U.S. Treasury bond rates (where 1 basis point is equal to one-hundredth of 1 percent, or 0.01 percent). The weighted average interest rate is calculated by dividing a company's total interest obligations on an annual basis by the debt outstanding:

$$\text{Weighted average interest rate} \; = \; \frac{\text{Effective annual interest payments}}{\text{Debt outstanding}}$$

### 2.2.1    Pretax Cost of Debt

The *pretax cost of debt* represents the cost of debt before considering the tax shielding effects of the debt.

### 2.2.2    After-Tax Cost of Debt

Because interest on debt is tax deductible, the tax savings reduces the actual cost of debt. The formula for computing the after-tax cost of debt is:

$$\text{After-tax cost of debt} \; = \; \text{Pretax cost of debt} \times (1 - \text{Tax rate})$$

| Example 2 | After-Tax Cost of Long-Term Debt |
|---|---|

**Facts:** Assume that the long-term debt component of the weighted average cost of capital for a firm includes a pretax cost of debt of 12.5 percent and a 30 percent tax rate.

**Required:** Compute the after-tax cost of long-term debt.

**Solution:**

$$
\begin{aligned}
\text{After-tax cost of long-term debt} \; &= \; \text{Pretax cost of debt} \times (1 - \text{Tax rate}) \\
&= \; 0.125 \times (1 - 0.30) \\
&= \; 0.125 \times 0.7 \\
&= \; 0.0875 = 8.75\%
\end{aligned}
$$

Although the pretax interest rate is 12.5 percent, the after-tax interest rate, after considering the deductibility of the interest expense, is 8.75 percent. Note that if the tax rate increased to 40 percent, the cost of debt would decrease to 7.5 percent [12.5% × (1 − 0.40)].

## Pass Key

- Debt carries the lowest cost of capital and the interest is tax deductible.
- The higher the tax rate, the more incentive exists to use debt financing.

## 2.3 Cost of Preferred Stock

The cost of preferred stock is the dividends paid to preferred stockholders. After-tax considerations are irrelevant with equity securities because dividends are not tax deductible.

### 2.3.1 Formula

$$\text{Cost of preferred stock} = \frac{\text{Preferred stock dividends}}{\text{Net proceeds of preferred stock}}$$

### 2.3.2 Preferred Stock Dividends

Preferred stock dividends can be stated as a dollar amount or a percentage. For example, 5 percent preferred stock pays an annual dividend of 5 percent of par value, if dividends are declared by the corporation.

### 2.3.3 Net Proceeds of Preferred Stocks

The net proceeds from a preferred stock issuance can be calculated as the proceeds net of flotation costs (i.e., issuance costs).

### Example 3      Cost of Preferred Stock

**Facts:** Assume that the preferred stock component of the weighted average cost of capital for a firm is 10 percent, $100 par value preferred stock that was issued at par value with a flotation cost of $5 per share.

**Required:** Compute the cost of preferred stock.

**Solution:**

Preferred stock dividend = Dividend percentage times par value = 10% × $100 = $10

Cost of preferred stock = Dividends / Net proceeds

= $10 / ($100 − $5)

= $10 / $95

= 0.1053 = 10.53%

    

## 2.4    Cost of Retained Earnings

The cost of equity capital obtained through retained earnings is equal to the rate of return required by the firm's common stockholders. A firm should earn at least as much on any earnings retained and reinvested in the business as stockholders could have earned on alternative investments of equivalent risk. As mentioned above, after-tax considerations are irrelevant to equity securities because dividends are not tax deductible. Arriving at the components of the formula for the cost of retained earnings can be difficult and potentially subjective.

### 2.4.1   Three Common Methods of Computing the Cost of Retained Earnings

**1.**  Capital asset pricing model (CAPM)

**2.**  Discounted cash flow (DCF)

**3.**  Bond yield plus risk premium (BYRP)

### 2.4.2   The Capital Asset Pricing Model (CAPM)

**Key Assumptions**

- The cost of retained earnings is equal to the risk-free rate plus a risk premium.

- The market risk premium is equal to the systematic (nondiversifiable) risks associated with the overall stock market.

- The beta coefficient is a numerical representation of the volatility (risk) of the stock relative to the volatility of the overall market. A beta equal to 1 means the stock is as volatile as the market, and a beta greater (less) than 1 means the stock is more (less) volatile than the market.

- The risk premium is the stock's beta coefficient multiplied by the market risk premium.

- The market risk premium is the market rate of return minus the risk-free rate.

**Cost of Retained Earnings Formula (CAPM)**

Cost of retained earnings  =  Risk-free rate + Risk premium

=  Risk-free rate + (Beta × Market risk premium)

=  Risk-free rate + [Beta × (Market return − Risk-free rate)]

| Example 4 | Capital Asset Pricing Model |
|---|---|

**Facts:** Assume that a firm's beta is 1.25, the risk-free rate is 8.75 percent, and the market rate of return is 14.25 percent.

**Required:** Compute the cost of retained earnings using the capital asset pricing model (CAPM).

**Solution:** Cost of retained earnings using the capital asset pricing model (CAPM):

Cost of retained earnings  =  Risk-free rate + Risk premium

=  0.0875 + [1.25 × (0.1425 − 0.0875)]

=  0.0875 + [1.25 × 0.0550]

=  0.0875 + 0.0688

=  0.1563 = 15.63%

### 2.4.3　Discounted Cash Flow (DCF)

■　**Key Assumptions**

- Stocks are normally in equilibrium relative to risk and return.

- The estimated expected rate of return will yield an estimated required rate of return.

- The expected growth rate may be based on projections of past growth rates, a retention growth model, or analysts' forecasts.

■　**Formula**

$$\text{Cost of retained earnings} = \frac{D_1}{P_0} + g$$

Where:

$P_0$ = Current market value or price of the outstanding common stock

$D_1$ = The dividend per share expected at the end of one year

$g$ = The constant rate of growth in dividends

---

**Example 5　　Discounted Cash Flow**

**Facts:** Assume that a firm is a constant growth firm that just paid an annual common stock dividend of $2.00, has a dividend growth rate of 7.5 percent, and a current market price for common stock of $25.25 per share.

**Required:** Compute the cost of retained earnings using the discounted cash flow (DCF) method.

**Solution:** Compute the dividend per share expected at the end of the year as follows:

$D_1$　=　$D_0 \times (1 + g)$

$D_1$　=　$2.00 \times (1 + 0.075)$

$D_1$　=　$2.00 \times 1.075$

$D_1$　=　$2.15

Cost of retained earnings using the discounted cash flow (DCF) method:

$$\text{Cost of retained earnings} = (D_1 / P_0) + g$$
$$= (\$2.15 / \$25.25) + 0.075$$
$$= 0.0851 + 0.075$$
$$= 0.1601 = 16.01\%$$

---

### 2.4.4　The Bond Yield Plus Risk Premium (BYRP)

■　**Key Assumptions**

- Equity and debt security values are comparable before taxes.

- Risks are associated with both the individual firm and the state of the economy. Risk premiums depend on nondiversifiable risk.

- Risk estimation can be derived by using a market analysts' survey approach or by subtracting the yield on an average (A-rated) corporate long-term bond from an estimate of the return on the equity market.

■ **Formula**

> Cost of retained earnings = Pretax cost of long-term debt + Market risk premium

### Example 6 — Bond Yield Plus Risk Premium

**Facts:** Assume that a firm has estimated its market risk premium at 4.5 percent and has determined that the yield to maturity on its own bonds is 11.34 percent.

**Required:** Compute the cost of retained earnings using the bond yield plus risk premium (BYRP) method.

**Solution:** Cost of retained earnings using the bond yield plus risk premium method:

Cost of retained earnings = Firm's own bond yield + Market risk premium
= 0.1134 + 0.045
= 0.1584 = 15.84%

### 2.4.5 Comparison of the CAPM, DCF, and BYRP Methods

Each method is a valid method of calculating the cost of retained earnings.

The average of the three cost amounts could be used as the estimate of the cost of retained earnings if there is sufficient consistency in the results of the three methods.

### Example 7 — Cost of Retained Earnings

**Facts:** The cost of retained earnings under:

CAPM method = 15.63%
DCF method = 16.01%
BYRP method = 15.84%

**Required:** Compute the average cost of retained earnings.

**Solution:** Average cost of retained earnings:

$$\text{Average} = \frac{(CAPM + DCF + BYRP)}{3}$$

$$= \frac{(15.63\% + 16.01\% + 15.84\%)}{3}$$

$$= 15.83\%$$

| Question 1 | CPA-03385 |
|---|---|

DQZ Telecom is considering a project for the coming year, which will cost $50 million. DQZ plans to use the following combination of debt and equity to finance the investment.

- Issue $15 million of 20-year bonds at a price of 101, with a coupon rate of 8 percent, and flotation costs of 2 percent of par.

- Use $35 million of funds generated from (retained) earnings.

The equity market is expected to earn 12 percent. U.S. Treasury bonds are currently yielding 5 percent. The beta coefficient for DQZ is estimated to be 0.60. DQZ is subject to an effective corporate income tax rate of 40 percent. Assume that the after-tax cost of debt is 7 percent and the cost of equity is 12 percent. Determine the weighted average cost of capital.

    **a.** 10.50 percent

    **b.** 8.50 percent

    **c.** 9.50 percent

    **d.** 6.30 percent

| Question 2 | CPA-03420 |
|---|---|

Using the capital asset pricing model (CAPM), the required rate of return for a firm with a beta of 1.25 when the market return is 14 percent and the risk-free rate of 6 percent is:

    **a.** 14 percent.

    **b.** 7.5 percent.

    **c.** 17.5 percent.

    **d.** 16 percent.

**NOTES**

# 1  Optimal Capital Structure

The *optimal cost of capital* is the ratio of debt to equity that produces the lowest WACC. Required rates of return demanded by debt and equity holders fluctuate as the ratio of debt to equity changes. At some point as debt to equity increases, leverage becomes more pronounced and debtors will demand a greater return for the high level of default risk. In addition, equity holders also will require a greater return due to the negative effect of high leverage on their potential future cash flows.

## 1.1  Determination of Lowest WACC

The following graph displays an example of the cost of using equity financing, the cost of using debt financing, and the resulting WACC as debt and equity conditions change. In this example, the firm achieves its lowest WACC when its debt-to-equity ratio is at 4.0.

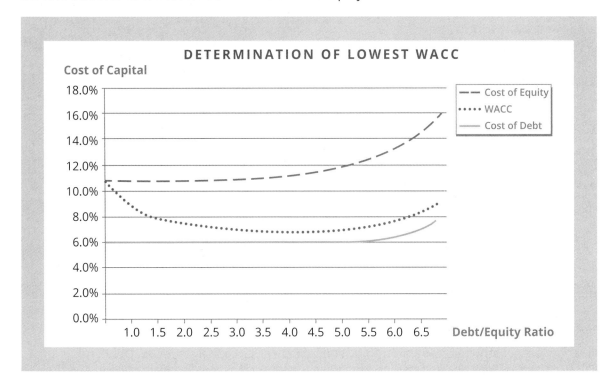

## 1.2 Application to Capital Budgeting

Generally, new projects are funded by sources of capital that maintain the optimum capital structure (ratio of debt to equity) and meet or exceed the hurdle rate implied by its cost. The historic weighted average cost of capital may not be appropriate for use as a discount rate for a new capital project unless the project carries the same risk as the corporation and results in identical leveraging characteristics. Appropriate application of the weighted average cost of capital as a hurdle rate for capital projects involves use of the weighted average cost of each additional new dollar of capital raised at the margin as that capital need arises.

# 2 Asset Structure

While a firm's capital structure relates to the debt and equity components of its balance sheet, the asset structure relates to the composition of assets on its balance sheet. Specifically, asset structure describes the dollar amounts in each line on the balance sheet and the proportions of the assets that are classified as current and long-term.

## 2.1 Current Assets

Current assets are expected to provide economic benefits to the company within the 12-month period following the balance sheet date. Examples of current assets include:

- Cash and cash equivalents
- Inventory
- Accounts receivable
- Notes receivable
- Prepaid expenses
- Marketable security investments classified as trading

## 2.2 Non-current Assets

Non-current assets represent probable economic benefits that will extend beyond the next 12 months. Examples of non-current assets include:

- Long-term investments
- Property, plant, and equipment
- Intangible assets
- Deferred tax assets

## 2.3 Influence of Capital Structure

An entity's asset structure is influenced by and influences its capital structure. Debt and equity issuances may be used to fund long-term assets such as building construction and the acquisition of other companies. When a company issues new debt or equity, it receives an immediate cash infusion that boosts current assets. With debt in the capital structure, cash (or other current assets that can easily be converted to cash) are needed to fund interest and principal payments when they come due. With equity, the company may choose to pay dividends, which require cash payments (typically each quarter).

# 3    Loan Covenants and Capital Structure

Lenders use debt covenants to protect their interests by limiting or prohibiting the actions of borrowers that might negatively affect the position of the lenders. An entity's capital structure influences the extent to which it is subjected to loan covenants. If a borrower's capital structure is heavily weighted toward equity, its financial leverage will be low and its fixed obligations associated with debt will be relatively minimal. In these situations, loan covenants may not be particularly stringent or difficult to maintain because there is less risk that the borrower will be unable to make its interest and principal payments. However, when a borrower has a significant amount of outstanding debt relative to equity, loan covenants will typically increase and become more stringent because there is more risk for the lender.

# 4    Growth and Profitability

Investors, creditors/lenders, and individuals who do business with a company want to see sustainable growth and profitability over time; this provides assurance that the company will meet its obligations and provide a positive return on investment for its stakeholders. Both growth and profitability are affected by an entity's capital structure.

## 4.1    Growth Rate

The growth rate associated with a company's earnings is a key component of financial valuation. A company's annual earnings are allocated between dividend payments to shareholders and retained earnings. The percentage that is retained is multiplied by the company's return on equity (ROE) to produce the growth rate.

> Growth rate (g) = Retention ratio (rr) × Return on equity (ROE)

| Example 1 | Growth Rate |
| --- | --- |

**Facts:** A company calculates return on equity of 7.5 percent in the current year.

**Required:** Calculate the expected growth rate if the company follows a policy of paying out 40 percent of all earnings as dividends.

**Solution:** The growth rate is 4.5 percent, which is equal to the ROE of 7.5 percent multiplied by the retention ratio of 60 percent. (If the dividend payout ratio is 40 percent the retention ratio is equal to 1 − 40 percent, or 60 percent).

### 4.1.1    Influence of Capital Structure

An entity's capital structure influences its growth rate. The retention ratio is influenced by the level of equity. Dividends paid to shareholders increase the dividend payout ratio and decrease the retention ratio and the overall growth rate. Return on equity is affected by an entity's net income (which is reduced by interest expense associated with a company's debt) and the amount of equity (relative to debt) in a firm's capital structure. Lower net income and/or higher equity decrease the growth rate.

## 4.2　Profitability

A key financial measure of success for a company is profitability. Measures of profitability include return on investment (ROI), return on assets (ROA), and return on equity (ROE). All else being equal, a higher profitability ratio (over time for a single company or relative to its peers when comparing companies) is desirable.

$$\text{Return on investment (ROI)} = \frac{\text{Net income}}{\text{Invested capital}}$$

$$\text{Return on assets (ROA)} = \frac{\text{Net income}}{\text{Assets}}$$

$$\text{Return on equity (ROE)} = \frac{\text{Net income}}{\text{Shareholders' equity}}$$

### 4.2.1　Influence of Capital Structure

ROI, ROA, and ROE measure profitability after accounting for capital structure decisions. Net income is the bottom line of the income statement after both interest expense and taxes are taken into account. The higher an entity's debt, the greater the impact of interest expense on net income. Dividend payments affect these ratios in the sense that dividend payments reduce assets and retained earnings (equity).

# 5　Leverage and Risk

Leverage affects the variability of company profits and, therefore, affects the risk assumed (and return required) by creditors and owners. Leverage is a significant consideration as a factor in designing capital structure. Financial managers must consider both operating leverage and financial leverage.

## 5.1　Operating Leverage

### 5.1.1　Definition

Operating leverage is the degree to which a company uses fixed operating costs rather than variable operating costs. Capital-intensive industries often have high operating leverage. Labor-intensive industries generally have low operating leverage.

### 5.1.2　Implications

A company with high operating leverage must produce sufficient sales revenue to cover its high fixed-operating costs. High operating leverage is beneficial when sales revenue is high. High contribution margin indicates high operating leverage.

A company with high operating leverage will have greater risk but greater possible returns. There is risk because the variability of profits is greater with higher operating leverage.

When sales decline, a company with high operating leverage may struggle to cover its fixed costs. However, beyond the breakeven point, a company with higher fixed costs will retain a higher percentage of additional revenues as operating income (earnings before interest and taxes or EBIT).

---

### Illustration 1    Operating Leverage

When Pat Jones compared his company's operating leverage with a competitor's operating leverage, Jones found that his company experienced a 21 percent increase in EBIT as a result of a 5 percent increase in sales, while the competitor experienced a 10 percent increase in EBIT as a result of a 5 percent increase in sales. Jones' company has higher operating leverage than the competitor, which implies that fixed costs constitute a higher proportion of his company's total costs compared with the competitor. As a result, Jones' company will need to generate more revenue to cover its fixed costs, but will be highly profitable once those fixed costs are met.

---

### Illustration 2    High Operating Leverage

Nursing homes and hospitals are required to meet minimum staffing levels to maintain bed capacity. Salaries represent a fixed cost of maintaining capacity and result in higher operating leverage.

---

### Illustration 3    Low Operating Leverage

Big box retailers have high variable operating costs in their cost of goods sold and part-time labor pool, resulting in low operating leverage.

---

## 5.2    Financial Leverage

### 5.2.1    Definition

When making financing decisions, a firm can choose to issue debt or equity. When debt is issued, the firm generally must pay fixed interest costs. Equity issuances do not result in an increase in fixed costs because dividend payments are not required. Financial leverage is the degree to which a company uses debt rather than equity to finance the company.

### 5.2.2    Implications

A company that issues debt must produce sufficient operating income (EBIT) to cover its fixed interest costs. However, once fixed interest costs are covered, additional EBIT will go straight to net income and earnings per share. A higher degree of financial leverage implies that a relatively small change in earnings before interest and taxes (increase or decrease) will have a greater effect on profits and shareholder value. Another benefit of financial leverage is that interest costs are tax deductible, whereas dividends are not.

Companies that are highly leveraged may be at risk of bankruptcy if they are unable to make payments on their debt. They also may be unable to find new lenders in the future.

### Illustration 4     Financial Leverage

If a firm with significant debt experiences a 42 percent increase in EPS as a result of a 21 percent increase in EBIT, the firm has more than enough operating income to cover its fixed interest costs. As a result, EPS has been magnified. If the firm had issued equity rather than debt, EPS most likely would have decreased because the number of shares outstanding would have increased. The higher a firm's financial leverage, the greater its potential profitability (but also the greater its risk).

### Illustration 5     Financial Leverage

Jax Company issues new common equity to obtain cash for the purchase of new equipment for $1,000,000. Jax is not using financial leverage, and has no fixed financing costs associated with this transaction. Jax may or may not pay dividends to the new stockholders.

Max Company borrows $900,000 and uses its own cash of $100,000 to buy equipment. Max is using financial leverage, and now must pay fixed interest costs annually.

In the next year, the economy enters recession, and profits do not materialize for Jax or Max as each had expected. Max must pay the fixed interest cost on the loan, which further erodes its already tight cash flow. Jax has no interest expense and protects its cash by not declaring a dividend.

In future years, as sales improve, Max Company will benefit from financial leverage because interest is a fixed charge and is tax deductible. Additional earnings in excess of the interest charges will go straight to EPS. Jax, however, has no such guarantee because dividends are not fixed and shareholders may require larger returns. In addition, Jax has more shares of stock outstanding, which dilutes EPS.

## 6     Impact of Capital Structure on Financial Ratios

An entity's solvency, or ability to meet its long-term obligations, is affected by the amount of debt in its capital structure. Solvency can be measured using ratios such as debt to total capital, debt to equity, and debt to assets. The times interest earned ratio measures the company's ability to meet its interest obligations on long-term debt.

### 6.1     Debt-to-Total-Capital Ratio

$$\text{Debt-to-total-capital ratio} = \frac{\text{Total debt}}{\text{Total capital*}}$$

*Total capital = Debt + Equity = Total assets

- **Interpretation:** The debt-to-total-capital ratio provides indications related to an organization's long-term debt-paying ability. The lower the ratio, the greater the level of solvency and the greater the presumed ability to pay debts. The debt-to-total-capital ratio is alternatively expressed as the debt-to-assets ratio.

▪ **Variations:** Some analysts adjust the debt-to-total capital ratio to exclude certain items from the denominator (such as reserves, deferred taxes, minority shareholder interests, and redeemable preferred stock) as a basis for refining the amount truly available to liquidate debt.

## 6.2    Debt-to-Equity Ratio

Although comprehensive ratios provide insights into the overall solvency, relationships between the elements of capital structure provide more refined views of solvency.

$$\text{Debt-to-equity ratio} \ = \ \frac{\text{Total debt}}{\text{Total shareholders' equity}}$$

▪ **Interpretation:** The debt-to-equity ratio relates the two major categories of capital structure to each other and indicates the degree of leverage used. The lower the ratio, the lower the risk involved.

▪ **Variations:** Some analysts use the reciprocal of this ratio (total shareholders' equity to total debt) to measure the amount of equity backing up every dollar of debt. Another alternative version of this ratio uses only long-term debt in the numerator to purely compare only the long-term elements of capital structure.

## 6.3    Times Interest Earned Ratio

The times interest earned ratio shows the number of times the interest charges are covered by net operating income.

$$\text{Times interest earned ratio} \ = \ \frac{\text{Earnings before interest and taxes (EBIT)}}{\text{Interest expense}}$$

▪ **Interpretation:** The times interest earned ratio measures the ability of the company to pay its interest charges as they come due. It is a measure of long-term solvency.

| Question 1 | CPA-03431 |
|---|---|

Sylvan Corporation has the following capital structure:

| Debenture bonds | $10,000,000 |
|---|---|
| Preferred equity | 1,000,000 |
| Common equity | 39,000,000 |

The financial leverage of Sylvan Corp. would increase as a result of:

    **a.**   Issuing common stock and using the proceeds to retire preferred stock.

    **b.**   Issuing common stock and using the proceeds to retire debenture bonds.

    **c.**   Financing its future investments with a higher percentage of bonds.

    **d.**   Financing its future investments with a higher percentage of equity funds.

# Working Capital Metrics

# 1 Working Capital

Working capital policy and working capital management involve managing cash so that a company can meet its short-term obligations, and include all aspects of the administration of current assets (CA) and current liabilities (CL). The goal of working capital management is shareholder wealth maximization. The optimal mix of current assets and current liabilities depends on the nature of the business and the industry and requires offsetting the benefit of CA and CL against the probability of technical insolvency.

## 1.1 Definition of Net Working Capital

Net working capital is defined as the difference between current assets (CA) and current liabilities (CL).

## 1.2 Balancing Profitability and Risk

Working capital must be financed either with long-term or short-term debt or with stockholders' equity. Adequate working capital reserves mitigate risk, and thereby increase profitability. Less working capital increases risk by exposing a company to the likelihood of a possible failure to meet current obligations and potentially reducing a firm's ability to obtain additional short-term financing.

## 1.3 Analysis of Working Capital

Working capital metrics should be evaluated regularly. A ratio on its own will have some value, but significant value lies in examining ratio trends and making comparisons for both a single entity across time and comparisons to industry/peers at a point in time. Ratios provide quantitative support for understanding and explaining trends and changes in financial and business operations.

# 2 Working Capital Ratios

## 2.1 Current Ratio

### 2.1.1 Formula

$$\text{Current ratio} = \frac{\text{Current assets}}{\text{Current liabilities}}$$

### 2.1.2 Interpretation

The net amount of working capital (CA minus CL) measures the amount by which current assets exceed current liabilities, and the current ratio (CA divided by CL) measures the number of times current assets exceed current liabilities and is a way of measuring short-term solvency. This ratio demonstrates a firm's ability to generate cash to meet its short-term obligations.

### 2.1.3  Analysis

In general, a higher current ratio is better. The current ratio is generally considered to be the best single indicator of a company's ability to meet short-term obligations. The current ratio measures liquidity at a point in time, but it is not indicative of future cash flows.

- **Deteriorating Current Ratio**

  A decline in the current ratio, which implies a reduced ability to generate cash, can be attributable to increases in short-term debt, decreases in current assets, or a combination of both.

- **Improving Current Ratio**

  An increase or improvement in the current ratio implies an increased ability to pay off current liabilities and may be attributable to using long-term borrowing to repay short-term debt (in cases in which a firm lacks cash to reduce current debts).

### 2.1.4  Limitations of the Current Ratio (and Other Liquidity Ratios)

Unless short-term liquidity is a relevant issue, the current ratio is not necessarily the best measure of the health of a business.

---

**Illustration 1     Current Ratio**

A restaurant might have low CA (e.g., accounts receivable and inventory) relative to CL (e.g., accounts payable and payroll obligations), but might otherwise be healthy in terms of increasing cash flows, growing reputation, good location, and limited long-term debt obligations.

A bookstore might have a high CA (e.g., inventory) relative to CL (e.g., accounts payable), but might otherwise be unhealthy in terms of diminishing cash flows, poor location, increased competition from Internet vendors, and low inventory turnover.

---

## 2.2    Quick (Acid-Test) Ratio

### 2.2.1  Formula

$$\text{Quick ratio} \ = \ \frac{\text{Cash + Marketable securities + Receivables}}{\text{Current liabilities}}$$

Some analysts elect to include prepaid assets in the numerator of the quick ratio, but it is more conservative to exclude such items.

### 2.2.2  Interpretation

The quick ratio is a more rigorous test of liquidity than the current ratio because inventory and prepaids are excluded from current assets. Inventory is the least liquid of current assets. The ability to meet current obligations without liquidating inventory is important.

### 2.2.3 Analysis

The higher the quick ratio (or acid-test ratio), the better.

## 2.3 Cash Ratio

### 2.3.1 Formula

$$\text{Cash ratio} = \frac{\text{Cash} + \text{Cash equivalents} + \text{Marketable securities}}{\text{Current liabilities}}$$

### 2.3.2 Interpretation

The cash ratio (also called the "cash coverage ratio") is the most conservative of the liquidity ratios. It measures the cash and cash equivalents a company has available to cover its short-term debts. All other current assets, such as inventory, marketable securities, and receivables, are excluded from the calculation.

### 2.3.3 Analysis

As is the case with the current ratio and the quick ratio, a higher cash ratio is better as it implies a greater ability to fund short-term debt obligations. While having a higher cash ratio demonstrates liquidity, excess idle cash may result in foregone opportunities to earn higher investment returns and enhance the growth of a company.

## 2.4 Cash Conversion Cycle

### 2.4.1 Formula

$$\text{Cash conversion cycle} = \begin{array}{c}\text{Inventory}\\\text{conversion}\\\text{period}\end{array} + \begin{array}{c}\text{Receivables}\\\text{collection}\\\text{period}\end{array} - \begin{array}{c}\text{Payables}\\\text{deferral}\\\text{period}\end{array}$$

### 2.4.2 Interpretation

The cash conversion cycle (sometimes called net operating cycle) is the length of time from the date of the initial expenditure for production to the date cash is collected from the customers offset by the length of time it takes to pay vendors for the initial expenditures.

### 2.4.3 Elements of the Cash Conversion Cycle Formula

The elements of the cash conversion cycle can most easily be calculated using the related turnover ratios.

■ **Inventory Conversion Period**

The inventory turnover ratio (the number of times a year inventory is sold) and the inventory conversion period (the average number of days inventory is held before it is sold) are measures of the effectiveness of an entity's inventory management. The inventory conversion period measures the degree to which resources have been devoted to inventory to support sales.

$$\text{Inventory turnover} = \frac{\text{Cost of goods sold}}{\text{Average inventory}}$$

$$\text{Inventory conversion period} = \frac{365}{\text{Inventory turnover}}$$

### Receivables Collection Period

The accounts receivable turnover ratio and the receivables collection period are measures of the effectiveness of a company's credit policy. The accounts receivable turnover ratio measures the number of times receivables are collected over an accounting period (typically one year). The receivables collection period measures the number of days after a typical credit sale is made until the firm receives payment:

$$\text{Accounts receivable turnover} = \frac{\text{Credit sales}}{\text{Average accounts receivable}}$$

$$\begin{array}{c}\text{Receivables}\\\text{collection}\\\text{period}\end{array} = \begin{array}{c}\text{Days sales}\\\text{outstanding}\\\text{(DSO)}\end{array} = \frac{365}{\text{Accounts receivable turnover}}$$

### Payables Deferral Period

The accounts payable turnover ratio (the number of times a year a company pays its suppliers) and the accounts payable deferral period (the average number of days it takes for a company to pay its suppliers) are measures of the effectiveness of a company's attempt to delay payment to creditors.

$$\text{Accounts payable turnover} = \frac{\text{Cost of goods sold}}{\text{Average accounts payable}}$$

$$\text{Accounts payable deferral period} = \frac{365}{\text{Accounts payable turnover}}$$

| Example 1 | Cash Conversion Cycle |
|---|---|

**Facts:** ABC Computers has annual sales of $36 million. On average, the company carries $5 million in inventory, $3 million in accounts receivable, and $3 million in accounts payable.

**Required:** If the annual cost of goods sold for ABC is $27 million, what is the length of the cash conversion cycle for the firm?

**Solution:** Inventory conversion period:

$$\text{Inventory turnover} = \frac{\$27,000,000}{\$5,000,000} = 5.4x$$

$$\text{Inventory conversion period} = \frac{365}{5.4} = 67.6 \text{ days}$$

Receivables collection period:

$$\text{AR turnover} = \frac{\$36,000,000}{\$3,000,000} = 12x$$

$$\text{Receivables collection period} = \frac{365}{12} = 30.4 \text{ days}$$

Payables deferral period:

$$\text{AP turnover} = \frac{\$27,000,000}{\$3,000,000} = 9x$$

$$\text{Payables deferral period} = \frac{365}{9} = 40.6 \text{ days}$$

$$\text{Cash conversion cycle} = 67.6 \text{ days} + 30.4 \text{ days} - 40.6 \text{ days} = 57.4 \text{ days}$$

### 2.4.4  Analysis

A company should minimize the amount of time it takes to convert inventory to cash while maximizing the amount of time it takes to pay vendors. Therefore, the lower the cash conversion cycle, the better. Each component of the cash conversion cycle should be analyzed individually.

▪ **Inventory Conversion Period**

A company is doing well when it quickly converts inventory into sales. A long inventory conversion period could mean that inventory becomes obsolete and ultimately a sunk cost to the entity. If the inventory conversion period is too short, the company may not have enough inventory on hand to support potential sales.

▪ **Receivables Collection Period**

A short receivables collection period is ideal, although a company may lose sales if its credit or collection policies are too strict. A long receivables collection period indicates that the company is struggling to collect from its customers.

▪ **Payables Deferral Period**

A company conserves cash by delaying payment to vendors for purchases on credit. Too short of a period presents the risk of not fully utilizing cash to the advantage of the company. Too long of a period may cause the company's relationship with its vendors to deteriorate.

## 2.5    Working Capital Turnover

### 2.5.1    Formula

$$\text{Working capital turnover} = \frac{\text{Sales}}{\text{Average working capital}}$$

Average working capital is the beginning-of-period plus end-of-period working capital divided by 2.

### 2.5.2    Interpretation

Working capital turnover is a measure of how effective a company is at generating sales based on funds used in operations.

### 2.5.3    Analysis

A higher working capital turnover ratio implies that a company is doing a relatively good job converting its working capital into sales. Too low of a ratio implies too much money is invested in current assets such as receivables and inventory relative to the amount of sales a company is generating from that capital. Too high of a ratio implies that there may not be enough capital in place to continue to support operations and sales.

| Question 1 | CPA-03528 |
| --- | --- |

Which one of the following would increase the working capital of a firm?

    **a.**   Cash collection of accounts receivable.

    **b.**   Refinancing of accounts payable with a two-year note payable.

    **c.**   Cash payment of accounts payable.

    **d.**   Payment of a 30-year mortgage payable with cash.

| Question 2 | CPA-03456 |
| --- | --- |

Which of the following transactions would increase the current ratio and decrease net profit?

    **a.**   A federal income tax payment due from the previous year is paid.

    **b.**   A long-term bond is retired before maturity at a discount.

    **c.**   A dividend is paid.

    **d.**   Vacant land is sold for less than the net book value.

## 1 Inventory Management

Inventory may represent the most significant current noncash resource of an organization. Inventory typically is most significant in businesses that involve the sale or manufacture of goods.

### 1.1 Types of Inventory

Inventory may be classified as raw materials, work-in-process, and finished goods.

- **Raw Materials:** Inventory held for use in the production process.
- **Work-in-Process:** Inventory in production but incomplete.
- **Finished Goods:** Production inventory that is complete and ready for sale.

### 1.2 Inventory Valuation

#### 1.2.1 Lower of Cost, Market, or Net Realizable Value

Inventory is generally accounted for at cost, which is the price paid to acquire an asset. When the value of the inventory falls below original cost, the inventory must be restated to the lower of market value or net realizable value. Inventory costed using LIFO or the retail inventory method is measured at the lower of cost or market value. Inventory costed using other methods is measured at the lower of cost or net realizable value.

#### 1.2.2 Market Value

Market value represents the median value of the item's replacement cost, the market ceiling, and the market floor.

- **Replacement Cost:** Replacement cost is equal to the cost to purchase the inventory on the valuation date.
- **Market Ceiling:** The market ceiling is the net selling price less the costs to complete and dispose of the inventory.
- **Market Floor:** The market floor is equal to the market ceiling less a normal profit margin.

#### 1.2.3 Net Realizable Value

Net realizable value is equal to the net selling price less costs to complete and dispose. This is also known as the market ceiling.

| Example 1 | Lower of Cost or Market |
| --- | --- |

**Facts:** Six months ago, Duffy Inc. purchased inventory for $55 per unit. The current replacement cost is $48 per unit, while the net selling price less costs to complete (net realizable value) is $51 and the normal profit margin is $5.

**Required:** Determine the value of the inventory on the balance sheet if the inventory is costed using LIFO and FIFO.

**Solution:** Under LIFO, the inventory is valued at the lower of cost or market:

     Cost  =  $55

   Market  =  $48

Market is the median value of the replacement cost ($48), market ceiling ($51), and market floor ($46 = $51 − $5).

The value of the inventory per unit on the balance sheet will be $48.

Under FIFO, the inventory is valued at the lower of cost and net realizable value:

         Cost  =  $55

  Net realizable value  =  $51

The value of the inventory per unit on the balance sheet will be $51.

## 1.3    Periodic vs. Perpetual Inventory Systems

### 1.3.1    Periodic Inventory System

In a periodic inventory system, inventory quantities are determined by physical counts performed at least annually. Inventory units are valued at the end of the accounting period and actual cost of goods sold for the period is determined after each physical inventory by calculating the difference between beginning inventory plus purchases less ending inventory.

### 1.3.2    Perpetual Inventory System

With a perpetual inventory system, the inventory balance is updated for each purchase and each sale, and is always current. Cost of goods sold is determined and recorded with each sale.

## 1.4    Cost Flow Assumptions

Inventory valuation depends on the inventory system employed and the cost flow assumption chosen by an entity.

### 1.4.1    Specific Identification Method

Under specific identification, the cost of each item in inventory is uniquely identified to that item. The cost follows the physical flow of the item in and out of inventory to cost of goods sold.

### 1.4.2    First In, First Out (FIFO) Method

Under FIFO, the first costs inventoried are the first costs transferred to cost of goods sold. Ending inventory on the balance sheet includes the most recently incurred costs and therefore approximates replacement cost. The periodic and perpetual inventory systems can be used with FIFO.

### 1.4.3   Last In, First Out (LIFO) Method

Under LIFO, the last costs inventoried are the first costs transferred to cost of goods sold. The ending inventory balance typically does not approximate replacement cost because ending inventory includes the oldest inventory. The periodic and perpetual inventory systems can be used with LIFO.

### 1.4.4   Weighted Average Method

The weighted average method calculates an average cost per item at the end of the period by dividing the total costs of inventory available by the total number of units of inventory available. This average cost is used for both the ending inventory balance and cost of goods sold. The weighted average method works with a periodic inventory system.

### 1.4.5   Moving Average Method

The moving average method computes the weighted average cost of the inventory after each purchase by dividing the total cost of inventory available after each purchase (inventory plus current purchase) by the total units available after each purchase. The moving average method requires the perpetual inventory system.

---

| Illustration 1 | Cost Flow Assumptions |
|---|---|

If a company chooses to use FIFO, the oldest costs inventoried are included in the cost of goods sold, leaving more recent purchases in the ending inventory balance on the balance sheet. When prices are falling, the older costs are the more expensive costs. Therefore, the cost of goods sold will be higher under FIFO and net income will be lower. In terms of working capital, current assets will be lower because inventory on the balance sheet will include the more recently purchased lower price inventory. As a result, working capital will be lower.

---

## 2   Inventory Management Strategies

### 2.1   Factors Influencing Inventory Levels

Inventory depends on the accuracy of sales forecasts. Lack of inventory can result in lost sales, and excessive inventory can result in burdensome carrying costs, including:

- Storage costs
- Insurance costs
- Opportunity costs of inventory investment
- Lost inventory due to obsolescence or spoilage

### Pass Key

The lower the carrying costs of inventory, the more inventory companies are willing to carry.

---

## 2.2 Optimal Levels of Inventory

Numerous factors affect the optimal level of inventory, including the usage rate of inventory per period of time, cost per unit of inventory, cost of placing orders for inventory, and the time required to receive inventory. Concepts related to the determination of the optimal level of inventory include:

- Inventory turnover
- Safety stock
- Reorder point
- Economic order quantity
- Materials requirements planning

## 2.3 Safety Stock

Many companies maintain safety stock to ensure that manufacturing or customer supply requirements are met. The determination of safety stock depends on the following factors:

- Reliability of sales forecasts
- Possibility of customer dissatisfaction resulting from back orders
- Stockout costs (the cost of running out of inventory), including loss of income, the cost of restoring goodwill with customers, and the cost of expedited shipping to meet customer demand
- Lead time (the time that elapses from the placement to the receipt of an order)
- Seasonal demands on inventory

## 2.4 Reorder Point

The reorder point is the inventory level at which a company should order or manufacture additional inventory to meet demand and to avert incurring stockout costs. The reorder point can be calculated using the following formula:

$$\text{Reorder point} = \text{Safety stock} + (\text{Lead time} \times \text{Sales during lead time})$$

### Example 2 | Reorder Point

**Facts:** Worldwide Widgets sells 8,000 widgets per year, manufactures widgets in groups of 1,500, and requires five weeks of lead time for widget production. Worldwide also maintains an absolute minimum safety stock of 1,200 widgets.

**Required:** Assuming a 50-week year and constant demand, compute Worldwide's reorder point for widgets.

**Solution:**

Worldwide sells an average of 160 widgets per week (8,000 widgets per year / 50 weeks).

Reorder point = Safety stock + (Lead time × Sales during lead time)

Reorder point = 1,200 widgets + (5 weeks × 160 widgets per week) = 2,000 widgets

Worldwide will manufacture additional widgets when its inventory of widgets falls to 2,000 units.

## 2.5   Economic Order Quantity

When managing inventory, there is a trade-off between carrying costs (the costs of holding inventory) and ordering costs (the costs of ordering additional inventory). For example, if the order quantity is small then carrying costs are low, but inventory must be ordered more frequently to meet demand, which increases ordering costs.

Ordering costs typically represent the costs of labor associated with order placement. The costs are driven by order frequency (rather than quantity per order) and they include the costs of entering the purchase order, processing the receipt of the inventory, inspecting the inventory to ensure that the goods received (typically a sample) are acceptable, and processing of the vendor invoice and consequent payment.

The *economic order quantity* (EOQ) inventory model attempts to minimize total ordering and carrying costs. The model can be applied to the management of any exchangeable good.

### 2.5.1   Assumptions

EOQ assumes that demand is known and is constant throughout the year, so EOQ does not consider stockout costs, nor does it account for costs of safety stock. EOQ also assumes that carrying costs per unit and ordering costs per unit are fixed.

### 2.5.2   The EOQ Equation and Equation Components

$$E = \sqrt{\frac{2SO}{C}}$$

◯ Order size (**EOQ**)

◯ Annual **Sales** (in units)

◯ Cost per Purchase **Order**

◯ Annual **Carrying** cost per unit

---

**Example 3**      **EOQ**

**Facts:** Maximus Company incurs carrying costs of $50 a month and each order costs the firm $5,625.

**Required:** Calculate Maximus' economic order quantity if Maximus goes through 100 units of inventory monthly.

**Solution:**

$$E = \sqrt{\frac{2SO}{C}}$$

$$E = \sqrt{\frac{2 \times 100 \times \$5,625}{\$50}}$$

$$E = 150 \text{ units}$$

When Maximus orders inventory, it should order 150 units to minimize total ordering costs and carrying costs.

**Note:** Although the formula calls for annual sales and carrying costs, using monthly sales in the numerator and monthly carrying costs in the denominator will produce the same result.

---

    

## 2.6    Other Inventory Management Issues

### 2.6.1    Just-in-Time Inventory Models

The *just-in-time (JIT) inventory model* was developed to reduce the lag time between inventory arrival and inventory use. JIT ties delivery of components to the speed of the assembly line. JIT reduces the need of manufacturers to carry large inventories, but requires a considerable degree of coordination between manufacturer and supplier. The benefits of JIT implementation include tying production scheduling with demand, more efficient flow of goods between warehouses and production, reduced setup time, and greater employee efficiencies.

### 2.6.2    Kanban Inventory Control

Kanban inventory control techniques give visual signals that a component required in production must be replenished. This technique prevents oversupply or interruption of the entire manufacturing process as the result of lacking a component.

### 2.6.3    Computerized Inventory Control

Computerized inventory control operates by establishing real-time communication links between the cashier and the stock room. Every purchase is recognized instantaneously by the inventory database, as is every product return. Computers are programmed to alert inventory managers as to reorder requirements. In some cases, company databases interface directly with supplier software to allow for instantaneous reorders, thereby removing the human element.

# 3    Supply Chain Management/Integrated Supply Chain Management (ISCM)

Integrated supply chain management (ISCM) exists when a firm and the entire supply chain (suppliers, producers, distributors, retailers, customers, and service providers) are able to reasonably predict the expected demand of consumers for a product and then plan accordingly to meet that demand. Integrated supply chain management is a collaborative effort between buyers and sellers.

## 3.1    Goal Is to Understand Needs and Preferences of Customers

The goal of ISCM is to better understand the needs and preferences of customers and cultivate the relationship with them. If the actual demand of the customer is met and excess supply does not exist in the market, the firm will be able to minimize costs all along the supply chain (e.g., raw materials, production, packaging, shipping, etc.).

## 3.2    Supply Chain Operations Reference (SCOR) Model

The SCOR model was developed by the Supply Chain Council, which attempted to create a generic model for supply chain analysis. The SCOR model assists a firm in mapping out its true supply chain and then configuring it to best fit the needs of the firm. There are four key management processes or core activities pertaining to SCOR: plan, source, make, and deliver.

### 3.2.1    Plan

The process of planning consists of developing a way to properly balance demand and supply within the goals and objectives of the firm and prepare for the necessary infrastructure. According to the Supply Chain Council, examples of activities associated with "plan" are:

- Determining the demand requirements
- Assessing the ability of the suppliers to supply resources
- Planning the inventory levels

- Planning the distribution of inventory
- Planning for the purchase of raw materials
- Assessing capacity concerns and capabilities
- Identifying viable distribution channels
- Configuring the supply chain
- Managing the product's life cycle
- Making make/buy decisions

### 3.2.2 Source

Once demand has been planned, it is necessary to procure the resources required to meet it and to manage the infrastructure that exists for the sources. According to the Supply Chain Council, this process deals with the following types of activities:

- Selecting vendors
- Obtaining vendor feedback and certification
- Overseeing and obtaining proper vendor contracts
- Collecting and processing vendor payments
- Ordering, inspecting, and storing inputs to the production process
- Overseeing the quality assurance process
- Assessing vendor performance

### 3.2.3 Make

The "make" process encompasses all the activities that turn the raw materials into finished products that are produced to meet a planned demand. According to the Supply Chain Council, the process includes the following types of activities:

- Managing the production process
- Implementing changes in engineering
- Requesting products for use in the production process
- Manufacturing the product
- Testing the product
- Packaging the product
- Releasing inventory for shipment
- Maintaining the production equipment and the facilities
- Performing quality assurance measures
- Scheduling production runs
- Analyzing capacity availability

### 3.2.4 Deliver

The "deliver" process encompasses all the activities of getting the finished product into the hands of the ultimate consumers to meet their planned demand. According to the Supply Chain Council, this process includes the following types of activities:

- Managing of orders (e.g., provide quotes, grant credit, enter orders, etc.)
- Forecasting
- Pricing

- Managing transportation (e.g., freight, import/export issues, truck coordination, etc.)

- Managing accounts receivable and collections

- Shipping of products

- Labeling of products

- Scheduling installation of products

- Delivering the inventory according to channel distribution rules

---

**Illustration 2      Supply Chain Operations Reference (SCOR) Model**

Steel Products Inc. (SPI) manufactures custom steel rolls and standardized cut steel sheets. Despite its relatively small size, the company uses the SCOR model to assist in its supply chain management. Key features of SPI's SCOR model are as follows:

**Plan:** Prior to each new operating year, the plant manager estimates specific demand for SPI's steel products. The manager then estimates year-end inventory levels for each of SPI's standardized products. Once this is determined, the manager develops a plan to purchase the generic steel inputs.

**Source:** The next step is for the plant manager to select the vendors for purchasing the steel inputs used for the upcoming year's production. The steel is ordered from the vendors and then stored in the receiving section of the main plant. As part of the receiving supervisor's responsibilities, he is required to inspect the quality of each of the steel shipments and assess the dependability of each vendor.

**Make:** The plant manager, along with an outside consultant, assesses the current year's production process to determine whether any production changes should be made for the current year. At the start of the new operating year, the company manufactures its steel products from customer orders received. As new orders are obtained from the sales department, the plant manager schedules the weekly production runs.

**Deliver:** Once the steel orders are completed, they are priced using a combination of market intelligence and production cost inputs. The products are then shipped using the company's semitrailer trucks for regional orders and a national trucking company for longer-distance deliveries.

---

## 3.3   Benefits of Implementing Supply Chain Management

Examples of benefits derived from implementing supply chain management include:

- Reduced costs in inventory management

- Reduced costs in warehousing

- Optimization of the distribution network and facility locations

- Enhanced revenues

- Improved service times

- Strategic shipment consolidation

- Reduced cost in packaging

- Improved delivery times

- Cross-docking (the minimization of handling and storage costs while receiving and processing of goods in the shortest time possible)

- Identification of inefficiencies in supply chain activities

- Integration of suppliers

- Management of suppliers

# 4  Accounts Payable Management

## 4.1  Trade Credit

Trade credit (or accounts payable) generally provides the largest source of short-term credit for small firms. Trade credit represents the purchases of goods and services as part of usual and customary business transactions for which payment is made 30 to 45 days after acquisition.

## 4.2  Accruals

Accruals represent routine transactions that remain unpaid at the end of an accounting period (e.g., wages payable and taxes payable) purely as a result of transaction timing. Accruals are another common form of short-term credit.

## 4.3  Discounts

Although extension of payments under trade credit arrangements can be very effective in preserving cash balances and financing current operations, the effective annual interest cost can be extremely high if discounts are offered and foregone as part of this working capital management strategy.

### 4.3.1  Calculating Payment Discounts

The formula for calculating the annual cost (APR) of a quick payment discount (assuming a 360-day year) follows:

$$\text{APR of quick payment discount} = \frac{360}{\text{Pay period} - \text{Discount period}} \times \frac{\text{Discount}}{100 - \text{Discount \%}}$$

---

**Example 4**  |  **Payment Discounts (APR)**

**Facts:** Terranova Company's main vendor offers a quick payment discount of 1/10, net 30 to its customers.

**Required:** Assuming a 360-day year, calculate the annual cost to Terranova of not taking advantage of the discount.

**Solution:**

$$\frac{360}{30 - 10} \times \frac{1\%}{100\% - 1\%} = \frac{360}{20} \times \frac{1\%}{99\%} = 18.2\%$$

---

### 4.3.2 Factors Affecting Discount Policy

As shown in the previous example, there can be a high cost associated with a customer not taking advantage of a discount offered by the vendor. The decision whether or not to pay early and take the discount depends on several factors, including whether:

- The company has the cash on hand to pay that particular vendor early.

- The company wants to preserve its cash position for other purposes (investments, projects, maintaining a reserve, etc.).

- There is potential to negotiate even more favorable terms with vendors, including greater discounts or longer discount periods.

## 4.4 Use of Electronic Funds Transfer

The electronic movement of funds from one institution to another is called electronic funds transfer, or EFT. Electronic funds transfer can be used to ensure timely payment.

## 4.5 Optimal Vendor Payment Schedule

Companies need to find an optimal balance between conserving cash and ensuring that vendors are paid in a timely manner. If a company is a regular buyer and/or a large volume buyer from a particular vendor, it may be able to negotiate more favorable terms in order to either take advantage of discounts or extend payment periods. If, for example, the discount period is 10 days, a company will want to pay on the 10th day. If the overall payment is due in 30 days and the discount is not taken, the company should pay on the 30th day. Setting up automatic payments to pay vendors at the end of the payment period is ideal, as it allows the company to conserve cash as long as it can and still pay in a timely manner.

---

### Illustration 3     Optimal Vendor Payment Schedule

Riggs Corp. pays for gas and electricity costs from Lancor, with monthly payments due on the 12th of each month. Rather than issuing paper checks from its Accounts Payable department, Riggs sets up the payments in its automated bill-pay system such that the amount due is automatically wired from Riggs' bank to Lancor on the morning of the 12th. Setting up the payments in this manner allows Riggs to conserve cash and meet the payment deadline without worrying about remembering to issue checks.

---

## 4.6 Methods to Delay Disbursements

### 4.6.1 Defer Payments

Postponing payment of accounts payable provides a spontaneous source of credit to which management can resort if the company is confronted with a short-term cash shortage. Communications to creditors that payments will arrive later than usual serve to mitigate possible damage to credit ratings.

### 4.6.2 Line of Credit

Establishing a line of credit with a bank serves to slow down payments. A line of credit extends the company's trade credit by paying off the company's trade accounts with borrowed funds and allowing the company a longer period to pay back that loan to the bank.

---

**Question 1**                                                                  **CPA-03458**

Garo Company, a retail store, is considering foregoing sales discounts in order to delay using its cash. Supplier credit terms are 2/10, net 30. Assuming a 360-day year, what is the annual cost of credit if the cash discount is *not* taken and Garo pays net 30?

    **a.**  24.0 percent

    **b.**  24.5 percent

    **c.**  36.0 percent

    **d.**  36.7 percent

---

**Question 2**                                                                  **CPA-06627**

An increase in which of the following should cause management to reduce the average inventory?

    **a.**  The cost of placing an order.

    **b.**  The cost of carrying inventory.

    **c.**  The annual demand for the product.

    **d.**  The lead time needed to acquire inventory.

## NOTES

# 1 Cash and Credit Management

## 1.1 Management of Cash and Cash Equivalents

Factors influencing the levels of cash include the volume of collections and their timing, the volume of disbursements and their timing, and the degree to which idle cash is invested in marketable securities.

Businesses use various techniques to maximize cash balances, including managing float, synchronizing cash inflows and outflows, speeding collections and deposits, and mitigating risks with overdraft systems or compensating balances.

### 1.1.1 Motives for Holding Cash

Companies hold cash to make routine payments for business transactions, to repay loans and other financing costs, to maintain compensating balances for banks, to prepare for future uncertainties, and to prepare for future opportunities. Motives for holding cash include:

- **Transaction Motive:** A company may hold cash to meet payments arising from the ordinary course of business.

- **Speculative Motive:** Cash may be needed to take advantage of temporary opportunities.

- **Precautionary Motive:** It is important to have enough cash on hand to maintain a safety cushion to meet unexpected needs.

### 1.1.2 Disadvantages of High Cash Levels

Maintaining high levels of cash can be a disadvantage because of:

- The "negative arbitrage" effect (i.e., interest obligations exceed interest income from cash reserves).

- Increased attractiveness as a takeover target.

- Investor dissatisfaction with allocation of assets (i.e., failure to pay dividends).

### 1.1.3 Primary Methods of Increasing Cash Levels (Reducing the Operating Cycle)

Either speeding up cash inflows or slowing down cash outflows increases cash balances. Improved rates of cash collection are generally achieved through faster accounts receivable collections. Reduced cash outflows are often achieved through delayed (or deferred) disbursements. The combination of current cash inflows and current cash outflows related to a business is called the operating cycle. The objective of financial managers is to shorten the operating cycle.

## 1.2    Management of Accounts Receivable

### 1.2.1   Credit Policy

Credit policy is one of the major determinants of demand for a firm's products or services, along with price, product quality, and advertising. The credit policy of a company is typically established by a committee of senior company executives. Credit policy variables include:

1.  **Credit Period:** Credit period is the length of time buyers are given to pay for their purchases. A commonly used credit period is 30 days. If the credit period is too long, the company may experience cash shortages. A credit period that is too short may damage relationships with customers and negatively affect future sales.

2.  **Credit Standards:** Credit standards refer to the required financial strength of credit customers. Extending credit to only financially strong customers minimizes uncollectible receivables, but also limits potential sales. Extending credit to a broader base of customers increases sales, but adds risk in that a greater percentage of receivables are likely to be written off.

3.  **Collection Policy:** Collection policy is measured by its stringency or laxity in collecting delinquent accounts. This is also a balancing act between wanting to collect cash owed quickly versus maintaining positive relationships with customers.

4.  **Discounts:** Discounts include the discount percentage and period. Offering discounts to customers who pay early may result in faster receivables collection, depending on the terms of the discount and the customer's own cash needs and capacity to pay early.

### 1.2.2   Accounts Receivable Ratios

Financial ratios can be used to evaluate the effectiveness of an entity's credit policy. The list below represents common metrics used to evaluate AR collections.

- **Accounts Receivable Turnover (ART):** The number of times (per year, typically) a company is converting its receivables into cash.

$$ART = \frac{\text{Credit sales}}{\text{Average accounts receivable}}$$

- **Days Sales Outstanding (DSO):** A key component of the cash conversion cycle, the DSO represents how many days on average it takes a company to convert its credit sales into cash.

$$DSO = \left( \frac{\text{Average accounts receivable}}{\text{Credit sales}} \right) \times \text{Number of days in the period}$$

### 1.2.3   Methods to Speed Collections

- **Customer Screening and Credit Policy:** A company can choose to extend credit to more responsible customers, who are more likely to pay bills promptly.

- **Prompt Billing:** Timely billing of charges to credit customers ultimately serves to speed collections.

- **Payment Discounts:** Offering payment discounts may influence customers to pay faster and can result in improved cash collections. Discounts foregone represent a higher cost to the customer than a bank loan for similar financing.

- **Expedite Deposits:** Financial managers not only must collect credit sales in a timely manner, but also must ensure that funds are deposited and credited to their account quickly. The following techniques reduce the time during which payments received by a firm remain uncollected (not yet credited as cash in the bank).

  - **Electronic Funds Transfer:** The electronic movement of funds from one institution to another is called electronic funds transfer, or EFT. Electronic funds transfer and credit cards ensure timely payment. Having funds sent electronically to a company's bank account facilitates immediate collection rather than waiting for checks to be deposited.

  - **Lockbox Systems:** Lockbox systems expedite cash inflows by having a bank receive payments from a company's customers directly via mailboxes to which the bank has access. Payments that arrive in these mailboxes are deposited into the company's account immediately.

- **Concentration Banking:** Concentration banking is characterized by the designation of a single bank as a central depository. Advantages of concentration banking include:

  - Improved controls over inflows and outflows of cash

  - Reduced idle balances

  - Improved effectiveness for investments

## 1.2.4 Factoring

Factoring accounts receivable entails turning over the collection of accounts receivable to a third-party factor in exchange for a discounted short-term loan. Cash is collected from the factor immediately rather than from the customer according to the credit terms.

---

| Example 1 | Factoring |
| --- | --- |

**Facts:** Radon Technologies enters into an agreement with a firm that will factor the company's accounts receivable. The factor agrees to buy the company's receivables, which average $50,000 a month, and have an average collection period of 30 days. The factor will advance up to 80 percent of the face value of receivables at an annual rate of 12 percent and charge a fee of 2 percent on all receivables purchased. The controller of the company estimates that the company would save $10,000 in collection expenses over the year. Fees and interest are not deducted in advance. Assuming a 360-day year, what is the annual cost of financing?

**Required:** Assuming a 360-day year, compute the annual cost of financing.

**Solution:**

|  | AR | × Fee | × (Days in year / Days in period) | Subtotals |
| --- | --- | --- | --- | --- |
| AR submitted | $ 50,000 | 2% | 360 / 30 | $ 12,000 |
| Amount withheld (20%) | (10,000) |  |  |  |
| Amount subject to interest | $ 40,000 | 12% / 12 | 360 / 30 | 4,800 |
| Cost to company |  |  |  | 16,800 |
| Less expense saved (due to outsourced collections) |  |  |  | (10,000) |
| Net cost |  |  |  | $ 6,800 |

Net cost/average amount advanced = $6,800 / $40,000 = 17% (APR)

---

# 2    Corporate Banking Arrangements

Debt involves risk, but it also provides management with the funds needed for operations and growth. One source of debt is borrowing from banks and other lending institutions that offer various forms of credit to companies.

## 2.1    Letter of Credit

A letter of credit represents a third-party guarantee, generally by a bank, of financial obligations incurred by the company. Letters of credit represent an external credit enhancement used by a company issuing otherwise unsecured debt to enhance its credit or can be required by a creditor to ensure payment.

---

**Illustration 1    Letter of Credit**

WUTFUN Toy Company is stocking up for its year-end inventory requirements and seeks to issue commercial paper to its suppliers upon delivery of stock. Toy wholesalers expect weak sales and are reluctant to accept unsecured debt. WUTFUN arranges for a letter of credit to guarantee payment of its indebtedness in order to ensure delivery of inventory.

---

## 2.2    Line of Credit

A line of credit represents a revolving loan with a bank, or group of banks, that is up to a specific dollar maximum amount for a defined term and is renewable upon the maturity date. Any outstanding balances under the line of credit reduce the future availability of funds that may be drawn by the company under that line. Lines of credit that are drawn represent a loan from the bank(s).

A company may also have a seasonal revolving credit facility that allows additional capital availability for a limited time period. Seasonal revolving credit facilities are used by companies during periods of high working capital needs.

---

**Illustration 2    Line of Credit**

Lacey's Stores Inc. is a soft goods general retailer. Through the first six months of the current operating year, the company has been able to cover its operating costs and working capital needs through its internal cash flow generation and the issuance of commercial paper. As the summer season begins to wind down, the retailer is planning a significant buildup of retail inventory for the upcoming holiday season. In order to obtain the necessary capital for this working capital expansion, the retailer draws down 80 percent of the availability under its master revolving line of credit facility. Several months later, Lacey's uses its seasonal revolving line of credit to cover its additional retail inventory needs. As the holiday season ends, the retailer pays down all outstanding balances under the master revolving credit facility and seasonal revolving line of credit (which is subsequently terminated at operating year-end).

---

## 2.3   Borrowing Capacity

A company's borrowing capacity, or borrowing limit, represents the amount of money in the form of credit or loans that a given lender, such as a bank, is willing to extend/lend to the company. Financial strength and stability (often summarized in the form of a credit rating) are key factors in this determination, as is the collateral a borrower has available to pledge toward the borrowed amount. In the event the borrower defaults on its obligation, the collateral is in place to protect the lender. Another key factor is the income level (and stability) of the borrower, as this will ultimately be the source of repayments to the lender.

Both lenders and borrowers have to manage their risk, and the borrowing capacity is protection for both sides such that the borrower does not take on more debt than it can reasonably manage and ultimately pay back. If a lender thinks that the borrower has no capacity to take on debt, the borrowing capacity is zero and no money will be lent.

## 2.4   Debt Covenants

Creditors use debt covenants in lending agreements to protect their interests by limiting or prohibiting the actions of debtors that might negatively affect the positions of the creditors. Covenants contained in a lending agreement may be positive or negative. A positive covenant may include the requirement that the issuer provides quarterly financial reporting (information) to the investors; a negative covenant may involve a restriction on asset sales for a stipulated time frame. When issuing debt instruments, company management should consider the potential effect of debt covenants on a firm's solvency, as highly restrictive covenants could hinder the company's basic operating decisions.

### 2.4.1   Common Debt Covenants

Debt covenants vary widely. Debt covenants may be positive (specifying something the borrower will do) or negative (specifying something the borrower will not do). Common debt covenants include:

- Limitations on issuing additional debt
- Restrictions on the payment of dividends
- Limitations on the disposal of certain assets
- Limitations on how the borrowed money can be used
- Minimum working capital requirements
- Maintenance of specific financial ratios, including:
  - Maximum debt-to-total-capital ratio (debt ratio)
  - Maximum debt-to-EBITDA ratio (cash flow coverage)
  - Minimum interest coverage ratio (times interest earned)
- Providing monthly, quarterly, or annual financial statements to bondholders (lenders)

### 2.4.2   Violation of Debt Covenants

When debt covenants are violated, the debtor is in technical default and the creditor can demand repayment of the entire principal. Most of the time, concessions are negotiated and real default, as opposed to technical default, is avoided. Concessions can result in the violated covenant(s) being waived temporarily or permanently. Concessions also can result in a change in the interest rate or other terms of the debt.

                 

# 3 Financing Decisions and Working Capital

Companies use a mix of short-term and long-term financing to meet their capital requirements. Short-term and long-term financing have different advantages and disadvantages, and different effects on working capital.

## 3.1 Short-Term Financing

### 3.1.1 Characteristics

Short-term financing is generally classified as current and will mature within one year.

- **Rates:** Rates associated with short-term financing tend to be lower than long-term rates and presume greater liquidity on the part of the organization using short-term financing.

- **Effect on Working Capital:** Short-term financing is classified as a current liability and decreases working capital. The extent to which an organization uses short-term financing is dependent on both the amount of current assets it maintains and the risk tolerance of management. Shorter-term financing strategies require current asset levels to be sufficient to meet short-term obligations.

### 3.1.2 Advantages

- **Increased Profitability:** Rapid conversion of operating cycle components (e.g., inventory, receivables) into cash in order to meet short-term obligations carries the potential of increased profitability (and improved liquidity).

- **Decreased Financing Cost:** Short-term interest rates are generally lower than long-term interest rates given the shorter duration of the financing instruments.

### 3.1.3 Disadvantages

- **Increased Interest Rate Risk:** Interest rates may abruptly change, and given shorter maturities, may require greater financing charges than anticipated on future refinancing.

- **Decreased Capital Availability:** Lender evaluation of creditworthiness may change and thereby make financing impossible or less favorable by virtue of increased rates and/or less favorable terms.

## 3.2 Long-Term Financing

### 3.2.1 Characteristics

Long-term financing is generally classified as non-current and will mature after one year.

- **Rates:** Rates associated with long-term financing tend to be higher than short-term rates and presume less liquidity on the part of the organization using long-term financing.

- **Effect on Working Capital:** Long-term financing is classified as non-current and is not included in the calculation of working capital. However, dividend, interest, and principal repayments all require cash, which can reduce working capital over time. The extent to which an organization uses long-term financing is dependent on both the amount of current assets it maintains and the risk tolerance of management. Long-term financing increases financial leverage.

### 3.2.2 Advantages

- **Decreased Interest Rate Risk:** For the borrower, long-term financing locks in an interest rate over a long period, thereby reducing the exposure to fluctuations in rates.

- **Increased Capital Availability:** Securing long-term debt guarantees financing over a long period and reduces the company's exposure to any risk that refinancing might be denied or modified with less favorable terms.

### 3.2.3 Disadvantages

- **Decreased Profitability:** Higher financing costs reduce profitability.

- **Increased Financing Costs:** Long-term debt generally carries a higher interest rate given the longer duration of the financing instruments.

  - **Interest Rate Risk: Lender's Perspective**

    For the lenders, a higher interest rate is charged for longer-term debt because the likelihood that interest rates will change over the period of the loan increases as the term of the loan increases. Higher financing charges compensate the lender for increased interest rate risk. Therefore, the lenders recognize their exposure to interest rate risk with long-term financing and charge a premium to the borrower in the form of higher rates.

  - **Interest Rate Risk: Borrower's Perspective**

    The borrowers, on the other hand, lock themselves into a long-term interest rate to reduce their exposure to interest rate risk, and pay a premium to do so.

| Question 1 | CPA-05315 |
|---|---|

What would be the primary reason for a company to agree to a debt covenant limiting the percentage of its long-term debt?

  **a.** To cause the price of the company's stock to rise.

  **b.** To lower the company's bond rating.

  **c.** To reduce the risk for existing bondholders.

  **d.** To reduce the coupon rate on the bonds being sold.

## NOTES

# Financial Valuation Methods: Part 1

## 1 Security Valuation

### 1.1 Absolute Value Models

Absolute value models assign an intrinsic value to an asset based on the present value of its future cash flows. Estimates of cash flows are derived and discounted based on interest rates applicable to the level of risk and required return associated with the asset and its projected cash flows.

#### 1.1.1 Annuities

An annuity is a series of equal cash flows to be received over a number of periods. The traditional approach to asset valuation is the annuity present value formula, which divides future cash flows by a rate of return in order to determine the value of the annuity in today's dollars.

- **Calculating the Present Value of an Annuity**

$$\text{Annuity present value} = C \times (1 - \text{Present value factor})/r$$

$$= C \times \frac{1 - \dfrac{1}{(1 + r)^t}}{r}$$

Terms are defined as follows:

$C$ = Amount of annuity (equal future cash flows)

$r$ = Rate of return

$t$ = Number of years

- **Assumptions:** Key assumptions implied by the variables of the formula include:

  - **Recurring Amount of the Annuity:** The amount of the periodic annuity must be specified (e.g., $10,000 per year).

  - **Appropriate Discount Rate:** Assumptions must specify the discount rate (e.g., the company requires a 15 percent return per year).

  - **Duration of the Annuity:** Assumptions must specify how long the annuity will continue (e.g., 2 years, 10 years, or even perpetuity, etc.).

  - **Timing of the Annuity:** An annuity may be received or paid in any number of ways. Assumptions must specify if the annuity payment occurs monthly, quarterly, annually, etc. The assumptions also must specify whether the annuity occurs at the beginning or the end of the period. The formula above assumes that annuity payments are made at the end of each period.

### 1.1.2 Perpetuities (Zero Growth Stock)

When the periodic cash flows paid by an annuity last forever, the annuity is called a perpetuity or perpetual annuity. The traditional annuity formula for perpetual cash flow streams is simplified, because no duration is known. When a company is expected to pay the same dividend each period, the perpetuity formula can be used to determine the value of the company's stock. This is the method used to value preferred stock.

- **Per-Share Valuation**

> Present value of a perpetuity = Stock value per share = $P = D/R$
>
> Terms are defined as follows:
>
> P  =  Stock price
>
> D  =  Dividend
>
> R  =  Required return

- **Assumptions**

  - The assumptions must specify the dividend (and assume that it will never change).

  - The assumptions must specify the required return.

---

**Example 1        Perpetuities**

**Facts:** Baker Corporation pays a constant annual dividend per share of $5 per year. Able wants to invest in Baker and earn a 20 percent return.

**Required:** Calculate the value of Baker's stock.

**Solution:**

$$P = D/R$$
$$P = \$5/20\%$$
$$P = \$25$$

Able should pay $25 for a share of Baker.

---

### 1.1.3 Constant (Gordon) Growth Dividend Discount Model (DDM)

The dividend discount model (DDM) assumes that dividend payments are the cash flows of an equity security and that the intrinsic value of the company's stock is the present value of the expected future dividends. If dividends are assumed to grow at a constant rate, the constant (Gordon) growth DDM can be used to determine the value of the company's stock.

- ▧ **Per-Share Valuation With Assumed Growth**

  - ● **Value (Price) of Equity Formula**

    $$P_t = D_{(t+1)}/(R - G)$$

    Terms are defined as follows:

    | | | |
    |---|---|---|
    | $P_t$ | = | Current price (price at period "t") |
    | $D_{(t+1)}$ | = | Dividend one year after period "t" |
    | $R$ | = | Required return |
    | $G$ | = | (Sustainable) Growth rate |

    The candidate may be given the dividend at time = 0 or $D_0$. To determine $D_1$, the numerator of the formula becomes: $D_0(1 + G)$

  - ● **Determining the Required Rate of Return (R)**

    The capital asset pricing model (CAPM) is often used to determine the required return for the DDM model as follows:

    $$R_{ce} = R_f + \beta_i[(E(R_m) - R_f]$$

    Where:

    | | | |
    |---|---|---|
    | $R_{ce}$ | = | Required rate of return on the (common) equity security |
    | $R_f$ | = | Risk-free rate of return |
    | $\beta_i$ | = | Beta on the security |
    | $E(R_m)$ | = | Expected return on market (portfolio) |

    Under the CAPM formula, the $[E(R_m) - R_f]$ term is also known as the equity risk premium.

- ▧ **Assumptions**

  - ● The assumptions must specify (or allow for the calculation of) dividends one year beyond the year in which you are determining the price.

  - ● The assumptions must include a required return.

  - ● The assumptions must include a constant growth rate of dividends.

  - ● The formula implies that the stock price will grow at the same rate as the dividend, in perpetuity.

  - ● The formula assumes that the required rate of return is greater than the dividend growth rate. If this relationship does not hold true, the formula will not work.

## Example 2 — Dividend Discount Model

**Facts:** Baker Corporation pays a current dividend per share of $5 per year and is projected to grow at 4 percent per year. Able wants to invest in Baker and earn a 20 percent return.

**Required:** Calculate the value of Baker's stock today.

**Solution:**

$$P_t = D_{(t+1)}/(R - G)$$
$$D_{(t+1)} = \$5 \times 1.04$$
$$D_{(t+1)} = \$5.20$$
$$P_t = \$5.20/(0.20 - 0.04)$$
$$P_t = \$5.20/(0.16)$$
$$P_t = \$32.50$$

The intrinsic value of Baker's stock today is $32.50.

## Example 3 — Dividend Discount Model

**Facts:** Baker Corporation pays a current dividend per share of $5 per year and is projected to grow at 4 percent per year. Able wants to invest in Baker and earn a 20 percent return.

**Required:** Calculate the amount that Able will pay for Baker's stock three years from today.

**Solution:**

$$P_t = D_{(t+1)}/(R - G)$$
$$D_{(t+1)} = \$5 \times 1.04 \times 1.04 \times 1.04 \times 1.04, \text{ or}$$
$$D_{(t+1)} = \$5 \times (1.04)^4$$
$$D_{(t+1)} = \$5 \times 1.1698586$$
$$D_{(t+1)} = \$5.85$$
$$P_t = D_{(t+1)}/(R - G)$$
$$P_t = (\$5.85)/(0.20 - 0.04)$$
$$P_t = \$5.85/(0.16)$$
$$P_t = \$36.56$$

In order to value Baker in three years, the dividend to be paid in the fourth year is required. Able should pay $36.56 for Baker in three years.

### 1.1.4   Introduction to Discounted Cash Flow Analysis

Discounted cash flow (DCF) analysis attempts to determine the intrinsic (true) value of an equity security by determining the present value of its expected future cash flows. To apply DCF analysis, an analyst takes the following steps:

▩ Choose an appropriate model.

- Dividend discount models (DDM) use the stock's expected dividends as the relevant cash flows. The Gordon constant growth model is an example of a simple dividend discount model.

- Free cash flow models including free cash flow to the firm (FCFF) and free cash flow to equity (FCFE). The free cash flow models discount the cash flow left over by the firm after satisfying certain required obligations including working capital needs and fixed capital investment.

  - Residual income models represent the income left over after the firm satisfies the investor's required return.

▩ Forecast the security's cash flows using one of the model approaches above.

▩ Select a discount rate methodology. The CAPM is a popular method used to estimate the required return for an equity security.

▩ Estimate the discount rate and apply to the appropriate DCF model.

▩ Calculate the equity security's intrinsic value and compare to its current market value.

## 1.2   Relative Valuation Models

Relative valuation models use the value of comparable stocks to determine the value of similar stocks. Price multiples are useful metrics in relative valuation.

Price multiples represent ratios of a stock's market price to another measure of fundamental value per share. Investors use price multiples to determine if a stock is undervalued, fairly valued, or overvalued.

### 1.2.1   Price-Earnings (P/E) Ratio

The P/E ratio is the most widely used multiple when valuing equity securities. The rationale for using this measure is that earnings are a key driver of investment value (stock price). This multiple is widely used by the investment community and empirical research has shown that changes in a company's P/E are tied to the long-run stock performance of that company.

▩ **Calculating the P/E Ratio**

$$P/E \text{ ratio} = P_0 / E_1$$

**Terms are defined as follows:**

$P_0$ = Stock price or value today

$E_1$ = EPS expected in one year (next four quarters)

**Note:** The above formula is termed the "forward P/E" as the denominator is based on expected earnings over the next year or four quarters.

■ **Valuing Equity With the P/E Ratio**

The P/E ratio, once calculated, can be multiplied by anticipated future earnings in order to determine the current stock price. It requires that earnings be greater than zero.

---

**Example 4**  ▸  **P/E Ratio**

**Facts:** Assume that Baker Corporation has current-year earnings per share of $1.50 and anticipates earnings per share in the coming year of $2.

**Required:** If the P/E ratio is 7.5x, calculate the expected value of Baker's shares.

**Solution:**

$(P_0)$ = $(P_0/E_1) \times E_1$

$(P_0)$ = $7.5 \times \$2$

$(P_0)$ = $\$15$

The P/E ratio of 7.5x implies that the current stock price should be 7.5x the anticipated earnings per share of $2. An investor would expect the current stock price to therefore be $15.

---

■ **Trailing vs. Forward P/E**

The numerator in the P/E ratio is unambiguous, as the stock price for publicly traded companies is readily available. This is not the case for the denominator of the ratio, as the earnings used in the P/E ratio can either be past earnings or expected future earnings.

When past earnings are used in the P/E ratio, such as earnings for the past four quarters or trailing 12-month EPS, the ratio calculated is the *trailing P/E*. When expected earnings of the company next year is used in the denominator, the ratio is the *forward P/E*.

The trailing P/E is the preferred calculation method when a company's forecasted earnings are unavailable, while the forward P/E is the preferred method when the company's historical earnings is not representative of its future earnings. The formula for the trailing P/E ratio is as follows:

> Trailing P/E ratio = $P_0 / E_0$
>
> Terms are defined as follows:
>
> $P_0$ = Stock price or value today
>
> $E_0$ = EPS for the past year (past four quarters)

### 1.2.2 PEG Ratio

The PEG ratio is a measure that shows the effect of earnings growth on a company's P/E, assuming a linear relationship between P/E and growth. Generally, stocks that have lower PEG ratios are more attractive to investors than stocks that have higher PEG ratios.

■   **Calculating the PEG Ratio**

$$PEG = (P_0/E_1)/G$$

Terms are defined as follows:

$P_0$ = Stock price or value today

$E_1$ = Expected EPS

$G$ = Growth rate = 100 × Expected growth rate

■   **Valuing Equity With the PEG Ratio**

The PEG ratio calculates the P/E ratio per unit of growth. The PEG ratio can be multiplied by both forecasted future earnings and the growth rate to determine the current price of the stock.

$$(P_0) = PEG \times E_1 \times G$$

Terms are defined as follows:

$P_0$ = Stock price or value today

$E_1$ = Expected EPS

$G$ = Growth rate = 100 × Expected growth rate

| Example 5 | PEG Ratio |
|-----------|-----------|

**Facts:** Baker wants to use the PEG ratio to estimate the price of its stock. The company's PEG ratio is 2.5x and its current earnings per share is $5. The growth rate for earnings is anticipated to be 4 percent.

**Required:** Calculate the current price of Baker's stock.

**Solution:**

$E_1$   =   5.00 × 1.04 = $5.20

$(P_0)$   =   PEG × $E_1$ × G

$(P_0)$   =   2.5 × $5.20 × 4

$(P_0)$   =   $52.00

### 1.2.3  Price-to-Sales Ratio

Similar to the P/E ratio, this price multiple ratio can be used to estimate the current stock price. The rationale for using the price-to-sales ratio is that sales are less subject to manipulation than earnings or book values; sales are always positive so this multiple can be used even when EPS is negative; and this ratio is not as volatile as the P/E ratio, which includes the effect of financial and operating leverage. Empirical studies have shown that P/S is an appropriate measure to value stocks that are associated with mature or cyclical companies.

- **Calculating the Price-to-Sales Ratio**

$$\text{Price-to-sales ratio} = P_0 / S_1$$

Terms are defined as follows:

$P_0$ = Stock price or value today

$S_1$ = Expected sales in one year

- **Valuing Equity With the Price-to-Sales Ratio**

    The value of equity can then be calculated as follows:

$$(P_0) = (P_0 / S_1) \times S_1$$

### 1.2.4  Price-to-Cash-Flow Ratio

The price-to-cash-flow ratio may also be used to calculate the current stock price. The rationale for using this price multiple is that cash flow is harder for companies to manipulate than earnings; P/CF is a more stable measure than P/E; and empirical research has shown that changes in a company's P/CF ratios over time are positively related to changes in a company's long-term stock returns.

- **Calculating the Price-to-Cash-Flow Ratio**

$$\text{Price-to-cash-flow ratio} = P_0 / CF_1$$

Terms are defined as follows:

$P_0$ = Stock price or value today

$CF_1$ = Expected cash flow in one year

- **Valuing Equity With the Price-to-Cash-Flow Ratio**

    The value of equity can then be calculated as follows:

$$(P_0) = (P_0 / CF_1) \times CF_1$$

### 1.2.5  Price-to-Book Ratio

The price-to-book (P/B) ratio is another price multiple used by analysts that focuses on the balance sheet rather than the income statement or statement of cash flows. The rationale for using this multiple is that a firm's book value of common equity (assets minus liabilities and preferred stock) is more stable than earnings per share, especially when a firm's EPS is extremely high or low for a given period. Because P/B is usually positive, this multiple can be used even when a firm's EPS is negative or zero. Research indicates that the P/B ratio can explain a firm's average stock returns over the long run.

- **Calculating the P/B Ratio**

$$\text{P/B ratio} = P_0 / B_0$$

Terms are defined as follows:

$P_0$ = Stock price or value today

$B_0$ = Book value of common equity

- **Valuing Equity With the P/B Ratio**

    The value of equity can then be calculated as follows:

$$(P_0) = (P_0 / B_0) \times B_0$$

| Example 6 | Price-to-Book Ratio |
| --- | --- |

**Facts:** An analyst assembles the following financial and market data for Bolden Corporation's most recent year-end. The analyst projects that the firm's operating cash flow will increase 20 percent in the upcoming year.

**Market Data**

| | |
| --- | --- |
| Common stock price | $18 |
| Common shares outstanding | 10,000,000 |

**Financial Data**

| | |
| --- | --- |
| Total assets | $250,000,000 |
| Total liabilities | 110,000,000 |
| Preferred stock | 20,000,000 |
| Common stock | 25,000,000 |
| Additional paid-in capital | 45,000,000 |
| Retained earnings | 50,000,000 |
| Total stockholders' equity | 140,000,000 |
| Cash flow from operations | 25,000,000 |

**Required:** Using the previous data, calculate the P/B and P/CF multiples.

(continued)

(continued)

**Solution:**

The P/B multiple for Bolden Corporation's current year is derived as follows:

1. Determine book value of common equity

   $25,000,000 (CS) + $45,000,000 (APIC) + $50,000,000 (RE) = $120,000,000

2. Determine book of common equity per share

   $120,000,000 / 10,000,000 shares = $12

3. Calculate P/B multiple

   $P_0/B_0$ = $18/$12

   $\phantom{P_0/B_0}$ = 1.5

Based on the previous data and the analyst's operating cash flow forecast, the P/CF multiple is derived as follows:

1. Determine the firm's expected cash flow per share

   $CF_1$ = $25,000,000 × 1.20 = $30,000,0000

   $CF_1/Sh.$ = $30,000,000/10,000,000 shares = $3

2. Calculate P/CF multiple

   $P_0/CF_1$ = $18/$3

   $\phantom{P_0/CF_1}$ = 6.0

### 1.2.6 Assumptions

The price multiple ratios have similar assumption requirements, each of which can be influenced by management behaviors, including:

- Future earnings
- Future cash flows
- Future sales
- Future growth rate
- The duration of sales, earnings, or cash flow trends

### 1.2.7 Relative Valuation

Once an analyst calculates a set of price multiple ratios for a given company (stock), these ratios are used as a method of comparison to the same corresponding ratios calculated for similar companies (stocks) within that industry sector to determine a ranking for each price multiple ratio and ultimately provide important input into a particular company's stock valuation.

| Example 7 | Relative Valuation Models |
|---|---|

**Facts:** An investor is comparing market ratios for the XLX Company to those of its industry. The following ratios were calculated at the end of the current fiscal year:

| Ratio | XLX Company | Industry |
|---|---|---|
| P/E | 16.2 | 14.9 |
| PEG | 4.8 | 5.3 |
| P/S | 18.1 | 19.4 |
| P/CF | 13.6 | 13.7 |
| P/B | 19.2 | 17.8 |

**Required:** Discuss what each ratio indicates regarding XLX stock valuation and how the numbers can be interpreted.

**Solution:**

- **P/E Ratio:** XLX has a higher P/E ratio than its industry peer group. This measure, on its own, would indicate that the stock price for XLX is overvalued relative to that of its peers. Investors would expect the price of XLX stock to decline in order to align the P/E ratio with that of its peers.

- **PEG Ratio:** XLX has a lower PEG ratio than its industry. For XLX, the growth rate is equal to 3.38 percent (PE of 16.2 divided by PEG of 4.8). For the industry, the growth rate is equal to 2.81 percent (PE of 14.9 divided by PEG of 5.3). Given the higher level of growth for XLX versus its industry, the PEG ratio indicates that XLX stock may actually be undervalued relative to that of its peers.

- **P/S Ratio:** This is another indicator that XLX stock may actually be undervalued relative to that of its peers. However, this ratio alone does not account for cost structure, capital structure, or tax effects that should be evaluated before determining whether a stock is relatively overvalued or undervalued.

- **P/CF Ratio:** XLX and the industry have very similar P/CF ratios. This metric alone would indicate that the stock price for XLX is fairly valued.

- **P/B Ratio:** Relative to the value of its equity, XLS's stock price is higher than that of its peers. The stock may not necessarily be overvalued, as a higher P/B may indicate that the market thinks that XLX's net assets are undervalued.

---

### Question 1                                                          CPA-06137

Fernwell wants to buy shares of Gurst Company in two years. Fernwell uses a constant growth dividend discount model with a presumed dividend growth rate of 5 percent. If Fernwell's discount rate is 10 percent and Gurst's current year dividend is $20, what is the approximate price Fernwell will pay?

    **a.** $400

    **b.** $420

    **c.** $441

    **d.** $463

---

### Question 2                                                          CPA-06131

Coldwell is using a constant growth dividend discount model to forecast the value of a share of common stock. Inherent in Coldwell's assumptions is the idea that:

    **a.** Compounding growth is linear.

    **b.** Dividends will grow at a rate faster than the presumed discount rate.

    **c.** Stock price will grow at the same rate as the dividend.

    **d.** Stock price will grow at the same amount as the dividend.

---

### Question 3                                                          CPA-06133

Investors are likely to view a high price-earnings (P/E) ratio as an indication that:

    **a.** Earnings have growth potential.

    **b.** Earnings have peaked and will remain flat.

    **c.** Earnings have peaked and will likely fall.

    **d.** There is no logical conclusion to reach about the relationship between price and earnings.

---

# 1 Option Pricing Models

## 1.1 Definition of an Option

An option is a contract that entitles the owner (holder) to buy (call option) or sell (put option) a stock (or some other asset) at a given price within a stated period of time. American-style options can be exercised at any time prior to their expiration. European-style options can be exercised only at the expiration or maturity date of the option.

## 1.2 Valuing Options: The Black-Scholes Model

Different factors enter into the determination of the value of an option. A commonly used method for option valuation is the Black-Scholes model. The calculation is extremely complex and beyond the scope of the CPA Exam. However, you do need a high-level understanding of the concepts and assumptions that underlie Black-Scholes. Accountants may use this method in valuing stock options when accounting for share-based payments. Option price calculators are widely available, so you do not need to understand the complexity of the actual calculations to apply this method.

- Inputs into the Black-Scholes model (determinants of the call option value)

  - Current price of the underlying stock (higher price → higher option value)

  - Option exercise price

  - Risk-free interest rate (higher rate → higher option value)

  - Current time until expiration (longer time → higher call option value)

  - Some measure of risk for the underlying stock (higher risk → higher option value)

- Assumptions underlying the Black-Scholes model

  - Stock prices behave randomly.

  - The risk-free rate and volatility of the stock prices are constant over the option's life.

  - There are no taxes or transaction costs.

  - The stock pays no dividends, although the model can be adapted to dividend-paying stock.

  - The options are European-style (exercisable only at maturity).

- Limitations of the Black-Scholes model

  Despite its current use, the Black-Scholes model does have several limitations:

  - Due to the model's assumptions, results generated from the Black-Scholes model may differ from real prices.

  - It assumes instant, cost-less trading, which is unrealistic in today's markets.

  - The model tends to underestimate extreme price movements.

  - The model is not applicable to pricing American-style options.

## 1.3    Valuing Options: Binomial Model

Another option pricing model is the binomial or Cox-Ross-Rubinstein model. It is a variation of the original Black-Scholes model. The binomial model considers the underlying security over a period of time, as compared to the value at one point in time under the Black-Scholes model. This model is useful for valuing American-style options, which can be exercised over a period of time.

■    The assumptions of the binomial model are:

●    a perfectly efficient stock market; and

●    the underlying security price will move up or down at certain points in time (called nodes) during the life of the option.

■    The result of applying the model is a tree diagram showing the possible values of the options at different points in time or nodes. The math for this approach is also beyond the scope of the CPA Exam.

■    The benefits of the binomial method are:

●    it can be used for American-style options; and

●    it can be used for stocks that pay dividends without modifying the model, as is necessary with Black-Scholes.

# 2    Valuing Debt Instruments

The value of a bond is equal to the present value of its future cash flows (which consist of interest payments and the principal payment at maturity). The cash flows may be discounted using a single interest rate or multiple interest rates aligned with the degree of risk for each cash flow.

Bonds paying a fixed coupon rate equal to the market rate for comparable bonds are issued at par (face) value. If a bond's coupon rate at issuance is less (more) than the market rate, the bond will be issued at a discount (premium). As market interest rates change, the market value of the bond will also change. For fixed-rate bonds, when market interest rates rise the market value of the bond falls, and vice versa.

| Example 1 | Debt Instruments |
| --- | --- |

**Facts:** A $1,000 face value bond maturing in three years pays annual interest of 4 percent.

**Required:** Calculate the bond's price If the market rate at the time of issuance is 5 percent.

**Solution:** Because the bond pays a lower coupon rate than market rate, it will be issued at a discount to par. The calculation for the bond's price is as follows:

Year 1 payment: 40 / 1.05 = $38.10

Year 2 payment: $40 / (1.05)^2 = \$36.28$

Year 3 payment: $(40 + 1{,}000) / (1.05)^3 = \$898.39$

Total value: $38.10 + $36.28 + $898.39 = $972.77

# 3    Valuing Tangible Assets

Fixed assets represent the property (land), plant (buildings), and equipment (PP&E) held by a company to provide the infrastructure needed to support operations. GAAP and IFRS dictate how PP&E is reported on the balance sheet; the actual value of these assets can be determined using the following methods:

## 3.1    Cost Method

The value of the assets is based on the original cost paid to acquire the asset. Adjustments may be made for depreciation in order to reduce the value of the asset to reflect current utility.

## 3.2    Market Value Method

This method requires that similar assets be available in the marketplace in order to find a comparable value. Two iterations of the market value method are the replacement cost method (what it would cost to replace the valued asset) and the net realizable value method (the price at which the asset could be sold in the marketplace, reduced by any costs associated with selling the asset).

---

**Illustration 1    Market Value Method**

A company is assessing the value of the equipment at its headquarters. Using the market value method, the company determines that it would cost $6,200,000 today to replace all of its equipment. The company also determines that selling its equipment in the marketplace would generate $5,900,000 after accounting for selling/disposal costs. Either value may be used as a reasonable proxy for market value.

---

## 3.3    Appraisal Method

Under this method, a professional appraiser determines the value of the asset, assuming that the company can find an appraiser with knowledge and experience working with the specific asset(s) in question.

## 3.4    Liquidation Value

If the asset had to be sold today, the liquidation value represents the amount that the company would get upon sale assuming that there is an active market for the asset.

# 4    Valuing Intangible Assets

Intangible assets do not have a physical form, but like any asset, they provide probable future economic benefit to the entity that owns them. Intangible assets include patents, trademarks, intellectual property, copyrights, etc. The following methods may be used to value intangible assets.

## 4.1    Market Approach

This approach requires that actual arm's-length transactions (sales, transfers, licenses) in similar markets be used as a reference for the asset to be valued. Although this is a preferred approach to valuation, the unique nature of individual intangible assets and relative trading infrequency present challenges.

### Illustration 2     Market Approach

A company has a patent in its intangibles portfolio that it is looking to monetize. In looking at recent transactions for comparable patent sales, the company discovers four within the last couple of years.

- Sale 1: $18.5 million
- Sale 2: $16.2 million
- Sale 3: $16.8 million
- Sale 4: $15.1 million

The company will look to assign a value within a range of $15.1 million to $18.5 million, perhaps using the median value of $16.5 million; or, the company may identify the transaction involving the asset that is closest to the nature of the patent the company is looking to sell and use that value.

## 4.2   Income Approach

Using this approach, future expected cash flows over the estimated useful life of the intangible asset are discounted to present value using discount rates reflecting the level of risk (including asset risk, industry risk, and market risk) associated with the income stream.

### Illustration 3     Income Approach

Eagle Road Enterprises owns a patent that is expected to generate $4 million each year for the next 10 years. Using a discount rate of 5.5 percent and a discounting factor of 7.5376, the patent is worth $30.15 million today ($4 million × 7.5376 = $30.15 million).

## 4.3   Cost Approach

When there are no similar assets or transactions involving similar assets, and no reasonable estimates of future income, the cost approach can be used. Iterations of the cost approach include replacement cost (expenses required to create a similar asset) and reproduction cost (the expenses needed to reproduce the same asset). Costs incorporated will include materials, labor, overhead, legal and other fees, development costs, production costs, and opportunity costs.

### Illustration 4     Cost Approach

Alpine Inc. looks to establish a value for the copyrights in its intangible asset portfolio. Using a valuation date of today, Alpine determines the following values for the costs associated with reproducing the same copyrights:

- Labor: $15,000
- Materials: $9,000
- Overhead: $11,000
- Legal and other fees: $22,000
- Development costs: $16,000
- Production costs: $13,000
- Opportunity costs: $26,000
- Total cost: $112,000

# 5   Valuation Using Accounting Estimates

Certain financial statement line items are valued using accounting estimates. For example:

- Accounts receivable is presented net of an allowance for uncollectible accounts.

- Inventory is reported at the lower of cost or market, or lower of cost and net realizable value, including write-downs of obsolete inventory.

- Fixed assets are offset by accumulated depreciation.

- Contingent liabilities are based on the best estimate of probable future losses.

## 5.1   Preparing Accounting Estimates

When preparing accounting estimates, management must consider the following data and factors:

- **Historical Information:** GAAP requires that the allowance for uncollectible accounts be estimated using historical information regarding the collectibility of a company's receivables from its customers. Historical patterns of fixed-asset usage may be used to justify the method used to depreciate fixed assets.

- **Market Information:** Information on the current value of inventory items should be used to determine the lower of cost or market and lower of cost and net realizable value, and should also be used to determine whether inventory should be written down or written off due to obsolescence.

- **Expected Usage:** Depreciation methods may be based on expected patterns of fixed-asset usage.

- **Estimates From Experts:** Attorneys are often used to provide estimates of probable future losses on pending or threatened litigation.

## 5.2   Review and Approval of Accounting Estimates

Accounting estimates should be supported by documentation that shows the assumptions and calculations upon which the estimates are based. Management should regularly review the support for material accounting estimates and should approve each estimate when reviewed.

Companies that use accounting estimates should expect their auditors to closely scrutinize the assumptions and support underlying the estimates. Auditors expect accounting estimates to be reasonable and look closely at any information that contradicts the assumptions made by management when preparing the estimates.

## NOTES

# Financial Decision Models: Part 1

## 1 Cash Flows Related to Capital Budgeting

Capital budgeting is a process for evaluating and selecting the long-term investment projects of the firm. Proper capital budgeting is crucial to the success of an organization. The amount of cash the company takes in and pays out for an investment affects the amount of cash the company has available for operations and other activities of the company.

### 1.1 Cash Flow Effects

#### 1.1.1 Direct Effect

When a company pays out cash, receives cash, or makes a cash commitment that is directly related to the capital investment, that effect is termed the direct effect. It has an immediate effect on the amount of cash available.

#### 1.1.2 Indirect Effect

Transactions which are indirectly associated with a capital project or which represent noncash activity that produces cash benefits or obligations are termed indirect cash flow effects.

---

**Illustration 1    Cash Flow Effects**

Depreciation is a noncash expense taken as a tax deduction. Depreciation reduces the amount of taxable income and, consequently, the related taxes. The reduced tax bill resulting from increased depreciation expense associated with a new project decreases the cash paid out. This type of effect is termed an indirect effect (or tax effect) of capital budgeting.

---

#### 1.1.3 Net Effect

The total of the direct and indirect effects of cash flows from a capital investment is called the net effect.

### 1.2 Stages of Cash Flows

Cash flows exist throughout the life cycle of a capital investment project. Cash flows are categorized in three general stages.

#### 1.2.1 Inception of the Project (Time Period Zero)

Both direct cash flow effects (the acquisition cost of the asset) and indirect cash flow effects (working capital requirements or disposal of the replaced asset) occur at the time of the initial investment. The initial cash outlay for the project is often the largest amount of cash outflow of the investment's life.

- **Working Capital Requirements:** Working capital is defined as current assets minus current liabilities. When a capital project is implemented, the firm may need to increase or decrease working capital to ensure the success of the project.

  - **Additional Working Capital Requirements:** A proposed investment may be expected to increase payroll, expenses for supplies, or inventory requirements. This may result in an indirect cash outflow that is recognized at the inception of the project because part of the working capital of the organization will be allocated to the investment project and will be unavailable for other uses in the organization.

  - **Reduced Working Capital Requirements:** Implementing a just-in-time inventory system (in which the amount of inventory required to be on hand is reduced) represents a decrease in current assets and is recognized as an indirect cash inflow at the inception of the project.

- **Disposal of the Replaced Asset**

  - **Asset Abandonment:** If the replaced asset is abandoned, the net salvage value is treated as a reduction of the initial investment in the new asset. The abandoned asset's book value is considered a sunk cost, and therefore not relevant to the decision-making process. The remaining book value (for tax purposes) is deductible as a tax loss, which reduces the liability in the year of abandonment. This tax liability decrease is considered a reduction of the new asset's initial investment.

  - **Asset Sale:** If a new asset acquisition requires the sale of old assets, the cash received from the sale of the old asset reduces the new investment's value. If a gain or loss (for tax purposes) exists, there is also a corresponding increase or decrease in income taxes. The amount of income tax paid on a gain on a sale is treated as a reduction of the sales price (which increases the initial expenditure). Conversely, a reduction in tax resulting from a loss on a sale is treated as a reduction of the new investment.

## 1.2.2 Operations

The ongoing operations of the project will affect both direct and indirect cash flows of the company.

- The cash flows generated from the operations of the asset occur on a regular basis. These cash flows may be the same amount every year (an annuity) or may differ.

- Depreciation tax shields create ongoing indirect cash flow effects.

## 1.2.3 Disposal of the Project

Disposal of the investment at the end of the project produces direct or indirect cash flows.

- If the asset is sold, there is a direct effect for the cash inflow created on the sale and an indirect effect for the taxes due (in the case of a gain) or saved (in the case of a loss).

- Certain direct expenses may be incurred for the disposal (e.g., severance pay).

- If the asset is scrapped or donated, there may be a tax savings (an indirect effect) if the net tax basis is greater than zero (i.e., the asset has not been fully depreciated).

- There may be indirect effects associated with changes in the amount of working capital committed once the project is disposed of (e.g., employees who worked on the project may no longer be needed). A working capital commitment that was recognized as an indirect cash outflow at the inception of a project is recognized as an indirect cash inflow at the end of the project when the working capital commitment is released.

## 1.3    Calculation of Pretax and After-Tax Cash Flows

### 1.3.1    Pretax Cash Flows

The traditional computation of an asset's value is based on the cash flows it generates. Thus an investment's value is often based on the present value of the future cash flows that investors expect to receive from the investment. Larger cash outflows than inflows may indicate that a project is unprofitable.

### 1.3.2    After-Tax Cash Flows

After-tax cash flows are relevant to capital budgeting decisions and are computed using either of the following methods. Operating cash flow differs from net income because noncash expenses like depreciation must be added-back to net income to get to cash flow.

- **Method 1**

    1. Estimate net operating cash inflows (cash inflows minus cash outflows).

    2. Subtract noncash tax deductible expenses to arrive at taxable income.

    3. Compute income taxes related to a project's income (or loss) for each year of the project's useful life.

    4. Subtract tax expense from net cash inflows to arrive at after-tax cash flows.

- **Method 2**

    1. Multiply net operating cash inflows by (1 − Tax rate).

    2. Add the tax shield associated with noncash expenses such as depreciation (depreciation multiplied by the tax rate).

    3. The sum of these two amounts will equal the after-tax cash flows.

---

| Illustration 2 | **Methods of Calculating After-Tax Cash Flows** |
|---|---|

Compute after-tax cash flows based on the following facts:

| | |
|---|---|
| Annual cash inflows | $40,000 |
| Depreciation | 10,000 |
| Tax rate | 40% |

| Transaction Data | Method 1 | | | | | Method 2 |
|---|---|---|---|---|---|---|
| Cash inflows | $ 40,000 | × | (1 − 40%) | = | | $24,000 |
| Depreciation | 10,000 | × | 40% | = | | + 4,000 |
| Pretax income | 30,000 | | | | | $28,000 |
| Tax rate | (12,000) | | | | | |
| Net income | $ 18,000 | | | | | |
| **After-Tax Cash Flows** | | | | | | |
| Cash inflows | $ 40,000 | | | | | |
| Taxes | (12,000) | | | | | |
| **After-Tax Cash Flows** | $ 28,000 | | | | | |

---

## Example 1     Cash Flows for Capital Budgeting

**Facts:** The divisional management of Carlin Company has proposed the purchase of a new machine that will improve the efficiency of the operations in the company's manufacturing plant. The purchase price of the machine is $425,000. Costs associated with putting the machine into service include $10,000 for shipping, $15,000 for installation, and $6,000 for the initial training.

Carlin expects the machine to last six years and to have an estimated salvage value of $7,000. The machine is expected to produce 4,000 units a year with an expected selling price of $800 per unit and prime costs (direct materials and direct labor) of $750 per unit.

Tax depreciation will be computed under the accelerated straight-line rules (not MACRS) for five-year property with no consideration for salvage value (i.e., the entire asset amount capitalized will be depreciated). Carlin has a marginal tax rate of 40 percent.

**Required:** Calculate cash flows at the beginning of the first year (Year 0), for Years 1–5, and for Year 6, which is the final year.

**Solution: Cash flow at the beginning of the first year for capital budgeting analysis**

The net cash outflow at the beginning of the first year is calculated as follows:

| | | |
|---|---|---|
| Initial investment | $(425,000) | |
| Shipping | (10,000) | |
| Installation | (15,000) | |
| Training | (6,000) | |
| Total | $(456,000) | [Outflow] |

**Sample year: Net cash flow for Years 1–5 for capital budgeting analysis**

| | | |
|---|---|---|
| Net cash flow from sales | $ 200,000 | [4,000 × ($800 − $750)] |
| Less: taxes on net sales | (80,000) | [$200,000 × 0.40] |
| Add: net indirect effect of depreciation on machine | 36,480 | [($456,000 / 5) × 0.40] |
| Total | $ 156,480 | [Inflow] |

**Net cash flow for the final year (Year 6) for capital budgeting analysis**

| | | |
|---|---|---|
| Net cash flow from sales | $200,000 | [per above] |
| Less: taxes on net sales | (80,000) | [per above] |
| Add: net indirect effect of depreciation on machine | -0- | No depreciation in Year 6 |
| Salvage value | 4,200 | [$7,000 gain × 0.60, which is net of tax] |
| Total | $ 124,200 | [Inflow] |

# 2    Discounted Cash Flow (DCF)

DCF valuation methods (including the net present value and the internal rate of return methods) are techniques that use time value of money concepts to measure the present value of cash inflows and cash outflows expected from a project.

## 2.1    Objective and Components of Discounted Cash Flow as Used in Capital Budgeting

The objective of the discounted cash flow (DCF) method is to focus the attention of management on relevant cash flows appropriately discounted to present value. The factors used to evaluate capital investments under discounted cash flow include the dollar amount of the initial investment, the dollar amount of future cash inflows and outflows, and the rate of return desired for the project.

### 2.1.1    Rate of Return Desired for the Project

The rate used to discount future cash flows may be set by management using several different approaches. Management may use a weighted average cost of capital (WACC) method, a specific target rate assigned to new projects, or a rate that relates to the risk specific to the proposed project. If the proposed project is similar in risk to the ongoing projects of the company, WACC is appropriate because it reflects the market's assessment of the average risk of the company's projects.

### 2.1.2    Limitation of Discounted Cash Flow: Simple Constant Growth Assumption

Discounted cash flow methods are widely viewed as superior to methods that do not consider the time value of money. However, discounted cash flow methods do have an important limitation—they frequently use a single interest rate assumption. This assumption is often unrealistic because, over time, as management evaluates its alternatives, actual interest rates or risks may fluctuate.

# 3    Net Present Value Method (NPV)

## 3.1    Objective

The objective of the net present value method is to focus decision makers on the initial investment amount that is required to purchase (or invest in) a capital asset that will yield returns in an amount in excess of a management-designated hurdle rate.

NPV requires managers to evaluate the dollar amount of return rather than either percentages of return (as with the internal rate of return method) or years to recover principal (as with the payback methods) as a basis for screening investments.

## 3.2    Calculation of Net Present Value

Net present value is calculated as follows:

1. **Estimate the Cash Flows**

    Estimate all direct and indirect after-tax cash flows (both inflows and outflows) related to the investment.

    - **Ignore Depreciation (Unless a Tax Shield)**

        As with DCF methods, depreciation is ignored except to the extent that it reduces tax payments (i.e., a tax shield). Use of accelerated (instead of straight-line) depreciation methods increases the present value of the depreciation tax shield.

    - **Ignore Interest Expense**

        The discounting process itself deals with the cost of financing the project, and therefore finance costs are excluded from the cash flow forecast.

2. **Discount the Cash Flows**

    Discount all cash flows (both inflows and outflows) to present value using the appropriate discount factor based on the hurdle rate and the timing of the cash flow. The net present value method assumes that the cash flows are reinvested at the same rate used in the analysis.

3. **Compare**

    Compare the present values of inflows and outflows.

### Pass Key

Discounted cash flow is the basis for net present value methods:

- **Step 1:** Calculate after-tax cash flows = Annual net cash flow × (1 − Tax rate)

- **Step 2:** Add depreciation benefit = Depreciation × Tax rate

- **Step 3:** Multiply result by appropriate present value of an annuity (assuming cash flows are an annuity)

- **Step 4:** Subtract initial cash outflow

*Result:* Net present value

## 3.3    Interpreting the NPV Method

The investment decision is based on whether the net present value is positive or negative. Note that if the net present value is equal to zero, management would be indifferent about accepting or rejecting the project. NPV is the theoretical dollar change in the market value of the firm's equity due to the project.

### 3.3.1   Positive Result = Make Investment

If the result is positive (greater than zero), the rate of return for the project is greater than the hurdle rate (the discount percentage rate used in the net present value calculation) and the investment should be made. If the company has unlimited funds, all projects with a net present value greater than zero should be accepted. Project ranking and acceptance techniques in circumstances involving limited capital are described below.

### 3.3.2   Negative Result = Do Not Make Investment

If the result is negative (less than zero), the rate of return for the project is less than the hurdle rate and the investment should not be made because it does not meet management's minimum rate of return. A negative NPV means that the internal rate of return on the investment is less than management's hurdle rate for the project.

## 3.4   Interest Rate Adjustments for Required Return

Net present value analysis may incorporate many types of hurdle rates, such as the cost of capital (the average rate of return demanded by investors), the interest rate of the opportunity cost, or some other minimum required rate of return. All rates are determined by management.

### 3.4.1   Adjustments to Rate

Rates may be modified (generally increased) to adjust for:

- **Risk:** Discount rates may be increased to further factor differences in risk into the analysis.

| Illustration 3     Interest Rate Adjustment for Risk |
| --- |
| Management would select a high hurdle rate for certain projects to factor risk into its consideration of acceptance of those projects. The higher hurdle rate discounts (reduces) future cash flows more, creating a smaller present value, which stands a larger chance of yielding an NPV below zero, with the project not being selected. By "devaluing" the cash flows for a project, the NPV model compensates for risk. |

- **Inflation (Also Affects Cash Flows):** Rates may be raised to compensate for expected inflation.

| Illustration 4     Interest Rate Adjustment for Inflation |
| --- |
| Assume that management anticipates higher-than-normal inflation. To compensate for the falling value of the dollars it anticipates from its cash flows, the interest rate (discount factor) may be increased. In addition, the future cash flows also should be increased to the extent of predicted inflation. If management anticipates no change in tax rates, cash flows generated from the effects of depreciation would not be adjusted because they relate to the original investment. |

### 3.4.2 Differing Rates

Different rates may be used for different time periods using the NPV method. For example, 12 percent might be the rate for the first three years, and 15 percent (which reflects a greater risk) might be the rate for subsequent years. If the NPV is greater than zero, the project will be acceptable.

## Pass Key

The NPV method of capital investment valuation is considered to be superior to the internal rate of return (IRR) method because it is flexible enough to handle inconsistent rates of return for each year of the project.

### 3.4.3 Discount Rate Applied to Qualitatively Desirable or Non-optional Investments

A project that meets qualitative management criteria for investment (e.g., mandated technology investments) is subject to financing, rather than capital budgeting, considerations. In this case, the discount rate used for NPV evaluation should be the after-tax cost of borrowing, sometimes called the incremental borrowing rate.

---

### Example 2      Net Present Value

**Facts:** McLean Inc. is considering the purchase of a new machine, which will cost $150,000. The machine has an estimated useful life of three years. Assume for simplicity that the equipment will be fully depreciated for tax purposes 30 percent, 40 percent, and 30 percent in each of the three years, respectively. The new machine will have a $10,000 resale value at the end of its estimated useful life. The machine is expected to save the company $85,000 per year in operating expenses. McLean uses a 40 percent estimated income tax rate and a 16 percent hurdle rate to evaluate capital projects.

Discount rates for a 16 percent rate are as follows:

| | Present Value of $1 | Present Value of an Ordinary Annuity of $1 |
|---|---|---|
| Year 1 | 0.862 | 0.862 |
| Year 2 | 0.743 | 1.605 |
| Year 3 | 0.641 | 2.246 |

**Required:** Calculate the net present value of the proposed purchase of the new machine.

(continued)

---

(continued)

**Solution:**

1.  **Annual Depreciation Shield**

    First, calculate the annual depreciation tax shield as follows (Depreciation × Tax rate):

    |                     | Years 1 and 3 (30%) | Year 2      |
    | ------------------- | ------------------- | ----------- |
    | Cost of asset       | $150,000            | $150,000    |
    | Depreciation %      | ×       30%         | ×       40% |
    | Annual depreciation | $ 45,000            | $ 60,000    |
    | Tax rate            | ×       40%         | ×       40% |
    | Tax shield          | $ 18,000            | $ 24,000    |

2.  **Annual Savings**

    Calculate the after-tax annual savings as follows [Savings × (1 − Tax rate)]:

    Annual savings = $85,000 [savings per year] × (1 − 0.40)

    Annual savings = $85,000 × 0.60

    Annual savings = **$51,000**

3.  **Salvage Value Inflow**

    Calculate the salvage value inflow as follows:

    | Proceeds from salvage | $10,000 |                          |
    | --------------------- | ------- | ------------------------ |
    | Less: Basis of machine | —      | [fully depreciated]      |
    | Gain on salvage       | $10,000 |                          |
    | Less: Taxes           | (4,000) | [$10,000 × 40%]          |
    | Cash inflow           | $ 6,000 | [$10,000 × (1 − 0.40)]   |

4.  **Net Present Value Schedule and Calculation**

    |                        | Year 0     | Year 1   | Year 2   | Year 3   |                  |
    | ---------------------- | ---------- | -------- | -------- | -------- | ---------------- |
    | Equipment cost         | $(150,000) |          |          |          |                  |
    | Depreciation tax shield|            | $18,000  | $24,000  | $18,000  | [from 1, above]  |
    | Annual savings         |            | 51,000   | 51,000   | 51,000   | [from 2, above]  |
    | Salvage value inflow   |            |          |          | 6,000    | [from 3, above]  |
    | After-tax cash flow    | (150,000)  | 69,000   | 75,000   | 75,000   |                  |
    | Discount rate          | ×    1.00  | × 0.862  | × 0.743  | × 0.641  |                  |
    | Present value          | (150,000)  | 59,478   | 55,725   | 48,075   | = **$13,278**    |

## 3.5 Advantages and Limitations of the Net Present Value Method

### 3.5.1 Advantages

The net present value method is flexible and can be used when there is no constant rate of return required for each year of the project.

### 3.5.2 Limitations

Even though NPV is considered the *best* single technique for capital budgeting, the net present value method of capital budgeting is limited by not providing the true rate of return on the investment. The NPV purely indicates whether an investment will earn the "hurdle rate" used in the NPV calculation.

## 3.6 Capital Rationing

The concept of capital rationing describes how limited investment resources are considered as part of investment ranking and selection decisions.

### 3.6.1 Unlimited Capital

Ideally, a company has virtually unlimited resources at its disposal, so the company may do everything (or nearly everything) that meets the company's screening criteria. Investments are undertaken in the order that they are ranked. If a company has unlimited capital, all investment alternatives with a positive NPV should be pursued.

### 3.6.2 Limited Capital

Realistically, a company has extremely limited resources that make its investment choices mutually exclusive (i.e., if one investment is chosen over another, the company does not have the option of "hedging its bet" with the second alternative because resources are entirely committed).

- **Importance:** Capital budgeting decisions involve a tremendous amount of money, time, and risk. If the company is down to two mutually exclusive choices, the importance of clearly defined calculations is just that much more critical.

- **Ranking and Acceptance:** If capital is limited and must be rationed, managers will allocate capital to the combination of projects with the maximum net present value. The ranking of projects from a group of qualifying investments (those that exceed the hurdle rate) is best accomplished using the profitability index (described below) and becomes especially important when projects are independent (i.e., mutually exclusive).

## 3.7 Profitability Index

The profitability index is the ratio of the present value of net future cash inflows to the present value of the net initial investment. The profitability index is also referred to as the excess present value index, or simply the present value index. Ranking and selection of investment alternatives anticipate positive net present values for all successfully screened investments. The profitability ratio likely will be over 1.0, which means that the present value of the inflows is greater than the present value of the outflows.

$$\text{Profitability index} = \frac{\text{Present value of net future cash inflow}}{\text{Present value of net initial investment}}$$

### 3.7.1 Application

The profitability index measures cash-flow return per dollar invested; the higher the profitability index, the more desirable the project. Projects that meet the screening criteria (e.g., positive NPV) are ranked in descending order by their profitability index. Limited capital resources are applied in the order of the index until resources are either exhausted or the investment required by the next project exceeds remaining resources.

---

| Example 3 | Capital Rationing |
|---|---|

**Facts:** Beaman Enterprises has $50,000 of capital to invest in new projects for the coming fiscal year. The company must decide which projects to invest in given its budget constraints. The chart below shows the initial cost of the five investment options, along with the calculated present value of the future cash inflows.

| Project | Initial Investment | PV Future Inflows |
|---|---|---|
| A | $16,000 | $25,000 |
| B | 4,000 | 7,000 |
| C | 30,000 | 38,000 |
| D | 8,000 | 11,000 |
| E | 25,000 | 42,000 |

**Required:** Rank the investments using the profitability index and determine which project options Beaman should choose to pursue.

**Solution:** The first step is to calculate the profitability index for each project, which is done by dividing the present value of future inflows by the present value of the initial investment.

| Project | PV Future Inflows | Initial Investment | Profitability Index |
|---|---|---|---|
| A | $25,000 | $16,000 | 1.5625 |
| B | 7,000 | 4,000 | 1.75 |
| C | 38,000 | 30,000 | 1.267 |
| D | 11,000 | 8,000 | 1.375 |
| E | 42,000 | 25,000 | 1.68 |

The second step is to rank the projects from highest profitability index to lowest. The order would then be: Projects B, E, A, D, C.

The third and final step is to add the initial investments until the company's $50,000 threshold is reached.

$$B + E + A = \$4,000 + \$25,000 + \$16,000 = \$45,000$$

The next best project, which is D, would cost Beaman $8,000 and would push the company over the threshold of $50,000. Therefore, the projects Beaman will choose are projects B, E, and A.

---

## Question 1        CPA-03283

In equipment-replacement decisions, which one of the following does *not* affect the decision-making process?

- **a.** Current disposal price of the old equipment.
- **b.** Original fair market value of the old equipment.
- **c.** Cost of the new equipment.
- **d.** Operating costs of the new equipment.

## Question 2        CPA-03358

When the risks of the individual components of a project's cash flows are different, an acceptable procedure to evaluate these cash flows is to:

- **a.** Compute the net present value of each cash flow using the firm's cost of capital.
- **b.** Compare the internal rate of return from each cash flow to its risk.
- **c.** Utilize the accounting rate of return.
- **d.** Discount each cash flow using a discount rate that reflects the degree of risk.

## Question 3        CPA-03337

If the net present value of a capital budgeting project is positive, it would indicate that the:

- **a.** Present value of cash outflows exceeds the present value of cash inflows.
- **b.** Internal rate of return is equal to the discount percentage rate used in the net present value computation.
- **c.** Present value index would be less than 100 percent.
- **d.** Rate of return for this project is greater than the discount percentage rate used in the net present value computation.

| **Question 4** | **CPA-06644** |
|---|---|

Salem Co. is considering a project that yields annual net cash inflows of $420,000 for Years 1 through 5, and a net cash inflow of $100,000 in Year 6. The project will require an initial investment of $1,800,000. Salem's cost of capital is 10 percent. Present value information is presented below:

Present value of $1 for five years at 10 percent is 0.62.

Present value of $1 for six years at 10 percent is 0.56.

Present value of an annuity of $1 for five years at 10 percent is 3.79.

What was Salem's expected net present value for this project?

    **a.**  $83,000

    **b.**  $(108,200)

    **c.**  $(152,200)

    **d.**  $(442,000)

## NOTES

# 1 Application of NPV: Lease-vs.-Buy Decisions

## 1.1 The Issue

A company may acquire an asset by purchasing the asset or through a leasing arrangement. There are two main types of leases:

1. **Operating Lease:** Property is rented over an insignificant portion of the asset's useful life with no obligation (or opportunity) to assume ownership of the property.

2. **Capital Lease:** Analogous to a lessee buying an asset and financing it with debt.

The important issue for financial decision-making is the *cash flows* created by a lease, as compared with purchasing the asset.

## 1.2 Decision-Making

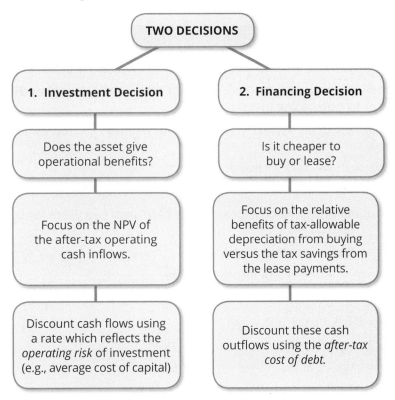

### 1.2.1 Investment Decision

- Discount the after-tax operating cash inflows at the firm's weighted average cost of capital (WACC).

### 1.2.2  Financing Decision

▪ Discount the cash flows specific to each financing option at the after-tax cost of debt.

▪ The preferred financing option is that with the lowest NPV of cost.

▪ The relevant cash flows to consider include:

- Buy asset or capital lease (same tax treatment—depreciation is tax deductible)
  - —Purchase cost or present value of lease payments
  - —Tax savings from depreciation
  - —Scrap proceeds
- Operating lease (lease payments are tax deductible)
  - —Lease payments
  - —Tax savings on lease payments

## Pass Key

If the PV of the cost of the best source of financing is less than the PV of the operating cash flows, then the project should be undertaken.

## Example 1     Lease or Buy

**Facts:** Boulder Inc. is considering the acquisition of a new machine, either through an operating lease or by purchasing the asset.

The asset will cost $200,000 on January 1, Year 1, and will have a scrap value of $25,000 at the end of Year 2.

Operating inflows are $150,000 for two years.

The tax rate is 30 percent and the company's weighted average cost of capital is 9 percent.

The machine is fully depreciated on a straight-line basis over two years for both book and tax purposes.

Boulder's financing options for the asset are:

- using a bank loan at a 10 percent interest rate; or

- leasing for $92,500 a year, with lease payments due on January 1 of each year.

Relevant PV factors include the following:

|  |  |
|---|---|
| PV of ordinary annuity at 9% | 1.759 |
| PV of annuity due at 7% | 1.935 |

| | **PV of $1 at 7%** |
|---|---|
| Year 1 | 0.935 |
| Year 2 | 0.873 |

(continued)

(continued)

**Required:**

1. Determine the operational benefit of the project.

2. Determine how the project should be financed.

3. Determine the NPV of the investment.

**Solution:**

1. Operational Benefit

    PV of annual after-tax cash inflow = [$150,000 × (1 − 30%)] × 1.759

    PV of annual after-tax cash inflow = $105,000 × 1.759 = $184,695

2. Financing Decision

    After-tax cost of debt = 10% × (1 − 30%) = 7%

    **a.** Borrow and buy asset

    Annual depreciation tax shield = $100,000 × 30% = $30,000

    After-tax cash inflow from scrap = $25,000 × (1 − 30%) = $17,500

    |  | Year 0 | Year 1 | Year 2 |
    |---|---|---|---|
    | Cost of machine | $(200,000) | | |
    | Depreciation tax shield | | $30,000 | $30,000 |
    | Scrap | – | – | 17,500 |
    | After-tax cash flow | (200,000) | 30,000 | 47,500 |
    | Discount rate | 1 | 0.935 | 0.873 |
    | Present value | $(200,000) | $28,050 | $41,468 = $(130,483) |

    **b.** Operating lease

    PV of annual after-tax cash outflow = [$92,500 × (1 − 30%)] × 1.935

    PV of annual after-tax cash outflow = $64,750 × 1.935 = $(125,291)

    Project should be financed using the operating lease because the NPV of the cost is lower.

3. Net Present Value

    | | |
    |---|---|
    | PV of operating inflows | $184,695 |
    | PV of lease financing | (125,291) |
    | Net present value | $ 59,404 |

## 1.3    Effect on the Financial Statements

Financial accounting implications must be considered when making a lease-versus-buy decision.

This is certainly relevant for the managers of a public company as key ratios may be influenced—particularly financial risk indicators such as the firm's debt-to-equity ratio and interest coverage ratio.

The implications of each financing option can be summarized as follows:

■   **Borrow to Buy**

The bank loan will be recorded in non-current liabilities and will increase the firm's debt-to-equity ratio. Interest on the debt will reduce the firm's interest coverage ratio. However, the overall effect also depends on the profits generated by the asset as these will increase earnings and equity.

■   **Operating Lease**

Neither the asset nor any related liability is shown in the statement of financial position. Operating leases are a form of off-balance sheet financing (although commitments under operating leases would be disclosed in the notes to the financial statements). Although rental expense decreases earnings, this should be offset by the returns generated by operating the asset.

■   **Capital Lease**

Both the asset and a related liability are recognized in the balance sheet (similar to the borrow to buy option). Therefore, the debt-to-equity ratio would initially rise. Lease payments are split between interest expense and repayment of principal and therefore the liability is amortized over time and ultimately falls to zero. Interest expense in early years is relatively high, decreasing the interest coverage ratio, but interest expense falls in later years as the liability decreases.

# 2    Internal Rate of Return (IRR)

The internal rate of return (IRR) is the expected rate of return of a project and is sometimes called the time-adjusted rate of return.

## 2.1    Objective

The IRR method determines the present value factor (and related interest rate) that yields an NPV equal to zero. (The present value of the after-tax net cash flows equals the initial investment on the project.)

The IRR method focuses the decision maker on the discount rate at which the present value of the cash inflows equals the present value of the cash outflows (usually the initial investment).

### Pass Key

Although the NPV method highlights dollar amounts, the IRR method focuses decision makers on percentages.

## 2.2    Interpreting IRR for Investment Decisions

The targeted rate of return or hurdle rate is predetermined and is compared with the computed IRR. Note that management would be indifferent about accepting or rejecting the project if the IRR were equal to the hurdle rate.

- **Accept When IRR > Hurdle Rate:** Projects with an IRR greater than the hurdle rate will be accepted.

- **Reject When IRR < Hurdle Rate:** Projects with an IRR less than the hurdle rate will be rejected.

## 2.3    Limitations of IRR

### 2.3.1    Unreasonable Reinvestment Assumption

Cash flows generated by the investment are assumed in the IRR analysis to be reinvested at the internal rate of return. If internal rates of return are unrealistically high or unrealistically low, assumed returns on reinvested cash flows based on IRR rates could lead to inappropriate conclusions.

### 2.3.2    Inflexible Cash Flow Assumptions

The timing or the amount of cash flows used to determine IRR can be misleading when compared with the NPV method. The IRR method is less reliable than the NPV method when there are several alternating periods of net cash inflows and net cash outflows or the amounts of the cash flows differ significantly.

### 2.3.3    Evaluates Alternatives Based Entirely on Interest Rates

The IRR method evaluates investment alternatives based on the achieved IRR and does not consider the dollar impact of the project.

---

**Illustration 1    Limitations of IRR**

If an investment of $50 earns $100, then there is a 200 percent return [100 / 50 = 200%]. If an investment of $50,000 earns $25,000, then there is a 50 percent return [25 / 50 = 50%]. The IRR method would suggest that it would be best to invest $50 to earn $100 and receive a 200 percent return, while the NPV method would favor the larger $25,000 NPV on the $50,000 investment.

---

# 3    Payback Period Method

The payback period is the time required for the net after-tax operating cash inflows to recover the initial investment in a project.

## 3.1    Objective

The payback period method focuses decision makers on both liquidity and risk. The payback period method measures the time it will take to recover the initial investment in the project, thereby emphasizing the project's liquidity and the time during which return of principal is at risk. The payback method is often used for risky investments. The greater the risk of the investment, the shorter the payback period that is expected (tolerated) by the company.

## 3.2 Calculation

The formula for calculating the payback period is as follows, assuming equal annual cash flows:

$$\text{Payback period} = \frac{\text{Net initial investment}}{\text{Annual net after-tax cash flow}}$$

## 3.3 Cash Flow Assumptions

### 3.3.1 Uniform Cash Inflows

The net cash inflows are generally assumed to be constant for each period during the life of the project. The payback period is computed at the point of initial investment using after-tax cash flows. Cash flows involve the following factors:

- **Project Evaluation:** In the case of a project, the net annual cash inflow would be the net cash receipts associated with the project.

- **Asset Evaluation:** In the case of the purchase of equipment, the net annual cash inflow will be the savings generated by use of the new equipment.

- **Depreciation Tax Shield:** Depreciation expense is not considered, except to the extent that it is a tax shield.

---

| Example 2 | Uniform Cash Flows |
|---|---|

**Facts:** Helena Company is planning to acquire a $250,000 machine that will provide increased efficiencies, thereby reducing annual operating costs by $80,000. The machine will be depreciated by the straight-line method over a five-year life with no salvage value at the end of five years.

**Required:** Assuming a 40 percent income tax rate, calculate the machine's payback period.

**Solution:**

1. Calculate the annual net cash savings (also referred to as the average expected cash flows) as follows:

| | | |
|---|---|---|
| Expected cash flow savings | | $ 80,000 |
| Net income increase | $ 80,000 | |
| Less: annual depreciation | (50,000) | |
| Net income before income taxes | $ 30,000 | |
| Multiplied by 40% tax rate | × 40% | (12,000) |
| Net cash savings | | $ 68,000 |

2. Calculate the payback period, as follows:

$$\frac{\text{Investment}}{\text{Net cash savings}} = \frac{\$250,000}{\$68,000} = 3.68 \text{ years}$$

---

### 3.3.2 Non-uniform Cash Flows (Use Cumulative Approach)

The standard payback formula shown above applies to uniform annual cash inflows. If cash flows are not uniform (i.e., they vary from period to period over the life of the project), a cumulative approach (rather than the standard payback formula) to determine the payback period is used. Net after-tax cash inflows are accumulated until the time they equal the initial net investment (at which point the end of the payback period is reached).

---

**Example 3**      **Non-uniform Cash Flows**

**Facts:** Radon Technologies is considering the purchase of a new machine costing $200,000 for its surfboard manufacturing plant in San Diego, CA. The management of Radon estimates that the new machine will last approximately four years and will be directly responsible for efficiencies that will increase the company's after-tax cash flows by the following amounts (non-uniform cash flow):

| | | **Cumulative Amounts** |
|---|---|---|
| Year 1 | $90,000 | $ 90,000 |
| Year 2 | 80,000 | 170,000 |
| Year 3 | 75,000 | 245,000 |
| Year 4 | 60,000 | 305,000 |

**Required:** Calculate the payback period for this investment.

**Solution:** The cumulative cash flows reach the initial investment amount of $200,000 sometime in Year 3.

Therefore, the payback period would be more than two years and less than three years. Assume that the cash flow is earned evenly throughout the year. The payback period is then calculated as follows:

1. Amount of cash flow in Year 3 needed to attain $200,000 cumulative cash flows:

    $200,000 − $170,000 (Year 2's cumulative amount) = $30,000

2. Percentage of Year 3 until cumulative amount of $200,000 is attained:

    $$\frac{\$30,000}{\$75,000} = 40\%$$

3. 2 + 0.40 = 2.40 years payback

---

## 3.4 Advantages and Limitations of Payback

### 3.4.1 Advantages of the Payback Method

■ **Easy to Use and Understand:** The simplicity of the objective and the absence of complex formulas or multiple steps make the payback method easy to use and understand.

■ **Emphasis on Liquidity:** The computation focuses management on return of principal. The method's emphasis on liquidity is a very important consideration when making capital budgeting decisions (e.g., most companies will prefer shorter payback periods, all other factors being equal).

                           

### 3.4.2 Limitations of the Payback Method

▪ The time value of money is ignored.

▪ Project cash flows occurring after the initial investment is recovered are not considered.

▪ Reinvestment of cash flows is not considered.

▪ Total project profitability is neglected.

# 4 Discounted Payback Method

Companies may use the discounted payback method as an alternative to the nondiscounted payback method. This variation computes the payback period using expected cash flows that are discounted by the project's cost of capital (the method considers the time value of money). Discounted payback is also referred to as the breakeven time method (BET).

## 4.1 Objective

The objective of the discounted payback method (or BET) is to evaluate how quickly new ideas are converted into profitable ideas.

▪ **Focus on Liquidity and Profit:** The measure focuses decision makers on the number of years needed to recover the investment from discounted net cash flows.

▪ **Evaluation Term:** The computation begins when the project team is formed and ends when the initial investment has been recovered (based on cumulative discounted cash flows).

▪ **Using Discounted Payback:** Discounted payback (or BET) is often used to evaluate new product development projects of companies that experience rapid technological changes. These companies want to recoup their investment quickly, before their products become obsolete.

## 4.2 Advantages and Limitations of Discounted Payback

The advantages and limitations of discounted payback are the same as the payback method (except that discounted payback incorporates the time value of money, a feature ignored by the payback method). Both focus on how quickly the investment is recouped rather than overall profitability of the entire project.

| Example 4 | Discounted Payback |
|-----------|--------------------|

**Facts:** Radon Technologies is considering the purchase of a new machine costing $200,000 for its surfboard manufacturing plant in San Diego, CA. The company's discount rate for projects of this type is 10 percent. The management of Radon estimates that the new machine will last approximately four years and will be directly responsible for efficiencies that will increase the company's after-tax cash flows by the following amounts (non-uniform cash flow):

| | |
|---|---|
| Year 1 | $90,000 |
| Year 2 | 80,000 |
| Year 3 | 75,000 |
| Year 4 | 60,000 |

The present value interest factors for 10 percent are as follows:

| | |
|---|---|
| Year 1 | 0.909 |
| Year 2 | 0.826 |
| Year 3 | 0.751 |
| Year 4 | 0.683 |

**Required:** Calculate the discounted payback period for this investment.

**Solution:**

1.  Calculate the present value of the future cash flows:

| Year | Cash Flow Increase | Discount Factor | 10% PV of Cash Flow | Cumulative PV |
|------|--------------------|-----------------|---------------------|---------------|
| Year 1 | $ 90,000 | 0.909 | $ 81,810 | $ 81,810 |
| Year 2 | 80,000 | 0.826 | 66,080 | 147,890 |
| Year 3 | 75,000 | 0.751 | 56,325 | 204,215 |
| Year 4 | 60,000 | 0.683 | 40,980 | 245,195 |
| | $305,000 | | $245,195 | |

2.  Determine the discounted payback period:

    The cumulative present value reaches the initial investment amount of $200,000 in Year 3. Therefore, the discounted payback period would be more than two years and less than three years. Assume that the cash flow is earned evenly throughout the year. The discounted payback period is then calculated as follows:

    - Amount of cash flow in Year 3 needed to attain $200,000 cumulative cash flows:

        $200,000 − $147,890 (Year 2's cumulative amount) = $52,110

    - Percentage of Year 3 until cumulative amount of $200,000 is attained:

        $$\frac{\$52,110}{\$56,325} = 92.5\%$$

    - 2 + 0.925 = 2.925 years discounted payback

## Pass Key

### Calculating Time Value of Money Without Factors

Although the CPA Exam often will provide factors for use in time value of money calculations, it is very helpful for candidates to understand how to calculate these factors in the event that they are not given on the exam.

### Present Value of $1

The formula to calculate present value is as follows:

$$PV = FV / (1 + r)^n$$

Where:

PV = Present value

FV = Future value

r = Interest rate

n = Number of years

Example: What is the factor for the present value of $1 to be received two years in the future at an interest rate of 6 percent?

$$
\begin{aligned}
PV &= \frac{FV}{(1 + r)^n} \\[2mm]
&= \frac{1}{(1.06)^2} \\[2mm]
&= 0.890
\end{aligned}
$$

### Present Value of Annuity

The formula to calculate the present value of an annuity is as follows:

$$PV = PMT \times \frac{\left[ 1 - \dfrac{1}{\left(1 + r\right)^n} \right]}{r}$$

Where:

PMT = Annuity payment

Example: What is the factor for the present value of $1 to be received in each of the next three years at an interest rate of 6 percent?

$$PV = 1 \times \frac{\left[ 1 - \dfrac{1}{(1.06)^3} \right]}{0.06}$$

$$= 2.673$$

---

**Question 1**                                                      CPA-05785

Which of the following statements about investment decision models is true?

    **a.** The discounted payback rate takes into account cash flows for all periods.

    **b.** The payback rule ignores all cash flows after the end of the payback period.

    **c.** The net present value model says to accept investment opportunities when their rates of return exceed the company's incremental borrowing rate.

    **d.** The internal rate of return rule is to accept the investment if the opportunity cost of capital is greater than the internal rate of return.

---

**Question 2**                                                      CPA-04836

Which of the following statements is true regarding the payback method?

    **a.** It does not consider the time value of money.

    **b.** It is the time required to recover the investment and earn a profit.

    **c.** It is a measure of how profitable one investment project is compared to another.

    **d.** The salvage value of old equipment is ignored in the event of equipment replacement.

---

**Question 3**                                                      CPA-05309

In considering the payback period for three projects, Fly Corp. gathered the following data about cash flows:

| | | | Cash Flows by Year | | |
| --- | --- | --- | --- | --- | --- |
| | Year 1 | Year 2 | Year 3 | Year 4 | Year 5 |
| Project A | $(10,000) | $ 3,000 | $ 3,000 | $ 3,000 | $ 3,000 |
| Project B | (25,000) | 15,000 | 15,000 | (10,000) | 15,000 |
| Project C | (10,000) | 5,000 | 5,000 | | |

Which of the projects will achieve payback within three years?

    **a.** Projects A, B, and C.

    **b.** Projects B and C.

    **c.** Project B only.

    **d.** Projects A and C.

---

## NOTES

# Operations Management: Cost Accounting and Performance Management

## Module

# 1 Cost Objects (or Objectives)

*Cost objects* (or cost objectives) are defined as resources or activities that serve as the basis for management decisions. Cost objects require separate cost measurement and may be products, product lines, departments, geographic territories, or any other classification that aids in decision making.

## 1.1 Focus of Cost Objectives

Integration of product costing with cost control measurement and assignment objectives maximizes the effectiveness of management accounting systems. Cost measurement and assignment may focus on valuation of product or inventory (i.e., product costing) or cost control (i.e., cost comparison to standards and budgets).

| Pass Key |
|---|

A single cost object can have more than one measurement. Inventory (product) costs for financial statements are usually different from costs reported for tax purposes. Both inventory (product) costs and costs reported for tax purposes are different from costs used by management to make decisions.

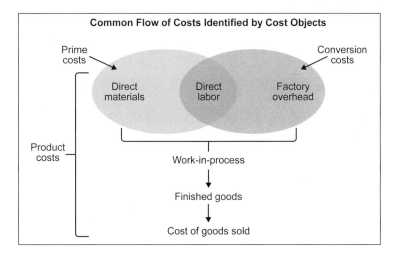

## 1.2 Common Cost Objects and Their Definitions

### 1.2.1 Product Costs

*Product costs* are all costs related to the manufacture of the product.

- **Inventory and Cost of Goods Manufactured and Sold:** Product costs are inventoriable (i.e., considered as assets before the product is sold). These costs attach to the units of output.

- **Components:** Product costs consist of direct materials, direct labor, and manufacturing overhead applied.

### 1.2.2 Period Costs

*Period costs* are expensed in the period in which they are incurred and are not inventoriable.

- **Expenses:** Period costs include selling, general, and administrative expenses as well as interest (financing) expense.

- **Components:** Period costs are the costs of selling the product and administering and managing the operations of the firm.

### 1.2.3 Manufacturing Costs (Treated as Product Costs)

*Manufacturing costs* include all costs associated with the manufacture of a product.

- **Inventory and Cost of Goods Manufactured and Sold:** Manufacturing costs are specifically capitalized to the cost of the manufactured product.

- **Components:** Manufacturing costs consist of both direct and indirect costs (described later).

### 1.2.4 Nonmanufacturing Costs (Treated as Period Costs)

*Nonmanufacturing costs* are costs that do not relate to the manufacture of a product. These costs (e.g., selling, general, and administrative expenses) are expensed in the period incurred.

## Pass Key

Cost accounting systems are designed to meet the goal of measuring cost objects or objectives. The most frequent objectives include:

- Product costing (inventory and cost of goods manufactured and sold)
- Income determination (profitability)
- Efficiency measurements (comparisons to standards)

## Example 1     Product Costs and Period Costs

**Facts:** Thompson Manufacturing incurred the following costs during its recent fiscal year:

| | |
|---|---:|
| Wages for factory employees | $ 5,700,000 |
| Wages for accounting department | 840,000 |
| Sales and promotion expense | 325,000 |
| Raw materials purchased | 4,950,250 |
| General and administrative costs | 675,500 |
| Manufacturing overhead | 1,100,000 |
| Interest expense | 195,000 |

(continued)

(continued)

**Required:** Compute Thompson's product costs and period costs for the year.

**Solution:**

Product costs:

| | |
|---|---:|
| Wages for factory employees | $ 5,700,000 |
| Raw materials purchased | 4,950,250 |
| Manufacturing overhead | 1,100,000 |
| Total product costs | **$11,750,250** |

Period costs:

| | |
|---|---:|
| Wages for accounting department | $ 840,000 |
| Sales and promotion expense | 325,000 |
| General and administrative costs | 675,500 |
| Interest expense | 195,000 |
| Total period costs | **$ 2,035,500** |

# 2 Tracing Costs to Cost Objects

## 2.1 Direct Costs

A *direct cost* can be easily (i.e., without excessive cost and without significant effort) traced to a cost pool or object, as the cost directly relates to that item. Common direct costs include:

### 2.1.1 Direct Raw Materials

*Direct raw materials* are the costs of materials purchased to be used in production (including freight-in net of any applicable purchase discounts) plus a reasonable amount for normal scrap created by the process.

### 2.1.2 Direct Labor

*Direct labor* is the cost of the labor that is directly related to the production of a product or the performance of a service plus a reasonable amount of expected "downtime" for the labor (e.g., breaks, setup, training, etc.).

---

**Illustration 1     Direct Costs**

---

Spud Furnishings Inc. manufactures custom couches. Raw materials (fabric or leather) used in the production process of a custom order (a couch) are considered direct materials and are easily traced to the cost object, the custom order. The time spent by the upholsterer to make the couch is considered direct labor and is also easily traced to the cost object, the custom order.

---

## 2.2    Indirect Costs

An *indirect cost* is not easily traceable to a cost pool or cost object. Indirect costs are typically incurred to benefit two or more cost pools or objects. The specific benefit each cost gives to the cost pool or object cannot be determined without making some sort of reasonable estimate or using an allocation methodology. Indirect costs are known as *overhead*. In the manufacturing business, such costs are classified as *manufacturing overhead*.

### 2.2.1    Indirect Materials

The category *indirect materials* covers the cost of materials that were not used specifically or could not be traced to the completed product with ease.

| Illustration 2      Indirect Materials |
| --- |
| Spud Furnishings Inc. manufactures custom couches. In addition to the direct material for fabric, wood for framing, and springs it uses in the couches, the company purchases cleaning supplies used in the manufacturing area and small replacement parts for the manufacturing machines. These items are *indirect materials* that do not directly benefit any specific cost object. These costs are included in overhead. |

### 2.2.2    Indirect Labor

*Indirect labor* is the cost of labor that is not easily traceable to a particular product, service, etc. Most often, this type of labor supports the manufacturing process but does not work directly on the specific job, etc.

| Illustration 3      Indirect Labor |
| --- |
| Spud Furnishings Inc. manufactures custom couches. In addition to upholsterers, Spud Furnishings employs forklift drivers, maintenance workers, shift supervisors, workers in the receiving department, janitorial staff, inspectors, engineers, training, and other human resources staff. These costs are *indirect labor* and are included in *manufacturing overhead*. |

### 2.2.3    Other Indirect Costs

*Other indirect costs* are indirect costs other than those for materials or labor.

| Illustration 4      Other Indirect Costs |
| --- |
| Spud Furnishings Inc. incurs costs for depreciation of the facility and machinery, rent of the production warehouse, machine maintenance, property taxes on the building, insurance, rent, utilities, etc. These miscellaneous facility costs are *other indirect costs* and are included in *manufacturing overhead*. |

## Pass Key

*Prime cost* = **Direct labor + Direct material**

*Conversion cost* = **Direct labor + Manufacturing overhead**

## 2.3    Overhead Allocation Using Cost Drivers

Indirect costs are allocated (assigned) to benefiting cost pools or cost objects using cost drivers that are considered to have a strong relationship to the incurrence of these costs.

- ▪ **Allocation Bases**

    The cost drivers that are used to allocate indirect costs are referred to as allocation bases.

- ▪ **Accounting for Overhead**

    When traditional costing is used, all indirect costs are allocated to a single cost pool (or account) called "overhead" and allocated as a single pool. Overhead may also be allocated using activity-based costing.

## Pass Key

When traditional costing is used, the application of overhead is accomplished in two steps:

**Step 1:** Overhead rate = Budgeted overhead costs ÷ Estimated cost drive

**Step 2:** Applied overhead = Actual cost driver × Overhead rate (from Step 1)

# 3    Cost Behavior (Fixed vs. Variable)

Costs can be classified by their behavior, the degree to which the costs are either fixed or variable. Direct material and direct labor are generally variable costs, and indirect costs consist of both fixed and variable components.

*Cost behaviors* are graphically illustrated as follows:

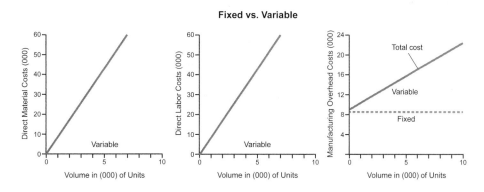

**Fixed vs. Variable**

Module 1        B3–7

## 3.1 Variable Cost

- **Behavior:** A variable cost changes proportionally with the cost driver (e.g., typical cost drivers include sales volume and production volume).

- **Amount (Constant per Unit, Total Varies):** Variable costs change in total, but they remain constant per unit. As production volume increases (or decreases), the total variable cost will increase (or decrease), but the variable cost per unit will always remain the same.

- **Long-Run Characteristics:** The short-run and long-run effects of variable costs are the same within relevant ranges (the range of production over which cost behavior assumptions are valid).

## 3.2 Fixed Cost

- **Behavior:** In the short term and within a relevant range, a fixed cost does not change when the cost driver changes.

- **Amount (Varies per Unit, Total Remains Constant):** Fixed costs remain constant in total, but they vary per unit. As production volume increases (or decreases), fixed costs remain the same, but the cost per unit will decrease (or increase), respectively.

### Pass Key

The distinction between variable costs and fixed costs allows managers to determine the effect of a given percentage change in production output on costs. *Be careful!* The examiners often attempt to trick candidates by providing a fixed cost per unit for a given volume of production. As fixed costs are "fixed," the candidate must convert this format to a dollar amount that will not change as production volume changes within a relevant range.

- **Long-Run Characteristics:** Given enough time (and a long enough relevant range), any cost can be considered variable.

### Illustration 5     Long-Run Characteristics

Depreciation is typically a fixed cost in a relevant manufacturing range of units or up to production capacity but can be considered variable in the long run. A new building will have to be purchased if the production levels exceed plant capacity (thus possibly increasing depreciation expense, depending on the extent to which other facilities have been depreciated).

## 3.3 Semi-variable Costs (Mixed Costs)

Costs frequently contain both fixed and variable components. Costs that include components that remain constant over the relevant range and include components that fluctuate in direct relation to production are classified as *semi-variable*.

                              

| Example 2 | Cost Behavior |
|---|---|

**Facts:** Quality Ornaments Inc. (QOI) manufactures collector porcelain figurines and holiday ornaments in its single manufacturing facility. During the recently completed operating year, the company incurred manufacturing labor costs of $3,200,000 (including indirect labor of $200,000, which includes a base annual contractual amount and a variable rate amount for hours worked above a contractual threshold), raw material costs of $6,000,000, plant depreciation costs of $440,000 (straight-line method used), electricity costs of $250,000 (directly tied to hours of production), heating costs of $100,000 (annual rate), and delivery expenses of $25,000 (based on a formula per customer order). Additionally, QOI incurred $10,000 in building and equipment maintenance and repair expense that includes both a fixed contractual amount for weekday maintenance and a variable rate amount for maintenance performed on Saturdays and holidays.

**Required:** Based on the above scenario, calculate the company's variable costs, fixed costs, and semi-variable costs for the year.

**Solution:**

| Cost Item | Variable Costs | Fixed Costs | Semi-variable Costs |
|---|---|---|---|
| Direct labor | $3,000,000 | | |
| Indirect labor | | | $200,000 |
| Raw materials | 6,000,000 | | |
| Depreciation | | $440,000 | |
| Electricity | 250,000 | | |
| Heating | | 100,000 | |
| Maintenance and Repair | | | 10,000 |
| Deliveries | 25,000 | | |
| **Total Costs** | **$9,275,000** | **$540,000** | **$210,000** |

## 3.4 Relevant Range

The *relevant range* is the range for which the assumptions of the cost driver (i.e., linear relationship with the costs incurred) are valid. When the cost driver activity is no longer within the relevant range, the variable and fixed cost assumptions for that cost driver cannot be used to allocate costs to cost objects. Relevant range is graphically illustrated as follows:

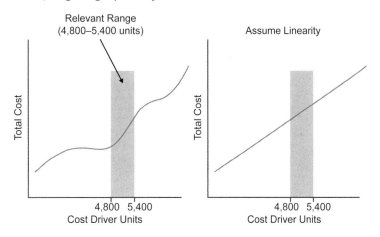

## Illustration 6     Cost Behaviors

| | Variable | Fixed | Semi-variable |
|---|:---:|:---:|:---:|
| **Sales** | x | | |
| Less: returns and allowances | x | | |
| | | | |
| **Cost of sales** | | | |
| Direct material | x | | |
| Direct labor | x | | |
| Indirect labor | | | x |
| Fringe benefits (15% of labor) | x | | x |
| Royalties (1% of product sales) | x | | |
| Maintenance and repairs of building | | | x |
| Factory production supplies | x | | |
| Depreciation: straight-line | | x | |
| Electricity: used in the mfg. process | x | x | |
| Scrap and spoilage (normal) | x | | |
| | | | |
| **Selling, general, and administrative expense** | | | |
| Sales commissions | x | | |
| Officers' salaries | | x | |
| Fringe benefits (relate to labor) | x | x | |
| Delivery expenses | x | | |
| Advertising expenses (annual contract expenses) | | x | |

## Question 1                                                    CPA-07083

If a product required a great deal of electricity to produce, and crude oil prices increased, which of the following costs most likely increased?

    a.   Direct materials.

    b.   Direct labor.

    c.   Prime costs.

    d.   Conversion costs.

# 1 Cost Accumulation Systems

*Cost accumulation systems* are used to assign costs to products. The system used is driven by the cost object involved. If the cost object is a custom order, job costing is used. If the cost object is a mass-produced, homogeneous product (e.g., steel), process costing is used.

## Pass Key

Although the most commonly tested cost accumulation systems are job-order costing and process costing, there are many variations of cost accumulation systems that may appear on your examination:

- Operations costing uses components of both job-order costing and process costing.

- Backflush costing accounts for certain costs at the end of the process in circumstances in which there is little need for in-process inventory valuation.

Life-cycle costing seeks to monitor costs throughout the product's life cycle and expand on the traditional costing systems that focus only on the manufacturing phase of a product's life.

# 2 Cost of Goods Manufactured and Sold

Production costs may be summarized in a cost of goods manufactured statement and a cost of goods sold statement. These statements may be prepared separately or combined as a cost of goods manufactured and sold statement.

## 2.1 Cost of Goods Manufactured

The *cost of goods manufactured* statement accounts for the manufacturing costs of the products completed during the period. These costs consist of direct material, direct labor, and manufacturing overhead costs. The manufacturing costs incurred during the period are increased or decreased by the net change in work-in-process inventory (beginning WIP minus ending WIP) to equal cost of goods manufactured.

| XYZ Company **Cost of Goods Manufactured** For the Month Ended November 30, Year 1 | | |
|---|---:|---:|
| Work-in-process inventory, beginning | | $ 40,000 |
| Add: direct material used | $ 30,000 | |
| Direct labor | 50,000 | |
| Manufacturing overhead applied | 40,000 | |
| Total manufacturing costs incurred | | 120,000 |
| Total manufacturing costs available | | 160,000 |
| Less: work-in-process inventory, ending | | (10,000) |
| Cost of goods manufactured | | $ 150,000 |

## 2.2 Cost of Goods Sold

A *cost of goods sold* statement for a manufacturer is very similar to one prepared for a retailer except that cost of goods manufactured is used in place of purchases made during the period.

| XYZ Company **Cost of Goods Sold** For the Month Ended November 30, Year 1 | |
|---|---:|
| Finished goods inventory, beginning | $ 20,000 |
| Add: cost of goods manufactured | 150,000 |
| Cost of goods available for sale | 170,000 |
| Less: finished goods inventory, ending | (50,000) |
| Cost of goods sold | $120,000 |

# 3  Job-Order Costing

*Job-order costing* (or job costing) is the method of product costing that identifies the job (or individual units or batches) as the cost objective and is used when relatively few units are produced and when each unit is unique or easily identifiable.

## 3.1 Cost Objective Is the Job (or Unit)

Under job-order costing, cost is allocated to a specific job as it moves through the manufacturing process. Record keeping for job costing emphasizes the job as the cost objective.

## 3.2 Job-Cost Records

*Job-cost records* are maintained for each product, service, or batch of products, and they serve as the primary records used to accumulate all costs for the job. Job-cost records are also referred to as job-cost sheets or job orders. Job-cost records accumulate data from the following internal documents:

- **Materials Requisitions:** *Materials requisitions* are documents showing materials requested for use on the job.

- **Labor Time Tickets (Time Cards):** *Labor time tickets* (time cards) are documents that show the labor hours and labor rate associated with the time applied to the job.

- **Job-Order Costing:** *Job-costing systems* require a limited number of work-in-process accounts.

### Pass Key

Job-costing systems are best suited for customized production environments such as construction, aircraft assembly, printing, etc. A new job-cost record would be started every time a new job (building project, airplane, or print job) is started.

---

| Question 1 | CPA-05321 |
|---|---|

Jonathon Manufacturing adopted a job-costing system. For the current year, budgeted cost driver activity levels for direct labor hours and direct labor costs were 20,000 and $100,000, respectively. In addition, budgeted variable and fixed factory overhead were $50,000 and $25,000, respectively.

Actual costs and hours for the year were as follows:

| | |
|---|---|
| Direct labor hours | 21,000 |
| Direct labor costs | $110,000 |
| Machine hours | 35,000 |

For a particular job, 1,500 direct-labor hours were used. Using direct-labor hours as the cost driver, what amount of overhead should be applied to this job?

    **a.** $3,214

    **b.** $5,357

    **c.** $5,625

    **d.** $7,500

## Overview: Job-Order Costing

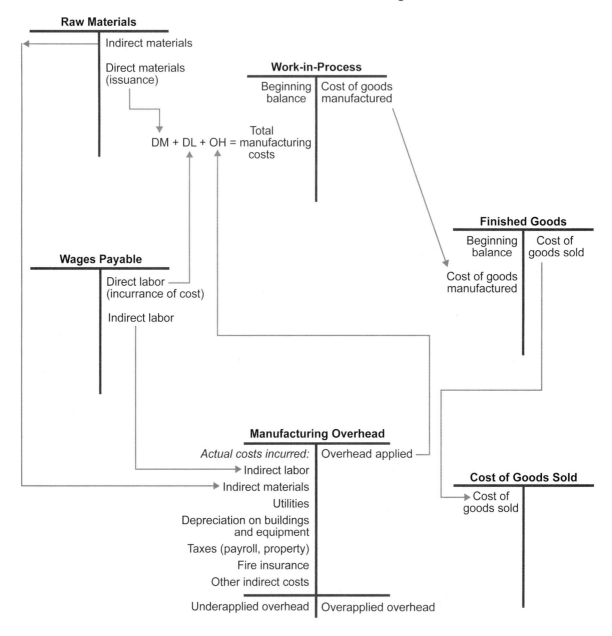

# 4 Process Costing

*Process costing* is a method of product costing that averages costs and applies them to a large number of homogeneous items using the following steps:

1. Summarize the flow of physical units (beginning with the production report).

2. Calculate "equivalent unit" output.

3. Accumulate the total costs to be accounted for (production report).

4. Calculate the average unit costs based on total costs and equivalent units.

5. Apply the average costs to the units completed and the units remaining in ending work-in-process inventory.

## 4.1 Units and Costs Collected on a Production Report

Costs incurred for a period as well as all units produced during that period are accumulated on a production report that accounts for the physical flow of units. The report includes the beginning inventory, the number of units started, the number of units completed, and the number of units remaining in inventory.

▪ **Unit (Quantity) Accounting**

The number of units accounted for must equal the number of units charged to the department (or separate process).

▪ **Cost Accounting**

The amount of costs accounted for must also equal the amount of costs charged to the department (or separate process).

| Pass Key |
|---|

The following shows the flow of inventory from beginning raw materials to ending finished goods inventory:

| Inventory: Raw Materials | Inventory: Work-in-Process | Inventory: Finished Goods |
|---|---|---|
| Beginning inventory of raw materials | Beginning inventory of work-in-process | Beginning inventory of finished goods |
| Add: purchases of raw materials | Add: raw materials used plus direct labor and overhead used | Add: inventory transferred from work-in-process |
| Raw materials available for use | Work-in-process inventory available to be finished | Finished goods inventory available-for-sale |
| Subtract: raw materials used | Subtract: inventory transferred to finished goods | Subtract: cost of goods sold |
| Ending inventory of raw materials | Ending inventory of work-in-process | Ending inventory of finished goods |

| **Illustration 1** | **Production Report** |
| --- | --- |

**Quantities**

| | |
| --- | --- |
| Charged to department: | |
| In process, beginning | 5,000 |
| Transferred in | 20,000 |
| Total units charged to department | 25,000 |
| Units accounted for: | |
| Transferred out | 15,000 |
| In process, end | 10,000 |
| Total units accounted for | 25,000 |

**Costs**

| | |
| --- | --- |
| Charged to department: | |
| In process, beginning | $12,000 |
| During the period | 85,000 |
| Total units charged to department | $97,000 |
| Costs accounted for: | |
| Transferred out | $60,000 |
| In process, end | 37,000 |
| Total costs accounted for | $97,000 |

## 4.2   Equivalent Units

Costs must be attached to the completed units as well as to the units that are partially complete at the end of each period. This calculation is made by taking into account the partially completed units and by making use of equivalent units.

### Pass Key

Accounting for the physical flow of units is an important step in process costing. Remember, however, that the pure physical flow of units will be different from the equivalent units of production.

### 4.2.1   Equivalent Unit Defined

An equivalent unit of direct material, direct labor, or conversion costs (direct labor plus factory overhead) is equal to the amount of direct material, direct labor, or conversion costs necessary to complete one unit of production.

---

### Illustration 2     Equivalent Units

Company X would like to produce 10,000 units during the first quarter. The company obtains the raw material inputs prior to the production of each unit and has applied the necessary direct labor and manufacturing overhead to complete 75 percent of the production during the first two months (with the remaining production process to be performed during the third month).

When preparing its internal monthly production reports, Company X would indicate that it has 10,000 units 100 percent complete as to direct materials and 7,500 equivalent units of production as to direct labor and overhead at the February 28 month end.

### 4.2.2   Process Costing Assumptions

■ **Transfers In Are 100 Percent Complete**

*Transfers in* from other departments are always considered 100 percent complete. The transfer in costs of direct material from a previous department are treated as direct materials (DM), even though they are called "transfer in" costs or "previous department" costs.

■ **Timing of Addition of Direct Material**

● **Addition at the Beginning or During a Process**

Direct material added at the beginning of or during a second or later process may either be 100 percent complete or "partially complete," depending on how much work has been done on that component of the process.

● **Addition at the End of a Process**

Any material added at the (very) end of a process will not be in work-in-process inventory at the month end.

## 4.3   Calculations of Average Unit Costs

The calculation of average unit costs and the application of those costs to various segments of the process is complicated by a number of issues.

### 4.3.1   Averaging of Costs From Prior Month's WIP

Frequently, costs from the previous month's work-in-process inventory are different from costs of the current month. These costs must be averaged.

### 4.3.2   Cost Flow Assumptions

Cost averaging computations depend on FIFO and/or weighted (or moving) average cost flow assumptions. These computations require a well-labeled account analysis format for each unit of direct material, direct labor, or overhead.

## 4.4   Calculation Using First In, First Out (FIFO)

Under FIFO accounting, the ending inventory is priced at the cost of manufacturing during the period, assuming that the beginning inventory was completed during the period.

---

### 4.4.1   Equivalent Unit Components

The *equivalent units* are composed of three elements:

**1.**   Completion of units on hand at the beginning of the period

**2.**   Units started and completed during the period (Units completed − Beginning WIP)

**3.**   Units partially complete at the end of the period

### 4.4.2   Cost Components

Current costs incurred during the period are allocated to the equivalent units produced during the period.

## 4.5   Calculation Using Weighted Average

The weighted average cost method averages the cost of production during the period with the costs in the beginning work-in-process inventory.

### 4.5.1   Equivalent Unit Components

The *equivalent units* are composed of two elements:

**1.**   Units completed during the month (Beginning WIP + Units started and completed during the month)

**2.**   Units partially complete at the end of the period

### 4.5.2   Cost Components

Total costs, including both the costs of beginning inventory and current costs, are allocated to equivalent units to arrive at a weighted average unit cost.

| Example 1 | Equivalent Units of Production |
| --- | --- |

**Facts:** Assume the following information:

| | |
| --- | --- |
| Work-in-process, beginning | 100 units, 25% complete |
| Units completed and transferred out | 600 units |
| Work-in-process, ending | 200 units, 40% complete |

**Required:** Compute the equivalent units of production using the FIFO method and the weighted average cost method.

**Solution:**

**Weighted average equivalent units of production**

| | |
| --- | --- |
| Units completed and transferred out (always 100%) | 600 |
| Work-in-process, ending | |
| 200 units × 40% | 80 |
| Equivalent units of production | 680 |

(continued)

(continued)

**FIFO equivalent units of production**

| | | |
|---|---:|---:|
| Work-in-process, beginning | | |
| 100 units × 75% (to complete) | | 75 |
| Units started and completed this period | | |
| Units completed and transferred out | 600 | |
| Units in beginning inventory | (100) | 500 |
| Work-in-process, ending | | |
| 200 units × 40% | | 80 |
| Equivalent units of production | | 655 |

## 4.6   Comparison of FIFO and Weighted Average

### 4.6.1   Equivalent Unit Calculation

Equivalent unit calculation under FIFO consists of three elements representing current period production, whereas the calculation under the weighted average method consists of only two elements, units completed and units available in beginning inventory.

### 4.6.2   Cost Components

FIFO represents only costs incurred in the current period. The weighted average approach includes both current period units plus prior period units.

| Pass Key |
|---|

Equivalent units of production may be computed using either the FIFO or weighted average methods. The FIFO method specifically accounts for work to be completed, and the weighted average method blends the units, as follows:

**1.** Weighted average (two steps)

| | | |
|---|---|---:|
| Units completed | | XXX |
| Ending WIP × % completed | + | XXX |
| *Equivalent units* | | XXX |

**2.** FIFO (three steps)

| | | |
|---|---|---:|
| Beginning WIP × % to be completed | | XXX |
| Units completed—Beginning WIP | + | XXX |
| Ending WIP × % completed | + | XXX |
| *Equivalent units* | | XXX |

## Pass Key

Cost per equivalent unit is computed by dividing total costs by equivalent units. FIFO uses only current costs, and the weighted average method uses both beginning inventory and current costs.

**1.** Weighted average

$$\text{Weighted average} = \frac{\text{Beginning cost} + \text{Current cost}}{\text{Equivalent units}}$$

**2.** FIFO

$$\text{FIFO} = \frac{\text{Current cost only}}{\text{Equivalent units}}$$

---

| Example 2 | Process Costing |
|---|---|

**Facts:**

Comprehensive Example
**Process Costing Under FIFO and Weighted Average**
May of Year 1

| | Percent Complete | Materials | Conversion | Total |
|---|---|---|---|---|
| **1.** Units in process, May 1 | | | | |
|     Materials | 100% | 4,000 | | |
|     Conversion | 40% | | 4,000 | |
| **2.** Units started and completed in May | | | | |
|     Materials | 100% | 10,000 | | |
|     Conversion | 100% | | 10,000 | |
| **3.** Units in process, May 31 | | | | |
|     Materials | 100% | 2,000 | | |
|     Conversion | 80% | | 2,000 | |
| **4.** Costs associated with May 1 WIP | | | | |
|     Materials | | $ 1,000 | | $ 1,000 |
|     Conversion | | | $ 3,000 | 3,000 |
| **5.** Costs associated with May production | | | | |
|     Materials | | $24,000 | | $24,000 |
|     Conversion | | | $49,000 | 49,000 |
| **6.** Total Costs | | | | **$77,000** |

(continued)

(continued)

**Required:**

1. Compute equivalent units of production using FIFO and weighted average.

2. Compute production costs using FIFO and weighted average.

3. Compute equivalent cost per unit using FIFO and weighted average.

**Solution:**

1. Equivalent units of production

|  | First In, First Out | | | | Weighted Average | | | |
| --- | --- | --- | --- | --- | --- | --- | --- | --- |
|  | Materials (%) | | Conversion (%) | | Materials (%) | | Conversion (%) | |
| Units in process, May 1 | – | (0%) | 2,400 | (60%) | 4,000 | (100%) | 4,000 | (100%) |
| Units started and completed in May | 10,000 | (100%) | 10,000 | (100%) | 10,000 | (100%) | 10,000 | (100%) |
| Units in process, May 31 | 2,000 | (100%) | 1,600 | (80%) | 2,000 | (100%) | 1,600 | (80%) |
| Total Units | **12,000** | | **14,000** | | **16,000** | | **15,600** | |

2. Production costs

|  | | | | |
| --- | --- | --- | --- | --- |
| Costs in WIP, May 1 | $ – | $ – | $ 1,000 | $ 3,000 |
| Costs during May | 24,000 | 49,000 | 24,000 | 49,000 |
| Total Costs | **$24,000** | **$49,000** | **$25,000** | **$52,000** |

3. Equivalent cost per unit

|  | | | | |
| --- | --- | --- | --- | --- |
| Equivalent cost per unit | **$ 2.00** | **$ 3.50** | **$ 1.56** | **$ 3.33** |

## 4.7 Spoilage (or Shrinkage)

*Spoilage* (or shrinkage) is generally taken care of automatically because the equivalent units added for the month are generally less than the actual units added during the month due to problems with the production process.

### 4.7.1 Normal Spoilage (Inventory Cost)

*Normal spoilage* occurs under regular operating conditions and is included in the standard cost of the manufactured product.

▪ **Computation**

For normal spoilage (or shrinkage), per unit cost is automatically increased as a result of spoilage because actual costs are spread over fewer equivalent good units rather than actual units produced.

▪ **Accounting Treatment**

Normal spoilage is capitalized as part of inventory cost. Normal spoilage costs, if accounted for separately, are allocated to good units produced.

### 4.7.2 Abnormal Spoilage (Period Expense)

*Abnormal spoilage* should not occur under normal operating conditions and is excluded from the standard cost of a manufactured product.

- ## Computation

  For abnormal spoilage (or shrinkage), the per unit cost is based on actual units. Equivalent units of production include spoiled units.

- ## Accounting Treatment

  The cost of abnormal spoilage is normally expensed separately on the income statement as a period expense.

---

| Example 3 | Spoilage Application |
|---|---|

**Facts:** Fresh Baked Company produces ready-to-serve fruit pies for local restaurants and supermarkets. During the month of April, the company had the following costs related to the production of 20,000 pies:

| | |
|---|---:|
| Pie ingredients | $45,000 |
| Baking labor | 24,000 |
| Plant production overhead | 11,000 |
| Sales and marketing expenses | 500 |
| General and administrative expenses | 1,200 |
| Normal spoilage | 400 |
| Abnormal spoilage | 200 |

**Required:**

1. What is the per unit cost of the pies assigned to inventory for April?

2. What amount will the company assign as a period expense for April?

**Solution:**

1. Unit cost

   **Step 1:** Determine inventory costs.          **Step 2:** Determine per unit cost.

| | | | |
|---|---:|---|---|
| Pie ingredients | $45,000 | Per unit cost (of pies) = | $80,400 ÷ 20,000 pies |
| | | | **$4.02** |
| Baking labor | 24,000 | | |
| Plant production overhead | 11,000 | | |
| Normal spoilage | 400 | | |
| Total inventory costs | **$80,400** | | |

2. Period expense

   The period expenses assigned to April are as follows:

| | |
|---|---:|
| Sales and marketing expenses | $    500 |
| General and administrative expenses | 1,200 |
| Abnormal spoilage | 200 |
| Total period expenses | **$ 1,900** |

## Question 2 CPA-05798

Merry Co. has two major categories of factory overhead: material handling and quality control. The costs expected for these categories for the coming year are as follows:

| | |
|---|---|
| Material handling | $120,000 |
| Quality inspection | 200,000 |

The plant currently applies overhead based on direct labor hours. The estimated direct labor hours are 80,000 per year. The plant manager is asked to submit a bid and assembles the following data on a proposed job:

| | |
|---|---|
| Direct materials | $4,000 |
| Direct labor (2,000 hours) | 6,000 |

What amount is the estimated product cost on the proposed job?

   a. $8,000

   b. $10,000

   c. $14,000

   d. $18,000

## Question 3 CPA-03601

Kerner Manufacturing uses a process costing system to manufacture laptop computers. The following information summarizes operations relating to laptop computer model No. KJK20 during the quarter ending March 31:

| | Units | Direct Materials |
|---|---|---|
| Work-in-process inventory, January 1 | 100 | $ 70,000 |
| Started during the quarter | 500 | |
| Completed during the quarter | 400 | |
| Work-in-process inventory, March 31 | 200 | |
| Costs added during the quarter | | $750,000 |

Beginning work-in-process inventory was 50 percent complete for direct materials. Ending work-in-process inventory was 75 percent complete for direct materials. What were the equivalent units of production using the FIFO method, with regard to materials for the quarter ended March 31?

   a. 450

   b. 500

   c. 550

   d. 600

| Question 4 | CPA-03644 |
|---|---|

Kimbeth Manufacturing uses a process cost system to manufacture Dust Density Sensors for the mining industry. The following information pertains to operations for the month of May:

|  | *Units* |
|---|---|
| Beginning work-in-process inventory, May 1 | 16,000 |
| Started in production during May | 100,000 |
| Completed production during May | 92,000 |
| Ending work-in-process inventory, May 31 | 24,000 |

The beginning inventory was 60 percent complete for materials and 20 percent complete for conversion costs. The ending inventory was 90 percent complete for materials and 40 percent complete for conversion costs.

Costs pertaining to the month of May are as follows:

- Beginning inventory costs are: materials, $54,560; direct labor, $20,320; and factory overhead, $15,240.

- Costs incurred during May are: materials used, $468,000; direct labor, $182,880; and factory overhead, $391,160.

Using the weighted average method, the equivalent unit cost of materials for May is:

    **a.** $4.50

    **b.** $4.60

    **c.** $5.03

    **d.** $5.46

# 1 Activity-Based Costing (ABC)

## 1.1 Types of Operational Cost Drivers

### 1.1.1 Volume-Based

Traditional costing systems assign overhead as a single cost pool with a single plant-wide overhead application rate using a single allocation base. These rates generally use volume-based cost drivers such as direct labor hours or machine hours. Assigning overhead costs based on volume can distort the amount of costs assigned to various product lines because all overhead costs do not fluctuate with volume.

### 1.1.2 Activity-Based

*Activity-based costing* (ABC) refines traditional costing methods and assumes that the resource-consuming activities (tasks, units of work, etc.) with specific purposes cause costs. ABC assumes that the best way to assign indirect costs to products (cost objects) is based on the product's demand for resource-consuming activities (i.e., costs are assigned based on the consumption of resources). Application of activity-based costing techniques attempts to improve cost allocation by emphasizing long-term product analysis.

## 1.2 Introduction to Activity-Based Costing

### 1.2.1 Terminology

- **Activity:** An *activity* is any work performed inside a firm. Activities are identified for ABC.

- **Resource:** A *resource* is an element that is used to perform (or applied to perform) an activity.

- **Cost Drivers:** *Cost drivers* used in ABC are activity bases that are closely correlated with the incurrence of manufacturing overhead costs in an activity center, and they are often used as allocation bases for applying overhead costs to cost objects.

### Pass Key

A cost driver is a factor that has the ability to change total costs. Cost drivers (including nonfinancial, statistical measurements of activities such as sales or production volume) are identified by ABC and are related to one of multiple cost pools for cost allocation.

- **Resource Cost Driver:** A *resource cost driver* is the amount of resources that will be used by an activity.

- **Activity Cost Driver:** An *activity cost driver* is the amount of activity that a cost object will use, and it is used to assign the costs to the cost objects.

- **Activity Centers:** An operation necessary to produce a product is an *activity center*.

| Illustration 1 | ABC Terminology |
| --- | --- |

Hope Hospital applies ABC to costing its services. The surgical unit is identified as an activity center that includes various professional service (surgeon and nurse) functions as well as facilities (operating room) functions. Resources used include hours of staff time for surgery and operating room preparation as well as for facilities maintenance. Resource drivers may include the complexity of surgical procedures (including setup time) and activity drivers may be purely admissions or scheduled surgeries.

- **Cost Pool:** A *cost pool* is a group of costs (e.g., raw material or direct labor) or a specially identified cost center (e.g., a department or a manager) in which costs are grouped, assigned, or collected.

### 1.2.2 Characteristics of ABC

ABC applies a more focused and detailed approach than using a department or plant as the level for gathering costs. ABC focuses on multiple causes (activities) and effects (costs) and then assigns costs to them. The cost of activities is used to "build up" the engineered cost of products using increased cost pools and allocations.

- ABC can be part of a job order system or a process cost system.
- ABC can be used for manufacturing or service businesses.
- ABC takes a long-term viewpoint and treats production costs as variable.
- The cost driver is often a nonfinancial variable.
- ABC may be used for internal but not for external purposes.

### 1.2.3 Transaction-Based Costing

Activity-based costing is also referred to as *transaction-based costing*. The cost driver is typically the number of transactions involved in a particular activity.

### 1.2.4 Focuses on Cost/Benefit of Activities

ABC focuses management on the cost/benefit of activities. Value-added activities increase the product value or service.

- **Value Chain (Value-Added Activities):** A *value chain* is a series of activities in which customer usefulness is added to the product. Support activities directly support value-added activities.

- **Non-Value-Added Activities:** *Non-value-added activities* do not increase product value or service and are targeted for elimination. Often, these types of activities (e.g., warehousing) should be eliminated.

## 1.3 Basic Operation of Activity-Based Costing

Activity-based costing is done using the following steps:

1. **Identify the Cost Drivers**
   Identify the activity centers and the activities that drive the costs in each activity center.

2. **Accumulate the Costs in Cost Pools**
   Many small cost pools are accumulated.

3. **Trace Indirect Costs to Activity Centers**
   Trace any indirect costs to the activity centers that can be assigned without allocation.

### 4. Allocate Remaining Indirect Cost Pools

Costs of each activity are applied to cost objects based on the most appropriate cost drivers.

### 5. Divide Assigned Costs by Level of Activity for the Cost Center

Divide the costs assigned to the activity center by the estimated level of activity for the center to derive an application rate for that center.

### 6. Cost the Product

Cost the product by multiplying its demand for the resources of an activity center by the rate for that activity center.

## 1.4 Effects of Activity-Based Costing

An ABC system will apply high amounts of overhead to a product that places high demands on expensive resources. If a product places few demands on expensive resources, the system will assign little of that cost to the product. This will remove much of the cost distortion caused by traditional, volume-based overhead systems.

## 1.5 ABC and Standard Cost Systems

*Standard cost systems* are a natural extension of activity-based costing. Standards are set at activity levels based on cost drivers. Useful variances are calculated by comparing actual and standard costs that consider levels of activity. These variances can be due to price (rate for labor), usage (efficiency), or other factors. Further, flexible budgets are derived at the activity level.

▪ Normal and abnormal scrap or spoilage is estimated for activity levels.

▪ Standards may be difficult to set on a per unit basis.

- Per unit costs are often inversely proportional to volume.

- Assumption of a relevant range may be necessary to set a per unit standard.

---

### Illustration 2     ABC Costing

Iowa Products makes two products at its Boone factory. The company has used a traditional cost accounting system for the application of overhead to the products. Currently it uses direct labor hours as an application base. One product, Can, incurred 150,000 direct labor hours and the other product, Bottle, incurred 45,000 direct labor hours. The company is considering converting to an activity-based costing system. The estimated data for its Year 1 operations is summarized below:

|                     |            |                              | Activity Level ||
| Activity Center     | Costs      | Cost Driver                  | Cans    | Bottles |
|---------------------|------------|------------------------------|---------|---------|
| Units               |            |                              | 500,000 | 150,000 |
| Material handling   | $  480,000 | Pounds                       | 100,000 | 60,000  |
| Production orders   | 90,000     | Number of production orders  | 100     | 100     |
| Product redesign    | 250,000    | Number of changes            | 50      | 200     |
| Plant utilities     | 2,300,000  | Machine hours                | 150,000 | 80,000  |

(continued)

---

(continued)

1. Illustration of the overhead application rate under a *traditional system* using direct labor hours as an application base:

| | |
|---|---:|
| Material handling | $ 480,000 |
| Production orders | 90,000 |
| Product redesign | 250,000 |
| Plant utilities | 2,300,000 |
| Total overhead costs | **$3,120,000** |

$$\text{Overhead application rate} = \frac{\text{Total overhead costs}}{\text{Total direct labor hours}}$$

$$= \$3,120,000 / (150,000 + 45,000)$$

$$= \$16 \text{ per direct labor hour}$$

**Cans:**　150,000 direct labor hours × $16　= $2,400,000
　　　　　$2,400,000 / 500,000 cans　　　= $4.80 per can
**Bottles:**　45,000 direct labor hours × $16　= $720,000
　　　　　$720,000 / 150,000 bottles　　　= $4.80 per bottle

2. Illustration of the overhead application rate under an *activity-based costing system* using each activity as a cost pool:

| | | |
|---|---|---|
| Material handling: | $480,000 / 160,000 pounds | = $3 per pound |
| Production orders: | $90,000 / 200 orders | = $450 per order |
| Product redesign: | $250,000 / 250 changes | = $1,000 per change |
| Plant utilities: | $2,300,000 / 230,000 machine hr. | = $10 per machine hour |

**Cans:**

| | |
|---|---:|
| Material handling, 100,000 lb. × $3 | $ 300,000 |
| Production orders, 100 orders × $450 | 45,000 |
| Product redesign, 50 changes × $1,000 | 50,000 |
| Plant utilities, 150,000 machine hr. × $10 | 1,500,000 |
| Total overhead costs | **$1,895,000** |

$1,895,000 / 500,000 cans = $3.79 per can

**Bottles:**

| | |
|---|---:|
| Material handling, 60,000 lb. × $3 | $ 180,000 |
| Production orders, 100 orders × $450 | 45,000 |
| Product redesign, 200 changes × $1,000 | 200,000 |
| Plant utilities, 80,000 machine hr. × $10 | 800,000 |
| Total overhead costs | **$1,225,000** |

$1,225,000 / 150,000 bottles = $8.167 per bottle

Bottle cost significantly increased with activity-based costing. This resulted because bottles required a large amount of the redesign resource. Redesign is a very costly resource and not related to volume. Because bottles required a large amount of this resource, a high amount of indirect cost was assigned to bottles. The cost of cans decreased significantly because that used comparatively little redesign resource.

## 1.6 Service Costs Allocation Using ABC

Companies in all sectors of the economy allocate service department costs to production or user departments and ultimately the final products produced.

---

### Illustration 3    Service Cost Allocation

Hospitals use complex methods to allocate service-related costs such as patient admissions or housekeeping to the various hospital departments that ultimately affect patient billing. By allocating these service department costs to the individual production departments and the final product, the entity is recognizing that these service costs are an input into the production process.

---

### 1.6.1 Direct Method

- The *direct method* is the most widely used (and least complex) method to allocate service costs.

- Each service department's total costs are directly allocated to the production departments without recognizing that service departments themselves may use the services from other service departments.

### 1.6.2 Step-Down Method

- The *step-down method* or sequential method is a more sophisticated approach to allocate service costs in more complex situations.

- Service department costs are also allocated to other service departments as well as production departments.

- Step-down allocations assume that once a service department's costs have been allocated to another service department, there can be no subsequent costs allocated back to the other service department(s).

---

### Example 1    Direct Method

**Facts:** Remington Company has two production departments, Division A and Division B. The company also has two service departments, which consist of Information Systems (IS) and Human Resources (HR). During the most recently completed operating year, the IS and HR departments had total service costs of $2,220,000 and $975,000, respectively.

| Dept. | Activity Center | Cost Driver | Division A | Division B |
|-------|-----------------|-------------|------------|------------|
| IS | Planning and reporting | Computing hours | 9,000 | 6,000 |
| HR | Division administration | Performance appraisals | 2,800 | 2,200 |

**Required:** Allocate the IS and HR departments' service costs to the two production divisions.

(continued)

---

(continued)

**Solution:**

### Application rate using ABC system

| | |
|---|---|
| Planning and reporting | $2,220,000 ÷ 15,000 hours = $148/hr. |
| Division administration | $975,000 ÷ 5,000 appraisals = $195/appraisal |

### Division A: Service cost allocation

| | |
|---|---|
| IS—Planning and reporting: 9,000 hours × $148 | $1,332,000 |
| HR—Division administration: 2,800 appraisals × $195 | 546,000 |
| **Total service costs** | **$1,878,000** |

### Division B: Service cost allocation

| | |
|---|---|
| IS—Planning and reporting: 6,000 hours × $148 | $  888,000 |
| HR—Division administration: 2,200 appraisals × $195 | 429,000 |
| **Total service costs** | **$1,317,000** |

---

| Example 2 | Step-Down Method |
|---|---|

**Facts:** Assume the same facts as the Remington Company direct-method example, above, with the exception that the Information Systems (IS) department also uses the services of the Human Resources (HR) department. Specifically, performance appraisals administered by the HR department to the IS department accounted for an additional 200 appraisals during the recent operating year. Further, assume that because of data privacy issues, the HR department uses an outside contractor for its information technology needs instead of the IS department.

**Note:** The allocation of IT computing service hours to the other two production divisions remains the same as above, as there is no IT service allocation to HR.

| Dept. | Activity Center | Cost Driver | Division A | Division B |
|---|---|---|---|---|
| HR | Division administration | Performance appraisals | 2,800 | 2,200 |

**Required:** Allocate the service costs for performance appraisals from HR to IT and the two production divisions using ABC.

**Solution:**

### HR application rate using ABC system

| | |
|---|---|
| HR—Division administration | $975,000 ÷ 5,200 appraisals = $187.50/appraisal |

### IT service department: Service cost allocation (of HR)

| | |
|---|---|
| HR—Division administration | 200 appraisals × $187.50 = $37,500 |

(continued)

(continued)

### IT application rate using ABC system

IT—Planning and reporting    ($2,220,000 + $37,500) ÷ 15,000 hours = $150.50 per hour

### Division A: Service cost allocation

| | |
|---|---|
| IT—Planning and reporting: 9,000 hours × $150.50 | $1,354,500 |
| HR—Division administration: 2,800 appraisals × $187.50 | 525,000 |
| **Total service costs** | **$1,879,500** |

### Division B: Service cost allocation

| | |
|---|---|
| IT—Planning and reporting: 6,000 hours × $150.50 | $   903,000 |
| HR—Division administration: 2,200 appraisals × $187.50 | 412,500 |
| **Total service costs** | **$1,315,500** |

It should be noted that under the step-down method, the HR (performance appraisal) allocation is lower to both Division A and Division B under ABC costing, given that HR costs are also allocated to the IS department.

# 2 Joint Product Costing and By-product Costing (Common Cost Allocation)

Accountants face the problem of allocating the cost of a single process (*joint costs*) among several final products (or by-products) if two or more final products are produced from the same raw material or input.

| Illustration 4 | Joint Costing |
|---|---|

The meat-packing industry takes a single input, a steer, and produces many final products. Each product must be assigned a cost, including the different cuts of meat for human consumption, different food products for animal consumption (pet food), and basic ingredients for glue (by-product).

## 2.1 Terminology

- **Joint Products:** *Joint products* are two or more products that are generated from a common input.

- **By-products:** *By-products* are minor products of relatively small value that incidentally result from the manufacture of the main product.

- **Split-off Point:** The *split-off point* is the point in the production process at which the joint products can be recognized as individual products.

- **Joint Product Costs (or Joint Costs):** *Joint product costs* are costs incurred in producing products up to the split-off point.

- **Separable Costs:** *Separable costs* are costs incurred on a product after the split-off point.

- **Joint Products:** *Joint products* represent outputs of significant value that are the object of a manufacturing process.

## 2.2 Allocation by Unit Volume Relationships

| Example 3 | Joint Cost Allocation by Unit Volume |
|---|---|

**Facts:** Simple Manufacturing Company produces two products, Product A and Product B. Direct costs associated with manufacturing Product A and Product B were $25,000 and $50,000, respectively, with joint costs of production representing $10,000. In order to allocate joint costs, the company used the proportional gallons of production for its two products as follows:

|  | **Volume** |
|---|---|
| Product A | 10,000 gal |
| Product B | 20,000 gal |
| **Total** | **30,000 gal** |

**Required:** Determine the portion of *joint costs* that will be allocated to each product and the total cost of each product.

**Solution:**

**Joint cost allocation**

| Product A: | (10,000/30,000) × $10,000 | = | $ 3,333 |
|---|---|---|---|
| Product B: | (20,000/30,000) × $10,000 | = | 6,667 |
|  |  |  | $10,000 |

**Total cost**

| Product A: | $25,000 (direct) + $3,333 (joint) | = | $28,333 |
|---|---|---|---|
| Product B: | $50,000 (direct) + $6,667 (joint) | = | $56,667 |

## 2.3    Relative Net Realizable Values at Split-off Point

Net realizable value equals sales value less cost of completion and disposal. Relative sales value at split-off point is used purely for inventory costing and is of little use for cost planning and control purposes.

### 2.3.1    Sales Price Quotations Available at Split-off

The relative sales value at split-off point can be used to allocate joint costs if sales price quotations are known or can be determined. The relative sales value approach assigns costs to the separate joint products in relation to their market values.

---

**Example 4**          **Joint Cost Allocation: Sales Values Known at Split-off**

**Facts:** Brown Company produces two products, A and B. Joint production costs incurred in the production of A and B totaled $1,000. At the split-off point, 100 units of A had a sales value of $20/unit and 400 units of B had a sales value of $15/unit.

**Required:** Compute the joint costs to be allocated to A and B using relative sales values at split-off.

**Solution:**

Allocation based on relative sales value:

| | |
|---|---:|
| Product A: 100 units @ $20 | $2,000 |
| Product B: 400 units @ $15 | 6,000 |
| | **$8,000** |

| | | |
|---|---|---:|
| Joint cost allocated to A:  $1,000 × ($2,000 ÷ $8,000) | = | $  250 |
| Joint cost allocated to B:  $1,000 × ($6,000 ÷ $8,000) | = | 750 |
| Total allocated joint cost | | **$1,000** |

---

### 2.3.2    Sales Values Not Available at Split-off

If sales values at split-off are not available because there are no markets for the joint products at split-off, then sales values at split-off must be derived using the following formula:

> **Sales value at split-off ≈ Final selling price − Identifiable costs incurred after split-off**

| Example 5 | Joint Cost Allocation: No Sales Value at Split-off |
|---|---|

**Facts:** Smith Company produces two joint products: F and G. Joint production costs for October were $30,000. During October, further processing costs beyond the split-off point (separable costs), needed to convert the products into saleable form, were $16,000 and $24,000 for 1,600 units of F and 800 units of G, respectively. F sells for $25 per unit and G sells for $50 per unit. Smith uses the net realizable value method for allocating joint product costs.

**Required:** Determine the joint costs to be allocated to F and G during October.

**Solution:**

| | | |
|---|---|---|
| Product F: Net realizable value | | |
| Sales value, $25 per unit × 1,600 units | $40,000 | |
| Further processing costs | (16,000) | |
| Net realizable value | | $24,000 |
| Product G: Net realizable value | | |
| Sales value, $50 per unit × 800 units | $40,000 | |
| Further processing costs | (24,000) | |
| Net realizable value | | 16,000 |
| Total net realizable value | | **$40,000** |
| Joint costs allocated to F: $30,000 × ($24,000 / $40,000) | $18,000 | |
| Joint costs allocated to G: $30,000 × ($16,000 / $40,000) | 12,000 | |
| Total joint costs | **$30,000** | |

## 2.4 Service Departments Cost Allocation to Joint Products

The allocation of service department costs to joint products can be accomplished by using the joint products unit-volume relationship.

| Example 6 | Service Department Joint Cost Allocation |
|---|---|

**Facts:** Simple Manufacturing Company manufactures two products (Product A and Product B) and allocates its joint costs using the proportional gallons of production for its two products as follows:

| | Volume |
|---|---|
| Product A | 10,000 gal |
| Product B | 20,000 gal |
| Total | **30,000 gal** |

The company's lone service department is Janitorial Services. Costs incurred for this department were $6,000 for the operating year.

**Required:** Determine the portion of service department costs that will be allocated to each product based on the joint products unit-volume relationships.

**Solution:**

| | | | |
|---|---|---|---|
| Product A: | (10,000/30,000) × $6,000 | = | $2,000 |
| Product B: | (20,000/30,000) × $6,000 | = | 4,000 |
| | | | **$6,000** |

## 2.5    By-products

*By-products* represent outputs of relatively minor value that are incidental to a manufacturing process. By-products have relatively low sale values that are not sufficient to cover their share of common costs (otherwise, they would be joint products). Revenue accounting can take one of two forms:

**1.   Applied to Main Product**

Any proceeds from the sale of by-products are a reduction to common costs for joint product costing. The revenue earned from their sale is credited to joint costs incurred either at the time of production or the time of sale.

**2.   Miscellaneous Income**

As an alternative, revenue from the sale of by-products may be credited to miscellaneous income.

## 2.6    By-product Costing vs. Joint Costing

Decisions regarding whether to use by-product costing or joint costing are practical ones, and they depend on relative demand.

---

**Illustration 5    Joint vs. By-product Costing**

Before the invention of the automobile, gasoline produced when oil was refined had no value and was scrap for disposal. After the invention of the automobile, gasoline was first priced as a by-product and then priced as a joint product (when demand for gasoline increased).

---

**Question 1**                                                          **CPA-08307**

A manufacturing company has several product lines. Traditionally, it has allocated manufacturing overhead costs between product lines based on total machine hours for each product line. Under a new activity-based costing system, which of the following overhead costs would be most likely to have a new cost driver assigned to it?

   **a.**   Electricity expense

   **b.**   Repair and maintenance expense

   **c.**   Employee benefits expense

   **d.**   Depreciation expense

| Question 2 | CPA-03477 |
|---|---|

A processing department produces joint products Ajac and Bjac, each of which incurs separable production costs after split-off. The following details pertain to a batch produced at a $60,000 joint cost before split-off:

| Product | Separable costs | Sales value |
|---|---|---|
| Ajac | $ 8,000 | $ 80,000 |
| Bjac | 22,000 | 40,000 |
| | $30,000 | $120,000 |

What is the joint cost assigned to Ajac if costs are assigned using the relative net realizable value?

    **a.** $16,000

    **b.** $40,000

    **c.** $48,000

    **d.** $52,000

# 1 Financial and Nonfinancial Performance Measures

Both *financial* and *nonfinancial measures* are ultimately designed to provide feedback that will motivate appropriate employee behaviors. Feedback tied to self-interest is most effective. The issue associated with any performance measurement system is the appropriate linkage of measures, incentives, and goals.

## 1.1 Financial Measures

Financial measures of performance include financial scorecards (including the balanced scorecard), costs of quality, return on investment, return on assets, return on equity, residual income, and economic value added.

## 1.2 Nonfinancial Measures

### 1.2.1 External Benchmarks: Productivity Measures

Productivity is defined as the measure of the ratio of the outputs achieved to the inputs of production. Productivity is a measure of efficiency and uses the relationships derived from actual performance in comparison to similar organizations over time. Two types of productivity ratios are generally recognized.

- **Total Factor Productivity Ratios (TFP)**

  *Total factor productivity ratios* (TFPs) reflect the quantity of all output produced relative to the costs of all inputs used. This ratio can be used to compare actual cost per unit production levels to budgeted (or a prior year's) production levels.

- **Partial Productivity Ratios (PPRs)**

  *Partial productivity ratios* (PPRs) reflect the quantity of output produced relative to the quantity of individual input(s) used. This ratio can be used to compare the actual levels of a production input needed to produce a given output, which may be used for a comparison with a budgeted (or a prior year's) input level. It is the most frequently used productivity measure.

| Example 1 | Productivity Ratios |
|---|---|

**Facts:** Garden Furnishings Inc. produces outdoor garden sculptures for its high-end niche market. Each garden sculpture manufactured by the company includes two raw materials, with plastic being the largest product input. During the previous month, the company used 20,000 pounds of plastic and 5,000 pounds of cement to produce 1,000 garden sculptures. Material prices at time of production were $1.25/lb. and $1.75/lb. for plastic and cement, respectively.

**Required:** Calculate the partial productivity ratio for plastic and the total factor productivity ratio.

**Solution:**

Based on the above, the direct material (plastic) *partial productivity ratio* is calculated as follows:

PPR = Quantity of output produced / Quantity of input used
= 1,000 units of garden sculptures / 20,000 lb. of plastic
= 0.05 sculpture units per lb. of plastic

Using the above, the *total factor productivity* ratio is calculated as follows:

TFP = Quantity of output produced / Costs of all inputs used
= 1,000 garden sculptures / (20,000 × $1.25) + (5,000 × $1.75)
= 1,000 garden sculptures / $33,750
= 0.02963 units of output per dollar of input cost

## 1.2.2 Internal Benchmarks: Techniques to Find and Analyze Problems

Internal benchmarks include a variety of techniques to find and analyze problems or measure performance. Among the most common quality-monitoring and investigative techniques are the procedures described below.

- **Control Charts**

  *Control charts* are an important tool used in statistical quality control (SQC). This graphical tool is used to plot a comparison of actual results by batch or other suitable constant interval to an acceptable range. Control charts show whether there is a trend toward improved quality conformance or deteriorating quality conformance.

**Illustration 1     Control Chart**

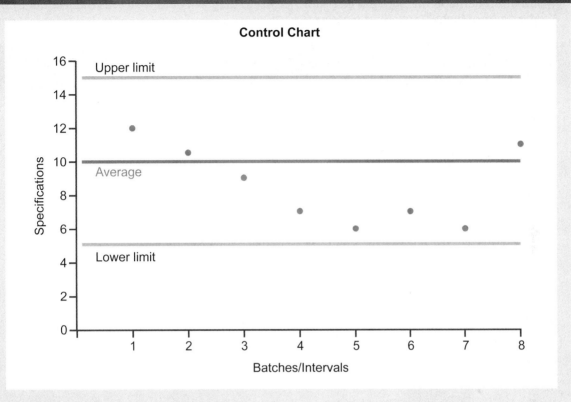

1. The control chart above demonstrates how individual batches/intervals of production fall within a range of quality specifications, from an acceptable upper limit of 15 occurrences to an acceptable lower limit of 5 occurrences, with production management establishing an average quality specification of 10 occurrences per batch/interval.

2. To further extrapolate the results of the control chart above, assume that the company's machine makes batches of rubber tires, with each batch consisting of 10,000 truck tires. Given management's historical experience with this production line, the company has set an upper-end defect rate of 15 tires per batch. The company has also established a lower-end defect rate of 5 tires per batch, as any amount set lower could result in production machine breakdown and repairs.

3. The results graphically displayed on the control chart above indicate that the individual tire production batches/intervals are all within the upper (15) and lower (5) limit tire defect specifications for production. Furthermore, the pattern of production shows a general decline in defects as more batches were produced for each subsequent monthly time interval; the very last batch (No. 8) is an outlier with more tire defects (11) than the average of 10.

### Pareto Diagrams

*Pareto diagrams* are used to determine the quality-control issues that are most frequent and often demand the greatest attention. A Pareto diagram demonstrates the frequency of defects from highest to lowest frequency.

---

**Illustration 2     Pareto Diagram**

The Pareto diagram below shows the individual and cumulative frequency of six types of quality issues. Addressing half of the types of defects (Type 3, Type 2, and Type 1) would address three quarters (75 percent) of all defects.

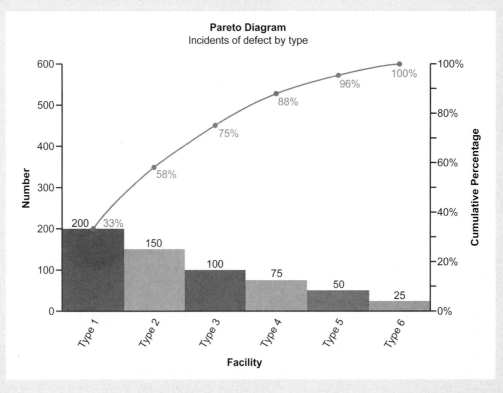

---

### Cause-and-Effect (Fishbone) Diagram

Once the most frequently recurring and costly defects/problems are identified by the Pareto diagram, a cause-and-effect diagram may be used to further analyze the defect.

Cause-and-effect diagrams provide a framework for managers to analyze the problems that contribute to the occurrence of defects. Production processes that lead to the manufacture of an item are displayed along a production line in a manner that looks like a fishbone. Managers use the diagram to identify the sources of problems in the production process by resource and take corrective action.

---

**Illustration 3     Fishbone Diagram**

This fishbone diagram indicates that the main categories of potential causes of the defect (called "large bones") are machinery, method used, materials, and use of manpower. Individual factors under each primary factory can be added on ("bones") and provide more detailed reasons for the higher-level ("large bone") cause of the defect. For example, under "machinery," the diagram indicates that incorrect settings may be a specific cause for the defect. Although not shown here, additional "bones" may be added to the machinery "large bone," such as functional obsolescence and lack of sufficient machine downtime.

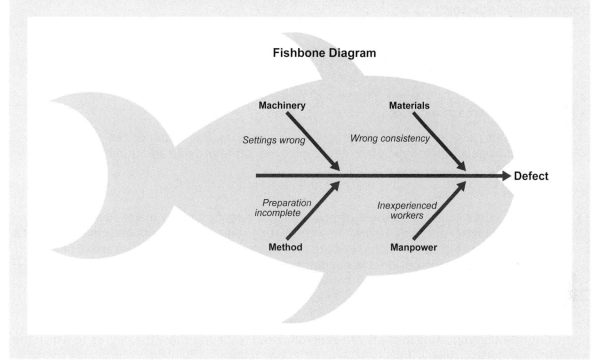

**Fishbone Diagram**

# 2    Financial Scorecards

Financial scorecards take many forms, including budget versus actual and other variance reports, as well as overall analysis of business performance. Financial performance is often a function of organizational decisions and the performance objectives given to each segment.

## 2.1    Types of Responsibility Segments

Responsibility segments, sometimes referred to as strategic business units (SBUs), are generally classified by four financial measures (performance objectives) for which managers may be held accountable. SBUs are highly effective in organizing performance requirements and in establishing accountability for financial responsibility.

1.   **Cost SBU**

     Managers are held responsible for controlling costs.

2.   **Revenue SBU**

     Managers are held responsible for generating revenues.

---

**3.  Profit SBU**

Managers are held responsible for producing a target profit (accountability for both revenues and costs).

**4.  Investment SBU**

Managers are held responsible for return on the assets invested to produce the earnings generated by the SBU.

## 2.2  Areas of Accountability in Financial Scorecards

The effectiveness of each strategic business unit is often subdivided into additional areas of accountability, including:

■ **Product Lines**

Some strategic business units involve multiple products. Costs, sales, profits, or returns associated with each of these products can be analyzed for further insight into the sources of profits or losses.

■ **Geographic Areas**

Strategic business units also cross geographic boundaries. Performance can generally be traced by geographic location or geographic market to provide additional insight into results.

■ **Customer**

Often the most significant segment classification is a classification by major customer. The relative profitability or losses associated with any one customer may influence management's decisions to either drop the customer or to reevaluate the relationship in regard to any marginal benefits to the business (e.g., contribution of the customer to fixed costs, etc.).

## 2.3  Contribution Reporting

Profit SBUs are normally responsible for generating a level of profit in relation to controllable costs. Contribution reporting formats are generally used to clearly show the degree to which the profit that strategic business units have generated has covered variable or controllable costs.

### 2.3.1  Contribution Margin

Contribution margin measures the excess of revenues over variable costs (or the contribution to fixed costs) for a company or division.

### 2.3.2  Controllable Margin

Contribution by SBU is a refinement of contribution margin reporting and represents the difference between contribution margin and controllable fixed costs. Controllable fixed costs are costs that managers can influence in less than one year (e.g., advertising and sales promotion).

### 2.3.3  Allocation of Common Costs

Managers have control over variable costs and over controllable fixed costs. Financial scorecards that use contribution reporting factor in these costs. Common costs are not controllable. Approaches to the rational allocation of central administrative costs must be understood by responsible managers and must be fair and logical. Employees are more motivated to achieve corporate goals if they believe that common costs do not represent an arbitrary burden.

### Illustration 4    Contribution Reporting

Delta Manufacturing has four regions that it has organized into profit strategic business units. Delta's management has designed a financial performance evaluation report that focuses on contribution margin and controllable margins. The report is designed as follows:

*Delta Manufacturing Performance Evaluation*

|  | Region 1 | Region 2 | Region 3 | Region 4 | Untraceable Costs | Total |
|---|---|---|---|---|---|---|
| Revenues | $ 200 | $ 300 | $ 150 | $450 | $  – | $1,100 |
| Variable costs | (150) | (250) | (125) | (350) | – | (875) |
| Contribution margin | 50 | 50 | 25 | 100 | – | 225 |
| Controllable fixed costs | (25) | (25) | (10) | (50) | – | (110) |
| Controllable margin | 25 | 25 | 15 | 50 | – | 115 |
| Noncontrollable fixed costs | (15) | (15) | (6) | (44) | – | (80) |
| Contribution by SBU | 10 | 10 | 9 | 6 | – | 35 |
| Untraceable costs | – | – | – | – | (20) | (20) |
| Operating Income | $ 10 | $ 10 | $ 9 | $ 6 | $(20) | $ 15 |

## 2.4   Balanced Scorecard

The *balanced scorecard* gathers information on multiple dimensions of an organization's performance defined by critical success factors necessary to accomplish the firm's strategy. Critical success factors are classified as:

- Financial

- Internal business processes

- Customer satisfaction

- Advancement of innovation and human resource development (learning and growth)

Typically, the scorecard describes the classifications of critical success factors, the strategic goals, the tactics, and the related measures associated with strategic and tactical goals.

## Illustration 5    Balanced Scorecard

Instafab Manufacturing is building its business using a cost leadership strategy. The management of Instafab has identified four strategic goals, one associated with each classification of critical success factors, to help its business grow. The strategic goals are:

1.  Capturing additional market share

2.  Maintaining low costs that are supported by low prices

3.  Becoming a low-price leader

4.  Linking strategy with reward and recognition

Help Instafab design tactics to achieve its strategic goals, define measures it might use, and organize them in the manner of a balanced scorecard.

**Legend:**

|  | **Tactics** | **Measures** |
|---|---|---|
| **Financial Perspective** | | |
| *Strategic goals* | Capture increasing market share | Company vs. industry growth |
| *Critical success factors* | Maintain customer base | Volume trend line |
| *Tactics and measures* | Steadily expand services | Percentage of sales from new products |
| **Internal Business Processes** | | |
| *Strategic goals* | Maintain low costs that are supported by low prices | Costs compared to competitor |
| *Critical success factors* | Maintain consistent production | First pass rates |
| *Tactics and measures* | Improve distribution efficiency | Percentage of perfect orders |
| **Customer Perspective** | | |
| *Strategic goals* | Become a low-price leader | Our cost vs. competition |
| *Critical success factors* | Anticipate customer needs before competitors | Percentage of products in R&D being test-marketed |
| *Tactics and measures* | Increase customer satisfaction | Customer surveys |
| **Advance Learning and Innovation (Human Resources)** | | |
| *Strategic goals* | Link strategy with reward and recognition | Net income per dollar of variable pay |
| *Tactics and measures* | Promote entrepreneurial culture | Annual reports |

# 3  Costs of Quality

*Quality* is broadly defined by the marketplace as a product's ability to meet or exceed customer expectations.

The cost of quality includes costs associated with activities related to conformance with quality standards and opportunity costs or activities associated with correcting nonconformance with quality standards.

## 3.1  Conformance Costs

The costs of ensuring *conformance* with quality standards are classified as prevention and appraisal costs.

### 3.1.1  Prevention Costs

*Prevention costs* are incurred to prevent the production of defective units. This includes such cost elements as:

- Employee training
- Inspection expenses
- Preventive maintenance
- Redesign of product
- Redesign of processes
- Search for higher-quality suppliers

### 3.1.2  Appraisal Costs

*Appraisal costs* are incurred to discover and remove defective parts before they are shipped to the customer or the next department. These costs include:

- Statistical quality checks
- Testing
- Inspection
- Maintenance of the laboratory

## 3.2  Nonconformance Costs

The costs of nonconformance with quality standards are classified as internal and external costs. *Nonconformance costs* are often difficult to compute because most of these costs are in the form of opportunity costs (e.g., lost sales or reputation damage).

### 3.2.1  Internal Failure

*Internal failure* costs are the costs to cure a defect discovered before the product is sent to the customer. These costs include:

- Rework costs
- Scrap
- Tooling changes
- Costs to dispose
- Cost of the lost unit
- Downtime

### 3.2.2 External Failure

*External failure* costs are the costs to cure a defect discovered after the product is sent to the customer. These costs include:

- Warranty costs

- Cost of returning the good

- Liability claims

- Lost customers

- Reengineering an external failure

## 3.3 Quality Reporting

"Cost of quality" reports display the financial result of quality. An inverse relationship between conformance and nonconformance costs exists. Increased investment in conformance costs should result in decreases in nonconformance costs, while the consequence of reduced investment in conformance costs may result in increased nonconformance costs.

- **Appraisal** includes the costs incurred (e.g., statistical quality control, inspection, and testing) to identify defective products or services.

- **Prevention** includes the costs incurred (e.g., engineering or training) to prevent the production or delivery of defective products or services.

- **Internal** failure is the cost of defective parts or lost production time (e.g., scrap and rework).

- **External** failure is the cost of returns and lost customer loyalty due to defective products or services.

| Illustration 6 | Costs of Quality |
| --- | --- |

Glass Products Inc. (GPI) experienced several internal failure costs in the past operating year, including significant production downtime and batch rework costs. Additionally, GPI had external failure costs after shipping glass products to its customers, including material costs pertaining to product returns and lost customers.

At the beginning of the current operating year, the company's production manager was replaced. The new manager, in his first week on the job, hired a statistical quality technician to test the products as they exited the production line. The new production manager then implemented quarterly employee training, preventive maintenance measures, and weekly inspections by line supervisors. Through the first half of the year, these appraisal and prevention measures have reduced production downtime by 90 percent and have reduced the company's scrap costs by 50 percent. As a result of these prevention measures, the company has also experienced fewer glass product returns and has lost no customers in the current operating year.

---

### Question 1                                                          CPA-03883

Listed below are selected line items from the Cost of Quality Report for Watson Products for last month.

| Category | Amount |
|----------|--------|
| Rework | $ 725 |
| Equipment maintenance | 1,154 |
| Product testing | 786 |
| Product repair | 695 |

What is Watson's total prevention and appraisal cost for last month?

- **a.** $786
- **b.** $1,154
- **c.** $1,849
- **d.** $1,940

---

### Question 2                                                          CPA-03890

In a quality control program, which of the following is (are) categorized as internal failure costs?

I.   Rework.
II.  Responding to customer complaints.
III. Statistical quality control procedures.

- **a.** I only.
- **b.** II only.
- **c.** III only.
- **d.** I, II, and III.

---

## NOTES

# 1 Return on Investment

Return on investment (ROI) provides for the assessment of a company's percentage return relative to its capital investment risk. The ROI is an ideal performance measure for investment strategic business units (SBUs). In simplest terms, ROI is expressed as income divided by invested capital; however, ROI is also expressed as a product of profit margin and investment turnover.

> ROI = Income / Investment capital
>
> *Or:*
>
> ROI = Profit margin × Investment turnover

## 1.1 Components of ROI

Return on investment (ROI) can be disaggregated as indicated in the following flowchart, in which income is expressed as a percentage of sales (i.e., the profit margin calculation) and sales are expressed as a percentage of invested capital (i.e., the investment turnover calculation). The higher the percentage return, the better.

**ROI Flowchart**

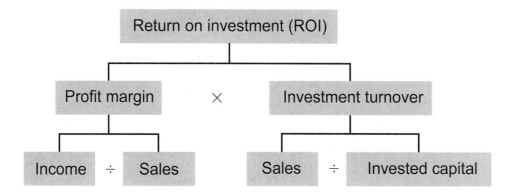

---

### Example 1     ROI

**Facts:** Assume that sales are $1,000,000, net income is $40,000, and invested capital is $250,000. The organization's required rate of return (hurdle rate) is 12 percent.

**Required:** Determine whether the organization is meeting performance expectations using ROI.

**Solution:**

$$\frac{\$40,000}{\$1,000,000} \times \frac{\$1,000,000}{\$250,000} = \frac{\$40,000}{\$250,000} = 16\%$$

The organization is meeting its requirements based on ROI computations. The ROI of 16 percent exceeds the required rate of return of 12 percent.

---

## 1.2    Return on Assets

Return on assets (ROA) is similar to ROI, except that ROA uses average total assets in the denominator rather than invested capital.

$$ROA = \frac{\text{Net income}}{\text{Average total assets}}$$

## 1.3    ROI/ROA Issues

### 1.3.1   Variations on Asset Valuation

Asset valuations used in the ROI and ROA computations affect the results. The appropriate asset valuation depends on the strategic objectives of the company and the direction that leadership wants to give its managers. The following terms define different asset valuations.

- **Net Book Value:** Assets valued at net book value represent historical cost less accumulated depreciation.

- **Gross Book Value:** Assets valued at gross book value represent historical cost prior to the reduction for accumulated depreciation.

- **Replacement Cost:** Assets valued at replacement cost represent the cost to replace assets at their current level of utility.

- **Liquidation Value:** Assets valued at liquidation value represent the selling price of productive assets.

   

### 1.3.2 Limitations of ROI

ROI, like any performance measure, is designed to direct managers to achieve corporate objectives and provide a basis for incentives. ROI computations have the following limitations:

- **Short-Term Focus:** Use of ROI exclusively as a measure of the performance can inadvertently focus managers purely on maximizing short-term returns. The overemphasis of managers on investment return targets is referred to as investment myopia.

- **Disincentive to Invest:** Profitable units are reluctant to invest in additional productive resources because they could reduce ROI in the short term.

# 2 Return on Equity and the DuPont Model

## 2.1 Return on Equity

A critical measure for determining a company's effectiveness is its return on equity (ROE).

$$\text{ROE} = \frac{\text{Net income}}{\text{Equity}}$$

The advantage of this ROE formula is that it is simple to compute. However, additional breakouts of the components of ROE provide management with a much clearer picture of the efficiencies and leverage of a given company's operations.

## 2.2 DuPont Analysis

### 2.2.1 Components of DuPont ROE

The three-step DuPont model breaks ROE into three distinct components: Net profit margin, asset turnover, and financial leverage.

- **Net Profit Margin**

  Net profit margin is a measure of operating efficiency.

$$\text{Net profit margin} = \frac{\text{Net income}}{\text{Sales}}$$

### Asset Turnover

Asset turnover is a measure of the degree of efficiency with which a company is using its assets.

$$\text{Asset turnover} = \frac{\text{Sales}}{\text{Assets}}$$

### Financial Leverage

Financial leverage measures the extent to which a company uses debt in its capital structure.

$$\text{Financial Leverage} = \frac{\text{Assets}}{\text{Equity}}$$

## 2.2.2 Calculating DuPont ROE

The formula for DuPont ROE is:

$$\text{DuPont ROE} = \text{Net profit margin} \times \text{Asset turnover} \times \text{Financial leverage}$$

$$= \frac{\text{Net income}}{\text{Sales}} \times \frac{\text{Sales}}{\text{Assets}} \times \frac{\text{Assets}}{\text{Equity}}$$

Note that net profit margin and asset turnover can be multiplied to calculate return on assets (ROA). Therefore, DuPont ROE can also be calculated as:

$$\text{DuPont ROE} = \text{ROA} \times \text{Financial leverage}$$

## 2.2.3 Extended DuPont Model

The extended DuPont model further breaks out net profit margin into three distinct components: Tax burden, interest burden, and the operating income margin.

### Tax Burden

The *tax burden* is the extent to which a company retains profits after paying taxes.

$$\text{Tax burden} = \frac{\text{Net income}}{\text{Pretax income}}$$

■ **Interest Burden**

The *interest burden* reflects how much in pretax income a company retains after paying interest to debt holders.

$$\text{Interest burden} = \frac{\text{Pretax income}}{\text{Earnings before interest and taxes (EBIT)}}$$

■ **EBIT Margin**

The *EBIT margin* is a measure of company profits earned on sales after paying operating and nonoperating costs (other than interest and taxes).

$$\text{EBIT margin} = \frac{\text{EBIT}}{\text{Sales}}$$

■ **Extended DuPont ROE Formula**

The last two components of the ROE calculation remain the same, with the extended model shown below:

$$
\begin{array}{ccccccccc}
\text{Extended} & = & \text{Tax} & \times & \text{Interest} & \times & \text{EBIT} & \times & \text{Asset} & \times & \text{Financial} \\
\text{DuPont ROE} & & \text{burden} & & \text{burden} & & \text{margin} & & \text{turnover} & & \text{leverage}
\end{array}
$$

$$
= \frac{\text{Net income}}{\text{Pretax income}} \times \frac{\text{Pretax income}}{\text{EBIT}} \times \frac{\text{EBIT}}{\text{Sales}} \times \frac{\text{Sales}}{\text{Assets}} \times \frac{\text{Assets}}{\text{Equity}}
$$

## Pass Key

Average assets and average equity should be used when calculating ROE. However, if a CPA Exam question only gives ending assets and/or ending equity, these amounts may be used to calculate ROE.

## Example 2 ▶ ROE

**Facts:** Blake Co. reports the following in its Year 5 financial statements:

| | | | | |
|---|---|---|---|---|
| Sales | $500,000 | | Assets | $900,000 |
| COGS | 275,000 | | Liabilities | 300,000 |
| Gross profit | 225,000 | | Equity | 600,000 |
| SG&A | 150,000 | | | |
| EBIT | 75,000 | | | |
| Interest expense | 15,000 | | | |
| Pretax income (EBT) | 60,000 | | | |
| Tax (30% rate) | 18,000 | | | |
| Net income | $ 42,000 | | | |

**Required:** Calculate each of the individual component ratios for Blake, as well as the ROE for Blake using both the DuPont model and the extended DuPont model.

**Solution:**

Net profit margin = Net income / Sales
= $42,000 / $500,000
= **0.084**

Tax burden = Net income / Pretax income
= $42,000 / $60,000
= **0.70**

Interest burden = Pretax income / EBIT
= $60,000 / $75,000
= **0.80**

EBIT margin = EBIT / Sales
= $75,000 / $500,000
= **0.15**

Asset turnover = Sales / Assets
= $500,000 / $900,000
= **0.56**

Financial leverage = Assets / Equity
= $900,000 / $600,000
= **1.50**

DuPont ROE = Net profit margin × Asset turnover × Financial leverage
= 0.084 × 0.56 × 1.50
= **0.07 or 7%**

Extended DuPont ROE = Tax burden × Interest burden × EBIT margin × Asset turnover × Financial leverage
= 0.70 × 0.80 × 0.15 × 0.56 × 1.50
= **0.07 or 7%**

## Pass Key

It is important to note that both methods of calculating ROE (DuPont and extended DuPont) produce the same number. By breaking out the calculation into different components, management can get a better understanding of what factors are driving ROE and how those factors compare relative to competing companies and to the industry overall.

# 3 Residual Income

The residual income method measures the excess of actual income earned by an investment over the return required by the company. The rate of return/hurdle rate for the company may be its WACC, cost of equity, or it may simply be the return established by management as a target rate. Although ROI provides a percentage measurement, residual income provides an amount. Like ROI, residual income is a performance measure for investment SBUs.

## 3.1 Formula

The formula for residual income is as follows:

> Residual income = Net income (from the income statement) − Required return
>
> Where:
>
> Required return  =  Net book value (Equity) × Hurdle rate

## 3.2 Interpretation

A positive residual income indicates that performance is meeting standards, and a negative residual income indicates that performance is not meeting standards.

### Example 3     Residual Income

**Facts:** Instafab Manufacturing has an investment in its Southeast regional plant with a net book value of $200,000. Instafab's expected hurdle rate is 10 percent, and the division produces net income of $30,000.

**Required:** Calculate residual income.

**Solution:**

| | | |
|---|---|---|
| Net income | | $ 30,000 |
| Net book value | $200,000 | |
| Hurdle rate | × _____10%_ | |
| Required return | | _(20,000)_ |
| Residual income | | **$ 10,000** |

## 3.3    Benefits of Residual Income Performance Measures

Advantages of using residual income include the ease of measurement of actual dollars earned by an investment above its required amount.

### 3.3.1    Realistic Target Rates

Usually, the target rate in the residual income method will be less than the highest return rates actually earned by the best-performing investment centers in a company. Historical weighted average cost of capital is often used as the target or hurdle rate; however, the rate optimally used is the target return set by the company's management.

### 3.3.2    Focus on Target Return and Amount

Residual income controls and performance measures encourage managers to invest in projects that generate income in excess of the target or calculated rate, thereby improving company profits and promoting the congruence of individual and corporate goals. Divisions with high *rates* of return do not fear dilution of their rates and, therefore, do not avoid investments that demonstrate strong residual income performance.

## 3.4    Weaknesses of Residual Income Performance Measures

### 3.4.1    Reduced Comparability

Use of an absolute amount to compute performance distorts comparison of units with unequal size. Larger units of an organization may produce larger dollar volumes of residual income even though their performance is identical to a smaller unit on a percentage basis.

### 3.4.2    Target Rates Require Judgment

Reliance on computing a target rate of return may sometimes be difficult to establish.

# 4    Economic Value Added

The Economic Value Added™ (EVA™) method of performance evaluation is very similar to the residual income method. The residual income method computes required return based on a hurdle rate determined by management, and the EVA measures the excess of income after taxes (not counting interest expense) earned by an investment over the return rate defined by the company's overall cost of capital (WACC). The amount used to represent income after taxes is the firm's net operating profit after taxes (NOPAT), and it often incorporates several accounting adjustments prior to application into the model. Economic value added ensures that performance is measured in comparison to changes associated with all capital, debt, and equity. EVA is expressed as an amount and is considered a form of economic profit.

## 4.1    Formula

The formula for EVA is:

> **Economic value added = Net operating profit after taxes (NOPAT) − Required return**
>
> **Where:**
>
> **Required return   =   Investment × WACC**

## 4.2    Interpretation

- **Positive EVA:** A *positive EVA* indicates that performance is meeting standards.
- **Negative EVA:** A *negative EVA* indicates that performance is not meeting standards.

## 4.3    Economic Value Added Component Issues

*Economic value added* can be refined using investment or income adjustments to produce a more accurate analysis of economic profit (value added).

### 4.3.1    Investment Valuation Issues

- **Capitalization of Research and Development:** The organization may *capitalize research and development* costs as part of its asset base along with other value-adding investments in advertising and training.
- **Current Valuation of the Balance Sheet:** *Balance sheet* accounts are generally revalued to represent current cost.

### 4.3.2    Income Determination

NOPAT may be adjusted to eliminate the effect of certain transactions and thereby create a nearly cash basis income statement.

- Adjustments to the balance sheet affect the income statement.
- Deferred taxes are ignored.

---

| Example 4 | EVA |
| --- | --- |

**Facts:** Instafab Manufacturing has an investment in its Southeast regional plant with an investment of $300,000 after adjustments for capitalization of research and development costs and revaluation of certain assets. The company's cost of capital is 12 percent, and its division produces a net operating profit after taxes of $50,000 after adjustments for current-year research and development, asset revaluations, and other accounting considerations.

**Required:** Calculate the economic value added.

**Solution:**

| | | |
| --- | --- | --- |
| NOPAT | | $50,000 |
| Investment | $300,000 | |
| Cost of capital | ×        12% | |
| Required return | | (36,000) |
| Economic value added | | **$14,000** |

Instafab's economic value added is positive. Instafab has added to shareholder value.

---

---

**Question 1**                                                                        CPA-06645

SkyBound Airlines provided the following information about its two operating divisions:

|                        | Passenger | Cargo     |
|------------------------|-----------|-----------|
| Operating profit       | $ 40,000  | $ 50,000  |
| Investment             | 250,000   | 500,000   |
| External borrowing rate| 6%        | 8%        |

Measuring performance using return on investment (ROI), which division performed better?

   **a.** The Cargo division, with an ROI of 10 percent.

   **b.** The Passenger division, with an ROI of 16 percent.

   **c.** The Cargo division, with an ROI of 18 percent.

   **d.** The Passenger division, with an ROI of 22 percent.

---

**Question 2**                                                                        CPA-04809

Minon Inc. purchased a long-term asset on the last day of the current year. What are the effects of this purchase on return on investment and residual income?

|       | Return on Investment | Residual Income |
|-------|----------------------|-----------------|
| **a.**| Increase             | Increase        |
| **b.**| Decrease             | Decrease        |
| **c.**| Increase             | Decrease        |
| **d.**| Decrease             | Increase        |

---

**Question 3**                                                                        CPA-08378

Spear Corp. had sales of $2,000,000, a profit margin of 11 percent, and assets of $2,500,000. Spear decided to reduce its debt ratio to 0.40 from 0.50 by selling new common stock and using the proceeds to repay principal on some outstanding long-term debt. After the refinancing, what is Spear's return on equity?

   **a.** 3.5 percent

   **b.** 5.3 percent

   **c.** 14.7 percent

   **d.** 22.9 percent

---

| Question 4 | CPA-04818 |
|---|---|

Zig Corp. provides the following information:

| | |
|---|---:|
| Pretax operating profit | $  300,000,000 |
| Tax rate | 40% |
| Capital used to generate profits 50% debt, 50% equity | 1,200,000,000 |
| Cost of equity | 15% |
| Cost of debt (after tax) | 5% |

Which of the following represents Zig's year-end economic value-added amount?

- **a.** $0
- **b.** $60,000,000
- **c.** $120,000,000
- **d.** $180,000,000

## NOTES

# BEC
# 4

# Operations Management: Planning Techniques

## Module

# 1 Projection Techniques

Projections are prepared to show multiple, hypothetical ("what-if") scenarios and courses of action that a business might follow. Projections serve as the precursor to actual forecasts. Projections are typically prepared for internal use and can assist managers in making decisions regarding products, acquisitions, revenues, expenses, etc.

Sensitivity and scenario analyses are frequently used to project revenues, costs, and profitability.

## 1.1 Sensitivity Analysis

*Sensitivity analysis* is the process of experimenting with different parameters and assumptions regarding a model and cataloging the range of results to view the possible consequences of a decision. Sensitivity models often use probabilities to approximate reality.

Also called "what-if" analysis, sensitivity analysis is a risk management tool that is used to test the effect of specific variables on overall profitability. Managers incorporate sensitivity analysis into the budgeting process to determine which variables are the most sensitive to change and therefore will have the biggest effect on the bottom line.

The biggest drawback of sensitivity analysis is the implicit assumption that variables are independent. The reality is that variables do not typically operate in a vacuum, and a change in one will often result in changes in others that are difficult to predict with accuracy.

---

**Example 1** ▶ **Sensitivity Analysis**

**Facts:** July sales for Besser Company are projected to be $100,000, with cost of goods sold of $60,000 and general/administrative expenses of $25,000. The CFO has determined that variability in sales has the biggest impact on profitability and she wants to determine the effect on operating income if sales dollars are over-/underestimated by 25 percent.

In order to estimate the change in operating income, the CFO assumes that cost of goods sold will consistently be 60 percent of sales and general/administrative expenses will stay constant at $25,000.

**Required:** Project operating income using the assumptions that sales at $100,000 are overestimated by 25 percent, correct, or underestimated by 25 percent.

(continued)

---

(continued)

**Solution:**

|  | Sales Overestimated by 25% | Sales Correctly Estimated | Sales Underestimated by 25% |
|---|---|---|---|
| Sales | $75,000 | $100,000 | $125,000 |
| Cost of goods sold | (45,000) | (60,000) | (75,000) |
| General/administrative | (25,000) | (25,000) | (25,000) |
| Operating Income | $ 5,000 | $ 15,000 | $ 25,000 |

Because cost of goods sold remains a fixed percentage of sales, and general/administrative expenses remain constant (and therefore independent of sales), the biggest impact on operating income will result from sales being different from estimates.

## 1.2   Scenario Analysis

In preparing models for future periods, managers may prepare multiple different scenarios which represent alternative possible outcomes. Budgets will be prepared under each scenario and then probabilities may be assigned in order to come up with weighted totals.

| Example 2 | Scenario Analysis |
|---|---|

**Facts:** In preparing its budgets for the coming year, Ridge Company projects three scenarios for revenues:

- Optimistic scenario (30 percent likelihood): 5 percent sales growth
- Pessimistic scenario (20 percent likelihood): 5 percent sales decline
- Most likely scenario (50 percent likelihood): No sales growth/decline

**Required:** If sales in the previous fiscal year were $40 million, project sales for next year.

**Solution:**

- Expected sales growth/decline: (30% × 5%) + (20% × –5%) + (50% × 0%) = 0.5% growth.
- $40 million × (1.005) = $40.2 million in projected sales for next year.

# 2 Forecasting Techniques

Forecasting is driven by historical data and actual expectations rather than hypothetical scenarios. Projections are typically used internally, and forecasts are prepared for both internal and external audiences.

Forecasting techniques generally can be broken out into qualitative and quantitative methods. Qualitative forecasts are based on the opinions and judgment of management and other experts, and do not require historical data. Quantitative forecasts use historical data and are categorized as either time series methods or causal methods. Time series methods use past trends to predict future variables, and causal methods are based on cause-and-effect relationships between variables.

## 2.1 Forecasting Analysis

*Forecasting (probability/risk) analysis* is an extension of sensitivity analysis.

### 2.1.1 Purpose

Forecasting involves predicting future values of a dependent variable (the variable that one is trying to explain) using information from previous time periods. Historical relationships may be examined in order to use predictions about independent variables to forecast changes in dependent variables.

- **Forecasting Revenues:** On the revenue side, sales are a dependent variable that may be a by-product of independent variables such as expectations regarding the economy, personal income, product competition, growth of the industry, etc.

- **Forecasting Expenses:** On the expense side, total costs are a by-product of specific independent variables such as overall fixed costs and per-unit variable costs.

### 2.1.2 Application

Various quantitative methods (including regression analysis, explained below) are used in forecasting.

# 3 Regression Analysis

Linear regression is a method for studying the relationship between two or more variables. One use of linear regression is to predict the value of a dependent variable [e.g., total cost ($y$)] corresponding to given values of the independent variables [e.g., fixed costs (a), variable cost per unit (B), and production expressed in units ($x$)].

## 3.1 Simple Linear Regression Model

Regression analysis explains variation in a dependent variable as a linear function of one or more independent variables. Simple regression involves only one independent variable. Multiple regressions involve more than one independent variable.

▪ **Components of the Simple Linear Regression Model:** The simple linear regression model takes the following form:

$$y = a + Bx$$

Where:

$y$ = The dependent variable (the variable we are trying to explain). For example, $y$ might be total costs measured in dollars for a cost function.

$x$ = The independent variable (the regressor). The variable that explains $y$. For example, in a cost function, $x$ would be total activity (or output).

$a$ = The $y$-axis intercept of the regression line. For example, if $y$ is total costs, $a$ would measure total fixed costs.

$B$ = The slope of the regression line. For example, if $y$ is total costs, and $x$ is output, $B$ measures the change in total costs due to a one-unit change in output (variable cost per unit).

▪ **Application:** If $y$ is total costs and $x$ is total activity or output, one goal of regression analysis would be to predict total costs ($y$, the dependent variable) based on observed total activity or output. Questions on the CPA Exam expect you to predict total cost.

## 3.2    Statistical Measures to Evaluate Regression Analysis

### 3.2.1    The Coefficient of Correlation ($r$)

▪ **Definition:** The coefficient of correlation measures the strength of the linear relationship between the independent variable ($x$) and the dependent variable ($y$). In standard notation, the coefficient of correlation is "$r$."

▪ **Interpretation:** The range of "$r$" is from −1.00 to +1.00, as follows:

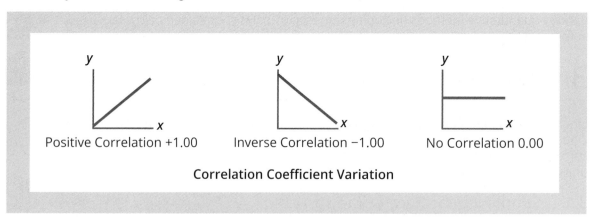

Positive Correlation +1.00          Inverse Correlation −1.00          No Correlation 0.00

**Correlation Coefficient Variation**

• **Perfect Positive Correlation (+1.00):** The dependent and independent variables move together in the same direction. An increase (decrease) in the independent variable produces an equivalent increase (decrease) in the dependent variable.

• **Perfect Inverse Correlation (−1.00):** The dependent and independent variables move in equivalent opposite directions. An increase (decrease) in the independent variable produces an equivalent decrease (increase) in the dependent variable.

• **No Correlation (0.00):** The dependent and independent variables are not related in a linear fashion. Movement in the independent variable cannot be used to predict the movement in the dependent variable.

- **Projecting Total Cost:** When predicting total cost (the dependent variable) as a function of fixed costs, variable costs, and volume (the independent variable), management's expectation is that the correlation coefficient will be somewhere between 0.00 and 1.00. As more units of a given product are produced, a reasonable expectation is that total costs will increase.

### 3.2.2  The Coefficient of Determination ($R^2$)

- **Definition:** The coefficient of determination ($R^2$) is the proportion of the total variation in the dependent variable ($y$) explained by the independent variable ($x$). Its value lies between zero and one.

- **Interpretation:** The higher the $R^2$, the greater the proportion of the total variation in $y$ that is explained by the variation in $x$. That is, the higher the $R^2$, the better the fit of the regression line.

---

**Illustration 1       Coefficient of Determination**

Based on looking at five years of data on fixed costs and variable costs per unit, Raxan Inc. determines that its fixed and variable costs in the next year will be $16,000 and $4.50 per unit, respectively. Raxan has determined that the correlation coefficient between the independent and dependent variable is equal to 0.90. The $R^2$ for the regression equation $y$ (total costs) = $16,000 + $4.50$x$, with $x$ being volume, is equal to 0.81. An $R^2$ of 0.81 means that 81 percent of the change in total cost during a period can be attributed to changes in volume.

---

# 4     High-Low Method

The *high-low method* is a simple technique that is used to estimate the fixed and variable portions of cost, usually production costs.

## 4.1    Procedures

### 4.1.1   Gather Data

Compare the high and low volumes and costs (ignoring any obvious aberrations). Outliers, which are unusually high or low volumes, are eliminated.

### 4.1.2   Analyze Data

- Divide the difference between the high and low dollar total costs by the difference in high and low volumes to obtain the variable cost per unit.

- Use either the high volume or the low volume to calculate the variable costs by multiplying the volume times the variable cost per unit.

- Subtract the total calculated variable cost from total costs to obtain fixed costs.

### 4.1.3   Formulate Results

The result enables preparation of a flexible/performance budget by identifying total fixed costs and variable costs per unit. This may be used to estimate total costs at any volume.

## 4.2 Flexible Budget Formula

The result of the high-low method is called a total cost formula and, sometimes, a flexible budget formula (or equation).

### 4.2.1 Flexible Budget

A *flexible budget* is a series of budgets that are prepared for a range of activity levels rather than a single activity (in which variable costs are adjusted to the level of activity and fixed costs are held constant).

### 4.2.2 Formula

This formula defines total costs as equal to the fixed costs plus the variable costs per unit times the units. The flexible budget formula is then used to estimate total cost at any volume.

$$\text{Total cost} = \text{Fixed cost} + \left[ \frac{\text{Variable cost}}{\text{per unit}} \times \frac{\text{Number}}{\text{of units}} \right]$$

---

**Illustration 2     High-Low Method**

| Period | Units/Volume | Cost |
|---|---|---|
| January | 1,200 | $9,000 |
| February | 1,000 | 8,450 |
| March | 1,050 | 8,600 |
| April | 1,130 | 8,750 |
| May | 1,400 | 9,550 |
| June | 1,200 | 9,000 |
| High | 1,400 | 9,550 |
| Low | (1,000) | (8,450) |
| Difference between high and low | 400 | $1,100 |

Variable cost per unit = $1,100 / 400 units = $2.75 per unit

Using either the high or the low will produce the same total fixed-cost result:

| | High | Or: | Low |
|---|---|---|---|
| Units | 1,400 | | 1,000 |
| Total cost of units | $9,550 | | $8,450 |
| Variable costs @ $2.75 per unit | (3,850) | | (2,750) |
| Total fixed costs | $5,700 | = | $5,700 |

Total costs = Fixed costs + [Variable costs per unit × Number of units]

Total costs = $5,700 + [$2.75 × Number of units]

---

# 5  Learning Curve

*Learning curve* analysis is based on the premise that as workers become more familiar with a specific task, the per-unit labor hours will decline as experience is gained and production becomes more efficient.

- This analysis is used to set standards and to project costs, as variable costs per unit should decline until a steady-state period is achieved. Once steady state occurs, labor hours per unit will remain constant.

- In order for learning curve analysis to be applied, the activity itself must be repetitive in nature, involve intense labor, and have little to no labor force turnover or breaks in production.

- The calculation begins with the first unit/batch. As cumulative production doubles (from one unit to two units, to four units, to eight units, etc.), cumulative average time per unit falls to a fixed percentage (the learning curve rate) of the previous average time.

| Example 3 | Learning Curve |
|---|---|

**Facts:** It takes the Jones Production Company 50 hours to produce the first unit of its only product.

**Required:** Assuming a 70 percent learning curve, estimate the average time and total to produce 2 units, 4 units, and 8 units.

**Solution:**

*2 Units*

What is the average time it takes Jones to produce 2 units?

　　Average time (2 units) = 50 hours × 0.70 = 35 hours

What is the total time it takes Jones to produce 2 units?

　　Total time (2 units) = 35 hours × 2 units = 70 hours

*4 Units*

What is the average time it takes Jones to produce 4 units?

　　Average time (4 units) = 35 hours × 0.70 = 24.5 hours

What is the total time it takes Jones to produce 4 units?

　　Total time (4 units) = 24.5 hours × 4 units = 98 hours

*8 Units*

What is the average time it takes Jones to produce 8 units?

　　Average time (8 units) = 24.5 hours × 0.70 = 17.15 hours

What is the total time it takes Jones to produce 8 units?

　　Total time (8 units) = 17.15 hours × 8 units = 137.2 hours

| Example 4 | Learning Curve |
|---|---|

**Facts:** It takes the Jones Production Company 50 hours to produce the first unit, and 70 total hours to produce the first two units.

**Required:** Calculate the learning curve rate.

**Solution:** 70%. (70 total hours for 2 units)/(50 hours × 2 units) = 70/100 = 70%.

| Example 5 | Learning Curve |
|---|---|

**Facts:** It takes the Jones Production Company 50 hours to produce the first unit, and 35 hours, on average, to produce each of the first two units.

**Required:** Calculate the learning curve rate.

**Solution:** 70%. (35 hours on average for each unit) / (50 hours for the first unit).

| Question 1 | CPA-07088 |
|---|---|

The coefficient of determination, $R^2$, in a multiple regression equation is the:

    **a.** Percentage of variation in the independent variables explained by the variation in the dependent variable.

    **b.** Percentage of variation in the dependent variable explained by the variation in the independent variables.

    **c.** Measure of the proximity of actual data points to the estimated data points.

    **d.** Coefficient of the independent variable divided by the standard error of regression coefficient.

| Question 2 | CPA-04642 |
|---|---|

Trijonis Company estimated its material handling costs at two activity levels, as follows:

| Kilos Handled | Cost |
|---|---|
| 80,000 | $160,000 |
| 60,000 | $132,000 |

What is Trijonis' estimated cost for handling 75,000 kilos?

    **a.** $150,000

    **b.** $153,000

    **c.** $157,500

    **d.** $165,000

# 1 Cost-Volume-Profit (CVP) Analysis

*Cost-volume-profit (CVP) analysis* is used by managers to forecast profits at different levels of sales and production volume. The point at which revenues equal total costs is called the breakeven point. Cost-volume-profit analysis is synonymous with breakeven analysis.

## 1.1 Assumptions

### 1.1.1 General Assumptions

- All costs can be separated into either variable or fixed costs, depending on the behavior of the cost.

- Volume is the only relevant factor affecting cost.

- All costs behave in a linear fashion in relation to production volume.

- Cost behaviors are anticipated to remain constant over the relevant range of production volume because there is an assumption that the efficiency of production does not change.

- Costs show greater variability over time. The longer the time period, the greater the percentage of variable costs. The shorter the time period, the greater the percentage of fixed costs.

### 1.1.2 Use of Single Product

Although cost-volume-profit analysis can be performed for more than one product, in its simplest form, the model assumes that the product mix remains constant.

### 1.1.3 Contribution Approach (Direct Costing) Is Used Rather Than Absorption Approach

The contribution approach to the income statement is used for breakeven analysis. Identifying each element of cost as fixed or variable defines its relationship to volume and to the computation of breakeven.

### 1.1.4 Selling Prices Remain Unchanged

The volume of transactions produces a uniform contribution margin per unit and a predictable projected contribution margin based on volume.

# 2 Absorption Approach vs. Contribution Approach

## 2.1 Absorption Approach

The *absorption approach,* which is required for financial reporting under U.S. GAAP, does not segregate fixed and variable costs.

The equation for the absorption approach follows:

Revenue

Less: cost of goods sold

Gross margin

Less: operating expenses

Net income

## 2.2    Contribution Approach

The *contribution approach* to the income statement uses *variable costing* (also called *direct costing*). Although it does not represent generally accepted accounting principles, the contribution approach is extremely useful for internal decision making.

The equation for the contribution approach follows:

Revenue

Less: variable costs

Contribution margin

Less: fixed costs

Net income

### Pass Key

Variable costs include direct labor, direct material, variable manufacturing overhead, shipping and packaging, and variable selling expenses.

Fixed costs include fixed overhead, fixed selling, and most general and administrative expenses.

- ◼ **Total or Per Unit:** Revenue, variable costs, and contribution margin may be expressed in total and on a per-unit basis.
- ◼ **Unit Contribution Margin:** *Unit contribution margin* is the unit sales price minus the unit variable cost.
- ◼ **Contribution Margin Ratio:** The *contribution margin ratio* is the contribution margin expressed as a percentage of revenue.

## Pass Key

The contribution ratio formula is expressed as follows:

Contribution margin ratio = Contribution margin ÷ Revenue

## 2.3 Absorption Approach vs. Contribution Approach

The difference between the *absorption approach* and the *contribution approach* is the treatment of fixed factory overhead. Selling, general, and administrative expenses are period costs under both methods.

### 2.3.1 Treatment of Fixed Factory Overhead

■ **Absorption Approach—Product Cost:** Under the *absorption approach* (absorption costing), all fixed factory overhead is treated as a product cost and is included in inventory values. Cost of goods sold includes both fixed costs and variable costs.

■ **Contribution Approach—Period Cost:** Under the *contribution approach* (variable costing), all fixed factory overhead is treated as a period cost and is expensed in the period incurred. Inventory values include only the *variable manufacturing costs*, so cost of goods sold includes only variable manufacturing costs.

### 2.3.2 Treatment of Selling, General, and Administrative Expenses

*Selling, general, and administrative expenses* are *period costs* used in the determination of net income under both methods.

■ **Absorption Approach:** Under the *absorption approach*, both variable and fixed selling, general, and administrative expenses are part of operating expenses and are reported on the income statement separately from cost of goods sold.

■ **Contribution Approach:** Under the *contribution approach*, the variable selling, general, and administrative expenses are part of the total variable costs for the contribution margin calculation.

## Pass Key

| Absorption Costing | Variable (Direct) Costing |
|---|---|
| **Product costs** | **Product costs** |
| • Direct materials | • Direct materials |
| • Direct labor | • Direct labor |
| • Variable manufacturing overhead | • Variable manufacturing overhead |
| • Fixed manufacturing overhead | |
| **Period costs** | **Period costs** |
| • Variable and fixed selling, general, and administrative expenses | • Fixed manufacturing overhead |
| | • Variable and fixed selling, general, and administrative expenses |

### 2.3.3   Gross Margin vs. Contribution Margin

The general income statement formats of both methods are presented below:

| **Gross Margin** *Absorption (Full Cost) Method* | | **Contribution Margin** *Variable (Direct) Cost Method* | |
|---|---|---|---|
| Sales | $XX | Sales | $XX |
| Less: cost of goods sold | (X) | Less: variable cost of goods sold (excludes fixed overhead) | (X) |
| Gross margin* | XX | Less: variable selling and administrative expense | (X) |
| Less: variable selling and administrative expenses | (X) | Contribution margin | $XX |
| Fixed selling and administrative expenses | (X) | Less: fixed expenses | |
| Operating income | $XX | Fixed manufacturing overhead | (X) |
| | | Fixed selling and administrative expenses | (X) |
| | | Operating income | $XX |

*Gross profit margin may also be stated as a percentage, which is calculated as gross margin (or profit) divided by net sales.

## 2.4   Effect on Income

If all production is sold every period, both methods produce the same operating income figures. However, if the number of units sold is more or less than the number of units produced, the operating income figures will be different.

### 2.4.1   Production Greater Than Sales

If units produced exceed units sold, then some units are added to ending inventory and income is higher under absorption costing than under variable costing.

- Under absorption costing, a portion of the fixed manufacturing overhead is included with each unit in ending inventory.
- Under variable (direct) costing, all fixed manufacturing overhead is considered a period cost and is expensed during the period.

### 2.4.2   Sales Greater Than Production

If units sold exceed units produced, then ending inventory is less than beginning inventory and income is lower under absorption costing than under variable costing.

- Under absorption costing, the fixed manufacturing overhead carried over from a previous period as a part of beginning inventory is charged to cost of sales.
- Under variable (direct) costing, those fixed costs were charged to income in a prior period (when they were incurred).

## Pass Key

Examiners frequently ask about the difference between variable costing net income and absorption costing net income. Follow the simple steps below to compute the difference:

- **Step 1:** Compute fixed cost per unit (Fixed manufacturing overhead / Units produced)

- **Step 2:** Compute the change in income (Change in inventory units × Fixed cost per unit)

- **Step 3:** Determine the impact of the change in income:

**No change in inventory:** Absorption net income = Variable net income

**Increase in inventory:** Absorption net income > Variable net income

**Decrease in inventory:** Absorption net income < Variable net income

## 2.5    Benefits and Limitations of Each Method

### 2.5.1    Absorption (GAAP) Costing

■ **Benefits**

- *Absorption costing* is GAAP.

- The Internal Revenue Service requires the use of the absorption method for financial reporting.

■ **Limitations**

- The level of inventory affects net income because fixed costs are a component of product cost.

- The net income reported under the absorption method is less reliable (especially for use in performance evaluations) than under the variable method because the cost of the product includes fixed costs and, therefore, the level of inventory affects net income.

### 2.5.2    Variable (Direct) Costing

■ **Benefits**

- Variable and fixed costs are separated and can be easily traced to and controlled by management.

- The net income reported under the contribution income statement is more reliable (especially for use in performance evaluations) than under the absorption method because the cost of the product does not include fixed costs and, therefore, the level of inventory does not affect net income.

- Variable costing isolates the contribution margins in financial statements to aid in decision making (the contribution margin is defined as sales price less all variable costs, including variable sales and administrative costs, and breakeven analysis is often based on contribution margins).

■ **Limitations**

- Variable costing is not GAAP.

- The Internal Revenue Service does not allow the use of the variable cost method for financial reporting.

| Illustration 1 | Absorption vs. Variable Costing | | | |

| Costs | Total Costs | Absorption Method Product Cost | Contribution Method Product Cost |
|---|---|---|---|
| Direct materials | $1.00 | $1.00 | $1.00 |
| **Labor** | | | |
| Direct | 4.00 | 4.00 | 4.00 |
| Indirect (fixed building maintenance) | 0.50 | 0.50 | – |
| **Overhead** | | | |
| Variable | 1.50 | 1.50 | 1.50 |
| Fixed | 2.00 | 2.00 | – |
| Commissions to salesman | 1.00 | – | – |
| Freight out | 0.80 | – | – |
| Total | $10.80 | $9.00 | $6.50 |

# 3   Breakeven Analysis

Breakeven analysis determines the sales required (in dollars or units) to achieve zero profit or loss from operations. In determining the amount in revenues required to break even, management must estimate both fixed costs overall and variable costs on a per-unit basis.

| Example 1 | Breakeven Analysis |

**Facts:** The following information is applicable to Green Grass Industries and will be used for all of the examples in the next several sections:

- Sales price per unit of $125 and variable costs per unit of $50. The contribution margin per unit is $75 ($125 – $50) and the contribution margin ratio is 60% ($75 / $125).

- Fixed costs of $150,000.

- Desired pretax profit of $60,000, a tax rate of 40%, and desired after-tax profit of $36,000.

- Potential unit sales of 2,500 at the current sales price, and a maximum of 3,000 in unit sales to reach market saturation.

## 3.1    Breakeven Point in Units

The contribution approach to the income statement makes it easy to calculate the breakeven point in either units or sales dollars.

The breakeven point in units can be determined by dividing the unit contribution margin into the total fixed costs:

$$\text{Breakeven point in units} = \frac{\text{Total fixed costs}}{\text{Contribution margin per unit}}$$

### Example 1 ▶ Breakeven Analysis (continued)

**Facts:** The same as the first part of Example 1.

**Required:** Calculate Green Grass' breakeven point in units.

**Solution:** Breakeven point in units = $150,000 / $75 = 2,000 units

The company will need to sell 2,000 units in order to recover its variable costs of $75 per unit and its total fixed costs of $150,000.

## 3.2    Breakeven Point in Dollars

There are two approaches to computing breakeven in sales dollars.

1.  **Contribution Margin per Unit:** Compute the breakeven point in units using the contribution margin per unit, and then multiply those breakeven units by the selling price per unit:

$$\text{Breakeven point in dollars} = \text{Unit price} \times \text{Breakeven point (in units)}$$

### Example 1 ▶ Breakeven Analysis (continued)

**Facts:** The same as the first part of Example 1.

**Required:** Calculate Green Grass' breakeven point in dollars, using breakeven units.

**Solution:** Breakeven point in dollars = $125 × 2,000 units = $250,000

The company will need sales of $250,000 in order to cover total variable costs of $100,000 (2,000 units × $50 per unit) and total fixed costs of $150,000.

2. **Contribution Margin Ratio:** Divide total fixed costs by the contribution margin ratio (i.e., the contribution margin as a percentage of revenue per unit or unit price):

$$\text{Breakeven point in dollars} = \frac{\text{Total fixed costs}}{\text{Contribution margin ratio}}$$

| Example 1 | Breakeven Analysis (continued) |
|---|---|

**Facts:** The same as the first part of Example 1.

**Required:** Calculate Green Grass' breakeven point in dollars, using the contribution margin ratio.

**Solution:** Breakeven point in dollars = $150,000 / 60% = $250,000

## 3.3 Required Sales Volume for Target Profit

Breakeven analysis can be extended to calculate the unit sales or sales dollars required to produce a targeted profit. Although profit figures are most relevant on an after-tax basis, the amount that must be added to the breakeven computation in order to calculate the required sales dollars/units must be a before-tax profit amount. This is done for the purposes of maintaining consistency with the pretax sales and pretax cost figures used in the calculation.

### 3.3.1 Sales Units Needed to Obtain a Desired Profit

The formula is modified to treat the desired net income before taxes as another fixed cost.

$$\text{Sales (units)} = (\text{Fixed cost} + \text{Pretax profit}) / \text{Contribution margin per unit}$$

| Example 1 | Breakeven Analysis (continued) |
|---|---|

**Facts:** The same as the first part of Example 1.

**Required:** Calculate Green Grass' unit sales needed in order to achieve its desired pretax profit of $60,000.

**Solution:** Sales (units) = ($150,000 + $60,000) / $75 = 2,800 units

Green Grass must sell 2,800 units in order to cover its fixed and variable costs and to achieve its desired pretax profit of $60,000.

### 3.3.2   Sales Dollars Needed to Obtain a Desired Profit

There are two approaches to computing the sales dollars needed to achieve a desired profit.

**1.   Summation of Total Costs and Profits**

> Sales dollars = Variable costs + Fixed costs + Pretax profit

---

**Example 1          Breakeven Analysis (continued)**

**Facts:** The same as the first part of Example 1.

**Required:** Calculate Green Grass' sales (in dollars) needed in order to achieve its desired pretax profit.

**Solution:** Total variable costs = 2,800 units × $50 per unit = $140,000

Sales (dollars) = $140,000 + $150,000 + $60,000 = $350,000

Green Grass must have sales of $350,000 in order to cover its variable and fixed costs and achieve its desired $60,000 pretax profit.

---

**2.   Contribution Margin Ratio**

$$\text{Sales} = \frac{\text{Fixed cost} + \text{Pretax profit}}{\text{Contribution margin ratio}}$$

---

**Example 1          Breakeven Analysis (continued)**

**Facts:** The same as the first part of Example 1.

**Required:** Calculate Green Grass' sales (in dollars) needed in order to achieve its desired pretax profit.

**Solution:** Sales (dollars) = ($150,000 + $60,000)/60% = $350,000

---

### 3.4 Predicting Profits Based on Volume

After breakeven has been achieved, each additional unit sold will increase net income by the amount of the contribution margin per unit.

---

**Example 1**     **Breakeven Analysis (continued)**

**Facts:** The same as the first part of Example 1.

**Required:** Calculate Green Grass' profit if the company sells 2,500 units.

**Solution:** Profit = Units above the breakeven point × Contribution margin per unit
= 500 × $75 = $37,500.

The breakeven point calculated earlier was 2,000 units. For every unit sold above 2,000, the company will book a $75 profit. If it sells 2,500 units, that is 500 additional units above breakeven; those 500 units will provide a total profit of $37,500.

---

### 3.5 Setting Selling Prices Based on Assumed Volume

This analysis also may be used to derive a per-unit selling price necessary to cover all costs and the desired pretax profit given a specific volume limit.

> Sale price per unit = (Fixed costs + Variable costs + Pretax profit) / Number of units sold

---

**Example 1**     **Breakeven Analysis (continued)**

**Facts:** The same as the first part of Example 1.

**Required:** Calculate Green Grass' per-unit sales price needed to produce its desired pretax profit given the market saturation level of 3,000 units.

**Solution:** Per-unit sales price = [$150,000 + (3,000 units × $50 per unit) + $60,000]/3,000
= $120 per unit.

If the company can sell 3,000 units at $120 per unit, it will cover all fixed costs, variable costs, and the desired pretax profit.

---

### 3.6 Margin of Safety Concepts

The margin of safety is the excess of sales over breakeven sales, and generally is expressed as either dollars or a percentage.

#### 3.6.1 Sales Dollars

The margin of safety expressed in dollars is calculated as follows:

> Margin of safety (in dollars) = Total sales (in dollars) – Breakeven sales (in dollars)

### 3.6.2 Percentage

The margin of safety also can be expressed as a percentage of sales, as indicated below:

$$\text{Margin of safety percentage} = \frac{\text{Margin of safety in dollars}}{\text{Total sales}}$$

## 3.7 Breakeven Charts

Breakeven charts graphically display the results of breakeven analysis.

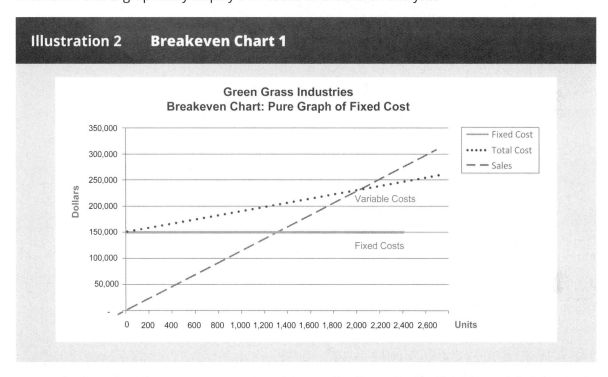

**Illustration 2    Breakeven Chart 1**

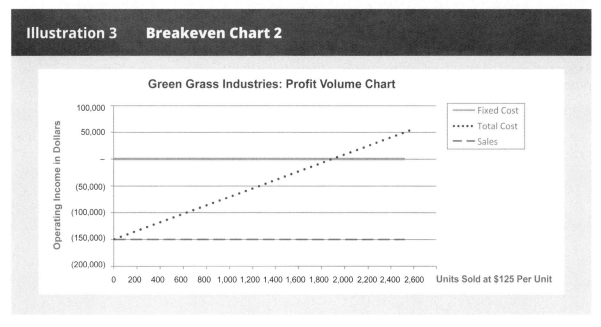

**Illustration 3    Breakeven Chart 2**

# 4 Target Costing (Used for Target Pricing)

Target costing is a technique used to establish the product cost allowed to ensure both profitability per unit and total sales volume.

## 4.1 Cost Determination

The concept of target costing uses the selling price of the product to determine the production costs to be allowed.

### 4.1.1 Market Circumstances Creating Target Costing

As competition (typically from a "cost leader") sets prices, any change in price could easily cause a customer defection. Target costing is the first step in establishing cost controls to ensure ongoing profitability.

### 4.1.2 Target Cost Computation

The target cost of the product is the market price minus profit calculated as follows:

$$\text{Target cost} = \text{Market price} - \text{Required profit}$$

## 4.2 Implications of Target Costing

If management commits to a target cost, serious measures must be employed to reduce costs. Although the mechanics are simple, the implications can be far-reaching.

### 4.2.1 Compromised Quality

The firm may have to sacrifice quality (by reducing costs), but this can have the effect of loss of sales.

### 4.2.2 Increased Marketing and Downstream Costs

Firms competing in this type of environment may incur increased downstream costs in an attempt to differentiate their products and create brand loyalty (and a competitive advantage).

### 4.2.3 Increased Complexity in Cost Measurement

Advanced cost management techniques may have to be employed to attain a higher productivity level.

### 4.2.4 Product Redesign

The product may have to be redesigned to provide for the reduction of costs throughout the life cycle of a product (referred to as the Kaizen method).

---

**Question 1**
CPA-03709

Breakeven analysis assumes that over the relevant range:

- **a.** Unit revenues are nonlinear.
- **b.** Unit variable costs are unchanged.
- **c.** Total costs are unchanged.
- **d.** Total fixed costs are nonlinear.

---

**Question 2**
CPA-04798

Waldo Company, which produces only one product, provides its most current month's data as follows:

| | | |
|---|---:|---:|
| Selling price per unit | $ | 80 |
| *Variable costs per unit:* | | |
| Direct materials | | 21 |
| Direct labor | | 10 |
| Variable manufacturing overhead | | 3 |
| Variable selling and administrative | | 6 |
| *Fixed costs:* | | |
| Manufacturing overhead | $76,000 | |
| Selling and administrative | 58,000 | |
| *Units:* | | |
| Beginning inventory | | 0 |
| Month's production | | 5,000 |
| Number sold | | 4,500 |
| Ending inventory | | 500 |

Based on the above information, what is the total contribution margin for the month under the variable costing approach?

- **a.** $46,000
- **b.** $180,000
- **c.** $207,000
- **d.** $226,000

---

| Question 3 | CPA-04815 |
|---|---|

At the end of a company's first year of operation, 2,000 units of inventory are on hand. Variable costs are $100 per unit, and fixed manufacturing costs are $30 per unit. The use of absorption costing, rather than variable costing, would result in a higher net income of what amount?

    **a.** $60,000

    **b.** $140,000

    **c.** $200,000

    **d.** $260,000

| Question 4 | CPA-03676 |
|---|---|

At annual sales of $900,000, the Ebo product has the following unit sales price and costs:

| | | |
|---|---|---|
| Selling price per unit | | $20 |
| Prime cost | 6 | |
| *Manufacturing overhead:* | | |
| Variable | 1 | |
| Fixed | 7 | |
| *Selling and administrative costs:* | | |
| Variable | 1 | |
| Fixed | 3 | |
| | | 18 |
| Profit | | $ 2 |

What is Ebo's breakeven point in units?

    **a.** 25,000 units

    **b.** 31,500 units

    **c.** 37,500 units

    **d.** 45,000 units

# 1 Ratio Analysis: An Overview

Ratios are a quick and easy way to evaluate a company's past, current, and future performance and financial standing. The results of forecasts and projections can be analyzed using ratio analysis and by looking for correlations to and variations from key financial ratios.

Many of the ratios in this module are also presented elsewhere in the text. In this section, they are defined and interpreted in the context of projections and forecasts (with these terms used interchangeably for simplicity).

---

**Illustration 1 Gi Company Forecast**

Gi Company has used its Year 1 financial results and other information on the historical performance of the company to forecast its Year 2 financial results and has prepared the following forecasted financial statements for Year 2.

The company will use ratio analysis to determine the financial implications of the forecasted results.

### Gi Company Balance Sheet

|  | 12/31/Year 2 | 12/31/Year 1 |
|---|---|---|
| **Current assets** | | |
| Cash and cash equivalents | $ 50,000 | $ 35,000 |
| Trading securities (at fair value) | 75,000 | 65,000 |
| Accounts receivable | 300,000 | 390,000 |
| Inventory (at lower of cost or market) | 290,000 | 275,000 |
| Total current assets | 715,000 | 765,000 |
| Investments available for sale (at fair value) | 350,000 | 300,000 |
| Fixed assets: | | |
| Property, plant, and equipment (at cost) | 1,900,000 | 1,800,000 |
| Less: accumulated depreciation | (180,000) | (150,000) |
|  | 1,720,000 | 1,650,000 |
| Goodwill | 30,000 | 35,000 |
| Total assets | $2,815,000 | $2,750,000 |

(continued)

---

(continued)

Current liabilities:

| | | |
|---|---|---|
| Accounts payable | $ 150,000 | $ 125,000 |
| Notes payable | 325,000 | 375,000 |
| Accrued and other liabilities | 220,000 | 200,000 |
| Total current liabilities | $ 695,000 | $ 700,000 |
| **Long-term debt** | | |
| Bonds and notes payable | 650,000 | 700,000 |
| Total liabilities | 1,345,000 | 1,400,000 |
| **Stockholders' equity** | | |
| Common stock (100,000 shares outstanding) | 500,000 | 500,000 |
| Additional paid-in capital | 670,000 | 670,000 |
| Retained earnings | 300,000 | 180,000 |
| Total equity | 1,470,000 | 1,350,000 |
| Total liabilities and equity | $2,815,000 | $2,750,000 |

## Gi Company Income Statement

| | Year 2 (Forecasted) | Year 1 (Actual) |
|---|---|---|
| Sales | $1,800,000 | $1,700,000 |
| Cost of goods sold | (1,000,000) | (940,000) |
| Gross profit | 800,000 | 760,000 |
| Operating expenses | (486,970) | (476,970) |
| Interest expense | (10,000) | (10,300) |
| Net income before income taxes | 303,030 | 272,730 |
| Income taxes (34%) | (103,030) | (92,730) |
| Net income after income taxes | $ 200,000 | $ 180,000 |
| Earnings per share | $ 2.00 | $ 1.80 |
| **Other financial information** | | |
| Operating cash flows | $275,000 | $265,000 |
| Dividends for the year | $0.80 per share | $0 for Year 1 |
| Market price per share | $12 | $11 |

Assumptions for forecast:

Sales: A forecasted increase of 100,000 in sales from 1,700,000 to 1,800,000.

COGS: A forecasted increase of 60,000 in COGS from 940,000 to 1,000,000 due to rising inventory costs.

Operating expenses: A forecasted increase of 10,000 tied to annual wage increases.

Interest expense: A forecasted decline of 300 due to pay down of a small amount of debt.

Operating cash flows: increase of $10,000.

# 2  Liquidity Ratios

The focus of liquidity ratios is on the current liabilities side of a company's balance sheet, and on whether a company will have enough in current assets and other funds to pay the liabilities when they are due. Key liquidity ratios include the current ratio, quick ratio, cash ratio, operating cash flow ratio, and working capital turnover ratio.

## 2.1  Working Capital

Working capital = Current assets – Current Liabilities

Year 2: $715,000 – $695,000  =  $20,000
Year 1: $765,000 – $700,000  =  $65,000

## 2.2  Current Ratio

$$\text{Current ratio} = \frac{\text{Current assets}}{\text{Current liabilities}}$$

$$\text{Year 2} = \frac{\$715,000}{\$695,000} = 1.03$$

$$\text{Year 1} = \frac{\$765,000}{\$700,000} = 1.09$$

(Industry average = 1.50)

The ratio, and therefore Gi's ability to meet its short-term obligations, is forecasted to decrease slightly and it is low compared with the industry average. The only components (current assets and current liabilities) needed to calculate this ratio come straight from totals on the balance sheet.

■ **Projection Interpretations:** All else being equal, a higher current ratio is better because it implies that more current assets are available to pay short-term liabilities. If a company expects either decreases in current assets or increases in current liabilities, this will result in a lower forecasted current ratio, which can have a potential negative effect on future funding opportunities and business operations.

## 2.3 Quick (Acid-Test) Ratio

$$\text{Quick (acid-test) ratio} = \frac{\text{Cash} + \text{Cash equivalents} + \text{Marketable securities} + \text{Receivables}}{\text{Current liabilities}}$$

$$\text{Year 2} = \frac{\$50{,}000 + \$75{,}000 + \$300{,}000}{\$695{,}000} = 0.61$$

$$\text{Year 1} = \frac{\$35{,}000 + \$65{,}000 + \$390{,}000}{\$700{,}000} = 0.70$$

(Industry average = 0.80)

This ratio is similar to the current ratio, except that it only includes the more liquid components of current assets such as cash, marketable securities (investments), and receivables. Gi's ratio is forecasted to decrease from Year 1 to Year 2 and the industry average of 0.80 is higher than Gi's ratio, which together indicate that Gi may have trouble meeting short-term needs.

■ **Projection Interpretations:** Like the current ratio, a higher quick ratio is better because it implies that more current liquid assets are available to pay short-term liabilities. Projected shifts in dollars from liquid current assets to more illiquid assets or increases in current liabilities will result in a lower forecasted ratio.

## Pass Key

When current assets are used to pay down current liabilities, the numerator and denominator of the current ratio and quick ratio decrease by the same amount. If the current ratio or quick ratio is already less than one, this will result in a lower ratio amount.

## 2.4 Cash Ratio

$$\text{Cash ratio} = \frac{\text{Cash} + \text{Cash equivalents} + \text{Marketable securities}}{\text{Current liabilities}}$$

$$\text{Year 2} = \frac{\$50{,}000 + \$75{,}000}{\$695{,}000} = 0.18$$

$$\text{Year 1} = \frac{\$35{,}000 + \$65{,}000}{\$700{,}000} = 0.14$$

(Industry average: 0.25)

The cash ratio is more conservative than the quick ratio, as only cash, cash equivalents and marketable securities from the current assets section of the balance sheet are used. Although there is a forecasted improvement in this ratio for Year 2, Gi is still showing a lower number than the industry average. In an extreme situation in which Gi may need to use highly liquid assets to meet its current liabilities, the company will have a more difficult time doing so than its peers.

■ **Projection Interpretations:** Cash and cash equivalents are the most liquid assets a company can have, so a higher ratio here implies that a company can easily cover its current obligations. A ratio that is too high may indicate that a company is holding too much in cash and not investing enough in projects that can potentially generate a high return. Projected future cash flow needs will have a large impact on this ratio.

## 2.5    Operating Cash Flow Ratio

$$\text{Operating cash flow ratio} = \frac{\text{Cash flow from operations}}{\text{Current liabilities}}$$

$$\text{Year 2} = \frac{\$275,000}{\$695,000} = 0.40$$

$$\text{Year 1} = \frac{\$265,000}{\$700,000} = 0.38$$

(Industry average: 0.45)

This ratio measures how much cash a company has generated from operating activities to cover current liabilities. Gi forecasts an increase in this ratio from 0.38 to 0.40, which means that it expects to generate more from its core operations to cover its current liabilities. Although the output is still lower than the industry average, it is moving in the right direction and presumably strong for a relatively new company going into its second year.

■ **Projection Interpretations:** A higher ratio is desired, as it implies that a company is generating more cash from its core activities to pay its current liabilities. Positive and sustainable cash flows from operations are crucial for the ongoing success of a company. If operating cash flows are projected to decline in the future, the company will have to look to investing and financing sources to cover the shortfall.

## 2.6    Working Capital Turnover

$$\text{Working capital turnover} = \frac{\text{Sales}}{\text{Average working capital}}$$

$$\text{Year 2} = \frac{\$1,800,000}{\left[(\$715,000 - \$695,000) + (\$765,000 - \$700,000)\right]/2}$$

$$= 42.4 \text{ times}$$

(Industry average: 48.5 times)

The sales amount comes from the income statement, while working capital is calculated as the difference between current assets and current liabilities. This measure is used to evaluate the money used to fund the company's operations and the sales derived from the operations. Gi's forecasted working capital turnover ratio is slightly below industry average, indicating that the company is not doing as well as its peers at converting its working capital into sales. The expectation is that as the company matures, this ratio will improve.

- **Projection Interpretations:** All else being equal, a higher working capital turnover ratio is better. Higher projected net sales in future years will cause this ratio to increase. The ratio will also increase with projected declines in current assets or increases in current liabilities. A ratio that is too high could indicate a working capital amount that is too low.

# 3 Activity Ratios

Activity ratios are used to assess how efficient a company is at utilizing its resources to generate sales and profits. Key activity ratios include the inventory conversion period, receivables collection period, payables deferral period, operating cycle, and cash conversion cycle.

## 3.1 Inventory Conversion Period (Inventory Turnover in Days)

$$\text{Inventory conversion period} = 365 \times \frac{\text{Average inventory}}{\text{Cost of goods sold}}$$

$$= 365 \times \frac{(\$290{,}000 + \$275{,}000)\,/\,2}{\$1{,}000{,}000}$$

$$= 103.11 \text{ days}$$

(Industry average: 78 days)

This ratio indicates the average number of days required to sell inventory. Inventory will typically be averaged in this ratio in order to align the time period to cost of goods sold. Gi is forecasting a Year 2 inventory conversion ratio that is significantly higher than the industry average, which means that it will take the company longer to convert its inventory into sales. This ratio will need to be reduced over the next several years, or the company will risk its inventory becoming obsolete (as well as potentially incurring higher carrying costs in order to sustain the inventory).

- **Projection Interpretations:** This ratio reflects how long it takes on average to turn inventory into sales. The output will be in days, with a lower number of days indicating a company is more efficient in converting inventory into sales. Projected sales will affect projected inventory, which will influence the projected inventory conversion period.

## 3.2 Receivables Collection Period (Accounts Receivable Turnover in Days)

$$\text{Receivables collection period} = 365 \times \frac{\text{Average net receivables}}{\text{Net credit sales}}$$

$$= 365 \times \frac{(\$300{,}000 + \$390{,}000)\,/\,2}{\$1{,}800{,}000}$$

$$= 69.96 \text{ days}$$

(Industry average: 55 days)

This ratio indicates the receivables' quality and the success of the firm in collecting outstanding receivables. The net sales number from the income statement is equal to gross sales less sales returns and allowances. Receivables are often averaged in this ratio to align to the period covered by net sales on the income statement. Although Gi is forecasting a 70-day receivables collection period (relative to the industry average of 55), it is forecasting an increase in sales along with a decrease in the receivables balance, implying that it expects to collect on much of its outstanding receivables while boosting revenue. Gi is still unfavorable relative to the industry, but it is moving in the right direction.

- ▥ **Projection Interpretations:** This measure provides an average number of days to convert sales into cash. A shorter number of days indicates that a company is doing a good job collecting on its outstanding receivables. Future expected growth in sales will likely tie to increases in receivables, unless a company projects a change in the percentage of credit sales relative to cash sales.

## 3.3    Payables Deferral Period (Accounts Payable Turnover in Days)

$$\text{Payables deferral period} = 365 \times \frac{\text{Average accounts payable}}{\text{Cost of goods sold}}$$

$$= 365 \times \frac{(\$150,000 + \$125,000) \,/\, 2}{\$1,000,000}$$

$$= 50.19 \text{ days}$$

(Industry average: 62 days)

Accounts payable will typically be averaged to align with the time period associated with cost of goods sold. Here, Gi is forecasting a little over 50 days to pay its vendors, whereas the industry takes 62 days. As long as the company is meeting the payment terms of its vendors, it should look to extend this period in order to conserve cash.

- ▥ **Projection Interpretations:** This is a measure of how long it takes for a company to pay its vendors for goods purchased on credit. If a company wishes to conserve cash, it will project longer average time periods to pay its vendors.

## 3.4    Operating Cycle

$$\text{Operating cycle} = \text{Inventory conversion period} + \text{Receivables collection period}$$

$$= 103.11 \text{ days} + 69.96 \text{ days}$$

$$= 173.07 \text{ days}$$

The operating cycle indicates the number of days between acquisition of inventory and realization of cash from selling the inventory. The inventory conversion period and receivables collection period calculations are shown earlier in this section.

- ▥ **Projection Interpretations:** The operating cycle represents the amount of time it takes a company to convert inventory into cash. Changes to inventory management policies and receivables collection processes will affect whether this cycle increases or decreases in the future.

## 3.5    Cash Conversion Cycle

$$\text{Cash conversion cycle} = \frac{\text{Inventory}}{\text{conversion period}} + \frac{\text{Receivables}}{\text{collection period}} - \frac{\text{Payables}}{\text{deferral period}}$$

$$= 69.96 \text{ days} + 103.11 \text{ days} - 50.19 \text{ days}$$

$$= 122.88 \text{ days}$$

(Industry average: 71 days)

Gi is forecasting a cash conversion cycle that is double that of its industry. Although it is expected that a relatively new company such as Gi will take some time to develop efficiencies and procedures designed to maximize its cash position, there is room for improvement in all three components that make up this cycle. Gi will have to address how fast it converts inventory into sales, how fast it collects outstanding receivables, and how long it takes Gi to pay its vendors. The biggest area for improvement is inventory conversion.

- **Projection Interpretations:** All else being equal, a lower cash conversion cycle is better because a company would want to minimize the number of days it takes to convert inventory into sales and sales into cash, while taking as long as possible to pay its vendors. Similar to the operating cycle, policy and forecasted cash flow decisions will influence this cycle time.

| Example 1 | Cash Conversion Cycle |
|---|---|

**Facts:** A company expects to reduce its operating cycle by five full days as a result of new sales initiatives and more aggressive collection policies.

**Required:** If the cash conversion cycle is projected to be three days shorter than before, compute the change in the payables deferral period.

**Solution:** The operating cycle consists of the inventory conversion period and receivables collection period, which represents two-thirds of the cash conversion cycle. If the overall cash conversion cycle is projected to be three days shorter and the operating cycle will be five days shorter, it must be a case that the payables deferral period is decreasing by two days.

# 4    Debt Ratios

Debt ratios measure the extent to which a company employs financial leverage in its capital structure. Although debt is cheaper than equity from a cost standpoint because of the tax benefits and lower interest rates, too much debt is risky for the borrowing company. Key debt ratios include the debt-to-equity ratio, debt-to-assets ratio, debt-to-total-capital ratio, interest coverage ratio, and debt service coverage ratio.

## 4.1   Debt-to-Equity Ratio

$$\text{Debt-to-equity ratio} = \frac{\text{Total liabilities}}{\text{Common stockholders' equity}}$$

$$\text{Year } 2 = \frac{\$1,345,000}{\$1,470,000} = 0.91$$

$$\text{Year } 1 = \frac{\$1,400,000}{\$1,350,000} = 1.04$$

(Industry average = 0.75)

This ratio indicates the degree of protection to creditors in case of insolvency. A lower ratio is better. Gi is forecasting a reduction in this ratio, which is positive as both current and long-term liabilities are forecasted to decline and equity is forecasted to increase due to net income from Year 2. The goal for the company should be to get this ratio closer to the industry average, which can be accomplished by paying down debt. If new debt is added, there should be at least as much growth in equity to cover the debt increase.

- **Projection Interpretations:** A higher debt-to-equity ratio indicates that the company employs more risk. If a company anticipates issuing debt in the future or reducing the amount of outstanding stock, this ratio will increase. Ideally, a company will choose the mix of liabilities and equity that will minimize its overall cost of capital.

## 4.2   Debt-to-Assets Ratio

$$\text{Debt-to-assets ratio} = \frac{\text{Total liabilities}}{\text{Total assets}}$$

$$\text{Year } 2 = \frac{\$1,345,000}{\$2,815,000} = 47.8\%$$

$$\text{Year } 1 = \frac{\$1,400,000}{\$2,750,000} = 50.9\%$$

(Industry average: 40%)

Gi's debt-to-assets ratio is forecasted to improve due to an increase in assets and a decrease in liabilities. Because a higher ratio indicates higher risk, this forecast shows a positive trend and will get the company closer to the industry average.

- **Projection Interpretations:** Very similar to the debt-to-equity ratio, a company's risk level increases as this ratio increases. Forecasted future year asset and liability totals are compared to produce a projected debt-to-assets ratio. If a company wishes to lower its risk levels, it will have to reduce total liabilities or increase total assets without incurring more debt.

## 4.3    Times Interest Earned (Interest Coverage) Ratio

$$\text{Times interest earned ratio} = \frac{\text{Earnings before interest and taxes}\left(\text{EBIT}\right)}{\text{Interest expense}}$$

$$\text{Year 2} = \frac{\$303{,}030 + \$10{,}000}{\$10{,}000} = 31.3 \text{ times}$$

$$\text{Year 1} = \frac{\$272{,}730 + \$10{,}300}{\$10{,}300} = 27.5 \text{ times}$$

(Industry average: 24.5 times)

Gi has a more favorable ratio than its peers. The ratio of 27.48 days for Year 1 is forecasted to increase to 31.30 days, which shows the company can cover its debt expenses.

- **Projection Interpretations:** A higher number implies that a company has more funding to cover its required interest expense associated with debt. By paying down old debt or replacing old debt with new debt carrying lower interest rates, interest expense can be lowered in the future, which will increase this ratio.

# 5    Profitability Ratios

The focus of profitability ratios is on determining how profitable a company is at various levels of its business. Although the bottom line is very important, cost controls earlier in the process can be extremely beneficial for a company. Common profitability ratios include the margins (gross, operating, and net), return on equity, and return on assets.

## 5.1    Gross Margin

$$\text{Gross margin} = \frac{\text{Sales} - \text{Cost of goods sold}}{\text{Sales}}$$

$$\text{Year 2} = \frac{\$1{,}800{,}000 - \$1{,}000{,}000}{\$1{,}800{,}000} = 44.4\%$$

$$\text{Year 1} = \frac{\$1{,}700{,}000 - \$940{,}000}{\$1{,}700{,}000} = 44.7\%$$

(Industry average: 48%)

This ratio is looking at profitability at the highest level. Gi is forecasting relatively flat gross margins in Year 2 relative to Year 1. As the company becomes more efficient in its operations and reduces costs relative to sales, this ratio should improve such that it meets or exceeds the industry average.

- **Projection Interpretations:** All profitability margins are interpreted the same way: All else being equal, higher is better. Sales are forecast to grow at a certain percentage each year based on a variety of factors described earlier in the text. For ease of calculation purposes, cost of goods sold is often forecast to remain a specific percentage of sales—keeping the gross margin constant.

## 5.2    Operating Margin

$$\text{Operating margin} = \frac{\text{Operating income}}{\text{Sales}}$$

$$\text{Year 2} = \frac{\$313{,}030}{\$1{,}800{,}000} = 17.4\%$$

$$\text{Year 1} = \frac{\$283{,}030}{\$1{,}700{,}000} = 16.6\%$$

(Industry average: 19%)

This ratio represents profitability after all nonfinancing and nontax costs are taken into account. Gi's operating margin is forecasted to increase from Year 1 to Year 2. Gi should continue to find ways to increase sales while controlling costs.

■  **Projection Interpretations:** A higher ratio is better, as higher operating income indicates more sales generated using fewer costs. This represents the profitability of a company taking into account everything other than financing decisions (issuance of debt and equity) and tax effects over which the company has very little control. Projected changes in sales, cost of goods sold, and/or SG&A expenses will affect this ratio.

## 5.3    Net Profit Margin

$$\text{Net profit margin} = \frac{\text{Net income}}{\text{Sales}}$$

$$\text{Year 2} = \frac{\$200{,}000}{\$1{,}800{,}000} = 11.1\%$$

$$\text{Year 1} = \frac{\$180{,}000}{\$1{,}700{,}000} = 10.6\%$$

(Industry average: 13%)

As with all margins, the goal is to increase the ratio. Gi is forecasting an increase in the net profit margin. Controlling growth in costs while continuing to increase sales will get the company closer to the industry average.

■  **Projection Interpretations:** The higher the net profit margin the better, as this means a company is profitable after taking into account all costs associated with generating sales and operating its business. This is one of the key measures a company evaluates in making projections, as this will likely impact future capital structure decisions and stock growth.

## 5.4    Return on Equity (ROE)

$$\text{Return on equity} \left( \text{ROE} \right) = \frac{\text{Net income} - \text{Preferred dividends}}{\text{Average shareholders' equity}}$$

$$= \frac{\$200{,}000 - \$0}{(\$1{,}470{,}000 + \$1{,}350{,}000) \, / \, 2}$$

$$= 14.2\%$$

(Industry average: 15%)

Gi's forecasted ROE for Year 2 is very close to the industry average. Continued growth in profitability while managing dividend outflows will boost this ratio. Because net income comes from the income statement and shareholders' equity comes from the balance sheet, it is common practice to use average shareholders' equity in the denominator.

- **Projection Interpretations:** A higher ROE is desirable, as higher net income for shareholders means greater profitability, higher earnings per share, and probable future stock growth. While equity is a by-product of future capital structure decisions, future net income (which also affects equity) will be a result of forecasted sales and costs.

## 5.5    Return on Assets (ROA)

$$\text{Return on assets} \left( \text{ROA} \right) = \frac{\text{Net income}}{\text{Average total assets}}$$

$$= \frac{\$200{,}000}{\$2{,}782{,}500}$$

$$= 7.2\%$$

(Industry average: 8%)

In line with other profitability and return measures, Gi's ROA is slightly below the industry average. As long as Gi can continue to increase its bottom-line profits at a rate faster than overall asset growth, this measure will improve. Similar to ROE, common practice is to take the average balance of assets at the beginning and end of the period in order to align with the period covered by net income.

- **Projection Interpretations:** A higher ROA implies that a company is generating more profits relative to its base of assets. Projected net income should be compared with projected assets to determine whether this ratio is increasing or decreasing in the future.

| **Question 1** | **CPA-03991** |
|---|---|

Which of the following transactions does not change the current ratio or total current assets?

    **a.**  A cash advance is made to a divisional office.

    **b.**  A cash dividend is declared.

    **c.**  Short-term notes payable are retired with cash.

    **d.**  Equipment is purchased with a three-year note and a 10 percent cash down payment.


| **Question 2** | **CPA-04009** |
|---|---|

An increase in sales collections resulting from an increased cash discount for prompt payment would be expected to cause a(n):

    **a.**  Increase in the operating cycle.

    **b.**  Increase in the average collection period.

    **c.**  Decrease in the cash conversion cycle.

    **d.**  Increase in bad debt losses.

## NOTES

# Module 4 Marginal Analysis

## 1 Terms Related to Marginal Analysis

The operational decision method, referred to as *marginal analysis*, is used when analyzing business decisions such as the introduction of a new product or changes in output levels of existing products, acceptance or rejection of special orders, making or buying a product or service, selling or processing further, and adding or dropping a segment. Marginal analysis focuses on the relevant revenues and costs that are associated with a decision.

### 1.1 Relevant Revenues and Costs

When making business decisions that will affect future periods, revenues and costs related to those decisions are deemed to be relevant only if they change as a result of selecting different alternatives. Although variable costs are more likely to be relevant because they change with production volume and output, relevant costs can be either fixed or variable.

Relevant costs often share similar characteristics, including their specific traceability to cost objects that may change as a result of selecting different alternatives. Ultimately, a cost's relevance pertains to its potential to affect the decision.

- **Direct Costs:** Costs that can be identified with or traced to a given cost object. Direct costs are usually relevant (variable costs are generally direct costs).

- **Prime Costs:** Direct material and direct labor costs, which are generally relevant.

- **Discretionary Costs:** Costs arising from periodic (usually annual) budgeting decisions by management to spend in areas not directly related to manufacturing. Discretionary costs are generally relevant.

---

**Illustration 1    Discretionary Costs**

Costs to maintain landscaping at a corporation's headquarters are generally viewed as discretionary.

---

- **Incremental Costs:** Also known as marginal costs, differential costs, or out-of-pocket costs, the additional costs incurred to produce an additional amount of the unit over the present output. Incremental costs are relevant costs and include all variable costs and any avoidable fixed costs associated with a decision.

- **Opportunity Costs:** The cost of foregoing the next best alternative when making a decision. Opportunity costs are relevant costs.

## Illustration 2  Opportunity Costs

1.  Costs related to a special device that is necessary if a special order is selected are relevant.

2.  Costs associated with alternative uses of plant space are relevant.

- **Irrelevant Costs:** Costs that do not differ among alternatives are irrelevant and should be ignored in a marginal cost analysis.

- **Sunk Costs:** Costs that are unavoidable because they were incurred in the past and cannot be recovered as a result of a decision. Sunk costs are not relevant costs.

## Illustration 3  Sunk Costs

Electramag Corporation is evaluating whether to replace a piece of equipment. The cost of the old equipment is a sunk cost and is not relevant to the replacement decision. Additionally, under either alternative (keep the old equipment or replace it), the anticipated cost of electricity remains the same. The cost of electricity is a variable cost. Even so, the cost of electricity is not relevant because it does not change regardless of the selected alternative.

- **Controllable Costs:** Costs that are authorized by the business unit manager or the decision maker. The ability to control cost is evaluated when analyzing business decisions. By classifying a cost as either controllable or uncontrollable, the specific level of management responsible for the cost is identified. Controllable costs are relevant if they will change as a result of selecting different alternatives.

- **Uncontrollable Costs:** Costs that were authorized at a different level in the organization. Uncontrollable costs are not relevant costs because they cannot be changed by the manager making the decision.

## Illustration 4  Controllable vs. Uncontrollable Costs

A manufacturing department manager has control over the materials and supplies used in the manufacturing department (i.e., controllable costs), but that manager has no control over the fixed asset depreciation allocated to the department (i.e., uncontrollable costs).

- **Avoidable Costs and Revenues:** Costs and revenues that result from choosing one course of action instead of another. As a result, the firm avoids the cost and revenue associated with the course of action not selected. They are relevant to the decision.

- **Unavoidable Costs:** Costs that are the same regardless of the chosen course of action are unavoidable costs that are not relevant to future decisions. These costs will continue regardless of the course of action taken. They have no effect on the decision.

# 2 Special Order Decisions

Special order decisions are defined as opportunities that require a firm to decide whether a specially priced order should be accepted or rejected. Decisions of this character involve a comparison of the special order price to the relevant costs of the decision and an analysis of the strategic issues that relate to the acceptance or rejection of the order.

## 2.1 Determining Relevant Costs

### 2.1.1 Capacity Issues

Special orders are short-term decisions that often assume excess capacity. Fixed costs are generally not relevant to these decisions unless the special order will change total fixed costs.

■ **Presumed Excess Capacity**

If there is excess capacity, a comparison should be made of the incremental costs of the order to the incremental revenue generated by the order. The special order should be accepted if the selling price per unit is greater than the variable cost per unit.

■ **Presumed Full Capacity**

If the company is operating at full capacity, the opportunity cost of producing the special order should be included in the analysis.

● The production that is forfeited to produce the special order is the next best alternative use of the facility.

● The opportunity cost is the contribution margin that would have been produced if the special order were not accepted.

| Example 1 | Special Order With Excess Capacity |
| --- | --- |

**Facts:** Kator Company is a manufacturer of industrial components. Product KB-96 is normally sold for $150 per unit and has the following costs per unit:

| | |
| --- | --- |
| Direct materials | $20 |
| Direct labor | 15 |
| Variable manufacturing overhead | 12 |
| Fixed manufacturing overhead | 30 |
| Shipping and handling costs | 3 |
| Fixed selling costs | 10 |
| Total cost | $90 |

Kator has received a special, one-time order for 1,000 units of KB-96.

**Required:** Assuming that Kator has excess capacity, calculate the minimum acceptable price for this one-time special order.

**Solution:** The fixed manufacturing overhead and the fixed selling costs are not relevant to the decision. The incremental per-unit production cost is the total variable cost per unit of $50. Kator should accept the special order only if the selling price per unit is greater than $50.

| Example 2 | Special Order With No Excess Capacity |
|---|---|

**Facts:** Assume the same costs as in the previous example. Kator has received a special, one-time order for 1,000 units of KB-96. Assume that Kator is operating at full capacity. Also assume that the next best alternative use of the capacity is the production of LB-64, which would produce a contribution margin of $10,000.

**Required:** Calculate the minimum acceptable price for this one-time special order.

**Solution:** Kator's next best alternative use of its capacity would produce a contribution margin of $10,000. If Kator produces 1,000 units of KB-96, this $10-per-unit ($10,000 / 1,000 units) opportunity cost would be added to the variable cost of $50 to determine the minimum justifiable price for the special order. Kator should accept the special order only if the selling price per unit is greater than $60.

## 2.2 Strategic Factors

The acceptance of a special order also requires consideration of a number of strategic factors, including:

- The effect on regular-priced sales and other long-term pricing issues.
- The possibility of future sales to this customer.
- The possibility of exceeding plant capacity or the complexities of the order itself.
- The pricing of the special order.
- The impact of income taxes.
- The effect on machinery and/or the scheduled machine maintenance program.

# 3 Make vs. Buy

The decision to make or buy a component (also referred to as insourcing versus outsourcing) is similar to the special order decision. Managers should select the lowest-cost alternative.

## 3.1 Determining Relevant Costs and Other Make-or-Buy Issues

### 3.1.1 Capacity Issues

- **Excess Capacity:** If there is excess capacity, the cost of making the product internally is the cost that will be avoided (or saved) if the product is not made. This will be the maximum outside purchase price.

- **No Excess Capacity:** If there is no excess capacity, the cost of making the product internally is the cost that will be avoided (saved) if the product is not made plus the opportunity cost associated with the decision.

| Example 3 | Make vs. Buy Decisions |
|---|---|

**Facts:** Offset Manufacturing produces 20,000 units of part No. 125. The production costs are:

| | Total Cost | Cost per Unit |
|---|---|---|
| Direct materials | $ 10,000 | $ .50 |
| Direct labor | 40,000 | 2.00 |
| Variable manufacturing overhead | 20,000 | 1.00 |
| Fixed factory overhead | 40,000 | 2.00 |
| Total cost | $110,000 | $5.50 |

An outside manufacturer approaches Offset Manufacturing and offers to sell it the same part for $5 per unit. Offset has excess capacity. The $10,000 factory floor supervisor's salary is the only fixed cost that will be eliminated if Offset purchases the part.

**Required:** Determine whether Offset Manufacturing should make or buy the part.

**Solution:**

| | Make Total | Make Per Unit | Buy Total | Buy Per Unit |
|---|---|---|---|---|
| Purchase cost | | | $100,000 | $5.00 |
| Direct materials | $10,000 | $0.50 | | |
| Direct labor | 40,000 | 2.00 | | |
| Variable factory overhead | 20,000 | 1.00 | | |
| Fixed factory overhead (avoidable) | 10,000 | 0.50 | | |
| Total relevant costs | $80,000 | $4.00 | $100,000 | $5.00 |
| Difference | $20,000 | $1.00 | | |

Offset will choose to make the part because it is the lowest-cost alternative when relevant costs are considered.

## 3.2 Strategic Factors

The following strategic factors should be considered when analyzing a make-or-buy decision:

- The quality of the product purchased compared with the quality of the product manufactured.
- The reliability of the purchased product.
- The value of service contracts or other warranties.
- The risks associated with outsourcing or buying outside the organization, including inflexibility, loss of control, and less confidentiality.
- The most efficient use of the entity's resources.

                                        

# 4 Sell or Process Further

The decision regarding *additional processing* is made based on profitability.

## 4.1 Joint Costs

*Joint costs* are the costs of a single process that yields multiple products (e.g., the processing of a pig to produce ham, bacon, and pork chops). Joint costs cannot be traced to an individual product. Joint costs are sunk costs that are not relevant to decisions of whether to sell or to process further.

## 4.2 Separable Costs

*Separable costs* are costs incurred after the split-off point that can be traced to individual products and are relevant to decisions of whether to sell or to process further.

## 4.3 Deciding Factors to Sell or Process Further

The decision on whether to sell at the split-off point is made by comparing the incremental cost and the incremental revenue generated after the split-off point.

If the incremental revenue exceeds the incremental cost, the organization should process further.

If the incremental cost exceeds the incremental revenue, the organization should sell at the split-off point.

---

### Example 4 Sell or Process Further

**Facts:** Jackson Inc. processes raw materials into beauty products. The Soap Division (Soap) processes fats and lye at a cost of $200 per batch, which yields 2,000 bars of soap. Soap can sell the soap for $0.50 per bar at this point. Alternatively, various fragrances and oils can be added to produce fine soaps for the high-end retail market from a given batch of raw materials. Soap could incur an additional cost of $1.20 per bar of soap for the perfumes and attractive packaging and create lavender-scented soap. Or, for an additional cost of $1.75 per bar, Soap could create rose-scented soap. The high-end soap would sell for $1.30 per bar for the lavender scent and $3 per bar for the rose scent.

**Required:** Determine whether the soap division will produce the lavender soap, rose-scented soap, or both.

**Solution:** The Soap Division will not produce the lavender soap because the costs after the split-off point are $1.20 per bar and the incremental revenue is only $0.80 ($1.30 for lavender soap minus the $0.50 revenue for basic soap). Incremental revenue is less than incremental costs.

If the company decides to produce rose-scented soap, incremental costs are $1.75 per bar and incremental revenue is $2.50 ($3 minus $0.50) per bar. Because the incremental revenue exceeds incremental costs, Soap would produce rose soap.

---

# 5    Keep or Drop a Segment

Relevant costs should be used to determine whether to *keep or drop a business* segment.

## 5.1    Classification of Costs

The fixed costs associated with the segment must be identified as either avoidable (relevant) or unavoidable, even if the segment is discontinued.

## 5.2    Decision Factors

A firm should compare the fixed costs that can be avoided if the segment is dropped (i.e., the cost of running the segment) to the contribution margin that will be lost if the segment is dropped.

- Keep the segment if the lost contribution margin exceeds avoided fixed costs.

- Drop the segment if the lost contribution margin is less than avoided fixed costs.

---

**Example 5**    **Fixed Costs Are Unavoidable**

**Facts:** The executives at Chowderhead Industries are evaluating each of their product lines. A variable costing analysis by product shows that the company's clam and corn chowder products are profitable but its conch chowder product is not.

| Description | Clam | Conch | Corn | Total |
|---|---|---|---|---|
| Sales | $125,000 | $75,000 | $50,000 | $250,000 |
| Variable costs | 90,000 | 60,000 | 25,000 | 175,000 |
| Contribution margin | 35,000 | 15,000 | 25,000 | 75,000 |
| Fixed costs | 20,000 | 20,000 | 20,000 | 60,000 |
| Operating Income | $ 15,000 | $ (5,000) | $ 5,000 | $ 15,000 |

The conch chowder fixed costs are unavoidable.

**Required:** Determine whether Chowderhead should eliminate its conch chowder product line.

**Solution:** If the conch chowder fixed costs are unavoidable, they will be incurred even if conch chowder is eliminated.

| Description | Clam | Conch | Corn | Total |
|---|---|---|---|---|
| Sales | $125,000 | – | $50,000 | $175,000 |
| Variable costs | 90,000 | – | 25,000 | 115,000 |
| Contribution margin | 35,000 | – | 25,000 | 60,000 |
| Fixed costs | 20,000 | 20,000 | 20,000 | 60,000 |
| Net Income | $ 15,000 | $(20,000) | $ 5,000 | – |

The conch chowder product line should not be eliminated. Elimination of the product would eliminate company-wide profits because the product makes a positive contribution to covering the entity's fixed costs.

---

## Example 6 — Some Fixed Costs Are Avoidable

**Facts:** Assume that $16,000 of the Conch Chowder fixed costs are avoidable advertising costs that will not be incurred if the product is eliminated.

**Required:** Given these new facts, determine whether Chowderhead Industries should eliminate its conch chowder product line.

**Solution:** If $16,000 of the fixed costs are avoidable, then only $4,000 are unavoidable and will be incurred even if conch chowder is eliminated.

| Description | Clam | Conch | Corn | Total |
|---|---|---|---|---|
| Sales | $125,000 | – | $50,000 | $175,000 |
| Variable costs | 90,000 | – | 25,000 | 115,000 |
| Contribution margin | 35,000 | – | 25,000 | 60,000 |
| Unavoidable fixed costs | 15,000 | 4,000 | 16,000 | 35,000 |
| Avoidable fixed costs | 5,000 | – | 4,000 | 9,000 |
| Operating Income | $ 15,000 | $ (4,000) | $ 5,000 | $ 16,000 |

The Chowderhead executives should eliminate the conch chowder product line because the avoidable fixed costs exceed the contribution margin that is lost when the product is eliminated. In this case, elimination of the conch chowder product line improves overall productivity from $15,000 to $16,000.

## 5.3 Strategic Factors

Important strategic factors to consider include:

- The complementary character of products and their relationship to the sales of other products. Manufacturers might produce and price certain products as loss leaders to promote sales of more profitable products.

- The impact of product addition or deletion on employee morale.

- The growth potential of each product regardless of individual profitability.

- Opportunity costs associated with available capacity.

---

### Question 1                                                          CPA-06169

The Danforth Corp. circuit production plant has a 12,000-unit capacity and currently produces 10,000 circuits per year. The company incurs $50,000 in variable costs for its current production and carries a $40,000 fixed cost burden.

If Danforth has an opportunity to fill a special order for 1,000 circuits, the price per unit for the order should exceed:

    **a.**   $4.00

    **b.**   $5.00

    **c.**   $8.33

    **d.**   $9.00

---

### Question 2                                                           CPA-06170

The Danforth Corp. circuit production plant has a 10,000-unit capacity and currently produces 10,000 circuits per year. The company incurs $50,000 in variable costs for its current production and carries a $40,000 fixed cost burden.

Danforth has explored other alternatives and knows that the next best alternative would produce a $2,000 contribution margin for a 1,000-unit run. If Danforth has an opportunity to fill a special order for 1,000 circuits, the price per unit of the order should exceed:

    **a.**   $2.00

    **b.**   $5.00

    **c.**   $7.00

    **d.**   $11.00

                                    

## NOTES

# 1 Operational and Tactical Planning

*Operational and tactical planning* is the process of determining the specific objectives and means by which strategic plans will be achieved. Tactical plans are short term and cover periods up to 18 months.

## 1.1 Single-Use Plans

Tactical plans are also called *single-use plans* because they are developed to apply to specific circumstances during a specific time frame.

## 1.2 Annual Budget

An *annual budget* is a (type of) single-use tactical plan. Budgets translate the strategic plan and implementation into a period-specific operational guide. Placing responsibility for achievement of strategic goals in the hands of managers promotes routine accomplishment of strategy as part of the manager's job function.

# 2 Budget Policies

To effectively budget, an organization should implement formal *budget policies* that include the following key features.

## 2.1 Management Participation

Typically, a budget will extend for a period of one year and involve numerous individuals. The budget process normally involves a budget committee, which includes members of senior management. The budget committee is charged with resolving disputes and making final decisions regarding major budget changes.

## 2.2 Budget Guidelines

Top management should provide *guidelines* for budget preparation based on the entity's strategic goals and long-term plan. These guidelines should include:

### 2.2.1 Evaluation of Current Conditions

- Consideration of the changes to the environment since the adoption of the strategic plan.
- Organizational goals for the coming period.
- Operating results year-to-date.

### 2.2.2 Management Instructions

- Setting the tone for the budget (e.g., cost containment, innovation, etc.).
- Corporate policies (e.g., mandated downsizing).

# 3  Standards and Benchmarking

Budgets frequently revolve around the development of standards. Standards have been referred to as per-unit budgets and are integral to the development of flexible budgets.

## 3.1  Ideal and Currently Attainable Standards

Standards are often set below expectations to motivate productivity and efficiency, but those standard costs must be revised periodically (generally once a year) to reflect changes in previously determined standards. The best standard is the standard that leads to the accomplishment of strategic goals.

### 3.1.1  Ideal Standards

*Ideal standards* represent the costs that result from perfect efficiency and effectiveness in job performance. Ideal standards are generally not historical; they are forward-looking. No provision is made for normal spoilage or downtime.

- **Advantage:** An advantage of using ideal standards is the implied emphasis on continuous quality improvement (CQI) to meet the ideal.

- **Disadvantage:** A disadvantage is the demotivation of employees by the use of unattainable standards.

### 3.1.2  Currently Attainable Standards

*Currently attainable* standards represent costs that result from work performed by employees with appropriate training and experience but without extraordinary effort. Provisions are made for normal spoilage and downtime.

- **Advantage:** Fosters the perception that standards are reasonable.

- **Disadvantage:** Required use of judgment and potential manipulation.

## 3.2  Authoritative and Participative Standards

### 3.2.1  Authoritative Standards

*Authoritative standards* are set exclusively by management.

- **Advantage:** Authoritative standards can be implemented quickly and will likely include all costs.

- **Disadvantage:** Workers might not accept imposed standards.

### 3.2.2  Participative Standards

*Participative standards* are set by both managers and the individuals who are held accountable to those standards.

- **Advantage:** Workers are more likely to accept participative standards.

- **Disadvantage:** Participative standards are slower to implement.

# 4 Master Budgets

A *master budget* (or "annual business plan") documents specific short-term operating performance goals for a period, normally one year or less. The plan normally includes an operating (nonfinancial) budget as well as a financial budget that outlines the sources of funds and detailed plans for their expenditure.

## 4.1 Overview

### 4.1.1 Purpose

Annual business plans are prepared to provide comprehensive and coordinated budget guidance for an organization consistent with overall strategic objectives.

- **Control Objective:** The master budget serves to communicate the criteria for performance over the period covered by the budget.

- **Terminology:** Master budgets are alternatively referred to as static budgets, annual business plans, profit planning, or targeting budgets.

- **Use:** Annual business plans are appropriate for most industries but are particularly useful in manufacturing settings that require coordination of financial and operating budgets.

### 4.1.2 Components

A master budget generally comprises operating budgets and financial budgets prepared in anticipation of achieving a *single level of sales volume* for a specified period.

- **Pro Forma Financial Statements:** The ultimate output of the annual business plan is a series of pro forma financial statements, including a balance sheet, an income statement, and a statement of cash flows.

- **Assumptions:** Pro forma financial statements are supported by schedules that reflect the underlying operating assumptions that produce those statements.

### 4.1.3 Limitations of the Annual Plan

- **Master Budget Confined to One Year at a Single Level of Activity:** Budget amounts may be much different from actual results, even though the relationship between expenses and revenues is consistent. An annual static budget divided by 12 (to establish a monthly budget) may exaggerate variances due to seasonal or volume fluctuations.

- **Reporting Output:** The product of the process is a set of pro forma financial statements. Although familiar, pro forma financial statements may not provide the type of management information most useful to decision making.

## 4.2 Mechanics of Master Budgeting

The annual business-plan process produces the following budgets and reports:

### 4.2.1 Operating Budgets

*Operating budgets* are established to describe the resources needed and the manner in which those resources will be acquired. Operating budgets include:

- Sales budgets
- Production budgets
- Selling and administrative budgets
- Personnel budgets

### 4.2.2   Financial Budgets

*Financial budgets* define the detailed sources and uses of funds to be used in operations. Financial budgets include:

- Pro forma financial statements
- Cash budgets

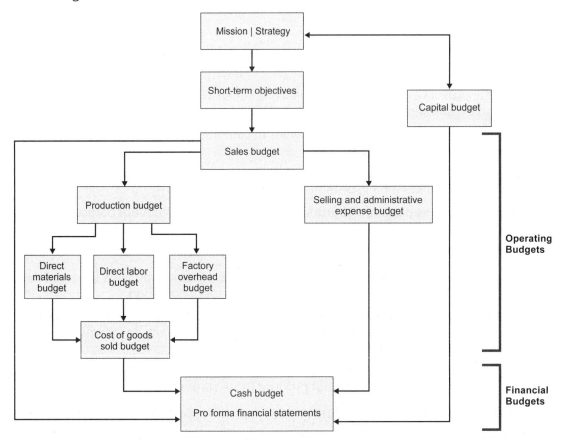

# 5   Operating Budgets: Sales Budget

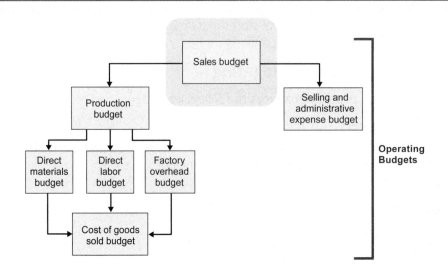

The sales budget is the foundation of the entire budget process. The sales budget represents the anticipated sales of the organization in units and dollars. The sales budget is the first budget prepared and it drives the development of most other components of the master budget. Sales budget units drive the number of units required by the production budget. Sales budget dollars drive the anticipated cash and revenue figures. Inventory levels, purchases, and operating expenses are coordinated with sales levels.

## 5.1    Sales Forecasting and Budgeting

The *sales budget* is based on the sales forecast. Sales forecasts are derived from input received from numerous organizational resources, including the opinions of sales staff, statistical analysis of correlation between sales and economic indicators, and opinions of line management. Sales forecasts are developed after consideration of the following factors:

- Past patterns of sales
- Sales force estimates
- General economic conditions
- Competitors' actions
- Changes in the firm's prices
- Changes in product mix
- Results of market research studies
- Advertising and sales promotion plans

---

### Example 1    Sales Budget

**Facts:** Blanchforte Stereo is a retailer of audio equipment. Blanchforte's sales manager is working with the controller to develop the sales budget for the next year. Blanchforte's sales manager knows that sales volume is seasonal and that it can be influenced by price and by promotions. The sales manager has developed the following sales forecasts based on units to be sold and average selling price.

**Assumptions for Forecasts**

First-quarter sales are often weak. The sales manager projects the following sales volumes for aggregate units and average prices.

- 2,000 units at full retail of $75
- 2,500 units assuming discounts down to $60

Second-quarter sales strengthen somewhat for graduation and Father's Day promotions. A greater volume and ability to collect full retail can be anticipated based on promotions.

- 3,000 units at full retail of $75
- 4,000 units assuming discounts down to $60

Third-quarter sales historically decline despite summer vacation and back-to-school promotions.

- 1,500 units at full retail of $75
- 2,000 assuming discounts down to $50

(continued)

---

(continued)

Fourth-quarter sales spike in response to holiday spending.

- 7,000 units at full retail of $75

- 10,000 units at discounts down to $60

**Required:** Use the sales forecasts to develop the sales budget, assuming that the company has selected a cost-leadership strategy.

**Solution:**

|  | Q1 | Q2 | Q3 | Q4 | Total |
|---|---|---|---|---|---|
| Sales (units) | 2,500 | 4,000 | 2,000 | 10,000 | |
| Average price | × $60 | × $60 | × $50 | × $60 | |
| Total | $150,000 | + $240,000 | + $100,000 | + $600,000 | = $1,090,000 |

# 6  Operating Budgets: Production Budget

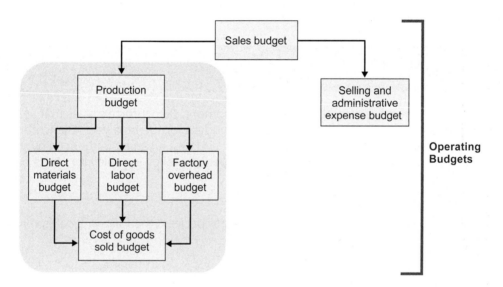

*Production/inventory budgets* are prepared for each product or each department based on the amount that will be produced, stated in units. The production budget is made up of the amounts spent for direct labor, direct materials, and factory overhead. The amount of the production budget is based on the amounts of inventory on hand and the inventory necessary to sustain sales.

## 6.1 Establishing Required Levels of Production

■ The relationship between production, sales, and inventory levels is displayed in the following formula:

> Budgeted sales
>
> + Desired ending inventory
>
> – Beginning inventory
> _____
>
> Budgeted production

■ Desired levels of inventory are normally a function of sales volume and seek to balance the risk of stockouts with the cost of maintaining inventory.

| Example 2 | Production Budget |
|---|---|

**Facts:** Carlisle Manufacturing is trying to estimate the level of production for the month of June. Assume that Carlisle wants safety stock in beginning inventory of 30 percent of estimated sales and that estimated sales for June and July are as follows:

June ⟶ 40,000
July ⟶ 30,000

**Required:** Compute the estimated inventory amounts and estimated production for June.

**Solution:**

Estimated inventory amounts:

| | June | July |
|---|---|---|
| Sales | 40,000 | 30,000 |
| Safety stock percentage | × 30% | × 30% |
| Beginning inventory required | 12,000 | 9,000 |

Estimated production for June:

| | |
|---|---|
| Budgeted sales for June | 40,000 |
| Desired ending inventory | + 9,000 |
| Estimated beginning inventory | – 12,000 |
| Budgeted production | 37,000 |

■ **Other Factors Affecting the Production Budget**

- Company policies regarding stable production
- Condition of production equipment
- Availability of productive resources
- Experience with production yields and quality

## 6.2   Direct Materials Budgets

The direct materials required to support the production budget are defined by the direct materials purchases budget and the direct materials usage budget.

### 6.2.1   Direct Materials Purchases Budget

The *direct materials purchases budget* represents the dollar amount of purchases of direct materials required to sustain production requirements.

- **Number of Units to Be Purchased:** The number of units of direct materials to purchase is calculated from the production budget. The formula is:

> Units of direct materials needed for a production period
> \+   Desired ending inventory at the end of the period
> –   Beginning inventory at the start of the period
> _____
> Units of direct materials to be purchased for the period

- **Cost of Direct Materials to Be Purchased:** The cost of direct materials purchased is calculated by applying the anticipated cost per unit of direct materials to the computed amount of direct materials to be purchased.

> Units of direct materials to be purchased for the period
> ×   Cost per unit
> _____
> Cost of direct materials to be purchased for the period (purchases at cost)

### 6.2.2   Direct Materials Usage Budget (Cost of Direct Materials Used)

The direct materials usage budget represents the number of units of direct materials required for production along with the related cost of those direct materials.

- The extended costs associated with direct materials are derived as follows:

> Beginning inventory at cost
> \+   Purchases at cost
> –   Ending inventory at cost
> _____
> Direct materials usage (cost of materials used)

### 6.2.3   Impact of Purchasing Policies

Purchases budgets are influenced by management's philosophy regarding required inventory levels, including safety stock and stockout decisions.

## 6.3   Direct Labor Budget

*Direct labor budgets* anticipate the hours and rates associated with workers directly involved in meeting production requirements. Direct labor hours are computed based on the hours necessary to produce each unit of finished goods.

|  | |
|---|---|
| **Budgeted production (in units)** | |
| × **Hours (or fractions of hours) required to produce each unit** | |
| **Total number of hours needed** | |
| × **Hourly wage rate** | |
| **Total wages** | |

---

### Example 3     Direct Materials and Labor Budgets

**Facts:** Carlisle Manufacturing computed its budgeted production at 37,000 units to sustain budgeted sales of 40,000 units in the month of June. Four pounds of direct material are needed to produce each unit of finished product. We assume that new direct materials cost $10 per pound and that they were previously acquired for $9 per pound. Carlisle has 48,000 pounds on hand at the beginning of June and has a desired direct materials ending inventory of 36,000.

Two hours of direct labor at $20 per hour are needed to convert the direct materials to finished goods.

**Required:** Prepare the direct materials and direct labor budgets for the month of June.

**Solution:**

**Direct materials purchases**

*Units of direct materials needed for a production period*

| | | |
|---|---:|---|
| Budgeted production | 37,000 | units |
| Pounds of direct material per unit | × 4 | pounds |
| Total pounds needed | 148,000 | pounds |

*+ Desired ending inventory at the end of the period*

| | | |
|---|---:|---|
| Pounds of direct material | 36,000 | pounds |

*− Beginning inventory at the start of the period*

| | | |
|---|---:|---|
| Pounds of direct material | (48,000) | pounds |
| Direct material to be purchased | 136,000 | |
| Cost per pound | × $10 | |
| Direct material purchases | $1,360,000 | |

(continued)

(continued)

**Direct materials usage budget (cost of direct materials used)**

| | |
|---|---|
| Beginning inventory at cost (48,000 × $9) | $432,000 |
| + Purchases at cost | 1,360,000 |
| − Ending inventory at cost (36,000 × $10) | (360,000) |
| = Direct materials usage (cost of materials used) | $1,432,000 |

**Direct labor budget**

| | | |
|---|---|---|
| Budgeted production | 37,000 | units |
| Hours of direct labor per unit | ×          2 | hours |
| Total hours needed | 74,000 | hours |
| Rate per hour | ×      $20 | |
| Direct labor budget | $1,480,000 | |

## 6.4 Factory Overhead Budget

*Factory overhead* includes the fixed and variable production costs that are not direct labor or direct materials. Factory overhead is applied to inventory (cost of goods manufactured and sold, below) based on a representative statistic (cost driver). Frequently, the rate is applied using direct labor hours.

| Example 4 | Factory Overhead Budget |
|---|---|

**Facts:** Carlisle Manufacturing uses direct labor hours to apply variable factory overhead and has determined that its variable overhead rate is $5 per hour. Assume that the company used 74,000 direct labor hours according to the direct labor budget.

**Required:** Compute the variable overhead to be applied to the cost of goods manufactured in the month of June.

**Solution:** Budgeted overhead = 74,000 direct labor hours × $5 per hour = $370,000

## 6.5 Cost of Goods Manufactured and Sold Budget

The *cost of goods manufactured and sold budget* accumulates the information from the direct labor, direct material, and factory overhead budgets.

### 6.5.1 Components of the Costs of Goods Manufactured and Sold Budget

The cost of goods manufactured represents the sum of the budgets for each element of manufacturing as follows:

- Direct labor
- Direct material
- Factory overhead

Cost of goods sold considers cost of goods manufactured in relation to beginning and ending inventories of finished goods as follows:

> Cost of goods manufactured
> + Beginning finished goods inventory
> – Ending finished goods inventory
> _____
> Cost of goods sold

---

### Example 5    Cost of Goods Manufactured and Sold

**Facts:** Carlisle Manufacturing is preparing its budgeted cost of goods manufactured and budgeted cost of goods sold schedules for the month of June. It has developed the following information:

| | |
|---|---|
| Direct materials used | $1,432,000 |
| Direct labor | 1,480,000 |
| Factory overhead (variable) | 370,000 |
| Factory overhead (fixed) | 300,000 (given) |
| Finished goods (beginning) | 1,000,000 (given) |
| Finished goods (ending) | 750,000 (given) |

**Required:** Compute the cost of goods manufactured.

**Solution:**

| | |
|---|---|
| Direct materials used | $1,432,000 |
| Direct labor | 1,480,000 |
| Factory overhead (variable) | 370,000 |
| Factory overhead (fixed) | 300,000 |
| Total cost of goods manufactured | 3,582,000 |
| | |
| Plus finished goods, beginning | 1,000,000 |
| Goods available | 4,582,000 |
| Less finished goods, ending | (750,000) |
| Cost of goods sold | $3,832,000 |

---

### 6.5.2   Cost of Goods Sold and the Pro Forma Financial Statements

The budgeted cost of goods sold amount feeds directly into the pro forma income statement. Budgeted cost of goods sold is matched with budgeted sales as a basis for budgeted gross margin.

# 7 Operating Budgets: Selling and Administrative Expense Budget

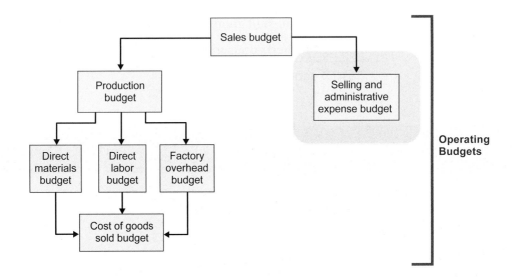

Selling and administrative expenses represent the fixed and variable nonmanufacturing expenses anticipated during the budget period.

## 7.1 Components of Selling and General Administration Expense

### 7.1.1 Variable Selling Expenses

■ Sales commissions

■ Delivery expenses

■ Bad-debt expenses

### 7.1.2 Fixed Selling Expenses

■ Sales salaries

■ Advertising

■ Depreciation

### 7.1.3 General Administrative Expenses (All Fixed)

■ Administrative salaries

■ Accounting and data processing

■ Depreciation

■ Other administrative expenses

## 7.2 Selling and Administrative Expenses and the Pro Forma Financial Statements

*Selling and administrative expenses* are not inventoried and are budgeted as period costs. Budgeted selling and administrative expenses are matched in their entirety against budgeted sales.

---

**Question 1**                                                                CPA-05829

Which of the following listings correctly describes the order in which the four types of budgets must be prepared?

    **a.**   Production, direct materials purchases, sales, cash disbursements.

    **b.**   Sales, production, direct materials purchases, cash disbursements.

    **c.**   Cash disbursements, direct materials purchases, production, sales.

    **d.**   Sales, direct materials purchases, production, cash disbursements.

---

**Question 2**                                                                CPA-04793

Johnson Co. is preparing its master budget for the first quarter of next year. Budgeted sales and production for one of the company's products are as follows:

| Month | Sales | Production |
|-------|-------|------------|
| January | 10,000 | 12,000 |
| February | 12,000 | 11,000 |
| March | 15,000 | 16,000 |

Each unit of this product requires 4 pounds of raw materials. Johnson's policy is to have sufficient raw materials on hand at the end of each month for 40 percent of the following month's production requirements. The January 1 raw materials inventory is expected to conform with this policy.

How many pounds of raw materials should Johnson budget to purchase for January?

    **a.**   11,600

    **b.**   46,400

    **c.**   48,000

    **d.**   65,600

---

## NOTES

# 1 Financial Budgets: Cash Budgets

Cash budgets represent detailed projections of cash receipts and disbursements. The cash budget is derived from other budgets based on cash collection and disbursement assumptions. Cash budgets provide management with information regarding the availability of funds for distribution to owners, for repayment of debt, and for investment. Cash budgets are generally divided into three major sections:

- Cash available
- Cash disbursements
- Financing

## 1.1 Cash Available

Cash available for use by the organization is normally associated with both balances available at the beginning of the period and cash collections.

### 1.1.1 Cash Balances

*Cash balances* are the amounts of cash on hand that can be used to liquidate expenses. Cash balances that are available for use are limited by management policies relative to minimum cash on hand and compensating balance agreements.

### 1.1.2 Cash Collections

*Cash collection* budgets specify the amounts of cash that will be received from sales, based on the sales budget and from anticipated loan proceeds.

- Cash collection budgets set standards for collections based on current-period sales (usually monthly) and prior-period sales (also usually monthly).

- Cash collection budgets make assumptions regarding the percentage of credit sales and the speed at which those collections will occur.

| Example 1 | Cash Collections |
|---|---|

**Facts:** Beck-Con Inc. is a U.S. retailer creating its cash budget for September. Based on historical data, it assumes the following information regarding collections:

- 80 percent of credit sales collected in the next month after sale.

- 18 percent of credit sales collected in the second month after sale.

- The remaining 2 percent will not be collected.

| Month | Type | Sales Dollars |
|---|---|---|
| July | Credit | $850,000 |
| August | Credit | $925,000 |
| September | Credit | $700,000 |
| September | Cash | $170,000 |

**Required:** Calculate cash collections for September.

**Solution:**

|  |  |  |
|---|---|---|
| July credit sales ($850,000 × 18%) | $ | 153,000 |
| + August credit sales ($925,000 × 80%) | | 740,000 |
| + September cash sales | | 170,000 |
| Total cash collections | | $1,063,000 |

## 1.2 Cash Disbursements

*Cash disbursements* budgets represent the cash outlays associated with purchases and with operating expenses.

### 1.2.1 Purchases

Cash disbursements budgets (for purchases) indicate the amount that is expected to be paid for *purchases*.

- Cash disbursements budgets include:

  - Cash purchases for the current period (generally the current month).

  - Credit purchases (accounts payable) for the current period.

  - Cash disbursements required to pay accounts payable during the current period.

- Cash disbursements budgets are developed using the percentage of goods bought on credit, the age of payables liquidated, and the percentage of goods purchased for cash.

## 1.2.2   Operating Expenses

Cash disbursements budgets (for operating expenses) specify the amounts paid out to defray the costs of *operating expenses*.

- Cash disbursements budgets eliminate noncash operating expenses (such as depreciation).

- Cash disbursements budgets include:

  - Percentage of prior month expenses to be paid in the current month.

  - Current month expenses for which disbursement is deferred until the following month.

  - Current month expenses paid in cash in the current month.

- Cash disbursements consider the effect of accounts payable (other operating expenses) and accrued payroll (wages).

---

### Example 2    Cash Disbursements

**Facts:** To forecast its cash disbursements for September, Beck-Con divided its outflows into the following categories:

| Cost Category | Applicable Dollar Amounts |
|---|---|
| Direct materials | $425,000 to be purchased in August, payable in September |
| Direct labor | $310,000 to be incurred and payable in September |
| Overhead | $150,000 in actual costs to be incurred and payable in September |
| Operating expenses | $145,000 in actual costs to be incurred and payable in September |
| Capital expenditures | $120,000 (from the capital expenditure budget) |
| Tax payments | None in September |
| Dividends | $35,000 payable in September, for the last quarter of the fiscal year |

**Required:** Calculate Beck-Con's cash disbursements for September.

**Solution:** September cash disbursements are calculated as follows:

|   | | |
|---|---|---:|
|   | Direct materials | $ 425,000 |
| + | Direct labor | 310,000 |
| + | Overhead | 150,000 |
| + | Operating expenses | 145,000 |
| + | Capital expenditures | 120,000 |
| + | Dividends | 35,000 |
|   | Total cash disbursements | $1,185,000 |

---

## 1.3  Financing

*Financing budgets* consider the manner in which operating (line of credit) financing will be used to maintain minimum cash balances or the manner in which excess or idle cash will be invested to ensure liquidity and adequate returns.

---

### Illustration 1     Financing Budget

Beck-Con forecasts a beginning cash balance for September 1 of $80,000. The company would like to ensure that the ending cash balance is at least $50,000. In order to accomplish this, it plans to borrow $95,000 at the end of September from its established line of credit at an annual interest rate of 6 percent. The first interest payment would not be due until October 31.

---

## 1.4  Cash Budget Formats

*Cash budgets* represent statements of planned cash receipts and disbursements and are primarily affected by the amounts used in the budgeted income statement. Cash budgets consider:

- Beginning cash
- Cash collections from sales (add)
- Cash disbursements for purchases and operating expenses (subtract)
- Computed ending cash
- Cash requirements to sustain operations (subtract)
- Working capital loans to maintain cash requirements

---

### Example 3     Combined Cash Budget

**Facts:** Beck-Con's cash budget includes a beginning balance of $80,000; cash collections of $1,063,000; cash payments of $1,185,000; and a letter of credit borrowing of $95,000.

**Required:** Prepare the cash budget that will allow the company to end September with a cash balance of $53,000.

**Solution:**

| | |
|---|---:|
| Beginning cash balance: | $  80,000 |
| + Cash collections | 1,063,000 |
| Total cash available | 1,143,000 |
| Less cash payments: | (1,185,000) |
| Ending cash balance (before financing) | $  (42,000) |
| | |
| Financing: | |
| Borrowings | $  95,000 |
| Interest payments | 0 |
| Repayments | 0 |
| Ending cash balance | $   53,000 |

---

# 2 Financial Budgets: Pro Forma Financial Statements

## 2.1 Pro Forma Income Statement

Key components of the budgeted income statement include the data described in the operating budgets:

- Sales budget
- Cost of goods sold budget (derived from the production budgets)
- Selling and administrative expense budget
- Interest expense budget (taken from the cash budget)

## 2.2 Pro Forma Balance Sheet

Budgeted balance sheets display the balances of each balance sheet account in a manner consistent with the income statement and cash budget plans developed above. Balance sheet accounts are adjusted for the cash collections and disbursements associated with the cash budget and the noncash transactions accounted for in the income statement.

## 2.3 Pro Forma Statement of Cash Flows

The budgeted statement of cash flows is derived from the budgeted income statement, the current and previous budgeted balance sheets, and then reconciled to the cash budget. Cash budgeting has the benefits of displaying the cash effects of the master budget on actual cash flows, assisting in the determination of whether additional sources of financing are required, and evaluating the optimal use of trade credit.

| Example 4 | Pro Forma Income Statement |
| --- | --- |

**Facts:** The CFO for Packer Company is creating a pro forma income statement for the upcoming fiscal year. The estimated current-year income statement shows:

| | |
| --- | --- |
| Sales | $500,000 |
| Cost of goods sold | (320,000) |
| SG&A | (60,000) |
| Interest expense | (20,000) |
| Pretax profit (EBT) | $100,000 |

For the next fiscal year, the CFO forecasts the following:

- Sales growth of 5 percent.
- An inventory increase of $25,000, along with projected cost of goods manufactured of $365,000.
- An increase in SG&A expenses of $10,000.
- A pay down of a substantial amount of debt, reducing interest expense by $15,000.

(continued)

(continued)

**Required:** Create a pro forma income statement for the upcoming fiscal year.

**Solution:**

| | | |
|---|---|---|
| Sales | $525,000 | 5 percent growth over prior year's $500,000. |
| Cost of goods sold | (340,000) | COGM of $365,000—Increase in inventory balance of $25,000. |
| SG&A | (70,000) | Increase of $10,000 over prior year's $60,000. |
| Interest expense | (5,000) | Decrease of $15,000 over prior year's $20,000. |
| Pretax profit (EBT) | $110,000 | Overall $10,000 increase over prior year's $100,000. |

# 3 Capital Budgets

*Capital purchases budgets* identify and allow management to evaluate the capital additions of the organization, often over a multiyear period. Financing is a significant component of the capital purchases budget. Capital budgets detail the planned expenditures for capital items (e.g., facilities, equipment, new products, and other long-term investments). Capital budgets are highly dependent on the availability of cash or credit, and they generally involve long-term commitments by the organization.

## 3.1 Pro Forma Balance Sheet

Planned additions of capital equipment and related debt from the capital budget are added to the balance sheet.

## 3.2 Pro Forma Income Statement

Planned additions of capital equipment are considered in developing budgeted depreciation expense; interest expense associated with planned financing is included as an expense.

## 3.3 Cash Budget

Planned financing expenses and principal repayments are included as disbursements on the cash budget.

# 4 Flexible Budgeting

A *flexible budget* is a financial plan prepared in a manner that allows for adjustments for changes in production or sales and accurately reflects expected costs for the adjusted output. Analysis focuses on substantive variances from standards rather than just simple changes in volume or activity. Flexible budgets represent adjustable economic models that are designed to predict outcomes and accommodate changes in actual activity. Revenues and expenses are adjusted to display anticipated levels for achieved outputs.

## 4.1 Assumptions and Uses

Flexible budgets include consideration of revenue per unit, variable costs per unit, and fixed costs over the relevant range within which the relationship between revenues and variable costs will remain unchanged and fixed costs will remain stable.

### 4.1.1 Yield

Flexible budgets consider the amount of cost per unit allowed for units of output.

### 4.1.2  Variance Analysis

Flexible budgets derive the expenses and revenues allowed from the output achieved for purposes of comparison to actual activity and performance evaluation.

## 4.2    Benefits and Limitations of the Flexible Budget

### 4.2.1  Benefits

Flexible budgets can display different volume levels within the relevant range to pinpoint areas in which efficiencies have been achieved or waste has occurred.

### 4.2.2  Limitations

Flexible budgets are highly dependent on the accurate identification of fixed and variable costs and the determination of the relevant range.

---

**Example 5**   **Flexible Budgeting**

**Facts:** The Flex-o-matic Corp. produces the Flex-o-matic, a piece of exercise equipment. Corporate Controller Felix Flexmeister is developing a flexible budget. Felix has already developed a master budget but estimates that the relevant range extends 20 percent above and below the master budget.

**Required:** Calculate income over the relevant range in dollars assuming a selling price of $60 per unit, variable costs of $40 per unit, fixed costs of $100,000, and anticipated output according to the master budget of 5,000 units.

**Solution:**

|                       | 80% of Master | Master Budget | 120% of Master |
|-----------------------|---------------|---------------|----------------|
| Sales                 | $240,000      | $300,000      | $360,000       |
| Variable costs        | (160,000)     | (200,000)     | (240,000)      |
| Contribution margin   | 80,000        | 100,000       | 120,000        |
| Fixed costs           | (100,000)     | (100,000)     | (100,000)      |
| Operating income      | $ (20,000)    | $        0    | $  20,000      |

---

**Question 1**                                                                              **CPA-03813**

The basic difference between a master budget and a flexible budget is that a master budget is:

    **a.**  Only used before and during the budget period and a flexible budget is only used after the budget period.

    **b.**  For an entire production facility and a flexible budget is applicable to single departments only.

    **c.**  Based on one specific level of production, and a flexible budget can be prepared for any production level within a relevant range.

    **d.**  Based on a fixed standard and a flexible budget allows management latitude in meeting goals.

---

| **Question 2** | **CPA-05867** |

A company's controller is adjusting next year's budget to reflect the effect of an expected 5 percent inflation rate. Listed below are selected items from next year's budget before the adjustment:

| | |
|---|---|
| Total salaries expense | $250,000 |
| Health costs | 100,000 |
| Depreciation expense | 65,000 |
| Interest expense on 10-year fixed-rate notes | 37,750 |

After adjusting for the 5 percent inflation rate, what is the company's total budget for the selected items before taxes for next year?

    **a.** $470,250

    **b.** $472,138

    **c.** $473,500

    **d.** $475,388

# 1 Actual vs. Plan

Variance analysis is a tool for comparing some measure of performance to a plan, budget, or standard for that measure. Variance analysis is used for planning and control purposes, and can be used to evaluate revenues and costs. Comparison of actual results to the annual business plan is the first and most basic level of control and evaluation of operations.

## 1.1 Performance Report

Actual results may be easily compared with budgeted results. However, usefulness is limited by the existence of budget variances that may be strictly related to volume.

---

**Example 1**  |  **Budget vs. Plan Performance Report**

**Facts:** Neostar Corporation has prepared its annual business plan for Year 1. The organization anticipated that it would sell 10,000 units of its product at $15 apiece, that its contribution margin percentage would be 20 percent, and that its fixed costs would be $25,000. Actual units sold numbered only 8,000 (totaling $112,000 in revenue); variable expenses materialized at $100,800 and fixed costs materialized at $24,000.

**Required:** Prepare a performance report comparing actual versus budgeted results.

**Solution:**

|  | Budget | Actual | Variance | |
|---|---|---|---|---|
| Revenue | $150,000 | $112,000 | $(38,000) | Unfavorable |
| Variable expenses | (120,000) | (100,800) | 19,200 | Favorable |
| Contribution margin | 30,000 | 11,200 | (18,800) | Unfavorable |
| Fixed costs | (25,000) | (24,000) | 1,000 | Favorable |
| Operating income | $ 5,000 | $ (12,800) | $(17,800) | Unfavorable |

Variances need significant analysis before they are useful. The favorable variance in variable expenses, for example, does not represent efficiencies. Budgeted contribution margin ratios are 20 percent; actual contribution margin ratios are 10 percent. Sales in units were off budget by 20 percent, yet revenue was down by 25 percent. Something is very wrong at Neostar, but what?

---

## 1.2 Use of Flexible Budgets to Analyze Performance

*Budget variance analysis* becomes progressively more sophisticated as managers review flexible budget comparisons. The flexible budget allows managers to identify how an individual change in a cost or revenue driver affects the overall cost of a process.

---

**Example 2** | **Flexible Budget Performance Report**

**Facts:** Management at Neostar has heard that flexible budgeting can provide more meaningful information.

**Required:** Prepare a flexible budget using the same information described in Example 1.

**Solution:**

Neostar Corporation
**Flexible Budget Performance Report**
For the year ended December 31, Year 1

| | Actual Results @ Actual | Flexible Budget Variances | Flexible Budget @ Actual (Planned Cost) | Sales Activity (Volume) Variances | Master Budget |
|---|---|---|---|---|---|
| Units | 8,000 | | 8,000 | | 10,000 |
| Sales | $112,000 | $ (8,000) | $120,000 | $(30,000) | $150,000 |
| Variable costs | (100,800) | (4,800) | (96,000) | 24,000 | (120,000) |
| Contribution margin | 11,200 | (12,800) | 24,000* | (6,000) | 30,000* |
| Fixed costs | (24,000) | 1,000 | (25,000) | – | (25,000) |
| Operating income | $ (12,800) | $(11,800) | $ (1,000) | $ (6,000) | $ 5,000 |
| | | | | | |
| Flexible budget variances | | (11,800) | | | |
| Sales activity (volume) variances | | | | (6,000) | |
| Total master budget variances | | | | | (17,800) |

*24,000 / 120,000 = 20%
 30,000 / 150,000 = 20%

Flexible budget variances show that revenue per unit was less than expected and variable costs per unit were greater than expected. The company has performed $11,800 worse than expected. Meanwhile, differences in volume produced a $6,000 unfavorable variance, yielding a total variance from the budget of $17,800.

Although we still do not know what is wrong with Neostar, we know where to look. Revenue is not materializing as expected despite efforts to discount our selling price (producing an unfavorable sales price variance of $8,000), and expenses are over budget (producing an unfavorable variable cost variance of $4,800 despite a favorable fixed-cost variance of $1,000).

---

# 2   Variance Analysis Using Standards

Variance analysis becomes increasingly sophisticated as the investigation of differences between budgeted and actual performance moves from the aggregate examinations associated with either performance reporting or flexible budget analysis to the computation of per-unit variances normally associated with the use of standard costing systems.

## 2.1   Standard Costing Systems

Standard costing systems are the most common cost-measurement systems. Standard costs, in the aggregate, measure the costs the firm expects that it *should* incur during production. In a standard costing system, standard costs are used for all manufacturing costs (i.e., raw materials, direct labor, and manufacturing overhead).

### 2.1.1   Calculations

■ **Direct Costs**

> Standard direct costs = Standard price × Standard quantity

■ **Indirect (Overhead) Costs**

> Standard indirect costs = Standard (predetermined) application rate × Standard quantity

### 2.1.2   Purposes of Standard Costing Systems

■ Cost control

■ Data for performance evaluations (variance analysis)

■ Ability to learn from standards and improve various processes

## 2.2   Variance Calculations Using Standards

### 2.2.1   Standard Cost Objectives

The objective of using a standard costing system is to attain a realistic predetermined or budgeted cost for use in planning and decision making. It also greatly simplifies bookkeeping procedures.

### 2.2.2   Evaluating Variances From Standard

The differences between actual amounts and standard amounts are called variances.

■ **Evaluating Results:** An actual cost lower than standard cost is called a *favorable* variance, and an actual cost higher than standard cost is called an *unfavorable* variance.

■ **Evaluating Control:** If a variance from standard could have been prevented, it is called a controllable variance; if not, the variance is known as an *uncontrollable* variance.

### 2.2.3  Product Costs Subject to Variance Analysis

Product costs generally consist of direct materials, direct labor, and manufacturing overhead. A favorable or unfavorable variance in total is a composite of a number of variances. Variances are typically calculated for the following cost elements:

- Direct materials (DM)
- Direct labor (DL)
- Variable manufacturing overhead (VOH)
- Fixed manufacturing overhead (FOH)

## 2.3  Direct Materials and Direct Labor Variance

For direct materials and direct labor, two variances are typically calculated: a price (or rate) variance and a quantity (or efficiency) variance. The variance calculations may be approached in either an equation or a tabular format. Both are presented below:

### 2.3.1  Equation Format

> DM price variance = Actual quantity purchased × (Actual price − Standard price)
>
> DM quantity usage variance = Standard price × (Actual quantity used − Standard quantity allowed)
>
> DL rate variance = Actual hours worked × (Actual rate − Standard rate)
>
> DL efficiency variance = Standard rate × (Actual hours worked − Standard hours allowed)

Materials and labor variances are expense variances. When actual price/rate or actual quantity/ hours exceed standards, variances are unfavorable. If standards exceed actuals, variances are favorable.

### 2.3.2  Tabular Format

The variance is computed by comparing two totals. If a figure on the left (actual) is larger than a figure on the right (standard), then the variance is unfavorable; if the figure on the left is smaller, the variance is favorable. The specific variances follow:

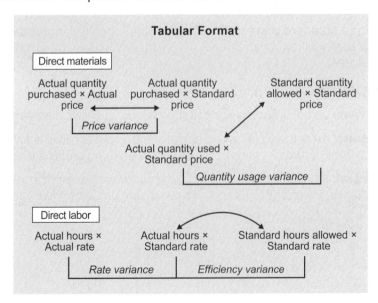

## Illustration 1     Materials Variances Using Equation and Tabular Formats

Actual quantity purchased          200 units
Actual quantity used               110 units
Units standard quantity            100 units
Actual price paid                    $8 per unit
Standard price                      $10 per unit

$$DM\ price\ variance = AQ_{purchased} \times (AP - SP)$$
$$= 200\ units \times (\$8/unit - \$10/unit)$$
$$= \$400\ Favorable$$

$$DM\ quantity\ variance = SP \times (AQ_{used} - SQ_{allowed})$$
$$= \$10/unit \times (110\ units - 100\ units)$$
$$= \$100\ Unfavorable$$

| Actual quantity purchased × Actual price | Actual quantity purchased × Standard price | Standard quantity allowed × Standard price |
|---|---|---|
| 200 × $8 = $1,600 | 200 × $10 = $2,000 | 100 × $10 = $1,000 |

Price variance = $400 F

Actual quantity used × Standard price

Quantity usage variance
110 × $10 = $1,100
= $100 U

## Illustration 2     Labor Variances Using Equation and Tabular Formats

Actual hours worked               450 hours
Standard hours                    500 hours
Actual paid rate                   $20 per hour
Standard rate                      $15 per hour

$$DL\ rate\ variance = AH_{worked} \times (AR - SR)$$
$$= 450\ hours\ worked \times (\$20/hour - \$15/hour)$$
$$= \$2,250\ Unfavorable$$

$$DL\ efficiency\ variance = SR \times (AH_{worked} - SH_{allowed})$$
$$= \$15/hour \times (450\ hours\ worked - 500\ hours\ allowed)$$
$$= \$750\ Favorable$$

| Actual hours × Actual rate | Actual hours × Standard rate | Standard hours allowed × Standard rate |
|---|---|---|
| 450 × $20 = $9,000 | 450 × $15 = $6,750 | 500 × $15 = $7,500 |

Rate variance = $2,250 U      Efficiency variance = $750 F

## 2.4    Manufacturing Overhead Variance

At a high level, the analysis of manufacturing overhead compares the actual overhead incurred in a period to the applied overhead in that same period. Overhead is estimated and applied based on a predetermined overhead application rate.

### 2.4.1    Underapplied and Overapplied Overhead

If the actual amount of overhead incurred in the period exceeds the amount applied, overhead will be considered underapplied and the overhead account will have a net debit balance. This will result in an unfavorable variance because the actual amount of overhead incurred is higher than expected.

If the actual amount of overhead incurred is less than the amount applied, overhead will be considered overapplied and the overhead account will have a net credit balance. The variance will be favorable because the actual overhead incurred is less than expected.

### 2.4.2    Variable and Fixed Overhead Variances

The overall manufacturing overhead variance can be broken into variable and fixed overhead variances. The variable overhead (VOH) variance can be further broken into a rate (spending) variance and an efficiency variance. The fixed overhead (FOH) variance can be divided into a budget (spending) variance and a volume variance. Although the variable and fixed overhead spending variances can be combined for calculation purposes, they serve different functions from a strategic/analytical perspective.

### Pass Key

The equations for the four overhead variances are as follows:

- VOH rate (spending) variance = Actual hours × (Actual rate – Standard rate)

- VOH efficiency variance = Standard rate × (Actual hours – Standard hours allowed for actual production volume)

- FOH budget (spending) variance = Actual fixed overhead – Budgeted fixed overhead

- FOH volume variance = Budgeted fixed overhead – Standard fixed overhead cost allocated to production*

*Based on Actual production × Standard rate

### 2.4.3    Establishing Overhead Application Rates

Overhead rates are applied using various cost drivers that most appropriately assign the components of overhead cost pools to production. Predetermined fixed and variable overhead rates are established by dividing planned fixed and variable overhead amounts by a suitable cost driver.

### 2.4.4    Application of Overhead

Overhead is applied to production based on the predetermined rate per cost driver times the standard cost driver allowed for the actual level of activity (hours worked, units produced, etc.).

## Pass Key

When standard costing is used, the application of overhead is accomplished in two steps:

- **Step 1:** Calculated overhead rate = Budgeted overhead costs ÷ Estimated cost driver
- **Step 2:** Applied overhead = Standard cost driver for actual level of activity × Overhead rate (from Step 1)

### 2.4.5 Interpretation

Overhead variances represent the analysis of balance in the overhead account after overhead has been applied. Overapplied overhead (more credit) is favorable, as it will ultimately result in a credit to cost of goods sold at the end of the period and therefore a reduction in expenses (and increase in profits). Underapplied (more debit) is unfavorable, as the eventual debit to cost of goods sold will increase expenses and therefore decrease profits. Each component of the variance computation follows the same logic.

- If the number on the right is greater than the number on the left (more credit), then the variance is favorable.

- If the number on the left is greater than the number on the right (more debit), then the variance is unfavorable.

- The sum of all variances equals the net balance in the overhead account.

### 2.4.6 Variable Manufacturing Overhead Variances

- **Variable Overhead Rate (Spending) Variance**

> VOH rate (spending) variance = Actual hours × (Actual rate – Standard rate)

This variance tells managers whether more or less was spent on variable overhead than expected. A favorable variance occurs when the standard rate exceeds the actual rate, which is beneficial to a company because it means that it paid less per labor hour than anticipated. An unfavorable variance occurs when the actual rate exceeds the standard rate, which means that the company paid more per labor hour than it expected to spend.

- **Variable Overhead Efficiency Variance**

> $$\text{VOH efficiency variance} = \text{Standard rate} \times (\text{Actual hours} - \text{Standard hours allowed for actual production volume})$$

This variance is tied to the efficiency with which labor hours are utilized. The efficiency variance isolates the amount of total variable overhead variance that is due to using more or fewer direct labor hours than what was budgeted (assuming that direct labor hours is the cost driver). In other words, given what was produced in terms of output, did it require more or fewer labor hours than anticipated? A favorable variance results from using fewer labor hours than budgeted, and an unfavorable variance stems from using more labor hours than budgeted.

### 2.4.7   Fixed Manufacturing Overhead Variances

■ **Fixed Overhead Budget (Spending) Variance**

$$\text{FOH budget (spending) variance} = \text{Actual fixed overhead} - \text{Budgeted fixed overhead}$$

Companies budget an amount for fixed overhead costs every period, and this variance focuses at a high level on whether more or less was spent than budgeted. All of the actual fixed overhead costs are summed for the period and the total actual overhead is compared with the budgeted amount of fixed overhead. A favorable variance occurs when actual fixed overhead costs are less than budgeted, and an unfavorable variance results from actual fixed overhead costs exceeding the budgeted amount.

■ **Fixed Overhead Volume Variance**

$$\text{FOH volume variance} = \text{Budgeted fixed overhead} - \text{Standard fixed overhead cost allocated to production*}$$

*Based on actual production × Standard rate

Fixed overhead costs are typically applied using a rate derived from budgeted fixed overhead costs and expected volume (the cost driver). When the actual volume produced differs from the amount used to calculate the fixed overhead application rate, there will be a variance. A favorable variance occurs when volume is higher than anticipated, which implies that more units were produced using the same amount of fixed resources. An unfavorable variance occurs when volume is lower than anticipated, as fewer units were produced using a fixed amount of resources.

| Example 3 | Manufacturing Overhead Variance |
|---|---|

**Facts:** Lucy Inc. produces widgets and applies overhead costs based on direct labor hours. The table below provides budgeted and actual information on the number of widgets, labor hours, variable overhead costs, and fixed overhead costs for January.

**Required:** Using this information, calculate the rate and efficiency variable overhead variances, the budget and volume fixed overhead variances, and the overall overhead variance.

(continued)

(continued)

**Solution:**

| Number of Widgets | | |
|---|---|---|
| Budgeted number of widgets | 4,000 widgets | |
| Actual number of widgets | 3,800 widgets | |
| **Labor Hours** | | |
| Standard labor hours required per widget | 1.00 labor hour | |
| Standard labor hours total (based on actual production) | 3,800 hours | (3,800 widgets × 1.00 labor hour per widget) |
| Actual labor hours used | 3,900 hours | |
| **Variable Overhead** | | |
| Standard VOH Rate | $1.50 per hour | |
| Actual VOH Rate | $1.60 per hour | |
| Actual VOH Costs | $6,240 | (3,900 hours × $1.60 per hour) |
| **Fixed Overhead** | | |
| Standard FOH per widget | $3.00 per hour | |
| Budgeted FOH Costs | $12,000 | (4,000 budgeted widgets × 1.00 labor hour per widget × $3.00 per hour) |
| Actual FOH Costs | $10,560 | |

**VOH rate (spending):** 3,900 hours × ($1.60 – $1.50) = $390 Unfavorable

**VOH efficiency:** $1.50 × [3,900 hours – (3,800 × 1.00 hour)] = $150 Unfavorable

**FOH budget (spending):** $10,560 – $12,000 = $1,440 Favorable

**FOH volume:** $12,000 – *$11,400 = $600 Unfavorable

*3,800 hours budgeted (for production of 3,800 widgets) × $3 per hour

**Adding all of the variances produces a total overall favorable variance of $300:** $390U + $150U – $1,440F + $600U = $300F

**Overall variance:** $16,800 actual – $17,100 applied = $300 Favorable

**Actual overhead (FOH + VOH):** $16,800

   *Actual FOH:* $10,560

   *Actual VOH:* $6,240

**Applied overhead (FOH + VOH):** $17,100

   *Applied FOH:* $11,400 [3,800 standard labor hours (to produce 3,800 widgets) × $3.00 per hour]

   *Applied VOH:* $5,700 [3,800 standard labor hours (to produce 3,800 widgets) × $1.50 per hour]

| Interpretation | Driver |
|---|---|
| • Spending (VOH and FOH) | |
| —VOH rate: $390 Unfavorable | VOH rate was higher than anticipated |
| —FOH budget: $1,440 Favorable | Spent less than anticipated on FOH |
| • Efficiency (VOH only) | |
| —VOH efficiency: $150 Unfavorable | Took longer per unit than anticipated |
| • Volume (FOH only) | |
| —FOH volume: $600 Unfavorable | Produced fewer units than budgeted |

## 2.5 Sales and Contribution Margin Variances

Sales and contribution margin variance analyses can be used to evaluate the effectiveness of an entity's identification of target markets and its strategies to capture those markets. The sales variance (the difference between actual sales revenue and budgeted sales revenue) has various components, as described below.

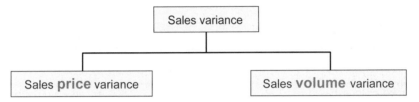

### 2.5.1 Sales Price Variance (or Sales Revenue Flexible Budget Variance)

The *sales price variance* measures the aggregate effect of a selling price different from the budget.

$$\text{Sales price variance} = \left[\frac{\text{Actual SP}}{\text{Unit}} - \frac{\text{Budgeted SP}}{\text{Unit}}\right] \times \text{Actual sold units}$$

- **Strategy and Mission:** Firms might reduce prices in an effort to move into a cost leadership strategy or increase prices in an effort to put a differentiation strategy into place. Variance results have specific implications in analyzing the effectiveness of a firm in reaching its target markets.

- **Interpretation:** A favorable variance in price (the actual sales price exceeds the budgeted sales price) can result in untapped profit potential for a firm. If a firm plans to increase its market share or sales volume simply by reducing sales prices, however, it can risk reducing the profitability of the firm if the expected volume increase is not enough to cover the reduction in price.

| Example 4 | Sales Price Variance |
|---|---|

**Facts:** In Cascade Company's January budget, the company shows 3,000 budgeted units sold, a sale price of $16 per unit, and variable costs of $10 per unit. The company actually sells 4,000 units at a price of $14 per unit.

**Required:** Calculate Cascade's sales price variance for January.

**Solution:** Sales price variance = ($14 – $16) × 4,000 = $8,000 unfavorable. This variance is unfavorable because the per-unit selling price was less than anticipated.

### 2.5.2 Sales Volume Variance

The *sales volume variance* is a flexible budget variance that distills volume activity from other sales performance components. The basic sales volume variance is:

$$\text{Sales volume variance} = \left[\begin{array}{c}\text{Actual} \\ \text{sold units}\end{array} - \begin{array}{c}\text{Budgeted} \\ \text{sales units}\end{array}\right] \times \text{Standard contribution margin per unit}$$

A favorable variance exists when more units are sold than budgeted, and an unfavorable variance occurs when budgeted units exceed actual units.

| Example 5 | Sales Volume Variance |
|---|---|

**Facts:** In Cascade Company's January budget, the company shows 3,000 budgeted units sold, a sale price of $16 per unit, and variable costs of $10 per unit. The company actually sells 4,000 units at a price of $14 per unit.

**Required:** Calculate Cascade's sales volume variance for January.

**Solution:** Sales volume variance = (4,000 − 3,000) × $6 = $6,000 Favorable. This variance is favorable because the company sold more units than it anticipated.

| Question 1 | CPA-03836 |
|---|---|

The standard direct material cost to produce a unit of Lem is 4 meters of material at $2.50 per meter. During May of the current year, 4,200 meters of material costing $10,080 were purchased and used to produce 1,000 units of Lem. What was the material price variance for May?

- **a.** $400 favorable
- **b.** $420 favorable
- **c.** $80 unfavorable
- **d.** $480 unfavorable

| Question 2 | CPA-05251 |
|---|---|

A company produces widgets with budgeted standard direct materials of 2 pounds per widget at $5 per pound. Standard direct labor was budgeted at 0.5 hour per widget at $15 per hour. The actual usage in the current year was 25,000 pounds and 3,000 hours to produce 10,000 widgets. What was the direct labor usage variance?

- **a.** $25,000 favorable
- **b.** $25,000 unfavorable
- **c.** $30,000 favorable
- **d.** $30,000 unfavorable

---

**Question 3**                                                                      CPA-05874

A company uses a standard costing system. At the end of the current year, the company provides the following overhead information:

*Actual overhead incurred:*

| | |
|---|---|
| Variable | $90,000 |
| Fixed | 62,000 |
| Budgeted fixed overhead | 65,000 |
| Variable overhead rate (per direct labor hour) | 8 |
| Standard hours allowed for actual production | 12,000 |
| Actual labor hours used | 11,000 |

What amount is the variable overhead efficiency variance?

    **a.** $8,000 favorable

    **b.** $8,000 unfavorable

    **c.** $6,000 favorable

    **d.** $2,000 unfavorable

---

**Question 4**                                                                      CPA-03831

Baby Frames Inc. evaluates manufacturing overhead by using variance analysis. The following information applies to the month of May:

| | *Actual* | *Budgeted* |
|---|---|---|
| Number of frames manufactured | 19,000 | 20,000 |
| Variable overhead costs | $ 4,100 | $ 2 per direct labor hour |
| Fixed overhead costs | 22,000 | 20,000 $1 per unit |
| Direct labor hours | 2,100 hours | 0.1 hour per frame |

What is the production volume variance?

    **a.** $1,000 favorable

    **b.** $1,000 unfavorable

    **c.** $2,000 favorable

    **d.** $2,000 unfavorable

| **Question 5** | **CPA-06165** |
| --- | --- |

Anderson Corporation budgeted sales of 6,250 at $12 per unit but achieved sales of 5,000 at $15 per unit. Anderson would compute a selling price variance of:

    **a.**  $0

    **b.**  $3,750

    **c.**  $15,000

    **d.**  $18,750

## NOTES

# BEC
# 5

# Economic Concepts and Analysis

**Module**

# 1 Economics

*Economics* is defined as a science that studies human behavior as the relationship between ends and scarce means that have alternative uses. In essence, economics is about people (e.g., individuals, corporations, governments) and the choices they make. Because economics is a crucial component of the business environment which ultimately affects an individual's, company's, or government's performance (and financial reporting), it is considered an important area of study in the Business Environment and Concepts (BEC) curriculum.

# 2 Business Cycles

## 2.1 Introduction

Business cycles refer to the rise and fall of economic activity relative to long-term growth trends (i.e., the swings in total national output, income, and employment over time). Although the economy tends to grow over time, the growth in economic activity is not stable. Rather, economic activity is characterized by fluctuations, and these fluctuations are known as business cycles. Business cycles vary in duration and severity. The analysis of business cycles is part of the field of macroeconomics. Macroeconomics is the study of the economy as a whole. It examines the determinants of national income, unemployment, inflation, and how monetary and fiscal policies affect economic activity.

## 2.2 Measuring Economic Activity (Gross Domestic Product)

Because business cycles refer to the rise and fall of economic activity, it is important to first examine how economic activity is measured. The most common measure of the economic activity or output of an economy is gross domestic product (GDP). GDP is the total market value of all final goods and services produced within the borders of a nation in a particular period. The term "final goods and services" *excludes used* goods that have been resold; GDP is the nation's output of goods and services. Note that GDP includes all final goods and services produced by resources *within* a country regardless of who owns the resources. Thus, U.S. GDP includes the output of foreign-owned factories in the United States but excludes the output of U.S.-owned factories operating abroad.

## 2.3 Nominal vs. Real GDP

### 2.3.1 Nominal GDP

Nominal GDP (unadjusted) measures the value of all final goods and services in prices prevailing at the time of production. That is, nominal GDP measures the value of all final goods and services in current prices.

### 2.3.2 Real GDP

Real GDP (adjusted) measures the value of all final goods and services in constant prices. That is, real GDP is adjusted to account for changes in the price level (i.e., it removes the effects of inflation by using a price index). Real GDP is the most commonly used measure of economic activity and national output (i.e., the total output of an economy).

The price index used to calculate real GDP is called the GDP deflator. It is a price index for all goods and services included in GDP. Using the GDP deflator, real GDP is calculated as the ratio of nominal GDP to the GDP deflator times 100.

$$\text{Real GDP} = \frac{\text{Nominal GDP}}{\text{GDP deflator}} \times 100$$

---

| Example 1 | Application of Price Index to Determine Real GDP |
|---|---|

**Facts:** Assume that a local economist is attempting to measure an economy's real GDP and the change in real GDP from the prior year. Based on his research, the following economic data is gathered on the economy's production:

|  | Current Year | Prior Year |
|---|---|---|
| Nominal GDP ($ billions) | $3,450.3 | $3,286.0 |
| GDP deflator | 107.0 | 105.0 |

**Required:** Using the table above, calculate the real GDP for the current year and prior year and the change in real GDP for the economy.

**Solution:** The following formula is used to measure real GDP:

$$\text{Real GDP} = \frac{\text{Nominal GDP}}{\text{GDP deflator}} \times 100$$

$$\text{Current year} = \frac{\$3,450.3}{107.0} \times 100$$

$$= \textbf{\$3,224.6 billion}$$

$$\text{Prior year} = \frac{\$3,286.0}{105.0} \times 100$$

$$= \textbf{\$3,129.5 billion}$$

The following formula is used to measure the change in real GDP:

$$\%\,\Delta\,\text{Real GDP} = \frac{\text{Current year real GDP}}{\text{Past year real GDP}} - 1$$

$$= \frac{\$3,224.6}{\$3,129.5} - 1$$

$$= \textbf{+3.04\%}$$

### 2.3.3   Real GDP per Capita and Economic Growth

Real GDP per capita is real GDP divided by population. Real GDP per capita is typically used to compare standards of living across countries or across time. Real GDP per capita is also used to measure economic growth. Economic growth is the increase in real GDP per capita over time.

## 2.4    Summary Composition of Business Cycles

As noted previously, economic activity is characterized by fluctuations, and these fluctuations are known as business cycles. Business cycles typically comprise the following:

- **Expansionary Phase:** An expansionary phase is characterized by rising economic activity (real GDP) and growth. During an expansionary phase, economic activity is rising above its long-term growth trend. Firms' profits are likely to be rising during an expansionary phase as the demand for goods and services increases. Firms also are likely to increase their workforces during an expansion, and the prices of goods and services are likely to be rising.

- **Peak:** A peak is a high point of economic activity. It marks the end of an expansionary phase and the beginning of a contractionary phase in economic activity. At the peak of a business cycle, firms' profits are likely to be at their highest levels. Firms also are likely to face capacity constraints and input shortages (raw material and labor), leading to higher costs and higher overall price levels.

- **Contractionary Phase:** A contractionary phase is characterized by falling economic activity and growth, and follows a peak. During a contractionary phase, firms' profits are likely to be falling from their highest levels.

- **Trough:** A trough is a low point of economic activity. At this point of the business cycle, firms' profits are likely to be at their lowest levels. Firms also are likely to experience significant excess production capacity, leading them to reduce their workforces and cut costs.

- **Recovery Phase:** A recovery phase follows a trough. During a recovery phase, economic activity begins to increase and return to its long-term growth trend. Further, firms' profits typically begin to stabilize as the demand for goods and services begins to rise.

**Business Cycles**

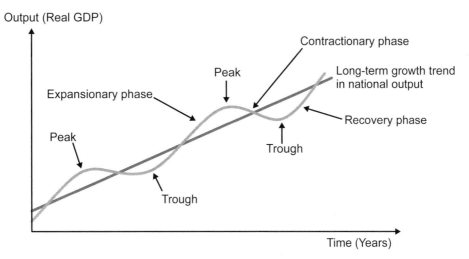

## 2.5    Terminology Used in Describing Business Cycles

### 2.5.1    Recession

A recession occurs when the economy experiences negative real economic growth (declines in national output). Economists define a recession as two consecutive quarters of falling national output. During a recession, firms' profits tend to fall and many firms incur losses. Firms also are likely to have excess capacity. As a result, during a recession, resources (including labor) are likely to be underutilized and unemployment is likely to be high.

### 2.5.2    Depression

A depression is a very severe recession. It is characterized by a relatively long period of stagnation in business activity and high unemployment rates. As a result, firms experience significant excess capacity. Furthermore, due to the significant reduction in the demand for goods and services, it is likely that many firms will go out of business during a depression.

# 3    Economic Indicators

Although business cycles tend to be irregular and unpredictable, economists nevertheless attempt to predict business cycles and their severity and duration using economic indicators. Economic indicators (gathered by The Conference Board) are statistics that historically have been highly correlated with economic activity. They can be "leading indicators," "lagging indicators," or "coincident indicators."

## 3.1    Leading Indicators

Leading indicators tend to predict economic activity. They change before the economy starts to follow a certain trend. The government routinely revises the numbers as more data becomes available. Thus, leading indicators are subject to change.

Leading indicators include:

- Average new unemployment claims
- Building permits for residences
- Average length of the workweek
- Money supply (M2)
- Standard & Poor's 500 stock index
- Orders for goods
- Price changes of materials
- Index of consumer expectations
- Interest rate spread
- Index of supply deliveries

## 3.2    Lagging Indicators

Lagging indicators tend to follow economic activity; i.e., they change after a given economic trend has already started. They give signals after the fact. Economists measure lagging indicators to confirm or dispute previous forecasts and the effectiveness of policy directives.

Lagging indicators include:

- Prime rate charged by banks
- Average duration of unemployment
- Commercial and industrial loans outstanding
- Consumer price index for services
- Consumer debt-to-income ratio
- Changes in labor cost per unit of manufacturing output
- Inventories-to-sales ratio

## 3.3 Coincident Indicators

Coincident indicators change at approximately the same time as the whole economy, thereby providing information about the current state of the economy. A coincident indicator may be used to identify, after the fact, the timing of peaks and troughs in a business cycle.

Coincident indicators include:

- Industrial production
- Manufacturing and trade sales
- Industrial production (GDP)
- Personal income less transfer payments

# 4 Reasons for Fluctuations

Although there are a variety of theories regarding the cause of business cycles, economists generally agree that business cycles result from shifts in aggregate demand and/or aggregate supply. Aggregate demand and aggregate supply curves can be used to illustrate the relationship between a country's output (real GDP) and price level (the GDP deflator). They also are used to examine the causes of economic fluctuations.

## 4.1 Aggregate Demand (AD) Curve

The aggregate demand (AD) curve illustrates the maximum quantity of all goods and services that households, firms, and the government are willing and able to purchase at any given price level. The curve shows the relationship between total output (real GDP) of the economy and the price level. Note that this "aggregate" demand curve is the macroeconomic demand curve of the "total" demand in the economy as a whole. The x-axis is real GDP and the y-axis is the price level.

## 4.2 Aggregate Supply (AS) Curve

The aggregate supply (AS) curve illustrates the maximum quantity of all goods and services producers are willing and able to produce at any given price level. Note that this "aggregate" supply curve is the macroeconomic supply curve of the "total" supply in the economy as a whole.

### 4.2.1 Short-Run Aggregate Supply Curve

The short-run aggregate supply (SRAS) curve is upward sloping, illustrating that as the price level rises, firms are willing to produce more goods and services.

### 4.2.2   Long-Run Aggregate Supply Curve

The long-run aggregate supply (LRAS) curve is vertical, illustrating that in the long run, if all resources are fully utilized, output is determined solely by the factors of production. This curve corresponds to the potential level of output in the economy.

### 4.2.3   Potential Level of Output (Potential GDP)

Potential GDP refers to the level of real GDP (national output) that the economy would produce if its resources (capital and labor) were fully employed. When real GDP is below the potential level of output, the economy will typically be experiencing a recession. Similarly, when real GDP rises above the potential level of output, the economy typically will be experiencing an expansion.

**Aggregate Demand and Aggregate Supply Curves**

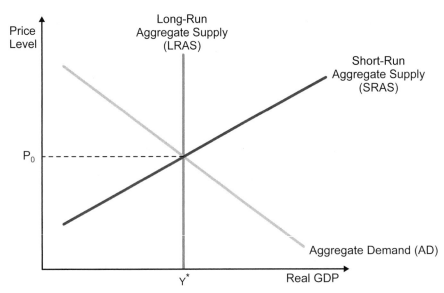

The intersection of the short-run aggregate supply (SRAS) curve and the aggregate demand (AD) curve determines the level of output (real GDP) and price level in the short run. The position of the long-run aggregate supply (LRAS) curve determines the level of output in the long run. The LRAS curve is vertical at the economy's potential level of output.

$Y^*$ = GDP at the potential (equilibrium) level of output

## 4.3   Aggregate Demand, Aggregate Supply, and Economic Fluctuations

Business cycles, or economic fluctuations, result from shifts in aggregate demand and short-run aggregate supply (note that shifts in the long-run aggregate supply curve are associated with long-run growth in the economy and do not affect business cycles).

### 4.3.1   Reduction in Demand

If circumstances cause individuals, businesses, or governments to reduce their demand for goods and services, economic activity (real GDP) will decline, leading to a contraction in economic activity and possibly a recession. As a result, a reduction in demand tends to cause firms' profits to decline. Firms also are likely to experience an increase in excess capacity, leading them to reduce their workforces.

### 4.3.2   Increase in Demand

In contrast, if circumstances cause individuals, businesses, and governments to increase their demand for goods and services, economic activity will rise, leading to a recovery or an expansion in economic activity. As a result, an increase in demand tends to cause firms' profits to rise. Firms also are likely to experience a reduction in excess capacity, leading them to increase their workforces.

### 4.3.3   Reduction of Supply

If circumstances cause firms to reduce their supply of goods and services, economic activity will fall, leading to a contraction or possibly a recession. As firms reduce their supply, they also are likely to reduce their workforces, leading to higher unemployment.

### 4.3.4   Increase in Supply

If circumstances cause firms to increase their supply of goods and services, economic activity will rise, leading to an expansionary phase of economic activity. As firms increase their supply, they also are likely to increase their workforces, leading to lower unemployment.

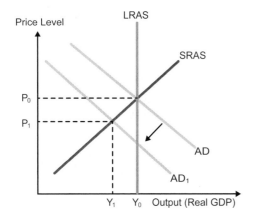

**Shift in Aggregate Demand**

**A recession caused by a shift in the aggregate demand curve:** A decrease in aggregate demand causes actual GDP to fall below potential GDP. This is illustrated as the leftward shift in aggregate demand. As a result, real GDP falls from $Y_0$ to $Y_1$.

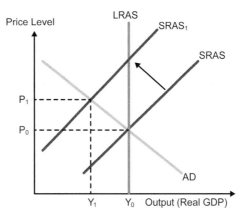

**Shift in Short-Run Aggregate Supply**

**A recession caused by a shift in the short-run aggregate supply curve:** A decrease in short-run aggregate supply causes actual GDP to fall below potential GDP. This is illustrated as the leftward shift in the short-run aggregate supply curve. As a result, real GDP falls from $Y_0$ to $Y_1$.

## 4.4   Factors That Shift Aggregate Demand

The primary factors that shift aggregate demand are:

### 4.4.1   Changes in Wealth

- **Increase in Wealth:** An increase in real wealth causes the aggregate demand curve to shift to the right. Thus, an increase in wealth causes the economy to expand and leads to an increase in national output (real GDP).

- **Decrease in Wealth:** A decrease in wealth causes the aggregate demand curve to shift to the left. A decrease in wealth does the opposite of an increase in wealth. For example, a large decline in stock prices would decrease consumer wealth and therefore shift the aggregate demand curve to the left. As a result, national output would fall, causing a contraction and possibly a recession.

### 4.4.2    Changes in Real Interest Rates

- **Increase in Real Interest Rates:** An increase in interest rates increases the cost of capital and, therefore, tends to reduce consumer demand for durable goods, such as new cars and homes, and firms' demand for new plants and equipment. Therefore, an increase in real interest rates causes the cost of capital to rise and shifts the aggregate demand curve to the left, causing national output to fall.

- **Decrease in Real Interest Rates:** A decrease in real interest rates reduces the cost of borrowing, thereby increasing the demand for investment goods and shifting the aggregate demand curve to the right, causing national output to rise.

### 4.4.3    Changes in Expectations About the Future Economic Outlook (Consumer Confidence)

- **Confident Economic Outlook:** If households become confident about the economic outlook (consumer confidence increases), their willingness to acquire investments and consumer goods increases and the aggregate demand curve shifts right, causing national output to rise.

- **Uncertain Economic Outlook:** When the economic outlook appears more uncertain, consumers tend to reduce current spending, shifting aggregate demand to the left and causing national output to fall.

### 4.4.4    Changes in Exchange Rates

- **Appreciated Currencies:** If the currency of a country appreciates in real terms relative to the currencies of its trading partners, its goods will become relatively more expensive for foreigners, while foreign goods will become relatively less expensive for its residents. As a result, net exports (exports minus imports) will fall, shifting the aggregate demand curve to the left and causing national output to fall.

- **Depreciated Currencies:** If the currency of a country depreciates in real terms relative to the currencies of its trading partners, its goods will become relatively less expensive for foreigners, while foreign goods will become relatively more expensive for its residents. As a result, net exports (exports minus imports) will rise, shifting the aggregate demand curve to the right and causing national output to rise.

### 4.4.5    Changes in Government Spending

- **Increase in Government Spending:** An *increase* in government spending shifts the aggregate demand curve to the right, causing national output to rise.

- **Decrease in Government Spending:** A *decrease* in government spending shifts the aggregate demand curve to the left, causing national output to fall.

### 4.4.6    Changes in Consumer Taxes

- **Increase in Consumer Taxes:** An *increase* in consumer taxes (e.g., the personal income tax) reduces the disposable income (gross income minus taxes) of consumers and, therefore, shifts the aggregate demand curve to the left, causing national output to fall.

- **Decrease in Consumer Taxes:** A *decrease* in consumer taxes increases the disposable income of consumers and therefore shifts the aggregate demand curve to the right, causing national output to rise.

### Expansionary Fiscal Policy

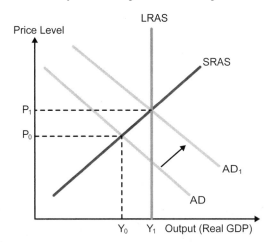

The economy is initially in a recession, illustrated as output level $Y_0$, which is below the potential level of output $Y_1$. The government can stimulate the economy by increasing government spending or decreasing taxes (or both), shifting the aggregate demand curve to the right and causing national output (real GDP) to rise.

### Contractionary Fiscal Policy

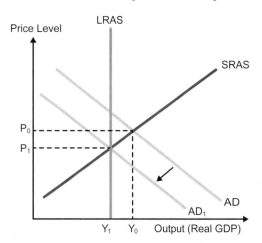

The economy is initially in an expansionary phase, illustrated as output level $Y_0$, which is above the potential level of output $Y_1$. The government can contract the economy by decreasing government spending or increasing taxes (or both), shifting the aggregate demand curve to the left and causing national output (real GDP) to fall.

## Pass Key

Remember the factors that shift aggregate demand as **TWICE G**overnment:

**Taxes**

**Wealth**

**Interest** rates

**Consumer** confidence

**Exchange** rates

**Government** spending

## 4.5 Multiplier Effect

The *multiplier effect* refers to the fact that an increase in consumer, company, or government spending produces a multiplied increase in the level of economic activity. For example, a $1 increase in government spending results in a greater than $1 increase in real GDP. The multiplier effect stems from the fact that increases in spending generate income for firms, which in turn spend that income. Their spending gives other households and firms income, and so on. Therefore, the effect of a $1 increase in spending is magnified by the multiplier effect. The multiplier effect results from the marginal propensity to consume (MPC). The MPC is the change in consumption due to a $1 increase in income. Because people tend to save part of their income, the MPC is typically less than one.

Using the MPC, the size of the multiplier effect can be calculated using the following formulas:

$$\text{Multiplier} = \frac{1}{(1 - \text{MPC})}$$

$$\text{Change in real GDP} = \text{Multiplier} \times \text{Change in spending}$$

**Note:** The examiners could refer to "1 – MPC" as the marginal propensity to save (MPS), so be aware of this terminology as well.

| Example 2 | Multiplier Effect |
|---|---|

**Facts:** Suppose that the MPC is 0.8 (i.e., the change in consumption due to a $1 increase in income is 80 cents) and that spending increases by $100.

**Required:** Calculate the change in real GDP.

**Solution:**

$$\text{Change in real GDP} = \frac{1}{(1 - 0.8)} \times \$100 = \$500$$

Thus, a $100 increase in spending results in a $500 increase in real GDP.

## 4.6    Factors That Shift Short-Run Aggregate Supply

Recall that shifts in long-run aggregate supply are associated with economic growth, not business cycles. Therefore, when discussing business cycles, we focus on shifts in the short-run aggregate supply curve.

The primary factors that shift short-run aggregate supply are:

### 4.6.1   Changes in Input (Resource) Prices

■ **Increase in Input Prices:** An *increase* in input prices (raw material prices, wages, etc.) causes the short-run aggregate supply curve to shift left. Thus, an increase in input prices causes the economy to contract and leads to a decrease in national output (real GDP).

| Illustration 1 | Increase in Input Prices |
|---|---|

A large increase in oil prices (oil is a primary input in production) would shift the short-run aggregate supply curve to the left. As a result, national output would fall, causing a contraction and possibly a recession.

- **Decrease in Input Prices:** A *decrease* in input prices causes the short-run aggregate supply curve to shift to the right. A decrease in input prices causes the economy to expand and leads to an increase in national output (real GDP).

### 4.6.2   Supply Shocks

- **Supplies Are Plentiful:** If resource supplies become more plentiful, the short-run aggregate supply curve will shift to the right, causing national output to increase.

- **Supplies Are Curtailed:** If resource supplies are curtailed (e.g., crop failures, damage to infrastructure caused by earthquakes, etc.), the short-run supply curve will shift to the left, causing national output (real GDP) to decline.

| Question 1 | CPA-03291 |
| --- | --- |

Which of the following is *not* likely to cause a rightward shift in the aggregate demand curve?

- **a.** An increase in wealth.
- **b.** An increase in the level of real interest rates.
- **c.** An increase in government spending.
- **d.** An increase in the general level of confidence about the economic outlook.

| Question 2 | CPA-05318 |
| --- | --- |

Which of the following statements is correct if there is an increase in the resources available within an economy?

- **a.** More goods and services will be produced in the economy.
- **b.** The economy will be capable of producing more goods and services.
- **c.** The standard of living in the economy will rise.
- **d.** The technological efficiency of the economy will improve.

# 1 Overview

Economists and policy makers rely on a host of economic measures or indicators to determine the overall state of economic activity. Some of the most commonly cited economic measures are:

- Real gross domestic product (real GDP)
- Unemployment rate
- Inflation rate
- Interest rates

It is important to remember that these economic measures tend to move together. For example, when real GDP is rising, unemployment tends to be falling. Similarly, when the unemployment rate is rising, the inflation rate tends to be falling.

# 2 National Income Accounting System

The National Income and Product Accounting (NIPA) system was developed by the U.S. Department of Commerce to monitor the health and performance of the U.S. economy. The two methods for measuring GDP, expenditure approach and income approach, are calculated using NIPA. The combined economic output of the following four sectors is called gross domestic product (GDP), the total dollar value of all new final goods and services produced within the economy in a given period.

- Households (or consumers)
- Businesses
- Federal, state, and local governments
- Foreign sector

## 2.1 Two Methods of Measuring GDP

The two methods of measuring GDP are the *expenditure approach* and the *income approach*.

### 2.1.1 Expenditure Approach

Under the expenditure approach, GDP is the sum of the following four components:

- **Government** purchases of goods and services
- Gross private domestic **investment** (nonresidential fixed investment, residential fixed investment, and change in business inventories)
- Personal **consumption** expenditures (durable goods, nondurable goods, and services)
- Net **exports** (exports minus imports)

The first letters of the words in bold form the mnemonic **GICE**.

### 2.1.2 Income Approach

The income approach accounts for GDP as the value of resource costs and incomes generated during the measurement period. The income approach includes business profits, rent, wages, interest, depreciation, and business taxes. Under the income approach, GDP is the sum of the following eight components:

- **Income** of proprietors

- **Profits** of corporations

- **Interest** (net)

- **Rental** income

- **Adjustments** for net foreign income and miscellaneous items

- **Taxes** (indirect business taxes)

- **Employee** compensation (wages)

- **Depreciation** (also known as capital consumption allowance)

The first letters of the words in bold form the mnemonic **I PIRATED.**

## 2.2 Comparison of Approaches

The two different approaches are used to prepare an "income statement" for the domestic economy (the GDP), as shown in the following table.

- The aggregate expenditures approach on the left is a flow of product approach (at market prices).

- The income approach on the right is a flow of earnings and other resources that generate domestic income.

| Comparison of Approaches (in Billions of Dollars) | | | |
|---|---|---|---|
| *Expenditure Approach (Flow-of-Product)* | | *Income Approach (Earnings and Costs)* | |
| **Government** purchases | $1,314.70 | **Income** of proprietors | $ 450.90 |
| **Investment** | 1,014.40 | **Profits** of corporations | 526.50 |
| **Consumption** | 4,698.70 | **Interest** (net) | 392.80 |
| **Exports** (net) | (96.40) | **Rental** income | 116.60 |
| | | **Adjustments** for net foreign income/ miscellaneous | 45.00 |
| | | **Taxes** (indirect business) | 572.50 |
| | | **Employee** compensation | 4,008.30 |
| | | **Depreciation** (consumption of fixed capital) | 818.80 |
| Aggregate expenditure | $6,931.40 | Domestic Income | $6,931.40 |

## 2.3    Other Measures of National Income

Although GDP is the most common measure of national income and an economy's output and performance, there are several other noteworthy measures.

- **Net Domestic Product (NDP):** *Net domestic product* is GDP minus depreciation (the capital consumption allowance).

- **Gross National Product (GNP):** *Gross national product* is defined as the market value of final goods and services produced by residents of a country in a given time period. GNP differs from GDP because GNP includes goods and services that are produced overseas by U.S. firms and excludes goods and services that are produced domestically by foreign firms.

- **Net National Product (NNP):** *Net national product* is defined as GNP minus economic depreciation (i.e., losses in the value of capital goods due to age and wear).

- **National Income (NI):** *National income* is NNP less indirect business taxes (e.g., sales tax).

- **Personal Income (PI):** *Personal income* is the income received by households and noncorporate businesses.

- **Disposable Income (DI):** *Disposable income* is personal income less personal taxes. It is the amount of income households have available either to spend or to save.

---

### Illustration 1    GNP vs. GDP

If BMW produces cars in the United States, that production is counted as part of U.S. GDP, but it is not counted as part of U.S. GNP because BMW is a foreign-owned company.

---

# 3    Unemployment Rate

The *unemployment* rate measures the ratio of the number of people classified as unemployed to the total labor force. The total labor force includes all non-institutionalized individuals 16 years of age or older who either are working or are actively looking for work. (An unemployed person is defined as a person 16 years of age or older who is available for work and who has actively sought employment during the previous four weeks.) Note that to be counted as unemployed, a person must be actively looking for work. The unemployment rate can be expressed as:

$$\text{Unemployment rate} = \frac{\text{Number of unemployed}}{\text{Total labor force}} \times 100$$

## 3.1    Types of Unemployment

### 3.1.1    Frictional Unemployment

*Frictional unemployment* is normal unemployment resulting from workers routinely changing jobs or from workers being temporarily laid off. It is the unemployment that arises because of the time needed to match qualified job seekers with available jobs.

### 3.1.2  Structural Unemployment

*Structural unemployment* occurs when:

- jobs available in the market do not correspond to the skills of the workforce; and

- unemployed workers do not live where the jobs are located.

### 3.1.3  Seasonal Unemployment

*Seasonal unemployment* is the result of seasonal changes in the demand and supply of labor. For example, shortly before Christmas, the demand for labor in some industries increases and then decreases again after Christmas.

### 3.1.4  Cyclical Unemployment

*Cyclical unemployment* is the amount of unemployment resulting from declines in real GDP during periods of contraction or recession or in any period when the economy fails to operate at its potential. When real GDP is below the potential level of output, cyclical unemployment is positive. When real GDP is above the potential level of output, cyclical unemployment is negative. Thus, cyclical unemployment rises during a recession and falls during an expansion.

## 3.2  Natural Rate of Unemployment and Full Employment

### 3.2.1  Natural Rate of Unemployment

The *natural rate of unemployment* is the "normal" rate of unemployment around which the unemployment rate fluctuates due to cyclical unemployment. Thus, the natural rate of unemployment is the sum of frictional, structural, and seasonal unemployment or the employment rate that exists when the economy is at its potential output level.

### 3.2.2  Full Employment

*Full employment* is defined as the level of unemployment when there is no cyclical unemployment. Full employment does not mean zero unemployment. When the economy is operating at full employment, there is still frictional, structural, and seasonal unemployment.

# 4  Price Level and Inflation

## 4.1  Definitions

### 4.1.1  Inflation

*Inflation* is defined as a sustained increase in the general prices of goods and services. It occurs when prices on average are increasing over time.

### 4.1.2  Deflation

*Deflation* is defined as a sustained decrease in the general prices of goods and services. It occurs when prices on average are falling over time.

Most economists believe that deflation is a much bigger economic problem than inflation. During periods of deflation, firms are likely to experience significant excess production capacity. This occurs because consumers tend to hold off purchasing goods and services during a period of deflation because they realize that the price of goods and services is likely to continue to fall. Consequently, firm profits are likely to be falling during periods of deflation.

### 4.1.3 Inflation/Deflation Rate

The *inflation* or *deflation rate* is typically measured as the percentage change in the consumer price index (CPI) from one period to the next.

▪ **Consumer Price Index (CPI):** The *consumer price index* (CPI) is a measure of the overall cost of a fixed basket of goods and services purchased by an average household. The CPI is computed as follows:

$$CPI = \frac{\text{Current cost of market basket}}{\text{Base year cost of market basket}} \times 100$$

---

| Example 1 | **Consumer Price Index** |
|---|---|

**Facts:** A doctoral student in economics is working on her dissertation. As part of her research, she selects four goods (products) that are consumed by college students on the local campus and then collects data to determine the average price changes for these products over the past 10 years. She gathers the following data for the four products.

|  | Time = 0 (Base year) | Time = Year 10 (Current year) |
|---|---|---|
| Product A | $ 3.00 | $ 4.80 |
| Product B | 25.00 | 39.00 |
| Product C | 17.00 | 22.00 |
| Product D | 6.00 | 8.20 |
| Total | $51.00 | $74.00 |

**Note:** The prices for each product above are the average prices for T = 0 and T = 10.

**Required:** Compute the (consumer) price index for these four products.

**Solution:**

$$CPI = \frac{\$74.00 \times 100}{\$51.00}$$

$$= 145.1$$

---

▪ **Inflation Rate:** Using the CPI, the inflation rate is calculated as the percentage change in the CPI from one period to the next:

$$\text{Inflation rate} = \frac{CPI_{\text{this period}} - CPI_{\text{last period}}}{CPI_{\text{last period}}} \times 100$$

▪ **Producer Price Index (PPI):** The *producer price index* (PPI) measures the overall cost of a basket of goods and services typically purchased by firms.

      

## 4.2    Causes of Inflation and Deflation

Inflation and deflation are caused by shifts in the aggregate demand and short-run aggregate supply curves.

A rightward shift in the *aggregate demand* curve will cause the price level to rise, leading to inflation. Similarly, a leftward shift in the *short-run aggregate supply* curve will also cause the price level to rise, leading to inflation.

### 4.2.1    Demand-Pull Inflation

*Demand-pull inflation* is caused by increases in aggregate demand. Thus, demand-pull inflation could be caused by factors such as:

▨    increases in government spending;

▨    decreases in taxes;

▨    increases in wealth; or

▨    increases in the money supply.

### 4.2.2    Cost-Push Inflation

*Cost-push inflation* is caused by reductions in short-run aggregate supply. Thus, cost-push inflation could be caused by factors such as:

▨    an increase in oil prices; or

▨    an increase in nominal wages.

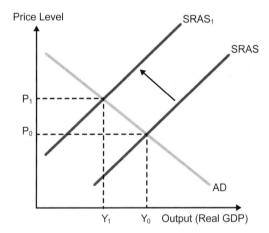

**Demand-Pull Inflation**

An increase in aggregate demand causes the short-run equilibrium price level to rise from $P_0$ to $P_1$.

**Cost-Push Inflation**

A decrease in short-run aggregate supply causes the short-run equilibrium price level to rise from $P_0$ to $P_1$.

### 4.2.3 Deflation

*Deflation* is also caused by shifts in aggregate demand or short-run aggregate supply. A shift left in aggregate demand (perhaps brought about by a stock market crash or a large increase in taxes) will cause the aggregate price level to fall. Similarly, a shift right in the short-run aggregate supply curve will also cause the aggregate price level to fall.

## 4.3 Inflation and the Value of Money

Inflation has an inverse relationship with purchasing power. As the price level rises, the value of money (purchasing power) declines.

### 4.3.1 Definitions

- **Monetary Assets and Liabilities:** *Monetary assets and liabilities* (e.g., cash, accounts receivable, notes payable, etc.) are fixed in dollar amounts regardless of changes in specific prices or the general price level.

- **Nonmonetary Assets and Liabilities:** The value of nonmonetary assets (e.g., a building, land, machinery, etc.) and nonmonetary liabilities (e.g., rent collected in advance) will fluctuate with inflation and deflation.

### 4.3.2 Holding Monetary Assets

During a period of inflation, those with a fixed amount of money or income (e.g., retired persons) will be hurt (i.e., their purchasing power will be eroded). Similarly, firms that loan money at fixed interest rates are likely to be hurt by inflation.

### 4.3.3 Holding Monetary Liabilities

During a period of inflation, those with a fixed amount of debt (e.g., those with home mortgages) will be aided (i.e., the debt will be repaid with inflated dollars). Thus, inflation also tends to benefit firms with large amounts of outstanding debt.

---

### Illustration 2     OPEC and the Stagflation of the 1970s

From 1973 to 1974, OPEC (Organization of the Petroleum Exporting Countries) substantially curtailed its production of crude oil. As a result, the price of a barrel of crude oil rose from about $2 a barrel in late 1973 to $10 a barrel in late 1974.

This increase in the price of crude oil had a substantial effect on the U.S. economy. Specifically, rising crude oil prices represented an increase in input costs for U.S. firms. As a result, firms cut back production and the short-run aggregate supply curve shifted left.

As the short-run aggregate supply curve shifted left, national output (real GDP) began to decline, unemployment began to rise, and the aggregate price level began to rise (cost-push inflation).

The combination of falling national output and a rising price level is known as *stagflation*. The actions of OPEC in 1973–74 led to a recession in the U.S. that was particularly harsh because not only was the unemployment rate rising, but the newly unemployed were facing higher prices for goods and services due to inflation.

---

## Illustration 3    The Great Depression and Deflation

The Great Depression began with the stock market crash of Oct. 29, 1929. By 1932, the Dow Jones Industrial Average had fallen 89 percent from its peak in 1929. In addition, shortly before the stock market crash, the Federal Reserve (the central bank of the U.S.) increased interest rates in an attempt to control inflation. It then increased interest rates again in early 1931.

Although the stock market crash was not the only cause of the Great Depression, it did mark the beginning of the Great Depression. The Great Depression was caused by a number of factors, including ill-timed interest rate hikes by the Federal Reserve and protectionist trade policies, as well as the stock market crash. The table below shows what happened to real GDP, the unemployment rate, and the price level (as measured by the CPI) from 1929 through 1933.

| Year | Real GDP (Billions of 1987 Dollars) | Unemployment Rate | Price Level (CPI) |
|------|-------------------------------------|-------------------|-------------------|
| 1929 | 821.8 | 3.15% | 17.1 |
| 1930 | 748.9 | 8.71% | 16.7 |
| 1931 | 691.3 | 15.91% | 15.2 |
| 1932 | 599.7 | 23.65% | 13.7 |
| 1933 | 587.1 | 24.87% | 13.0 |

As the table illustrates, the Great Depression was characterized by falling output (falling real GDP), rising unemployment, and deflation. The deflation that occurred can be seen by noting that from 1929 through 1933, the price level fell continuously. Furthermore, at the height of the Great Depression, one out of every four workers was unemployed.

The data suggest that the Great Depression was caused by a shift left in aggregate demand. Specifically, the stock market crash reduced household wealth, which shifted the aggregate demand curve to the left. In addition, the interest rate hikes orchestrated by the Federal Reserve increased the cost of capital, thereby decreasing the demand for investment goods and shifting the aggregate demand curve even further to the left. As aggregate demand fell, the price level also fell and the nation experienced a period of deflation.

## 4.4    Inverse Relationship Between Inflation and Unemployment

The *Phillips curve* illustrates the inverse relationship between the rate of inflation and the unemployment rate. It illustrates the trade-off that exists in the short run between inflation and unemployment. Unemployment and inflation have historically moved in opposite directions, but during the oil shocks of the 1970s, the Phillips curve broke down. The oil crisis (a supply shock) caused a decrease in short-run aggregate supply that caused both unemployment and inflation.

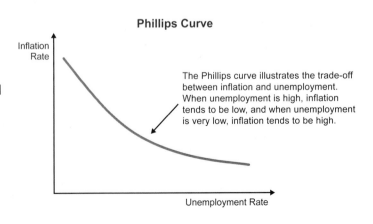

**Phillips Curve**

The Phillips curve illustrates the trade-off between inflation and unemployment. When unemployment is high, inflation tends to be low, and when unemployment is very low, inflation tends to be high.

# 5    Budget Deficits and Surpluses

The budget is the federal government's plan for spending funds and raising revenues through taxation, fees, and other means (and for borrowing funds if necessary). The budget deficit and the budget surplus are important indicators of the current and future health of an economy.

## 5.1    Budget Deficits

A budget deficit occurs when a country spends more than it takes in (mostly in the form of taxes during the year).

### 5.1.1    Financing Budget Deficits

*Budget deficits* are usually financed by government borrowing, which affects interest rates. The government could also finance budget deficits by printing new money. Financing budget deficits by printing money, however, causes inflation.

### 5.1.2    Cyclical Budget Deficit

A *cyclical budget deficit* is caused by temporarily low economic activity. For example, a cyclical budget deficit might be caused by a recession and the resulting lower level of national output.

### 5.1.3    Structural Budget Deficit

A *structural budget deficit* is one that is caused by a structural imbalance between government spending and revenue. Structural deficits are not caused by temporarily low economic activity.

## 5.2    Budget Surpluses

A *budget surplus* occurs when government revenues exceed government spending during the year.

# 6    Interest Rates and the Money Supply

## 6.1    Nominal and Real Interest Rates

### 6.1.1    Nominal Interest Rate

The *nominal interest rate* is the amount of interest paid (or earned) measured in current dollars. When the economy experiences inflation, nominal interest rates are not a good measure of how much borrowers really pay or lenders really receive when they take out or make a loan. A more accurate measure of the interest borrowers pay or lenders receive is the *real interest rate*.

### 6.1.2    Real Interest Rate

The *real interest rate* is defined as the nominal interest rate minus the inflation rate. It is a measure of the purchasing power of interest earned or paid.

$$\text{Real interest rate} = \text{Nominal interest rate} - \text{Inflation rate}$$

## Illustration 4    Real Interest Rate

If you take out a loan with a 10 percent nominal interest rate and the inflation rate is 3 percent, then your real interest rate is only 7 percent. That is, after adjusting for the fact that the dollars with which you will repay the loan in the future are worth less than current dollars due to inflation, you are really only paying 7 percent to borrow the money.

### 6.1.3   Relationship Between Nominal Interest Rates and Inflation

Nominal interest rates and inflation naturally move together. When the inflation rate increases, so does the nominal interest rate. The relationship between nominal interest rates and inflation may be shown by rearranging the above equation for real interest rates as follows:

$$\text{Nominal interest rate } = \text{ Real interest rate } + \text{ Inflation rate}$$

Thus, if *real interest rates* do not change, a one percent increase in the inflation rate will lead to a one percent increase in *nominal interest rates*.

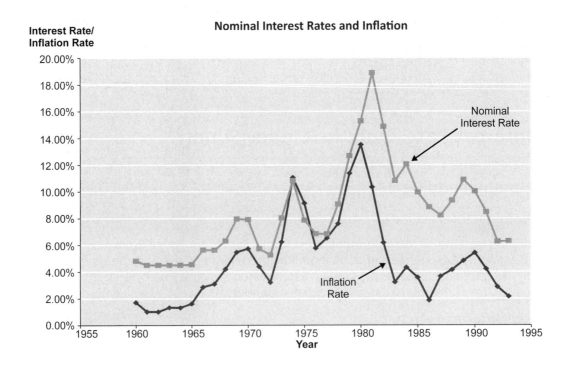

Note the close relationship between nominal interest rates and the inflation rate. As the inflation rate increases, the nominal interest rate also increases. Also note that about 1974–1975, the inflation rate was actually higher than the nominal interest rate, implying real interest rates were negative.

## 6.2    Definition of Money and the Money Supply

Money is the set of liquid assets generally accepted in exchange for goods and services. The money supply is defined as the stock of all liquid assets available for transactions in the economy at any given point in time. There are several definitions of money supply. M1 and M2 are the most common measures of money supply and are reported (periodically) in financial publications (for example, The Wall Street Journal).

### 6.2.1    M1

*M1* is defined broadly as money that is used for purchases of goods and services. It typically includes coins, currency, checkable deposits (accounts that allow holders to write checks against interest-bearing funds within them), and traveler's checks. M1 does not include savings accounts or certificates of deposit (CDs).

### 6.2.2    M2

*M2* is defined broadly as M1 plus liquid assets that cannot be used as a medium of exchange but that can be converted easily into checkable deposits or other components of M1. These include time certificates of deposit less than $100,000, money market deposit accounts at banks, mutual fund accounts, and savings accounts.

### 6.2.3    M3

*M3* includes all items in M2 as well as time certificates of deposit of $100,000 or more.

---

| Example 2 | The Money Supply |
|---|---|

**Facts:** Assume that at year-end, an economy had the following liquid assets (in billions of dollars):

| | |
|---|---|
| Money market deposit accounts | $10,500 |
| Checkable deposits | 42,100 |
| Certificates of deposits > $100,000 | 3,435 |
| Traveler's checks | 700 |
| Mutual funds | 24,650 |
| Currency | 85,284 |
| Savings accounts | 37,169 |

**Required:** Calculate the economy's M1, M2, and M3 money measures.

**Solution:**

**M1** = Checkable deposits + Traveler's checks + Currency

$42,100 + $700 + $85,284 = **$128,084 billion**

**M2** = M1 + Money market deposits + Mutual funds + Savings accounts

$128,084 + $10,500 + $24,650 + $37,169 = **$200,403 billion**

**M3** = M2 + Certificates of deposits > $100,000

$200,403 + $3,435 = **$203,838 billion**

---

## 6.3 Interest Rates and the Demand for and Supply of Money

### 6.3.1 Demand for Money Is Inversely Related to Interest Rates

Changes in the money supply have a direct effect on interest rates because interest rates are determined by the supply of and demand for money. The demand for money is the relationship between how much money individuals want to hold and the interest rate. The demand for money is inversely related to the interest rate—as interest rates rise, it becomes more expensive to hold money (because holding money rather than saving or investing it means you do not earn interest), thus reducing the demand for money.

### 6.3.2 Supply of Money Is Fixed at a Given Point in Time

As noted above, the supply of money is determined by the Federal Reserve and is therefore fixed at any given point in time at the level set by the Federal Reserve.

### 6.3.3 The Money Market

The graph below illustrates the demand for and supply of money. The intersection of the money demand curve and the money supply line determines the interest rate.

- An increase in the money supply will cause interest rates to fall.

- Conversely, a decrease in the money supply will cause interest rates to rise.

**The Money Market**

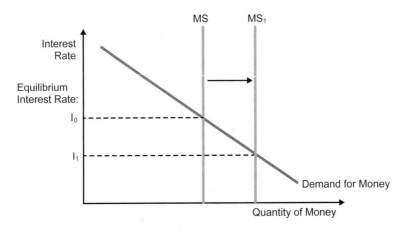

The equilibrium interest rate is found where the demand for money intersects the supply of money. The money supply curve is vertical since the Federal Reserve controls the supply of money (thus it is independent of the interest rate). If the Fed increases the money supply, interest rates will fall, as illustrated by the fall in interest rates from $I_0$ to $I_1$.

# 7 The Federal Reserve and Monetary Policy

*Monetary policy* is the use of the money supply to stabilize the economy. The Federal Reserve uses monetary policy to increase or decrease the money supply in an effort to promote price stability and full employment. Understanding the effects of changes in the money supply is important because changes in the money supply lead to changes in interest rates, changes in the price level, and changes in national output (real GDP).

## 7.1 Tools of the Federal Reserve

The Federal Reserve controls the money supply through the following mechanisms.

### 7.1.1 Open Market Operations (OMO)

*Open market operations* consist of the purchase and sale of government securities (Treasury bills and bonds) in the open market by the Federal Reserve as a means to expand or contract the existing money supply. Open market operations are the most common method used by the Federal Reserve to impact monetary policy.

- When the Federal Reserve purchases government securities, it increases the money supply (that is, puts money into circulation to pay for the securities). Specifically, the money supply is increased when the Federal Open Market Committee (FOMC) of the Federal Reserve decides to purchase government securities.

- When the Federal Reserve sells government securities, it decreases the money supply (that is, takes money out of circulation).

### 7.1.2 Changes in the Discount Rate

The *discount rate* is the interest rate the Federal Reserve charges member banks for short-term (normally overnight) loans. Member banks may borrow money from the Federal Reserve to cover liquidity needs, increase reserves, or make investments.

- Raising the discount rate discourages borrowing by member banks and decreases the money supply.

- Lowering the discount rate encourages borrowing by member banks and increases the money supply.

### 7.1.3 Changes in the Required Reserve Ratio (RRR)

The *required reserve ratio* is the fraction of total deposits banks must hold in reserve.

- Raising the reserve requirement decreases the money supply.

- Lowering the reserve requirement increases the money supply.

## 7.2 Expansionary Monetary Policy (Increase in the Money Supply)

Expansionary monetary policy results when the Fed increases the money supply, affecting the economy through the following chain of events:

1. An increase in the money supply causes interest rates to fall.

2. Falling interest rates reduce the cost of capital and hence stimulate the desired levels of firm investment and household consumption.

3. Increases in desired investment and consumption cause an increase in aggregate demand.

4. Aggregate demand shifts to the right, causing real GDP to rise, the unemployment rate to fall, and the price level to rise.

## 7.3   Contractionary Monetary Policy (Decrease in the Money Supply)

Contractionary monetary policy results when the Fed decreases the money supply. The effect is the exact opposite of expansionary monetary policy. Specifically:

1.   A decrease in the money supply causes interest rates to rise.

2.   Rising interest rates reduce the desired levels of firm investment and household consumption.

3.   Decreases in desired investment and consumption cause a decrease in aggregate demand.

4.   Aggregate demand shifts to the left, causing real GDP to fall, the unemployment rate to rise, and the price level to fall.

---

**Question 1**                                                                                               CPA-03396

Assume the following data for the U.S. economy in a recent year:

| | |
|---|---:|
| Personal consumption expenditures | $5,015 billion |
| Exports | 106 billion |
| Government purchases of goods/services | 1,040 billion |
| M1 | 262 billion |
| Imports | 183 billion |
| Gross private domestic investment | 975 billion |
| Open market purchases by Federal Reserve | 5 billion |

Based on this information, which of the following was the U.S. GDP for the year in question?

   **a.**   $6,953 billion

   **b.**   $6,958 billion

   **c.**   $6,691 billion

   **d.**   $7,215 billion

---

**Question 2**                                                                                               CPA-03404

What type of unemployment is shown when individuals do not have the qualifications or skills necessary to fill available jobs?

   **a.**   Frictional

   **b.**   Natural

   **c.**   Cyclical

   **d.**   Structural

---

| Question 3 | CPA-05857 |
|---|---|

Which of the following individuals would be most hurt by an unanticipated increase in inflation?

    **a.** A retiree living on a fixed income.

    **b.** A borrower whose debt has a fixed interest rate.

    **c.** A union worker whose contract includes a provision for regular cost-of-living adjustments.

    **d.** A saver whose savings was placed in a variable rate savings account.

| Question 4 | CPA-05869 |
|---|---|

Assume an economy is at the peak of the business cycle. Which of the following policy combinations is the most effective way to dampen the economy and prevent inflation?

    **a.** Increase government spending, reduce taxes, increase money supply, and reduce interest rates.

    **b.** Reduce government spending, increase taxes, increase money supply, and increase interest rates.

    **c.** Reduce government spending, increase taxes, reduce money supply, and increase interest rates.

    **d.** Reduce government spending, reduce taxes, reduce money supply, and reduce interest rates.

## NOTES

# 1 The Laws of Demand and Supply

While macroeconomics focuses on how human behavior affects outcomes in highly aggregated markets (e.g., products, labor), microeconomics focuses on how human behavior affects the conduct of more narrowly defined units, including a single individual, household, or business firm. Basic principles of microeconomic theory are very important on the CPA Exam, but understanding the fundamentals is also important to the business manager. Managers are more likely to be successful if they understand how their actions and various governmental policies or collusive actions (for example, cartels) affect their market and firm. A market is simply a collection of buyers and sellers *meeting or communicating* in order to trade goods or services.

## 1.1 Demand

### 1.1.1 Definitions

- **Demand Curve**

  The *demand curve* illustrates the maximum quantity of a good that consumers are willing and able to purchase at each and every price (at any given price), all else being equal. Note that this demand curve is similar to the aggregate demand curve, except that the *x*-axis here is quantity and not real GDP. It does, however, illustrate the same kind of relationship. This demand curve is the microeconomics demand curve for a certain good or product and not the total demand in the economy as a whole.

- **Quantity Demanded**

  *Quantity demanded* is defined as the quantity of a good (or service) individuals are willing and able to purchase at each and every (given) price, all else being equal.

- **Change in Quantity Demanded (Movement Along the Demand Curve)**

  A *change in quantity demanded* is a change in the amount of a good demanded resulting solely from a change in price. Changes in quantity demanded are shown by *movements along the demand curve* (D). When assumptions regarding price or quantity change, the "demand point" will change along this demand curve. For example, if the price of a product increases, there will be a move up the demand curve.

- **Change in Demand (Movement of the Demand Curve)**

  A *change in demand* is a change in the amount of a good demanded resulting from a change in something other than the price of the good. A change in demand cannot be due to a change in price. A change in demand causes a shift in the demand curve.

### 1.1.2 Fundamental Law of Demand

The *fundamental law of demand* states that the price of a product (or service) and the quantity demanded of that product (or service) are inversely related. As the price of the product increases (decreases), the quantity demanded decreases (increases). Quantity demanded is inversely related to price for two reasons:

■ **Substitution Effect**

The *substitution effect* refers to the fact consumers tend to purchase more (less) of a good when its price falls (rises) in relation to the price of other goods. The substitution effect exists because people tend to substitute one similar good for another when the price of a good they usually purchase increases. For example, if the price of Pepsi decreases, it will be used as a substitute for Coca-Cola (a similar good).

■ **Income Effect**

The *income effect* means that as prices are lowered with income remaining constant (i.e., as purchasing power or real income increases), people will purchase more or all of the lower-priced products. For example, a decrease in the price of a good increases a consumer's real income even when nominal income remains constant. As a result, the consumer can purchase more of all goods.

### 1.1.3 Factors That Shift Demand Curves (Factors Other Than Price)

○ ■ **Changes in Wealth**

A positive or negative change in wealth for people will result in a shift in the demand curve. For example, if people become wealthier it may increase (shift) their demand for luxury items (e.g., high-end sports cars).

○ ■ **Changes in the Price of Related Goods (Substitutes and Complements)**

If the price of a similar good (a substitute good) increases, the demand curve will shift to the right (increase) for the original good, now perceived as a bargain. If the price of a good used in conjunction with the original good (referred to as a complementary good) decreases, the demand for the original good will increase (e.g., if personal computer prices fall, demand increases for peripherals, such as monitors and printers).

○ ■ **Changes in Consumer Income**

An increase in consumers' incomes will shift the demand curve to the right (depicted as the shift from $D_1$ to $D_2$). Assume, for example, that employment in a local community is primarily retail-based. Because employees' commissions rise during the Christmas season, those employees will have additional consumer income and will demand more goods (demand curve shifts to right).

○ ■ **Changes in Consumer Tastes or Preferences for a Product**

When consumers' preferences (tastes) for a given product increase or decrease, there is a shift in the demand curve. For example, if the clothing industry experiences a revival of the 1960s era, the demand for bell-bottom jeans (retro clothing) will increase. This is also depicted as the shift from $D_1$ to $D_2$.

○ ■ **Changes in Consumer Expectations**

If consumers anticipate that there will be a future price increase, immediate demand will increase for that product (at the current, lower price). For example, if commuters expect that the price of a monthly or annual bus pass will increase 10 percent in the near term, there should be a spike in demand for bus passes.

○ ■ **Changes in the Number of Buyers Served by the Market**

An increase in the number of buyers will shift the demand curve to the right. This is evident in a community in which there has been a steady rise in the population of people 65 and older. As the number of senior citizens grows, there will be more buyers of prescription drugs, resulting in a shift in the demand curve to the right.

## Change in Quantity Demanded vs. Change in Demand

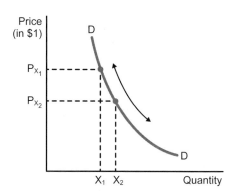 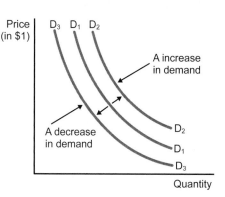

**Change in quantity demanded:**
Changes in price cause movements along the demand curve.

**Change in demand:**
Shift in demand curve caused by external influences (other than the price of the good).

## 1.2 Supply

### 1.2.1 Definitions

The fundamental law of supply states that price and quantity supplied are positively related (i.e., they have a positive correlation). The higher the price received for a good, the more sellers will produce (higher quantity).

- **Supply Curve**

  The *supply curve* illustrates the maximum quantity of a good that sellers are willing and able to produce at each and every price (at any given price), all else being equal. Note that this supply curve is similar to the aggregate supply curve, except that the *x*-axis here is quantity and not real GDP. It does, however, illustrate the same kind of relationship. This is the microeconomics supply curve for a certain good or product and not the total supply in the economy as a whole.

- **Quantity Supplied**

  *Quantity supplied* is the amount of a good that producers are willing and able to produce at each and every (given) price, all else being equal.

- **Change in Quantity Supplied (Movement Along the Supply Curve)**

  A *change in quantity* supplied is a change in the amount producers are willing and able to produce resulting solely from a change in price. A change in quantity supplied is represented by a *movement along the supply curve*. When price changes, there will be movement up or down the supply curve to find the new quantity that will be supplied.

- **Change in Supply (Movement of the Supply Curve)**

  A *change in supply* is a change in the amount of a good supplied resulting from a change in something other than the price of the good. A change in supply *cannot be due to a change in price*. A change in supply causes a shift in the supply curve.

### 1.2.2   Factors That Shift Supply Curves

■   **Changes in Price Expectations of the Supplying Firm**

If prices are expected to decrease, the firm will supply more now at each price level to take advantage of the currently higher prices. For example, Coffee Products Inc. produces gourmet coffee (in cans) sold primarily to the restaurant industry. Given expected favorable crop and market conditions, the company believes that the average price of gourmet coffee will decline by $1 a can in the next six months. Based on this forecast, the company will increase the supply of gourmet coffee now to maximize profitability. This is represented by the shift in the supply curve from $S_1$ to $S_2$.

■   **Changes in Production Costs (Price of Inputs)**

When production costs are expected to decline (rise) there will be a shift in the supply curve to the right (left). A decrease in wages paid to workers would cause a shift to the right in the supply curve because for a lower amount of production dollars, the firm is willing to supply more products. This is represented by the shift in the supply curve from $S_1$ to $S_2$.

■   **Changes in the Price or Demand for Other Goods**

A decrease (increase) in the demand for another good supplied by a firm would cause the firm to shift its resources and increase (decrease) the supply of its remaining goods. Assume that a firm produces two products, butter and margarine. If there is an industry-wide increase in the price of butter that also lowers butter demand, the firm will shift its production to make more margarine, causing a shift in the supply curve for margarine to the right.

■   **Changes in Subsidies or Taxes**

A decrease in taxes or an increase in subsidies would increase the amount supplied at each price level. In contrast, assume that a local company produces cigarettes and that a tax is levied on the sale of cigarettes in the state. If the company believes that this tax increase will negatively affect the demand for cigarettes, it will decrease the supply of cigarettes, which will shift the supply curve to the left.

■   **Changes in Production Technology**

An improvement in technology would cause a shift to the right of the supply curve. For example, a company has introduced a state-of-the art technology that would significantly increase the finished bottle output for a production day. Under this scenario, the company would increase supply, resulting in a shift in the supply curve to the right.

#### Change in Quantity Supplied vs. Change in Supply

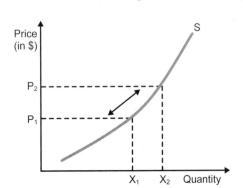

**Change in quantity supplied:**
Changes in price cause movements along the supply curve.

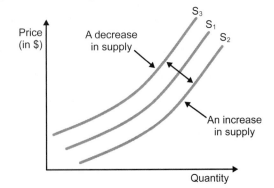

**Change in supply:**
Shift in supply curve caused by external factors (other than price).

## 1.3    Market Equilibrium

A market is in equilibrium when there are no forces acting to change the current price/quantity combination. The market supplies just as much as is demanded, and there is no pressure to change prices.

- ◼ The market's equilibrium price and output (quantity) is the point at which the supply and demand curves intersect. This is sometimes called the market clearing price.

- ◼ The interaction of demand and supply determines equilibrium price.

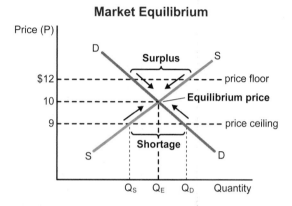

**Market Equilibrium**

- Price (P) is $10 at equilibrium, and the quantity supplied (Q) is $Q_E$.
- If the price is set below the equilibrium price, the quantity demanded will exceed the quantity supplied, and a shortage will result.
- If the price is set above the equilibrium price, the quantity demanded will be less than the quantity supplied, and a surplus will result.

### 1.3.1    Changes in Equilibrium

If supply and/or demand curves shift, the equilibrium price and quantity will change.

- ◼ **Effects of a Change in Demand on Equilibrium**

    A rightward shift (increase) in demand from curve D to curve $D_1$ (below, left) will result in an increase in price (from P to $P_1$) and an increase in market clearing quantity (from Q to $Q_1$). Conversely, a leftward shift (decrease) in demand from curve D to curve $D_1$ (below, right) will result in a decrease in price (from P to $P_1$) and a decrease in market clearing quantity (from Q to $Q_1$).

**Effects of a Change in Demand on Equilibrium**

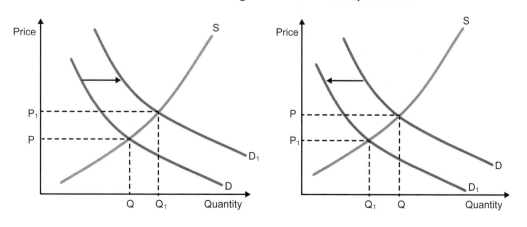

### ■ Effects of a Change in Supply on Equilibrium

A rightward shift (increase) in supply from curve S to curve $S_1$ (below, left) will result in a decrease in price (from P to $P_1$) and an increase in market clearing quantity (from Q to $Q_1$). Conversely, a leftward shift (decrease) in supply from curve S to curve $S_1$ (below, right) will result in an increase in price (from P to $P_1$) and a decrease in market clearing quantity (from Q to $Q_1$). Market clearing quantity is the equilibrium quantity. Market clearing is the idea that the market will "eventually" be cleared of all excess supply and demand (all surpluses and shortages), assuming that prices are free to change.

**Effects of a Change in Supply on Equilibrium**

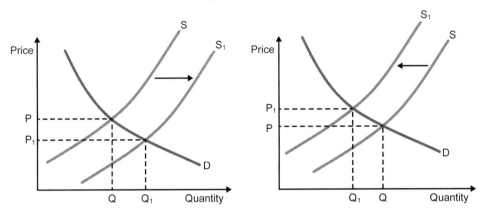

| Illustration 1 | Effects of Changes in Demand and Supply on Equilibrium |

Consider the situation in the northeastern U.S. seaboard states during a recent hurricane. Prior to the hurricane, the market for generators was most likely in a state of equilibrium. However, as a result of the hurricane, residents began to demand more generators, causing a shortage. Suppliers of generators were motivated to increase the price of generators so fewer people wanted to purchase them. The price increase could potentially "clear" the market (both demand and supply), resulting in a state of equilibrium at the higher price.

### ■ General Effects of Changes in Demand and Supply on Equilibrium

- An increase in demand and supply results in an increase in equilibrium quantity, but the effect on price is indeterminate.

  It is certain that the effect is an increase of equilibrium quantity (because both an increase in demand and an increase in supply cause quantity to increase); however, the effect on equilibrium price is indeterminate because an increase in demand and supply could cause an increase, decrease, or no change (if equal changes) in equilibrium price.

  —If the increase in demand is larger than the increase in supply, the equilibrium price will rise.

  —Conversely, if the increase in supply is larger than the increase in demand, the equilibrium price will fall.

- The effect of other complex scenarios such as 1) a decrease in demand and an increase in supply, 2) an increase in demand and a decrease in supply, or 3) a decrease in demand and a decrease in supply can be analyzed in a similar manner. The table below summarizes the effect of all four scenarios discussed above on equilibrium price and quantity. To understand them more fully, you should draw supply and demand diagrams for each case to verify the effects listed.

| Change in Demand | Change in Supply | Effect on Equilibrium Quantity | Effect on Equilibrium Price |
|---|---|---|---|
| Increase | Increase | Increase | Indeterminate |
| Increase | Decrease | Indeterminate | Increase |
| Decrease | Decrease | Decrease | Indeterminate |
| Decrease | Increase | Indeterminate | Decrease |

## 1.4    Government Intervention in Market Operations

Sometimes, the government will intervene in a market by mandating a price different from the "market price" (causing either a surplus or a shortage). This most often is accomplished by using *price ceilings* and *price floors*.

### 1.4.1   Price Ceilings

A *price ceiling* is a maximum price that is established *below* the equilibrium price which causes shortages to develop. Price ceilings cause prices to be artificially low, creating a greater demand than the supply available.

### 1.4.2   Price Floors

A *price floor* is a minimum price set *above* the equilibrium price which causes surpluses to develop. Price floors are minimum prices established by law, such as minimum wages and agricultural price supports.

---

**Illustration 2      Government Intervention in Market Operations**

**Price Ceiling:** Rent-controlled apartments exist in some places. The price is required by government mandate to remain at a certain level below the market price. The result is an artificially high demand for those apartments. (There may be policy reasons for having rent controls, but the economic result is that there is a shortage of apartments.)

**Price Floors:** You can always find supporters of increasing the minimum wage in the United States. However, businesses hiring minimum-wage workers counter that they will be able to hire fewer people at the higher rates, thus creating a higher unemployment rate among those workers. Again, there is competition between the social policy and the economic policy in this case.

---

# 2 Elasticity of Demand and Supply

Elasticity is a measure of how sensitive the demand for, or the supply of, a product is to a change in price.

## 2.1 Price Elasticity of Demand

*The price elasticity of demand is the percentage change in quantity demanded divided by the percentage change in price.*

$$E_p = \text{Price elasticity of demand} = \frac{\text{\% change in quantity demanded}}{\text{\% change in price}}$$

- In a normal demand curve, the price elasticity of demand is usually negative. This negative price elasticity reflects the downward sloping demand curve; as price goes up (positive percentage change), the quantity demanded goes down (negative percentage change). A negative price elasticity coefficient results if the demand curve is normal.

- Generally, the absolute value of the elasticity coefficient (positive value) is considered when elasticity problems are posed on the examination, because it is presumed that price elasticity is negative for a demand curve.

---

| Example 1 | Elasticity of Demand |
|---|---|

**Facts:** Suppose that when the price of a product increases from $100 to $120, quantity demanded decreases from 1,000 units to 900 units.

**Required:** Using the point method, calculate the price elasticity of demand.

**Solution:**

$$\frac{\text{\% change}}{\text{in quantity}} = \frac{900 \text{ [new demand]} - 1,000 \text{ [old demand]}}{1,000 \text{ [old demand]}} = \frac{-100 \text{ units}}{1,000 \text{ units}} = -10\%$$

*Divided by:*

$$\frac{\text{\% change}}{\text{in price}} = \frac{\$120 \text{ [new price]} - \$100 \text{ [old price]}}{\$100 \text{ [old price]}} = \frac{\$20}{\$100} = 20\%$$

$$E_p = \text{Price elasticity of demand} = \frac{-10}{20}, \text{ or } = -0.5 \text{ [absolute value} = 0.5]$$

---

### 2.1.1 Price Inelasticity (Absolute Price Elasticity of Demand < 1.0)

Demand for a good is *price inelastic* if the absolute price elasticity of demand is less than 1.0. The smaller the number the more inelastic the demand for the good.

- If price inelasticity is zero, demand is perfectly inelastic. Note also that perfectly inelastic demand curves are vertical, depicting that the quantity demanded stays the same no matter how the price changes (e.g., in the pharmaceutical industry, the demand for insulin by diabetics).

- The calculation above with a 0.5 value is an example of inelastic demand.

### 2.1.2 Price Elasticity (Absolute Price Elasticity of Demand > 1.0)

Demand is *price elastic* if the absolute price elasticity of demand is greater than 1.0. When the value is greater than 1.0 (defined as elastic), the greater the number, the more elastic the demand.

### 2.1.3 Unit Elasticity (Absolute Price Elasticity of Demand = 1.0)

Demand is *unit elastic* if the absolute price elasticity of demand is equal to exactly 1.0. Demand is unit elastic if the percentage change in the quantity demanded caused by a price change equals the percentage change in price.

### 2.1.4 Factors Affecting Price Elasticity of Demand

- Product demand is more elastic with more substitutes available but is inelastic if few substitutes are available. (Demand for soft drinks and fast-food restaurant meals are price elastic. Purveyors of those products must be careful in raising their prices.)

- The longer the time period, the more product demand becomes elastic because more choices are available.

### 2.1.5 Price Elasticity Effects on Total Revenue

If we know the price elasticity of demand for a good, we can determine how a change in price will affect a firm's total revenue. Total revenue is simply the price of a good multiplied by the quantity of the good sold.

- **Effects of Price Inelasticity on Total Revenue (Positive Relationship)**

  When demand is price inelastic, an increase in price results in a decrease in quantity demanded that is proportionally *smaller* than the increase in price. As a result, total revenue (equal to price times quantity) will increase.

- **Effects of Price Elasticity on Total Revenue (Negative Relationship)**

  When demand is price elastic, an increase in price results in a decrease in quantity demanded that is proportionally *larger* than the increase in price. As a result, total revenue (equal to price times quantity) will decrease.

- **Effects of Unit Elasticity on Revenue (No Effect)**

  If demand is unit elastic, a change in price will have no effect on total revenue.

- **Summary**

  The table below summarizes the relationship between the price elasticity of demand and total revenue.

| Price Elasticity of Demand | Implied Elasticity | Impact of a Price Increase on Total Revenue | Impact of a Price Decrease on Total Revenue |
|---|---|---|---|
| Elastic | Greater than 1 | Total revenue decreases | Total revenue increases |
| Inelastic | Less than 1 | Total revenue increases | Total revenue decreases |
| Unit Elastic | Equal to 1 | Total revenue is unchanged | Total revenue is unchanged |

## 2.2 Price Elasticity of Supply

The *price elasticity of supply* is calculated the same way as the price elasticity of demand, except that we now measure the change in quantity supplied.

$$E_p = \text{Price elasticity of supply} = \frac{\%\ \text{change in quantity supplied}}{\%\ \text{change in price}}$$

---

### Illustration 3 — Elasticity of Supply

$$\frac{\%\ \text{change}}{\text{in quantity}} = \frac{600\ (\text{new supply}) - 500\ (\text{old supply})}{500\ (\text{old supply})} = \frac{100}{500} = 20\%$$

*Divided by:*

$$\frac{\%\ \text{change}}{\text{in price}} = \frac{\$11\ (\text{new price}) - \$10\ (\text{old price})}{\$10\ (\text{old price})} = \frac{1}{10} = 10\%$$

$$E_p = \text{Price elasticity of supply} = \frac{20\%}{10\%} = 2.0$$

---

### 2.2.1 Price Inelasticity (Supply < 1.0)

Supply is *price inelastic* if the absolute price elasticity of supply is less than 1.0. If supply is perfectly inelastic, the price elasticity of supply equals zero. Perfectly inelastic supply curves are vertical, which reflects that quantity supplied is insensitive to price changes.

### 2.2.2 Price Elasticity (Supply > 1.0)

Supply is *price elastic* if the absolute price elasticity of supply is greater than 1.0.

### 2.2.3 Unit Elasticity (Supply = 1.0)

Supply is *unit elastic* if the absolute price elasticity of supply is equal to 1.0.

### 2.2.4 Factors Affecting Price Elasticity of Supply

- The feasibility of producers storing the product will affect the price elasticity of supply. For example, a product that can be produced and stored until needed may have a high elasticity of supply. When the prices increase, the product is available to sell. Perishables, such as fresh flowers, cannot be stored very long and may have a low elasticity because it is more difficult to increase supply when prices rise.

- The time required to produce and supply the good will affect the price elasticity of supply. For example, longer production time leads to lower price elasticity.

## 2.3 Cross Elasticity

*Cross elasticity* of demand (or supply) is the percentage change in the quantity demanded (or supplied) of one good caused by the price change of another good. A producer of butter might want to know the cross elasticity of demand or supply for margarine.

$$C_e = \text{Cross elasticity of demand (supply)}$$

$$= \frac{\text{\% change in number of units of X demanded (supplied)}}{\text{\% change in price of Y}}$$

### 2.3.1 Substitute Goods (Positive Coefficient)

If the coefficient is positive (i.e., the price of Product Y goes up, causing the demand for Product X to go up), the two goods are substitutes (people stop buying the higher-priced goods and begin to buy the substitute). For example, some consumers would consider ground beef and ground turkey to be substitutes.

### 2.3.2 Complementary Goods (Negative Coefficient)

If the coefficient is negative (i.e., an increase in the price of Product A results in a decrease in quantity demanded for Product B), the commodities are complements. For example, peanut butter and jelly are complementary goods (assuming you like PB&J sandwiches). Printers and ink cartridges are complementary goods.

### 2.3.3 Unrelated Goods

If the coefficient is zero, the goods are unrelated.

| Example 2 | Cross Elasticity |
|---|---|

**Facts:** The table below indicates how the price of sirloin steak will affect the quantity of steak sauce demanded (sold) at a local supermarket in a given week.

**Required:** Calculate the cross elasticity of demand for steak sauce if the price of sirloin steak (per pound) is increased from $6.50 to $7.00 this week (and the supermarket only carries sirloin steak and no hamburger).

**Solution:**

| Price (lb.) Sirloin Steak | Quantity Steak Sauce Sold |
|---|---|
| $6.00 | 80 |
| 6.50 | 60 |
| 7.00 | 38 |
| 7.50 | 23 |

$$C_{\text{Steak Sauce}} = \text{Cross elasticity of demand/supply of steak sauce}$$

$$= \frac{\text{\% change in quantity demanded of sauce}}{\text{\% change in price of steak}}$$

% change in quantity demanded of sauce = (38 − 60)/60 = −0.3667

% change in the price of steak = ($7.00 − $6.50)/$6.50 = 0.0769

Cross elasticity of demand/supply of steak sauce = −0.3667/0.0769 = −4.77

**Interpretation:** The cross elasticity is negative; the goods are complementary.

## 2.4    Income Elasticity of Demand

The *income elasticity of demand* measures the percentage change in quantity demanded for a product for a given percentage change in income.

$$I_e = \text{Income elasticity of demand (supply)}$$

$$= \frac{\% \text{ change in number of units of X demanded (supplied)}}{\% \text{ change in income}}$$

### 2.4.1    Positive Income Elasticity (Normal Good)

If the income elasticity of demand is *positive* (e.g., demand increases as income increases), the good is a normal good. A *normal good* is a product whose demand is positively related to income. As income goes up, demand for normal goods increases (e.g., premium foods such as steak and lobster).

### 2.4.2    Negative Income Elasticity (Inferior Good)

If the income elasticity of demand is *negative* (e.g., demand decreases as income increases), the good is an *inferior good*. An inferior good is a product whose demand is inversely related to income (opposite of a normal good). As income goes up, demand for inferior goods decreases (e.g., generic-labeled vegetables or hamburger).

| Example 3 | Income Elasticity of Demand |
|-----------|------------------------------|

**Facts:** Assume that the level of family annual income increases from $100,000 to $120,000, resulting in the following change in attendance at professional sports events:

| Annual Family Income | Number of Sporting Events Attended |
|:---:|:---:|
| $ 80,000 | 3 |
| 100,000 | 5 |
| 120,000 | 9 |
| 140,000 | 11 |

**Required:** Using the data above, calculate the income elasticity of demand for sporting events attended in a year in which income increases from $100,000 to $120,000.

**Solution:**

$I_e$ = Income elasticity of demand for attendance at sporting events

$$= \frac{\% \text{ change in quantity demanded of sporting events}}{\% \text{ change in income}}$$

% change in quantity demanded = (9 – 5) / 5 = 0.8

% change in income = ($120,000 – $100,000) / $100,000 = 0.2

Income elasticity of demand for sporting events = 0.8 / 0.2 = 4

**Interpretation:** Income elasticity of demand is positive; this is a normal good.

### Question 1                                                                 CPA-03667

Which one of the following changes will cause the demand curve for gasoline to shift to the left?

  **a.** The price of gasoline increases.
  **b.** The supply of gasoline decreases.
  **c.** The price of cars increases.
  **d.** The price of cars decreases.

### Question 2                                                                 CPA-05577

A city ordinance that freezes rent prices may cause:

  **a.** The demand curve for rental space to fall.
  **b.** The supply curve for rental space to rise.
  **c.** The quantity demanded of rental space exceeds the quantity supplied.
  **d.** The quantity supplied of rental space exceeds the quantity demanded.

### Question 3                                                                 CPA-05770

Which of the following characteristics would indicate that an item sold would have a high price elasticity of demand?

  **a.** The item has many similar substitutes.
  **b.** The cost of the item is low compared to the total budget of the purchasers.
  **c.** The item is considered a necessity.
  **d.** Changes in the price of the item are regulated by governmental agency.

## NOTES

# Module 4 The Impact of Market Influences: Part 1

## 1 Market Structures and Pricing

Operating environments influence a firm's strategic plan. Following is a brief discussion of the overall market structures in which firms may operate.

### 1.1 Perfect (Pure) Competition

In a perfectly competitive market, no individual firm can influence the market price of its product, nor shift the market supply sufficiently to make a good scarcer or more abundant.

#### 1.1.1 Assumptions and Market Conditions

- A large number of suppliers and customers act independently. Firms are small relative to the industry.
- There are no barriers to entry because firms exert no influence over the market or price (thus, goods and services are produced at the lowest cost to the consumer in the long run).
- Very little product differentiation (homogeneous products).
- Firms are price takers. Price is set by the market.
- Firms control only the quantity produced. Each firm can sell as much or as little as it wants at the given market price.
- Demand is perfectly elastic.
- Because there are no barriers to entry, the entry and exit of new firms ensures that economic profits are zero in the long run; thus, firms earn a normal rate of return.

#### 1.1.2 Strategies Under Perfect Competition

Under *perfect competition*, strategic plans may include maintaining the market share and responsiveness of the sales price to market conditions.

### 1.2 Monopolistic Competition

Monopolistic competition exists when many sellers compete to sell a differentiated product in a market into which the entry of new sellers is possible (e.g., brand-name cosmetic products).

#### 1.2.1 Assumptions and Market Conditions

- There are numerous firms with differentiated products. Firms are small relative to the industry.
- Few barriers to entry exist.
- Firms exert some influence over the price and market through differentiation, but have more control over quantity produced than over price.
- Differentiation results in a highly elastic but downward-sloping demand curve.

■　Because there are few barriers to entry under monopolistic competition, in the long run, monopolistically competitive firms will earn zero economic profits. If profits are positive in the short run, more firms will enter and drive down profits to zero. If firm profits are negative in the short run, firms will exit and drive up profits to zero.

### 1.2.2　Strategies Under Monopolistic Competition

Under *monopolistic competition*, strategic plans may include maintaining the market share (as with pure competition) but also will likely include a plan for enhanced product differentiation and extensive allocation of resources to advertising, marketing, product research, etc.

## 1.3　Oligopoly

An oligopoly is a market structure in which a few sellers (e.g., the "Big Three" U.S. automotive manufacturers) dominate the sales of a product and entry of new sellers is difficult or impossible.

### 1.3.1　Assumptions and Market Conditions

■　Relatively few firms with differentiated products. Firms are large relative to the industry.

■　There are fairly significant barriers to entry (e.g., high capital cost of designing a safety-tested car and building an auto plant).

■　Products are differentiated and firms have control over both the quantity produced and the price charged.

■　Firms are strongly interdependent.

■　Oligopolists face a kinked demand curve because firms match price cuts of competitors but ignore price increases. This causes the demand curves to have different slopes above and below the prevailing price.

■　Because of high barriers to entry, economic profits are positive in the long run.

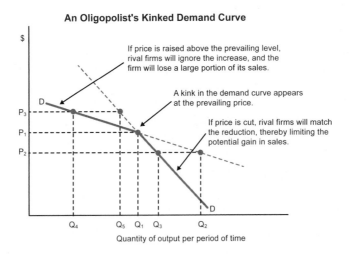

The matching of price cuts and the ignoring of price increases by rival firms has the effect of making an oligopolist's demand curve highly elastic above the ruling (prevailing) price. This causes the demand curve to be kinked, illustrating that there is not a direct relationship between price and quantity at all points on the demand curve. Firms would be foolish to engage in price cutting because rivals merely match the price reduction (e.g., the airline industry).

### 1.3.2　Strategies Under Oligopoly

Under an oligopoly, strategic plans focus on market share and call for the proper amount of advertising (to ensure appropriate product differentiation) and ways to properly adapt to price changes or required changes in production volume.

## 1.4 Monopoly

Monopoly (e.g., the classic utility company, which was a "regulated" monopoly) represents concentration of supply in the hands of a single firm.

### 1.4.1 Assumptions and Market Characteristics of Monopoly

▪ There is a single firm with a unique product.

▪ Insurmountable barriers to market entry exist.

▪ Monopolies are "price setters," as opposed to firms in perfect competition (which are "price takers"). The firm sets both output and prices (e.g., through patents or regulatory restrictions against competition).

▪ There are no substitute products (the firm's demand curve is the same as the industry's demand curve). Demand is inelastic.

▪ Because of insurmountable barriers to entry, economic profits are positive in the long run.

### 1.4.2 Strategies Under Monopoly

Under a *monopoly*, strategic plans will likely ignore market share and focus on profitability from production levels that maximize profits.

---

### Example 1 — Market Structure

**Facts:** ABC Company ("ABC") and XYZ Company ("XYZ") operate in different industries. ABC is a relatively small firm in the men's clothing industry that focuses on the young men's niche by continuously producing and offering new fashion items to its retail customers. Although ABC has significant control over the quantity of fashion items produced, the pricing of these products to its retail customer base is more a function of the market.

XYZ manufactures hubcaps and wheel covers for the U.S. auto industry. XYZ is one of many competitors in this industry, in which the standard products offered are commodity-like and the prices offered to wholesalers for its products are driven entirely by market forces. XYZ's management continues to be concerned about the expansion of firms competing against XYZ in this industry.

**Required:**

1. Identify the most likely market structure for ABC and XYZ.

2. Identify one characteristic that is common to both ABC and XYZ.

3. Indicate a market strategy that should be used by ABC and XYZ.

**Solution:**

1. The market structures for ABC and XYZ are monopolistic competition and perfect competition, respectively.

2. Both ABC and XYZ would seek a zero economic profit over the long run.

3. ABC's market strategy would focus on maintaining its market share primarily through continued enhanced product differentiation. XYZ would also focus on maintaining its market share despite a continued saturation of new firms entering this market. To accomplish this, XYZ needs to ensure that its pricing of its products continuously responds to existing market conditions.

---

## 1.5    Market Assumptions and Conditions

- Regardless of the model that represents the industry, the firm will operate best when marginal revenue equals marginal cost (MR = MC).

- Microeconomic theory holds that firms make decisions based on marginal cost and marginal revenue (essentially ignoring fixed or sunk costs).

- The following table summarizes the market assumptions and conditions underlying perfect competition, monopolistic competition, oligopoly, and monopoly.

| Summary Table: Market Structure | | | | |
|---|---|---|---|---|
| *Characteristic* | *Perfect Competition* | *Monopolistic Competition* | *Oligopoly* | *Monopoly* |
| *Number of firms in the industry* | Many (Highly competitive) | Many (Highly competitive) | Few (Moderately competitive) | One (No competition) |
| *Size of firms relative to industry* | Small | Small | Large | 100% of industry |
| *Barriers to entry* | None (Easy to enter industry) | Low (Easy to enter industry) | High (Difficult to enter industry because of economies of scale) | Insurmountable (No entry is possible) |
| *Differentiation of product* | None (All firms sell the same commodity product) | Some (Firms sell slightly different products that are close substitutes) | Various (Firms usually sell differentiated products) | None (One firm sells only one product) |
| *Firm's control over price and quantity* | Firm has control over quantity produced only; price is set by the market, firm must accept the market price | Firm has control mostly over quantity produced; price is primarily set by the market | Firm has control over both the quantity produced and the price charged | Firm has control over both price and quantity |
| *Elasticity of demand* | Perfectly elastic (Firm sells as much, or as little, as it wants at the given market price) | Highly elastic but downward sloping (Firm can adjust quantity of products sold without affecting the price very much) | Inelastic (Firms face a kinked downward-sloping demand curve) | Inelastic (Firm faces the entire demand curve for the product, which slopes downward) |
| *Long-run profitability* | Zero economic profit | Zero economic profit | Positive economic profit | Positive economic profit |
| *Strategies* | Maintaining market share and responsiveness of sales price to market conditions | Maintaining market share, enhanced product differentiation, and allocation of resources to advertising, marketing, and product research | Maintaining or enhancing market share, proper spending on advertising, and proper adaptation to price changes and changes in production volume | Ignore market share and focus on profitability from production levels that maximize profits |

# 2    The Economy as a System of Markets

## 2.1    Production and Demand for Economic Resources

### 2.1.1    Factors of Production (Resources)

Businesses use resources to make final products. The primary resources from which final products are made consist of *land* (natural resources), *labor* (human capital), and *capital* (nonhuman physical capital accumulated through past investment). These resources are known as *factors of production*. Factors of production are bought and sold in markets just as final goods and services are bought and sold in markets.

■    To maximize profits, firms need to decide on the optimal levels of inputs to employ.

■    The price firms must pay for the factors of production is determined by the interaction of supply and demand in the input market.

### 2.1.2    Types of Inputs

■    **Complementary Inputs:** Inputs are *complementary inputs* if an increase in the usage of one input results in an increase in the usage of the other input.

| Illustration 1    Complementary Inputs |
| --- |
| A firm opens two new factories (capital) and will need to hire more employees (human capital). |

■    **Substitute Inputs:** Inputs are *substitute inputs* if an increase in the usage of one input results in a decrease in the usage of the other input.

| Illustration 2    Substitute Inputs |
| --- |
| A firm that invests in production line automation (capital) may need fewer employees (human capital). |

### 2.1.3    Derived Demand

Derived demand is the demand for factors of production. A firm's demand for inputs is derived from its decision to produce a good or service. Therefore, the demand for inputs is directly related to the demand for the goods and services those inputs produce.

■    **Demand for Inputs Depends on Demand for Outputs**

The demand for any input depends on the demand for the product the input produces (i.e., the firm's output) and the marginal product of the input itself. (Recall that marginal product, or MP, is the change in total product resulting from a one-unit change in an input.)

•    If the demand for a firm's output increases, the demand for the inputs used to produce that output will also increase.

•    Similarly, if the marginal product of an input increases, the demand for that input will also increase.

■ **Examples of Derived Demand**

- The demand for labor is directly related to the demand for the goods and services that labor produces.

- If the demand for medical services increases, the derived demand for doctors, nurses, and medical equipment will also increase.

## 2.2 The Labor Market

In modern economies, workers sell their services to employers in labor markets, where workers independently offer skills of a given quality to employers who compete for the workers' services. Just as in any other market, the supply of labor and demand for labor determines the price, or wage, of workers. Thus, in the labor market, wages are the price paid for labor. The laws of demand and supply prevail in labor markets as they do in product markets. The lower the wage, the greater the quantity of labor service demanded by employers.

The following graph illustrates equilibrium in the labor market. The equilibrium wage depends on the supply of and demand for labor. The equilibrium wage is found where the demand curve for labor intersects the supply curve for labor.

**The Labor Market**

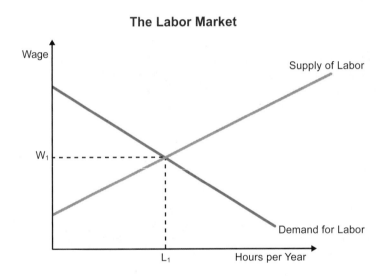

### 2.2.1 Labor Demand and Supply Under Monopsony

A *monopsony* occurs when there is only one employer in a market. For example, if a town contains a single firm, that firm is known as a monopsonist. Much like a monopolist has market power in the product market, a monopsonist has market power in the input (labor) market. Relative to a purely competitive labor market, a monopsony results in lower wages and lower levels of employment.

### 2.2.2 Unions and Wages

■ **Effect on Unionized Workers**

By forming a union and acting collectively, workers gain market power much in the same way that a monopoly or cartel has market power. The union may use its market power to bargain collectively for higher wages or restrict the supply of labor. As a result, wages of unionized workers increase.

■ **Effect on Nonunionized Workers**

Unions may also affect the wages of nonunionized workers. Suppose there are two worker sectors in an economy, one unionized and the other not. Because employment falls in the unionized sector, displaced workers may seek employment in the nonunion sector. As a result, wages in the nonunion sector may fall as the supply of labor in that sector increases. Thus, while wages rise in the unionized sector, they may fall in the sector that is not unionized.

### 2.2.3 Minimum Wage Laws

The use of minimum wage laws to increase the wages of low-skilled labor is controversial. If the minimum wage is set above the equilibrium wage, an excess supply of labor will result. In other words, if the minimum wage is above the equilibrium wage, the result is unemployment.

Furthermore, the imposition of a minimum wage increases the income of those workers who have a job, but it decreases the income of workers who find themselves unemployed as a result of the imposition of the minimum wage. The effect of a minimum wage is illustrated in the following graph.

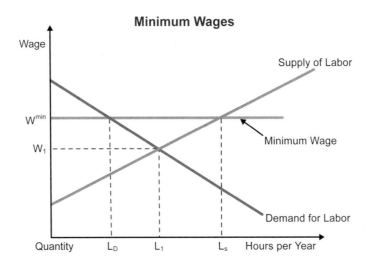

When the minimum wage is set at $W^{min}$, the quantity of labor demanded decreases from $L_1$ to $L_D$ and the quantity of labor supplied increases from $L_1$ to $L_s$. As a result, the minimum wage causes unemployment, or an excess supply of labor, of $L_s - L_D$.

# 3    Factors That Influence Strategy

When determining the effects of the market on business strategy, a look at the overall macro-environment in which the firm operates is essential because it can significantly assist the company in developing and choosing the best strategy to meet its goals.

## 3.1    General Types of Factors That Influence Strategy

Firms use SWOT (Strengths, Weaknesses, Opportunities, and Threats) analysis to assist in developing their appropriate strategic plans. Any strategy must consider these factors in its development.

### 3.1.1 Internal Factors (Strengths and Weaknesses)

Factors internal to the organization that affect strategy are sources of strengths and weaknesses and include:

- Innovation of product lines
- Competence of management
- Core competencies (outstanding skills that are better than those of the competitors)
- Influence of high-level managers
- Capital improvements
- Leadership in research and development
- Cohesiveness of the values of the organization
- Marketing effectiveness
- Effectiveness of communication
- Clarity of the strategic mission

### 3.1.2 External Factors (Opportunities and Threats)

Factors external to the organization are sources of opportunities in the market and threats to the firm's ability to continue with its strategic plan.

- **Factors That Affect the Overall Industry and Competitive Environment of the Industry**
  - The economy
  - Regulations and laws
  - Demographics of the population
  - Technological advances and existing technology
  - Social values
  - Political issues

- **Factors That Affect the Competitive Environment of the Firm**
  - Barriers to market entry
  - Market competitiveness
  - Existence of substitute products
  - Bargaining power of the customers
  - Bargaining power of the suppliers

## Illustration 3    SWOT Analysis

Diverse Company (DC) is an international firm that produces bottles and pumps for its three distinct business segments, including food, healthcare, and fragrance. The following SWOT analysis was prepared by an equity analyst to further understand the factors which affect the company's business strategy.

Strengths **(S):** Diverse Company has developed strong business relationships in many of its international markets, which has resulted in steadily increasing market shares for its product offerings. The company has been successful in implementing production efficiencies, which has led to improved operating margins.

Weaknesses **(W):** Despite its diversification, the company has significant exposure to the European market, which has been in a recession. The company's net earnings are also subject to foreign-exchange risk (exposure) as DC has operations in 12 countries.

Opportunities **(O):** There has been increased demand for personal healthcare products in emerging market countries. Although DC currently has limited product sales to emerging markets, management considers this a significant opportunity to expand its global market share.

Threats **(T):** While barriers to entry in the company's product markets are moderate, DC will have to increase its already significant investment in R&D to maintain its customer base. These additional operating costs, along with expected further compliance and regulatory costs, may erode the company's impressive operating margins.

---

### Question 1                                                                           CPA-06642

Which of the following is an assumption in a perfectly competitive financial market?

- **a.** No single trader or traders can have a significant impact on market prices.
- **b.** Some traders can impact market prices more than others.
- **c.** Trading prices vary based on supply only.
- **d.** Information about borrowing/lending activities is only available to those willing to pay market prices.

---

### Question 2                                                                           CPA-03493

Under an oligopoly structure, strategic plans focus on:

- **a.** Profitability from production levels that maximize profits.
- **b.** Maintaining the market share and being responsive to market conditions related to sales price.
- **c.** Maintaining the market share and planning for enhanced product differentiation.
- **d.** Maintaining the market share, ensuring product differentiation, and adapting to changes in price and/or production volume.

# 1 Porter's Five Forces

The following five forces identified by Michael Porter of Harvard University have a significant effect on the competitive environment and profitability of the firm.

## 1.1 Barriers to Entry

The firm faces the threat of new firms entering the market in which it operates.

- **Types of Barriers to Entry**

  Often, rival firms face barriers to entry in the form of government regulation, supplier access, high up-front capital requirements, preexisting customer preferences and loyalties, economies of scale, learning-curve issues, and other up-front competitive cost disadvantages, including patents, trade barriers, and other restrictions.

- **When New Companies Will Attempt to Enter**

  New companies will attempt to enter the competition when barriers to entry are low, potential high profits exist in the market, and the risk of retaliation by other firms is low. If the industry as a whole is earning a profit, other firms will desire to enter the market. Unless barriers to entry exist, firms will enter until profits fall to a competitive level. It is also possible that the simple threat of new entrants will scare existing firms into keeping their prices at competitive levels.

## 1.2 Market Competitiveness (Intensity of Competition)

The existence of competition from rival firms is often the most significant of the five forces of competition.

- **Ability of Rival Firms to Respond to Change**

  If a firm is in competition with other firms that are all able to respond to changes in various components affecting business (e.g., regulation, input costs, labor issues, technology changes, consumer desires for improved quality and service, etc.), the firm faces a strong competitive force.

- **Advertising of Rival Firms**

  If rival firms are likely to spend large amounts of money on advertising aimed at changing customer preferences and creating loyalty, the impact of this competitive factor is increased.

- **Research and Development of Rival Firms**

  When rival firms spend large amounts of money on research and development to improve their products or create innovations in technology, the effect of this competitive factor is increased.

■ **Alliances of Rival Firms and Suppliers**

Often, rival firms focus on developing strong alliances with suppliers. This could affect the firm's ability to obtain its inputs to the production process at advantageous prices and, thus, reduce its competitive advantage. When alliances are created, the impact of this competitive factor is increased.

■ **Other Factors Increasing Competition**

Competition becomes an even stronger force affecting the firm when: the market is not growing fast (in contrast, in fast-growing markets, competitors are usually able to sustain profitability without having to take market share from their rivals); several equal-sized firms exist in the market; customers do not have strong brand preferences; the cost of exiting the market exceeds the cost of continuing to operate; some firms profit from making certain moves to increase market share; and the various firms employ different types of strategic plans.

## 1.3    Existence of Substitute Products

If the firm faces heavy competition from substitute products, the ability of a firm to sustain profits is significantly affected by the maximum amount that buyers are willing to pay for a product. This is especially true if the substitutes are readily available to consumers, have equal performance, and are priced at or below the price of the firm's product. The effect is further intensified when the costs of the buyer switching to the substitute product are low. If few substitutes exist, buyers have little choice of products and may be willing to pay a higher price for the products that are available. If close substitutes exist, buyers may have a limit on the maximum price that they are willing to pay, and this has a direct effect on the profits of the firm.

---

**Illustration 1    Existence of Substitute Products**

Both Chevrolet and Ford have strong market positions in the U.S. pickup truck market. If Ford is able to lower its model prices due to increased efficiencies in its production process, and consumers view their pickup truck models as comparable, there is a legitimate threat that Chevrolet could lose market share because switching costs are virtually nonexistent.

---

## 1.4    Bargaining Power of the Customers

If buyers are in the position to bargain with suppliers on the conditions of service, price, and quality, they are a strong force in the competitive market in which the firm operates. For example, Wal-Mart Stores Inc. is a retailer that is known to have a strong position when it comes to bargaining with its suppliers.

Buyers may be quite price sensitive and change products solely based on price, or they may have such brand loyalty and strong preferences that they will stay with a product regardless of price (oftentimes depending on the elasticity of demand).

■ **Large Volume of a Firm's Business (High Buyer Concentration)**

If one group of customers makes up a large volume of the firm's business, the bargaining power (negotiating power) of the customer will significantly affect the competitive environment of the firm, and the strategy of firms should focus on pleasing this group of customers.

■ **Availability of Information**

The more information that is available to the buyer, the more the buyer will be able to compare and contrast features of a product and choose one over the other.

▪ **Buyer's Low Cost of Switching Products**

If the costs of switching from one product to another are low, the impact on the competitive environment from buyers is increased. This result is intensified if the firm cannot easily change production without incurring high costs to begin producing another product.

▪ **High Number of Alternative Suppliers**

When many suppliers exist to serve the customers, the bargaining power of the buyer is increased.

## 1.5    Bargaining Power of the Suppliers

When the bargaining power of the suppliers of inputs to the production process is high, suppliers can take profits away from a firm simply by increasing the cost of the inputs to the firm's production process.

▪ **Firm Is Unable to Change Suppliers**

If the firm is unable to use different suppliers or cannot change its inputs (i.e., no substitutes are available), changes in the operations of the supplier, and thus the price of the input, will affect the profitability of firms, especially when those input costs are a significant part of the overall product cost.

▪ **Reputation of Supplier and Demand for Its Goods**

If the reputation of the supplier (e.g., the quality of its product) is excellent and crucial to the success of the firm's product, and the demand for its goods from other firms is high, the firm could be placed in a difficult situation, especially if the firm is not a large client of the supplier or if strategic alliances have been formed between the supplier and a competitor.

# 2    Types of Competitive Strategies

Building a successful competitive strategy requires being able to attain some sort of competitive advantage while still holding customer loyalty and having value for the customer.

## 2.1    Competitive Advantage in General

The overall competitive advantage of a firm is determined by the value the firm offers to its customers minus the cost of creating that value. Firms that seek to achieve competitive advantage with respect to products will choose from two basic forms of advantage.

### 2.1.1    Cost Leadership Advantage

The *cost leadership advantage* stems from the fact that the buyers of the product are better off because the firm has been able to produce and sell its product for less than its rivals. If the total costs of the firm are less than those of rival firms, the firm has a competitive market advantage. This advantage may be used by the firm in one of two ways:

▪ **Build Market Share**

If the firm lowers the price of its product below the price of its competitors, it may be able to gain market share by securing a larger part of the market as its customer base while still maintaining the profits that are required.

▪ **Match the Price of Rivals**

If a firm enjoys a low-cost competitive advantage, it will be able to match the price of its rivals and, because it has overall lower total costs, beat the profitability of its rivals.

### 2.1.2 Differentiation Advantage (Offering Advantage)

The *differentiation advantage* (product differentiation) stems from the fact that buyers are better off because the customer perceives the firm's product to be superior in some way to those of its rivals. Therefore, they are willing to pay a higher price for its uniqueness.

All parts of the buying decision are affected by the perceived value of the product (e.g., higher quality, timeliness of delivery, superior service, wide range of goods, fewer risks, performance measures, etc.). After the product has been differentiated, the firm must always be sure to remain profitable and recoup the cost of the "premium" included with the product. This advantage may be used by the firm in one of two ways:

- **Build Market Share**

  The firm may attempt to build market share by pricing its product below what it would charge to recoup the premium with a standard number of buyers and try to recover its costs because it captures more than an average share of the market.

- **Increase Price**

  The firm may increase the price of its product to the point at which it exactly offsets the value the customer perceives in the product.

## 2.2 Five Basic Types of Competitive Strategies

There are five types of competitive strategies that firms can employ:

1. Cost leadership focused on a broad range of buyers.
2. Cost leadership focused on a narrow range (niche) of buyers.
3. Differentiation focused on a broad range of buyers.
4. Differentiation focused on a narrow range (niche) of buyers.
5. Best cost provider.

## 2.3 Cost Leadership Strategies

Organizations may choose to achieve their organizational missions by selling their product or service for less than any other participant in the marketplace. Cost leaders undermine the profitability of their competitors as a means of achieving overwhelming market share.

---

**Illustration 2     Cost Leadership Strategies**

Toys-Only Company is an online toy retailer that sells toys to the mass consumer market. In order to increase its market share and to compete with the "brick and mortar" stores, the company's strategy has been focused on offering a complete line of toys at the lowest prices. This cost leadership strategy has been successful for Toys-Only given that it sells commodity-like products to the general U.S. toy retail market.

---

■ **When Cost Leadership Strategies Work Well**

Cost leadership strategies work well in markets in which buyers have large amounts of bargaining power and are able to switch between competitive products without incurring significant cost.

Such strategies also are successful in markets with heavy price competition and where firms (especially new entry firms) can influence buyers to switch to their product and then increase their customer base simply by cutting the price of the product for a period.

■ **When Cost Leadership Strategies Fail**

If firms focus too much on cutting costs of the current process, they may overlook technological advances that could help lower costs (especially those that rivals have latched onto) or overlook the fact that consumers may want improvements to the product or may not care as much about the existence of a lower price in the desired product.

## 2.4   Differentiation Strategies (Product Differentiation)

Organizations may choose to achieve their organizational missions by creating the perception that their product is better or has a unique quality that differentiates it from competitors in the marketplace. Firms that successfully differentiate their products are able to command higher prices.

---

### Illustration 3     Differentiation Strategies

Quality Bathroom Inc. sells high-end bathtubs and accessories to a regional market. Because the company offers unique features, designs, and materials, its bathtubs sell at premium prices. This strategy has been successful for the company given its ability to clearly offer value-added products (at higher prices) to its retail customer market.

---

■ **When Differentiation Strategies Work Well**

Differentiation strategies work well when customers are able to see value in a product, when the product appeals to different people for different reasons, and when the firms that are competing in the market choose different features to differentiate their products.

■ **When Differentiation Strategies Fail**

When a firm attempts to differentiate in an area without properly assessing the requirements of the consumer for desired features and preferences, or without creating value for the consumer, a differentiation strategy can fail.

Further, firms that focus too much on one area (or the wrong area) may end up creating a product whose value does not exceed the higher price that must be charged for the feature.

If a firm is in a market in which customers do not care about differentiation, will not pay extra for unique features, and are happy with paying a lower price for a more generic product, a differentiation strategy can fail.

## 2.5   Best Cost Strategies

The best cost strategy combines the cost leadership strategy with the differentiation strategy to give customers higher value for their purchase price (i.e., a high-quality product at a reasonable price). If a firm is able to achieve the lowest cost among its closest competitors while matching them on features desired by consumers, it will succeed.

**Illustration 4     Best Cost Strategies**

Wal-Mart Stores Inc. is a mass merchandiser that uses a best cost strategy to increase its market share. Because of sheer economies of scale (e.g., purchasing, distribution), the company is able to offer the lowest prices on its vast product lines, which include many name brands as well as its own generic brands. Wal-Mart's business strategy continues to be focused on offering customers superior products at the overall lowest prices.

- **When Best Cost Strategies Work Well**

    Best cost strategies work well when generic products are not acceptable to the varied needs and preferences of the buyers, but the buyers are still sensitive to the value that they are receiving for the money they are spending and the overall price they are paying.

- **When Best Cost Strategies Fail**

    Because the best cost strategist plays the "middle," it faces the risk of losing customers to other firms that are using cost leadership strategies or those that are specifically focused on differentiation.

## 2.6    Focus/Niche Strategies

Firms with cost leadership or differentiation strategies may choose to focus their chosen strategy on a select, small group of consumers, or a niche. Rather than having to address the needs and preferences of a broad range of consumers, these firms are able to focus on market niches where consumers have specialized needs and preferences.

**Illustration 5     Focus/Niche Strategies**

All-Star Baseball Gloves Inc. makes premium baseball gloves for the collegiate/professional niche market, which includes collegiate baseball, minor league baseball, and major league teams. The company has been successful because it uses the highest-quality leather materials and includes special features in each of the player position baseball gloves it manufactures and sells to the collegiate/professional niche market.

- **When Focus/Niche Strategies Work Well**

    The focus/niche strategy works well, provided the niche has a large enough demand to create a profit for the firm, the firm has the proper resources to adequately serve the needs of the niche group, and when few firms are focusing in an area where others cannot compete in price or are not addressing a particular feature.

- **When Focus/Niche Strategies Fail**

    When other firms see that the niche has been successful for those serving it, they will attempt to enter the market as competitors and take away some of the sales of the firm, likely reducing the firm's profits and its competitive advantage. The firm also faces a risk that those consumers in the current niche may find that they actually prefer the features of products that the overall market desires. If the firm is not easily responsive to change (flexible) for whatever reason, the focus/niche strategies can fail.

# 3   Value Chain Analysis

Value chain analysis is a *strategic tool* that assists a firm in determining how important its value is (as perceived by buyers) with respect to the market in which the firm operates. Managers must determine the flow of activities undertaken by the organization to produce a service or product and critique the value added to the customer by each link in the value chain. Once the firm is aware of how its product is perceived, value chain analysis is invaluable in assessing the ability of the firm to obtain a competitive advantage.

## 3.1   Approach of Value Chain Analysis

Firms must assess every part of the value chain to allow them to provide their customers with maximum value; they must determine the parts of the value chain that will provide them with the largest competitive advantage. Three major forms of analysis are performed.

### 3.1.1   Internal Costs Analysis

In order to determine the internal value-creating ability of a firm, the sources of profit and costs of the internal activities within the firm must be analyzed.

### 3.1.2   Internal Differentiation Analysis

The firm may analyze its ability to create value through differentiation (e.g., what are the sources of differentiation and what are the related costs?) when the customer perceives that the firm's product is superior to those of its rivals.

### 3.1.3   Vertical Linkage Analysis

Analyzing the vertical linkage of the firm means understanding the activities of the suppliers and buyers of the product (i.e., all links from the sources of the raw materials through the recycling and disposal of the product after use) and determining where value can be created external to the firm's operations.

## 3.2   Steps in Value Chain Analysis

There are four general steps in value chain analysis:

1.  **Identify Value Activities**

    Organizations must *identify value activities* performed as part of their business. Value activities are generally those processes that are involved with *designing, preparing, manufacturing,* and *delivering* a good or service.

2.  **Identify Cost Drivers Associated With Each Activity**

    *Cost drivers* represent factors that increase total cost. Identification of cost drivers assists the organization in determining those areas in which it has a competitive advantage. Organizations might also identify those areas in which outsourcing is valuable.

3.  **Develop a Competitive Advantage by Reducing Cost or Adding Value**
    - **Identify Competitive Advantage:** Firms with cost leadership strategies will look at cost-saving opportunities, and firms with differentiation strategies will look at opportunities for innovation.

    - **Identify Opportunities for Added Value:** Product innovation for those organizations that depend on differentiation and reduced prices for those organizations that are focused on cost leadership will be the drivers of value chain analysis.

- **Identify Opportunities for Reduced Cost**: Analysis of the cost drivers should show where the organization is not competitive. Elimination or outsourcing of those items for which the organization is not cost competitive is generally proposed from this step in value chain analysis.

4. **Exploit Linkages Among Activities in the Value Chain**

   Analysis of the value chain may also show synergies or connections that can be used to create greater efficiencies or greater value. Each step of the value chain should produce some value.

   In some cases, that value not only benefits the specific activity in the chain, but also benefits other activities. For example, in-house customer service departments handle customer complaints in an efficient and courteous manner that establishes organizational responsiveness to the customer and creates loyalty. In-house customer service staff also can be alert for patterns of complaints that may influence product design.

---

**Illustration 6     Value Chain Analysis**

Boat Motors Inc. (BMI) is a low-cost manufacturer of motor boat engines for recreational fishing boats. Company management has prepared the following value chain analysis blueprint for the upcoming operating year.

BMI *Value Activities* include state-of-the-art design, production of low-cost efficient engines, and superior delivery and installation of boat engines.

BMI's primary *cost drivers* are focused on using high-quality raw materials, outsourcing certain production labor costs, lowering assembly and repair costs, and minimizing delivery costs.

BMI's *competitive advantage* will focus on further lowering product costs by expanding its outsourcing of direct and indirect labor, and designing a more efficient assembly production process. Given the company's extensive trucking network, BMI will attempt to maximize its economies of scale in trucking while reducing redundancies in delivery routes.

BMI will continue to strive to *improve the linkage* of its key production functions, including basic motor part production/purchases, motor design, motor assembly, and motor installation. In order to effectively reduce costs to the customer end-user, each production function will have a goal of lowering costs by a minimum of 5 percent in the upcoming year. The head of operations will accomplish this production goal by initiating monthly meetings between the production-function department heads and holding the managers more accountable for their goal achievement by restructuring their compensation packages.

---

## 3.3    Global Competitive Advantage and Value Chain Analysis

In addition to Michael Porter's look at the "five forces" that affect the profits and competitive environment of an industry, Porter focused on the competitive forces that exist globally by studying the ability of a nation to attain and sustain worldwide competitive advantage. When the various parts of the value chain exist in different parts of the world, this may pose problems of costs of transportation and lack of control and communication, which can negatively affect the overall customer value.

Porter identified four major factors that impact global competitive advantage:

1. **Conditions of the Factors of Production**

   If the nation has a strong set of factors of production (e.g., a skilled labor force) that are required in a given industry, it will fare better with regard to global competitive advantage.

2. **Conditions of Domestic Demand**

   If the nation's domestic demand for the product is high, the nation will fare better with regard to global competitive advantage.

3. **Related and Supporting Industries**

   If suppliers of material inputs exist within the nation, it may help the nation fare better with regard to global competitive advantage (unless the costs are prohibitively high). If other rival domestic firms that are competitive in the international environment exist, the nation's competitive advantage is increased.

4. **Firm Strategy, Structure, and Rivalry**

   The practices of a nation with respect to how companies are managed and organized, along with the laws of the nation that regulate the formation of companies and the intensity of rivalry among competing firms, all influence the ability of the nation to attain and sustain competitive advantage.

| Question 1 | CPA-04830 |
|---|---|

Under which of the following conditions is the supplier most able to influence or control buyers?

  a.  When the supplier's products are not differentiated.

  b.  When the supplier does not face the threat of substitute products.

  c.  When the industry is controlled by a large number of companies.

  d.  When the purchasing industry is an important customer to the supplying industry.

| Question 2 | CPA-03609 |
|---|---|

When do differentiation strategies fail?

  a.  The firm's product appeals to different people for different reasons.

  b.  The value of the firm's differentiation premium does not exceed its cost.

  c.  Customers are able to see (or perceive) a value in the firm's product compared with products of other firms.

  d.  The various rival firms have chosen different features on which to differentiate their products.

## NOTES

# 1 Globalization

*Globalization* is defined as the distribution of industrial and service activities across an increasing number of nations. Globalization produces deeper integration of the world's individual national economies and makes them more interdependent. Reduced barriers to trade have created opportunities to conduct operations in multiple countries or conduct import/export operations within the context of a traditional domestic operation. Entities that conduct business outside the country in which they are organized are frequently referred to as *multinational corporations* (MNC).

Globalization is often measured by world trade as a percentage of GDP—the greater the percentage, the greater the degree of globalization.

## 1.1 Factors That Drive Globalization

■ **Improvements in Transportation:** Increased efficiencies in transportation enhance the competitive status of importers in domestic markets.

■ **Technological Advancements:** Knowledge-based products (such as technical support for software, etc.) eliminate the importance of location.

■ **Deregulation of International Financial Markets:** Elimination of capital controls increases the options for direct foreign investment, although political and legal limitations are still an inherent risk of international commerce.

■ **Organizational/Operational Options for International Business:** When conducting business internationally, an entity must decide whether to centralize or decentralize certain business operations or functions. The availability of human labor, raw materials, or transportation channels for a business region can affect the type of production, distribution, and marketing activities performed by a region.

# 2 Motivations for International Business Operations

Entities are encouraged to look beyond the political borders in which they were organized to maximize shareholder value. Several economic theories support international trade as a means of achieving improved shareholder value.

## 2.1 Comparative Advantage

Specialization in the production and trade of specific products produces a *comparative advantage* in relation to *trading* partners. Companies and countries use comparative advantage to maximize the value of their efforts and resources.

---

**Illustration 1      Comparative Advantage**

The island nation of Bermuda produces no gasoline or vehicles, yet its roadways are filled with vehicles of all types. The country specializes in tourism and uses the money it earns from its visitors to buy (import) vehicles and petroleum products. The country maximizes its resources by specializing in tourism and buying transportation resources elsewhere.

## 2.2    Imperfect Markets

Resource markets are often deemed to be *imperfect*. The ability to trade freely between markets is often limited by the physical immobility of the resource or regulatory barriers. In order to retrieve more resources, companies must trade outside their borders.

---

**Illustration 2      Imperfect Markets**

Hi-Tech Components Inc. requires special electronic components to build its state-of-the art antenna systems. Although the company purchases 50 percent of these components domestically, Hi-Tech has historically purchased 35 percent and 15 percent of the remaining specialized components from Asia and Europe, respectively.

Over the past six months, Hi-Tech has faced a significant increase in prices for these international components due to production shortages, higher shipping costs, and political tensions with several of the exporting countries. In order to remedy this risk, Hi-Tech is currently seeking other international trading partners for these specialized components.

---

## 2.3    Product Cycle

Product manufacture or delivery is subject to a definable cycle, starting with the initial development of the product to meet needs in the domestic markets. Product cycle theory predicts that domestic success will result in domestic competition, encouraging the export of products or services to meet foreign demand and to maintain efficient use of capacity. Foreign success will in turn promote foreign competition. The entity is then motivated to establish a business outside its boundaries to differentiate itself more effectively and to compete with foreign business rivals.

# 3    Methods of Conducting International Business Operations

Multinational operations are structured in any number of ways. The following terms help define different methods of organization:

- **International Trade:** Companies (and nations) conduct international trade by exporting/ importing products or services.

- **Licensing:** Entities that provide the right to use processes or technologies in exchange for a fee are engaged in licensing activities.

> **Illustration 3     Licensing**
>
> Wireless Inc., a U.S. corporation, obligates itself to establishing and maintaining cellular telephone systems in Mexico in exchange for a licensing fee to use its technology.

- **Franchising:** Franchisors are entities whose marketing service or delivery strategy provides training and related service delivery resources in exchange for a fee.

> **Illustration 4     Franchising**
>
> Flip-a-Burger Inc., a U.S. corporation, obligates itself to providing training and the use of unique company logos to businesses that operate in Peru.

- **Joint Ventures:** *Joint ventures* take advantage of comparative advantage of one or both of the participants in marketing or delivering a product.

> **Illustration 5     Joint Ventures**
>
> Engulf & Devour Food Products, a U.S. corporation, teams with Chez Brule, a French concern, to distribute U.S. confections throughout France using Chez Brule's distribution network.

- **Direct Foreign Investment (DFI):** An entity may establish international operations by purchasing a foreign company as a subsidiary or by starting a subsidiary operation within the borders of a foreign country.

- **Global Sourcing:** *Global sourcing* is the synchronization of all levels of product manufacturing, including research and development, production, and marketing, on an international basis. Global sourcing is frequently implemented through a range of organizational and business arrangements (e.g., import/export operations, licensing, franchises, joint ventures).

# 4     Relevant Factors of Globalization

Factors relevant to assessing the effect of globalization on a company include:

- **Political and Legal Influences:** Conducting business internationally may involve certain political risks that could be potentially disruptive to an entity. The legal requirements for conducting business in a given foreign country should also be assessed.

- **Potential for Asset Expropriation:** Nations may expropriate (take) assets from the international companies that own the assets. Assessing the risk of political intervention is integral to business planning and financial reporting.

- **Taxes and Tariffs:** Governments may attempt to control economic activity through taxes and tariffs. Mitigation of this risk is typically handled through transfer pricing.

■ **Limitations on Asset Ownership or Joint Venture Participation:** Governments may limit the amount of ownership or entirely restrict any ownership of business ventures within their borders, thereby limiting joint ventures and direct investments.

■ **Content or Value Added Limits:** Sometimes referred to as sourcing requirements, governments may provide tariff reductions to companies whose imports include specified percentages of material and labor in their products.

■ **Foreign Trade Zones:** Governments may establish trade zones in which tariffs are waived until the goods leave the zone. The creation of foreign trade zones affects the government's control of imports and the location of import facilities.

■ **Economic Systems**

• **Centrally Planned Economies:** Some economies (such as China) are centrally planned. Factors of production (capital, land, etc.) are owned by the government and subject to restriction.

• **Market Economies:** Most industrialized economies (such as the United States and Japan) are market economies. The factors of production are owned by individuals.

• **Conglomerates:** Establishment of integrated conglomerates (e.g., the Japanese keiretsu or the Korean chaebol) creates self-sustaining entities that could not exist in the United States (fully integrated financing, manufacturing, and supplying organizations would likely violate antitrust laws).

■ **Culture:** Different *cultures* affect international business. *Culture* can be defined as the shared values and attitudes of a group. The cultures of nations or regions typically involve the following issues.

• **Individualism vs. Collectivism:** Some cultures (such as that of the United States) place a high value on individualism, and others (often Asian) are more likely to place a higher value on the collective.

• **Uncertainty Avoidance:** Certain cultures have difficulty dealing with *uncertainty*. The United States typically has a guarded ability to accept uncertainty, while Asian and South American cultures may be highly averse to dealing with uncertainty.

• **Short-Term vs. Long-Term Orientation:** Certain cultures are traditional, adapting more slowly to change, while others are more focused on immediate gratification. The United States tends to have a short-term orientation, and many Asian cultures have a longer-term focus.

• **Acceptance of Leadership Hierarchy:** Cultures have varying degrees of acceptance of vast differences between leadership and the rank and file. Some accept large differences in power and others anticipate greater levels of equality. The United States has a balanced view on this issue, although former European monarchies may be more accepting of wide differences in power. Less-developed former colonial counterparts in Asia and South America are often more distrustful of wide dispersions of power.

• **Technology and Infrastructure:** International business may require factoring in wide differences in:

—Communications systems

—Transportation systems

—Power and water sources

—Training of staff

—Differences in accounting practices

# 5    Inherent Risks of International Business Operations

The risks associated with conducting international business operations are generally categorized by the following:

## 5.1    Exchange Rate Fluctuation

*Exchange rate* or currency risks (and mitigation techniques) are generally divided into three categories:

- Transaction risk
- Economic risk
- Translation risk

## 5.2    Foreign Economies

An operation within a *foreign economy* carries the risk of functioning within the general health or weakness of a particular economy. Domestic economies may be booming while international economies may be suffering and acting as a drag on a multinational company's overall performance. The state of the foreign economy in which the company operates is highly significant to risk evaluation.

### 5.2.1    Foreign Demand

A multinational corporation exporting to a foreign country is vitally concerned with demand within that country. Demand is directly affected by the health of the economy of the country in which it operates.

- Weakening demand may cause the foreign government to implement tariffs or other regulatory measures that reduce foreign penetration.

- Measures to reduce foreign penetration may require either curtailment of foreign operations or export of goods produced by the multinational inside the foreign country instead of selling within the foreign country.

### 5.2.2    Interest Rates

- Higher interest rates in the foreign country are indicators of slower economic growth and reduced demand.

- Lower interest rates in the foreign country may be indicative of increased growth and demand.

### 5.2.3    Inflation

- Higher local (economy) inflation reduces purchasing power, making imported goods more expensive and reducing local demand.

- Lower local (economy) inflation increases the purchasing power for imported goods, resulting in higher local demand.

### 5.2.4    Exchange Rates

- Weak local currency reduces demand for imported goods.

- Strong local currency increases demand for imported goods.

## 5.3 Political Risk

Political risks represent noneconomic events or environmental conditions that are potentially disruptive to financial operations. Ultimately, political climates or actions can disrupt cash flows. Although expropriation of productive resources represents the most extreme political risk, other features of political risk also must be considered, including:

- Bureaucracies and related inefficiencies or barriers to trade
- Corruption
- The host government's attitude toward foreign firms
- The attitude of consumers toward foreign firms
- Inconvertibility of foreign currency
- War

---

### Question 1                                                          CPA-08364

Each of the following is an effect from opening markets to foreign investment, *except*:

    **a.** An increase in the correlation of emerging stock markets with world markets.

    **b.** A change in the volatility of emerging stock market returns.

    **c.** A decrease in local firms' cost of capital.

    **d.** A decrease in investment growth rates.

---

### Question 2                                                          CPA-08365

Global companies that deal with the political and financial risks of conducting business in a particular foreign location face which of the following types of risk?

    **a.** Country risk

    **b.** Principal risk

    **c.** Interest rate risk

    **d.** Commodity price risk

---

# 1  Business Combinations

An entity can expand its operations by entering into a business combination. The four primary types of combinations include horizontal, vertical, circular, and diagonal combinations. Transactions include mergers, acquisitions, consolidations, tender offers, purchases of assets, and management acquisitions.

## 1.1  Types of Business Combinations

### 1.1.1  Horizontal Combination

A horizontal combination occurs when companies in the same industry that produce the same goods or provide the same services join together under single management/leadership. Both horizontal and vertical combinations (described next) offer benefits, such as reduced competition, economies of scale leading to reduced costs, expertise at various levels of production, minimized overproduction, and maximized profits.

### Illustration 1    Horizontal Combination

Heinz and Kraft Foods, both in the business of selling processed food to consumers, merged into one company—the Kraft Heinz Company—in 2015. The expectation at the time of the merger was that the new company would become one of the largest food and beverage companies in both the United States and the world. The new company projected annual revenues of approximately $28 billion, along with an expected $1.5 billion in cost savings.

### 1.1.2  Vertical Combination

A vertical combination involves the combination of companies at different stages of the production process. The companies can be from the same industry or multiple industries. A vertical combination can assure the supply of raw materials (backward integration) or provide a stable market for products sold (forward integration).

### Illustration 2    Vertical Combination

In 1996, Time Warner Inc. merged with Turner Broadcasting to create a massive, worldwide entertainment conglomerate. This merger provided Time Warner access to many of the basic cable television channels (and historical films) that were owned previously by Turner. Federal Trade Commission concerns about the merger's effect on competition in the cable industry kept the deal in limbo for months.

### 1.1.3 Circular Combination

A circular combination occurs when different business units with relatively remote connections come together under single management. The relationship could come from using similar distribution or advertising channels, or requiring similar production processes. Having one management group over the combined units reduces overall administrative and other operational costs.

| Illustration 3 | Circular Combination |
| --- | --- |

Pharma Inc. is a leading company in the U.S. pharmaceuticals industry. In order to expand its business within its current consumer market and to take advantage of potential cost reductions, it acquires Letson Watson—a company specializing in building residential real estate for adult communities 55 and older.

### 1.1.4 Diagonal Combination

A diagonal combination occurs when a company that engages in an activity integrates with another company that provides ancillary support for that primary activity. The purpose is to ensure that the ancillary support is delivered in a timely and effective manner, which is crucial to the mission of the primary activity and business.

| Illustration 4 | Diagonal Combination |
| --- | --- |

Landbright Farms breeds organic livestock and sells the meat to high-end grocery stores. Fresh Meats Inc. transports Landbright's products to market in refrigerated trucks. If Landbright were to merge with Fresh Meats, this would be an example of a diagonal combination.

## 1.2 Transactions

### 1.2.1 Merger

In a merger, two (or more) entities combine to form a single new corporation, with the stocks of all merging companies surrendered and replaced with new stock in the name of the new company. Mergers often involve the combination of like-sized companies.

| Illustration 5 | Merger |
| --- | --- |

In 2016, Dell Inc. and EMC Corp. will merge to become Dell Technologies. The deal is expected to be worth close to $60 billion and will bring together two powerful technology franchises with strong capabilities in storage, servers, PCs, hybrid cloud, converged infrastructure, mobile, and security.

## 1.2.2   Acquisition

The acquisition of one company by another involves no new company. Only the acquirer remains after the acquisition. The acquired firm, which is generally smaller than the acquiring firm, may retain its legal structure and name, or it may be subsumed by the acquirer and cease to exist.

### Illustration 6   Acquisition

In 1984, the U.S. Department of Justice instructed AT&T to divest its regional telephone companies. Twenty-two years later, AT&T reacquired Bell South in a deal worth more than $85 billion dollars. The company retained the name AT&T.

## 1.2.3   Tender Offer

In a tender offer, a company makes an offer directly to shareholders to buy the outstanding shares of another company at a specified price. The offer may be in the form of cash or securities of the acquiring corporation (stocks, warrants, debt issuances). Shareholders of the target company have the option of accepting or rejecting the offer.

### Illustration 7   Tender Offer

Biltmore Inc. offers $13 per share to buy the stock directly from the shareholders of Alexander Co. (the target company). Alexander stock is currently selling at $11 per share, making the Biltmore offer very attractive to the target's shareholders. Assuming that the majority of shareholders agree to the terms, Biltmore will provide $13 per share. This is an example of a tender offer.

## 1.2.4   Purchase of Assets

A purchase of assets transaction occurs when a portion (or all) of the selling company's assets are purchased by the acquiring company, which may result in the dissolution of the selling company. As with a tender offer, shareholder approval must be obtained.

### Illustration 8   Purchase of Assets

Lox Industries enters into an asset purchase agreement with Bright Star Inc. to purchase approximately 80 percent of the latter's buildings and equipment. As part of the agreement, Lox agrees to assume the liabilities associated with mortgages outstanding on the buildings and capital leases on the equipment purchased.

# 2   Divestiture

A divestiture involves the partial or full disposal of a component or business unit of a company. Divestiture transactions include sell-offs, spin-offs, and equity carve-outs.

## 2.1   Sell-off

A sell-off is an outright sale of a subsidiary because, for example, the subsidiary's core competencies do not align with the overall company's or because there is a lack of synergy between the company and its subsidiary. Legal action stemming from anticompetitive or antitrust practices may also require a sell-off.

> **Illustration 9     Sell-off**
>
> Management and shareholders of BeckCo Industries think that its ownership of Blended Ltd. is causing the overall entity to be undervalued from a market perspective. As a result, the company sells the assets and liabilities of Blended to another entity in the hopes that investors will react favorably to the sale, which will lead to an increase in the stock price.

## 2.2   Spin-off

A spin-off creates a new, independent company by separating a subsidiary business from a parent company. A spin-off can be completed by distributing stock in the new entity as a stock dividend to existing shareholders or by offering shareholders stock in the new company in exchange for their stock in the parent company. Spin-offs typically occur when a unit is less profitable and/or unrelated to the core parent business. The assumption is that the operations of the unit after a spin-off are expected to have more value than they did as part of the larger operation.

> **Illustration 10     Spin-off**
>
> In 1994, Eli Lilly and Company (a large, U.S.-based global pharmaceutical company) shifted its focus purely to pharmaceuticals and other similar businesses. As a result, Lilly spun off its medical devices division, which went public later that year under the name Guidant. Guidant focused on cardiovascular medical products, such as artificial pacemakers, stents, and cardioverter-defibrillators.

## 2.3   Equity Carve-out

An equity carve-out occurs when a subsidiary is made public through an initial public offering (IPO), thereby creating a new publicly listed company. Unlike a spin-off, in which no cash comes to the parent company, the sale of shares in the new company generates cash for the parent as well as providing the parent with a controlling interest in the subsidiary. The hope is this strategy will unlock the independent value of the subsidiary previously contained within the merged entity.

## Illustration 11    Equity Carve-out

Teco Industries is a multinational company with several divisions specializing in unique product lines. Fearing that Teco is not focusing enough on its core business, management would like to divest one of the company's units. Management is interested in both a cash infusion from the divestiture and maintaining some degree of control. The equity carve-out is the most likely choice because it would provide cash while allowing management to retain a controlling interest.

---

### Question 1                                                                    CPA-03934

Which of the following situations best illustrates a potential horizontal merger between Companies X and Y?

- **a.** Companies X and Y are competitors in the same industry.
- **b.** Company X supplies raw materials to the production processes for Company Y.
- **c.** Company X is a textile manufacturer, whereas Company Y operates as a wholesaler for Company X products.
- **d.** Company X operates in the financial services industry, whereas Company Y operates in the scientific research and development industry.

---

### Question 2                                                                    CPA-03935

Gerard Incorporated is a leader in the home health services industry with operations primarily in the western United States. Gerard owns 100 percent of Brighton Greens, a company that operates nursing care facilities in the same region. Wanting to devote all of its corporate resources to home health care and hoping to generate cash, Gerard should look to divest its operation under which of the following mechanisms?

- **a.** Sell-off
- **b.** Spin-off
- **c.** Tender offer
- **d.** Equity carve-out

# BEC
# 6

# Process Management and Information Technology

## Module

# 1 Introduction to Business Process Management

## 1.1 Approaches

Business process management (BPM) is a management approach that seeks to coordinate the functions of an organization toward an ultimate goal of continuous improvement in customer satisfaction. Customers may be internal or external to an organization. Process management seeks effectiveness and efficiency through promotion of innovation, flexibility, and integration with technology.

Business process management attempts to improve processes continuously. By focusing on processes, an organization becomes more nimble and responsive than hierarchical organizations that are managed by function.

## 1.2 Activities

Business process management activities can be grouped into five categories: design, modeling, execution, monitoring, and optimization.

- **Design:** The design phase involves the identification of existing processes and the conceptual design of how processes should function once they have been improved.
- **Modeling:** Modeling introduces variables to the conceptual design for what-if analysis.
- **Execution:** Design changes are implemented and key indicators of success are developed.
- **Monitoring:** Information is gathered and tracked and compared with expected performance.
- **Optimization:** Using the monitoring data and the original design, the process manager continues to refine the process.

## 1.3 Techniques

The general technique or approach to process management is as follows:

- **Define:** The original process is defined as a baseline for current process functioning or process improvement.
- **Measure:** The indicators that will show a change to the process (e.g., reduced time, increased customer contacts, etc.) are determined.
- **Analyze:** Various simulations or models are used to determine the targeted or optimal improvement.
- **Improve:** The improvement is selected and implemented.
- **Control:** Dashboards and other measurement reports are used to monitor the improvement in real time and apply the data to the model for improvement.

## 1.4    Plan, Do, Check, Act (PDCA)

Process management also has been commonly referred to as plan, do, check, act (PDCA).

- **Plan:** Design the planned process improvement.
- **Do:** Implement the process improvement.
- **Check:** Monitor the process improvement.
- **Act:** Continuously commit to the process and reassess the degree of improvement.

---

### Illustration 1    PDCA

Brakes-Only Company (BOC) manufactures car brakes for each of the big three U.S. automakers. Over the past several years there has been an increase in the return of new brake systems by these automakers due primarily to the failure to meet all required design specifications.

In order to reverse this negative trend, the head of production at BOC has implemented the PDCA approach at the company. In the first quarter of the operating year, he designed a **plan** to ensure that all brake specifications are carefully reviewed prior to the production and shipment processes as well as to improve the communication among internal departments through enhanced internal reporting.

During the second quarter, the production manager implemented the process **(do)** at the company.

At the end of each the next two operating quarters, the production manager monitored **(check)** the effectiveness of the process by comparing year-to-date brake returns to the prior year.

This process continued the following operating year with BOC achieving a 10 percent reduction in brake system returns over an 18-month period. To further reduce the number of brake system returns, the production manager hired a full-time quality control manager. As part of his ongoing responsibilities, the quality control manager will continue to monitor **(act)** the effectiveness of the process and recommend any technological improvements to the production manager.

---

## 1.5    Measures

Measures or process metrics can be financial or nonfinancial and should correlate directly to the managed process. The measures are compared with expectations to monitor progress. Examples of measures include:

- **Gross Revenue:** *Gross revenue* is an appropriate measure for sales or other measures of revenue volume in sales-driven organizations.
- **Customer Contacts:** *Customer contacts* can be used in sales-driven organizations.
- **Customer Satisfaction:** Organizations using relationship marketing techniques may consider *customer satisfaction* measures.
- **Operational Statistics:** Manufacturing operations might use *operational statistics* such as throughput times, delivery times, or other logistical measures to determine the efficiency of a process.

## 1.6    Benefits

The benefits of a studied and systematic approach to process management allow the company to monitor the degree to which process improvements have been achieved. The benefits often mentioned for process management are:

▪ **Efficiency:** Fewer resources are used to accomplish organizational objectives.

▪ **Effectiveness:** Objectives are accomplished with greater predictability.

▪ **Agility:** Responses to change are faster and more reliable.

# 2    Shared Services, Outsourcing, and Offshore Operations

## 2.1    Shared Services

*Shared services* refers to seeking out redundant services, combining them, and then sharing those services within a group or organization. The distinguishing feature of shared services is that they are shared within an organization or group of affiliates.

---

**Illustration 2     Shared Services**

Financial Group Inc. is a financial services company with three distinct businesses including accounting, tax, and consulting. Currently, each division operates as a separate company with its own human resources, payroll, and legal departments. In order to more effectively manage the organization and reduce costs, the new CEO implements a shared services plan whereby all human resources, payroll, and legal department services will be consolidated into one centralized function. The CEO thinks that this shared services approach will eliminate redundant back-office functions and will reduce annual operating costs by $750,000.

---

Consolidation of redundant services creates efficiency but might also result in the following issues:

▪ **Service Flow Disruption:** The consolidation of work to a single location can create waste in the transition, rework, and duplication as well as increases in the time it takes to deliver a service.

▪ **Failure Demand:** The demand for a shared service caused by a failure to do something or to do something right for a customer is called failure demand. Failure demand results when a task must be performed for a second time because it was incorrectly performed the first time.

## 2.2    Outsourcing

*Outsourcing* is defined as the contracting of services to an external provider. Examples might include a payroll service or even a call center to provide support or back-office services for a fee. A contractual relationship exists between the business and its service provider.

Outsourcing can provide for efficiencies, but there are also risks. Those risks include:

▪ **Quality Risk:** An outsourced product or service might be defective. Suppliers might provide substandard products or services.

▪ **Quality of Service:** Poorly designed service agreements may impede the quality of service.

■ **Productivity:** Real productivity may be reduced even though service provider employees are paid less.

■ **Staff Turnover:** Experienced and valued staff whose functions have been outsourced may leave the organization.

■ **Language Skills:** Outsourced services may go offshore. Language barriers may reduce the quality of service.

■ **Security:** Security of information with a third party might be compromised.

■ **Qualifications of Outsourcers:** Credentials of service providers may be flawed. Offshore degrees may not include the same level of training as domestic degrees.

■ **Labor Insecurity:** Labor insecurity increases when jobs move to an external service provider or, as a result of globalization, out of the country.

## 2.3    Offshore Operations

*Offshore operations* relate to outsourcing of services or business functions to an external party in a different country. A computer manufacturer in the United States, for example, might have its call center in India. The most common types of offshore outsourcing are:

■ Information technology

■ Business process (call centers, accounting operations, tax compliance)

■ Software research and development (software development)

■ Knowledge process (processes requiring advanced knowledge and specialized skill sets, such as reading x-rays, etc.)

Business risks of offshore outsourcing are generally the same as outsourcing, but with greater emphasis on the lack of controls associated with proximity, as well as potential language issues.

# 3    Selecting and Implementing Improvement Initiatives

## 3.1    Selecting Improvement Initiatives

Rational and irrational methods may be used to select improvement initiatives.

### 3.1.1    Irrational

*Irrational* methods are intuitive and emotional. They lack structure and systematic evaluation. The irrational methods are based on fashion, fad, or trend. They may result from an immediate need for cost reduction, and stem from a very short-term viewpoint.

### 3.1.2    Rational

*Rational* assessments are structured and systematic and involve the following:

■ **Strategic Gap Analysis:** External (environmental) assessments and internal (organizational) assessments performed to create a strategic gap analysis.

■ **Review Competitive Priorities:** Review of price, quality, or other considerations.

■ **Review Production Objectives:** Review of performance requirements.

■ **Choose Improvement Program:** Decide how to proceed for improvement.

## 3.2    Implementing Improvement Initiatives

There are several crucial features of successful implementation activities.

- **Internal Leadership:** Senior management must provide direction and commit resources to the implementation.

- **Inspections:** Ongoing implementation must be monitored and measured.

- **Executive Support:** Executive management must be visibly supportive of the initiative.

- **Internal Process Ownership:** The individuals most deeply involved with process management must be committed to the need for process improvement and have the resources to carry it out.

# 4    Business Process Reengineering

*Business process reengineering* (BPR) refers to techniques to help organizations rethink how work is done to dramatically improve customer satisfaction and service, cut costs of operations, and enhance competitiveness. Development of sophisticated information technology systems and networks have driven many reengineering efforts.

Business process reengineering is not synonymous with business process management. Business process management seeks incremental change, and business process reengineering seeks radical changes.

## 4.1    Fresh Start

The basic premise of business process reengineering is the idea that management will "wipe the slate clean" and reassess how business is done from the ground up. Reengineering uses benchmarking and best practices to evaluate success.

## 4.2    Current Status

Reengineering is not as popular as it was when introduced in the mid-1990s. The technique has been criticized for what some believe was overaggressive downsizing. In addition, the programs have not produced the benefits that were originally anticipated.

---

### Illustration 3    Business Process Reengineering

Decorations Inc. manufactures holiday ornaments and decorative lawn figurines. Over the past several years, rising manufacturing costs have significantly eroded the company's operating profit margins. Currently, the automated manufacturing process and manual labor process represent 30 percent and 70 percent of the total production costs, respectively.

In order to combat this negative operating trend, company management hired an outside consulting firm that will consider both business process management and business process reengineering.

(continued)

---

(continued)

After performing due diligence, the consultants recommended a business process management plan that involved cutting 10 percent of the production workforce over the next three years and replacing 15 percent of the manual production process with newly designed machines. After severance and machine upgrade costs, it is estimated that this business process management program will reduce annual operating costs by $1,000,000 in three years.

The consulting firm also completed a business process reengineering study (plan) that would eliminate 80 percent of the current production workforce over the next three years and fully automate the production process, with the exception of the quality control function and packaging supervision. Although the up-front costs to implement the business process reengineering program are more significant than the BPM, the BPR plan is expected to reduce annual operating costs by $2,500,000 in three years.

The consulting firm submits both plans to company management, who must decide whether incremental change or radical change is more appropriate given the up-front costs to execute the plans and the expected annual cost savings associated with each plan.

# 5 Management Philosophies and Techniques for Performance Improvement

Performance improvement philosophies and techniques seek to provide the highest-quality goods and services in the most efficient and effective manner possible.

## 5.1 Just-in-Time (JIT)

*Just-in-time management* anticipates achievement of efficiency by scheduling the deployment of resources just-in-time to meet customer or production requirements.

### 5.1.1 Inventory Does Not Add Value

The underlying concept of JIT is that *inventory does not add value*. The maintenance of inventory on-hand produces wasteful costs.

### 5.1.2 Benefits

The *benefits* of JIT implementation include:

- Synchronization of production scheduling with demand.
- Arrival of supplies at regular intervals throughout the production day.
- Improved coordination and team approach with suppliers.
- More efficient flow of goods between warehouses and production.
- Reduced setup time.
- Greater efficiency in the use of employees with multiple skills.

## 5.2   Total Quality Management

*Total quality management* (TQM) represents an organizational commitment to customer-focused performance that emphasizes both quality and continuous improvement. Total quality management identifies seven critical factors, outlined below.

### 5.2.1   Customer Focus

The TQM organization is characterized by the recognition that each function of the corporation exists to satisfy the customer. Customers are identified as both external customers and internal customers.

- **External Customers:** The external customer is the ultimate recipient or consumer of an organization's product or service.

- **Internal Customers:** Each link in the value chain (and within the value chain) represents an internal customer.

---

**Illustration 4      TQM**

Supplies inventory managers provide services to internal customers, such as production managers. A TQM organization will demand that the supplies inventory manager value the satisfaction of production managers in the timely delivery of supplies adequate to meet production requirements.

---

### 5.2.2   Continuous Improvement

Quality is not viewed as an achievement in a TQM organization. The organization constantly strives to improve its product and processes. Quality is not just the goal; it is embedded in the process.

### 5.2.3   Workforce Involvement

TQM organizations are characterized by team approaches and worker input to process development and improvement. Small groups of workers that use team approaches to process improvement are called *quality circles.*

### 5.2.4   Top Management Support

*Top management* must actively describe and demonstrate support for the quality mission of the organization. Management can communicate support by meaningful delegation of authority to quality circles and involvement of suppliers.

### 5.2.5   Objective Measures

*Measures* of quality must be unambiguous, clearly communicated, and consistently reported.

### 5.2.6   Timely Recognition

Acknowledgement of TQM achievements (in terms of compensation and general recognition) must occur to encourage the ongoing involvement of the workforce.

### 5.2.7   Ongoing Training

*TQM training* should occur on a recurring basis to ensure workforce understanding and involvement.

## 5.3    Quality Audits and Gap Analysis

### 5.3.1   Quality Audits

*Quality audits* are a technique used as part of the strategic positioning function in which management assesses the quality practices of the organization. Quality audits produce the following:

- Analysis that identifies strengths and weaknesses.

- A strategic quality improvement plan that identifies the improvement steps that will produce the greatest return to the organization in the short term and long term.

### 5.3.2   Gap Analysis

*Gap analysis* determines the gap, or difference, between industry best practices and the current practices of the organization. Gap analysis produces the following:

- Target areas for improvement.

- A common objective database from which to develop strategic quality improvement.

## 5.4    Lean Manufacturing

*Lean manufacturing* or lean production requires the use of only those resources required to meet the requirements of customers. It seeks to invest resources only in value-added activities.

### 5.4.1   Waste Reduction

The focus of *lean* is on waste reduction and efficiency. The concept of preserving value while expending only the effort necessary is not uncommon and has a long history in business and economics. Kaizen- and activity-based management initiatives are waste-reduction methodologies that use empirical data to measure and promote efficiencies.

### 5.4.2   Continuous Improvement (Kaizen)

"Kaizen" refers to *continuous improvement* efforts that improve the efficiency and effectiveness of organizations through greater operational control.

Kaizen occurs at the manufacturing stage, where the ongoing search for cost reductions takes the form of analysis of production processes to ensure that resource usage stays within target costs.

### 5.4.3   Process Improvements/Activity-Based Management

Activity-based costing (ABC) and activity-based management (ABM) are highly compatible with process improvements and total quality management (TQM).

- **Cost Identification**

  Activity-based costing and management systems highlight the costs of activities. The availability of cost data by activity makes the identification of costs of quality and value-added activities more obvious.

- **Implementation**

  Organizations with ABC and ABM programs are more likely to have the information they need to implement a TQM program. Process improvement results from a detailed process management program (sometimes referred to as an activity-based management system, or ABM).

## 5.5 Demand Flow

*Demand flow* manages resources using customer demand as the basis for resource allocation. Demand flow contrasts with resource allocations based on sales forecasts or master scheduling.

### 5.5.1 Relationship to Just-in-Time

Demand flow is akin to *just-in-time* processes that focus on the efficient coordination of demand for goods in production with the supply of goods in production. Kanban systems, which visually coordinate demand requirements on the manufacturing floor with suppliers, are used to coordinate demand flow.

### 5.5.2 Relationship to Lean

Demand flow is designed to maximize efficiencies and reduce waste. One-piece flow manufacturing environments, in which components move progressively from production function to production function, benefit from demand flow ideas.

## 5.6 Theory of Constraints (TOC)

*Theory of constraints* states that organizations are impeded from achieving objectives by the existence of one or more constraints. The organization or project must be consistently operated in a manner that either works around or leverages the constraint.

### 5.6.1 Constraints

A *constraint* is anything that impedes the accomplishment of an objective. Constraints for purposes of TOC are limited in total and, sometimes, organizations may face only one constraint.

- **Internal Constraints**

    Internal constraints are evident when the market demands more than the system can produce.

    - Equipment may be inefficient or used inefficiently.

    - People may lack the necessary skills or mind-set necessary to produce required efficiencies.

    - Policies may prevent the efficient use of resources.

- **External Constraints**

    External constraints exist when the system produces more than the market requires.

### 5.6.2 Five Steps

TOC generally involves five steps:

1. **Identification of the Constraint:** Use of process charts or interviews results in identification of the constraint that produces suboptimal performance.

2. **Exploitation of the Constraint:** Planning around the constraint uses capacity that is potentially wasted by making or selling the wrong products, improper procedures in scheduling, etc.

3. **Subordinate Everything Else to the Above Decisions:** Management directs its efforts to improving the performance of the constraint.

4. **Elevate the Constraint**: Add capacity to overcome the constraint.

5. **Return to the First Step:** Reexamine the process to optimize the results. Remain cognizant that inertia can be a constraint.

### 5.6.3 Buffer

The concept of *buffers* is used throughout TOC. Managers add buffers before and after each constraint to ensure that enough resources to accommodate the constraint exist. Buffers, therefore, eliminate the effect of the constraint on work flow.

---

**Illustration 5      Internal Constraints**

Advanced Printing Co. purchased several state-of-the art printing presses in the fourth quarter of last year. Despite this significant capital investment, the company's year-to-date production output and costs have not changed. Company management attributes this production trend to several internal constraints, including a lack of sufficient training for employees operating the new presses and the fact that the machines were used inefficiently during the production process.

In order to improve the new machines' productivity and generate a positive return on capital investment, management will begin scheduling periodic training sessions for operating them and will hire an outside consultant to determine the most effective way to maximize productivity. Once the study is completed, each machine line supervisor will meet with the outside consulting firm to go over the study's results, share ways to further improve productivity, and provide an effective way to monitor employees' ongoing production performance. Each Saturday after a weekly production run is completed, every machine line supervisor will be required to submit a weekly production report to the production manager, explaining any negative cost and production variances greater than 2 percent from the plan. Management believes that these buffers will eliminate the internal constraints identified from the current year's operating results.

---

## 5.7   Six Sigma

*Six Sigma* uses rigorous metrics in the evaluation of goal achievement. Six Sigma is a continuous quality-improvement program that requires specialized training. The program expands on the *Plan-Do-Check-Act* model of process management described earlier, and outlines methodologies to improve current processes and develop new processes.

### 5.7.1   Existing Product and Business Process Improvements (DMAIC)

- **Define the Problem:** Based on customer comments, failed project goals, or other issues, determine the existence of a problem.

- **Measure Key Aspects of the Current Process:** Collect relevant data.

- **Analyze Data:** Examine the relationships between data elements.

- **Improve or Optimize Current Processes:** Use models and data to determine how the process can be optimized.

- **Control:** Develop a statistical control process to monitor results.

### 5.7.2   New Product or Business Process Development (DMADV)

- **Define Design Goals:** Design goals that are consistent with customer demands.

- **Measure CTQ (Critical to Quality Issues):** Analyze the value chain to determine the features that provide value to the customer and the production capabilities that are available.

- **Analyze Design Alternatives:** Develop different methodologies to produce the new product.

- **Design Optimization:** Use modeling techniques to determine optimization of the proposed process.

- **Verify the Design:** Implement and test the plan.

| Question 1 | CPA-03895 |
|---|---|

The benefits of a just-in-time system for raw materials usually include:

  **a.** Elimination of non-value adding operations.

  **b.** Increase in the number of suppliers, thereby ensuring competitive bidding.

  **c.** Maximization of the standard delivery quantity, thereby lessening the paperwork for each delivery.

  **d.** Decrease in the number of deliveries required to maintain production.

## NOTES

# 1 Overview

The role of information technology (IT) in an organization has evolved. The early focus was on automating transactions and reducing costs. Decision support systems (DSS) improved managers' decision making. Historically, IT was viewed as a support function for an organization. Today, IT is a strategic driver, making the IT governance function even more crucial and elevating it to the executive and board levels.

IT governance is a formal structure for how organizations align IT and business strategies, ensuring that companies stay on track to accomplish their strategies and goals, and implementing performance measures for IT.

An IT governance framework should answer key questions, such as how is the IT department functioning, what key metrics does management need, and what does IT return to the business.

# 2 Vision and Strategy

Technology and an entity's objectives are interconnected. The design of an information technology department's strategy has traditionally supported that of the overall organization. Technology decisions should be an input to the strategic process, defining innovations and helping to increase revenue.

---

### Illustration 1  IT Strategy and Corporate Strategy

Bell, a computer manufacturer, wants to expand to global markets. IT strongly influences how management can accomplish this. Without the investment in technology for e-commerce, customer service, inventory management, market research, etc., this strategy would not be viable. IT should be viewed as a critical component of strategy development, and not simply a back-office support function.

---

### Illustration 2  Technology-Driven Strategy

A brokerage firm was able to leverage faster computers and grid computing (large number of connected computers) to develop faster responses to customers who make inquiries online. Rather than have customers enter questions and data online and wait several hours to receive a response by e-mail, the response could be generated within seconds. This product innovation was extremely popular with customers.

---

# 3 Definition of IT Governance

IT governance is about how leadership accomplishes the delivery of mission-critical business capability using IT strategies, goals, and objectives. IT governance is concerned with the strategic alignment between the goals and objectives of the business and the utilization of its IT resources to effectively achieve the desired results. IT governance is the duty of executive management and the board of directors.  IT governance is crucial to the governance of the entire organization. IT governance comprises leadership, organizational structures, policies and processes, IT strategy, and IT objectives. IT governance establishes chains of responsibility, authority, and communication. It also establishes measurement, policy, standards, and control mechanisms to enable people to carry out their roles and responsibilities.

## 3.1 Five Areas of Focus

According to the IT Governance Institute, there are five areas of focus, which follow.

### 3.1.1 Strategic Alignment

Linking business and IT so they work well together. Typically, the starting point is the planning process, and true alignment can occur only when the corporate side of the business communicates effectively with line-of-business leaders and IT leaders about costs, reporting, and effects.

### 3.1.2 Value Delivery

Making sure that the IT department does what is necessary to deliver the benefits promised at the beginning of a project or investment. The best way to get a handle on everything is by developing a process to ensure that certain functions are accelerated when the value proposition is growing, and eliminating functions when the value decreases.

### 3.1.3 Resource Management

One way to manage resources more effectively is to organize staff more efficiently—for example, by skills rather than by line of business. This allows organizations to deploy employees to various lines of business on a demand basis.

### 3.1.4 Risk Management

Instituting a formal risk framework that puts some rigor around how IT measures, accepts, and manages risk, as well as reporting on what IT is managing in terms of risk.

### 3.1.5 Performance Measures

Putting structure around measuring business performance. One popular method involves instituting an IT balanced scorecard, which examines where IT makes a contribution in terms of achieving business goals, being a responsible user of resources, and developing people. This method uses both qualitative and quantitative measures to find those answers.

# 4 IT Strategy

IT strategy should intersect with the overall strategies of the corporation.

## 4.1 Corporate-Level Strategy

Corporate-level strategy is developed by senior management. It encompasses new business opportunities, the closing of old business units, and the allocation of resources among departments.

## 4.2    Business-Level Strategy

Business-level strategy is found in organizations that have autonomous departments with the need to develop their own strategies. Business strategy should function within the broader aims of the corporate strategy. This level of strategy is typically not found in small businesses.

## 4.3    Functional-Level Strategy

Functional-level strategy involves establishing strategies for marketing, manufacturing, IT, and finance. An effective strategy at the functional level improves the entity's ability to execute its business-level and corporate-level strategies.

| Illustration 3    Interaction of IT and Corporate Strategy |
| --- |
| Development of e-commerce or a well-designed website as an IT strategy should improve the market share and performance of the overall entity. |

# 5    Principles of Technology-Driven Strategy Development

1.   Technology is a core input to the development of strategy, just as much as customers, markets, and competitors.

2.   Because of the speed with which technology changes, strategy development must be a continual process, rather than something that is revisited every three to five years.

3.   Innovative emerging business opportunities must be managed separately and differently from core businesses.

4.   Technology has the power to change long-held business assumptions; managers and executives must be open to this.

5.   Technology must be managed from two perspectives:

   - The ability of technology to create innovation in existing businesses; and

   - The ability of emerging technologies to create new markets/products.

6.   The focus should be on customer priorities, internal efficiencies, and ways that IT can be maximized for the advantage of the entity.

# 6    Organization of IT Governance Structure

The IT governance structure within an organization must encompass the tone at the top; key stakeholders, including the steering committees; governance objectives and policies; and IT strategies and oversight.

## 6.1    The Tone at the Top

Technology plays a crucial role in enabling the *flow of information* in an organization. The selection of specific technologies to support an organization typically is a reflection of the:

1.   entity's approach to risk management and its degree of sophistication;

2.   types of events affecting the entity;

3.   entity's overall information technology architecture; and

4.   degree of centralization of supporting technology.

## 6.2 Stakeholders or Participants in Business Process Design

The participants in business process design form the project team, which typically includes the following parties:

### 6.2.1 Management

One of the most effective ways to generate systems development support is to send a clear signal from top management that user involvement is important. Top management's most important roles are providing support and encouragement for IT development projects and aligning information systems with corporate strategies. Because business process design often takes time away from other duties, management must ensure that team members are given adequate time and support to work on the project.

### 6.2.2 Accountants

*Accountants* may play three roles during systems design:

1. As users of an *accounting information system* (AIS), the accountants should determine their information needs and system requirements, and communicate these to system developers.

2. As members of the project development team or information systems steering committee, they can help manage system development.

3. As accountants, they should take an active role in designing system controls, and periodically monitor and test the system to verify that the controls are implemented and functioning properly.

### 6.2.3 Information Systems Steering Committee

An executive-level *information systems steering committee*, also known as the project steering committee, should plan and oversee the information systems function and address the complexities created by functional and divisional boundaries.

1. The committee often consists of high-level management, such as the controller and the systems and user-department management.

2. Functions of the steering committee include:

    * setting governing policies for the various information systems within the company;

    * ensuring top-management participation, guidance, and control; and

    * facilitating the coordination and integration of information systems activities to increase goal congruence and reduce goal conflict.

### 6.2.4 Project Development Team

The team members planning each project are responsible for the successful design and implementation of the business system. The team should work to ensure both technical implementation and user acceptance. Their tasks include:

1. Monitoring the project to ensure timely and cost-effective completion.

2. Managing the human element (e.g., resistance to change).

3. Frequently communicating with users and holding regular meetings to consider ideas and discuss progress so there are no surprises at project completion.

4. Risk management and escalating issues that cannot be resolved within the team.

### 6.2.5 External Parties

Many people outside an organization play a role in systems development, including customers, vendors, auditors, and governmental entities. For example, a major retailer may require that its vendors implement and use *electronic data interchange* (EDI).

## 6.3    Governance Objectives

### 6.3.1    Strategic Alignment

The linkage between business and IT plans is referred to as *strategic alignment* and includes defining, maintaining, and validating the IT value proposition, with a focus on customer satisfaction.

### 6.3.2    Value Creation

*Value creation* is the key governance objective of any enterprise. It includes the provision by IT of promised benefits to the organization, while satisfying its customers and optimizing costs and risks.

### 6.3.3    Resource Management

*Resource management* focuses on the optimization of knowledge and infrastructure.

### 6.3.4    Risk Management

*Risk management* is defined as risk awareness by senior management, characterized by understanding risk appetite and risk management responsibilities (e.g., event identification, risk assessments, and responses).

Risk management begins with identification of risks faced followed by determining how the company will respond to the risk. The company can avoid the risk, mitigate the risk, share the risk, or ignore the risk.

---

**Illustration 4    Dealing With Risk**

A health care provider might *avoid* risk by not providing certain high-risk medical procedures, and instead focusing on low-risk basic care. An online retailer might *mitigate* risk by implementing strict controls over customer account information. Companies share risk by purchasing insurance. *Ignoring* risk would be an option only if the risk presents low impact and small probability.

---

### 6.3.5    Performance Measurement

Features of *performance measurement* include tracking and monitoring strategy implementation, project completion, resource usage, process performance, and service delivery. It is important to define milestones and/or deliverables throughout the project so that progress toward completion can be measured.

# 7    Risk Assessment Process

## 7.1    Prepare a Business Impact Analysis

The purpose of the *business impact analysis* (BIA) is to identify which business units, departments, and processes are essential to the survival of an entity. The BIA will identify how quickly essential business units and/or processes need to return to full operation following a disaster situation. The BIA will also identify the resources required to resume business operations.

For example, the department may utilize some special hardware/software, some special locations may be involved, or there may even be a dependence on someone else's information resources.

The objectives of the BIA are as follows:

- Estimate the financial impacts for each business unit, assuming a worst-case scenario.

- Estimate the intangible (operational) impacts for each business unit, assuming a worst-case scenario.

- Identify the organization's business unit processes and the estimated recovery time frame for each business unit.

## 7.2 Identify Information Resources

This includes any hardware, software, systems, services, people, databases, and related resources important to the department. These resources should be identified in a manner such that overlap is minimized. It might also be appropriate to have some clear point of accountability (that is, an individual who is responsible for specific hardware, a software package, or an office process).

## 7.3 Categorize Information Resources by Impact

This step helps to determine the criteria for categorizing the list of information resources as high, medium, or low related to the effect on day-to-day operations. Criteria include characteristics such as criticality, costs of a failure, publicity, legal and ethical issues, etc. It is important to agree upon and establish a common understanding of the criteria and their meaning. Resources can be categorized as follows:

### 7.3.1 High Impact (H)

Under a high-impact category, the department:

- cannot operate without this information resource for even a short period of time;

- may experience a high recovery cost;

- may realize harm or obstruction to achieving one's mission or to maintaining one's reputation.

### 7.3.2 Medium Impact (M)

Under a medium-impact category, the department:

- could work around the loss of this information resource for days or perhaps a week, but eventually restoration of the resource must occur;

- may experience some cost of recovery;

- may realize harm or obstruction to achieving one's mission or to maintaining one's reputation.

### 7.3.3 Low Impact (L)

Under a low-impact category, the department:

- could operate without this information resource for an extended (although perhaps finite) period of time, during which particular units or individuals may be inconvenienced and/or need to identify alternatives;

- may notice an effect on achieving one's mission or maintaining one's reputation.

## 7.4 Identify and Categorize Risks by Likelihood

"Risks," as used here, includes problems as well as threats. Risks must be tangible and specific with respect to one or more resources. When finalizing the list, eliminate duplicates, combine risks as appropriate, and include only the risks that team members agree are valid. Categorize the identified risks by likelihood of occurrence. The definitions for likelihood are as follows:

### 7.4.1 High Likelihood (H)

The risk (threat) source is highly motivated and sufficiently capable, and controls to prevent the vulnerability are ineffective.

### 7.4.2 Medium Likelihood (M)

The risk (threat) source is motivated and capable, but controls are in place that may impede successful exercise of the vulnerability.

### 7.4.3 Low Likelihood (L)

The risk (threat) source lacks motivation or capability, or controls are in place to prevent or significantly impede successful exercise of the vulnerability.

## 7.5 Information Resources, Associated Risks, and Corrective Actions

- List the high-impact information resources and document the risks associated with each information resource.

- Supply comments where needed to clarify a specific situation. Denote the risk likelihood.

- Finally, indicate the action decision by the team to mitigate each specified risk. Definitions for risk actions are as follows:

  1. High Action (H): Take corrective action as soon as possible.

  2. Medium Action (M): Implement corrective actions within a reasonable time frame.

  3. Low Action (L): Take no corrective action. Accept the level of risk.

## 7.6 Recommendations for Mitigating Risks

All high- and medium-risk actions associated with high-impact information resources need a documented recommendation or plan for mitigating each risk. If no high-impact information resources exist, the team should review identified high and medium risks and develop recommendations to mitigate those risks. The process for developing appropriate recommendations is as follows:

1. *Identify* each recommendation that might be implemented (this includes technical and manual solutions, as well as policies and procedures) and appropriately documented. It may be obvious at this early point only one recommendation is applicable. Document that fact and include documentation regarding the dismissal of other recommendations.

2. *Provide a justification* for each proposed recommendation: this may be the same for each or it could be different, in which case it will be useful in any evaluation. The obvious justification is that the recommendation will handle the problem, but a specific solution may not handle all risks.

3. *Develop a cost-benefit analysis* for each proposed recommendation (in some cases this may involve other departments or units). This should include (but not be limited to) capital and direct costs, staff costs, training and support, and any ongoing operating costs.

4. *Specify any known implementation plans or specific dates* for the recommendations. This could be an important consideration depending on the severity of the risk and the time frame involved for implementation.

---

**Question 1**  CPA-06442

Which of the following is the responsibility of an information technology steering committee?

**a.** A steering committee plan shows how a project will be completed, including the modules or tasks to be performed and who will perform them, the dates they should be completed, and project costs.

**b.** A steering committee must develop clear specifications. Before third parties bid on a project, clear specifications must be developed, including exact descriptions and definitions of the system, explicit deadlines, and precise acceptance criteria.

**c.** A steering committee should be formed to guide and oversee systems development and acquisition.

**d.** Steering committee must assess the operations of IT using system performance measurements. Common measurements include: throughput (output per unit of time), utilization (percentage of time the system is being productively used), and response time (how long it takes the system to respond).

---

**Question 2**  CPA-07042

The IT Governance Institute identifies five focus areas for IT governance, including which of the following:

**a.** Systems analysis

**b.** Programming

**c.** Operations

**d.** Value delivery

---

# 1 The Role of Big Data/Data Analytics and Statistics in Supporting Business Decisions

Most companies store digital versions of documents on servers and storage devices. These documents become instantly available within a company, regardless of an employee's geographical location. Companies are able to store and maintain a tremendous amount of historical data economically, and employees benefit from immediate access to the documents they need.

## 1.1 What Is Big Data?

"Big data" is a fast-evolving concept in data management and in information technology in general. There is no single, widely accepted definition of "big data," or even "big," in this context.

Rapid advances in software technology and data management systems allow companies to build more individual relationships with customers and even predict what customers want before they ask for it. Think about the times you receive recommendations for products as soon as you sign into a website, or even in a personal e-mail you receive. Big data analytics is focused on finding marketing and sales patterns, discovering previously unknown relationships, detecting new market trends, and being able to ferret out actual customer preferences.

For any business, there are boundless ways in which the processing of big data can improve the company's results. In order to benefit from "big data," companies must have the systems and people to mine it and refine it so that it is useful for making decisions. Increasingly, the individuals who work with "big data" are not just the typical accountant, but are data scientists, statisticians, programmers, data analysts, and database engineers, among other professionals.

## 1.2 Dimensions of Big Data

IBM Corp. describes four dimensions of big data:

### 1.2.1 Volume

The volume of data is too large for traditional database software to store. Storage is a huge challenge usually solved by a distributed system in which there is a network of interconnected databases, possibly even globally.

### 1.2.2 Velocity

The flow of data is continuous, so the real value is in being able to analyze data in real time.

### 1.2.3 Variety

The best "big data" comes from a variety of sources, including customer relationship management systems, social media feedback, point-of-sale records, and other sources.

### 1.2.4 Veracity

Biases or irrelevant data must be mined from big data in order to minimize the chance of making decisions based on the wrong data.

## 1.3 Data Analytics Processes

The three main data analytics processes are the following:

### 1.3.1 Descriptive Analytics

Descriptive analytics describes events that have already occurred, such as financial reports and historical operations reports, which enable learning from past behaviors.

### 1.3.2 Predictive Analytics

Predictive analytics use statistical techniques and forecasting models to predict what could happen.

### 1.3.3 Prescriptive Analytics

Prescriptive analytics use optimization and simulation algorithms to affect future decisions. This is the most complex of the three types of analytics to implement.

## 1.4 Uses of Data Analytics

Some of the top uses of data analytics in businesses currently are the following:

### 1.4.1 Customer Analytics

Customer analytics supports digital marketing, and allows the company to deliver timely, relevant, and anticipated offers to customers.

### 1.4.2 Operational Analytics

Operational analytics uses data mining and data collection tools to plan for more effective business operations; normally used to observe and analyze business operations in real time.

### 1.4.3 Risk and Compliance Analytics

Risk and compliance analytics are used in Enterprise Risk Management activities such as continuous monitoring, continuous auditing, and fraud detection.

### 1.4.4 New Products and Services Innovation Analytics

New products and services innovation analytics are used to determine where innovation is needed, and to isolate product qualities that are most important to customers.

# 2 Role of Information Systems in Key Business Processes Within an Entity

One of the most basic and vital information technology components of any business is the set of software referred to as the "business information system." Information technology is the enabler of business functions, processes, and outcomes. Below are some of the key components of information technology used in most businesses today.

## 2.1 Communication

For many companies, e-mail is the principal means of communication between employees, suppliers, and customers. Other communications tools have also evolved, such as live chat systems, online meeting tools, and videoconferencing systems. Voice over Internet Protocol (VoIP) telephones and smartphones offer additional ways to facilitate communication within the organization.

## 2.2    Management Information Systems

*Management information systems* (MIS) enable companies to use data as part of their strategic planning process as well as the tactical execution of that strategy. Management information systems often have subsystems called decision support systems (DSS) and executive information systems (EIS).

A management information system provides users predefined reports that support effective business decisions. MIS reports may provide feedback on daily operations, financial and nonfinancial information to support decision making across functions, and both internal and external information.

## 2.3    Decision Support Systems (DSS)

A *decision support system* is an extension of an MIS that provides interactive tools to support decision making. A DSS may provide information, facilitate the preparation of forecasts, or allow modeling of various aspects of a decision. It is sometimes called an expert system.

| Illustration 1    DSS |
| --- |
| Examples of decision support systems include production planning, inventory control, bid preparation, revenue optimization, traffic planning, and capital investment planning systems. |

## 2.4    Executive Information Systems (EIS)

*Executive information systems* provide senior executives with immediate and easy access to internal and external information to assist in strategic decision making. An EIS consolidates information internal and external to the enterprise and reports it in a format and level of detail appropriate to senior executives.

| Illustration 2    EIS |
| --- |
| Examples of executive information systems include sales forecasting, profit planning, key performance indicators, macro-economic data, and financial reports. |

## 2.5    Accounting Information Systems (AIS)

The business information system that is most important to an accountant is the *accounting information system* (AIS). An accounting information system is a type of management information system; it also may be partly a transaction processing system and partly a knowledge system.

There may be separate systems (often called modules) for each accounting function, such as accounts receivable, accounts payable, etc., or there may be one integrated system that performs all of the accounting functions, culminating in the general ledger and the various accounting reports.

A well-designed AIS creates an audit trail for accounting transactions. The audit trail allows a user to trace a transaction from source documents to the ledger and to trace from the ledger back to source documents. The ability to trace in both directions is important in auditing.

An example of a basic accounting audit trail follows. Source documents are often stored as electronic documents, thus alleviating the need to file paper documents. Sophisticated scanning systems can turn paper documents into electronic documents before they are processed.

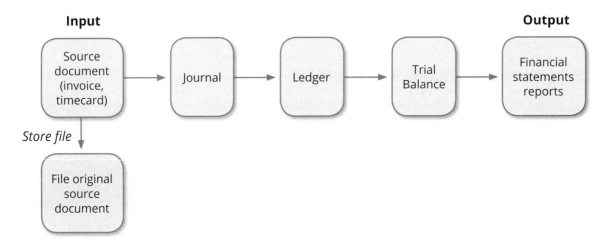

### 2.5.1   Objectives of an AIS

1.  Record valid transactions;

2.  Properly classify those transactions;

3.  Record the transactions at their proper value;

4.  Record the transactions in the proper accounting period; and

5.  Properly present the transactions and related information in the financial statements of the organization.

### 2.5.2   Sequence of Events in an AIS

1.  The transaction data from source documents is entered into the AIS by an end user. Alternatively, an order may be entered through the Internet by a customer.

2.  The original source documents, if they exist, are filed.

3.  The transactions are recorded in the appropriate journal.

4.  The transactions are posted to the general and subsidiary ledgers.

5.  Trial balances are prepared.

6.  Adjustments, accruals, and corrections are entered. Financial reports are generated.

## 2.6   Inventory Management

Inventory management systems track the quantity of each item a company maintains, triggering an order when quantities fall below a predetermined level. These systems are best used when the inventory management system is connected to the point-of-sale (POS) system. The POS system ensures that each time an item is sold, one of that item is removed from the inventory count.

## 2.7    Customer Relationship Management System (CRM)

### 2.7.1    Purpose

*Customer relationship management systems* (CRM) provide sales force automation and customer services in an attempt to manage customer relationships. CRM systems capture every interaction a company has with a customer. CRM systems record and manage customer contacts; manage salespeople; forecast sales; manage sales leads; provide and manage online quotes, product specifications, and pricing; and analyze sales data.

If a customer contacts a call center with an issue, a customer support representative will be able to see what the customer purchased, view shipping information, call up the training manual for that item, and effectively respond to the issue. The entire interaction is stored in the CRM system, ready to be recalled if the customer calls again.

### 2.7.2    CRM Benefits

The objective of CRM (and of CRM systems) is to increase customer satisfaction and thus increase revenue and profitability. CRM attempts to do this by appearing to market to each customer individually. The assumptions are that 20 percent of customers generate 80 percent of sales and that it is 5 to 10 times more expensive to acquire a new customer than to obtain repeat business from an existing customer.

CRM also attempts to reduce sales costs and customer support costs. It attempts to identify the best customers and possibly provide those best customers with increased levels of service or simply drop the worst customers.

### 2.7.3    Categories of CRM

CRM is sometimes divided into two categories:

1.  **Analytical CRM**

    Creates and exploits knowledge of a company's current and future customers to drive business decisions.

2.  **Operational CRM**

    This is the automation of customer contacts or contact points.

## 2.8    Enterprise Resource Planning Systems (ERP)

An *enterprise resource planning system* (ERP) is a cross-functional enterprise system that integrates and automates the many business processes and systems that must work together in the manufacturing, logistics, distribution, accounting, project management, finance, and human resource functions of a business.

ERP software comprises a number of modules that can function independently or as an integrated system to allow data and information to be shared among all of the different departments and divisions of large businesses.

ERP software manages the various functions within a business (enterprise) related to manufacturing, from entering sales orders to coordinating shipping and after-sales customer service. In spite of the name, ERP normally does not offer anything in the way of planning. The enterprise part, however, is correct. ERP is often considered a back-office system, from the customer order to fulfillment of that order.

### 2.8.1 ERP Operations

1. ERP systems store information in a central repository so that data may be entered once and then accessed and used by the various departments.

2. ERP systems act as the framework for integrating and improving an organization's ability to monitor and track sales, expenses, customer service, distribution, and many other business functions.

3. ERP systems can provide vital cross-functional information quickly to managers across the organization in order to assist them in the decision-making process.

## 2.9 Supply Chain Management Systems (SCM)

### 2.9.1 Characteristics

*Supply chain management* (SCM) is concerned with the four important characteristics of every sale: what, when, where, and how much. For example, all customers, whether business or consumer, expect all of the following:

1. The goods received should match the goods ordered.

2. The goods should be delivered on or before the date promised.

3. The goods should be delivered to the location requested.

4. The cost of the goods should be as low as possible.

### 2.9.2 Integration

Supply chain management is the integration of business processes from the original supplier to the customer and includes purchasing, materials handling, production planning and control, logistics and warehousing, inventory control, and product distribution and delivery. SCM systems may perform some or all of these functions.

### 2.9.3 Objectives and Functions

The overall objectives of SCM are achieving flexibility and responsiveness in meeting the demands of customers and business partners. SCM might incorporate the following functions:

1. Planning (e.g., demand forecasting, product pricing, and inventory management)

2. Sourcing (e.g., procurement and credit and collections)

3. Making (e.g., product design, production scheduling, and facility management)

4. Delivery (e.g., order management and delivery scheduling)

# 3  E-Commerce Technologies

Electronic commerce, commonly written as e-commerce, is the trading or facilitation of trading in products or services using computer networks, such as the Internet.

## 3.1 Electronic Funds Transfer(s)

*Electronic funds transfer systems* (EFT) are a form of electronic payment for banking and retailing industries. EFT uses a variety of technologies to transact, process, and verify money transfers and credits between banks, businesses, and consumers. The Federal Reserve's financial services systems are used frequently in EFT to reduce the time and expense required to process checks and credit transactions.

EFT service is often provided by a *third-party vendor* who acts as the intermediary between the company and the banking system. That third party might accept transactions from a business and perform all of the translation services. EFT security is provided through various types of data encryption. EFT reduces the need for manual data entry, thus reducing the occurrence of data entry errors.

## 3.2    Application Service Providers (ASP)

*Application service providers* (ASP) provide access to application programs on a rental basis. They allow smaller companies to avoid the extremely high cost of owning and maintaining today's application systems by allowing them to pay only for what is used. The ASPs own and host the software and users access it via a Web browser. The ASP is responsible for software updates and usually will also provide backup services for the users' data. The provided software may be referred to as software as a service, apps on tap, or on-demand software.

### 3.2.1   Advantages of ASP

The benefits of utilizing an ASP are lower costs, from a hardware, software, and people standpoint, and greater flexibility. Small businesses especially benefit because they do not need to hire systems experts to provide the services performed by the ASP.

### 3.2.2   Disadvantages of ASP

The drawbacks of utilizing an ASP are the possible risks to the security and privacy of the organization's data, the financial viability or lack thereof of the ASP, and possible poor support by the ASP (a concern anytime anything is outsourced).

## 3.3    Web Stores

### 3.3.1   Stand-Alone Web Stores

Many small companies have stand-alone Web stores that are not integrated with larger accounting systems. Such stores are typically hosted by shopping cart software that manages a product catalog, user registrations, orders, e-mail confirmations, and so on.

Financial reports, such as order summaries, are generated as needed by the software. The reports are then imported into general accounting software.

### 3.3.2   Integrated Web Stores

Many larger companies and an increasing number of small companies have turned to ERP systems that integrate all the major accounting functions, as well as the Web store, into a single software system. Such systems process Web orders and then automatically update cash and revenue accounts, handle inventory reordering, and so on. In effect, such systems treat Web-store sales the same as sales made in retail stores.

## 3.4    Dynamic Content

Web 2.0 is associated with an increase in Web pages with dynamic content. Such content is often linked to databases, such as price lists and catalog product lists. Such data can be dynamically embedded in Web pages through XML, with the data stored in a database separate from the Web page.

Dynamic content is any content that changes frequently and can include video, audio, and animation. Dynamic content in the context of HTML and the World Wide Web refers to website content that constantly or regularly changes based on user interactions, timing, and other parameters that determine what content is delivered to the user. This means that the content of the site may differ for every user because of different parameters. Facebook is an example of a site that delivers dynamic content, as every user gets different content based on friends and social interactions, although the layout generally stays the same.

## 3.5 Mash-ups

*Mash-ups* are Web pages that are collages of other Web pages and other information. Google Maps (*maps.google.com*) is an example of a mash-up. Google Maps allows the user to view various sources of information (e.g., places of interest and street names) superimposed on a single map.

## 3.6 Cloud Computing

*Cloud computing* is defined as virtual servers available over the Internet. Cloud computing includes any subscription-based or pay-per-use service that extends an entity's existing information technology capabilities on a real-time basis over the Internet. A public cloud sells services to anyone on the Internet. A private cloud is a private network or data center that provides services to a limited number of customers.

Cloud computing can offer the advantage of professional management of hardware and software. Cloud providers generally will have sophisticated backup procedures as well as high level security for customer data.

### 3.6.1 Services

Cloud computing services can be divided into three categories:

1. **Infrastructure-as-a-Service (IaaS):** Also known as Hardware-as-a-Service (HaaS), outsources storage, hardware, services, and networking components to customers, generally on a per-use basis. Amazon, Microsoft, Google, and Rackspace are providers in this market.

2. **Platform-as-a-Service (PaaS):** Allows customers to rent virtual servers and related services that can be used to develop and test new software applications.

3. **Software-as-a-Service (SaaS):** A method of software distribution in which applications are hosted by a vendor or service provider and made available to customers over the Internet. This is another name for the ASP (application service provider). An example is Salesforce.com.

| Question 1 | CPA-03682 |
|---|---|

Which of the following is usually a benefit of using electronic funds transfer for international cash transactions?

    **a.** Improvement of the audit trail for cash receipts and disbursements

    **b.** Creation of self-monitoring access controls

    **c.** Reduction of the frequency of data entry errors

    **d.** Off-site storage of source documents for cash transactions

| Question 2 | CPA-07012 |
|---|---|

An enterprise resource planning system is designed to:

    **a.** Allow nonexperts to make decisions about a particular problem.

    **b.** Help with the decision-making process.

    **c.** Integrate data from all aspects of an organization's activities.

    **d.** Present executives with the information needed to make strategic plans.

# 1 Protection of Information

Information security is a strategy including the processes, tools, and policies necessary to detect, prevent, document, and counter threats to both digital and physical information. Processes and policies often involve both digital and non-digital security measures to protect data from unauthorized access, use, replication, or destruction. Information security management can include various components such as mantraps, encryption, and malware detection.

Information security management programs are key for protecting the confidentiality, integrity and availability of IT systems and business data. Many large entities employ a dedicated security group to implement and maintain the organization's information security management program. The group is often led by a chief information security officer.

## 1.1 Security Policy Defined

An entity's information security policy is a document that states how an organization plans to protect its tangible and intangible information assets. Security policies include:

1.  Management instructions indicating a course of action, a guiding principle, or an appropriate procedure.

2.  High-level statements that provide guidance to workers who must make present and future decisions.

3.  Generalized requirements that must be written and communicated to certain groups of people inside and, in some cases, outside the organization.

## 1.2 Security Policy Goal

The goal of a good information security policy is to require people to protect information, which in turn protects the organization, its employees, and its customers.

## 1.3 Types of Policies

Computer security policies start out at a high level and become more specific (granular) at the lower levels.

### 1.3.1 Program-Level Policy

*Program-level policies* are used for creating a management-sponsored computer security program. A program-level policy, at the highest level, might prescribe the need for information security and may delegate the creation and management of the program to a role within the IT department. This is the mission statement for the IT security program.

### 1.3.2 Program-Framework Policy

*A program-framework policy* establishes the overall approach to computer security (i.e., a computer security framework). A framework policy adds detail to the program by describing the elements and organization of the program and department that will carry out the security mission. This is the IT security strategy.

- **Issue-Specific Policy:** *Issue-specific policies* address specific issues of concern to the organization (e.g., cloud computing).

- **System-Specific Policy:** *System-specific policies* focus on policy issues that exist for a specific system (e.g., the payroll system).

# 2 Development and Management of Security Policies

A three-level model can be used to develop a comprehensive set of security policies:

## 2.1 Security Objectives

The first step is to define the *security objectives*. The objectives should consist of a series of statements to describe meaningful actions about specific resources. These objectives should be based on system functionality or mission requirements and also state the security actions to support the requirements. Security objectives might relate to confidentiality, data integrity, authorization, access, resource protection, and other issues.

## 2.2 Operational Security

*Operational security* should define the manner in which a specific data operation would remain secure (e.g., operational security for data integrity might consider a definition of authorized and unauthorized modification: the individuals authorized to make modifications, by job category, by organization placement, by name, etc.).

## 2.3 Policy Implementation

Security is normally enforced through a combination of technical and traditional management methods. Although technical means are likely to include the use of access control technology, other automated means of enforcing or supporting security policy exist. For example, technology can be used to block telephone system users from calling certain numbers. Intrusion detection software can alert system administrators to suspicious activity or take action to stop the activity. Personal computers can be configured to prevent booting from an external drive.

# 3 Policy Support Documents

Policies are defined as statements of management's intent. Documents that serve to support policies include:

## 3.1 Regulations

*Laws, rules, and regulations* generally represent governmentally imposed restrictions passed by regulators and lawmakers (i.e., the Sarbanes-Oxley Act of 2002, HIPPA, etc.).

## 3.2 Standards and Baselines

Topic-specific and system-specific documents that describe overall requirements for security are called, respectively, standards and baselines.

## 3.3    Guidelines

*Guidelines* provide hints, tips, and best practices in implementation.

## 3.4    Procedures

*Procedures* are step-by-step instructions on how to perform a specific security activity (configure a firewall, install an operating system, and others).

# 4    Logical and Physical Access Controls

Data and procedural controls are implemented to ensure that data is recorded, errors are corrected during processing, and output is properly distributed.

## 4.1    Logical Controls

Logical controls use software and data to monitor and control access to information and computing systems.

### 4.1.1    User Access

Because user accounts are the first target of a hacker, care must be used when designing procedures for creating accounts and granting access to information.

### 4.1.2    Initial Passwords and Authorization for System Access

The first point of contact for a new employee is generally the human resources (HR) department. HR should generate the request for a user account and system access rights. Depending on the level of access being granted, the information security officer also may need to approve the account.

### 4.1.3    Changes in Position

*Changes in position* require coordination of effort between HR and IT.

- It is important to have procedures to address changes in jobs/roles and to remove access that is no longer needed.

- There must be a mechanism to disable accounts when an employee leaves an organization. The ideal scenario is for HR to alert IT prior to termination, or otherwise, as soon as possible.

### 4.1.4    Managing Passwords

Passwords are designed to protect access to secure sites and information. The first rule in password policy is that every account must have a password. A strong password management policy must address the following password characteristics:

- **Password Length:** Longer passwords are generally more effective. Many organizations require a minimum of seven or eight characters.

- **Password Complexity:** Complex passwords are more effective and generally feature three of the following four characteristics:

    1. Uppercase characters

    2. Lowercase characters

    3. Numeric characters

    4. ASCII characters (e.g., !, @, #, $, %, ^, &, *, or ?)

- **Password Age**

  Although there is no true standard, passwords should be changed frequently in order to be effective; every 90 days is considered a good policy. Administrative passwords should be changed more frequently.

- **Password Reuse**

  Although there is no true standard, passwords should not be reused until a significant amount of time has passed. The goal is to prevent users from alternating between their favorite two or three passwords.

- **Two-Factor Authentication**

  This method allows for a second authentication key from a secondary device such as a smartphone or other key generator that is based on the time of log-in.

### 4.1.5 Network and Host-Based Firewalls

- **Default-Deny Policy**

  The firewall administrator lists the allowed network services, and everything else is denied.

- **Default-Allow Policy**

  The firewall administrator lists network services that are not allowed, and everything else is accepted.

  A default-deny approach to firewall security is by far the more secure, but due to the difficulty in configuring and managing a network in that fashion, many networks instead use a default-allow approach.

### 4.1.6 Network Intrusion Detection Systems

These systems comprise devices or software programs that monitor network or system activities for malicious activities or policy violations and produce electronic reports for management.

### 4.1.7 Access Control Lists

These specify which users or system processes are granted access to objects, as well as what operations are allowed on given objects.

### 4.1.8 Data Encryption

*Encryption* is an essential foundation for electronic commerce. Encryption involves using a password or a digital key to scramble a readable (plaintext) message into an unreadable (ciphertext) message. The intended recipient of the message then uses another digital key to decrypt or decipher the ciphertext message back into plaintext.

With encryption keys, the longer the length of the key, the less likely is the message or transaction to be decrypted by the wrong party and the less likely the key is to be broken by a *brute-force attack*. In a brute-force attack, the attacker simply tries every possible key until the right one is found.

If encrypted content is communicated by an entity (a person or a machine) using cryptography, the sender is the entity that encrypts and the receiver is the entity that decrypts the content. Between the sender and the receiver lies the unsecured environment where the garbled message travels.

When encrypted content is stored, rather than transferred between a sender and a receiver, authorized users have the ability to encrypt and decrypt the content so they can use it for authorized purposes.

## Illustration 1    Encryption

A local bank uses encryption methods and hashing in all of its online banking transfers. (Hashing is the process of changing a series of characters into a shorter, fixed length that represents the original string of characters. It is commonly used with encryption.)

The bank has previously used a digital certificate from a trusted certificate authority (CA), such as Symantec or Network Solutions. A bank customer wants to make an online transfer between accounts. The encrypted transaction will be processed as follows:

**Step 1:** When a bank customer visits the bank's website, the customer will notice the lock icon displayed at the bottom of the screen once he or she clicks on a "Money Transfer" button or its equivalent. The bank customer's browser software will then obtain the website's digital certificate, verify its validity, and open it to get the bank's public key. The bank's website software follows the same concept to acquire the user's public key.

**Step 2:** Once the bank customer clicks on the "money transfer" button to view his or her online banking transactions, the encryption software performs the following steps:

**a.** It creates a hash of the money transfer by using a hashing algorithm.

**b.** It creates a digital signature for the money transfer by encrypting the hash using the bank customer's private key.

**c.** It encrypts the money transfer using the advanced encryption standard (AES) symmetric key in order to protect the confidentiality of the bank customer because only those with the AES key can decrypt the transfer.

**d.** The AES key is encrypted by using the bank's public key in order to ensure that only the intended recipient (bank) will be able to decrypt the AES key needed for the money transfer.

**Step 3:** The encrypted money transfer (created in Step 2 c), the AES key needed to decrypt the money transfer (created in Step 2 d), and the user's digital signature (created in Step 2 b) are all sent over the Internet to the bank.

**Step 4:** Once the bank's computer system receives the package of information via the Internet, it performs the following steps:

**a.** The system uses the user's public key, obtained in Step 1, to decrypt the digital signature created in Step 2 b, in order to yield the hash of the money transfer that was created by the bank customer.

**b.** The system uses its own private key to decrypt the AES key sent by the customer in Step 2 d.

**c.** The system uses the AES key from Step 4 b to decrypt the encrypted money transfer created in Step 2 c in order to produce the plaintext version of the customer's transfer.

**d.** The system uses the same hashing algorithm used on the user's computer in Step 1 to hash the plaintext copy of the money transfer created in Step 4 c.

The system compares the hash created in Step 4 d with the one produced in Step 4 a. If there is a match, the bank's system knows that the money transfer has not been changed or corrupted during transmission.

**Step 5:** The bank sends the customer an acknowledgement that the money transfer has been received.

### 4.1.9 Digital Certificates

▪ *Digital certificates,* another form of data security, are electronic documents created and digitally signed by a trusted party that certify the identity of the owners of a particular public key. The digital certificate contains that party's public key.

▪ The term *public key infrastructure (PKI)* refers to the system and processes used to issue and manage asymmetric keys and digital certificates. The organization that issues public and private keys and records the public key in a digital certificate is called a certificate authority.

Digital certificates intended for e-business use are typically issued by commercial certificate authorities, such as Comodo and Verisign. The certificate authority hashes the information stored on a digital certificate and then encrypts that hash with its private key. That digital signature is then appended to the digital certificate, which provides the means for validating the authenticity of the certificate.

### 4.1.10 Digital Signatures vs. E-Signatures

*Digital signatures* use asymmetric encryption to create legally binding electronic documents. Web-based e-signatures are an alternative and are provided by vendors as a software product. The e-signature is a cursive-style imprint of a person's name that is applied to an electronic document. E-signatures are legally binding, just as if the user had really "signed" a paper copy of the document.

## 4.2  Physical Controls

Physical controls monitor and control the environment of the workplace and computing facilities. They also monitor and control access to and from such facilities.

### 4.2.1  Segregation of Duties

This ensures that an individual cannot complete a critical task by himself.

### 4.2.2  Monitoring and Control of Access to and From the Facilities

Can include the following examples: doors, locks with retina or fingerprint scanners, secure pass-throughs called mantraps, heating and air-conditioning, smoke and fire alarms, fire suppression systems, cameras, barricades, fencing, security guards, cable locks, etc. Separating the network and workplace into functional areas are also physical controls.

### 4.2.3  Backup Files

Data backups are necessary both for recovery in a disaster scenario and for recovery from processing problems. Copies of key master files and records should be stored in safe places located outside of the company. Copies of files kept on-site should be stored in fireproof containers or rooms.

▪ **Backup of Systems That Can Be Shut Down:** The backup process is relatively simple when a system can be shut down for backup and maintenance. When this is the case, files or databases that have changed since the last backup (or just all data) can be backed up, using the son-father-grandfather or similar concept.

▪ **Backups of Systems That Do Not Shut Down:** Effective backups are more difficult when an information system cannot be shut down. Recovery often includes applying a transaction log (a file of the transactions that had been applied to the databases) and reapplying those transactions to get back to the point immediately before the failure.

▪ **Mirroring:** Mirroring is the use of a backup computer to duplicate all of the processes and transactions on the primary computer. Mirroring, which can be expensive, is sometimes used by banks and other organizations for which downtime is unacceptable.

### 4.2.4 Uninterrupted Power Supply

An *uninterrupted power supply* (UPS) is a device that maintains a continuous supply of electrical power to connected equipment. A UPS is also called battery backup. A UPS is used to prevent a system from shutting down inappropriately during an outage. A UPS can prevent data loss and can protect the integrity of a backup while it is being performed. When a power failure occurs, the UPS switches to its own power source instantaneously so that there is no interruption in power to the system.

A UPS is not a backup standby generator; the battery will run out sooner or later. Because a backup generator will not provide protection from a momentary power interruption, it is critical that the UPS be able to provide power without any interruption so that data will not be corrupted.

### 4.2.5 Program Modification Controls

*Program modification controls* are controls over changes to programs being used in production applications. Program modification controls include both controls designed to prevent changes by unauthorized personnel and controls that track program changes so that there is a record of what versions of what programs are running in production at any specific point in time.

### 4.2.6 Malware Detection

*Malware detection software* on servers and clients detects the threat of viruses, worms, and file infectors, to protect information.

# 5 General Controls and Application Controls

## 5.1 General Controls

*General controls* are designed to ensure that an organization's control environment is stable and well-managed, and include:

1. Systems development standards

2. Security management controls

3. Change management procedures

4. Software acquisition, development, operations, and maintenance controls

## 5.2 Application Controls

*Application controls* prevent, detect, and correct transaction error and fraud and are application-specific, providing reasonable assurance as to system:

1. Accuracy

2. Completeness

3. Validity

# 6 Disaster Recovery/Business Continuity Plans

*Disaster recovery* consists of an entity's plans for restoring and continuing operations in the event of the destruction of program and data files, as well as processing capability. Short-term problems or outages do not normally constitute disasters. If processing can be quickly reestablished at the original processing location, then disaster recovery is not necessary. If processing cannot be quickly reestablished at the original processing site (possibly because the original processing site no longer exists), then disaster recovery is necessary.

## 6.1    Major Players in Disaster Recovery

*Major players in a disaster recovery* plan are the organization itself and the disaster recovery services provider (e.g., IBM or SunGard). If application software packages are utilized, the package vendors may be involved. For distributed processing, hardware vendors may be involved. Senior management support is absolutely necessary for an effective disaster recovery plan.

## 6.2    Steps in Disaster Recovery

The *steps in a disaster recovery* plan are to:

**1.**   assess the risks;

**2.**   identify mission-critical applications and data;

**3.**   develop a plan for handling the mission-critical applications;

**4.**   determine the responsibilities of the personnel involved in disaster recovery; and

**5.**   test the disaster recovery plan.

Depending on the organization, the disaster recovery plan may be limited to the restoration of IT processing or may extend to restoration of functions in end-user areas (often called business continuity). One factor that must be considered in business continuity is the paper records that might normally be maintained in end-user areas and that might be lost in a disaster.

## 6.3    Advantages and Disadvantages of Disaster Recovery and Business Continuity

If an organization does not have a disaster recovery and business continuity plan and a disaster occurs, the organization may go out of business. The disadvantage is the cost and effort required to establish and maintain a disaster recovery plan.

## 6.4    Split-Mirror Backup

As the amount of data needed to support many large companies grows, so do the time and resources that it takes those companies to back up and recover their data. One often-used, effective backup method is known as a split-mirror backup, which is useful when the main systems must always be online. A split-mirror backup uses a remote server to back up large amounts of data offline that can be restored in the event of a disaster.

## 6.5    Data Backup and Recovery Procedures

### 6.5.1    Use of a Disaster Recovery Service

Some organizations contract with outside providers for disaster recovery services. Various levels and types of service can be provided, which could be one empty room or even complete facilities across the country where end users could be located. The major emphasis is on hardware and telecommunications services.

### 6.5.2    Internal Disaster Recovery

Some organizations with the requirement for instantaneous resumption of processing after a disaster (e.g., banks and houses) provide their own duplicate facilities in separate locations. Data might be mirrored (i.e., updated and stored in both locations), and processing can be switched almost instantaneously from one location to another. A duplicate data center and data mirroring are expensive, and most organizations adopt cheaper solutions.

### 6.5.3 Multiple Data Center Backups

▪ Using a data center to back up another or back up to a cloud provider, assuming that there is enough capacity to process the essential applications.

▪ Organizations also must decide what types of backups to perform in order to recover lost data.

1. *Full backup* is an exact copy of the entire database. Full backups are time consuming, so most organizations only do full backups weekly and supplement them with daily partial backups.

2. Two types of partial backups are possible:

—An *incremental backup* involves copying only the data items that have changed since the last backup. This produces a set of incremental backup files, each containing the results of one day's transactions. Restoration involves first loading the last full backup and then installing each subsequent incremental backup in the proper sequence.

—A *differential backup* copies all changes made since the last full backup. Thus, each new differential backup file contains the cumulative effects of all activity since the last full backup. Consequently, except for the first day following a full backup, daily differential backups take longer than incremental backups. Restoration is simpler, however, because the last full backup needs to be supplemented with only the most recent differential backup, instead of a set of daily incremental backup files. Many organizations make incremental and differential backups daily.

### 6.5.4 Alternative Processing Facilities

1. **Cold Site:** A *cold site* is an off-site location that has all the electrical connections and other physical requirements for data processing, but it does not have the actual equipment. Cold sites usually require one to three days to be made operational because equipment has to be acquired. Organizations that utilize a cold-site approach normally utilize generic hardware that can be readily (and quickly) obtained from hardware vendors. Cold sites are the cheapest form of off-site location.

2. **Hot Site:** A *hot site* is an off-site location that is equipped to take over the company's data processing. Backup copies of essential data files and programs may also be maintained at the location or a nearby data storage facility. In the event of a disaster, the organization's personnel need to be shipped to the disaster recovery facility to load the backup data onto the standby equipment.

   • **Telecommunications Network**

      The most difficult aspect of recovery is often the telecommunications network.

   • **Floor Space and Equipment Determination**

      Disaster recovery service providers normally have an extensive amount of floor space and an extensive amount of equipment, but they would have nowhere near enough if all customers (or even a significant number of similar customers) declare a disaster at the same time. How much is needed is determined on a probabilistic basis; to a disaster recovery services provider, geographic and industry diversification of customers is extremely important.

   • **Personnel Issues**

      Effective recovery, and especially rapid effective recovery, is often a function of having knowledgeable personnel involved.

3. **Warm Site:** A *warm backup site* is a facility that is already stocked with all the hardware that it takes to create a reasonable facsimile of the primary data center.

In order to restore the organization's service, the latest backups must be retrieved and delivered to the backup site. Next, a bare-metal restoration of the underlying operating system and network must be completed before recovery work can be done. The advantage of the warm backup site is that a restoration can be accomplished in a reasonable amount of time. The disadvantage is that there is still a continued cost associated with the warm backup site because a contract must be maintained with the facility to keep it up-to-date. The warm backup site is the compromise between the hot backup site and the cold backup site.

| Question 1 | CPA-06630 |
|---|---|

When a client's accounts payable computer system was relocated, the administrator provided support through a virtual private network (VPN) connection to a server. Subsequently, the administrator left the company. No changes were made to the accounts payable system at that time. Which of the following situations represents the greatest security risk?

    **a.** User passwords are *not* required to be in alphanumeric format.

    **b.** Management procedures for user accounts are *not* documented.

    **c.** User accounts are *not* removed upon termination of employees.

    **d.** Security logs are *not* periodically reviewed for violations.

| Question 2 | CPA-04813 |
|---|---|

Which of the following procedures is most important to include in the disaster recovery plan for an information technology department?

    **a.** Replacement personal computers for user departments

    **b.** Identification of critical applications

    **c.** Physical security of warehouse facilities

    **d.** Cross-training of operating personnel

# 1 The Role of Input, Processing, and Output Controls

## 1.1 Input Controls

The following source data controls regulate the integrity of input, which is crucial to accurate and complete output:

1. Data validation at the field level (edit checks, meaningful error messages, input masks, etc.).

2. Prenumbering forms, making it possible to verify that all input is accounted for and that no duplicate entries exist.

3. Well-defined source data preparation procedures, which are used to collect and prepare source documents. (Sometimes, no source documents exist because the data is entered automatically by way of a Web-based application or document scanning.)

## 1.2 Processing Controls

Important processing controls include the following:

### 1.2.1 Data Matching

Matching two or more items of data before taking an action improves transaction processing (e.g., controls should include matching information on the vendor invoice to both the purchase order and the receiving report before paying a vendor).

### 1.2.2 File Labels

Use of *file labels* ensures that the correct and most current files are updated. External labels are readable by humans, while internal labels are written in machine-readable form on the data recording media. Both internal and external labels should be used. External labels are easily altered so that internal labels are more secure. Two important types of internal labels are header and trailer records.

- The header record is at the beginning of each file and contains the file name, expiration date, and other identification data.

- The trailer record is at the end of a file and contains the batch totals calculated during input.

### 1.2.3 Recalculation of Batch Totals

Comparison of amounts input to amounts output ensures that the volume of transactions processed is correct. Hash totals (such as a sum of invoice numbers) also can be used to confirm that the correct source documents are included. If someone substituted a different invoice with the same amount, the batch total would agree but the hash total would not.

### 1.2.4 Cross-Footing and Zero-Balance Tests

Testing the sum of a column of row totals to the sum of a row of column totals to verify identical results provides some assurances as to accuracy. A zero-balance test requires the use of control accounts.

For example, the payroll clearing account is debited for the total gross pay of all employees. It is then credited for the amount of all labor costs allocated to various expense categories. The payroll clearing account should have a zero balance after these entries have been made; a nonzero balance indicates a processing error.

### 1.2.5 Write-Protection Mechanisms

Common file protections guard against the accidental writing over or erasing of data files stored on magnetic media. However, it is important to remember that although these provide protection from accidental erasure, most write-protection mechanisms are easily removed.

### 1.2.6 Database Processing Integrity Procedures

Database systems use database administrators, data dictionaries, and concurrent update controls to ensure processing integrity.

1.  The administrator establishes and enforces procedures for accessing and updating the database.

2.  The data dictionary ensures that data items are defined and used consistently.

3.  Concurrent update controls protect records from errors that occur when two or more users attempt to update the same record simultaneously. This is accomplished by locking out one user until the system has finished processing the update entered by the other.

## 1.3 Output Controls

Verification of system output provides additional control over processing integrity. *Output controls* include:

### 1.3.1 User Review of Output

Examination by users of system output for reasonableness, completeness, and verification that the output is provided to the intended recipient.

### 1.3.2 Reconciliation Procedures

Reconciliation of individual transactions and other system updates to control reports, file status, or update reports (e.g., reconcile input control totals to output control totals).

### 1.3.3 External Data Reconciliation

Reconciliation of database totals with data maintained outside the system (e.g., the number of employee records in the payroll file should be compared with the total from human resources to detect attempts to add fictitious employees to the payroll database).

### 1.3.4 Output Encryption

The authenticity and integrity of data outputs must be protected during transmission. Encryption techniques reduce the chance for data interception. Controls should be designed to minimize the risk of data transmission errors.

- When a receiving unit detects a data transmission error, it requests the sending unit to retransmit that data. Generally, the system will do this automatically, and the user is unaware that it has occurred.

- Parity checking and message acknowledgement techniques are two basic types of data transmission controls.

  - Parity checking is the process of taking the sum of the bits in a byte and adding either a zero or one to make the byte even for even parity or odd for odd parity.

  - If the message arrives and a bit has changed during transmission, then it is recognized and the message can be resent.

## 1.4    Correctly Functioning Controls

Completeness, accuracy, and continuous processing integrity are the goals of correctly functioning controls.

**1.**    Completeness means to be whole and have nothing missing.

**2.**    Accuracy means to be correct and precise.

**3.**    Continuous processing integrity means to have data integrity that is consistent and accurate throughout the processing cycle.

# 2    Design and Operating Effectiveness of Application Controls

## 2.1    Information Technology Controls

It is important to establish controls related to the use of information technology resources. Budgets should be established for the acquisition of equipment and software, for operating costs, and for usage. Actual costs should be compared with budgeted amounts, and significant discrepancies should be investigated. Specific information technology control procedures include:

- A plan of organization that includes appropriate segregation of duties to reduce opportunities for anyone to be in a position to both perpetrate and conceal errors or irregularities in the normal course of his or her duties.

| Illustration 1    Segregation of Duties |
| --- |
| Programmers should not have access to source code and production data. They should only make changes in a test environment with test data. Otherwise, a programmer could alter the program to commit fraud and then change the program back so the fraud would be undetected. |

- Procedures that include the design and use of adequate documents and records to help ensure the proper recording of transactions and events.

- Limits to asset access in accordance with management's authorization.

| Illustration 2    Access to Assets |
| --- |
| Only employees authorized to issue checks have access to the accounts payable module of the accounting system. |

- Effective performance management, with clear definitions of performance goals and effective metrics to monitor achievement of goals.

- Information processing controls are applied to check for proper authorization, accuracy, and completeness of individual transactions.

- The proper design and use of electronic and paper documents and records help ensure the accurate and complete recording of all relevant transaction data.

- Implementation of security measures and contingency plans.

  - Security measures focus on preventing and detecting threats. Data security controls should be designed to ensure that authorization is required to access, change, or destroy storage media.

  - Contingency plans detail the procedures to be implemented when threats are encountered. One goal of the contingency plan would be to minimize disruption of processing while ensuring the integrity of data input and processing.

  - It is a well-accepted concept in information system security that some active threats cannot be prevented without making the system so secure that it is unusable.

## 2.2 Effectiveness of Control Policies

Evaluating the ongoing *effectiveness* of control policies and procedures provides added assurance that controls are operating as prescribed and achieving their intended purpose. A diagnostic control system compares actual performance with planned performance.

### 2.2.1 Diagnostic Controls

*Diagnostic controls* are designed to achieve efficiency in operations of the firm to get the most from resources used.

### 2.2.2 Control Effectiveness

The following principles of control should be applied to systems development and maintenance:

- **Strategic Master Plan:** To align an organization's information system with its business strategies, a multiyear *strategic master plan* should be developed and updated annually. The plan should show the projects that must be completed to achieve long-range company goals and address the company's hardware, software, personnel, and infrastructure requirements.

- **Data Processing Schedule:** All data processing tasks should be organized according to a *data processing* schedule.

- **Steering Committee:** A *steering committee* should be formed to guide and oversee systems development and acquisition.

- **System Performance Measurements:** For a system to be evaluated properly, it must be assessed using *system performance measurements*. Common measurements include throughput (output per unit of time), utilization (percentage of time the system is being productively used), and response time (how long it takes the system to respond).

# 3 Roles and Responsibilities of Information Technology Professionals

*Information technology professionals* include administrators (for the database, the network, and the Web), librarians, computer operators, and developers (for systems and applications). The roles and responsibilities of IT professionals are defined individually by each organization, and, as indicated previously, job titles and responsibilities can vary widely depending on the needs of the organization and, in some cases, the personal preferences of IT management.

## 3.1    System Analyst

### 3.1.1    Internally Developed System

- Works with end users to determine system requirements.

- Designs the overall application system.

- Determines the type of network needed.

### 3.1.2    Purchased System

- Integrates the application with existing internal and purchased applications.

- Provides training to end users.

## 3.2    Computer Programmer

*Computer programmers* include application programmers and system programmers.

### 3.2.1    Application Programmer/Software Developer (Software Engineers)

- An *application programmer* is the person responsible for writing and/or maintaining application programs. A considerable number of the new ideas for the IT industry have been devoted to techniques to minimize or facilitate program maintenance.

- For internal control purposes, application programmers should not be given write/update access to data in production systems or unrestricted and uncontrolled access to application program change management systems.

### 3.2.2    System Programmer

- A *system programmer* is responsible for installing, supporting (troubleshooting), monitoring, and maintaining the operating system. System programmers also may perform capacity planning functions. In complex computing environments, a considerable amount of time can be spent testing and applying operating system upgrades.

- For internal control purposes, system programmers should not be given write/update access to data in production systems or access to change management systems.

## 3.3    Computer Operator

*Computer operators* are responsible for scheduling and running processing jobs. Much of the job of scheduling and running jobs can be automated and, in large computing environments, must be automated due to the sheer volume of information processed.

## 3.4    IT Supervisor

*IT supervisors* manage the functions and responsibilities of the IT department.

## 3.5    File Librarian

*File libraries* store and protect programs from damage and unauthorized use, and file librarians control the file libraries. In large computing environments, much of this work is automated.

## 3.6    Data Librarian

In large companies, the data librarian has custody of and maintains the entity's data and ensures that production data is released only to authorized individuals when needed.

## 3.7    Security Administrator

*Security administrators* are responsible for the assignment of initial passwords and often the maintenance of those passwords (if the end users do not maintain their own passwords). Security administrators are responsible for the overall operation of the various security systems and the security software in general.

## 3.8    System Administrator

### 3.8.1    Database Administrator (DBA)

- *Database administrators* are responsible for maintaining and supporting the database software and performing certain security functions. Database administrators perform functions for database software that are similar to those system programmers perform for the operating system as a whole.

- Database administrators differ from data administrators; a database administrator is responsible for the actual database software, and a data administrator is responsible for the definition, planning, and control of the data within a database.

### 3.8.2    Network Administrator

*Network administrators* support computer networks through performance monitoring and troubleshooting. Sometimes, network administrators are called telecommunication analysts or network operators.

### 3.8.3    Web Administrator

*Web administrators* are responsible for information on a website.

## 3.9    End User

*End users* are any workers in an organization who enter data into a system or who use the information processed by the system. End users now routinely enter much of their own data or transactions.

# 4    Segregation of Duties Within Information Technology

In a well-structured IT department, the duties discussed below are segregated. Because many transactions in an IT environment are actually performed by the application software, segregation of duties normally revolves around granting and/or restricting access to production programs and to production data.

## 4.1    System Analysts vs. Computer Programmers

System analysts design an information system to meet user needs, whereas computer programmers use that design to create an information system by writing computer programs. Analysts often are in charge of hardware and programmers are in charge of application software. Theoretically, if the same person is in charge of hardware and software, that person could easily bypass security systems without anyone knowing and steal organizational information or assets (e.g., embezzling of funds).

## 4.2    Computer Operators vs. Computer Programmers

It is important that *computer operators* and *computer programmers* be segregated because a person performing both functions could make unauthorized and undetected program changes.

## 4.3  Security Administrators vs. Computer Operators and Computer Programmers

*Security administrators* are responsible for restricting access to systems, applications, or databases to the appropriate personnel. If the security administrator were also a programmer or an operator for that system, that person could give himself or another person access to areas they are not authorized to enter. This security bypass also would allow that person to steal organizational information or assets.

# 5  Design and Effectiveness of Information Technology Control Activities

## 5.1  Manual vs. Automated Controls

A *manual control* is a control performed by a person without making direct use of automated systems.

---

### Illustration 3    Manual Control

When performing a quality assurance review, the reviewer evaluates the process and related requirements in order to confirm that the entire process was executed correctly.

---

An *automated control* is a control performed by an automated system, without interference of a person.

---

### Illustration 4    Automated Control

In a point-of-sale credit limit check at a retail store:

**Step 1:** Customer swipes a credit card at the register.

**Step 2:** The retail point-of-sale (POS) terminal communicates with the credit card issuer to verify credit limit and amount of available credit.

**Step 3:** If the transaction is within the credit limit, the system approves the transaction. If the transaction is above the credit limit, the system declines the transaction.

---

■ **Value of Automated Controls**

- Accuracy
- Timeliness
- Efficiency
- Security

## 5.2 Controls Can Be Preventive, Detective, and Corrective

### 5.2.1 Preventive

Preventive controls refers to using administrative controls such as security awareness training, technical controls such as firewalls, and anti-virus software to stop attacks from penetrating the network. Most industry and government experts agree that security configuration management is probably the best way to ensure the best security configuration allowable, along with automated patch management and updating anti-virus software.

### 5.2.2 Detective

Employing a blend of technical controls such as anti-virus, intrusion detection systems, system monitoring, file integrity monitoring, change control, log management, and incident alerting can help to track how and when system intrusions are being attempted.

### 5.2.3 Corrective

Applying operating system upgrades, backup data restore and vulnerability mitigation, and other controls to make sure that systems are configured correctly and can prevent the irretrievable loss of data.

| Question 1 | CPA-06984 |
|---|---|

What is the primary objective of data security controls?

- **a.** To establish a framework for controlling the design, security, and use of computer programs throughout an organization.
- **b.** To ensure that storage media are subject to authorization prior to access, change, or destruction.
- **c.** To formalize standards, rules, and procedures to ensure the organization's controls are properly executed.
- **d.** To monitor the use of system software to prevent unauthorized access to system software and computer programs.

| Question 2 | CPA-08305 |
|---|---|

A company's new time clock process requires hourly employees to select an identification number and then choose the clock-in or clock-out button. A video camera captures an image of the employee using the system. Which of the following exposures can the new system be expected to change the *least*?

- **a.** Fraudulent reporting of employees' own hours
- **b.** Errors in employees' overtime computation
- **c.** Inaccurate accounting of employees' hours
- **d.** Recording of other employees' hours

# 1 Fundamental Risks Related to Systems Development and Maintenance

Organizations constantly improve or replace information systems for any of the following reasons:

1. Changes in needs of a business unit (because of growth, downsizing, mergers, new regulations, etc.).

2. Technological advances resulting in more effective but less costly systems.

3. Improvements in business processes leading to shorter processing times.

4. Competitive advantages as the result of improvements in quality, quantity, and speed of information gathering.

5. Productivity gains due to automation of clerical tasks.

6. System age and need for replacement.

## 1.1 Technology Risk

The need for technology risk management has intensified in recent years due to the speed of technological change, the degree to which technology is driving business, and the adoption of emerging and disruptive technologies that change the way business is done, such as cloud, connected devices, and mobile.

There are four general types of risks associated with information technology systems, whether the system is in development or in use.

### 1.1.1 Strategic Risk

*Strategic risk* includes the risk of choosing inappropriate technology. For example, an organization may choose a Web-based program to share data between remote offices in different parts of the world. If one of the offices is in a location that does have access to high-speed Internet connections, it will not be able to enter data at the same speed as the other offices. This problem may lead to the generation of reports thought to be up-to-date but actually missing data from the office that does not have high-speed access.

### 1.1.2 Operating Risk

*Operating risk* includes the risk of doing the right things in the wrong way. For example, assume that a payroll manager is supposed to run the biweekly payroll after the human resources manager enters newly hired employees into the system. If the payroll manager runs the payroll too early (i.e., before the newly hired employees are entered), the newly hired employees do not get paid, and the payroll report is inaccurate.

### 1.1.3    Financial Risk

*Financial risk* includes the risk of having financial resources lost, wasted, or stolen. For example, an inventory report lists several laptop computers, but some of the laptops were not returned when employees left the organization. This problem could lead to inaccurate financial reports that report assets that no longer exist.

### 1.1.4    Information Risk

*Information risk* includes the risk of loss of data integrity, incomplete transactions, or hackers. If a network system that is connected to the Internet does not have a secure firewall or another type of security measure, hackers may enter the system and corrupt or destroy data.

# 2    Managing IT Risk

## 2.1    Risk IT Framework

ISACA (formerly known as the Information Systems Audit and Control Association) developed the Risk IT Framework, which can be used with other frameworks (e.g., ERM), to achieve the following three objectives:

1.   Integrate the management of IT risk into the overall risk management of the enterprise.

2.   Make well-informed decisions about the nature and extent of the risk, the risk appetite, and the risk tolerance of the enterprise.

3.   Develop a response to the risk.

## 2.2    IT Risk Defined

As defined in the Risk IT Framework, IT risk is the business risk associated with the use, ownership, operation, involvement, influence, and adoption of IT within an enterprise. It consists of IT-related events that could potentially affect the business. Examples are:

- Late project delivery

- Not achieving enough value from IT

- Compliance

- Obsolete or inflexible IT architecture

- IT service delivery problems

- Security issues

## 2.3    Categories of IT Risk

According to ISACA, there are three categories of IT risk, which are defined as separate from but interrelated to general business risks. These are:

1.   **IT Benefit/Value Enablement Risk:** Related to missed opportunities to use technology to improve business processes.

2.   **IT Program and Project Delivery Risk:** Related to the contribution of IT to new or improved business solutions.

3.   **IT Operations and Service Delivery Risk:** Related to all aspects of the performance of IT systems and services.

# 3 Risk Assessment

Before risks can be managed, they must be assessed. The steps in risk assessment are to:

1. identify threats;

2. evaluate the probability that the threat will occur;

3. evaluate the exposure in terms of potential loss from each threat;

4. identify the controls that could guard against the threats;

5. evaluate the costs and benefits of implementing controls; and

6. implement controls that are determined to be cost effective.

The following chart lists some of the major risks that could affect systems development, operation, and maintenance. New threats constantly arise, so the list is not considered to be complete.

| Sample of Potential Risks to IT | | | | |
|---|---|---|---|---|
| Risks From Nature | Risks From Current and Past Employees | Risks From Competitors | Risks From Hackers | Unintended Risks |
| 1. Earthquakes, volcanoes, fires, storms, and floods<br><br>2. Transportation accidents<br><br>3. Events related to hazardous materials | 1. Human error<br>2. Sabotage<br>3. Fraud<br>4. Professional misconduct<br>5. Negligence<br>6. Passive-aggressive behavior<br>7. Workplace revenge<br>8. Insurance fraud<br>9. Lawsuits against employer | 1. Intellectual property theft<br><br>2. Copyright infringement<br><br>3. Patent infringement<br><br>4. Price surveillance | 1. Viruses<br>2. Eavesdropping<br>3. Spam<br>4. Phishing<br>5. Spyware<br>6. Malware<br>7. Password cracking<br>8. Website defacement<br>9. Transmission control protocol and Internet protocol (TCP/IP) hijacking<br>10. System tampering | 1. Software defects<br>2. Loss of data due to hardware failure or employee error<br>3. Unavailability of key personnel due to disaster or illness<br>4. Failure to keep computers up-to-date with operating system, antivirus, or firewall software<br>5. Having insufficient personnel or personnel who are not adequately trained<br>6. Inadequate physical security<br>7. Employees sharing passwords or other access<br>8. Loss of outsourced services<br>9. Inadequate budgets to maintain appropriate software and hardware |

# 4 Risks Related to New Technology

Developing high-quality, error-free software is difficult, expensive, and time-consuming. An established fact in business is that most software projects deliver less, cost more, and take longer than expected. This does not address the projects that get canceled before completion.

The AICPA has published lessons learned by a major corporation in a recent system implementation that stressed the importance of the following points, adapted from the AICPA:

- **Defining the integration points to the governance processes.** Successfully moving a strategic plan from concept to reality depends on clear, well-defined integration points with the budgeting, governance, and decision-making processes within IT. Decision makers must understand the strategic directions and make decisions consistent with their intent. If localized, sub-optimal decisions will be made and the plan will not succeed.

- **Defining and managing planning data.** A wealth of data flows throughout the strategic planning process. To lend focus to the process and avoid wasted efforts, deliverables for each step of the process must be clearly defined from the start. This helps ensure that the correct data is developed for effective decision making and also builds support for the process by informing stakeholders of the expected output of each step.

- **Defining and publicizing the planning calendar.** When multiple levels of planning occur simultaneously, publicizing a planning calendar lets everyone know what's happening—and when—so that everyone involved is on the same page.

- **Realizing that timing is essential.** Each step in the planning process must support the next stage. Direct influence is lost if there are timing missteps along the way.

- **Clearly defining roles and responsibilities.** Core team members include a business process manager who defines, communicates, facilitates, and improves the process through each cycle. Subject matter experts develop the data, analysis, and ideas that are used throughout the process. It is best to have a broad, virtual team from across the organization participating in the process to make sure the output is challenged and supported from a number of different perspectives. Decision makers should review, discuss, and debate the strategic planning data and set the direction for the organization. Clearly defining the decision makers early on helps avoid organizational conflict later.

- **Communicating data and messages well.** Effectively communicating the strategic planning messages and associated data to middle and first-line managers helps them educate their personnel. Well-informed employees are most likely to commit to and support the plan.

# 5 Risks Related to Legacy Systems

The incentives to stick with legacy software do not negate the risks. One of the most powerful disincentives is the unguarded security vulnerabilities of legacy products. The cost of a breach that leaks Social Security or credit card information now averages more than $7 million.

## 5.1 Reasons for Persistence of Legacy Systems

Many entities choose to continue to use legacy systems due to:

- **Investment in Deployment:** The company already paid for the product, so there is an incentive to use it for as long as possible.

- **Investment in Training:** The employees have already invested time in learning the product, so again there is a built-in incentive to leverage that.

- **Dependencies on Supportive Technology:** The legacy software might only run on a legacy system, which would be burdensome to upgrade.

- **Dependencies Built on the Legacy Product:** The organization may have built custom products using the legacy software, creating a huge disincentive to abandon it and risk having to rebuild in-house software.

- **Risk Over Reward:** Saving time and money by continuing to use legacy software might seem like a reward, but it is often illusory. A security breach easily can result in a disaster, which is far more time-consuming and potentially costly than maintaining up-to-date software.

## 5.2 Risks of Legacy Systems

Using legacy systems exposes an entity to the following risks:

- **Lack of Vendor Support:** It costs money for a vendor to continue updating a product. Eventually, support may end and new vulnerabilities may not be caught. Vendors concentrate more of their resources on developing, updating, and promoting new products rather than maintaining old ones.

- **Old "Threatscape":** Older products possess less sophisticated security mechanisms. Legacy software was, by definition, developed at a time when the understanding of the security threatscape was less advanced than the present. Many of the techniques developed by hackers to compromise systems, as well as strategies created by security professionals to protect them, were less mature in the past.

- **Code Reutilization:** Often, software products incorporate some amount of code from a predecessor or other products. This can incorporate security vulnerabilities that predate even the legacy product.

- **Educated Hackers:** When security flaws are discovered in software, they are published so they can be known and acted on. This also educates the hackers, and for a legacy product the known vulnerabilities have been exposed for years, providing ample time for hackers to learn, understand, and develop tools to exploit them.

- **Patch Lag:** Many organizations are slow to install patches, allowing legacy products to remain exposed for a long period, during which the knowledge about those flaws is increasingly available.

- **Evolving Hacker Tools:** When a new security flaw is discovered in a contemporary product, many times it can be exploited only by the most sophisticated hackers with a high degree of technical savvy. Over time, the hacker toolkit evolves, and compromises which once required the most advanced knowledge can be executed by more rudimentary hackers using simple tools, often guided by online tutorials.

- **Dependency on Insecure Platform:** In some cases, a legacy product may only run in a legacy environment. Even if the legacy product in question does not itself pose a security risk, the fact that it forces you to continue using a highly exploited platform can put an organization in a vulnerable position.

## 5.3 Mitigating Risk in Legacy Systems

An entity can mitigate the risks related to its legacy systems by:

- **Isolating the System:** One of the many great uses of virtualization is to sandbox a risky platform to keep it isolated from your important systems. It is possible to run legacy apps within a self-contained window on a modern, secure system. In addition, the virtual system can be cut off from network access to the outside world.

■ **Virtual Patches:** Sometimes, no security patch is available to directly modify and harden a legacy product. But a so-called virtual patch can address a known vulnerability upstream of the insecure application. A virtual patch could consist of rules in a firewall packet inspector or Web server that look for and detect SQL injection syntax and block the request before it ever reaches the vulnerable legacy product.

# 6 Information System Testing Strategies

## 6.1 Purpose of Testing

Software testing is intended to accomplish the following:

1. Find defects created during the development of the software.

2. Determine the level of quality of the software.

3. Ensure that the end product meets the business and user requirements.

## 6.2 Guidelines for Successful Testing

■ Specify testing objectives explicitly. For example, load testing is a process of testing the behavior of software by applying maximum load in terms of accessing and manipulating large input data. This type of testing identifies the maximum capacity of software and its behavior at peak time.

■ Identify categories of users for the software and develop a profile for each. Develop a test plan that emphasizes rapid cycle testing. The goal of rapid testing is to identify major bugs early in the development process, requiring integration of test planning, execution, and reporting throughout the life cycle.

■ Build robust software that is designed to test itself.

■ Use effective formal reviews as a filter prior to testing.

■ Conduct formal technical reviews to assess the test strategy and test cases.

■ Develop a continuous improvement approach for the testing process.

## 6.3 Types of Tests

An effective testing strategy includes automated, manual, and exploratory tests to efficiently reduce risk and tighten release cycles. A discussion of some popular approaches to testing follows.

### 6.3.1 Unit Tests

Used to validate the smallest components of the system, ensuring that they handle known input and output correctly. This type of testing is performed by developers before the setup is handed over to the testing team to formally execute the test cases. The goal of unit testing is to isolate each part of the program and show that individual parts are correct in terms of requirements and functionality.

### 6.3.2 Integration Tests

Exercise an entire subsystem and ensure that a set of components operates smoothly together. Integration testing can be done in two ways:

1. **Bottom-Up Integration Testing:** This testing begins with unit testing, followed by tests of progressively higher-level combinations of units called modules or builds.

2. **Top-Down Integration Testing:** The highest-level modules are tested first and progressively lower-level modules are tested thereafter.

### 6.3.3   Validation Tests

Focus on visible user actions and user-recognizable outputs from the system. These tests answer the question, "Did we build the right thing?"

- Validation tests are based on the use-case scenarios, the behavior model, and the event flow diagram created in the analysis phase of the development.

  - Tests must ensure that each function or performance characteristic conforms to its specification.

  - Deviations (deficiencies) must be negotiated with the customer to establish a means for resolving the errors.

- Configuration review or audit is used to ensure that all elements of the software configuration have been properly developed, cataloged, and documented to allow its support during its maintenance phase.

### 6.3.4   Acceptance Tests

Make sure the software works correctly for the intended user in his or her normal work environment. This is arguably the most important type of testing, as it is conducted by a quality assurance (QA) team that gauges whether the application meets the intended specifications and satisfies the client's requirement. The QA team will have a set of prewritten scenarios and test cases that will be used to test the application.

- **Alpha Test:** Version of the complete software is tested by the customer under the supervision of the developer at the developer's site.

- **Beta Test:** Version of the complete software is tested by the customer at his or her own site without the developer being present.

### 6.3.5   System Testing

System testing tests the system as a whole. Once all the components are integrated, the application as a whole is tested rigorously to determine whether it meets the specified quality standards. This type of testing is performed by a specialized testing team.

**1.   Steps in System Testing**

- **Recovery Testing:** Checks the system's ability to recover from failures.

- **Security Testing:** Verifies that system protection mechanisms prevent improper penetration or data alteration.

- **Stress Testing:** Program is checked to see how well it deals with abnormal resource demands (i.e., quantity, frequency, or volume).

- **Performance Testing:** Designed to test the run-time performance of software, especially real-time software.

- **Deployment (or Configuration) Testing:** Exercises the software in each of the environments in which it is to operate.

**2.   Importance of System Testing**

- System testing is the first step in the software development life cycle, where the application is tested as a whole.

- The application is tested thoroughly to verify that it meets the functional and technical specifications.

- The application is tested in an environment that is very close to the production environment in which the application will be deployed.

- System testing enables QA to test, verify, and validate both the business requirements as well as the application architecture.

| Question 1 | CPA-03483 |
|---|---|

All of the following are different types of reporting risk that an accountant must recognize as threats to accuracy of reports, *except*:

    **a.**   Strategic risk.

    **b.**   Financial risk.

    **c.**   Information risk.

    **d.**   Data integrity risk.

| Question 2 | CPA-04827 |
|---|---|

Which of the following risks can be minimized by requiring all employees accessing the information system to use passwords?

    **a.**   Collusion

    **b.**   Data entry errors

    **c.**   Failure of server duplicating function

    **d.**   Firewall vulnerability

**NOTES**

## 1. CPA-06748

Choice "d" is correct. The principle of external communications asserts that matters affecting the achievement of financial reporting should be communicated with outside parties.

Choice "a" is incorrect. The principle of financial reporting information conveys the idea that information should be identified, captured, used at all levels of the company, and distributed in a manner that supports achievement of financial reporting objectives.

Choice "b" is incorrect. Internal control information is needed to facilitate the function of control components and is identified, captured, used, and distributed in a timely manner that enables personnel to fulfill their responsibilities.

Choice "c" is incorrect. The principle of internal communications asserts that communications should enable and support understanding and execution of internal control objectives, processes, and individual responsibilities.

## 2. CPA-06483

Choice "d" is correct. The financial reporting competencies principle of the control environment component of internal control integrated framework suggests stronger controls and encourages the company to retain qualified personnel to handle financial reporting.

Choice "a" is incorrect. The integrity and ethical values principle of the control environment component of internal control integrated framework suggests stronger controls with high standards of ethical conduct for top management, but does *not* address retention of qualified personnel to handle financial reporting.

Choice "b" is incorrect. The management philosophy and operating style principle of the control environment component of internal control integrated framework suggests strong controls and encourages management's attitudes to be congruent with strong financial controls, but does *not* address retention of qualified personnel to handle financial reporting.

Choice "c" is incorrect. The accountability principle of the control environment component of internal control integrated framework suggests strong controls and encourages management to hold individuals accountable for their internal control responsibilities, but does *not* address retention of qualified personnel to handle financial reporting.

## 1. CPA-06480

Choice "a" is correct. The governance and culture component of the enterprise risk management (ERM) framework includes foundational elements such as defining desired culture, establishing and operating structure, the organization's commitment to core values, and similar issues that influence the tone of the organization.

Choice "b" is incorrect. The strategy and objective-setting component of the ERM framework includes principles that relate to the definition of risk appetite and development of strategy and objectives, not core values.

Choice "c" is incorrect. The performance component of the ERM framework includes principles that relate to the evaluation of risk and development of appropriate responses, not to commitment to core values.

Choice "d" is incorrect. The review and revision component of the enterprise risk management framework includes principles that relate to the pursuit of improvements to enterprise risk management and reviews of risk and performance, not commitment to core values.

## 2. CPA-06754

Choice "c" is correct. Insuring against losses or entering into joint ventures to address risk is known as risk sharing.

Choice "a" is incorrect. A response to risk that involves the disposal of a business unit, product line, or geographical segment is called risk avoidance. Obtaining appropriate insurance is not avoidance.

Choice "b" is incorrect. A response to risk that involves the diversification of product offerings rather than elimination of product offerings is called reduction. Obtaining appropriate insurance is not reduction, it is sharing (the risk has not changed; it has been shifted to another party).

Choice "d" is incorrect. Self-insuring or simply tolerating the full exposure to risk is known as acceptance. Obtaining appropriate insurance is not acceptance of risk.

## 1. CPA-07014

Choice "c" is correct. The financial expert serving on the audit committee of an issuer must have experience with internal controls. The financial expert qualifies through education or past experience as an auditor or finance officer for an issuer of similar complexity.

Choice "a" is incorrect. The financial expert qualifies through education or past experience as an auditor or finance officer for an issuer of similar complexity. The expert should have an understanding of GAAP, application of GAAP, an understanding of internal controls, and an understanding of audit committee functions. There is no requirement to have a limited understanding of GAAS.

Choice "b" is incorrect. The financial expert qualifies through education or past experience as an auditor or finance officer for an issuer of similar complexity. The expert should have an understanding of GAAP, application of GAAP, an understanding of internal controls, and an understanding of audit committee functions. There is no requirement to have education and experience as a certified financial planner.

Choice "d" is incorrect. The financial expert qualifies through education or past experience as an auditor or finance officer for an issuer of similar complexity. The expert should have an understanding of GAAP, application of GAAP, an understanding of internal controls, and an understanding of audit committee functions. There is no requirement to have experience in tax return preparation.

## 2. CPA-06491

Choice "c" is correct. Issuers are generally prohibited from making personal loans to directors or executive officers under the Sarbanes-Oxley Act of 2002. Exceptions exist for loans made in the ordinary course of business.

Choice "a" is incorrect. Although there is no 10 percent cap on ownership, disclosures are required for persons who generally directly or indirectly own more than 10 percent of any class of most any equity security.

Choice "b" is incorrect. Although there is no 10 percent cap on ownership, disclosures are required for persons who generally directly or indirectly own more than 10 percent of any class of most any equity security.

Choice "d" is incorrect. There are no prohibitions on perquisite compensation but disclosures may be required.

## 1. CPA-05788

Choice "b" is correct. The effective rate of interest rate is 10 percent. The effective interest rate represents the actual finance charges associated with a borrowing after reducing loan proceeds for charges and fees.

The above scenario indicates that finance charges are $40,000 ($500,000 × 8%), and the net proceeds or amount available under the loan is $400,000 (the face value of $500,000 net of the 20 percent compensating balance of $100,000 [$500,000 × 20%]).

The effective rate of interest is the finance charge of $40,000 divided by the net proceeds of $400,000:

$40,000 ÷ $400,000 = 10%

Choice "a" is incorrect. The stated rate of the loan (8 percent) is not the effective rate of interest.

Choice "c" is incorrect. The compensating balance (20 percent) percentage is not the effective rate of interest.

Choice "d" is incorrect. The sum of the stated rate and the compensating balance (28 percent) is not the effective rate of interest.

## 1. CPA-05860

Choice "a" is correct. Foreign currencies are like anything else: their value can go up or down. If the dollar price of the euro rises, then the euro is getting more expensive. That means that the dollar is getting less expensive. Another way to say the same thing is that the dollar is depreciating against the euro.

Choice "b" is incorrect. This choice is backward.

Choice "c" is incorrect. The euro is the currency of Europe (or at least a large portion of Europe). If the price of the euro increases relative to the U.S. dollar, it will not buy fewer European goods. When the price of the euro rises, the price of European goods will also increase, and the euro will buy the same amount of European goods, but more U.S. goods.

Choice "d" is incorrect. When the price of the euro rises, the euro will buy more, not fewer, U.S. goods.

## 2. CPA-05590

Choice "a" is correct. As a foreign competitor's currency becomes weaker compared with the U.S. dollar, the product becomes less expensive in U.S. dollars. The less expensive product will increase demand and result in an advantage in the U.S. market.

Choice "b" is incorrect. The opposite effect occurs, as described in choice "a" above.

Choice "c" is incorrect. Foreign currency exchange rates affect both sales and possibly cost of goods sold of a competing domestic company. Sales within U.S. markets will deteriorate as the currency of foreign competitors deteriorates and makes the domestic company's goods more expensive. As a foreign competitor's currency appreciates, sales within U.S. markets by a domestic company should also increase as goods manufactured in the U.S. become less expensive. Cost of goods sold may fluctuate if foreign suppliers are used.

Choice "d" is incorrect. It is better for a U.S. company when the value of the U.S. dollar weakens, not strengthens. A weak U.S. dollar makes domestic goods relatively less expensive than imported goods.

## 3. CPA-05767

Choice "c" is correct. Because Platinum is going to receive euros in 30 days, it will want to lock in the price of euros now. The way to do that is to enter into a forward contract (referred to in the text as a forward hedge) to sell euros in 30 days. The price will be fixed now, but the transaction will not occur until the end of the 30-day period. A futures contract also might be able to be used. Note that, with the fixed price, Platinum will not be hurt if the price of euros in terms of dollars falls, but it will also not benefit if the price of euros in terms of dollars rises. In this question, the treasurer was concerned about the price of euros dropping.

Choice "a" is incorrect. Buying 30,000 euros now will not reduce the risk of a drop in the value of the euro. In fact, the risk will double because the company will have 60,000 euros in 30 days.

Choice "b" is incorrect. Buying an interest rate swap will do nothing to reduce the risk of a drop in the value of the euro. Interest rate swaps might reduce the risk of changes in interest rates.

Choice "d" is incorrect. Platinum can reduce the risk of a drop in the value of the euro by using the appropriate hedge. Hedges are often used to reduce currency risk.

## NOTES

## 1. CPA-03385

|  | Debt | | Equity | | Total |
|---|---|---|---|---|---|
| Investment dollars | $15 mil | + | $35 mil | = | $50 mil |
| Investment structure | 30% | | 70% | | 100% |
| Cost of investment | × 7% | | × 12% | | |
| Weighted avg. cost of capital | 2.1% | + | 8.4% | = | 10.5% |

Choice "a" is correct. 10.50 percent weighted average cost of capital.

Choices "b", "c", and "d" are incorrect, per the above calculation.

## 2. CPA-03420

Choice "d" is correct. The CAPM holds that:

Cost of retained earnings = Risk-free rate + [Beta × (Market return − Risk-free rate)]

Substituting

$$
\begin{aligned}
\text{Cost of retained earnings} &= 6\% + 1.25\,(14\% - 6\%) \\
&= 6\% + 10\% \\
&= 16\% \ (\text{Choice "d"})
\end{aligned}
$$

Choices "a", "b", and "c" are incorrect, per the above calculation.

## 1. CPA-03431

Choice "c" is correct. Financial leverage increases when the debt-to-equity ratio increases. Using a higher percentage of debt (bonds) for future investments would increase financial leverage.

Choice "a" is incorrect. This results in no change in total equity and, consequently, no change in financial leverage.

Choice "b" is incorrect. This would result in increased equity and decreased debt, which would decrease financial leverage.

Choice "d" is incorrect. This would increase equity, decrease the debt-to-equity ratio and decrease financial leverage.

## 1. CPA-03528

Choice "b" is correct. Working capital (WC) increases only if current assets are increased or current liabilities are decreased. Exchanging accounts payable (current liability) for a two-year note payable (long-term liability) would decrease current liabilities and increase working capital.

Choice "a" is incorrect. This would not impact WC.

Choice "c" is incorrect. This would not have an impact on WC (decrease of both CA and CL).

Choice "d" is incorrect. This would decrease WC.

## 2. CPA-03456

Choice "d" is correct. The current ratio is current assets divided by current liabilities. The sale of land would increase cash and therefore current assets without increasing current liabilities. This would increase the current ratio. Furthermore, the sale of land at a loss would decrease net profit.

Choice "a" is incorrect. The payment of a tax payment would not decrease net profit because the expense was accrued last year.

Choice "b" is incorrect. The use of cash to retire a long-term bond would reduce current assets without reducing current liabilities. This would reduce the current ratio.

Choice "c" is incorrect. As above, this would reduce cash without reducing current liabilities.

## 1. CPA-03458

Choice "d" is correct. 36.7% annual cost of credit if cash discount is not taken.

$$\frac{360}{(30-10)} \times \frac{2\%}{(100\% - 2\%)} = 36.7\%$$

Choices "a", "b", and "c" are incorrect, per the above calculation.

## 2. CPA-06627

Choice "b" is correct. An increase in the cost of carrying inventory would lead to a reduction in average inventory. Suppose item A is required to be refrigerated so that it will not spoil. If electricity prices are rising, management would prefer to have a lower inventory of item A on hand because of the electricity (i.e., carrying) cost of that item.

Choice "a" is incorrect. An increase in the cost of placing an order would lead to an increase in average inventory. Management would increase the amount of inventory per order to reduce the number of orders, thereby causing the company to on average hold more inventory.

Choice "c" is incorrect. Increased demand would likely increase average inventory to avoid stockout costs.

Choice "d" is incorrect. An increase in lead time would likely lead to an increase in average inventory. A higher safety stock likely would be needed to accommodate the lead time to ensure that requirements are met.

## 1. CPA-05315

Choice "d" is correct. The primary reason for a company to agree to a debt covenant limiting the percentage of its long-term debt is to reduce the coupon rate on NEW bonds being sold. A debt covenant is a provision in a bond indenture (contract between the bond issuer and the bond holders) that the bond issuer will either do (affirmative covenants) or not do (negative covenants) certain things. In this question, the issuer would agree not to issue bonds in the future over a certain percentage of its long-term debt. Such a provision would be good for the potential bondholders and would probably reduce the coupon rate on the bonds being sold.

Choice "a" is incorrect. The primary reason for a company to agree to a debt covenant limiting the percentage of its long-term debt is not to cause the price of the company's stock to rise. Bond covenants affect bonds, not equity (at least not directly).

Choice "b" is incorrect. The primary reason for a company to agree to a debt covenant limiting the percentage of its long-term debt is not to lower the company's bond rating. Such a covenant might raise, not lower, a company's bond rating because there would be less risk.

Choice "c" is incorrect. The primary reason for a company to agree to a debt covenant limiting the percentage of its long-term debt is not to reduce the risk of existing bondholders, although a reduction in the risk of the existing bondholders certainly might result from such a covenant. As a general rule, more debt means more risk, and less debt means less risk. So less debt would reduce the risk of all bondholders.

## 1. CPA-06137

Choice "d" is correct. Fernwell will pay approximately $463, computed as follows:

**Step 1, Compute dividend in subsequent year:**

$$P_t = D_{(t+1)} / (R - G)$$
$$D_{(t+1)} = \$20 \times 1.05^2$$
$$D_{(t+1)} = \$20 \times 1.1025$$
$$D_{(t+1)} = \$22.05$$

**Step 2, Apply growth rate to computed dividend:**

$$P_t = D_{(t+1)} / (R - G)$$
$$P_t = \$22.05 \times 1.05 / (0.10 - 0.05)$$
$$P_t = \$23.15 \times 0.05$$
$$P_t = \$463$$

**Terms are defined as:**

$P_t$ = Current price (price at period "t")

$D_{(t+1)}$ = Dividend one year after period "t"

R = Required return

G = Growth rate

Choice "a" is incorrect. $400 presumes a zero growth model.

Choice "b" is incorrect. $420 presumes only one year of growth, not two.

Choice "c" is incorrect. $441 does not properly account for growth. Specifically, it does not properly include the compounding in the year following the first two years of compounding.

## 2. CPA-06131

Choice "c" is correct. An underlying assumption of the constant growth model is the idea that the stock price will grow at the same rate as the dividend, thereby producing a constant growth rate.

Choice "a" is incorrect. Compounding growth is exponential, not linear.

Choice "b" is incorrect. The constant growth model assumes that the growth rate is less than the discount rate.

Choice "d" is incorrect. An underlying assumption of the constant growth model is the idea that the stock price will grow at the same rate (not amount) as the dividend as a means of producing a constant growth rate.

## 3. CPA-06133

Choice "a" is correct. The P/E ratio measures the amount that investors are willing to pay for each dollar of earnings per share. Higher P/E ratios generally indicate that investors are anticipating more growth and are bidding up the price of the shares in advance of performance.

Choice "b" is incorrect. High P/E ratios generally indicate investor confidence in earnings growth, not performance that has peaked.

Choice "c" is incorrect. High P/E ratios generally indicate investor confidence in earnings growth, not that performance will fall.

Choice "d" is incorrect. High P/E ratios give some insight into investor confidence of earnings growth.

### Business 2, Module 8

## 1. CPA-03283

Choice "b" is correct. The original FMV of the old equipment is a sunk cost that does not affect equipment-replacement decisions.

All of the following items affect the decision process:

- Current disposal price of the old equipment
- Cost of the new equipment
- Operating costs of the new equipment

## 2. CPA-03358

Choice "d" is correct. Discount rates may be adjusted to factor differences in risk into cash flow analysis. For example, a 12 percent discount rate may be used for the first three years of a project and a 15 percent discount rate for subsequent years to reflect the greater risk associated with the cash flows in the later time periods. Discount rates may also be adapted to compensate for expected inflation.

Choices "a", "b", and "c" are incorrect, per above.

### 3. CPA-03337

Choice "d" is correct. If the net present value of a project is positive, it would indicate that the rate of return for the project is greater than the discount percentage rate (hurdle rate) used in the net present value computation.

Choice "a" is incorrect. If the present value of cash outflows exceeds the present value of cash inflows, then the net present value is negative and the rate of return for the project is less than the discount percentage rate (hurdle rate).

Choice "b" is incorrect. If the internal rate of return is equal to the discount percentage rate (hurdle rate) used in the net present value computation, the net present value will be zero.

Choice "c" is incorrect. The present value index will be greater (not less) than 100 percent if the net present value of a project is positive.

### 4. CPA-06644

Choice "c" is correct. Net present value is computed as the difference between project inflows and outflows, discounted to present value as follows:

| Inflows | |
|---|---:|
| Years 1 through 5: $420,000 × 3.79 = | $1,591,800 |
| Year 6: $100,000 × 0.56 = | 56,000 |
| Present value of all inflows | 1,647,800 |
| Outflow (today, discount factor of 1.0) | 1,800,000 |
| Net present value | $ 152,200 |

Choices "a", "b", and "d" are incorrect, based on the above explanation.

Business 2, Module 9

### 1. CPA-05785

Choice "b" is correct. The payback period computation ignores cash flows after the initial investment has been recovered. The payback method focuses on liquidity and the time it takes to recover the initial investment.

Choice "a" is incorrect. The discounted payback period considers the time value of money but, like any other payback method, it ignores cash flows after the initial investment has been recovered.

Choice "c" is incorrect. The net present value method measures the amount of absolute return and not a rate. Although a positive net present value would confirm that the entity's investment exceeds the hurdle rate established by management, it neither measures the rate specifically nor assumes a hurdle rate equal to the incremental borrowing rate.

Choice "d" is incorrect. When using the internal rate of return, the analyst recommends acceptance of the investment in the event that the IRR is greater than the hurdle rate established by management.

## 2. CPA-04836

Choice "a" is correct. The payback method determines the number of years that it will take for a company to recoup or be paid back for its investment. The payback method does not consider the time value of money.

Choice "b" is incorrect. The payback method determines the number of years that it will take for a company to recoup or be paid back for its investment. Although the payback method focuses on liquidity, project cash flows after the initial investment are not considered; thus, profitability is ignored.

Choice "c" is incorrect. The payback method determines the number of years that it will take for a company to recoup or be paid back for its investment. Although the payback method focuses on liquidity, project cash flows after the initial investment are not considered; thus, profitability is ignored.

Choice "d" is incorrect. Salvage value is specifically considered as part of payback computations because it contributes to the incoming cash flow when the asset is sold.

## 3. CPA-05309

Choice "b" is correct. Projects B and C achieve payback by the end of Year 3. The payback period for Project A is somewhere between the end of Year 4 and Year 5. For all three projects, Year 1 appears to be a combination of cash outflows (initial cost) and cash inflows (return of investment), but it really does not make any difference. When the cumulative cash flow (both inflow and outflow) is zero, the project has paid back.

Choice "a" is incorrect. Project A does not pay back within three years even though Projects B and C do.

Choice "c" is incorrect. Projects B and C, *not* just Project B, pay back within three years.

Choice "d" is incorrect. Project A does *not* pay back within three years even though Project C does.

## BUSINESS 3

### 1. CPA-07083

Choice "d" is correct. Conversion costs include both direct labor and overhead. Increases in crude oil prices are likely to impact the cost of generating electricity (and, by extension, the rate for electricity). Electricity is significant in manufacture of the product in the fact pattern and would likely increase the overhead costs of the manufacturer.

Choice "a" is incorrect. Electricity is not included in direct materials. Direct material costs would likely not increase.

Choice "b" is incorrect. Electricity is not included in direct labor. Direct labor costs would likely not increase.

Choice "c" is incorrect. Prime costs are the sum of direct materials and direct labor. Electricity is not included in prime costs. Prime costs would likely not increase.

### 1. CPA-05321

Choice "c" is correct. Using direct labor hours, the overhead applied consists of both variable overhead and fixed overhead. The calculation is as follows:

Variable overhead rate = $50,000 / 20,000 hours = $2.50 per direct labor hour

Fixed overhead rate = $25,000 / 20,000 hours = $1.25 per direct labor hour

Total overhead rate = $2.50 + $1.25 = $3.75

Overhead applied to the job = $3.75 × 1,500 = $5,625

Choices "a" and "b" are incorrect, per the above calculation.

Choice "d" is incorrect. This answer incorrectly used a $5.00 overhead application rate, with the variable overhead rate applied twice instead of applying both a fixed and variable overhead rate.

### 2. CPA-05798

Choice "d" is correct. The estimated product cost is equal to the sum of prime costs and applied overhead or $18,000.

Prime costs are the sum of direct labor and direct material:

| | | |
|---|---|---|
| Direct labor | $ 6,000 | |
| Direct material | 4,000 | |
| Subtotal, prime costs | | $10,000 |

Applied overhead is equal to the overhead rate times the estimated hours:

| | | |
|---|---|---|
| Computations of rate—total overhead: | | |
| Material handling | $120,000 | |
| Quality inspection | 200,000 | |
| Total overhead | $320,000 | |
| Total cost driver | 80,000 | |
| Rate | $ 4.00 | |
| Applied overhead: | | |
| Estimated hours | 2,000 | |
| Rate | × 4.00 | |
| Applied overhead | | $ 8,000 |
| Estimated costs | | $18,000 |

Choice "a" is incorrect. The proposed solution incorrectly anticipates that the product cost is equal to only applied overhead, exclusive of prime costs.

Choice "b" is incorrect. The proposed solution incorrectly anticipates that the product cost is equal to only prime costs, exclusive of applied overhead.

Choice "c" is incorrect. The proposed solution incorrectly anticipates that the product cost is equal to the sum of only direct labor and applied overhead, exclusive of direct material.

### 3. CPA-03601

Choice "b" is correct. Under the FIFO method, the equivalent units of production is composed of three parts: (i) the completion of units on hand at the beginning of the period; (ii) the units started and completed during the period; and (iii) the units partially completed at the end of the period. Applying these principles to the given fact pattern, the total equivalent units of production for the quarter is determined as follows:

| | | |
|---|---|---|
| *Equivalent units for the first quarter:* | | |
| Work in process, beginning (100 units × 50% to complete) | | $50 |
| Units started and completed: | | |
| Units completed and transferred out | 400 | |
| Units in beginning inventory | (100) | 300 |
| Work in process, ending (200 units × 75% complete) | | 150 |
| Equivalent units of production | | $500 |

Choices "a", "c", and "d" are incorrect, per the above.

## 4. CPA-03644

Choice "b" is correct. $4.60 equivalent unit cost of materials using the weighted-average method, calculated as follows:

| | |
|---|---|
| Units completed | 92,000 |
| Ending WIP x % completed | 21,600 [ = 24,000 x 90%] |
| Equivalent units | 113,600 |

**Total costs:**

Beginning cost + Current cost = $54,560 + $468,000 = $522,560

Cost per equivalent unit = $522,560/113,600 = $4.60

Choices "a", "c", and "d" are incorrect, per the above explanation.

Business 3, Module 3

## 1. CPA-08307

Choice "c" is correct. Activity-based costing seeks to assign overhead costs in a manner that identifies consumption of resources. Employee salaries or even head count are more appropriate cost drivers than machine hours for employee benefits expense. Machine hours would be more likely identified as cost drivers for electric, repairs and maintenance, and depreciation expense.

Choice "a" is incorrect. Machine hours are likely an appropriate cost driver for electricity expense.

Choice "b" is incorrect. Machine hours are likely an appropriate cost driver for repairs and maintenance expense.

Choice "d" is incorrect. Machine hours are likely an appropriate cost driver for depreciation expense.

### 2. CPA-03477

Choice "c" is correct. Using the relative net realizable value method of allocating the joint costs, the net realizable value of both products is calculated as follows:

|                      | Ajac      | Bjac      |
|----------------------|-----------|-----------|
| Sales                | $80,000   | $40,000   |
| Separable costs      | (8,000)   | (22,000)  |
| Net realizable value | $72,000   | $18,000   |

The joint costs are allocated based on relative net realizable values. The two products together have a net realizable value of $90,000 ($72,000 + $18,000). Ajac contributes 80% of this total (72,000 / $90,000 = 80%). 80% of the joint costs are thus allocated to Ajac: 80% x $60,000 = $48,000.

Choice "a" is incorrect. This answer uses only the separable costs, not the net realizable value. The sales value must also be taken into consideration.

Choice "b" is incorrect. This answer uses only the sales value, not the net realizable value. The separable costs must also be taken into consideration.

Choice "d" is incorrect. The net realizable value (sales value less separable costs) must be computed in order to allocate the joint costs using the net realizable value method.

## Business 3, Module 4

### 1. CPA-03883

Choice "d" is correct. $1,940 total prevention and appraisal cost.

| Equipment maintenance (prevention) | $1,154 |
|------------------------------------|--------|
| Product testing (appraisal)        | 786    |
|                                    | $1,940 |

Rework is an internal failure cost.

Product repair (warranty) is an external failure cost.

Choices "a", "b", and "c" are incorrect, based on the above explanation.

### 2. CPA-03890

Choice "a" is correct. In a quality control program, internal failure costs are incurred because nonconforming products and services are detected prior to being shipped to customers. Examples are rework, scrap, reinspection, and retesting.

Choice "b" is incorrect. Responding to customer complaints is an external failure cost incurred because products or services failed to conform to requirements after being delivered to customers.

Choice "c" is incorrect. Statistical quality control procedures are appraisal costs incurred to detect defects.

Choice "d" is incorrect. Only rework represents an internal failure cost as described above.

## 1. CPA-06645

Choice "b" is correct. The passenger division has an ROI of 16% ($40,000 operating profit divided by $250,000 investment). The cargo division has ROI of 10% ($50,000 operating profit divided by $500,000 investment). The passenger division performed better than the cargo division based on ROI.

Notice that a performance measure based on ROI considers the amount invested to yield return rather than the absolute amount of operating profit. Also note that the rate associated with financing is not relevant.

Choice "a" is incorrect. The cargo division ROI is 10%. However, the cargo division's ROI is lower than the passenger division's ROI of 16%. The passenger division performed better than the cargo division as measured by ROI.

Choices "c" and "d" are incorrect. Both answers incorrectly add the external borrowing rate.

## 2. CPA-04809

Choice "b" is correct. The addition of an asset at year-end serves to reduce both return on investment and residual income. The addition of an asset increases the denominator in the ROI computation and increases the threshold earnings required using the residual income approach. Both measures would suffer as a result of addition of assets. See illustration below:

**Assumptions**

| | |
|---|---|
| Income | $ 100,000 |
| Assets | $1,000,000 |
| Required return | 10% |
| Additional asset | $ 200,000 |

| | Return on Investment | | | | Residual Income | | |
|---|---|---|---|---|---|---|---|
| | Before | Purchase | After | | Before | Purchase | After |
| Income | $ 100,000 | | $ 100,000 | Assets | $1,000,000 | $200,000 | $1,200,000 |
| Assets | $1,000,000 | $200,000 | $1,200,000 | Required Return | 10% | | 10% |
| Return | 10% | | 8% | Required Income | $ 100,000 | | $120,000 |
| | | | | Income | $ 100,000 | | $100,000 |
| | | | | Difference | $        - | | $(20,000) |

The purchase of the additional asset reduces ROI from 10% to 8% and produces negative residual income.

Choices "a", "c", and "d" are incorrect, per the above illustration.

### 3. CPA-08378

Choice "c" is correct. Return on equity (ROE) is calculated as follows:

$$ROE = \frac{\text{Net income}}{\text{Sales}} \times \frac{\text{Sales}}{\text{Assets}} \times \frac{\text{Assets}}{\text{Equity}}$$

The three terms in the calculation (in order) are known as the net profit margin, asset turnover, and financial leverage, respectively. For Spear, these amounts given in the question are reflected in the formula below:

$$ROE = 0.11 \times \frac{2,000,000}{2,500,000} \times \frac{2,500,000}{2,500,000\,(1-.40)} = .1467, \text{ or } 14.7\%$$

Note that equity is derived using the new debt ratio of 0.40. If debt represents 40 percent of total assets, equity must represent 60 percent.

Choices "a", "b", and "d" are incorrect, based on the above calculation.

### 4. CPA-04818

Choice "b" is correct. Economic value added (EVA) is computed as after-tax income in excess of required return. EVA is applied to the fact pattern as follows:

| | | | | |
|---|---|---|---|---|
| Pretax operating profit | | | | $300,000,000 |
| Less: taxes (40%) | | | | (120,000,000) |
| After tax income | | | | $180,000,000 |
| Less: required return | | | | |

| | Weight | Capital | Return | |
|---|---|---|---|---|
| Cost of equity | 50% | × $1,200,000,000 × | 15% | = $90,000,000 |
| Cost of debt | 50% | × $1,200,000,000 × | 5% | = 30,000,000 |
| Total required return | | | | 120,000,000 |
| Economic value added (EVA) | | | | $ 60,000,000 |

Earnings after taxes of $180,000,000 net of the required return of 15% on half of the investment funded by equity and 5% on the other half of the investment funded by debt ($120,000,000) yields an EVA of $60,000,000.

Choice "a" is incorrect, per the above computation.

Choice "c" is incorrect. The amount of the required return is not the EVA.

Choice "d" is incorrect. The amount of the after-tax income is not the EVA.

## BUSINESS 4

### 1. CPA-07088

Choice "b" is correct. The coefficient of determination ($R^2$) is the proportion of the total variation in the dependent variable ($y$) explained by the independent variable ($x$).

Choice "a" is incorrect. The independent variable is not explained by the dependent variable. Changes in the independent variable drive the variation in the dependent variable. The coefficient of determination ($R^2$) is the proportion of the total variation in the dependent variable ($y$) explained by the independent variable ($x$).

Choice "c" is incorrect. The measure of proximity of actual data points to estimated data points is not the coefficient of determination. The coefficient of determination ($R^2$) is the proportion of the total variation in the dependent variable ($y$) explained by the independent variable ($x$).

Choice "d" is incorrect. The coefficient of determination ($R^2$) is the proportion of the total variation in the dependent variable ($y$) explained by the independent variable ($x$), not the coefficient of the independent variable divided by the standard error of regression coefficient.

### 2. CPA-04642

Choice "b" is correct. Using the high-low method, the variable cost per kilo can be determined by dividing the change in cost ($160,000 − $132,000) by the change in volume (80,000 − 60,000):

$$\frac{\$160,000 - \$132,000}{80,000 - 60,000} = \$1.40 \text{ per kilo}$$

The fixed portion of the cost can be determined by substituting the volume and variable in the equation $Y = a + bx$, or

$$Y = a + bx$$
$$\$160,000 = a + \$1.40(80,000)$$
$$a = \$48,000$$

At 75,000 kilos, the total cost would be:

$$Y = \$48,000 + \$1.40x$$
$$Y = \$48,000 + \$1.40(75,000)$$
$$\mathbf{Y = \$153,000}$$

Choices "a", "c", and "d" are incorrect. Using the high-low method, the variable cost per kilo can be determined by dividing the change in cost by the change in volume. The fixed portion of the cost can be determined by substituting the volume and the variable in the equation $Y = a + bx$.

## 1. CPA-03709

Choice "b" is correct. Breakeven analysis assumes that all variable costs and revenues are constant on a per-unit basis and are linear over a relevant range. Fixed costs in total are constant.

Choice "a" is incorrect. Breakeven analysis assumes that all variable costs and revenues are constant on a per-unit basis and linear over a relevant range.

Choice "c" is incorrect. Total costs do change over a relevant range. Breakeven analysis assumes that all variable costs and revenues are constant per unit and linear within a relevant range.

Choice "d" is incorrect. Total fixed costs are assumed to be constant (representing a linear relationship) over a relevant range.

## 2. CPA-04798

Choice "b" is correct. Under variable costing, all fixed factory overhead is treated as a period cost and is expensed in the period incurred. The cost of inventory includes only variable manufacturing costs, so the cost of goods sold includes only variable costs. Also, the variable selling, general, and administrative expenses are part of total variable costs.

|  | Unit Price | Units |  | Total |
|---|---|---|---|---|
| Sales | $80.00 | 4,500 |  | $360,000 |
| Direct materials | $21.00 | 4,500 | $94,500 |  |
| Direct labor | $10.00 | 4,500 | 45,000 |  |
| Variable mfg. O/H | $3.00 | 4,500 | 13,500 |  |
| Variable S&A | $6.00 | 4,500 | 27,000 |  |
| Total variable costs |  |  |  | 180,000 |
| Contribution margin |  |  |  | 180,000 |
| Fixed mfg. O/H |  |  | 76,000 |  |
| Fixed S&A |  |  | 58,000 |  |
| Total fixed costs |  |  |  | 134,000 |
| Net income |  |  |  | $ 46,000 |

Choice "a" is incorrect. The net income is not the contribution margin.

Choice "c" is incorrect per the above computation.

Choice "d" is incorrect. The contribution margin is not the difference between sales and fixed costs ($360,000 − $134,000 = $226,000).

### 3.  CPA-04815

Choice "a" is correct. The difference between variable and absorption costing is the manner in which fixed manufacturing costs are treated. Under variable costing, only variable costs are included in inventory. Consequently, the difference in net income under variable costing rather than absorption costing is the amount of fixed manufacturing costs (accounted for in inventory under absorption costing) multiplied by the change in inventory. An increase in inventory indicates that a portion of the fixed costs associated with inventory under absorption costing are expensed under variable costing. Absorption costing, therefore, produces greater income than variable costing as inventory levels increase, as follows:

| | |
|---|---|
| Change in inventory (increase) | 2,000 units |
| Fixed manufacturing cost per unit (absorbed into inventory, excluded from cost of goods sold) | $      30 |
| Higher net income under absorption costing | $60,000 |

Choice "b" is incorrect. The difference between the fixed costs in inventory and the variable costs in inventory is not the difference in net income when comparing the two methods.

Choice "c" is incorrect. The change in inventory times the variable cost per unit does not define the difference in net income per above. Variable costs are included in inventory and, therefore, reduce cost of goods sold under both methods.

Choice "d" is incorrect. The change in inventory times total cost does not define the difference in net income. Inventory does receive a value under variable costing; however, it is limited to variable costs.

### 4.  CPA-03676

Choice "c" is correct.

**Step 1:**  Determine how many units were sold to generate the $900,000 in sales shown in the fact pattern: $900,000/$20 per unit = 45,000 units sold

**Step 2:**  Determine the total fixed costs:

Unit costs:

| | |
|---|---|
| Fixed manufacturing costs | $ 7 |
| Fixed selling and administrative costs | 3 |
| Total fixed cost per unit | $10 |

Total fixed costs = $10 per unit × 45,000 units = $450,000

**Step 3:**  Determine the contribution margin per unit:

| | |
|---|---|
| Selling price per unit | $20 |
| Prime costs | (6) |
| Variable overhead costs | (1) |
| Variable selling and administrative costs | (1) |
| Contribution margin per unit | $12 |

**Step 4:**  Determine the breakeven in units:

$$\text{Breakeven in units} = \frac{\text{Fixed costs}}{\text{C.M. per unit}}$$

$$\frac{450,000}{12} = 37,500 \text{ units}$$

Choices "a", "b", and "d" are incorrect, per the explanation above.

## 1. CPA-03991

Choice "a" is correct. This does not change the current assets or the current ratio because the reduction of cash is offset by an increase in accounts receivable.

Choice "b" is incorrect. A cash dividend increases current liabilities without increasing current assets. Although current assets remain unchanged (until the payment happens), the current ratio will change.

Choice "c" is incorrect. Cash is reduced and current liabilities are reduced. Total current assets will change (they will be reduced).

Choice "d" is incorrect. The payment of cash reduces current assets. Long-term assets are increased, as well as long-term and short-term liabilities. The current ratio is reduced.

## 2. CPA-04009

Choice "c" is correct. An increase in sales collections would decrease the cash conversion cycle.

Choice "a" is incorrect because the operating cycle (as well as the cash conversion cycle) would decrease.

Choice "b" is incorrect, as the average collection period would decrease.

Choice "d" is incorrect. Bad debt losses would decrease from an increase in sales collections.

## 1. CPA-06169

Choice "b" is correct. Assuming available capacity, the minimum cost per unit of a special order is equal to the variable cost per unit. Fixed costs are irrelevant.

Choice "a" is incorrect. The fixed cost per unit is not the minimum charge.

Choice "c" is incorrect. The variable cost per unit plus the fixed costs spread over available capacity is not the minimum charge. Fixed costs are irrelevant.

Choice "d" is incorrect. The variable cost per unit plus the fixed costs spread over current utilization is not the minimum charge. Fixed costs are irrelevant.

## 2. CPA-06170

Choice "c" is correct. At capacity, the minimum price for a special order is the sum of the variable costs of current utilization plus the contribution margin from the next best alternative.

| | |
|---|---|
| Variable costs ($50,000 ÷ 10,000) | $5 |
| Contribution margin, next best ($2,000 ÷ 1,000) | 2 |
| Total | $7 |

Choice "a" is incorrect. The minimum price is not purely the contribution margin on the next best alternative.

Choice "b" is incorrect. The minimum price is not purely the variable costs associated with existing capacity.

Choice "d" is incorrect. The minimum price is not the sum of the total cost plus the contribution from the next best alternative.

## 1. CPA-05829

Choice "b" is correct. The order of budget preparation begins with the sales budget, which logically drives the production budget (to support sales), which in turn drives the direct materials purchases (to support production), from which the cash disbursements budget is derived.

Choice "a" is incorrect. Budgets are driven by sales forecasts. To begin with, the production budget is illogical and presumes that the budget preparer can mandate sales levels based on production or is not constrained by inventory levels.

Choice "c" is incorrect. Budgets are driven by sales forecasts that ultimately determine cash flows. Beginning with cash disbursements is incorrect.

Choice "d" is incorrect. Although the order presented in this selection properly begins with sales, it does not logically support anticipated sales with production. The placement of direct materials before production appears to indicate that direct material purchases are determined independently of production as determined by sales. That relationship is generally not logical.

## 2. CPA-04793

Choice "b" is correct.

| | | Final Units | Safety Stock Percentage | WIP Conversion | WIP Units | |
|---|---|---|---|---|---|---|
| **B**eginning | Inventory | 12,000 | 40% | 4 | 19,200 | ↓ |
| **A**dditions | Purchases | N/A | N/A | N/A | **46,400** | Squeeze |
| **S**ubtractions | (Production) | 12,000 | N/A | 4 | 48,000 | ↑ |
| **E**nding | Inventory | 11,000 | 40% | 4 | 17,600 | |

The computation derives purchases using the BASE mnemonic where B is the beginning inventory computed at 40 percent of January's production requirements and E is the ending inventory at 40 percent of February's production requirements. Both are multiplied by the 4 pounds of raw material needed. Amounts subtracted from inventory, the "S," are the items produced in January, multiplied by the 4 pounds of raw materials needed. We then squeeze the purchases from the formula: Ending inventory of 17,600 + 48,000 units produced − Beginning inventory of 19,200, which equals 46,400.

Choice "a" is incorrect. It does not consider the raw material conversion of 4 pounds per unit.

Choice "c" is incorrect. This response simply considers the amount of units sold converted to raw materials.

Choice "d" is incorrect. This response is the sum of the units sold in February and the ending inventory requirements.

## 1. CPA-03813

Choice "c" is correct. A master budget is an overall budget, consisting of many smaller budgets, that is based on one specific level of production. A flexible budget is a series of budgets based on different activity levels within the relevant range.

Choice "a" is incorrect. The usefulness of master budgets and flexible budgets is not limited to specific periods.

Choice "b" is incorrect. The master budget includes the entire company, not just the production facility. The flexible budget can cover many levels of activity, not just one department.

Choice "d" is incorrect. Flexible budgets do not allow management latitude in meeting goals, but they do give management the opportunity to compare actual results to the budget for the activity level achieved.

## 2. CPA-05867

Choice "a" is correct. A 5 percent inflation rate would affect salary and health care costs but would not affect depreciation expense (based on historical cost), and would not affect interest expense (fixed based on amortization schedule). The budget would be computed as follows:

| | | |
|---|---|---|
| Salaries expense | $250,000 × 1.05 = | $262,500 |
| Health costs | 100,000 × 1.05 = | 105,000 |
| Depreciation expense | 65,000 × 1.00 = | 65,000 |
| Interest expense on 10-year fixed-rate notes | 37,750 × 1.00 = | 37,750 |
| **Total budget** | | **$470,250** |

Choice "b" is incorrect. The proposed solution improperly inflates interest expense.

Choice "c" is incorrect. The proposed solution improperly inflates depreciation expense.

Choice "d" is incorrect. The proposed solution improperly inflates all presented expenses.

## 1. CPA-03836

Choice "b" is correct. Material price variance is the difference between actual price and standard price times actual quantity.

$$
\begin{aligned}
\text{Material price variance} &= (AP - SP) \times AQ \\
&= [(\$10{,}080 \div 4{,}200) - \$2.50] \times 4{,}200 \\
&= (\$2.40 - \$2.50) \times 4{,}200 \\
&= \underline{420}
\end{aligned}
$$

The variance is favorable because the actual cost ($2.40) was less than the standard cost ($2.50).

Choice "a" is incorrect. The material price variance equals the difference in prices times the quantity purchased.

Choice "c" is incorrect. The total material variance is $80 unfavorable ($10,000 − $10,080). This total variance needs to be separated into price and quantity variances.

Choice "d" is incorrect. The material price variance equals the difference in prices times the quantity purchased.

## 2. CPA-05251

Choice "c" is correct. The direct labor usage (efficiency) variance is computed as follows:

Direct labor usage variance = Difference in standard and actual hours × Standard rate
Direct labor usage variance = [(10,000 units × 0.5 hour) − 3,000 hours] × $15 per hour
Direct labor usage variance = $30,000 favorable

The usage variance is favorable because the actual hours were less than the standard hours.

Choice "a" is incorrect. It is unclear how the $25,000 variance can be calculated in this question, but $25,000 favorable or unfavorable is certainly not correct.

Choice "b" is incorrect. It is unclear how the $25,000 variance can be calculated in this question, but $25,000 favorable or unfavorable is certainly not correct.

Choice "d" is incorrect. The variance was favorable, *not* unfavorable, because the actual hours were less than the standard hours.

## 3. CPA-05874

Choice "a" is correct. The efficiency variance compares the amount of the variable overhead applied (at standard) with the amount of variable overhead that would have been applied at actual. If more was applied than would have been incurred, the results are favorable.

| | |
|---|---|
| Standard hours allowed | 12,000 |
| Application rate | $ 8 |
| Total | 96,000 |
| Actual hours | 11,000 |
| Application rate | $ 8 |
| Total | (88,000) |
| Variable efficiency variance | $ 8,000 |

Choice "b" is incorrect. Results are favorable, not unfavorable.

Choice "c" is incorrect. The proposed amount is the budget variance, the amount applied compared with the amount spent.

Choice "d" is incorrect. The proposed answer is the variable spending variance (the actual amount spent compared with the amount applied at actual).

### 4. CPA-03831

**Rule:** The formula for the production volume variance component for overhead variances is computed as applied overhead minus budgeted overhead based on standard hours. The sole difference between these two calculated amounts is the application of fixed factory overhead.

Choice "b" is correct. Volume variances are computed as follows:

*Applied overhead:*

| | |
|---|---|
| (Standard variable overhead rate × Standard direct labor hours allowed) + (Standard fixed overhead rate × Actual production) | $22,800 |

*Budgeted overhead based on standard hours:*

| | |
|---|---|
| (Standard variable overhead rate × Standard direct labor hours allowed) + (Standard fixed overhead rate × Standard production) = ($2.00 × .1 × 19,000) + ($1.00 × 20,000) = | $23,800 |

*Difference:*

| | |
|---|---|
| Unfavorable variance | $ (1,000) |

Choices "a", "c", and "d" are incorrect, per the computation above.

### 5. CPA-06165

Choice "c" is correct. The selling price variance is computed as follows:

$$\text{Selling price variance} = \left[\frac{\text{Actual SP}}{\text{Unit}} - \frac{\text{Budgeted SP}}{\text{Unit}}\right] \times \text{Actual sold units}$$

Choice "a" is incorrect. Even though the budgeted and actual sales both compute to equal $75,000 ($15 × 5,000 for actual and $12 × 6,250 for budget), the selling price variance is not zero.

Choice "b" is incorrect. The selling price variance is not equal to the difference in price times the difference in volume.

Choice "d" is incorrect. The selling price variance is not equal to the difference in price multiplied by standard units.

## BUSINESS 5

Business 5, Module 1

### 1. CPA-03291

Choice "b" is correct. An increase in real interest rates increases the cost of capital, which shifts the aggregate demand curve to the left.

Choice "a" is incorrect. An increase in wealth shifts the aggregate demand curve to the right.

Choice "c" is incorrect. An increase in government spending shifts the aggregate demand curve to the right.

Choice "d" is incorrect. An increase in consumer confidence shifts the aggregate demand curve to the right.

### 2. CPA-05318

Choice "b" is correct. If there is an increase in the resources available in an economy, the economy will be capable of producing more goods and services. This increase is really an increase in the long-run aggregate supply (potential GDP). On the aggregate supply and demand chart, the long-run aggregate supply line (LRAS) is the vertical line that represents the potential or equilibrium level of output. If that line shifts to the right, then the economy is capable of expanding, but it will not automatically expand just because the line shifts to the right.

Choice "a" is incorrect. Just because there is an increase in the resources available in an economy, it does not mean that more goods and services will automatically be produced. There would have to be increased demand (a shift upward in the aggregate demand line) for more goods and services to actually be produced by suppliers.

Choice "c" is incorrect. If there is an increase in the resources available in an economy, the standard of living in the economy will not necessarily rise. It could rise, but it will not necessarily do that.

Choice "d" is incorrect. If there is an increase in the resources available in an economy, the technological efficiency of the economy will not automatically improve. This statement is backwards. An increase in technological efficiency of an economy will normally increase the resources available in the economy and potentially result in increased productivity.

Business 5, Module 2

### 1. CPA-03396

Choice "a" is correct. GDP = G + I + C + E (Exports − Imports)

|   | |
|---|---:|
|   | $1,040 billion |
| + | 975 billion |
| + | 5,015 billion |
| + | 106 billion |
| − | 183 billion |
|   | $6,953 billion |

### 2. CPA-03404

Choice "d" is correct. Structural unemployment occurs when the jobs available do not match the skills of the unemployed individuals or when the individuals do not live where jobs are available with their skills.

Choice "a" is incorrect. Frictional unemployment exists when workers are in the process of changing jobs or are temporarily laid off from their jobs.

Choice "b" is incorrect. The natural unemployment rate is the sum of frictional, structural, and seasonal unemployment or the unemployment rate that exists when the economy reaches its potential output level.

Choice "c" is incorrect. Cyclical unemployment is due to a downturn (recession) in the economy, which leads to a decline in real GDP and higher unemployment.

### 3. CPA-05857

Choice "a" is correct. Inflation is the sustained increase in the general price of goods and services. A retiree living on a fixed income would be most hurt by an unanticipated increase in inflation because the retiree's income would not increase to offset the negative effects of the inflation.

Choice "b" is incorrect. A borrower whose debt has a fixed interest rate would benefit from inflation because the borrower would be paying back the debt in cheaper dollars.

Choice "c" is incorrect. A union worker whose contract includes a provision for regular cost-of-living adjustments theoretically would have cost of living increases to offset the effects of the inflation. There would be a lag because the cost-of-living adjustments would be after-the-fact, but at least there would be some protection.

Choice "d" is incorrect. A saver whose savings were placed in a variable rate savings account would have the same kind of protection as the union worker (in choice "c"). The interest rate on the savings accounts would theoretically increase with the inflation. Again, there would probably be a lag, but at least there would be some protection.

### 4. CPA-05869

Choice "c" is correct. The economy can be dampened by reducing government spending and by increasing taxes (thus giving consumers less money to spend), both of which are fiscal policy. The economy can also be dampened by reducing the money supply (thus effectively decreasing prices) and increasing interest rates (thus giving consumers less money to spend because they are spending more money on interest), both of which are monetary policy.

Choice "a" is incorrect. All of these policies would stimulate the economy further.

Choice "b" is incorrect. Increasing money supply will stimulate the economy, not dampen it.

Choice "d" is incorrect. Reducing both taxes and interest rates will stimulate the economy, not dampen it.

## 1. CPA-03667

Choice "c" is correct. A shift left in any demand curve represents a decrease in demand (at all price levels) for that product. Because gasoline and cars are considered complementary goods, the demand for gasoline is directly impacted by the demand for cars. If the price for cars increases, the demand for cars will decrease, causing the demand for gasoline to decrease, and the gasoline demand curve to shift left.

Choice "a" is incorrect. An increase in the price for gasoline will decrease the quantity demanded but will not affect overall demand across all price levels and quantities (as represented by a left shift in the demand curve).

Choice "b" is incorrect. A change in the supply curve will not cause a shift in the demand curve.

Choice "d" is incorrect. A decrease in the price of cars would have the opposite effect and cause a right shift in the demand curve.

## 2. CPA-05577

Choice "c" is correct. A city ordinance that freezes rent prices (such as rent control and rent stabilization in New York City) may cause the quantity demanded for rental space to exceed the quantity supplied. This occurs if the rent controlled price is set below the market clearing price. At the controlled price, the quantity supplied will be constrained due to the low rent prices for the rent-controlled and rent-stabilized properties; builders will not want to build and rent properties for less than they are worth on the open market. The quantity demanded for the rental space will still be artificially high due to the city ordinance, which sets the controlled price below the market price. Thus, the quantity demanded will exceed the quantity supplied. New York City rent control is a perfect example of the effect of a price ceiling and the problems that it can cause.

Choice "a" is incorrect. A city ordinance that freezes rent prices will not cause the demand curve for rental space to fall. Price changes cause movements along the demand curve, not shifts in the demand curve.

Choice "b" is incorrect. A city ordinance that freezes rent prices will not cause the supply curve for rental space to rise. Price changes cause movements along the supply curve, not shifts in the supply curve.

Choice "d" is incorrect. A city ordinance that freezes rent prices will not cause the quantity supplied to exceed the quantity demanded; it would cause the reverse effect.

## 3. CPA-05770

Choice "a" is correct. If an item has many similar substitutes, its price elasticity of demand will be high. Customers can always switch to a substitute, so a change in price may affect demand substantially.

Choice "b" is incorrect. If the cost of an item is low compared to the total budget of the purchasers, it will make little difference how much it costs. For example, in a business the cost of paper clips will probably not be a significant factor.

Choice "c" is incorrect. If an item is considered a necessity (e.g., insulin to diabetics), the price elasticity of demand will be relatively low (i.e., inelastic). Purchasers will buy it regardless of the cost, and demand will not change all that much.

Choice "d" is incorrect. If the price of an item is regulated by a government agency, the demand may not be highly price elastic because any price changes (if made) will be controlled and implemented gradually over time.

### 1. CPA-06642

Choice "a" is correct. The inability of market participants (a single trader in this instance) to influence market prices is an attribute of perfect (pure) competition. Attributes of perfect competition also include a large number of suppliers, customers acting independently, very little product differentiation (homogeneous products), and no barriers to entry exist.

Choice "b" is incorrect. Market participants cannot influence prices in perfectly competitive markets.

Choice "c" is incorrect. Trading prices are based on both supply and demand in perfectly competitive markets.

Choice "d" is incorrect. Pricing information is available to all market participants in perfectly competitive markets.

### 2. CPA-03493

Choice "d" is correct. Under oligopoly, strategic plans focus on maintaining market share and call for the proper amount of advertising (to ensure product differentiation) and ways to properly adapt to price changes or required changes in production volume.

Choices "a", "b", and "c" are incorrect because they are characteristics of other types of market structures.

### 1. CPA-04830

Choice "b" is correct. When there are few good substitutes for a supplier's product, the supplier has market power (think of a monopoly). As a result, the supplier is better able to control buyers and act as a price setter rather than a price taker.

Choice "a" is incorrect. When supplier's products are not differentiated, buyers will be indifferent about which supplier they purchase from. In other words, if firms sell identical products (think of perfect competition) the product of one firm is a perfect substitute for the product of another firm. In this case, firms are price takers, not price setters.

Choice "c" is incorrect. When there are a large number of firms, no one firm has much market power. This is the case of either perfect competition (if all firms sell identical products) or monopolistic competition (if all firms sell slightly differentiated products).

Choice "d" is incorrect. If the purchasing industry is an important customer of the supplier, the *purchasing industry* (i.e., the buyer) will have some market power. This will diminish the ability of the supplier to influence or control the buyer.

### 2. CPA-03609

Choice "b" is correct. If a firm must pay a higher cost for the premium related to the differentiation than it is able to recoup in the market for that feature, then its profits will decrease, the firm will lose competitive advantage, and the differentiation strategy will fail.

Choices "a", "c", and "d" are incorrect, as these are all situations in which differentiation strategies work well.

### 1. CPA-08364

Choice "d" is correct. Opening markets to foreign investment is encompassed within globalization, which is the distribution of industrial and service activities across many nations. Investment growth rates will likely increase (rather than decrease) through globalization, as there are more opportunities for investment and growth.

Choice "a" is incorrect. Emerging markets will become more correlated (integrated) with world markets as globalization increases.

Choice "b" is incorrect. Emerging markets on their own tend to be highly volatile, but integration with world markets will help to reduce that volatility.

Choice "c" is incorrect. Local firms will likely see a decrease in their cost of capital because of an increase in growth and demand.

### 2. CPA-08365

Choice "a" is correct. Country risk encompasses the political risk, economic risk, transfer risk, sovereign risk, and exchange rate risk associated with engaging in business with foreign countries.

Choice "b" is incorrect. Principal risk relates to the risk of losing an investment (money).

Choice "c" is incorrect. Interest rate risk relates to the fluctuation in value of an investment as a result of changes in interest rates.

Choice "d" is incorrect. Commodity price risk relates to market values and future cash inflows that are affected by fluctuations in commodity prices.

### 1. CPA-03934

Choice "a" is correct. When two companies operating in the same industry merge, it represents a horizontal merger.

Choice "b" is incorrect. If a company merges with one of its suppliers, this represents a vertical merger.

Choice "c" is incorrect. This is likely to represent either a vertical or diagonal combination, depending on the extent of the relationship between the two companies.

Choice "d" is incorrect. This situation represents a circular combination, as the two companies appear to be in relatively unrelated industries.

### 2. CPA-03935

Choice "a" is correct. A sell-off would allow Gerard to raise cash while separating itself from Brighton Greens so that it can focus on its core business.

Choice "b" is incorrect. A spin-off would not result in cash for Gerard.

Choice "c" is incorrect. A tender offer is a form of business combination, not a divestiture.

Choice "d" is incorrect. An equity carve-out would allow Gerard to generate cash for the company through the sale of Brighton stock. However, equity carve-outs are typically used when the parent wants to retain control of the new entity, which is not the case in this question.

## NOTES

## 1. CPA-03895

Choice "a" is correct. The just-in-time system focuses on expediting the production process by having materials available as needed without having to store them prior to usage. Thus, the non-value adding operation of storing materials is eliminated.

Choice "b" is incorrect. A just-in-time system is designed to facilitate the flow of materials whether the materials come from one or more suppliers. Competitive bidding is not a major benefit of the just-in-time system.

Choice "c" is incorrect. Maximizing the delivery quantity of materials may increase the need to store the materials prior to using them. The just-in-time system focuses on minimizing storage time and storage costs. Lessening paperwork is not a focus of the just-in-time system.

Choice "d" is incorrect. With a just-in-time system, deliveries are made as materials are needed. A decrease in deliveries may increase the delivery quantity, thus increasing the need to store the materials prior to using them. The just-in-time system focuses on minimizing storage time and storage costs.

## 1. CPA-06442

Choice "c" is correct. A steering committee has broad objectives that include the oversight of systems development and acquisition after an assessment of data processing needs.

Choice "a" is incorrect. IT project planning and monitoring is the responsibility of the committee or group charged with project controls.

Choice "b" is incorrect. Development of specifications and acceptance criteria is the responsibility of the committee or group charged with post implementation review.

Choice "d" is incorrect. Evaluating IT performance using system performance measurements is the responsibility of managers involved in IT operations, not the direct responsibility of the information technology steering committee.

## 2. CPA-07042

Choice "d" is correct. Value delivery is one of the five focus areas identified by the IT Governance Institute for IT governance. Value delivery anticipates execution of the IT value proposition throughout the delivery cycle such that IT services consistently satisfy customer requirements. Other areas of IT governance include:

- Strategic alignment

- Resource management

- Risk management

- Performance measurement

Choice "a" is incorrect. Systems analysis is an important IT activity, but it is not a focus area of IT governance.

Choice "b" is incorrect. Programming is an important IT activity, but it is not a focus area of IT governance.

Choice "c" is incorrect. Operations are an important IT activity, but are not a focus area of IT governance.

### Business 6, Module 3

## 1. CPA-03682

Choice "c" is correct. Use of electronic funds transfer for any funds transfer reduces the need for manual data entry, thus reducing the occurrence of data entry errors.

Choice "a" is incorrect. Use of electronic funds transfer is likely to result in a reduction of the paper audit trail surrounding cash receipts and disbursements.

Choice "b" is incorrect. Use of electronic funds transfer creates a need for more stringent access controls.

Choice "d" is incorrect. Use of electronic funds transfer does not affect company policy regarding storage of source documents (e.g., an accounts payable invoice) for cash transactions.

## 2. CPA-07012

Choice "c" is correct. Enterprise resource planning (ERP) is designed to integrate data from all aspects of an organization's activity. ERP is defined as a cross-functional system that integrates and automates the many business processes that must work together in manufacturing, logistics, distribution, accounting, etc.

Choice "a" is incorrect. Although ERP systems can provide cross-functional information across the organization to assist managers in decision making, the system assumes a high level of sophistication among users and does not automate decision making. The focus of ERP is cross-functional information integration.

Choice "b" is incorrect. ERP provides integrated information that can assist with decision making; however, it is designed to automate the accumulation of cross-functional information.

Choice "d" is incorrect. ERP is primarily meant to provide integrated information for operational managers, not strategic information to executives.

## 1. CPA-06630

Choice "c" is correct. User accounts should immediately be disabled or removed upon termination of any employee. Enabled accounts for terminated employees present a great security risk since they allow unauthorized access to the system.

Choice "a" is incorrect. Passwords are usually required to be a combination of characters, but in comparison to failing to disable accounts for former employees, weak passwords do not present the greatest risk. Passwords, however weak they may be, provide at least some security.

Choice "b" is incorrect. Although management procedures should always be documented, lack of documentation does not present a high security risk as long as there are procedures in place that are being used.

Choice "d" is incorrect. Security logs should be reviewed periodically by the administrator regardless of whether employees have left the company. Although reviewing logs might detect unauthorized system access, allowing former employees to maintain active passwords has a high security risk of allowing the unauthorized access.

## 2. CPA-04813

Choice "b" is correct. The identification of critical applications will be found in almost all disaster recovery plans and thus is the best answer.

Choice "a" is incorrect. Replacement of PCs could be in some disaster recovery plans, but even when it is, the plan is more likely to be called a business continuity plan. PCs can be readily purchased, and many firms will decide to purchase replacements only when they need to.

Choice "c" is incorrect. Although the physical security of warehouses may be in another function's disaster recovery plan, it is not likely to be a part of the IT function's disaster recovery plan. It will most likely be included in a supply chain business continuity plan.

Choice "d" is incorrect. Cross-training could be included in some disaster recovery plans, assuming that the "operating personnel" means computer operations personnel (if it means something else, it will not be).

## 1. CPA-06984

Choice "b" is correct. The objective of data security controls is to ensure that storage media are only accessed, changed, or deleted after appropriate authorization. The objective is to protect information.

Choice "a" is incorrect. Policies establish an overall approach to computer security and are sometimes referred to as the IT security strategy. Data security controls are designed to protect information, not to establish strategy or policy.

Choice "c" is incorrect. Policy support documents, such as procedures, formalized standards, rules, and procedures to ensure the organization's controls are properly executed. Data security controls may be included in procedures, but development of procedures is not their objective.

Choice "d" is incorrect. Change management and related control activities anticipate monitoring the use of system software to prevent unauthorized access to system software and computer programs.

## 2. CPA-08305

Choice "b" is correct. Controls over time and attendance will not be effective in preventing or detecting errors in the computation of employee overtime. Miscalculation of the wage or overtime premium amount could occur even if hours worked are accurately controlled and captured by the time and attendance system.

Choice "a" is incorrect. Controls over time and attendance systems would be designed to be effective in preventing fraudulent reporting of an employee's own hours. The video image would be very helpful in this regard.

Choice "c" is incorrect. Controls over time and attendance systems would be designed to be effective in preventing inaccurate accounting for employees' hours. The video image would be very helpful in this regard.

Choice "d" is incorrect. Controls over time and attendance systems would be designed to be effective in preventing recording of other employees' hours. The video image would be very helpful in this regard.

Business 6, Module 6

## 1. CPA-03483

Choice "d" is correct. There is no separate data integrity risk category.

Choice "a" is incorrect. Strategic risk includes risks such as choosing inappropriate technology.

Choice "b" is incorrect. Financial risk includes risks such as having financial resources lost, wasted, or stolen.

Choice "c" is incorrect. Information risk includes risks such as loss of data integrity, incomplete transactions, or hackers.

## 2. CPA-04827

Choice "d" is correct. Because the primary purpose of a firewall is to prevent unauthorized access to a network, requiring all users to have a password helps to minimize vulnerability.

Choice "a" is incorrect. Collusion would not be minimized at all by requiring employees to have passwords; the employees conspiring to do bad things could merely share their passwords.

Choice "b" is incorrect. Passwords would not do anything about data entry errors.

Choice "c" is incorrect. The usage of passwords or the lack of passwords would have no effect on failure of the server duplicating function.

**Blueprint**

# BEC

## Summary blueprint

| Content area allocation | Weight |
| --- | --- |
| I. Corporate Governance | 17–27% |
| II. Economic Concepts and Analysis | 17–27% |
| III. Financial Management | 11–21% |
| IV. Information Technology | 15–25% |
| V. Operations Management | 15–25% |

| Skill allocation | Weight |
| --- | --- |
| Evaluation | — |
| Analysis | 20–30% |
| Application | 50–60% |
| Remembering and Understanding | 15–25% |

Business Environment and Concepts

# Area I – Corporate Governance (17–27%)

## A. Internal control frameworks

| Content group/topic | Skill | | | | Representative task |
|---|---|---|---|---|---|
| | Remembering and Understanding | Application | Analysis | Evaluation | |
| 1. Purpose and objectives | ✓ | | | | Define internal control within the context of the COSO internal control framework, including the purpose, objectives and limitations of the framework. |
| 2. Components and principles | ✓ | | | | Identify and define the components, principles and underlying structure of the COSO internal control framework. |
| | | ✓ | | | Apply the COSO internal control framework to identify entity and transaction level risks (inherent and residual) related to an organization's compliance, operations and reporting (internal and external, financial and non-financial) objectives. |
| | | ✓ | | | Apply the COSO internal control framework to identify risks related to fraudulent financial and non-financial reporting, misappropriation of assets and illegal acts, including the risk of management override of controls. |
| | | ✓ | | | Apply the COSO internal control framework to identify controls to meet an entity's compliance, operations and reporting (internal and external, financial and non-financial) objectives, throughout an entity's structure, from entity-wide through sub-units, down to the transactional level. |
| | | ✓ | | | Apply the COSO internal control framework to identify an appropriate mix of automated and manual application controls, (e.g. authorization and approval, verifications, physical controls, controls over standing data, reconciliations and supervisory controls) to prevent and detect errors in transactions. |
| | | ✓ | | | Describe the corporate governance structure within an organization (tone at the top, policies, steering committees, oversight, ethics, etc.). |

## Area I – Corporate Governance

**(17–27%)** (continued)

| Content group/topic | Skill | | | | Representative task |
|---|---|---|---|---|---|
| | Remembering and Understanding | Application | Analysis | Evaluation | |
| **B. Enterprise risk management (ERM) frameworks** | | | | | |
| 1. Purpose and objectives | ✓ | | | | Define ERM within the context of the COSO ERM framework, including the purpose and objectives of the framework. |
| 2. Components and principles | ✓ | | | | Identify and define the components, principles and underlying structure of the COSO ERM framework. |
| | ✓ | | | | Understand the relationship among risk, business strategy and performance within the context of the COSO ERM framework. |
| | | ✓ | | | Apply the COSO ERM framework to identify risk/opportunity scenarios in an entity. |
| **C. Other regulatory frameworks and provisions** | | | | | |
| | ✓ | | | | Identify and define key corporate governance provisions of the Sarbanes-Oxley Act of 2002 and other regulatory pronouncements. |
| | | ✓ | | | Identify regulatory deficiencies within an entity by using the requirements associated with the Sarbanes-Oxley Act of 2002. |

BEC8

Uniform CPA Examination Blueprints: Business Environment and Concepts (BEC)

# Area II – Economic Concepts and Analysis (17–27%)

| Content group/topic | Skill | | | | Representative task |
|---|---|---|---|---|---|
| | Remembering and Understanding | Application | Analysis | Evaluation | |
| **A. Economic and business cycles - measures and indicators** | | | | | |
| | ✓ | | | | Identify and define business cycles (trough, expansion, peak, recession) and conditions and government policies that impact an entity's industry or operations. |
| | | ✓ | | | Use appropriate inputs to calculate economic measures and indicators (e.g., Nominal and Real GDP, Consumer Price Index, Aggregate Demand Curve, Money Supply, etc.) and apply leading, coincident and lagging indicators (e.g., bond yields, new housing starts, personal income, unemployment, etc.). |
| | | ✓ | | | Use economic measures and indicators to explain the impact on an entity's industry and operations due to changes in government fiscal policy, monetary policy, regulations, trade controls and other actions. |
| | | ✓ | | | Use economic measures and indicators to explain the impact on an entity's industry and operations due to changes in business cycles and economic conditions, caused by factors such as exchange rates, inflation, productivity, state of the global economy, unemployment levels, etc. |
| **B. Market influences on business** | | | | | |
| | ✓ | | | | Identify and define the key factors related to the economic marketplace (e.g., competition, currencies, globalization, supply and demand, trade, etc.) and how they generally apply to a business entity. |
| | ✓ | | | | Identify and define market influences (e.g., economic, environmental, governmental, political, legal, social and technological, etc.). |
| | | | ✓ | | Determine the impact of market influences on the overall economy (e.g., consumer demand, labor supply, market prices, production costs, volatility, etc.). |
| | | | ✓ | | Determine the impact of market influences on an entity's business strategy, operations and risk (e.g., increasing investment and financial leverage, innovating to develop new product offerings, seeking new foreign and domestic markets, undertaking productivity or cost-cutting initiatives, etc.). |
| | | | ✓ | | Determine the business reasons for, and explain the underlying economic substance of, significant transactions (e.g., business combinations and divestitures, product line diversification, production sourcing, public and private offerings of securities, etc.). |

Business Environment and Concepts

## Area II – Economic Concepts and Analysis (17–27%) (continued)

### C. Financial risk management

| Content group/topic | Skill | | | | Representative task |
|---|---|---|---|---|---|
| | Remembering and Understanding | Application | Analysis | Evaluation | |
| 1. Market, interest rate, currency, liquidity, credit, price and other risks | | ✓ | | | Calculate and use ratios and measures to quantify risks associated with interest rates, currency exchange, liquidity, prices, etc. in a business entity. |
| 2. Means for mitigating/controlling financial risks | | ✓ | | | Identify strategies to mitigate financial risks (market, interest rate, currency, liquidity, etc.) and quantify their impact on a business entity. |

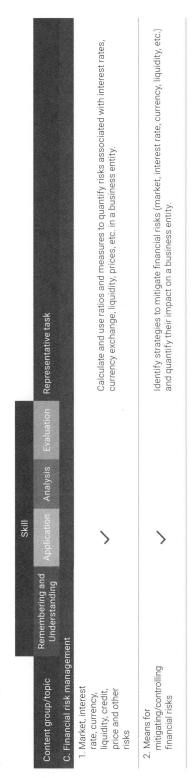

Business Environment and Concepts

# Area III – Financial Management (11–21%)

| Content group/topic | Skill | | | | Representative task |
|---|---|---|---|---|---|
| | Remembering and Understanding | Application | Analysis | Evaluation | |
| **A. Capital structure** | | | | | |
| | | ✓ | | | Describe an organization's capital structure and related concepts, such as cost of capital, asset structure, loan covenants, growth rate, profitability, leverage and risk. |
| | | ✓ | | | Calculate the cost of capital for a given financial scenario. |
| | | | ✓ | | Compare and contrast the strategies for financing new business initiatives and operations within the context of an optimal capital structure, using statistical analysis where appropriate. |
| **B. Working capital** | | | | | |
| 1. Fundamentals and key metrics of working capital management | | ✓ | | | Calculate the metrics associated with the working capital components, such as current ratio, quick ratio, cash conversion cycle, inventory turnover and receivables turnover. |
| | | | ✓ | | Detect significant fluctuations or variances in the working capital cycle using working capital ratio analyses. |
| 2. Strategies for managing working capital | | | ✓ | | Compare inventory management processes, including pricing and valuation methods, to determine the effects on the working capital of a given entity. |
| | | | ✓ | | Compare accounts payable management techniques, including usage of discounts, factors affecting discount policy, uses of electronic funds transfer as a payment method and determination of an optimal vendor payment schedule in order to determine the effects on the working capital of a given entity. |
| | | | ✓ | | Distinguish between corporate banking arrangements, including establishment of lines of credit, borrowing capacity and monitoring of compliance with debt covenants in order to determine the effects on the working capital of a given entity. |
| | | | ✓ | | Interpret the differences between the business risks and the opportunities in an entity's credit management policies to determine the effects on the working capital of a given entity. |
| | | | ✓ | | Analyze the effects on working capital caused by financing using long-term debt and/or short-term debt. |

Uniform CPA Examination Blueprints: Business Environment and Concepts (BEC)

BEC11

## Area III – Financial Management
### (11–21%) (continued)

| Content group/topic | Skill | | | | Representative task |
|---|---|---|---|---|---|
| | Remembering and Understanding | Application | Analysis | Evaluation | |
| C. Financial valuation methods and decision models | | | | | |
| | > | | | | Identify and define the different financial valuation methods and their assumptions, including but not limited to fair value, Black-Scholes, Capital Asset Pricing Model and Dividend Discount Model. |
| | > | | | | Identify and define the different financial decision models and assumptions involved in making decisions relating to asset and investment management, debt, equity and leasing. |
| | > | | | | Identify the sources of data and factors that management considers in forming the assumptions used to prepare an accounting estimate. |
| | > | | | | Describe the process and framework within which management exercises its responsibilities over the review and approval of accounting estimates. |
| | | > | | | Calculate the value of an asset using commonly accepted financial valuation methods. |
| | | | > | | Compare investment alternatives using calculations of financial metrics (payback period, net-present value, economic value added, cash flow analysis, internal rate of return etc.), financial modeling, forecasting, projection and analysis techniques. |
| | | | > | | Compare options in a lease vs. buy decision scenario. |

BEC12

Uniform CPA Examination Blueprints: Business Environment and Concepts (BEC)

Business Environment and Concepts

# Area IV – Information Technology (15–25%)

| Content group/topic | Skill | | | | Representative task |
| --- | --- | --- | --- | --- | --- |
| | Remembering and Understanding | Application | Analysis | Evaluation | |
| **A. Information technology (IT) governance** | | | | | |
| 1. Vision and strategy | ✓ | | | | Identify the role that the IT function plays in determining/supporting an organization's vision and strategy. |
| 2. Organization | | ✓ | | | Describe the IT governance structure within an organization (tone at the top, policies, steering committees, IT strategies, oversight, etc.). |
| 3. Risk assessments | | ✓ | | | Conduct an IT risk assessment, identify risks and suggest mitigation strategies. |
| **B. Role of information technology in business** | | | | | |
| | ✓ | | | | Recognize the role of big data/data analytics and statistics in supporting business decisions. |
| | | ✓ | | | Identify the role of information systems in key business processes within an entity. |
| | | ✓ | | | Identify the role of e-commerce in key business processes within an entity. |
| **C. Information security/availability** | | | | | |
| 1. Protection of information | | ✓ | | | Recognize the risks and controls associated with protecting sensitive and critical information within an organization's IT environment (the use of mobile technology, data storage devices, data transmission, cybersecurity, etc.). |
| 2. Logical and physical access controls | | ✓ | | | Identify weaknesses and mitigation strategies within an entity's IT environment in relation to logical and physical access controls. |
| | | ✓ | | | Identify weaknesses and mitigation strategies within an entity's IT environment in relation to IT general and application controls. |
| 3. System disruption/ resolution | | ✓ | | | Describe an entity's disaster recovery/business continuity plans, including threat identification and mitigation strategies, data backup and recovery procedures, alternate processing facilities, etc. |

BEC13

Uniform CPA Examination Blueprints: Business Environment and Concepts (BEC)

## Area IV – Information Technology
### (15–25%) (continued)

| Content group/topic | Skill | | | | Representative task |
|---|---|---|---|---|---|
| | Remembering and Understanding | Application | Analysis | Evaluation | |
| **D. Processing integrity (input/processing/output controls)** | | | | | |
| | ✓ | | | | Describe the role of input, processing and output controls within an entity to support completeness, accuracy and continued processing integrity. |
| | | ✓ | | | Determine the appropriateness of the design and operating effectiveness of application controls (authorizations, approvals, tolerance levels, input edits, etc.). |
| | | ✓ | | | Identify issues related to the design and effectiveness of IT control activities, including manual vs. automated controls, as well as preventive, detective and corrective controls. |
| **E. Systems development and maintenance** | | | | | |
| | ✓ | | | | Identify different information system testing strategies. |
| | | ✓ | | | Recognize the fundamental issues and risks associated with implementing new information systems or maintaining existing information systems within an entity. |

# Area V – Operations Management (15–25%)

| Content group/topic | Skill | | | | Representative task |
|---|---|---|---|---|---|
| | Remembering and Understanding | Application | Analysis | Evaluation | |
| **A. Financial and non-financial measures of performance management** | | | | | |
| | ✓ | | | | Calculate financial and non-financial measures appropriate to analyze specific aspects of an entity's performance (e.g., Economic Value Added, Costs of Quality-Prevention vs. Appraisal vs. Failure, etc.). |
| | | | ✓ | | Determine which financial and non-financial measures are appropriate to analyze specific aspects of an entity's performance and risk profile (e.g., Return on Equity, Return on Assets, Contribution Margin, etc.). |
| **B. Cost accounting** | | | | | |
| 1. Cost measurement concepts, methods and techniques | ✓ | | | | Apply cost accounting concepts, terminology, methods and measurement techniques within an entity. |
| | ✓ | | | | Differentiate the characteristics of fixed, variable and mixed costs within an entity. |
| | ✓ | | | | Compare and contrast the different costing methods such as absorption vs. variable and process vs. job order costing. |
| 2. Variance analysis | | | ✓ | | Determine the appropriate variance analysis method to measure the key cost drivers by analyzing business scenarios. |

Business Environment and Concepts

# Area V – Operations Management (15–25%) (continued)

| Content group/topic | Skill | | | | Representative task |
|---|---|---|---|---|---|
| | Remembering and Understanding | Application | Analysis | Evaluation | |
| **C. Process management** | | | | | |
| 1. Approaches, techniques, measures, benefits to process-management driven businesses | ✓ | | | | Identify commonly used operational management approaches, techniques and measures within the context of business process management. |
| 2. Management philosophies and techniques for performance improvement | ✓ | | | | Identify commonly used management philosophies and techniques for performance and quality improvement within the context of business process management. |
| **D. Planning techniques** | | | | | |
| 1. Budgeting and analysis | | ✓ | ✓ | | Prepare a budget to guide business decisions. |
| | | | ✓ | | Reconcile results against a budget or prior periods and perform analysis of variances as needed. |
| 2. Forecasting and projection | | ✓ | | | Use forecasting and projection techniques to model revenue growth, cost and expense characteristics, profitability, etc. |
| | | ✓ | | | Prepare and calculate metrics to be utilized in the planning process, such as cost benefit analysis, sensitivity analysis, breakeven analysis, economic order quantity, etc. |
| | | | ✓ | | Analyze results of forecasts and projections using ratio analysis and explanations of correlations to, or variations from, key financial indices. |
| | | | ✓ | | Compare and contrast alternative approaches (such as system replacement, make vs. buy and cost/benefit) proposed to address business challenges or opportunities for a given entity. |

Uniform CPA Examination Blueprints: Business Environment and Concepts (BEC)

BEC16

## NOTES

**Absorption Costing:** Absorption costing is a method of product costing that includes fixed manufacturing overhead costs, along with direct material, direct labor, and variable manufacturing costs, in the cost of the product. This method is also referred to as "full costing." Absorption costing is GAAP for financial statement purposes. Absorption costing is frequently contrasted with variable costing. The difference between absorption costing and variable costing methods is the treatment of fixed manufacturing overhead. Absorption costing includes fixed overhead as product costs, while variable costing treats all fixed costs as period costs. Fixed selling, general, and administrative costs are treated the same (as period costs) under both methods. *See also* variable costing *and* activity-based costing.

**Access Control List (ACL):** An access control list, in a computer security context, is a list of permissions attached to a piece of data. The access control list specifies who (which users or groups of users or roles) can access the data and what they can do to/with it (read, write, delete, and/or execute).

**Access Controls:** Access controls are controls that limit access to program documentation, data files, programs, and computer hardware to those who require it in the performance of their job responsibilities. These controls include physical access controls and electronic access controls. *See also* physical access controls *and* electronic access controls.

**Access Point:** An access point is a device that connects wireless communication devices to form a wireless network. An access point is often called a wireless access point (WAP, but different from the other WAP, wireless application protocol). The access point normally connects to a wired network. Several WAPs can link together to form a larger network that allows a larger roaming area. Wireless access points have IP addresses for configuration and management of the network.

**Accounting Costs:** Accounting costs are the explicit costs of operating a business (e.g., purchases of input services). *See also* explicit costs *and* accounting profit.

**Accounting Information System (AIS):** An accounting information system is a type of management information system; it may also be partly a transaction processing system and partly a knowledge system. There may be separate systems for each accounting function such as accounts receivable, accounts payable, etc., or there may be one integrated system that performs all of the accounting functions, culminating in the general ledger and the various accounting reports. *See also* decision support system *and* executive information system *and* management information system.

**Accounting Profit:** Accounting profit is the difference between total revenue and total explicit costs. No allowance is made for the opportunity cost of the equity capital of the firm's owners or other implicit costs. *See also* explicit costs *and* implicit costs *and* opportunity costs.

**Activity-Based Costing:** Activity-based costing is a costing system that divides production into activities where costs are accumulated into multiple cost pools and allocated to the product based on the level of activities (defined by cost drivers) demanded by the product. Activity-based costing is normally used as a supplement to, rather than a replacement for, a firm's absorption costing system. Activity-based costing normally allocates costs in addition to normal manufacturing costs, and the cost drivers are often nonfinancial activities. Absorption costing is frequently contrasted with traditional cost allocation, a method that assumes a single cost pool and a single cost driver. *See also* variable costing *and* absorption costing *and* cost pool.

**Ad Hoc Reports:** An ad hoc (done for a particular purpose) report is a report that does not currently exist but that can be created on demand, without involving a software developer or programmer. This capability is often called a user report writer.

**Aggregate Demand (AD):** Aggregate demand is the maximum quantity of all goods and services that households, firms, and governments are willing and able to purchase at any given price. The aggregate demand curve has the general price level on the y-axis and real GDP on the x-axis. The aggregate demand curve normally slopes down and to the right, indicating that the quantity of goods and services demanded increases as prices decline. Factors that shift the aggregate demand are changes in wealth, changes in real interest rates, changes in consumer confidence, changes in foreign currency exchange rates, changes in government spending, and changes in consumer taxes. *See also* aggregate supply *and* long-run aggregate supply.

**Aggregate Supply (AS):** Aggregate supply is the maximum quantity of all goods and services that providers are willing and able to produce at any given price. The aggregate supply curve has the general price level on the y-axis and the real GDP on the x-axis. The aggregate supply curve normally slopes upward and to the right, meaning that firms are willing to produce more goods and services at higher prices. The supply in this case is the short-run aggregate supply. Factors that shift aggregate supply are changes in resource prices and supply shocks. *See also* aggregate demand *and* long-run aggregate supply.

**Annual Percentage Rate (APR):** The annual percentage rate is the interest rate calculated by considering all of the added costs (points, application fee, closing costs, etc.) for a given loan. The calculation spreads these costs over the life of the loan, along with the interest rate, to arrive at a more accurate annualized percentage rate than the stated interest rate alone. The annual percentage rate for a given loan is equal to the stated interest rate if there are no added costs. The APR must be disclosed. *See also* stated interest rate.

**Application Controls:** Application controls are controls that apply to the processing of individual transactions and are built into the application itself. *See also* access controls *and* electronic access controls *and* physical access controls.

**Application Firewall:** An application firewall supplements the standard network firewall. A standard network firewall (which is what is meant when the word "firewall" is used by itself) inspects data in packet headers of packets that are coming from or going to certain ports (packet filtering) based on the set firewall access rules. An application firewall (also known as a proxy or an application layer gateway, if implemented hardware) examines data in the packets themselves. Note that the word "application" in this context does not refer to application software such as an accounts receivable application, but to the application layer in a network protocol.

**Application Service Provider (ASP):** Application service providers provide access to application programs on a rental basis. They allow smaller companies to avoid the extremely high cost of owning and maintaining more sophisticated application systems by allowing them to pay only for what is used. The ASPs own and host the software. *See also* on-demand computing.

**Application Software:** Application software includes the diverse group of systems and programs that an organization uses to accomplish its objectives. Application software can be generic (e.g., word processors, spreadsheets, or databases) or custom-developed for a specific application or a specific organization. Application software is made up of application programs. Application software can be purchased from an outside vendor or developed internally. *See also* system software.

**Appraisal Costs:** In quality control, appraisal costs are the costs to discover and remove defective parts before they are shipped to the customer. These costs include statistical quality checks, testing, and inspection. *See also* prevention costs.

**Artificial Intelligence:** Artificial intelligence is a field of study in which researchers attempt to develop software that can reason and think like humans.

**Asset Turnover:** Asset turnover is sales divided by total assets. *See also* investment turnover *and* return on assets.

**Attribute Standards:** Attribute standards published by the Institute of Internal Auditors (IIA) address many of the same issues as the general standards under generally accepted auditing standards. Issues related to auditor independence, technical proficiency, and professional care are addressed here.

**Audit Trail:** The path of a transaction through a data processing system from beginning to end. An audit trail provides a way to check the accuracy and validity of ledger postings and trace all changes in general ledger accounts from their initial balance to their final balance.

**Average Collection Period:** The (accounts receivable) average collection period is the year-end or average accounts receivable balance divided by the average daily sales. The average collection period is also called the number of days sales in receivables.

**Avoidable Costs:** Avoidable costs are costs that can be eliminated in whole or in part by choosing one alternative over another. *See also* incremental costs.

**B2B:** When a business sells its products or services to other businesses, it is called a Business-to-Business (B2B) transaction. *See also* B2C.

**B2C:** When a business sells its products or services to the public, it is called a Business-to-Consumer (B2C) transaction. *See also* B2B.

**Backdoor:** A backdoor is a means of access to a program or system that bypasses normal security mechanisms. A programmer will sometimes install a backdoor so that the program or system can be easily accessed for troubleshooting or other purposes. Backdoors should be eliminated. *See also* software vulnerability.

**Backflush Costing:** Backflush costing (or delayed costing) is a cost system that works backward from the final product to apply manufacturing costs. Backflush costing is used to simplify cost accounting when tracking work-in-process is not important. Backflush costing is often used with just-in-time systems to reduce inventory to very low levels. *See also* just-in-time.

**Backup:** Backup (or file backup) is the copying of data so that copies of the data will be available if the original data are damaged or destroyed. Backups are necessary in normal operations (where individual files or groups of files might be damaged by an incorrect application program, for example) or for disaster recovery. Backups may be full backups (where "all" of the data are backed up) or incremental backups (where only changed data after the last full backup or the last incremental backup are backed up). A hot backup is a backup of a database that is in use.

**Balanced Budget:** A balanced budget occurs when taxes and other governmental revenues equal governmental spending. *See also* budget surplus *and* budget deficit.

**Balanced Scorecard:** A balanced scorecard reports information on multiple dimensions of a firm's performance defined by the critical success factors necessary to accomplish the firm's business objective. A balanced scorecard normally includes both financial and nonfinancial data.

**Bandwidth:** Bandwidth is a measure of a communication medium's information-carrying capacity.

**Banker's Acceptance:** A banker's acceptance is a short-term credit investment created by a nonfinancial firm and guaranteed by a bank. Banker's acceptances are traded at a discount from face value in the secondary market. For corporations, a banker's acceptance acts as a negotiable time draft for financing imports, exports, or other transactions in goods. They are especially useful when the creditworthiness of a foreign trade partner is unknown. One advantage is that they do not need to be held until maturity. Instead they can be sold off in the secondary markets, where investors and institutions constantly trade them. *See also* trade acceptance *and* commercial paper *and* draft.

**Batch Processing:** With batch processing, input documents/transactions are collected and grouped by type of transaction. These groups (called batches) are processed periodically (e.g., daily, weekly, monthly, etc.). Batch processing systems may use either sequential storage devices (e.g., magnetic tape) or random access storage devices (i.e., disks).

**Batch Total:** A batch total is a total of a field in a transaction that might normally be added, such as dollar amounts. *See also* hash total.

**Benchmarking:** Benchmarking is the process of identifying standards for the critical success factors of the firm used in comparison to actual performance, determination of gaps in performance, and implementing improvements to meet or exceed the benchmark. Best practices represent world-class performance standards.

**Best Cost Strategy:** A best cost strategy is a competitive strategy that combines cost leadership strategies with differentiation strategies to give customers higher value for their money. *See also* cost leadership strategy *and* differentiation strategy *and* niche strategy.

**Beta Coefficient:** Beta coefficient is a statistical measure of an individual company's stock price variability in relation to the market as a whole. The beta coefficient is a key component of the capital asset pricing model (CAPM).

**Biases:** Biases, in the context of behavioral finance, anticipate human tendencies that distort financial analysis, including excessive optimism, overconfidence, and the illusion of control.

**Bill of Materials:** A bill of materials is a list that shows the quantity of each type of material in a unit of finished product. *See also* materials requirements planning.

**Biometric Authentication:** Biometric authentication (sometimes just biometrics) is the use of such things as fingerprints or eye-prints or voice-prints (physical characteristics of the user) in addition to or in place of access cards for physical or electronic access to a location or to a network. *See also* electronic access controls.

**Bit:** A bit is a binary digit (0 or 1) with which all computer data is stored. *See also* byte *and* field.

**Bond Indenture:** A bond indenture is the contract between a bond issuer/borrower and the bondholders that sets forth the obligations of the issuer and the rights of the bondholders. *See also* loan covenant.

**Bond Yield Plus Risk Premium Method:** The bond yield plus risk premium method is a method for determining the cost of equity capital (common stock or retained earnings) as the firm's cost of debt capital plus an equity risk premium (the compensation for taking the additional risk of equity ownership versus the holding of debt). *See also* capital asset pricing model *and* dividend yield plus growth rate method.

**Boycott:** A boycott is an organized group refusal to conduct market transactions with a target group or individual (using only social pressure, not legal obligation).

**Breakeven Point:** The breakeven point is the level of sales or the level of volume at which revenue equals expenses. It is also calculated as the ratio of fixed costs to the contribution margin. Profit is zero at the breakeven point because the total of fixed and variable expenses exactly equals sales revenue. *See also* cost-volume-profit analysis *and* contribution margin *and* margin of safety.

**BRIC:** The acronym BRIC refers to the four leading emerging economies of the world: Brazil, Russia, India and China.

**Budget (Controllable) Variance:** In a two-way overhead variance, the budget variance is the difference between the actual overhead and the budget based on the standard hours worked for the actual output. This budget variance is equal to the total of the spending variance and the efficiency variance in a three-way overhead variance. *See also* spending variance *and* efficiency variance *and* volume variance.

**Budget Deficit:** A budget deficit occurs when taxes and other governmental revenues are less than governmental spending. *See also* budget surplus *and* balanced budget.

**Budget Surplus:** A budget surplus occurs when taxes and other governmental revenues are greater than government spending. *See also* budget deficit *and* balanced budget.

**Bundling:** Bundling is the selling of a combination of products at a lower price than if the products were sold separately (e.g., a telecommunication company bundling a phone line, cable Internet, and cable TV).

**Business Continuity:** Business continuity planning deals with the safeguards for ensuring the continuity of a business as a whole.

**Business Cycle:** The business cycle is the rise and fall of economic activity (GDP) relative to the long-term growth trend of the economy. Business cycles typically comprise an expansionary phase, a peak, a contractionary phase, a trough, and a recovery phase. *See also* recession *and* depression.

**Business Information Systems:** A business information system is a set of interrelated components (hardware, software, networks, people, and data) that collect, process, store, transform, and distribute data and information to support decision making in an organization.

**Business Model:** A business model describes how a business produces, delivers, and sells its products or services so as to bring value to its customers.

**Business Process:** A business process is a unique set of tasks and actions that organizations develop and utilize to produce specific business results. A particular business process may or may not utilize information technology, but IT is becoming increasingly involved in most business processes.

**Business Process Reengineering (BPR):** Business process reengineering generally involves a comprehensive rethinking of how work is performed to emphasize customer service and reduce costs (improve effectiveness and efficiency). Implementation of new technologies is often a strong motivation for process reengineering.

**Business Strategy:** A business strategy is adopted by a company to both sustain and grow as a value-adding organization.

**Byte:** A byte is a group of normally 8 bits that can represent a number or a letter, with the specific form dependent on what internal representation format is being used. Sometimes, bytes are called characters. *See also* bit *and* field.

**Call Provision:** A call provision in a bond is a provision that allows the bond issuer to pay off part or all of a bond's principal before the maturity date. A call provision is beneficial to the bond issuer because it allows the issuer to pay off the bonds if interest rates decline (and to issue new debt at the lower interest rate). A call provision is thus detrimental to the bondholders since the bondholders will have to reinvest their proceeds at the lower interest rates. If callable, bonds are normally called at a (call) premium.

**Capacity Management:** Capacity management is the process of planning, sizing, and controlling computer processing or IT infrastructure capacity to satisfy user demand at a reasonable cost. The goal of capacity management is to optimize the capability of the IT infrastructure and supporting organization in order to deliver a cost-effective and sustained level of availability that enables a company to satisfy its business objectives.

**Capital Asset Pricing Model (CAPM):** The capital asset pricing model is a model for determining the cost of equity capital (common stock or retained earnings) or pricing risk. The CAPM assumes that investors must be compensated for the time value of money plus systematic risk, as measured by the stock's beta. The primary conclusion of the CAPM is that the risk of an individual stock is its contribution to the risk of a well-diversified portfolio. The CAPM can be used to determine the cost of common stock and retained earnings in determining the weighted average cost of capital. CAPM is computed as the risk-free rate plus (beta times the difference between the market rate and the risk-free rate). *See also* beta coefficient *and* nondiversifiable risk *and* bond yield plus risk premium method *and* dividend yield plus growth-rate method.

**Capital Budgeting:** Capital budgeting decisions are decisions that involve an outlay or outlays now (or soon) in order to obtain some return in the future. Capital budgeting decisions are often made for individual projects to determine if those projects will be undertaken. Capital investments that are independent should be made if they add value to a firm; otherwise, they should be rejected. Four common approaches to capital budgeting decisions are the payback method, the discounted payback method, the net present value method, and the internal rate of return method. Sometimes, the accounting rate of return method is also used. *See also* payback method *and* discounted payback method *and* net present value method *and* internal rate of return method.

**Capital Rationing:** Capital rationing is used when investment funding is limited. Capital is rationed among competing projects either by using a higher cost of capital or by setting a maximum for the entire capital budget. If capital is rationed, and there are no other constraints, capital is normally allocated to the projects with the highest net present value. A profitability index may be used to rank the projects. *See also* profitability index.

**Carrying Costs:** Carrying costs are the costs incurred to carry an asset (e.g., the costs incurred to carry inventory). Examples of carrying costs include the opportunity cost of the funds that are being used to carry the asset (i.e., the next best investment alternative), storage of the asset, insurance for loss of the asset, costs of obsolescence, various types of shrinkage, etc.

**Cartel:** A cartel is a group of firms acting together to coordinate output decisions and control prices so that the joint profit of the members of the cartel will be maximized. The cartel will attempt to create a monopoly. *See also* monopoly.

**Cash Conversion Cycle:** The cash conversion cycle, normally called the operating cycle, is the length of time between the date of the cash expenditures for production and the date of cash collection from customers (cash to cash). The cash conversion cycle is the inventory conversion period plus the receivables collection period less the payables deferral period. *See also* operating cycle *and* inventory conversion period *and* receivables collection period *and* payables deferral period.

**Cause-and-Effect Diagram:** In quality control, a cause-and-effect diagram identifies potential causes of failures or defects. *See also* Pareto diagram *and* statistical quality control.

**Centralized Processing:** Centralized processing environments maintain all data and perform all data processing at a central location. If end-user PCs are used merely to connect to a LAN to allow data entry from remote locations, and all editing and other such processing is accomplished by programs running on the central processors, the processing would be considered centralized. *See also* distributed processing.

**Change Control:** Change control (sometimes called program change control or change management if used in a more general context) is a formal process to ensure that a computer program is modified only with approved changes. Some system of change control (normally at least partly automated these days) is necessary to know exactly what versions of what programs are running in production at a particular point in time. In addition to normal planned changes, there are usually emergency changes (that bypass the normal change control procedure) to keep a system up and running.

**Check Digit:** Check digits exist when some kind of technique is used to compute a digit or digits to add to an existing number and other programs use the same computation when that number is used. *See also* field check *and* validity check.

**Cloud:** The cloud is the representation in network diagrams of the public switched data network (PSDN). Cloud computing involves information technology as a service rather than as a collection of products. Most carriers offer service-level agreements for transmission within the cloud.

**Coefficient of Correlation:** In regression analysis, the coefficient of correlation is the square root of the coefficient of determination. It measures the interdependence of the dependent variable and the independent variable. Its value lies between −1 and +1. The absence of correlation would be 0; perfect positive correlation would be +1; and perfect negative correlation would be −1. The algebraic sign of the correlation coefficient is the same as that of the regression coefficient b in the regression line equation. *See also* regression analysis *and* coefficient of determination *and* standard error of the estimate.

**Coefficient of Determination:** In regression analysis, the coefficient of determination ($R^2$) is the proportion of the total variation in the dependent variable explained by the independent variable. Its value lies between zero and 1. The greater the coefficient of determination, the better the fit of the regression line. *See also* regression analysis *and* coefficient of correlation *and* standard error of the estimate.

**Cold Site:** For disaster recovery, a cold site is an off-site location that has all the electrical connections and other physical requirements for data processing, but it does not have the actual equipment. Cold sites usually require one to three days to be made operational because equipment has to be acquired. Cold sites are the cheapest form of off-site location. *See also* hot site.

**Commercial Paper:** Commercial paper is short-term, unsecured promissory notes that are generally sold by large, creditworthy corporations on a discount basis to institutional investors and other corporations. Maturities of commercial paper are usually no longer than nine months, with maturities of one to two months common. Commercial paper is usually issued in denominations of $100,000 or more. *See also* banker's acceptance *and* trade acceptance.

**Committed Costs:** Committed costs are those costs that cannot be altered in the short run. Committed costs establish the present level of operating capacity. Committed costs are normally fixed costs. Committed costs can be contrasted to discretionary costs. *See also* discretionary costs.

**Committee of Sponsoring Organizations (COSO):** The COSO is an independent private sector initiative which was initially established to study the factors that can lead to fraudulent financial reporting. The private "sponsoring organizations" included the five major financial professional associations in the United States: the American Accounting Association, the American Institute of Certified Public Accountants, the Financial Executives Institute, the Institute of Internal Auditors, and the Institute of Management Accountants. The COSO has issued Internal Control–Integrated Framework, as well as Enterprise Risk Management–Integrated Framework, to assist organizations in developing comprehensive assessments of internal control effectiveness. The COSO is sometimes referred to as the Treadway Commission after its original chairman, James C. Treadway, Jr.

**Common Cost:** A common cost is a cost that is incurred to support a number of cost objects but that cannot be traced to them individually. Common costs are allocated to the cost objects on some basis. A common cost is a particular type of indirect cost. *See also* cost object *and* indirect costs *and* joint costs.

**Common Gateway Interface (CGI):** CGI is a standard protocol to interface external application software with a server such as a Web server, which allows the server to pass requests from a browser to the external application and for the external application to return output to the browser.

**Common Stock:** Common stock is a class of stock that will carry with it all rights of stock ownership and entitle the owner to rights of governance.

**Comparative Advantage:** When production possibility curves are drawn with the same products on the same axes, the country whose production possibility curve has the steepest slope has the comparative advantage in the product on the vertical axis and the other country has the comparative advantage in the product on the horizontal axis. Countries should concentrate on producing those products in which they have the comparative advantage. *See also* production possibility curve.

**Compensating Balance:** A compensating balance is a required minimum amount of funds (10 to 20 percent) that a firm receiving a loan or a line of credit must keep in a non-interest bearing checking account at the bank.

**Competitive Strategies:** Competitive strategies are (1) cost leadership focused on a broad range of buyers; (2) cost leadership focused on a narrow range of buyers; (3) product differentiation focused on a broad range of buyers; (4) product differentiation focused on a narrow range of buyers; and (5) best cost.

**Compilation:** The translation of a program from source code to object code so that the program can be executed. The source code is not necessarily translated line-by-line and is often optimized for execution speed. *See also* interpretation *and* source code *and* object code.

**Complements:** Complements or complementary products are products that are usually consumed jointly. Complements are related such that a decrease in the price of one product will cause an increase in demand of the other product. *See also* substitutes.

**Compound Interest:** Compound interest is interest computed with compounding (i.e., interest on principal and interest both). *See also* simple interest.

**Computer Operator:** In mainframe computing environments, computer operators are responsible for scheduling processing jobs, running or monitoring scheduled production jobs, hanging tapes, and possibly printing and distributing reports. Much of the job-scheduling and job-running work can be automated and, in large computing environments, must be automated due to the sheer volume of the processing that occurs. A computer operator is not a person entering data into a system. In most situations, computer operators have nothing to do with data. *See also* computer programmer *and* system programmer *and* end user.

**Computer Programmer:** A computer/application programmer is the person responsible for writing and/or maintaining application programs. The application programmer also normally handles the testing of application programs and the preparation of computer operator instructions, if there are any computer operators in the organization. Applications programmers are also sometimes called software engineers. *See also* system programmer *and* computer operator.

**Concentration Banking:** Concentration banking is a payment collection procedure in which payments are made to regionally dispersed collection centers. Checks are collected at these centers several times a day and deposited in local banks for quick clearing. *See also* zero balance account.

**Conceptual Design:** During the conceptual design phase, a company decides how to meet user needs.

**Constant Returns to Scale:** Constant returns to scale is the state in which the long-run average total cost stays the same as the quantity of output produced increases or decreases (i.e., the unit cost stays the same regardless of the number of units produced).

**Consumer Price Index (CPI):** The consumer price index is an index that is used to adjust for inflation. It is designed to measure the effect of price changes on the cost of a typical basket of goods purchased by urban consumer households. The current base (100) year for the consumer price index is 1982–1984. Inflation is the CPI of the current period less the CPI of the previous period, divided by the CPI of the previous period times 100. *See also* GDP deflator.

**Contractionary Monetary Policy:** Contractionary monetary policy is the reduction of the money supply by the Federal Reserve. *See also* monetary policy *and* expansionary monetary policy.

**Contribution Margin:** The contribution margin (also called marginal income) is sales minus variable costs or selling price per unit minus variable cost per unit. For this purpose, variable costs include variable manufacturing costs (direct material, direct labor, and variable manufacturing overhead) and variable selling costs. *See also* breakeven point *and* cost-volume-profit analysis and contribution margin ratio.

**Contribution Margin Ratio:** The contribution margin ratio is the contribution margin divided by sales. *See also* contribution margin.

**Control Activities:** As a component of the Internal Control–Integrated Framework (the Framework), control activities include the policies and procedures that will mitigate the risk of material misstatement of financial statements. As a component of Enterprise Risk Management–Integrated Framework (ERM), the concept is broadened to include the implementation of risk response strategies into operations through policies and procedures that consider not only a risk assessment but also a separate risk response component.

**Control Chart:** In quality control, a control chart is a graphical display of a quality characteristic that has been measured or computed from a sample versus the sample number or time. The chart contains a center line that represents the average value of the quality characteristic corresponding to the in-control state. Two other horizontal lines, called the upper control limit (UCL) and the lower control limit (LCL), are also drawn. These control limits are chosen so that if the process is in control, nearly all of the sample points will fall between them. As long as the sample points plot within the control limits, the process is assumed to be in control, and no action is necessary. *See also* statistical quality control *and* Pareto diagram *and* cause-and-effect diagram.

**Control Clerk:** In the old days of complete batch processing, control clerks logged or scheduled input and output and maintained error and correction logs. The control clerks also controlled the flow of batches through data entry and editing, monitored processing, and controlled distribution of reports and other output. In many large computing environments, this function is obsolete because the responsibilities have either been automated (and are now done by software and/or hardware) or have been distributed to the end users.

**Control Environment:** A component of the Internal Control–Integrated Framework (the Framework) that defines the "tone at the top" including integrity and ethical values, management operating styles, financial reporting competencies, etc.

**Conversion:** Conversion is the process of changing from an old application system to a new application system. There may be a direct cutover or some kind of parallel processing where both the old application system and the new application system are run and the results are compared (often a quite difficult comparison to make if the new and old systems do not perform the same functions in the same way).

**Conversion Costs (and Conversion Cost Pricing):** Conversion costs are direct labor and manufacturing overhead costs needed to convert raw materials into a finished product (i.e., they do not include raw materials). Pricing can be determined using conversion costs (i.e., "conversion cost pricing") when customers furnish the material to be used in the manufacturing process. *See also* prime costs.

**Core Competency:** A core competency is fundamental knowledge, ability, or expertise in a specific subject area or skill set.

**Corrective Control:** Corrective controls are controls that correct errors after they have occurred and have been detected. *See also* preventive control *and* detective control.

**Cost Assignment:** Cost assignment is the assignment of costs to either a cost pool or a cost object. Distinguishing between the direct and indirect components of a cost is required for proper cost assignment.

**Cost Driver:** A cost driver is a factor that has the ability to change total cost. Typically, cost drivers are activity bases that are closely correlated with the incurrence of manufacturing overhead costs in an activity center, and they are often used as allocation bases for applying overhead costs to cost objects. Cost drivers may be based on volume (output), activity, value added, or any other operational characteristics. *See also* cost object *and* cost pool.

**Cost Leadership Strategy:** A cost leadership strategy is a competitive strategy that emphasizes lowest overall cost. *See also* differentiation strategy *and* best cost strategy *and* niche strategy.

**Cost Object:** A cost object is the object of the assignment of a cost. Although a product is the object that many people think of first, a cost object can be customers, strategic business units (SBUs), services, etc. *See also* cost driver *and* strategic business unit.

**Cost of Goods Manufactured:** The cost of goods manufactured is beginning work-in-process inventory plus total manufacturing costs less ending work-in-process inventory. Manufacturing costs are the direct material used, the direct labor used, and the manufacturing overhead applied. *See also* direct material *and* direct labor *and* overhead.

**Cost of Goods Sold:** The cost of goods sold is beginning finished goods inventory plus cost of goods manufactured less ending finished goods inventory.

**Cost of Long-Term Debt:** The cost of long-term debt is the current yield prevailing in the market on newly issued par value bonds of equal risk to that already outstanding. The cost of long-term debt is computed on an after-tax basis as the product of the yield times (1 – the company's marginal tax rate). The after-tax cost of debt is used to compute the weighted average cost of capital. *See also* weighted average cost of capital *and* cost of preferred stock *and* cost of retained earnings.

**Cost of Preferred Stock:** The cost of preferred stock is the current yield prevailing in the market on newly issued preferred stock of equal risk to that already outstanding. The cost of preferred stock is computed as the preferred dividends divided by the net (of flotation cost) issuing price of the preferred stock. There is no pretax or after-tax cost of preferred stock since preferred dividends are not deductible for income tax purposed. The cost of preferred stock is used to compute the weighted average cost of capital. *See also* weighted average cost of capital *and* cost of long-term debt *and* cost of retained earnings.

**Cost of Retained Earnings:** The cost of retained earnings is the return prevailing in the market for common stock of equal risk to that already outstanding. The cost of retained earnings is also called the cost of internal capital or the cost of internal equity. The cost of retained earnings is computed using one of three methods: the capital asset pricing model, the dividend yield plus growth rate method (also called the discounted cash flow method), or the bond yield plus risk premium method. Since these various methods will normally provide different results, an average of the three results is often used for the weighted average cost of capital. *See also* weighted average cost of capital *and* cost of long-term debt *and* cost of preferred stock.

**Cost Pool:** A cost pool is a group of costs (e.g., raw material or direct labor) or a specially identified cost center (e.g., a department or a manager) in which costs are grouped, assigned, or collected. *See also* cost driver *and* cost assignment.

**Cost Push Inflation:** Cost push inflation is inflation caused by reductions in short-run aggregate supply (i.e., by a leftward shift in the short-run aggregate supply curve). *See also* demand pull inflation *and* aggregate supply.

**Cost-Volume-Profit Analysis:** Cost-volume-profit-analysis (sometimes called breakeven analysis) determines the effects of selling and production volume on revenues, costs, and net income. Assumptions of cost-volume-profit analysis are that the selling price is constant, costs are linear, the sales mix is constant, and inventories do not change. *See also* breakeven point *and* contribution margin.

**Country Risk:** Country risk is the risk of political and economic uncertainty in a foreign country that affects the value of loans or investments in that country.

**Coupon Interest Rate:** The coupon interest rate is the interest rate that will actually be paid on a bond. The coupon rate of interest is normally fixed and the interest is normally paid semiannually in the U.S. If the coupon rate is not fixed, then the bond is called a floating rate bond. *See also* effective interest rate *and* floating rate securities.

**Covered Interest Arbitrage:** In an interest arbitrage transaction, the foreign exchange risk can be covered (covered interest arbitrage) if, at the same time the investor exchanges the domestic currency for the foreign currency to make the foreign investment, the investor also engages in a forward sale of an equal amount of the foreign currency to coincide with the maturity of the investment. *See also* interest arbitrage *and* forward hedge.

**Credit Risk:** Credit risk is the risk of loss due to the "other" party, called a counterparty, defaulting on a contract or, more generally, the risk of loss due to some "credit event." Traditionally, credit risk is applied to bonds where the debt holders were concerned that the counterparty might default on a payment (coupon or principal). Credit risk is sometimes called default risk. *See also* interest rate risk *and* reinvestment risk.

**Cross Elasticity of Demand:** The cross elasticity of demand is the percentage change in the quantity demanded of one good divided by the percentage change in the price of a related good.

**Cross Elasticity of Supply:** The cross elasticity of supply is the percentage change in the quantity supplied of one good divided by the percentage change in the price of a related good.

**Cross Hedging:** Cross hedging is hedging the exposure in one currency by the use of futures, forwards, or other contracts in a second currency that is correlated with the first currency. *See also* currency variability.

**Currency Appreciation:** Currency appreciation is the strengthening of a currency in relation to another currency. Appreciation occurs when, because of a change in currency exchange rates, a unit of one currency buys more units of another currency.

**Currency Depreciation:** Currency depreciation is the weakening of a currency in relation to another currency. Depreciation occurs when, because of a change in currency exchange rates, a unit of one currency buys fewer units of another currency.

**Currency Variability:** Overall currency exposure can be assessed by considering each currency position together with that currency's variability and the correlations among the currencies (how much two currencies tend to increase and decrease together). The standard deviation of historical data serves as one measure of currency variability. Currency variability levels may change over time.

**Current Ratio:** The current ratio is current assets divided by current liabilities. *See also* working capital *and* quick ratio.

**Currently Attainable Standards:** Currently attainable standards represent standard costs that result from work performed by employees with appropriate training and experience but without extraordinary effort. Provision is made for normal spoilage and down time. *See also* ideal standards *and* standard costs.

**Customer Relationship Management (CRM):** Customer relationship management systems provide sales force automation and customer services in an attempt to manage customer relationships. CRM systems record and manage customer contacts, manage salespeople, forecast sales and sales targets and goals, manage sales leads and potential sales leads, provide and manage online quotes and product specifications and pricing, and analyze sales data. *See also* enterprise resource planning (ERP).

**Customization:** Customization is the changing of a purchased application software package to meet a customer's specific requirements. The software must be recustomized each time there is a new release of the software.

**Cyclical Unemployment:** Cyclical unemployment is unemployment resulting from business cycles, especially recessions or depressions. *See also* recession *and* depression *and* unemployment rate *and* structural unemployment *and* seasonal unemployment.

**Dashboard Reporting:** Reports provided to management with critical data presented in a summary format to quickly show the extent to which the entity's activities are operating within prescribed limits.

**Data:** Data are raw facts (e.g., a quantity, a name, or a dollar amount). Data are stored in computer systems in various ways. *See also* information.

**Data Administrator:** A data administrator is responsible for the definition, planning, and control of the data within a database or databases. *See also* database administrator *and* database.

**Data Encryption:** Data encryption offers a form of security, and it is based on the idea of keys. Each party has a public and private key for their data (public key encryption is one type of encryption). The public key is distributed to others in a separate transmission. The sender of a message uses the private key (which never goes anywhere) to encrypt the message, and the receiver uses the public key to decrypt the message. An encrypted message must properly process through the encryption algorithm after the keys are applied. As long as the private key is secure, the encryption scheme should provide a secure transmission. All encryption keys can be cracked, but the longer the key is, the harder it is. *See also* digital signature *and* digital certificate.

**Data Flow Diagram:** A data flow diagram is a graphic representation of information flow in a system.

**Data Matching:** Data matching is the combination of two or more data items that are combined to improve processing controls.

**Data Mining:** Data mining is the use of analytical techniques to identify trends, patterns, and relationships in data.

**Data Processing Cycle:** The data processing cycle is defined by four functional areas that affect the handling of data, including data input, data storage, data processing, and information output.

**Data Redundancy:** Data redundancy is the storage of the same data in more than one place in an organization. This can cause problems, because if data are stored in more than one place, reported values are likely to differ.

**Database:** A database is an integrated collection of data records and data files. It comprises nothing more than stored data. A database most often centralizes data and minimizes redundant data (think of the data as all being in one place, although it may or may not be physically stored that way). The structure of the data in the database often provides the data relationships that start to change the data into information. *See also* database management system *and* database administrator *and* schema *and* data administrator *and* structured query language (SQL).

**Database Administrator (DBA):** Within a database environment, database administrators are responsible for maintaining and supporting the database software. The database administrator may also perform some or all of the security functions for the database. Database administrators perform somewhat the same functions for database software as system programmers perform for the operating system as a whole. *See also* system programmer *and* data administrator *and* database.

**Database Management System (DBMS):** In organizations that employ mainframe and midrange computer systems, a database management system is a very important software package because it controls the development, use, and maintenance of the databases used by the organization. Quite often, the terms "database" and "DBMS" are used interchangeably. This usage is inaccurate. *See also* database *and* database administrator *and* data administrator.

**Database Structure:** Database structure is the structure of a database such as a hierarchical structure, relational structure, or object-oriented structure. *See also* database.

**Database Tuning:** Database tuning is the testing of a database to ensure that the database is operating effectively and efficiently. *See also* database.

**Debenture:** A debenture is an unsecured bond. *See also* subordinated debenture.

**Debt Securities:** Debt securities are bonds. A debt security represents a creditor-debtor relationship with the corporation whereby the corporation has borrowed funds from "outside investors" and promises to repay them.

**Debt-to-Assets Ratio:** The debt-to-assets ratio is debt divided by total assets.

**Debt-to-Equity Ratio:** The debt-to-equity ratio is another word for debt-to-total-capital ratio.

**Debt-to-Total-Capital Ratio:** The debt-to-total-capital ratio is debt divided by total capital. Total capital is total debt capital plus total equity capital and thus includes common stock, preferred stock, and retained earnings. The debt-to-total-capital ratio indicates what percentage of permanent capital is financed with debt and thus a firm's long-term debt-paying ability.

**Debugging:** Debugging is the process of removing as many bugs (programming errors) as possible. *See also* desk checking.

**Decision Support System (DSS):** A decision support system is a computer-based information system that provides interactive support for managers during the decision-making process. A DSS is an extension of an MIS and is useful for developing information directed toward making particular decisions. DSS do not automate decisions, but rather provide managers with interactive, computer-aided tools that combine their subjective judgments and insights with objective analytical data to guide the decision. DSS address problems where the procedure for arriving at a solution may not be fully predefined in advance. DSS may automate decision procedures, may provide information about certain aspects of the decision, may facilitate the preparation of forecasts based on the decision, or may allow the simulation of various aspects of the decision. DSS are often divided into data-driven and model-driven systems. DSS are sometimes called expert systems. *See also* accounting information system *and* executive information system *and* management information system *and* expert system *and* artificial intelligence.

**Default Risk:** Default risk is another word for credit risk. *See also* credit risk *and* liquidity risk *and* maturity risk premium.

**Defective Units:** Spoiled goods (goods that do not meet quality specifications or standards) that may be salvaged through rework or resale (at a reduced price) are termed defective units.

**Deflation:** Deflation is a sustained decrease in the general prices of goods and services. *See also* inflation.

**Demand Curve:** A demand curve is a curve that illustrates the relationship between the price of a good or service and the quantity demanded of that good or service. Price is plotted on the *y*-axis and quantity is plotted on the *x*-axis. *See also* supply curve.

**Demand Flow:** Demand flow is a management philosophy or business strategy that develops business processes in response to customer demand. (Demand pull is a similar concept.) At its most sophisticated level, demand flow uses quantitative techniques that connect processes in a flow and links them to daily changes in demand. Demand flow is the opposite of a schedule-push philosophy that would use sales forecasts to determine a production schedule.

**Demand Pull Inflation:** Demand pull inflation is inflation caused by increases in aggregate demand (i.e., by a rightward shift in the aggregate demand curve). *See also* cost push inflation.

**Demand Reporting:** Reports giving a user access to a report at any time. These reports are also referred to as response reports because an end user can log on to a workstation and obtain a response in the form of a report without waiting for the scheduled reporting time.

**Depreciation Tax Shield:** A depreciation tax shield is the tax reduction associated with depreciation. Depreciation is not considered in determining cash flows in capital budgeting models, except to the extent that it is a tax shield, since it is deductible for income tax purposes. The depreciation tax shield is the depreciation times the marginal tax rate. *See also* capital budgeting.

**Depression:** A depression is a very severe recession. *See also* recession *and* business cycle.

**Derived Demand:** Derived demand is the demand for the factors of production of a good caused by the demand for a final good.

**Desk Checking:** Traditionally, desk checking (reviewing printed listings of the program) was used to discover and eliminate bugs. *See also* debugging.

**Detective Control:** Detective controls are controls that discover errors after they have occurred. *See also* preventive control *and* corrective control.

**Differential Costs:** Differential costs are the difference in costs between two or more alternatives. Differential costs are also called incremental costs. The words differential and incremental can also be used for revenues to quantify the different revenues associated with two or more alternatives.

**Differentiation Strategy:** A (product) differentiation strategy is a competitive strategy that emphasizes the perception that a company's products are better or have a unique quality that differentiates them from competing products. *See also* cost leadership strategy *and* best cost strategy.

**Digital Cash:** Digital cash (also electronic cash or E-cash) is currency in an electronic form that moves outside the normal channels of money. Digital cash can be used to make purchases over the Internet without having to use credit cards. An example of digital cash is PayPal.

**Digital Certificate:** Digital certificates are a form of data security. An individual wishing to send an encrypted message applies for a digital certificate from a certificate authority. The certificate authority issues an encrypted digital certificate containing the applicant's public key and a variety of other identification information. The certificate authority makes its own public key readily available through print publicity or perhaps over the Internet. The recipient of an encrypted message uses the certificate authority's public key to decode the digital certificate attached to the message, verifies it as issued by the certificate authority, and then obtains the sender's public key and identification information contained in the certificate. With this information, the recipient can send an encrypted reply. *See also* data encryption *and* digital signature.

**Digital Checking:** Digital checking is an electronic check with a secure digital signature.

**Digital Signature:** Digital signatures, which authenticate a document by using a form of data encryption, are a form of data security. A mathematically condensed version of the message is produced and encrypted by the sender's private key. It is attached to the original message. The message and the digital signature can be unlocked by an authorized receiver (anybody with the public key). The original message can be compared with the condensed version to ensure that the original message has not been changed. *See also* data encryption *and* digital certificate.

**Direct Costs:** Direct costs are costs that can be identified with or traced to a given cost object in an economical manner. Direct costs are usually relevant to a costing decision. Variable costs are generally direct costs. *See also* indirect costs *and* cost object *and* variable costs *and* fixed costs.

**Direct Labor:** Direct labor is labor that can be identified with or traced to a given cost object in an economic manner. *See also* direct material *and* overhead *and* cost of goods manufactured.

**Direct Labor Efficiency Variance:** The direct labor efficiency variance is the standard rate times the difference between the actual hours worked and the standard hours allowed for the actual production. *See also* direct labor rate variance *and* direct material quantity variance.

**Direct Labor Rate Variance:** The direct labor rate variance is the actual hours worked times the difference between the actual rate and the standard rate. *See also* direct labor efficiency variance *and* direct material price variance.

**Direct Material:** Direct material is material that can be identified with or traced to a given cost object in an economical manner. *See also* direct labor *and* overhead *and* cost of goods manufactured.

**Direct Material Price Variance:** The direct material price variance is the actual quantity purchased times the difference between the actual price and the standard price, assuming that the price variances are isolated at the time of purchase. *See also* direct labor rate variance *and* direct material usage variance.

**Direct Material Usage Variance:** The direct material usage variance is the standard price times the difference between the actual quantity used and the standard quantity allowed for the actual production. *See also* direct material price variance *and* direct labor efficiency variance.

**Disaster Recovery:** Disaster recovery is the plan for or the actual resumption of computer processing after a disaster (which is more serious than just a temporary system outage).

**Discount Rate:** The discount rate is the interest rate that the Federal Reserve charges banks for short-term loans.

**Discounted Cash Flow Methods:** Discounted cash flow methods are capital budgeting methods that measure cash inflows and cash outflows at a single point in time, normally the current time, by incorporating the time value of money. Discounted cash flow methods, which include the net present value method and the internal rate of return method, are considered superior to methods that do not consider the time value of money. *See also* net present value method *and* internal rate of return method.

**Discounted Payback Method:** The discounted payback method is a capital budgeting method that calculates the amount of time to recover the initial investment for a project. The discounted payback method uses after-tax cash flows discounted at the project's cost of capital as the discount rate. *See also* payback method.

**Discretionary Costs:** Discretionary costs are costs that might or might not be incurred. They normally are fixed costs, have no causal relationship to the outputs of the costs, and are typically incurred because of an annual (or other periodic) decision regarding the amount of the cost to be incurred.

Examples of discretionary costs include human resource costs, advertising, training of executives, and other costs that are not generally crucial to the production process or other significant activity of the organization. Discretionary costs can be contrasted to committed costs. *See also* committed costs.

**Diseconomies of Scale:** Diseconomies of scale is the state in which the long-run average total cost increases as the quantity of output produced increases. *See also* economies of scale.

**Disintermediation:** Disintermediation is the removal of organizational or business process layers responsible for intermediate steps in a value chain. The process of shifting or moving intermediate steps in a value chain is called re-intermediation.

**Disposable Income:** Disposable income is personal income less personal taxes. *See also* personal income.

**Distributed Processing:** Distributed or decentralized processing occurs when computing power, applications, and work is spread out (or distributed) over many locations (i.e., via a LAN or WAN). Decentralized processing environments often use distributed processing techniques, where each remote computer performs a portion of the processing (e.g., a portion of the data validation), thus reducing the processing burden on the central computer or computers. *See also* centralized processing.

**Diversifiable Risk:** Diversifiable risk (also called unsystematic risk) is the risk of an individual stock (in a portfolio) that can be eliminated by diversification. Diversifiable risk is caused by such random events as lawsuits, strikes, successful and unsuccessful marketing programs, and other events that are unique to a particular firm. *See also* nondiversifiable risk.

**Dividend Yield Plus Growth Rate Method:** The dividend yield plus growth rate method is a method to determine the cost of common stock or retained earnings as the expected (at the end of the year) yield on the common stock plus the expected growth rate in the dividends per share after that. Unfortunately, this method is sometimes called the discounted cash flow method. *See also* capital asset pricing model *and* bond yield plus risk premium method.

**Dividends:** A dividend is a distribution of corporate profits as ordered by the directors and paid to the shareholders.

**Domain Name System (DNS):** The domain name system is the system of domain names that is employed by the Internet. The Internet is based on IP addresses, not domain names, and each Web server requires a domain name server to translate domain names into IP addresses.

**Draft:** A draft is an unconditional order in writing—signed by a person, usually an exporter in international trade financing—ordering the importer to pay, on demand or at a fixed future date (time draft), the amount specified on its face. *See also* banker's acceptance.

**Drill Down:** Drill down is moving from a piece of summary data to lower and lower levels of detail. The ability to drill down in this manner is a necessary function of an executive information system. *See also* executive information system.

**DSL:** DSL is an acronym for digital subscriber line, which is a mechanism to use high-speed access to the Internet through a regular telephone line.

**E-Business:** E-business refers to any use of information technology, particularly networking and communications technology, to perform business processes in an electronic form. The exchange of this electronic information may or may not relate to the purchase and sale of goods or services. E-commerce (by contrast) relates to buying and selling transactions. *See also* e-commerce.

**E-Commerce:** E-commerce is the electronic consummation of exchange (buying and selling) transactions. E-commerce uses a private network or the Internet as the communications provider. Certain types of e-commerce involve communication between previously known parties or between parties that have had no prior contracts or agreements with each other. *See also* e-business.

**Economic Costs:** Economic costs are accounting (explicit) costs plus implicit costs. *See also* explicit costs and implicit costs *and* opportunity costs.

**Economic Exposure:** Economic exposure is the risk that the present value of a firm's cash flows could increase or decrease as a result of changes in exchange rates. *See also* transaction exposure *and* translation exposure.

**Economic Order Quantity (EOQ):** The economic order quantity is the order quantity that minimizes the combination of the ordering and carrying costs of inventory.

**Economic Profit:** Economic profit is the difference between total revenue and total explicit costs and implicit costs. *See also* explicit costs *and* implicit costs *and* opportunity costs.

**Economic Value Added (EVA):** Economic value added is a firm's net operating profit after taxes less its after-tax cost of capital. Alternatively, it is operating capital times (the return on capital less the weighted average cost of capital). EVA is similar to residual income, which is the excess of a firm's net income over its required rate of return. Operating capital is the sum of interest-bearing debt, preferred stock, and common equity used to acquire the firm's net operating assets. *See also* residual income.

**Economies of Scale:** Economies of scale is the state in which long-run average total cost declines as the quantity of output produced increases. *See also* diseconomies of scale.

**Effective Interest Rate:** The effective interest rate is the market interest rate at the date bonds are issued. If the market interest rate is equal to the coupon rate, the bonds will sell at par; if the market interest rate is greater than the coupon rate, the bonds will sell at a discount; and if the market interest rate is less than the coupon rate, the bonds will sell at a premium. *See also* coupon interest rate *and* floating rate securities.

**Efficiency Variance:** The efficiency variance is the budget based on the actual hours worked less the budget based on standard hours allowed for the actual output. If variable overhead only is being analyzed, the formula can be expressed as the standard rate times the difference between the actual hours and the standard hours, and the formula corresponds to the direct material usage variance and the direct labor efficiency variance. *See also* direct material usage variance *and* direct labor efficiency variance *and* spending variance *and* budget variance *and* volume variance.

**Electronic Access Controls:** Electronic access controls are nonphysical controls over access to data and application programs such as user identification codes, assignment and maintenance of security levels, file attributes, firewalls, etc. *See also* access controls *and* physical access controls.

**Electronic Data Interchange (EDI):** EDI is computer-to-computer exchange of business transaction documents (e.g., purchase orders, confirmations, invoices, etc.) in structured formats that allow the direct processing of the data by the receiving system. Any standard business document (including an information request) that one organization can exchange with another can be exchanged via EDI, provided both organizations have made the proper preparations. *See also* value added network (VAN).

**Electronic Funds Transfer (EFT):** Electronic funds transfer systems are a form of electronic payment for the banking and retailing industries. EFT uses a variety of technologies to transact, process, and verify money transfers and credits between banks, businesses, and consumers. The Federal Reserve's financial services system is used frequently in EFT to reduce the time and expense required to process checks and credit transactions.

**E-mail Archiving:** E-mail archiving is a form of backup for the secure preservation of e-mail for regulatory compliance and other purposes. An e-mail archiving system normally extracts message contents and attachments, indexes them, and stores them in a read-only format so that they cannot be altered.

**Emerging Nations:** Emerging nations represent those economies outside the world's largest industrial nations that are experiencing rapid growth.

**Encryption:** Encryption is the use of a password or digital key to scramble a readable (plaintext) message into an unreadable (ciphertext) message. The intended recipient of the message then uses the same (or different, depending on encryption method) digital key to convert the ciphertext message back into plaintext.

**End User:** An end user is a person who actually uses a system or application.

**End User Computing (EUC):** EUC is the hands-on use of computers by end users.

**Engineered Costs:** Engineered costs (including direct and indirect costs and variable and fixed costs) typically have a causal relationship between the incurrence of the cost and the output associated with the cost.

**Enterprise Resource Planning (ERP):** An enterprise resource planning system is a cross-functional enterprise system that integrates and automates the many business processes that must work together in the manufacturing, logistics, distribution, accounting, finance, and human resource functions of a business. ERP software is composed of a number of modules that can function independently or as an integrated system to allow data and information to be shared among all of the different departments and divisions of large businesses. ERP is often considered a back office system, from the customer order to fulfillment of that order. *See also* customer relationship management (CRM).

**Enterprise Risk Management Integrated Framework:** The COSO publication Enterprise Risk Management–Integrated Framework (ERM) builds upon the COSO publication Internal Control–Integrated Framework (Framework) to provide a more extensive evaluation of the broader concept of enterprise risk management. ERM identifies four categories of business objectives including strategic operational, reporting and compliance and expands the five components in the internal control framework to include three additional components (objective setting, event identification and risk response) to support the risk assessment components of the framework and expand on the framework to embrace operations.

**Equity Securities:** Equity securities are stocks. An equity security is an instrument representing an investment in the corporation whereby its holder becomes a part owner of the business.

**Equivalent Unit (EQU):** An equivalent unit is the amount of work expressed in completed units of a product. For example, if 1,000 units are 80 percent complete as to direct material, direct labor, and manufacturing overhead, there are 800 equivalent units of production. Normally, however, there will be a different number of equivalent units for direct material, direct labor, and manufacturing overhead. For equivalent unit calculations, transfers in from previous departments are assumed to be 100 percent complete. Materials may be added either at the beginning or the end of the process in a particular department as is stated in the question. *See also* process costing.

**Escrow:** Escrow (of source code) is the holding of the source code of an application system by an independent third party (escrow agent) so that it can be made available to the purchaser if something happens to the vendor (e.g., filing for bankruptcy) or if the vendor fails to maintain the software as promised in the licensing agreement.

**Eurobonds:** A Eurobond is a bond issued in one country but denominated in the currency of some other country.

**Eurodollars:** Eurodollars are U.S. dollar-denominated time deposits at banks outside the U.S. The Eurodollar market evolved in Europe (specifically London), but Eurodollars can be held anywhere outside the U.S. Interest rates on Eurodollar deposits (and loans) are tied to LIBOR. *See also* LIBOR.

**Event Identification:** A component of the Enterprise Risk Management–Integrated Framework (ERM) that defines the process for identifying events that may positively or negatively impact the organization. Positive events are opportunities and negative events are risks.

**Exception Reporting:** Exception reports are produced when a specific condition or exception occurs. In other words, specific criteria are established, and any transaction or entity that meets the criteria is reported on the exception report.

**Exchange Rate:** An exchange rate is the price of one unit of foreign currency in terms of the domestic currency. These days most exchange rates are floating, which means that they are established in the foreign exchange market.

**Exchange Rate Risk:** Exchange rate risk (also called currency risk) is the risk that the exchange rate between the currency in which a cash flow is denominated (a bond denominated in Euros, for example) and the currency of the investor (the U.S. dollar, for example) might change.

**Executive Information System (EIS):** Executive information systems, or executive support systems, provide senior executives with immediate and easy access to internal and external information to assist the executives in monitoring business conditions in general. EIS assist in strategic, not daily, decision-making. EIS are collectors and synthesizers of business and economic information. A premium is normally placed on ease of use so that the systems can be used by executives who might lack full computer literacy. Extensive graphics are often used in presentation. A drill-down capability is often provided so that detail can be obtained in areas of interest. *See also* accounting information system *and* decision support system *and* management information system *and* drill down.

**Expansionary Monetary Policy:** Expansionary monetary policy is the expansion of the money supply by the Fed. *See also* monetary policy *and* contractionary monetary policy.

**Expected Value:** Expected value is the weighted average of the probable outcomes of a variable where the weights are the probabilities of each outcome occurring. Expected value is found by multiplying the probability of each outcome by its payoff and summing the results. *See also* probability *and* subjective probability *and* objective probability.

**Expenditure Approach:** One way to measure GDP is to measure expenditures for products bought by consumers, products bought by businesses, products bought by governments, and net exports, or exports minus imports (i.e., a flow of products approach). *See also* gross domestic product *and* gross domestic income *and* income approach.

**Expenditure Cycle:** The expenditure cycle is a transaction cycle characterized by the purchase of goods or services that use cash or produce debt or other obligations. *See also* transaction cycles.

**Experience Curve:** The experience curve is an extension of learning curve theory applied to groups of people undertaking a range of tasks. The experience curve anticipates that the amount of time required for a group of tasks will decrease as experience increases.

**Expert System:** An expert system is a class of computer programs. The programs are made up of a set of rules that analyze information about a specific class of problem and then provide an analysis of the problem or recommend a course of action. The problems solved by an expert system are the kind of problems that would be solved by a human "expert." *See also* decision support system *and* artificial intelligence.

**Expired Costs:** Expired costs are costs that cannot be justifiably carried forward because they have no benefit to future periods. *See also* sunk costs *and* unexpired costs.

**Explicit Costs:** Explicit costs are documented out-of-pocket expenses (e.g., wages, cost of raw materials, etc.). *See also* implicit costs *and* opportunity costs.

**External Factors:** In value chain analysis, external factors are sources of opportunities in the market and threats to the firm's ability to continue with its strategic plan. *See also* internal factors *and* value chain *and* value chain analysis.

**External Failure Costs:** External failure costs are costs to cure a defect discovered after a product is sent to the customer. These costs include warranty costs, costs of returning the goods, liability claims, and the cost of lost customers. *See also* internal failure costs.

**Extranet:** Extranets permit company suppliers, customers, and business partners (a general term for customers, suppliers, etc.) to have direct access to the company's network. *See also* intranet.

**Factoring:** Factoring is the selling of a firm's accounts receivable at a discount. Factoring may be on a recourse basis, where any uncollectible receivables can be returned, or nonrecourse, where the factor takes the risk of collectibility.

**Factors of Production:** Factors of production are the inputs or resources used to produce final goods and services. Factors of production are bought and sold in markets.

**Federal Reserve (Fed):** The Federal Reserve is the central bank of the United States.

**Field:** A field is a group of bytes in which a specific data element such as an employee number or name is stored. *See also* bit and byte *and* file and record.

**Field Check:** A field check is a data validation step performed on a data element to ensure that it is of the appropriate type (alphabetic, numeric, etc.). *See also* check digit *and* validity check.

**FIFO Method of Process Costing:** The FIFO method of process costing calculates equivalent units and production costs differently from the weighted average method of process costing. In the FIFO method, the equivalent units are the equivalent units in the beginning inventory plus the units started and completed during the period (100 percent) plus the equivalent units in the ending inventory. Production costs to be accounted for are the costs added during the month. Cost per equivalent unit is the production cost divided by the equivalent units. Normally, a separate cost per equivalent unit is calculated for direct materials and conversion costs (labor and overhead). *See also* weighted average method of process costing.

**File:** A file is a collection of related records often arranged in some kind of sequence, such as a customer file made up of customer records and organized by customer number. Traditionally, files were often classified as master files, which were stored permanently, and transaction files, which were used to update the master files and were normally not retained permanently. *See also* bit and byte *and* field and record.

**File Attribute:** File attributes are read/write indicators on files that restrict reading and writing/updating of the files. For example, if a file is marked read only, it cannot be updated.

**File Librarian:** File libraries store and protect programs and tapes from damage and unauthorized use. File librarians control the file libraries.

**Final Products:** In the computation of GDP, final products are products that do not undergo any further processing during the measurement period. Final products are either sold to end-users or remain as inventories. Intermediate products are products that are not final products. Total production is final products plus intermediate products. *See also* gross domestic product.

**Financial Leverage:** Financial leverage is defined as the degree to which a firm uses fixed financial costs to magnify the effects of a given percentage change in earnings before interest and taxes on the percentage change in its earnings per share. Financial leverage is an extension of operating leverage that purely focuses on one type of fixed cost, debt financing. A low financial fixed cost eliminates financial leverage as a consideration in operations. *See also* operating leverage.

**Financial Risk:** Financial risk includes the risk of having financial resources lost, wasted, or stolen. For example, an inventory report lists several laptop computers, but some of the laptops were not returned when employees left the organization. This problem could lead to inaccurate financial reports that are reporting assets that no longer exist. *See also* information risk *and* operating risk.

**Financing Cycle:** The financing cycle is a transaction cycle associated with equity and debt financing, including issuance of stock or debt, payment of dividends or debt service payments, etc. *See also* transaction cycles.

**Firewall:** A firewall is a system, often both hardware and software, of user identification and authentication that prevents unauthorized users from gaining access to network resources; acting as a gatekeeper, it isolates a private network from a public network. The term firewall may also be applied to a network node used to improve network traffic and to set up a boundary that prevents traffic from one network segment from crossing over to another. *See also* application firewall.

**Fiscal Policy:** Fiscal policy is the use of government spending and taxation policies to promote price stability, full employment, and economic growth. *See also* monetary policy.

**Fixed Costs:** Fixed costs are costs that remain constant in total over a relevant range of production activity (they may change from one relevant range to another). Fixed costs are fixed in total but variable on a per unit basis. *See also* variable costs *and* mixed costs *and* relevant range.

**Flexible Budget:** A flexible budget is a budget that is adjusted for changes in sales or production volumes. *See also* master budget.

**Float:** Float is the difference between a firm's cash account in its accounting records and the same account at the bank. Float, sometimes called net float, is the difference between collection float and disbursements float.

**Floating Rate Securities:** Floating rate securities are securities that pay coupon interest rates that are not fixed but that are set by a coupon formula based on some reference rate, such as LIBOR. *See also* Eurodollars *and* LIBOR.

**Flowchart:** A flowchart is a chart that depicts some aspect of a system. A flowchart may be a system flowchart or a program flowchart.

**Foreign Trade Zones:** Trade zones established by government in which tariffs are waived until the goods leave the zone. The creation of foreign trade zones has obvious implications on the government's control of imports and the location of import facilities.

**Forward Exchange Rate:** A forward exchange rate is the price at which foreign exchange can be bought or sold with payment/delivery set for some day in the future. Spot rates and forward exchange rates for the same currency are normally different. The term forward rate by itself, without the word exchange, is an interest rate that is expected to exist at some point in the future (and has nothing to do with currency or forward exchange). *See also* spot rate.

**Forward Hedge:** A forward hedge is a hedge transacted in the forward market for foreign currencies. A forward contract is a private agreement between two parties to enter into a transaction at some future date and at a price agreed to at the time the agreement is made. In terms of foreign currencies, a forward hedge entitles a firm to either purchase or sell units of an individual foreign currency for a negotiated price at a future time. Outside the foreign currencies market, the instrument is normally called a forward, without the word hedge. *See also* futures hedge *and* options hedge *and* money market hedge.

**Frictional Unemployment:** Frictional unemployment is unemployment resulting from workers routinely changing jobs or from workers being temporarily laid off. *See also* unemployment rate *and* structural unemployment *and* cyclical unemployment *and* seasonal unemployment.

**Full Employment:** Full employment is the level of unemployment when there is no cyclical unemployment. Full employment does not mean zero unemployment. *See also* cyclical unemployment *and* unemployment rate.

**Full Product Costing:** Full product costing is a product costing technique that considers all inputs in arriving at product costs, not just traditional inventoriable costs. Full product costs include such costs as research and development, product design, marketing, distribution, and customer service in product cost. Full product costs do not include finance or administrative costs. *See also* inventoriable costs.

**Functional Currency:** The functional currency is the currency of the primary economic environment in which a firm operates; normally that is the currency of the environment in which the firm primarily generates and expends cash. *See also* translation exposure.

**Functional Interdependence:** Functional interdependence (of nations and their economies) contemplates the participation of nations in world-wide institutions such as the United Nations (U.N.), World Trade Organization (WTO), and International Monetary Fund (IMF).

**Futures Hedge:** A futures hedge is a hedge transacted in the futures market for foreign currencies. A futures contract is an agreement between two parties to enter into a transaction at some future date and at a price agreed to at the time the agreement is made. For this purpose, the main difference between a forward hedge and a futures hedge is that futures are exchange traded and are much more standard than forward contracts. In terms of foreign currencies, a futures hedge entitles a firm to either purchase or sell units of an individual currency for a negotiated price at a future time. Outside the foreign currencies market, the instrument is normally called a future, without the word hedge. *See also* forward hedge *and* options hedge *and* money market hedge.

**G6:** The G6 is the group of the six largest industrial economies, including the United States, Japan, the United Kingdom, Germany, France, and Italy. The largest industrial nations are sometimes referred to as the G7, which comprises the G6 nations and Canada.

**Gateway:** A gateway is a combination of hardware and software that connect different types of networks by translating from one set of network protocols to another.

**GDP Deflator:** The GDP deflator is an index similar to the consumer price index. It is designed to measure the impact of price changes on the cost of a typical basket of goods purchased by consumers, businesses, governments, and foreigners (i.e., those goods that make up the GDP). *See also* consumer price index *and* real GDP *and* nominal GDP.

**General Controls:** General controls are controls over data center operations, system software acquisition and maintenance, access security, and application system development and maintenance. *See also* application controls.

**Gigabyte (GB):** A gigabyte is approximately 1 billion bytes (actually 1,073,741,824 bytes).

**Globalization:** Globalization represents the distribution of industrial and service activities across an increasing number of nations. Globalization makes the world's economies increasingly integrated and interrelated.

**Global Sourcing:** Synchronization of all levels of a product manufacture, from research and development to production, to marketing on an international basis.

**Gross Domestic Income (GDI):** Gross domestic income is the amounts that were paid for the resources that were used to make the products produced during the measurement cycle. The amounts that were paid are the same as the incomes of the owners of those resources. Gross domestic income is also wages plus interest plus rent plus indirect business taxes plus net income to foreigners plus depreciation plus the profits of producers. *See also* gross domestic product.

**Gross Domestic Product (GDP):** Gross domestic product is the total market value of all final goods and services produced within the borders of a nation within a particular time period. It is also the value added by work done by people and machines. *See also* final products *and* gross national product *and* gross domestic income.

**Gross National Product (GNP):** Gross national product is the total market value of all final goods and services produced by "residents" of a country within a particular time period. It includes goods and services that are produced overseas by U.S. firms (the residents) and excludes goods and services that are produced domestically by overseas firms (the nonresidents). *See also* gross domestic product *and* final products.

**Hacker:** Hacker is used to denote a person who gains unauthorized access to software or computer system, most often for nefarious purposes.

**Hardware:** Hardware is the actual physical computer or computer peripheral device. For example, a PC or some other kind of workstation, a mainframe, a disk drive, a tape drive, a monitor, a mouse, a printer, a scanner, and a keyboard are all considered hardware. *See also* software.

**Hash Total:** A hash total is a total of a field in a transaction that would not normally be added, such as a total of employee numbers. *See also* batch total.

**Hedge Transaction:** A hedge transaction is a transaction designed to protect against a price change that would negatively affect profits. There are two kinds of hedges: long hedges in which futures (or other) contracts are bought in anticipation of (or to protect against) price increases, and short hedges in which futures (or other) contracts are sold to guard against price declines. *See also* forward hedge *and* futures hedge *and* options hedge *and* money market hedge.

**Heuristic:** Heuristic means "rule of thumb" in common language. In finance, heuristics are generally agreed-upon benchmarks that can lead, dangerously, to poor decisions. In IT, heuristic has a technical meaning and can sometimes be used as an adjective and other times as a noun. Heuristic algorithms (heuristic used as an adjective) are algorithms that produce "good enough" answers. Algorithms are sets of detailed instructions that produce a predictable end from a known beginning (a computer program is an algorithm). In computer science, a heuristic (heuristic used as a noun) is a technique designed to solve a problem ignoring whether the solution can be proven to be correct but producing that "good enough" answer. An expert system might be called a heuristic system. *See also* expert system *and* decision support system.

**Heuristic (Behavioral Finance):** Heuristic means "rule of thumb" in common language. In behavioral finance it relates to assumptions that can distort the objective evaluation of financial evidence. Use of heuristics (e.g., a price earnings ratio should be at a certain level) promotes stereotyping, use of intuition instead of analysis, and exclusive use of easily available data.

**High-Low Method:** The high-low method is a technique to determine a regression line by using the high and low values of a set of data. It is one step up from using a ruler to determine the line. The method of least squares can be used to determine a more exact line. *See also* regression analysis *and* coefficient of correlation *and* coefficient of determination *and* standard error of the estimate *and* t-value.

**Hot Site:** For disaster recovery, a hot site is an off-site location that is equipped to take over the company's data processing. Backup copies of essential data files and programs may also be maintained at the location or a nearby data storage facility. *See also* cold site.

**Human Resources Cycle:** The human resources cycle is a transaction cycle associated with all phases of employee administration (hiring, determining compensation, paying employees, benefits administration and termination). *See also* transaction cycles.

**Hurdle Rate of Return:** The hurdle rate of return is the desired (or minimum) rate of return that is set to evaluate investments or projects. The hurdle rate of return is used to discount the various cash flows in the net present value method. The hurdle rate of return may be adjusted (increased) to reflect risk or to compensate for expected inflation. Different rates may be used for different time periods. *See also* net present value method *and* internal rate of return method.

**Hypertext Markup Language (HTML):** HTML is a tag-based formatting language used for Web pages. It provides a way to describe the structure of text-based information in a document and to replicate that information in a Web page by using tags in the text. An extension of HTML is XHTML (extensible HTML), which conforms to the extensible markup language (XML) format. The ability to read and work with HTML documents is built into browsers, and the ability to read XHTML is built into all new browsers. XML, on the other hand, needs a "parser" to translate it before it can be used in standard browsers.

**Ideal Standards:** Ideal standards are standard costs that result from perfect efficiency and effectiveness. *See also* currently attainable standards *and* standard costs.

**Implementation standards:** Implementation standards published by the Institute of Internal Auditors (IIA) are imbedded within the attribute and reporting standards to address the requirements of implementing both assurance and consulting activities.

**Implicit Costs:** Implicit costs are opportunity costs supplied by owners. *See also* explicit costs *and* opportunity costs.

**Importing Data:** Data files can be imported into a different program that can interpret the same data file (an inventory program "dumps" data concerning the latest inventory count into a data file that can be imported by the accounting program). In importing and exporting data, a standard format (e.g., a text file format) is used. Importing and exporting of data is not the same as data transfers from one application or system to another by data interface. With data interfaces, the transferor program and the transferee program both use a specialized format to transfer the data.

**Income Approach:** One way to measure GDP is to determine the gross domestic income (i.e., an earnings and cost approach). *See also* gross domestic product *and* gross domestic income *and* expenditure approach.

**Income Bonds:** Income bonds are bonds that pay interest only upon the achievement of target income levels (i.e., only if the interest is earned). *See also* debenture *and* subordinated debenture *and* junk bonds.

**Income Elasticity of Demand:** Income elasticity of demand is the percentage change in the quantity demanded of a good or service divided by the percentage change in consumer income.

**Incremental Costs:** Incremental costs are the difference in costs between two alternatives. In other words, they are also the additional costs incurred to produce an additional unit of product in excess of the current output. Incremental costs are also called differential costs. The words differential and incremental can also be used for revenues. *See also* differential costs.

**Indirect Costs:** An indirect cost is a cost that cannot be identified with or traced to a given cost object in an economic manner. Indirect material and indirect labor fit into this category. Indirect costs are accumulated in a cost pool and are then allocated to the various cost objects on some reasonable basis. Indirect costs are part of overhead and normally include both fixed and variable components. *See also* direct material *and* direct labor *and* overhead and common costs *and* cost pool.

**Inferior Good:** An inferior good is a good whose demand is negatively related to income (negative income elasticity of demand). *See also* normal good *and* income elasticity of demand.

**Inflation:** Inflation is a sustained increase in the general prices of goods and services. *See also* deflation.

**Information:** Information is organized and processed data that is meaningful to somebody. *See also* data.

**Information and Communication:** As a component of the Internal Control–Integrated Framework (the Framework), information and communication contemplates financial and internal control information as well as internal and external communication, while as a component of Enterprise Risk Management–Integrated Framework (ERM), the concept is broadened to include information and communication for general business operations.

**Information Risk:** Information risk includes the risk of loss of data integrity, incomplete transactions, or hackers. *See also* financial risk *and* operating risk.

**Information Technology Policy:** An information technology policy is management's formal notification to employees regarding the entity's technology objectives.

**Infrastructure:** Infrastructure (specifically IT infrastructure) is a collection of the shared hardware, software, storage technology, and network resources of an organization.

**Infrastructure Costs:** Infrastructure costs are those costs that exist because a firm has an infrastructure (e.g., a building, various machinery, etc.). Examples include depreciation and long-term leases. As these costs typically benefit a firm for a longer period of time than most other costs, capital budgeting is often necessary, and management pays particular attention to the outlay for these types of expenditures. Infrastructure costs can be contrasted to engineered costs and discretionary costs. *See also* engineered costs *and* discretionary costs.

**Input Controls:** Input controls are programmed controls that verify that transaction data is valid, complete, and accurate. *See also* processing controls.

**Intellectual Property:** Intellectual property is a term used to describe intangible products of the human intellect that have economic value (e.g., software and artistic works). Intellectual property can be protected as trade secrets or by copyrights or by patents.

**Interest Arbitrage:** Interest arbitrage is the transfer of funds from one currency to another to take advantage of higher rates of return. In order to make the foreign investment, the domestic (sometimes called home) currency must be converted into the foreign currency. Then, when the investment matures or is liquidated, the foreign currency must be reconverted back into the domestic currency. A foreign exchange risk arises because during the period of the investment, the spot exchange rate of the foreign currency may fall so that the investor gets back fewer domestic currency units than were originally paid. This fall may wipe out some or all of the extra interest earned on the foreign over the domestic investment and may even lead to an actual loss. *See also* covered interest arbitrage.

**Interest Rate Risk:** Interest rate risk is the risk that bond prices will decline when interest rates increase. When the coupon rate on a bond is equal to the market rate, the bond will sell at par. When the coupon rate on a bond is greater than the market rate (because the market rate has declined), the bond will sell at a premium. When the coupon rate is less than the market rate (because the market rate has increased), the bond will sell at a discount. The market rate adjusts the price of the bond to produce a market yield based on the coupon amount. Interest rate risk is a function of the bond's maturity (longer-term bonds are more volatile than short-term bonds), the bond's coupon rate (if a bond's coupon rate is lower, it will experience greater volatility), and the bond's yield (the higher the yield, the lower the volatility). Interest rate risk is measured by a calculated factor called duration. *See also* credit risk *and* default risk *and* reinvestment risk.

**Internal Control–Integrated Framework:** The COSO publication Internal Control–Integrated Framework (the Framework) describes internal control as a process that is designed to provide reasonable assurance in regard to the efficiency and effectiveness of operations, financial reporting, and compliance. The Framework identifies five major components, including control environment, risk assessment, control activities, information and communication, and monitoring.

**Internal Controls:** It is the process of directing, measuring and monitoring an organization's resources to provide reasonable assurance that the control objectives are achieved.

**Internal Environment:** A component of the Enterprise Risk Management–Integrated Framework (ERM) that defines the "tone at the top" including integrity and ethical values, risk appetite and risk management philosophy, and organizational structure.

**Internal Factors:** In value chain analysis, internal factors are the strengths and weaknesses of the firm. *See also* external factors *and* value chain *and* value chain analysis.

**Internal Failure Costs:** Internal failure costs are the costs to cure a defect before the product is sent to a customer. Internal failure costs include rework costs, scrap, tooling changes, and downtime. *See also* external failure costs.

**Internal Rate of Return Method:** The internal rate of return method is a capital budgeting method that determines the rate of return of an investment's or project's cash flows. The internal rate of return method is the inverse of the net present value method because it determines the rate at which the net present value of the investment is zero. *See also* net present value method *and* hurdle rate of return.

**International Monetary Fund (IMF):** The IMF is a global financial institution established to help stabilize exchange rates among the world's currencies and make loans as appropriate to improve the economies of member nations. Nearly 200 nations belong to the IMF, including the United States.

**Internet:** The Internet is a global network of computers. *See also* extranet *and* intranet.

**Internet-Based Networks:** Internet-based networks use Internet protocols and public communications channels to establish network communications.

**Interpretation:** The line-by-line translation of program source code to object code. Programs that are interpreted normally execute much more slowly than programs that are compiled because there is no optimization for execution speed. *See also* compilation.

**Intranet:** Intranets connect geographically separate LANs within a company. *See also* extranet *and* Internet.

**Inventoriable Costs:** Inventoriable costs are manufacturing costs (direct and indirect costs). *See also* full product costing.

**Inventory Conversion Period:** The inventory conversion period is the average inventory divided by the average cost of goods sold. *See also* cash conversion cycle *and* receivables collection period *and* payables deferral period.

**Inventory Turnover:** Inventory turnover is the cost of goods sold divided by the average inventory.

**Investment Turnover:** Investment turnover is another word for asset turnover. *See also* asset turnover.

**IP Address:** An IP address is an address assigned to users of a network or the Internet (assigned by the network information center [NIC]). IP addresses are written in dotted decimal notation (e.g., 123.11.1.123).

**Issue-Specific Policy:** An issue-specific policy addresses a specific issue of concern to the organization.

**Job Order Costing:** Job order costing, sometimes called job costing, is a cost accounting technique that involves the simple accumulation of all costs associated with a job, order, project, or activity. Job order costing is most effective for customized activities with easily traceable costs. Direct material and direct labor are traced to the individual jobs. Manufacturing overhead is applied to the individual jobs based on an overhead rate normally calculated at the beginning of the year based on the budgeted overhead costs divided by the estimated costs driver (such as the estimated number of units to be produced). *See also* process costing *and* cost driver.

**Joint Costs:** Joint costs are costs incurred in the production of two or more inseparable products from the same raw material or input. Joint costs stop at the split-off point where the products become separable; after that, the costs are called separable costs. The accounting treatment of joint costs depends on the character and value of the resulting products.

1. Joint products have relatively high values, and common costs must be allocated by some arbitrary means.

2. By-products have relatively low values, and any proceeds from their sale are a reduction of common costs or treated as miscellaneous income.

3. Scrap has little or no value, and any disposal cost adds to joint costs. Joint costs are often allocated using net realizable values at the split-off point.

**Junk Bonds:** Junk bonds are extremely risky bonds that are characterized by a high return to compensate for the risk. *See also* debenture *and* subordinated debenture *and* income bonds.

**Just-in-Time (JIT):** Just-in-time inventory systems, also called lean production systems, are inventory systems that minimize inventories by arranging for materials and sub-components to arrive just as they are needed and for goods to be made just in time to be shipped to customers. It is based on a "pull" approach, in which an item is produced only when it is requested further downstream in the production cycle. Raw materials are purchased in small quantities, enough only to meet immediate production demands.

**Kaizen:** Kaizen is continuous improvement. In practice, Kaizen can be implemented by improving every aspect of a business process in a step-by-step approach, while gradually developing employee skills through training, education, and increased involvement. The principles in Kaizen implementation are: (1) human resources are the most important firm asset; (2) processes must evolve by gradual improvement rather than by radical changes; and (3) improvement must be based on statistical/quantitative evaluation of process performance. *See also* statistical quality control.

**Kanban:** The Japanese refer to kanban as a simple parts-movement system that depends on cards and boxes/containers to take parts from one station to another on a production line. The essence of the kanban concept is that a supplier or the warehouse should deliver components to a production line only as they are needed so that there is no storage in the production area. Within a kanban system, stations located along production lines produce/deliver desired components only when they receive a card and an empty container indicating that more parts will be needed in production. *See also* just-in-time.

**Kilobyte (KB):** A kilobyte is approximately 1,000 bytes (actually 1,024 bytes).

**Kinked Demand Curve:** A kinked demand curve is the demand curve of an oligopolist. The kinked demand curve has different slopes above and below the prevailing price. *See also* oligopoly.

**Knowledge Management:** Knowledge management is gathering, management, and use of knowledge by an organization. It is also the process of improving an organization's management of its knowledge.

**Lagging Indicator:** A lagging indicator is an indicator (economic measure) that tends to follow economic activity. *See also* leading indicator.

**Law of Demand:** The law of demand is an economic proposition that states that the price of a product (or service) and the quantity demanded of that product (or service) are inversely related. *See also* law of supply.

**Law of Diminishing Returns:** The law of diminishing returns is the property by which output increases at a decreasing rate, as more and more units of an input are combined with a fixed amount of other inputs.

**Law of Supply:** The law of supply is an economic proposition that states that the price of a product or service and the quantity supplied of that product are positively related. *See also* law of demand.

**Leading Indicator:** A leading indicator is an indicator (economic measure) that tends to predict economic activity. *See also* lagging indicator.

**Lean:** Lean is shorthand for lean manufacturing or lean production. Lean anticipates that a production process can be made more efficient by identifying those efforts that add value to the customer and to limit efforts to those processes.

**Learning Curve:** Learning curve analysis is a step-by-step method of projecting costs for repetitive tasks where learning is a variable. The theory of learning recognizes that repetition of the same operation results in less time or effort expended on that operation. The direct labor hours necessary to complete a unit of production will decrease by a constant percentage each time the production quantity is doubled. While the learning curve emphasizes time, it can be easily extended to cost as well. The learning curve itself is a graphical representation of increased productivity per unit of time (e.g., per hour) as workers gain more experience with repetitive tasks.

**LIBOR:** LIBOR is a standard benchmark or reference rate for short-term interest rates. LIBOR stands for the London Interbank Offer Rate and is the rate of interest at which banks borrow funds from other banks in the London interbank market. *See also* Eurodollars.

**Line of Credit:** A line of credit is an informal agreement between a borrower and a bank indicating the maximum credit the bank will extend to the borrower. A revolving credit agreement is a formal line of credit.

**Liquidity Risk:** Liquidity risk is the risk that a security will not be able to be sold quickly without giving up a large price concession. *See also* default risk *and* maturity risk premium *and* interest rate risk.

**Loan Covenant:** Loan covenants are provisions in a bond indenture. The covenants can be either affirmative covenants or negative covenants. Affirmative covenants contain the activities that the issuer promises to do, such as a promise to pay interest and principal on a timely basis, a promise to keep certain assets (the collateral) in good condition and in working order, or a promise to submit periodic reports to the trustee. Negative covenants contain limitations and restrictions on the issuer's activities, such as restrictions on the issuer's ability to issue additional debt. *See also* bond indenture.

**Local Area Network (LAN):** LANs permit shared resources (software, hardware, and data) among computers within a limited area. LANs are normally privately owned, which means that they do not use telephone lines or that they use private lines leased from telecommunications providers. *See also* network *and* server *and* wide area network (WAN).

**Lockbox:** A lockbox system is a payment collection procedure in which payers send their payments to a nearby post office box that is emptied by the firm's bank several times a day. *See also* concentration banking *and* zero balance account.

**Long Run:** The long run is the period of time during which all of the costs of production are variable (i.e., a time frame that is long enough for fixed production facilities, technology, or institutional arrangements to be changed). *See also* short run.

**Long-Run Aggregate Supply (LRAS):** Long-run aggregate supply (potential GDP) is the economy's maximum rate of sustainable output given its current resource base, level of technology, and institutional arrangements. It is the optimal productive capacity of the economy that is dictated by the fixed plant and equipment assets currently in place. The long-run aggregate supply curve is vertical. Factors that shift the long-run aggregate supply curve are investment in new physical capital, improved technologies, additions to the raw materials resources, increases in the labor force, changes in institutional arrangements, and improvements in efficiency. The long-run aggregate supply is increased when people work harder and smarter. *See also* aggregate demand *and* aggregate supply.

**M1:** M1 is a measure of the money supply that includes cash, demand deposits, and traveler's checks. *See also* M2 *and* M3.

**M2:** M2 is a measure of the money supply that includes M1 plus savings deposits, time deposits less than $100,000, and money market mutual fund shares. *See also* M2 *and* M3.

**M3:** M3 is a measure of the money supply that includes M2 plus time deposits of more than $100,000. *See also* M1 *and* M2.

**Macro:** A macro is a series of prerecorded commands that will be executed on the occurrence of certain events.

**Magnetic Ink Character Reader (MICR):** A MICR reader is equipment that reads the magnetic ink characters on checks and similar documents.

**Maintenance:** Maintenance refers to both hardware maintenance (fixing the hardware) and software or application maintenance (fixing the software).

**Major Deficiency:** A material internal control deficiency or combination of deficiencies that significantly reduces the likelihood that an organization can achieve its objectives.

**Management by Objective:** Management by objective is a performance evaluation method that begins with the mutual development of goals for the upcoming performance evaluation period.

**Management Information System (MIS):** Management information systems, sometimes called management reporting systems, are a type of business information system. A management information system provides managerial and other end users with reports. *See also* accounting information system *and* decision support system *and* executive information system.

**Manufacturing Overhead:** Manufacturing overhead includes all costs associated with the manufacturing process that cannot easily be identified as part of the cost of the finished product. It can also be defined as all direct manufacturing costs other than direct materials and direct labor. Manufacturing overhead includes indirect material and indirect labor; factory rent; factory heat, light, and power; factory insurance; and factory depreciation. *See also* direct materials *and* direct labor.

**Margin of Safety:** The margin of safety is the excess of sales over sales at the breakeven point. *See also* breakeven point.

**Marginal Cost (MC):** Marginal cost is the change in total cost due to a one unit increase in output. *See also* marginal revenue *and* perfect competition.

**Marginal Product (MP):** Marginal product is the change in total product due to a one unit increase in the quantity of a variable input employed. *See also* marginal revenue product *and* total product.

**Marginal Propensity to Consume (MPC):** The marginal propensity to consume is the change in consumption due to a $1 increase in income. *See also* multiplier effect.

**Marginal Revenue (MR):** Marginal revenue is the change in total revenue due to a one unit increase in sales of the product. *See also* marginal cost *and* perfect competition.

**Marginal Revenue Product (MRP):** Marginal revenue product is the change in total revenue that results from employing an additional unit of input. It is computed as the marginal product of an input times the price of a firm's output. *See also* marginal product.

**Market Equilibrium:** Market equilibrium is the state in which there are no forces acting to change the current price/quantity combination of a good or service. It is the state of balance in a market.

**Market Risk:** Market risk is the risk of an individual stock or risk in a portfolio that cannot be eliminated by diversification. Market risk stems from factors that systematically affect most or all firms. Market risk is also called nondiversifiable risk. *See also* diversifiable risk *and* beta coefficient.

**Market Share Variance:** In target market analysis, market share variance is the budgeted contribution margin per unit times the actual units sold, times the difference between the actual market share and the budgeted market share. *See also* market size variance.

**Market Size Variance:** In target market analysis, market size variance is the budgeted contribution margin per unit times the budgeted market share, times the difference between the actual market size in units and the expected market size in units. *See also* market share variance.

**Master Budget:** A master budget is a budget for all of the planned activities of a firm. It normally is developed for a year at a time and normally includes an operating budget as well as a financial budget. The operating budget would include a sales budget; a production budget; and a selling, general, and administrative expenses budget. The financial budget would include a cash budget and pro forma (as if) financial statements. *See also* flexible budget.

**Materials Requirements Planning (MRP):** Materials resource planning systems extend the idea of computerized inventory control to manufacturing. Sales personnel estimate how many products will be sold in the future. The MRP system backtracks using estimated times to assemble each product. The system then explodes the product into lists of parts needed, using bills of materials for each product. The needed parts are ordered at times backdated from the assembly dates. *See also* bill of materials.

**Maturity Risk Premium:** A maturity risk premium is an interest premium to compensate investors for a longer maturity of bonds. *See also* credit risk *and* default risk *and* liquidity risk.

**Mbps:** Megabits per second (Mbps) is a measurement of data transmission speed. A megabit is 1 million bits. A T1 communications line is rated at 1.544 Mbps. Other common measures are kilobits per second (kbps), gigabits per second (Gbps), and terabits per second (Tbps).

**Megabyte:** A megabyte is approximately 1 million bytes (actually 1,048,576 bytes).

**Merger:** A merger involves one or more corporations merging into another corporation. One corporation survives the merger and continues in existence and the other merging corporations cease to exist following the merger.

**Mirroring:** Mirroring is the use of a backup computer to duplicate all of the processes and transactions on the primary computer. If the primary computer fails, the backup computer immediately takes its place without any interruption in service. Mirroring is often used by banks and other such organizations where any downtime is not acceptable.

**Mixed Costs:** Mixed costs are semi-variable costs and include both a fixed and a variable component. *See also* fixed costs *and* variable costs *and* relevant range.

**Monetary Assets and Liabilities:** Monetary assets and liabilities are assets and liabilities that are fixed in dollar amounts regardless of changes in specific prices or the general price level. *See also* nonmonetary assets and liabilities.

**Monetary Policy:** Monetary policy is the setting of the money supply by the Fed through the use of monetary policy tools to promote full employment and price stability. *See also* fiscal policy *and* contractionary monetary policy *and* expansionary monetary policy.

**Money Market Hedge:** A money market hedge is the simultaneous borrowing and lending transactions in two different currencies to lock in the domestic currency value of a foreign currency transaction. *See also* forward hedge *and* futures hedge *and* options hedge.

**Money Supply:** The money supply is the stock of all liquid assets (currency, checking account funds, and traveler's checks) available for transactions in the economy at any given point in time. *See also* M1 *and* M2 *and* M3.

**Monitoring:** As a component of the Internal Control–Integrated Framework (the Framework), monitoring contemplates ongoing and separate evaluations of the effectiveness of controls over financial reporting as well as reports of deficiencies, while as a component of Enterprise Risk Management–Integrated Framework (ERM) the concept is broadened to include general business operations.

**Monopolistic Competition:** Monopolistic competition is a market structure that consists of many firms each selling a slightly differentiated product. Under monopolistic competition, there are few barriers to entry but significant non-price competition in the market. *See also* perfect competition *and* monopoly.

**Monopoly:** A monopoly is a market structure that consists of one firm that is the only seller of a product. Under monopoly there are significant barriers to entry and no close substitutes for the good sold by the monopolist. Monopolists are price setters. *See also* price setter *and* oligopoly *and* natural monopoly.

**Monopsony:** A monopsony is a market in which there is only one buyer. In a labor market, there is only one employer. A monopsony, where there is only one buyer, is similar to a monopoly, where there is only one seller. *See also* monopoly.

**Mortgage Bond:** Mortgage bonds are bonds that are secured by liens on real assets of the issuer. *See also* debentures *and* subordinated debentures *and* junk bonds *and* income bonds.

**Multiplier Effect:** The multiplier effect is the magnified effect that an increase in household, firm, or government spending has on real GDP (i.e., a $1 increase in spending by households, firms, or the government results in a greater than $1 increase in real GDP). *See also* GDP *and* real GDP *and* nominal GDP *and* marginal propensity to consume.

**Multipolar:** The term multipolar is used to describe a world economy in which several nations have significant and potentially competing power. The growth of the world's emerging economies creates a multipolar environment.

**Multipolarity:** Multipolarity anticipates distributed power among nations and their economies.

**Multiprocessing:** Multiprocessing is the coordinated processing of programs by more than one processor. Multiprocessing is a general term that is divided into symmetric multiprocessing (in which one operating system controls the processing) and parallel processing (in which each processor has its own operating system). When multiple processors or computers process the same program, there is an efficiency loss to provide the control of the overall processing. *See also* multiprogramming *and* parallel processing.

**Multiprogramming:** Multiprogramming is several parts of a program running at the same time on a single processor. *See also* multiprocessing *and* parallel processing.

**National Income:** National income is net national product less indirect business taxes (sales taxes). *See also* net national product.

**National Income Accounting:** The national income accounting system is the process by which economic activity is measured on a national scale. *See also* national income.

**Natural Monopoly:** A natural monopoly is a monopoly that arises because economic and/or technical conditions permit only one efficient supplier. *See also* monopoly.

**Natural Rate of Unemployment:** The natural rate of unemployment is the normal rate of unemployment around which unemployment fluctuates due to cyclical unemployment. *See also* unemployment rate *and* cyclical unemployment.

**Net Book Value:** Net book value is the historical cost of an asset less its accumulated depreciation.

**Net Domestic Product:** Net domestic product is gross domestic product less depreciation. *See also* gross domestic product.

**Net National Product:** Net national product is gross national product less depreciation. *See also* gross national product *and* national income.

**Net Present Value Method (NPV):** The net present value method is a capital budgeting method that measures cash inflows and cash outflows of an investment at a single point in time by incorporating the time value of money and discounting each of the cash flows to that single point in time. One discount rate or different discount rates to reflect risk or inflation may be used. If the net present value is greater than zero (which means that the investment will at least earn the hurdle rate of return), the investment should be accepted; if the net present value is less than zero (which means that the investment will not earn the hurdle rate of return), the investment should not be accepted. *See also* internal rate of return method *and* hurdle rate of return.

**Network:** A network is an interconnected group of interconnected computers and terminals. The components of a network are computers, terminals, communications channels, communications processors, and communications software.

**Network Administrator:** Network administrators support computer networks. A network administrator sets up and configures a computer network so that multiple computers can share the same data and information. After a network is established, the work is mostly monitoring and troubleshooting. Sometimes, network administrators are called telecommunication analysts or network operators. *See also* security administrator.

**Network Monitoring:** Network monitoring is the monitoring of networks and the systems attached to them for slow or failing systems. Normally networks are monitored by a network management/monitoring system, with a network administrator checking for notifications and addressing problems. Intrusion detection software monitors the network for outside intrusions.

**Network Operating System (NOS):** A network operating system manages communication over a network. It may be either a peer-to-peer system (in which all nodes share in communications management) or a client/server system (in which a central machine serves as the mediator of communication on the network). *See also* operating system.

**Network Protocol:** Various pieces of hardware and software perform the various functions, all of which communicate by adhering to a common set of rules that allow them to communicate. The set of rules is called a communication or network protocol.

**Niche Strategy:** A niche strategy is a competitive strategy that focuses on a select group of consumers. *See also* cost leadership strategy *and* differentiation strategy *and* best cost strategy.

**Nominal GDP:** Nominal GDP is GDP measured in current (nominal) dollars (i.e., with current prices). *See also* GDP *and* real GDP *and* GDP deflator.

**Nominal Interest Rate:** The nominal interest rate is the amount of interest paid (or earned) measured in current dollars. Interest rates that are quoted in the financial press are nominal interest rates. *See also* real interest rate *and* inflation.

**Noncumulative Preferred Shares:** Shares with a preference usually are entitled to a fixed amount of money before distributions can be made with respect to nonpreferred shares. Unless the dividend is cumulative, the right to a dividend preference is extinguished if it is not declared for that year.

**Nondiversifiable Risk:** Nondiversifiable risk is another word for market or systematic risk. *See also* diversifiable risk.

**Nonmonetary Assets and Liabilities:** Nonmonetary assets and liabilities are assets and liabilities whose values fluctuate due to changes in specific prices or the general price level. *See also* monetary assets and liabilities.

**Normal Good:** A normal good is a good whose demand is positively related to income (positive income elasticity of demand). *See also* income elasticity of demand *and* inferior good.

**Normalization:** Normalization is the process of separating data into logical tables. Often, a process of data modeling is used. Before a relational database can be designed, a process of normalization has to occur. *See also* database *and* database administrator.

**Number of Days Sales in Inventory:** The number of days sales in inventory is ending inventory divided by cost of goods sold times 360 or 365.

**Objective Probability:** An objective probability is a probability based on past outcomes/historical data. The objective probability of an event is equal to the number of times that the event will occur divided by the total number of possible outcomes. Objective probabilities are also called empirical probabilities. Most people would assign approximately the same values to them. *See also* probability *and* subjective probability *and* expected value.

**Objective Setting:** A component of the Enterprise Risk Management–Integrated Framework (ERM) that defines the process for setting objectives, including strategic objectives, related objectives, and selected objectives, within the context of the risk appetite and tolerance of organization leadership.

**Oligopoly:** An oligopoly is a market structure that consists of a small number of firms selling similar products. Under an oligopoly, there are significant barriers to entry and strong interdependence among the firms within the market. *See also* monopoly *and* monopolistic competition.

**On-Demand Computing:** On-demand computing (also called utility computing) is the off-loading of peak demand processing to other data processing centers. Organizations can purchase and pay for computing power from central computing centers as that computing power is needed.

**Open Market Operations:** Open market operations are the buying and selling of government securities (Treasury bills and bonds) by the Fed.

**Operating Agreement:** An operating agreement is the internal document signifying the agreement between members of a limited liability company.

**Operating Cycle:** Operating cycle is another term for cash conversion cycle. *See also* cash conversion cycle.

**Operating Leverage:** Operating leverage is the degree to which a firm uses fixed operating costs (as opposed to variable operating costs) to magnify the effects of a given percentage change in sales on the percentage change in earnings before interest and taxes. It is calculated by the ratio of fixed operating costs to variable operating costs. *See also* financial leverage.

**Operating Risk:** Operating risk includes the risk of doing the right things in the wrong way. For example, assume that a payroll manager is supposed to run the biweekly payroll after the human resources manager enters newly hired employees into the system. If the payroll manager runs the payroll too early (i.e., before the newly hired employees are entered), the newly hired employees do not get paid, and the payroll report generated is inaccurate. *See also* financial risk *and* information risk.

**Operating System:** An operating system provides the interface between the user and the hardware. It defines what commands can be issued and how they are issued (e.g., typing in a command, pointing at an icon and clicking, issuing a verbal command, etc.). The operating system also controls all input and output to main memory, and it may include certain utility programs that might be used stand-alone or in application software. *See also* system programmer *and* network operating system *and* Unix.

**Operational Audit:** An operational audit provides a three-dimensional look at a company. Financial statements can illustrate problems, but normally cannot pinpoint the causes of the problems. During an operational audit, an objective third party probes deep inside the company, reviewing its operational and financial objectives, processes, tools, and controls, and focusing on the efficient or inefficient use of resources.

**Operational Costing:** Operational costing is a technique that blends concepts from job order costing and process costing and is applied to a batch production of homogeneous units processed through a sequence of activities. Work is organized by batch, similar to job order costing. Each activity (or each unit within a batch) is treated exactly the same, similar to process costing. Work orders initiate production for each job in operational costing. Materials are specific to the work order. Conversion costs (direct labor and manufacturing overhead) are applied on an average cost per unit basis, similar to process costing. *See also* job order costing *and* process costing.

**Opportunity Costs:** Opportunity costs are costs that would have been saved or the profit that would have been earned if another decision alternative had been selected. Accounting records do not record opportunity costs.

**Optimal Capital Structure:** The optimal or target capital structure is the capital structure that produces the lowest weighted average cost of capital and maximizes the price of a firm or at least of the firm's stock.

**Options Hedge:** An options hedge is a hedge transacted in the options market for foreign currencies. An option contract is an agreement between two parties where the purchaser of the option has the right, but not the obligation, to enter into a transaction at some future date and at a price agreed to at the time the agreement is made. In terms of foreign currencies, an options hedge entitles the option purchaser the right to either purchase or sell units of an individual currency for a negotiated price on a certain date. Outside the foreign currencies market, the instrument is normally called an option, without the word hedge. *See also* futures hedge *and* forward hedge *and* money market hedge.

**Output Controls:** Controls where system outputs are verified to enhance processing integrity.

**Outstanding Shares:** Outstanding shares are shares in shareholder's hands.

**Overapplied Overhead:** Overapplied overhead is manufacturing overhead applied to products that is greater than the actual overhead cost incurred. Depending on materiality, overapplied overhead is either allocated between ending inventory and cost of goods sold or just written off to cost of goods sold. *See also* underapplied overhead *and* overhead.

**Overhead:** Overhead is any manufacturing cost that is not material or labor. Overhead includes both fixed and variable components and is "applied" to the products. *See also* direct material *and* direct labor *and* overapplied overhead *and* underapplied overhead.

**Packet:** Packets are small pieces of data that travel over a network; they are normally small parts of the complete message. Each packet has a packet header to identify the packet and to indicate its sending and receiving locations. The whole thing is called the packet. *See also* packet filtering *and* firewall *and* application firewall.

**Packet Filtering:** Packet filtering examines packets of data as they pass through the firewall according to the rules that have been established for the source of the data, the destination of the data, and the network ports the data was sent from. Packet filtering is the simplest type of firewall configuration, but it can be circumvented by an intruder who forges an acceptable address (called IP spoofing). *See also* packet *and* firewall *and* application firewall.

**Par Value:** Par value is a specific face value placed on stock.

**Parallel Processing:** Parallel processing is the simultaneous use of more than one computer to execute a program, which first has to be divided into parts that can be executed separately. *See also* multiprocessing *and* multiprogramming.

**Pareto Diagram:** A Pareto diagram plots data in a hierarchical order, which allows the most significant or most frequent problems to be corrected first; it is a combination of a histogram with a line graph that displays the cumulative occurrence of the problems. The Pareto analysis technique is used primarily to identify and evaluate nonconformities, although it can summarize all types of data. Most quality problems result from a small number of problems, the so-called 80–20 rule (80 percent of the quality problems can be traced to 20 percent of the output). *See also* control chart *and* statistical quality control *and* cause-and-effect diagram.

**Payables Deferral Period:** The payables deferral period is the average accounts payable divided by the average daily purchases. *See also* cash conversion cycle *and* inventory conversion period *and* receivables collection period.

**Payback Method:** The payback method is a capital budgeting method that calculates the amount of time to recover the initial investment for an investment or project (i.e., the payback period). The shorter the payback period, the better. The normal payback method uses nondiscounted after-tax cash flows. *See also* discounted payback method.

**Perfect Competition:** Perfect competition is a market structure that consists of a very large number of sellers, each of which sells a nearly identical product. Under perfect competition, there are few barriers to entry and firms are price takers. Under perfect competition, short-run profits are maximized when prices are set so that marginal revenue equals marginal cost (Price = MR = MC). *See also* marginal revenue *and* marginal cost.

**Performance Standards:** Performance standards published by the Institute of Internal Auditors (IIA) address many of the same issues as fieldwork standards and reporting standards under GAAS. Issues related to planning and supervision of the engagement and documentation of evidence or basis for conclusions are addressed here along with generic reporting requirements.

**Period Costs:** Period costs are costs that are not the costs of producing the product manufactured and are thus not inventoriable. Period costs are charged to the period in which they are incurred. Selling and general and administrative costs are almost always period costs. *See also* product costs.

**Permanent File:** Master files represent data at a certain point in time. There are many different iterations of a master file; one for each point in time the master file is updated. Master files are permanent files and may be retained permanently or semi-permanently. Older iterations of a master file are often needed if significant processing problems are discovered and data has to be reconstructed. Master files that are kept permanently are called permanent files. *See also* temporary file.

**Personal Income:** Personal income is the income received by households and noncorporate businesses.

**Phillips Curve:** The Phillips curve is a curve that illustrates the typical inverse relationship between the rate of inflation and the unemployment rate. In the Phillips curve, the inflation rate is plotted on the y-axis and the unemployment rate is plotted on the x-axis. The curve normally slopes down to the right. *See also* inflation *and* unemployment rate.

**Phishing:** Phishing is the sending of phony e-mails to try to lure people to phony websites asking for financial information.

**Physical Access Controls:** Physical access controls encompass the physical security of IT assets, including access to facilities and access to programs and data. *See also* access controls *and* electronic access controls *and* application controls.

**Physical Design:** During the physical design phase, a company uses the conceptual design to develop detailed specifications to code and test the computer programs.

**Portal:** A portal (also corporate portal or enterprise portal) is a browser-based application that allows knowledge workers and other workers in an organization to gain access to, collaborate with, make decisions on, and take other actions on a wide variety of business-related information over a network. Web portals (e.g., Yahoo) are another type of portal that collect Web information and provide it to individual users.

**Practical Capacity:** Practical capacity is the maximum production that can be reached during normal operations with an allowance for normal downtime.

**Preventive Control:** Preventive controls are controls that reduce the occurrence of errors in the first place, i.e., they prevent errors from happening. *See also* corrective control *and* detective control.

**Prevention Costs:** In quality control, prevention costs are costs to prevent the production of defective units. These costs include inspection costs, preventive maintenance, redesign of products, redesign of processes, and the search for higher-quality suppliers. *See also* appraisal costs.

**Price Ceiling:** A price ceiling is a maximum price for a good or service established by law (e.g., rent control). If the price ceiling is set below the equilibrium price in a market, a shortage will develop. *See also* price floor.

**Price Elastic Demand:** Price elastic demand is when a 1 percent increase in price results in a greater than 1 percent decrease in the quantity demanded (i.e., when the absolute value of the price elasticity of demand is greater than 1). *See also* price inelastic demand.

**Price Elasticity of Demand:** Price elasticity of demand is the percentage change in quantity demanded divided by the percentage change in the price of a good or service.

**Price Elasticity of Supply:** Price elasticity of supply is the percentage change in quantity supplied divided by the percentage change in the price of a good or service.

**Price Floor:** A price floor is a minimum price for a good or service established by law (e.g., minimum wage). If the price floor is set above the equilibrium price in a market, a surplus will develop. *See also* price ceiling.

**Price Inelastic Demand:** Price inelastic demand is when a 1 percent increase in price results in a less than 1 percent decrease in quantity demanded (i.e., when the absolute value of the price elasticity of demand is less than 1). *See also* price elastic demand.

**Price Inelastic Supply:** Price inelastic supply is when a 1 percent increase in price results in a less than 1 percent increase in quantity supplied (i.e., when the price elasticity of supply is less than 1). *See also* price elasticity of supply.

**Price Searcher:** A price searcher is a firm that faces a downward sloping demand curve for its products. The amount that the firm will be able to sell is inversely related to the price that it charges. *See also* price taker *and* perfect competition.

**Price Setter:** The opposite of a price taker, a price setter has the power to set prices. For instance, a firm that faces a downward sloping demand curve can choose its price. *See also* price taker *and* monopoly.

**Price Taker:** A price taker is a firm that must take the market price in order to sell its products. Because each price taker's output is small in relation to the total market, price takers can sell all of their output at the market price, but they are unable to sell any of their output at a price higher than the market price. *See also* price searcher *and* perfect competition.

**Primary Market:** The primary market is where securities are created/initially issued. For stocks, this market is also called the initial public offering (IPO market). *See also* secondary market.

**Prime Costs:** Prime costs include direct material and direct labor. Prime costs are generally relevant to a costing decision. *See also* direct costs *and* indirect costs *and* cost object *and* variable costs *and* fixed costs.

**Probability:** A probability is the chance that an event will occur. Probabilities are assigned values between zero (0) and one (1). A zero probability indicates that there is no chance the event will ever occur (i.e., an impossibility). A probability of one indicates that the event will always occur (i.e., a certainty). *See also* objective probability *and* subjective probability *and* expected value.

**Process Costing:** Process costing is a cost accounting technique that is used when products are produced in a more-or-less continuous basis and when the products are indistinguishable from each other. Costs are accumulated by department, rather than by order as in job order costing, and are applied uniformly to all units that pass through the process during a period. Process costing is normally FIFO or weighted average. *See also* job order costing *and* cost driver *and* FIFO method of process costing *and* weighted average method of process costing.

**Process Management:** Process management represents a collection of different contemporary business concepts that include planning and monitoring the performance of a process to continuously improve the process and the resulting product to achieve objectives. Project management and business process reengineering are related to the concept of process management.

**Processing Controls:** Processing controls are programmed controls that verify that all transactions are processed correctly (completely and accurately) during file maintenance. *See also* input controls.

**Product Costs:** Product costs are the costs of producing the product manufactured and are thus inventoriable. Direct material, direct labor, and manufacturing overhead are product costs. Product costs normally become part of the cost of goods manufactured when the products are completed and the cost of goods sold when the products are sold. *See also* period costs.

**Production Cycle:** The production cycle is a transaction cycle characterized by the conversion of resources (e.g., raw material or time) into products or services. *See also* transaction cycles.

**Production Function:** The production function is the relationship between the firm's input of productive resources and its output of goods and services.

**Production Possibilities Curve:** A production possibilities curve identifies the amount of two different goods or services that can be produced with a given amount of resources when those resources are fully employed. Production possibilities curves are often used in the analysis of international trade. *See also* comparative advantage.

**Profit:** Profit is total revenue less total cost.

**Profitability Index:** The profitability index is used to rank qualifying investments. The index is the present value of the future cash flows divided by a project's or an investment's initial cost (or the present value of the cash outflows if the investment is not all at time 0). Mathematically, for independent investments, if the net present value of a project or an investment is greater than zero, its internal rate of return will be greater than the hurdle rate of return and the profitability index will be greater than 1.0.

**Program-Framework Policy:** A program-framework policy establishes an organization's approach to computer security (i.e., a computer security framework).

**Program-Level Policy:** A program-level policy is used to create a management-sponsored computer security program.

**Programming Language:** Programming languages allow programmers to write programs in source code. The programs are then translated into object code for execution. There are many different programming languages, each with strengths and weaknesses.

**Project:** A project is a temporary undertaking intended to produce a unique service, product, or result. Unlike continuing operations, a project has a definite beginning and an end.

**Push Reporting:** Under push reporting, information can actually be "pushed" and sent to a computer screen or computer desktop. Push reporting requires determination of the data that is to be selected for an end user, selection of the specified data by the push reporting software, and delivery of the specified data to the end user, but it can be more automated, even from the Internet. Delivery of the information can be to a PC, a PDA, or a cellular phone, depending on volume of the response. Push reports can be specific internal reports of a particular organization, or they can be general industry reports or information downloaded and possibly aggregated from the Internet.

**Quality:** Quality embraces a wide variety of concepts, including the perceived quality of products to consumers that result from enhanced features (a luxury vs. an economy car) or the engineering or manufacturing definitions of quality that pertain to conformance of goods to manufacturing specifications within tolerable limits.

**Quantity Demanded:** The quantity demanded is the maximum quantity of a good or service that consumers are willing and able to purchase at each and every price.

**Quantity Supplied:** The quantity supplied is the maximum amount of a good or service that a firm is willing and able to produce at each and every price.

**Quick Ratio:** The quick ratio is cash plus marketable securities plus receivables divided by current liabilities. *See also* current ratio *and* working capital.

**Real GDP:** Real GDP is GDP measured in dollars adjusted for inflation (i.e., in dollars of constant purchasing power). Inflation is measured by the GDP deflator, which is a measure of inflation somewhat like the more widely known consumer price index. *See also* GDP deflator *and* consumer price index.

**Real Interest Rate:** The real interest rate is the amount of interest paid (or earned) adjusted for inflation. The real interest rate is the nominal interest rate minus the inflation rate. *See also* nominal interest rate *and* inflation.

**Receivables Collection Period:** The receivables collection period is average accounts receivable divided by average daily sales. *See also* cash conversion cycle *and* inventory conversion period *and* payables deferral period.

**Recession:** A recession occurs when the economy experiences negative real economic growth for two consecutive quarters. *See also* depression *and* business cycle.

**Record:** A record is a group of fields that represents the data that is being stored for a particular entity, such as a customer or an account receivable. *See also* bit and byte *and* file and field.

**Referential Integrity:** In a relational database, referential integrity prevents the deletion of key values in related records (tables). For instance, if there is a relational database with customer records (tables) and invoice records (tables), the invoice records normally contain a customer number that references back to the customer record. If a customer is deleted, the invoice records with that customer's numbers should be updated or deleted. Referential integrity is enforced by the database management system.

**Regression Analysis:** Regression analysis is a method for determining the relationship between two or more variables. Simple regression analysis involves one dependent variable and one independent variable. Multiple regression analysis involves more than one independent variable. Often, the determination of whether there is a relationship, and the strength of that relationship if there is one, is called correlation analysis. Regression analysis is purely the determination of the actual regression equation (the intercept and slope coefficients of the regression line). *See also* coefficient of correlation *and* coefficient of determination *and* standard error of the estimate *and* high-low method.

**Reinvestment Risk:** Reinvestment risk is the risk that intermediate cash flows from a bond (interest payments or proceeds from a bond refunding) will have to be invested at a lower interest rate than the original bond (if interest rates have decreased in the meantime). *See also* interest rate risk *and* credit risk.

**Relevant Costs:** Relevant costs are future costs that will change as a result of selecting different alternatives. Costs that will not change as a result of selecting different alternatives are not relevant because they will not impact the total costs that will result from the decision. *See also* sunk costs.

**Relevant Range:** The relevant range is a range of activity levels in which cost behavior characteristics (fixed or variable) are valid. Within a relevant range, fixed costs are assumed to remain the same (i.e., they do not change). *See also* fixed costs *and* variable costs *and* mixed costs.

**Replication:** Replication (file or database replication) is the duplication of files or databases in their entirety, normally in different physical locations.

**Reporting Currency:** The reporting currency is the currency in which an entity prepares its financial statements, normally the U.S. dollar. *See also* functional currency.

**Required Reserves Ratio (RRR):** The required reserves ratio is the fraction of total deposits the Fed requires banks to hold in reserve (not be loaned). The required reserves ratio is the inverse of the multiplier.

**Residual Income:** Residual income is the excess of a firm's net income over its required rate of return. *See also* economic value added.

**Responsibility Accounting:** Responsibility accounting is an accounting system that provides information to management about the performance of other parts of the organization by the type of responsibility assigned to each part of the organization (e.g., responsibility for cost containment in cost centers and responsibility for revenue production in revenue centers). *See also* strategic business unit.

**Return on Assets (ROA):** Return on assets is a firm's profit margin multiplied by its asset turnover. Return on assets can also be calculated as net income divided by total assets. *See also* asset turnover.

**Return on Investment (ROI):** Return on investment is a firm's operating income divided by its average operating assets. Net operating income is income before interest and taxes (EBIT). Operating assets are cash, accounts receivable, inventory, plant and equipment, and all other assets held for productive use in the firm. Operating assets are normally measured at net book value, but they may be measured at cost.

**Revenue Cycle:** The revenue cycle is a transaction cycle characterized by the sales of goods or services that produce cash or other assets (e.g., receivables). *See also* transaction cycles.

**Rework:** The process and related cost of converting defective units into goods meeting production specifications is termed rework. Some imperfections are anticipated as part of the manufacturing process. Normal rework is included in standards and is included in manufacturing overhead.

**Risk Assessment:** As a component of the Internal Control–Integrated Framework (the Framework), risk assessment includes the risk of material misstatement of financial statements. As a component of Enterprise Risk Management–Integrated Framework (ERM), the concept is broadened to embrace the evaluation of risk as part of overall operational management and the criteria and techniques that might be used to fully assess risk.

**Risk Averse:** Risk averse means that the investor does not seek out risk and thus will demand a higher return for accepting risk in an investment.

**Risk-Free Rate:** The risk-free rate is the interest rate that would be paid on a riskless security. It is approximated by the interest rate on short-term U.S. Treasury securities. The real risk-free rate assumes no inflation; the nominal risk-free rate assumes inflation so that the nominal risk-free rate is the real risk-free rate plus an inflation risk premium.

**Risk Response:** A component of the Enterprise Risk Management–Integrated Framework (ERM) that defines the process for identifying the range of responses to enterprise risk.

**Safety Stock:** A safety stock is the level of inventory that is maintained to ensure that supply requirements are met.

**Sales Mix Variance:** In target market analysis, sales mix variance is the budgeted contribution margin per unit times the actual units sold times the difference between the actual sales mix and the budgeted sales mix. The sales mix variance is also the sales volume variance less the sales quantity variance.

**Sales Quantity Variance:** In target market analysis, sales quantity variance is the budgeted contribution margin per unit times the budgeted sales mix times the difference between the actual units sold and the budgeted sales volume. The sales quantity variance is also the sales volume variance less the sales mix variance.

**Sales Volume Variance:** In target market analysis, sales volume variance is the standard contribution margin per unit times the difference between the actual units sold and the budgeted sales volume.

**Sarbanes-Oxley Act of 2002:** Legislation that amended federal securities laws after a series of corporate financial scandals exposed serious weaknesses in the self-regulating system that had been intended to provide reliable company financial statements. Provisions of the act expand the responsibility of both auditors and corporate financial managers to annually assess the adequacy of internal controls.

**Scalability:** Scalability is the ability of a computer, computer product, or system to expand to serve a greater amount of users.

**Schema:** A description of the types of data elements that are in a database, the relationships among the data elements, and the structure used to organize the data. *See also* database.

**Scorched Earth Policy:** When a corporation is faced with the prospect of being taken over and the board of directors wants to resist the takeover attempt, it will sell off assets or take out loans that would make the company less financially attractive.

**Scrap:** Materials remaining after the manufacturing process that have a minor value in relation to primary products. Scrap is generally either sold or reused.

**Seasonal Unemployment:** Seasonal unemployment is the unemployment that arises from seasonal changes in the demand and supply of labor. *See also* structural unemployment *and* unemployment rate.

**Secondary Market:** Secondary markets are markets other than the primary market, where securities are traded among investors. *See also* primary market.

**Secondary Storage:** Secondary storage devices (e.g., hard drives or magnetic disks, flash drives, CD-ROM disks, optical disks, and magnetic tape) are a means to permanently store programs and data. With sequential storage devices (such as tapes), data is accessed sequentially. With random storage devices, data is normally accessed randomly.

**Security Administrator:** Security administrators are responsible for the assignment of initial passwords and often the maintenance of those passwords (if the end users do not maintain their own passwords). Security administrators are responsible for the overall operation of the various security systems and the security software in general. *See also* database administrator *and* system programmer *and* network administrator.

**Segregation of Duties:** Segregation of duties is defined as dividing responsibilities for different portions of a transaction (authorization, recording, and custody) among several different people or departments. The objective is to prevent any one person from having total control over all aspects of the transaction. Because many transactions in an IT environment are actually performed by the application software, segregation of duties in an IT environment normally revolves around granting and/or restricting access to production programs and to production data.

**Selling Price Variance:** In target market analysis, selling price variance is the actual units sold times (the actual selling price per unit less the budgeted selling price per unit). *See also* sales mix variance *and* sales volume variance.

**Sensitivity Analysis:** Sensitivity analysis is the process of experimenting with different parameters and assumptions regarding a model and recording the results.

**Server:** A server is a node dedicated to providing services or resources to the rest of the network (e.g., a file server maintains centralized application and data files, a print server provides access to high-quality printers, a database server provides access to a specific database, etc.). A server is generally not directly accessible by individual users but only through the network software. *See also* local area network (LAN).

**Service-Level Agreement:** From a telecommunications standpoint, a service-level agreement (SLA) is an agreement by a PSDN provider (carrier) to provide a certain level of service within the cloud. Service-level agreements can also be used wherever levels of service can be quantified and measured.

**Shareholder:** A shareholder is a party owning an interest in a corporation (also called a stockholder). A shareholder has a limited right to manage.

**Shareware:** Terminology for some types of application software includes groupware/shareware (which is short for group working software), software that lets different people work on the same documents and coordinate their work activities.

**Shifts in the Economic Balance of Power:** The ability of the world's emerging nations to contend with the economies of the industrialized world for power, resources, influence, etc., is a change or shift in the economic balance of power from previous decades. Balance of power theory holds that the states that are members of the global economy can either engage in balancing or bandwagoning behavior. An emerging nation might side with the United States or other industrialized nations in adopting standards that reduce greenhouse emissions that contribute to global warming (bandwagoning) or could join with other emerging nations in ignoring the leadership of the United States (balancing). The significance of an emerging nation's possible decision to change the impact of the effectiveness of environmental controls represents an important shift in the balance of economic power.

**Short Run:** The short run is a period of time during which some of the costs of production are fixed (i.e., a time frame that is not long enough for fixed production facilities, technology, or institutional arrangements to be changed). *See also* long run.

**Simple Interest:** Simple interest is interest computed without any compounding. *See also* compound interest.

**Six Sigma:** Six Sigma is a process improvement strategy initially adopted in manufacturing. The name Six Sigma is based on a statistical quality measurement that indicates near zero defects. The foundational premise of Six Sigma is the idea that product defects can be removed by improving business processes and eliminating variability of the manufacturing process. Quality management methods that utilize statistical techniques characterize Six Sigma. Methods are so technical that they often require specially trained individuals to fully implement the ideas. Degrees of expertise in Six Sigma are identified by titles borrowed from the martial arts (e.g., Black Belts, Green Belts, etc.). Six Sigma projects follow a defined sequence of steps and have quantified targets.

**Software:** Software is the systems and programs that process data and turn that data into information. Software can be very general and be used by any organization (e.g., a word processing program such as WordPerfect® or Microsoft Word®). Software also can be very specific (e.g., an internal auditing program). Software can be developed internally by the organization or can be purchased as an application package from an outside vendor. Software can be divided into the categories of system software, programming languages, and application software. *See also* system programmer.

**Software Distribution:** Software distribution refers to the process of distributing software updates and also to the various parts of an organization that use the software (e.g., an organization with multiple branch offices using the same software at each branch will want to have the same version of the software running at each office).

**Software Piracy:** Software piracy is the illicit copying of software and selling it. Software piracy is a subset of copyright infringement of software.

**Software Vulnerability:** A software vulnerability is a weakness in a system that allows attacks on the system.

**Source Code:** Source code is the program instructions written by a programmer. Source code is compiled (to produce object code) or interpreted.

**Spam:** Spam is unsolicited commercial e-mail, sent in bulk to many users in substantially the same form at the same time.

**Spending Variance:** The spending variance is the actual overhead less the budget based on the actual hours worked. If variable overhead only is being analyzed, the formula can be expressed as the actual hours times (the difference between the actual rate and the standard rate), and the formula corresponds to the direct material price variance and the direct labor rate variance. *See also* direct material price variance *and* direct labor rate variance *and* efficiency variance *and* budget variance *and* volume variance.

**Spoilage:** Spoilage is generally defined as waste. Accounting treatment for spoilage depends on the character of the spoilage. Normal spoilage is waste that cannot be avoided; it occurs under normal efficient operations. Normal spoilage is a product cost. Equivalent units of production include spoiled units (normal spoilage). Abnormal spoilage is waste that is not expected to occur during normal operations. Abnormal spoilage is a period cost as a separate component of cost of goods sold.

**Spoiled Goods:** Spoiled goods are products that fail to meet quality specifications or standards.

**Spot Rate:** The spot rate, sometimes called the spot exchange rate, is the price at which foreign exchange can be bought or sold with payment set for the same day. The term spot rate also means the current interest rate for a bond of a specific maturity (and has nothing to do with currency or forward exchange). *See also* forward exchange rate.

**Spyware:** Spyware is a broad category of malicious software designed to take control or partial control of a computer's operation without the informed consent of the computer's owner and gather information with the user's consent (e.g., keystroke loggers and screen capture programs).

**Standard Costs:** Standard costs are a firm's target costs, or the costs it hopes to attain or expects to incur in a production process, based on the information used to determine the standards. In a standard costing system, standard costs are used for all manufacturing costs. *See also* ideal standards *and* currently attainable standards.

**Standard Error of the Estimate:** In regression analysis, the standard error of the estimate is a measure of how good the estimate is. The standard error indicates the closeness of the estimate to the actual results (i.e., how perfect the regression line is in predicting the dependent variable). *See also* regression analysis *and* coefficient of correlation *and* coefficient of determination.

**Stated Interest Rate:** The stated interest rate is the coupon rate on the bond. *See also* effective interest rate *and* annual percentage rate.

**Statistical Quality Control:** Statistical quality control, or statistical process control, is a formal means of distinguishing between random variations and nonrandom variations in an operating or production process. *See also* control chart *and* Pareto diagram *and* Kaizen.

**Steering Committee:** A steering committee is a committee formed by organizations to guide and oversee systems development and acquisition.

**Step-Variable Costs:** The term step-variable costs is a synonym for semi-variable or semi-fixed costs and contemplates an increase in costs with an increase in capacity. Step-variable costs behave like fixed costs over a portion of the relevant range and then increase incrementally in a stairstep manner as capacity increases. For example, insurance expense may be fixed over a particular range of production within the overall relevant range but may increase incrementally as the number of locations or number of hours worked increases.

**Stockout Cost:** The cost of a stockout, which includes loss of income from product unavailability, the cost of restoring customer goodwill, and additional expenses to expedite shipping.

**Strategic Business Unit (SBU):** A strategic business unit, sometimes called a responsibility center, is any part of an organization whose manager has control over cost, revenue, or investment funds. SBUs are divided into cost SBUs (managers are responsible for controlling costs), revenue SBUs (managers are responsible for generating revenues), profit SBUs (managers are responsible for producing a target profit), and investment SBUs (managers are responsible for producing a target return on investment). *See also* responsibility accounting.

**Strategic Risk:** Strategic risk includes the risk of choosing inappropriate technology. For example, an organization may choose a Web-based program to share data between remote offices in different cities. If one of the offices does not have a high-speed Internet connection and cannot enter data at the same speed as the other offices, this problem could lead to the generation of reports thought to be up-to-date but in reality missing data from the office with the slow Internet connection. *See also* financial risk *and* information risk *and* operating risk.

**Structural Unemployment:** Structural unemployment is the unemployment that arises when the skills of workers do not match the skills demanded by employers and when qualified workers do not live where jobs they are qualified for are located. *See also* seasonal unemployment *and* cyclical unemployment *and* frictional unemployment *and* unemployment rate.

**Structured Query Language (SQL):** Database query is most often provided in a relational database by a language called SQL. SQL provides the ability to "select" data from individual tables in a database based on the data satisfying certain conditions (customers who had ordered more than a certain amount in a certain period) and to "join" certain tables such as suppliers and part numbers, etc. SQL consists of a data definition language (DDL), which is used to define the database; a data manipulation language (DML), which is used to query the database; and a data control language (DCL). *See also* database.

**Subjective Probability:** A subjective probability is the probability based on an individual's belief about the likelihood that a given event will occur. It is estimated based on judgment and past experience of the likelihood of future events. *See also* probability *and* objective probability *and* expected value.

**Subordinated Debenture:** A subordinated debenture is a debenture that is subordinated to (lower than) other debt in terms of payment in the event of bankruptcy. Subordinated debentures may be subordinated to certain types of debt or to all other debt. *See also* debenture.

**Substitutes:** Substitutes or substitute products are products that serve similar purposes. They are related such that an increase in the price of one will cause an increase in demand for the other. *See also* complements.

**Sunk Costs:** Sunk costs are previously incurred costs that have already been incurred and that cannot be avoided regardless of what a decision maker might decide. Sunk costs are irrelevant to a particular decision. For example, depreciation on existing equipment is a sunk cost as long as the equipment is retained. Ignoring a change in accounting principle, sunk costs can be changed only if the equipment is disposed of. *See also* expired costs *and* unexpired costs *and* committed costs.

**Supply Chain Management (SCM):** Supply chain management is the integration of business processes from the customer to the original supplier and includes purchasing, materials handling, production planning and control, logistics and warehousing, inventory control, and product distribution and delivery. SCM systems may perform some or all of these functions. *See also* ERP *and* CRM.

**Supply Curve:** A supply curve is a curve that illustrates the relationship between the price of a good or service and the quantity supplied of that good or service. Price is plotted on the *y*-axis and quantity is plotted on the *x*-axis. *See also* demand curve.

**Supply Shock:** A supply shock is a surprise occurrence that temporarily increases or decreases current output. Supply shocks will thus decrease short-run aggregate supply without directly affecting long-run aggregate supply. *See also* short-run aggregate supply *and* long-run aggregate supply.

**System Access Log:** System access logs are electronic lists of who has accessed or attempted to access systems or parts of systems or data or subsets of data. *See also* electronic access controls *and* system access log.

**System Analysis:** System analysis is the phase of the system development life cycle where management gathers information needed to purchase or develop a new system.

**System Analyst:** The information technology professional charged with design of an internally developed application system and, depending on the application system, the type of computer network needed, and changes to the overall network. The system analyst's responsibility is to work with the end users to determine the requirements for a system, and then design the specifics of the system to satisfy those requirements. The roles of system analysts are sometimes combined with that of programmers to create programmer/analysts. If an application package is purchased from an outside vendor and installed, system analysts may be called system integrators. In that case, his/her responsibilities may be to learn the purchased application (so that the system can be maintained after it is installed), to integrate that application with existing internal and package applications by designing interfaces with the existing applications, to determine how to convert the initial data for the application from other applications or manually, and to provide training to end users.

**System Design:** System design is the phase of the system development life cycle that includes specifying the input, processing, output, user interface, and file or database design. It is also when controls and security should be developed.

**System Development Life Cycle (SDLC):** SDLC is a framework for planning and controlling the detailed activities associated with system development.

**System Programmer:** A system programmer is responsible for installing, supporting (troubleshooting), monitoring, and maintaining the operating system (and often the related hardware if that function is not performed by a separate hardware technician). System programmers may also forecast hardware capacity and perform other capacity planning functions. In complex computing environments, a considerable amount of time can be spent testing and applying operating system upgrades. *See also* application software *and* application service provider.

**System Software:** System software consists of the programs that run the computer and support system management operations. *See also* application software *and* system programmer.

**Systematic Interdependence:** Systematic interdependence (of nations and their economies) acknowledges that all members of the global community share planet Earth. Actions of governments that adversely affect the climate or reduce our safety (nuclear proliferation) affect all nations.

**System-Specific Policy:** A system-specific policy is a policy that management has decided to implement for a specific system (e.g., the payroll system).

**Target Costs:** Target costs are standard costs developed in connection with a known selling price. Target costing backs into the level of costs that can be allowed for a given product in order to meet profitability objectives.

**TCP:** Transport control protocol (TCP) is the transmission protocol of the Internet protocol suite.

**TCP/IP:** TCP/IP is the network protocol used on the Internet. TCP/IP creates a packet-switching network, where a message is split into pieces by the sending end and put back together by the receiving end. The sending end attaches a header to each piece of each message, and the header information (which includes the destination address) is used to put the message back together again.

**Temporary File:** Temporary files are files that are not permanent files. *See also* permanent file.

**Terabyte (TB):** A terabyte is approximately 1 trillion bytes (actually 1,099,511,627,776 bytes).

**Theory of Constraints (TOC):** The theory of constraints is a management philosophy that contends that manageable systems and processes are limited from achieving their goals by one or more identifiable constraints. The TOC process seeks to identify the constraint(s) and restructure the business operations around the constraint(s). Business process improvement using theory of constraints anticipates the use of five focusing steps to work around the constraint, including identifying the constraint; taking organization-wide measures to exploit, leverage, or eliminate the constraint; and then verify that the process is working.

**Threat:** A threat is any eventuality that represents a danger to an asset or a capability linked to hostile intent. *See also* vulnerability.

**Throughput Costing (Super-Variable Costing):** Throughput costing is a relatively recent development in costing methods. This method assumes that the only truly variable costs are the costs for direct materials, so these are the only costs assigned to the product. All other costs (including direct labor) are expensed on the throughput contribution margin statement in the period in which they occur. *See also* absorption costing *and* variable costing.

**Token:** A token is a physical device similar to an identification card that identifies a particular user.

**Total Cost (TC):** Total cost is the amount a firm must pay for the resources used to produce its products. Total cost is the sum of the total fixed cost plus the total variable cost. *See also* total fixed cost *and* total variable cost.

**Total Cost of Ownership (TCO):** Total cost of ownership (TCO) is the total cost of hardware or software, including the original purchase price, ongoing maintenance, and support costs.

**Total Fixed Cost (TFC):** Total fixed cost is the total of the fixed costs of a firm. *See also* total variable cost.

**Total Leverage:** Total leverage is operating leverage plus financial leverage. *See also* operating leverage *and* financial leverage.

**Total Output (Q):** Total output is another name for total product.

**Total Product:** Total product is the total amount of output produced by a firm.

**Total Quality Management (TQM):** Total quality management represents an organizational commitment to customer performance that emphasizes both quality and continuous improvement. The factors of TQM are customer focus, continuous improvement, workforce involvement, top management support, objective measures of quality, timely recognition of achievements, and ongoing training.

**Total Revenue (TR):** Total revenue is the price of a product times the number of units sold.

**Total Variable Cost (TVC):** Total variable cost is the total of the variable costs of a firm. *See also* total fixed cost.

**Trade Acceptance:** A trade acceptance is a draft drawn by the seller of goods on the buyer and accepted by a commercial enterprise at a specified future date. The trade acceptance may be marketable at a discount depending on the buyer's creditworthiness. *See also* banker's acceptance.

**Trade Credit:** Trade credit is the use of credit from suppliers to finance current operations. It includes accounts payable, accrued expenses (expenses that have not become accounts payable yet), notes payable (accounts payable that have been formalized in notes), and trade acceptances.

**Transaction Cycles:** Similar economic events are typically grouped for repetitive processing into five transaction cycles. Transaction cycles are most frequently revenue, expenditure, production, human resources, and financing. Individual industries might have additional or customized transaction cycles.

**Transaction Exposure:** Transaction exposure is the risk that a firm could suffer economic loss or experience economic gain upon settlement of individual transactions as a result of change in foreign exchange rates. *See also* translation exposure *and* economic exposure.

**Transaction Processing System:** Transaction processing systems are the systems that process and record the routine daily transactions necessary to conduct the business. The functions of such a system are normally predefined and highly structured. *See also* decision support system *and* executive information system *and* management information system.

**Transfer Price:** A transfer price is the price charged for a good or service by one division (or segment) of a business to another division (or segment) of a business. Transfer prices may be based on market price, cost, or a negotiated amount.

**Translation Exposure:** Translation exposure is the risk that a company's equity, assets, or income will change in value as a result of foreign exchange rate changes. Translation exposure is also known as accounting exposure. *See also* transaction exposure *and* economic exposure.

**Treasury Bills:** Treasury bills, or T-Bills, are short-term securities that can be purchased either directly from the U.S. Treasury or through a bank or broker. Treasury bills are sold at a discount and are issued at maturities of one year or less.

**Treasury Bonds:** Treasury bonds are coupon securities (they pay interest) issued by the U.S. Treasury and whose original maturities are more than 10 years.

**Treasury Notes:** Treasury notes are coupon securities (they pay interest) issued by the U.S. Treasury and whose original maturities are more than one year and up to 10 years.

**Treasury Shares:** Treasury shares are issued shares that are sometimes repurchased by the corporation (called "issued but not outstanding").

**Trojan Horse:** A Trojan horse is a seemingly innocuous program in which malicious or harmful program code is hidden.

**T-Value:** In sampling with a normal distribution, a factor called the z-value is used for determining confidence intervals around a sample mean. The z-value is used when the data in the population are normally distributed with a known standard deviation. When the data in the population are not normally distributed or the standard deviation of the population is not known, the appropriate factor to use for the same purpose is called a t-value. It is based on the t-distribution, which approximates the normal distribution, especially as the sample size increases. *See also* regression analysis *and* coefficient of correlation *and* coefficient of determination *and* standard error of the estimate.

**Underapplied Overhead:** Underapplied overhead is manufacturing overhead applied to products that is less than the actual overhead cost incurred. Depending on materiality, underapplied overhead is either allocated between ending inventory and cost of goods sold or just written off to cost of goods sold. *See also* overapplied overhead.

**Unemployment Rate:** The unemployment rate is the ratio of the number of people classified as unemployed to the total labor force. The total labor force includes all noninstitutionalized individuals 16 years of age or older who are either working or actively looking for work. An unemployed person is defined as a person 16 years of age or older who is available for work and who has actively sought employment during the previous four weeks.

**Unexpired Costs:** Unexpired costs are costs that are reasonably expected to benefit future periods and should be carried forward as an asset. *See also* expired costs *and* sunk costs.

**Uniform Resource Locator (URL):** A uniform resource locator (URL) is a string of characters that refers to specific resources on a computer. URLs consist of three parts: (1) the protocol that will be used (e.g., the http in http://); (2) the computer on which the requested resource is located (e.g., www.beckerreview.com/); and (3) the resource (file) requested (e.g., students).

**Uninterruptible Power Supply (UPS):** A UPS is a device that maintains a continuous supply of electrical power to connected equipment. UPS is also called battery backup.

**Unipolar:** The term unipolar is used to describe a system (such as the world economy) with one dominant power. Currently the United States is the lone super power in the world. U.S. dominance is an illustration of unipolarity.

**Unipolarity:** Unipolarity anticipates concentration of economic power in one nation and its economy.

**Unit Elastic Demand:** Unit elastic demand is when a 1 percent increase in price results in a 1 percent decrease in quantity demanded (i.e., when the absolute value of the price elasticity of demand is equal to 1). *See also* price elasticity of demand.

**United Nations (U.N.):** The United Nations consists of nearly 200 countries. The goals of the U.N. include facilitating cooperation in international law and security, economic development, and the achievement of world peace.

**UNIX:** UNIX is an operating system designed for minicomputers.

**Unshielded Twisted Pair (UTP):** UTP is the standard telephone wiring (two strands of wire twisted together).

**Validity Check:** A validity check is a validation step performed on a data element to ensure that it is in a valid code table, such as product numbers, or that the data is within an appropriate range or that the data is otherwise valid in combination with other data elements. *See also* check digit *and* field check.

**Value Added Activities:** Value added activities in a value chain are those activities that increase product value. Non-value added activities are activities that do not add value. *See also* value chain.

**Value Added Network (VAN):** Value added networks are privately owned and managed communications networks that provide additional services beyond standard data transmission. VANs are often used for electronic data interchange. *See also* electronic data interchange (EDI).

**Value at Risk:** Value at risk is a calculation that allows a firm to estimate the maximum amount that it might expect to lose in an asset portfolio in a given time period with a given probability. It is a measure used to estimate how the value of the portfolio might decrease over a certain time period under usual conditions. It has two parameters: the time period and the confidence level at which the estimate is made. The time period is usually one day or 10 days. Confidence levels are usually 99 or 95 percent.

**Value Chain:** The value chain defines each major activity that adds value to the products or services produced by a firm. Comprehensive value chains typically begin with product development and end with product delivery. *See also* value added activities.

**Value Chain Analysis:** The value chain defines each of the major activities that add value to the products or services produced by an organization. Comprehensive value chains are typically represented as beginning with product development and ending with product delivery. Value chain analysis is the determination of what constitutes the value chain. Steps in value chain analysis are (1) identifying the value chain activities; (2) identifying the cost drivers associated with each activity; and (3) developing a competitive advantage by reducing cost or adding value.

**Value Engineering:** Value engineering is the identification of the functions of a product or service with the objective of providing those functions at the lowest total cost. Value engineering incorporates the systematic application of recognized techniques to identify product and service functions.

**Variable (Direct) Costing:** Variable costing is a method of product costing that includes only variable manufacturing costs (i.e., direct materials, direct labor, and variable manufacturing overhead) as part of product costs. All other costs, including fixed manufacturing overhead, are treated as period costs. Variable costing is not GAAP for financial statement purposes.

**Variable Cost Ratio:** The variable cost ratio is defined as variable costs divided by total sales.

**Variable Costs:** Variable costs are costs that change proportionately in total relative to changes in production within the relevant range. Variable costs per unit remain constant, but vary directly in total with changes in units. Almost any cost is variable in the long term (because the relevant range will change over time). *See also* fixed costs *and* mixed costs *and* relevant range.

**Variance Analysis:** Variance analysis is an analysis of the variances between standard costs and actual costs for direct material, direct labor, and overhead. *See also* standard costs.

**Vertical Integration:** Vertical integration is the improvement of a value chain through the supply end and the demand end in the same industry (i.e., when a firm expands its business into areas that are at different points of the same production path).

**Virtual Memory:** Virtual memory or virtual storage is not real memory. Portions of a program that are not being executed are stored on a disk as virtual memory pages and are retrieved and brought into actual physical memory when they are needed. Virtual memory provides the capability to run programs that require more memory than is physically available.

**Virtual Private Network (VPN):** A virtual private network is a private network configured within a public network to take advantage of the economies of scale of the public network. A VPN hides data in the private network in a wrapper to hide its contents. VPNs can be either encrypted (secure) or unencrypted (trusted).

**Virus:** A virus is a self-replicating computer program or piece of program code that spreads by inserting copies of itself into other programs or data. A virus can enter a system as an e-mail attachment, a file downloaded from the Internet, or other infected media. Not all malicious software programs are viruses; worms and Trojan horses are also considered malicious software.

**VOIP:** VOIP means voice over Internet protocol. VOIP is used for making phone calls using a high-speed connection to the Internet.

**Volume Variance:** In a two-way or three-way analysis of overhead variance, the volume variance is the budget based on standard hours allowed for the actual units and the applied overhead. There will be a volume variance only when fixed and variable overhead are both being analyzed because, for variable overhead, the budget based on standard hours allowed will be the same as the applied overhead (which is based on the standard rate times the actual units). *See also* spending variance *and* efficiency variance *and* budget variance.

**Vulnerability:** For business information systems, a vulnerability is a characteristic of a design, implementation, or operation that renders the system susceptible to a threat.

**Warm Site:** A warm backup site is a facility that is stocked with all the hardware necessary to create a reasonable facsimile of a primary data center. It is the compromise between the hot backup site and the cold backup site.

**Waste:** Waste includes scrap with no value or productive materials lost in the production process. A certain amount of shrinkage is anticipated and considered a normal part of production.

**Web 2.0:** Web 2.0 refers to change and innovation in the ways that software developers and users utilize the Internet.

**Web Administrator:** Web administrators, often called webmasters, are responsible for information on a website. *See also* network administrator.

**Web Hosting Service:** A Web hosting service is an organization that maintains a number of Web servers and provides space to users to maintain their websites.

**Web Server:** A Web server is a computer that delivers Web pages upon request. Any computer can be turned into a Web server by installing Web server software and connecting it to the Internet.

**Weighted Average Cost of Capital (WACC):** The weighted average cost of capital is the weighted average of the costs of the various components of capital (debt, preferred stock, and common stock or retained earnings). The weights are the market values of the different securities.

**Weighted Average Method of Process Costing:** The weighted average method of process costing calculates equivalent units and production costs differently from the FIFO method of process costing. In the weighted average method, the equivalent units are the units transferred out plus the equivalent units of the ending work in process. Production costs to be accounted for are the cost of beginning work in process plus costs added during the month. Cost per equivalent units is the production cost divided by the equivalent units. Normally, a separate cost per equivalent units is calculated for direct materials and conversion costs (labor and overhead). *See also* FIFO method of process costing.

**Wide Area Network (WAN):** WANs allow national and international communications. They usually employ non-dedicated public communications channels (e.g., fiber optic, terrestrial microwave, or satellite) as their communications media. WAN communication services may be provided by value added networks, Internet-based networks, or point-to-point networks (direct private/proprietary network links normally using leased lines). *See also* local area network (LAN).

**Wi-Fi:** Wi-Fi is the set of standards for wireless LANs, also called the 802.11 standards.

**Working Capital:** Working capital is current assets minus current liabilities. *See also* current ratio *and* quick ratio.

**Workstation:** A workstation is a node (usually a PC) that is used by end users.

**World Trade Organization (WTO):** The World Trade Organization is an international institution that deals with regulation of trade between nations including formalizing trade agreements and assisting in the resolution of trade disputes. The WTO has more than 150 member nations.

**Worm:** A worm is a self-replicating computer program, similar to a virus. Worms are self-contained and do not need to be part of other programs to propagate. Worms are generally designed to travel over networks such as the Internet.

**XBRL (Extensible Business Reporting Language):** XBRL is a license-free means of communicating business and financial data between businesses and via the Internet through the use of, for example, identifying tags that are assigned to data. Advantages of this language include cost savings and improved efficiency, accuracy, and reliability. XBRL is a very flexible program, able to handle various languages and accounting standards.

**XML (Extensible Markup Language):** XML is a technology that is being developed to transmit data in flexible formats, instead of the standard formats of EDI. XML tells systems the format of data and also what kind of information the data is. XML utilizes user-defined tags similar to the data formatting tags that are used in HTML for the display of Web pages in browsers. *See also* hypertext markup language (HTML).

**Zero Balance Accounts:** A zero balance account is a bank account that allows for automatic same-day transfers to or from a concentration account. A zero balance account allows a firm to move excess cash balances into a single account or to control the disbursement of funds from a central pool of money. The balance in the account is maintained at zero by transferring money to a concentration account. *See also* concentration banking.

**Zero-Based Budget:** A zero-based budget is a budget that requires justification of all expenditures every year.

**Zero-Coupon Bonds:** Zero-coupon bonds are discount bonds that do not pay interest. They are purchased at a discount and mature at par.

## NOTES

# A

## Q

## R

## S